About the Author

Ghostly phenomena were a common occurrence in Brad Steiger's childhood home, and because these experiences were accepted by a mystically inclined mother and challenged by a skeptically inclined father, Steiger believes that he achieved a balanced attitude toward ghosts and hauntings that has served him well during his over fifty years as a psychical researcher. Since 1958, Steiger has been invited to dozens of private homes, office buildings, dormitories, hospitals, and sacred areas to investigate haunting manifestations. He has witnessed spirit materializations, heard spectral voices, felt ghostly touches on his person, and once was even lifted into the air by a hostile entity. In the early 1970s, the Steiger family moved into a haunted house that was home to several entities who tried every frightening method they could devise to drive them out.

His first book, *Ghost, Ghouls and Other Peculiar People*, a collection of his articles on ghosts and the paranormal, was published in 1965. Steiger has now authored or coauthored 170 books on the mysterious and unknown, including the classics *The Werewolf Book: The Encyclopedia of Shapeshifting Beings*, *Mysteries of Time and Space*, and *Real Vampires, Night Stalkers, and Creatures from the Darkside*.

He has continued to investigate and research haunted places throughout the United States and abroad, along with his wife, Sherry, with whom he coauthored *The Gale Encyclopedia of the Unusual and the Unexplained*; *Real Aliens, Space Beings, and Creatures from Other Worlds*; *Conspiracies and Secret Societies, the Complete Dossier*; and the "Miracle" series. Brad is a veteran of broadcast news magazines, ranging from *Nightline* to the *NBC Nightly News*. He is also a regular radio guest on numerous radio programs.

Other Visible Ink Press Books by Brad Steiger

Conspiracies and Secret Societies: The Complete Dossier, 2nd edition
With Sherry Hansen Steiger
ISBN: 978-1-57859-368-2

Real Aliens, Space Beings, and Creatures from Other Worlds,
With Sherry Hansen Steiger
ISBN: 978-1-57859-333-0

Real Miracles, Divine Intervention, and Feats of Incredible Survival
With Sherry Hansen Steiger
ISBN: 978-1-57859-214-2

Real Monsters, Gruesome Critters, and Beasts from the Darkside
With Sherry Hansen Steiger
ISBN: 978-1-57859-220-3

Real Vampires, Night Stalkers, and Creatures from the Darkside
ISBN: 978-1-57859-255-5

Real Zombies, the Living Dead, and Creatures of the Apocalypse
ISBN: 978-1-57859-296-8

The Werewolf Book: The Encyclopedia of Shape-Shifting Beings, 2nd edition
ISBN: 978-1-57859-367-5

Also from Visible Ink Press

Angels A to Z, 2nd edition
by Evelyn Dorothy Oliver and James R Lewis
ISBN: 978-1-57859-212-8

Armageddon Now: The End of the World A to Z
by Jim Willis and Barbara Willis
ISBN: 978-1-57859-168-8

The Astrology Book: The Encyclopedia of Heavenly Influences, 2nd edition
by James R Lewis
ISBN: 978-1-57859-144-2

The Dream Encyclopedia, 2nd edition
by James R Lewis and Evelyn Dorothy Oliver
ISBN: 978-1-57859-216-6

The Encyclopedia of Religious Phenomena
by J. Gordon Melton
ISBN: 978-1-57859-209-8

The Religion Book: Places, Prophets, Saints, and Seers
by Jim Willis
ISBN: 978-1-57859-151-0

The Spirit Book: The Encyclopedia of Clairvoyance, Channeling, and Spirit Communication
by Raymond Buckland
ISBN: 978-1-57859-172-5

Unexplained! Strange Sightings, Incredible Occurrences, and Puzzling Physical Phenomena, 3rd edition
by Jerome Clark
ISBN: 978-1-57859-344-6

The Vampire Book: The Encyclopedia of the Undead, 3rd edition
by J. Gordon Melton
ISBN: 978-1-57859-281-4

The Witch Book: The Encyclopedia of Witchcraft, Wicca, and Neo-paganism
by Raymond Buckland
ISBN: 978-1-57859-114-5

Please visit us at visibleink.com

REAL GHOSTS, RESTLESS SPIRITS, AND HAUNTED PLACES

BRAD STEIGER

VISIBLE INK PRESS

Detroit

REAL GHOSTS, RESTLESS SPIRITS, AND HAUNTED PLACES

Visible Ink Press®
43311 Joy Rd., #414
Canton, MI 48187-2075

Visible Ink Press is a registered trademark of Visible Ink Press LLC.

Most Visible Ink Press books are available at special quantity discounts when purchased in bulk by corporations, organizations, or groups. Customized printings, special imprints, messages, and excerpts can be produced to meet your needs. For more information, contact Special Markets Director, Visible Ink Press, www.visibleinkpress.com, or 734-667-3211.

Managing Editor: Kevin S. Hile
Art Director: Mary Claire Krzewinski
Typesetting: Marco Di Vita
Proofreaders: Sharon R. Gunton and Chrystal Rosza
Indexing: Shoshana Hurwitz

Cover images: Shutterstock.com.

Cataloging-in-Publication Data

Steiger, Brad.
Real ghosts, restless spirits, and haunted places / by Brad Steiger.
—2nd ed.
    p. cm.
Includes bibliographical references and index.
ISBN 978-1-57859-401-6 (alk. paper)
1. Ghosts. 2. Spirits. 3. Haunted places. I. Title.
BF1461.S834 2013
133.1--dc23   2012025849

Printed in the United States of America

10 9 8 7 6 5 4 3 2

CONTENTS

Acknowledgments   [vii]

Photo Credits   [vii]

Introduction   [ix]

REAL GHOSTS, RESTLESS SPIRITS, AND HAUNTED PLACES

ACKNOWLEDGMENTS

I wish to thank all those individual researchers and experiencers of ghost and haunting phenomena who contributed their personal accounts, photographs, and artwork for inclusion in this second edition of *Real Ghosts, Restless Spirits, and Haunted Places*. If I attempted to acknowledge each one of them individually, I would surely omit someone, so a hearty expression of gratitude to all who contributed to the quality and the authenticity of this book. Once again, I am grateful for the opportunity of working with the gifted staff of Visible Ink: Kevin Hile, my editor extraordinaire, always just an email away; Roger Janecke, my ever-supportive publisher; Mary Claire Krzewinski, who always delights with page and cover design; and Marco Di Vita, the magic typesetter. Next I must thank my agent, Agnes Birnbaum, who for many years has continued to provide marvelous support to me and my work. Finally, I owe a great debt to Sherry, my best friend, fellow researcher of the unexplained, wife, and life partner for her courage in journeying with me to those haunted places where real ghosts and restless spirits await our investigation and for her steadfast love that never fails to elevate my spirit.

PHOTO CREDITS

AP/Wide World Photos: 98, 134, 154, 223, 257, 288, 295, 312, 315, 317, 319, 324, 326, 327, 416, 445, 447, 448, 453, 484, 485, 515, 559, 570, 572, 583.
Rick Aiello: 18.
Loyd Auerbach: 578.
Gregory J. Avery (orbmasster@cox.net): 65, 67.
Henry and Tatyana Bailey: 426, 491, 493, 494, 498, 501
Merry Barrentine/Utah Paranormal Exploration & Research (www.uper.freewebspace.com): 528.
Clarisa Bernhardt: 263.
Cindy Blake/Michigan Ghost Watchers (www.ghostwatchers.org): 595, 595.

Barry Conrad: 640, 639.

Christina Crawford: 322.

Thomas B. Creager: 519

Patrick Cross: 635.

Lukas Davita:584

Fortean Picture Library: 5, 51, 58, 75, 79, 83, 87, 88, 101, 133, 161, 171, 179, 231, 233, 240, 245, 246, 255, 256, 259, 261, 264, 291, 292, 292, 293, 299, 301, 303, 338, 344, 347, 369, 376, 377, 379, 382, 384, 386, 396, 399, 409, 450, 455, 456, 457, 479, 480, 542, 543, 566, 575, 580, 590, 605.

Stacie Freeland: 105.

Terry Gambill/Ghosts and Haunts in Missouri (www.missourighosts.net): 15.

Rick Garner: 473.

Dale Kaczmarek (www.ghostresarch.org) and Jim Graczyk (www.ghostguides.com): 351, 408.

"Mark": 599.

Frank Lazzaro, L'Aura Hladik, NJ Ghost Hunters Society: 614, 616,617.

Maureen Nelson/Washington State Ghost Society (www.washingtonghostsociety.org): 463.

Dr. Dave Oester and Dr. Sharon Gill/International Ghost Hunters (www.ghostweb.com): 619, 623.

Bret and Gina Oldham: 418, 420, 522, 523, 524.

Bill Oliver: 374, 380, 424, 435, 442, 497.

Ricardo Pustanio: 111, 113, 128, 138, 643, 646.

Nick Redfern: 476.

Todd Roll/Wausau Paranormal Society (www.pat-wausau.org): 536.

Richard Senate: 19.

Shutterstock: 14, 44, 53, 364, 366.

Benjamin Smith: 511.

Dusty Smith/Daytona Beach Psychical Research Group (www.dbprginc.org): 341, 342, 343.

Sherry Hansen Steiger: 430, 431, 432.

The Steiger Archives: 32, 52, 228, 248, 321, 331, 486, 487.

The Steiger Archives/Benjamin Smith: 511.

Dave Van Slyke (www.ghosttoghost.com): 563.

Tim Swartz: 43.

Pastor Robin Swope: 389, 391, 393

Dave Van Slyke (www.ghosttoghost.com): 563.

Wikicommons: 280, 334.

INTRODUCTION

Working on the second edition of *Real Ghosts, Restless Spirits, and Haunted Places* has been extremely gratifying for me. Since the book was first published by Visible Ink Press in 2003, I have received dozens of emails and letters from men and women who have recounted their own encounters with real ghosts and restless spirits, and from those individuals who expressed their mixed emotions when they found themselves residing in haunted places.

Although numerous readers commented on the enormous size of the first edition, this new edition contains many new accounts of hauntings and firsthand interactions with paranormal manifestations that can only be identified as ghosts, as well as many new and compelling illustrations.

And what exactly is a ghost? A spirit that once occupied a human body? An ethereal being that travels multidimensionally in defiance of time and space? Will we all one day become ghosts? After more than sixty years researching the paranormal, and nearly that many investigating mediumship and haunted houses on site, I spend little time these days theorizing about what ghosts might be. I completely accept the existence of such phenomena, and I conclude that it is extremely multifaceted.

Although there might be a single source for all ethereal and ghostly manifestations, the human mind seems to be fond of placing natural and paranormal phenomena into multiple categories.

And now, dear reader, I invite you to follow me as we explore the many dark and shadowed pathways that will lead us to encounter real ghosts, restless spirits, and haunted places.

1
HAUNTED HOUSES AND APARTMENTS

Whenever the Steiger family gathers for a holiday or some other occasion, eventually, usually late at night, talk turns to stories about the haunted house that we moved into during the summer of 1973. Although the children are now in their late forties and fifties, each of them have deep-seated memories of the occasionally nasty ghost that tried to drive us out of the old farmhouse.

We should have been forewarned about the haunting when a relative of the previous owner said that we had purchased the perfect home for a peculiar fellow like me who chased around the country looking for spooks. Now, he laughed, I wouldn't have to go out the house to find a ghost, because the home had been haunted for many years.

The problem between our family and the ghost probably started when we began updating the house with indoor plumbing, modern toilets, and a variety of electrical appliances. We had been warned that the patriarch of the family that had lived in the farmhouse had been opposed to modernization, but since it was now our home, it seemed reasonable for us to make ourselves comfortable.

I received the first ghostly attack when I was alone one morning and heard a serious of mysterious thuds, thumps, and bumps sounding throughout the house. When I would go to the attic to investigate, the thunderous sounds would move to the basement, until I grew tired of running up and down three flights of stairs and decided to ignore the manifestations.

Bryan, our older son, was treated to a similar performance when a pounding on the front door distracted him from his homework one night when he was at home alone. Answering the knock and finding no one there, he was then summoned to the back door by another series of rapping. After playing a strange game of tag from front to back door, Bryan was dismayed to find the disturbance had increased, with the sound of simultaneous blows on both doors and all the downstairs windows. The absence of footprints in the freshly fallen snow proved that no human tricksters were playing a prank on him.

Kari, our older daughter, often heard her name being called in a whispery voice that came from the attic. Steven, our younger son, began staying out later and later at night after he left his after-school job because of the manifestations in his room, especially the rocking chair that would creak back and forth until nearly dawn. The children's mother often found herself locked out of the house when she stepped outside, and once she awakened to find herself being held down in bed by the specter of an old man.

> "We experienced direct proof that there really is something within us that survives physical death...."

Julie, the youngest and most vulnerable member of our family, became the victim of the haunting's most persistent and cruel phenomena—the cacophonous mix of voices and eerie music that would grow louder and louder until she would seek refuge at a neighbor's home until one of us would retrieve her.

I had grown up in a house with otherworldly manifestations and had seen my first ghosts when I was about three years old, but those entities in our old homestead were relatively quiet—and most certainly benign. By the time we moved into the farmhouse, I had been ghost hunting for years and had experienced a wide variety of paranormal phenomena. Once I had so angered a spirit that it smashed down a door and hoisted me and my fellow researchers into the air. I could not say that the entity in our home was evil, but it certainly was behaving in a decidedly negative manner toward my family. For months we underwent a supernatural barrage of mysterious lights appearing both inside and outside the house, footsteps coming up and down the stairs, and a noisy repertoire of assorted pounding, drumming, and tapping. Eventually, the phenomena seemed to grow more accustomed to our presences or to wear itself out to a degree where coexistence became possible.

Interestingly, about four years ago, Julie summarized the time that we lived in the haunted house as some of the most horrible days of her life, but now, in retrospect, she can see there was a positive aspect to the eerie ordeal. "We experienced direct proof that there really is something within us that survives physical death," she said.

And in her observation wrought from frightening experience, Julie has provided the theme that is common to every ghost story that has ever been told: To experience a haunting, to see a ghost, is to receive proof that life goes on beyond the grave. Accounts of haunting phenomena—no matter how terrifying they may be—provide evidence of a continued existence for the spirit, which can manifest in more than one dimension, and confirm that humans are multidimensional beings that consist of mind, body, and soul.

⊸ᴍᴍ∫ᴨᴍᴍ⊷

THE HAUNTING OF WILLINGTON MILL

For the last two months of 1834, the nursemaid employed by the Joseph Proctor family tried her best to ignore the eerie noises that she heard coming from the deserted room over the nursery. Each night when she was left alone to watch the child, she would hear the sounds—a dull, heavy tread, like someone slowly pacing back and forth.

Finally she decided that she had had enough of the strange sounds that so disturbed her evenings. She was convinced that a ghost occupied the upstairs room; in a state of great nervous agitation, she asked that she be discharged from service in the Proctor home.

Joseph Proctor saw no reason why he should attempt to talk the woman into staying with them. She was obviously a high-strung woman who had frightened herself by imagining visitations by supernatural beings.

It wasn't long, however, before he too heard the sound of heavy feet in the upstairs room, as did his wife and the other servants. Although puzzled by the eerie tread of invisible feet, the Proctors convinced themselves that there was undoubtedly some natural explanation for the strange sounds.

The Proctors refused to take the noises seriously and purposely omitted any mention of the disturbed room when they hired a new nursemaid on January 23, 1835. On her first evening in the nursery, the girl came down to the sitting room to inquire who was in the room above her. The Proctors evaded her question, putting the whole matter down to the usual night noises in an old house.

The next day, Mrs. Proctor heard the steps of a man with heavy boots walking about in the upstairs room. That same day, while the family was at dinner, the nursemaid came down the stairs and blinked incredulously at Mr. Proctor. She said that she had been hearing someone walking in the room above her for five minutes. She had come downstairs to assure herself that it wasn't the master of the house.

"But if it isn't you, sir, "she inquired, "who is it?"

Proctor inspected the room that night. Trickery seemed out of the question. The empty room was covered with a thin, undisturbed layer of soot, which in itself was proof that not even a mouse had been walking about on the floor. The window had been boarded up many years before with wooden laths and plaster, and the door to the room had been nailed shut for some time. Proctor descended even more mystified then when he had gone up to conduct his investigation.

On January 31, the Proctors heard the sound of a dozen loud thuds next to their bed as they were preparing to retire. On the next night, Joseph Proctor heard a metallic rapping on the baby's crib. There was a brief pacing overhead, and then the sound of footsteps, which were never heard again in the upper room.

But what followed for the next several years included such a remarkable range of visible and auditory manifestations that the initial plodding footsteps began to seem like a baby's first steps in comparison. What is nearly as remarkable as the intense haunting of Willington Mill is the fact that the Proctors persisted in living in the house for over eleven years before finally surrendering to some of the most eerie paranormal disturbances on record.

Thomas Mann, the foreman of the mill that was separated from the Proctor's house by a road and a garden, told Proctor that he had heard a peculiar noise moving across the lawn in the darkness. At first, Mann thought it came from the wooden cistern that stood in the mill yard, and he suspected that some pranksters were attempting to spill it. However, upon pursuing the noise with a lantern in hand, he found that the cistern had not been budged. Mann also told Proctor in the strictest confidence that even before this peculiar disturbance, he had on several occasions heard a sound as if someone were walking on the gravel path.

It was shortly after their confidential conversation that both Mann and another neighbor observed the luminous image of a woman in a window of Proctor's house. Both parties had seen the ghost independent of each other, and Mann had called his entire family to witness the phantasm, which was fully visible for over ten minutes.

About a year after the phenomena at Willington Mill were becoming increasingly frightening, Jane Carr, Mrs. Proctor's sister, arrived for a stay. A few minutes before midnight one evening, she was awakened by a noise very much like that of someone winding a large clock. After this bizarre noise, her bed began to shake, and she clearly heard a sound like that of a heavy sack falling on the floor above. Several strong knocks sounded about her bedstead, and the unmistakable shuffle of feet surrounded her bed.

One night, the phenomena added bed-lifting to the haunting repertoire. An invisible something manifested itself under the bed of one of the Proctor children and began to raise the mattress until the boy cried out. Next, the thing hoisted the mattress of the bed on which Mrs. Proctor and a new nursemaid were sleeping. Mrs. Proctor described the sensation as feeling as if a large man were underneath the bed, pushing it up with his back.

A Haunted House.

In addition to the sounds of thudding feet, the ghost had acquired fists with which to pound on walls and the ability to lift beds. Later, the haunting developed new skills: whistling, talking, and materializing into a number of grotesque phantoms.

The Proctors' sons, Joseph and Henry, were awakened one night by a loud shriek that emanated from under their beds. Upon investigating, Joseph, Sr. heard an eerie moan coming from somewhere in the room. A bed began to move and the voice uttered what sounded like the words, "chuck-chuck." These sounds were followed by a noise similar to that of a infant sucking at a bottle. The youngest child, Jane, was moved to another room, but this did not spare her the torment of having her bed levitated.

The phenomena then began to leave its domain on the upper floor and venture forth to the lower floors during the night. The kitchen seemed to be a favorite target for its nightly forays, and on several mornings the cook would find the kitchen chairs heaped in a disorderly pile, the shutters thrown open, and utensils scattered about the room.

Mrs. Proctor's brother, Jonathan Carr, came for a visit, and after spending a night filled with bed-shakings and whistlings, declared that he would not live in the house for any amount of money.

Jane, Mrs. Proctor's sister, obviously had stronger nerves than her brother; judging from the journal that Joseph Proctor kept, the young woman spent many evenings in the afflicted house. One night as she shared a room with Mary Young, the cook, the two women were terrified to hear the bolt in their door slide back, the handle turn, and the door open. Something rustled the curtains as it moved across the bed, then it lifted the bedclothes from the trembling figures. As it passed around the bed to Mary's side, both women distinctly saw a dark shadow against the curtain.

Little Jane Proctor was sleeping with her aunt Jane one night when she saw a strange head peeping out at her from the curtains at the foot of the bed. The four-year-old girl later described the head as being that of an old woman, but Jane was much too frightened to observe any more and tucked her own head under the covers.

> Footsteps were constantly thudding around his bed, and there were thumpings about his pillow and other bedclothes.

Joseph, Jr., was disturbed nearly every night by the phenomena. He reported hearing the words, "Never mind" and "Come and get" being repeated over and over but there never seemed to be a reason for the utterances. Footsteps were constantly thudding around his bed, and there were thumpings about his pillow and other bedclothes.

A medical doctor named Drury arrived and asked Proctor's permission to carry out an examination of the haunted upper room. Proctor consented, and allowed the doctor and his companion, a young chemist, to make preparations to spend the night in the disturbed room.

At about one o'clock in the morning, Proctor was awakened by a piercing scream of terror coming from the upper floor. Dr. Drury had come face-to-face with the ghost of the wizened old woman.

The two curious would-be investigators spent the rest of the dark hours drinking coffee in the kitchen. They left the house at dawn. Proctor noted in his journal that the doctor and the chemist had received a shock that they would not soon forget.

An entity that resembled a monkey proved to be one of the most incredible materializations of the Willington Mill haunting. Eight-year-old Joseph, Jr. was seated atop a chest of drawers, pretending that he was making a speech to his sister Jane and his brothers, Henry and Edmund. Suddenly, in full view of all the children, a monkeylike creature appeared and began to tug at Joseph's shoe strap.

By the time Joseph, Sr., came running in response to their excited cries, the children were scurrying about the floor, trying desperately to play with the mischievous monkey. Even after it had vanished, two-year-old Edmund, the youngest Proctor child, continued to look under chairs and tables until his bedtime, trying to locate the entity that he identified as a "funny-looking cat."

Years later, the memory of that incident was still vivid in Edmund Proctor's mind. In the December, 1892 issue of the *Journal of the Society for Psychical Research*, he wrote: "Now it so happens that this monkey is the first incident in the lugubrious hauntings, or whatever they may be termed, of which I have any recollection. I suppose it was, or might easily be, the first monkey that I had ever seen, which may explain my memory being so impressed that I have not forgotten it…. My parents have told me that no monkey was known to be owned in the neighborhood, and that after diligent inquiry no organ man or hurdy-gurdy boy, either with or without a monkey, had been seen anywhere about the place or neighborhood, either on that day or for a length of time … I have an absolutely distinct recollection of that monkey, and of running to see where it went to as it hopped out of the room and into the adjoining [room]. We saw it go under the bed in that room, but it could not be traced or found anywhere afterwards. We hunted and ferretted about that room, and every corner of the house, but no monkey, or any trace of one, was more to be found."

The white face of what appeared to be an old woman was seen more and more often, but Joseph, Jr., soon added an old man to the list of materializations. Aunt Jane Carr did not see the monkey, but she reported that she had heard what sounded like an animal jumping down off an easy chair.

An astonishing thing occurred when the haunting fashioned a double of Joseph, Jr., that materialized in his room. Imagine the boy's shock upon discovering his mirror image peeking at him from the shadows beside his bed. He was about ten years old when this facet of the phenomena manifested, so his powers of observation must be given some credence. Joseph, Jr., said that his spectral self-image, which was even dressed in a manner identical to the boy, walked back and forth between the window and the wardrobe before it gradually dematerialized.

Shortly after this dramatic episode, the Proctors decided that they had endured enough. Patient Quakers though they were, eleven years of living amidst incessant supernatural disturbances had been enough for them. They had also become fearful of permanent injury to the minds of their children should they remain longer in what they called a "plague-ridden dwelling."

In 1866, Proctor obtained a residence at Camp Villa, North Shields, and after returning to the mill to assist with the packing, he and his wife sent the servants and the children on ahead. The last night Mr. and Mrs. Proctor spent alone in Willington Mill was perhaps the most frightening of all.

Throughout the night they lay and listened to the sounds of boxes being dragged with heavy thuds down the stairs, nonhuman footsteps walking across the floors, and invisible furniture being dragged around by invisible beings. The Proctors were, in effect, hearing a ghostly recreation of all the noises made by the family and their servants as they were engaged in their various moving chores.

One dreadful thought kept running through the Proctors' minds: Were the ghosts packing to move along with them?

It was with indescribable relief that the Proctors arrived at the new residence to find it completely free of the former horror that had blemished eleven years of their lives. Their residency in the new home was blissfully untroubled by knocking, whistling, footsteps, and phantasms.

After the Proctors moved from Willington Mill, the house was divided into two apartments. According to later testimonies of the new occupants, they were only occasionally bothered by haunting phenomena. However, in around 1868, when two new families moved into the apartments, they were so greatly disturbed by ghostly manifestations that one family moved out and refused to return.

After a number of years had passed, the mill was closed and made into a warehouse and the old Proctor house was divided into a number of small tenements. When Edmund Proctor visited the place around 1890, none of the tenants claimed to be troubled by ghosts. It appeared that whatever ethereal beings had plagued the house at Willington Mill had moved on to create a haunting in some other location.

THE DANCING GHOST OF ORENSBURG

When he returned on November 16, 1870 to his large country estate near Orensburg in the province of Uralsk in Russia, a wealthy landowner named Shchapoff found his household in an uproar over a dancing ghost.

According to Helena, his twenty-year-old wife, their baby daughter had been fussy on the night of November 14 and had not been at all eager to go to sleep. Mrs. Shchapoff asked Maria, the cook, if she would see to the child. Maria entertained the girl with her harmonica while her mistress and the miller's wife gossiped in the living room.

When Mrs. Shchapoff heard the sounds of the cook's feet tapping the floor in a brisk three-step dance, she remarked that if all else failed, Maria danced for the child and that always put the little one to sleep.

The miller's wife was in the act of nodding her head in agreement when she suddenly opened her mouth in surprise and terror and screamed that there was someone looking in the window.

Mrs. Shchapoff turned and saw nothing to cause the woman so much alarm. The miller's wife was visibly shaken and disturbed and said that she thought that she had seen a horrid face looking in at them. Mrs. Shchapoff assured her that it was probably only a shadow of some sort.

Maria entered the room and told her mistress that the child was now sound asleep. Mrs. Shchapoff thanked the cook and dismissed her for the evening.

A few minutes later as the two women sat chatting, the miller's wife once again claimed that she saw something at the window. Mrs. Shchapoff rose from her chair to investigate, but she was halted in her journey to the window by the sound of an uproar in the attic above their heads. At first it seemed to be a flurry of wild rapping that had the two women staring at one another in wide-eyed confusion. Then the pace of the tapping slowed until they became an exact reproduction of the three-step that Maria had been dancing for the child.

Mrs. Shchapoff was perplexed. Whatever was that silly woman doing up in the attic? Did she never get her fill of dancing?

But the miller's wife questioned how the cook could have gotten up to the attic without passing by them in the process.

Without speaking another word, the two women left the sitting room and walked quietly back to the cook's quarters. Opening the door just a crack, they were able to see Maria sound asleep in her bed.

Determined to see who had gone unnoticed to the loft, Mrs. Shchapoff grabbed a lantern from a kitchen shelf and the two women walked up the stairs to the attic. Although the sounds of the dancing continued, their lantern plainly revealed that there was no one in the loft. Then, as the women beat a hasty retreat down the stairs, the rapping seemed to race ahead of them, rattling the windows and pounding at the walls.

The miller's wife fled out of the manor to get her husband and the gardener, and Mrs. Shchapoff went to the nursery to check on the welfare of her daughter.

By the time the miller's wife returned with her husband and the gardener, the rapping and the dancing had greatly increased in volume and Mrs. Shchapoff's mother and her mother-in-law, as well as Maria, had been awakened by the racket. The two men searched the house and the grounds and found nothing that could explain the bizarre tapping-rapping disturbance that continued until dawn.

At ten o'clock the next evening, the dancing ghost once again began its spirited interpretation of the three-step. The Shchapoff's servants patrolled

> The two men searched the house and the grounds and found nothing that could explain the bizarre tapping-rapping disturbance that continued until dawn.

the house and the grounds, but could find no trace of the invisible dancer who continued to perform and to evade the searchers until dawn.

When Mr. Shchapoff returned that next afternoon from his business trip, he scoffed at his young wife's account and jokingly accused her of getting into his brandy while he had been away. Shchapoff was a no-nonsense landowner who had little patience with superstitious folktales or accounts of ghosts, dancing or otherwise. He grew very impatient when his mother and his mother-in-law substantiated Helena's story of a dancing ghost and warned him that something supernatural had visited the house in his absence.

In a gruff and irritated manner, Shchapoff scolded the ladies for sitting around idly in the evenings, concocting a ghost story that had frightened the servants and distracted them from their work. He decided to send Maria to fetch the miller, a man he regarded as completely sensible and reliable, to set the matter straight.

The miller didn't disappoint him. While he admitted that there had been strange noises that had disturbed and confused the entire household, he had that very day removed a pigeon's nest that he found under a cornice of the house. It seemed likely to him that the bird had somehow been responsible for the weird noises that had so upset the women and the servants. For Shchapoff, this put an end to the wild tales of a dancing ghost.

That evening after the rest of the household had retired to their rooms quite early, exhausted from their nocturnal ordeals with the eerie tapping sounds, Shchapoff sat down in the easy chair in his study to read for a while before going to bed. At about ten o'clock, he was distracted by scratching noises sounding from above his head. Thinking at first that the pesky pigeon had come back to roost under the cornice, he became puzzled when he began to listen more closely to the sounds and realized that they were arranging themselves into mimicking the tapping of someone dancing the three-step.

Believing that Helena was having a bit of fun with him, Shchapoff put down his book and began climbing quietly up the stairs to his wife's room. He stood outside the door for a moment to be certain that he had accurately traced the sound of the dancing. Then, convinced that there was no doubt that the sounds were coming from Helena's room, he pushed open the door and stood ready to deliver a stern lecture to his young wife.

She lay in her bed, sleeping soundly. The sounds of dancing had ceased the moment that he had opened the door.

There was something strange going on here. Confused and more than a little baffled, Shchapoff started to close the door when a series of raps sounded from above his wife's bed. He walked quietly to the wall, thinking he might catch a hidden prankster in the act of hammering on the bedstead. Just as he bent to listen more carefully to the tapping, a rap sounded with such force next to his ear that it nearly deafened him.

His wife sat up in bed, screaming in shock and fear. She calmed when she saw her husband standing near her bedside. "What was that?" she demanded. "Did you hear it?"

Not wishing to alarm his wife, Shchapoff insisted that he had heard nothing. As if to call him a liar, two explosive knocks seemed to shake the house down to its very foundation.

The angry landowner took his pistol from a drawer, slipped on his coat, and declared that he was putting a stop to the nonsense. He got his dogs, roused the servants, and told them that they were going to get whoever was responsible for the outrage against his home.

However, Shchapoff found no prankster that night. To those on the outside of the house, the rapping seemed to come from the inside. But those who remained indoors shouted that someone was trying to batter the house down from the outside. At last, Shchapoff had to admit defeat, and he dismissed his men until the next morning.

The next day, he enlisted the help of his neighbors as well as his own servants. The crew searched the entire house and examined every foot of the grounds to no avail. That night, at Shchapoff's request, his neighbors stayed to witness the disturbances.

> The uninvited invisible guest performed spectacularly. It danced above the heads of the searchers all night long....

The uninvited invisible guest performed spectacularly. It danced above the heads of the searchers all night long—and, for a finale, it struck a door with such force that the heavy wooden planking was torn from the hinges.

By the next night, even the stubborn landowner had become a believer in the dancing ghost, and he waited for the onset of a new round of the phenomena with dread. He paced the floor nervously until ten o'clock, the time the manifestations usually began. But on this night, there was not a single scratch, rap, or spritely danced three-step. Nor was there any sound from the loft on the next night.

It appeared that the mysterious phenomena had quieted down in the Shchapoff country house. Or perhaps they might have if Shchapoff had been wise enough to leave well enough alone.

A month later, on December 20, the Shchapoffs were entertaining guests, who openly expressed their skepticism of the phenomena which their hosts had described. Angered that their guests would doubt his word, Shchapoff summoned Maria to the parlor and commanded her to perform a three-step, announcing in a loud voice that probably all the ghost needed was a little coaxing and it would come back.

At her master's insistence, Maria danced a brisk little three-step. The cook completed the dance, then looked around the room fearfully as a rapping began at the windows. The assembled visitors listened incredulously as they heard an exact replication of Maria's dance coming from the attic overhead.

Skeptical guests accused Shchapoff of having planted another servant up in the loft, but when a group of doubters went up into the attic to investigate, they found no one.

On New Year's Eve, 1871, Shchapoff again ordered Maria to dance a three-step in order to induce the dancing ghost to follow her with an act of its own. The country place was filled with guests who heard for themselves the echo of Maria's dance coming from the ceiling above their heads. The invisible performer became so animated and enthusiastic that for the first time it made some attempts at vocalization and sang some garbled snatches of Russian folk songs.

After such remarkable phenomena had been witnessed at two holiday parties, the stories about the mysterious goings-on at the Shchapoffs country place spread across Russia. Soon, scientists and spiritualists were seeking an audience with the dancing ghost using widely diverse methods of communicating with the strange force.

A Dr. Shustoff explained the whole phenomena by invoking the magic name of electricity. He maintained that the soil conditions at the country place had produced the weird goings-on. He also theorized that somehow the electrical vibrations might be coming from Mrs. Shchapoff.

Dr. Shustoff's theory of prankish electrical currents was doomed when the phenomena began to give evidence of a level of intelligence that could respond to conversation and answer questions advanced by investigators. A psychic investigator named Alekseeff devised a series of knocks which he claimed allowed him to communicate with the entity that was haunting the country estate. According to Alekseeff, Mr. Shchapoff had been cursed by the servant of a neighboring miller. For whatever reason, this angry servant so despised Shchapoff that he had maliciously set a devil on the wealthy landowner.

The provincial governor, General Vervekin, appointed Mr. Akutin, an engineer; the aforementioned Dr. Shustoff, an electrical theorist; and Mr. Savicheff, a magazine editor, to be the official investigators of the disturbances on the Shchapoff estate. This committee eventually decided that Mrs. Shchapoff had been producing the so-called supernatural effects by means of trickery, and Mr. Shchapoff received a sharply worded letter from the governor, warning him not to allow his wife to produce the phenomena again.

In spite of the governor's demands, the disturbances increased in violence at the Shchapoff country place. The ghost had acquired frightening incendiary abilities, and Helena Shchapoff was the one who bore the brunt of the attacks. Balls of fire circled the house and bounced against the windows of her room, as if seeking to smash into the house and set it aflame. Dresses that hung unattended in closets burst into flame. A mattress began burning from its underside as a guest readied himself for bed.

The ghastly climax of the haunting phenomena occurred when Mrs. Shchapoff appeared to become a veritable pillar of fire in front of the horrified eyes of a houseguest and the miller. A crackling noise had come from beneath the floor, followed by a long, high-pitched wailing. A bluish spark seemed to jump up at Mrs. Shchapoff, and her thin dress was instantly swathed in flames. She cried out in terror and collapsed into unconsciousness.

The houseguest leaped to his feet and valiantly beat the flames out with his bare hands. The most curious thing about the incident was that the courageous guest suffered severe burns while Mrs. Shchapoff received not a single blister, even though her dress was nearly completely consumed by the flames.

> A psychic investigator named Alekseeff devised a series of knocks which he claimed allowed him to communicate with the entity that was haunting the country estate.

The Shchapoffs had had enough of their encounters with the dancing ghost. When the entity had contented itself with a nightly performance of the three-step, it had merely been a noisy nuisance. Now it had become a vicious terror, quite capable of dealing out fiery destruction. Mr. Shchapoff closed up his country place and made arrangements for a permanent move to the city of Iletski.

The phenomena ceased at once after the Shchapoffs had taken up residence in their home in town. Although Helena Shchapoff recovered the health that had been rapidly waning under the onslaughts of the ghost, eight years after their move, she died in childbirth.

The Orensburg haunting is an unusual case in many ways. Perhaps, as some have theorized, there actually was a curse levied on Mr. Shchapoff by a disgruntled servant of a neighboring miller. The projected hatred of such an individual may somehow have intensified what had begun as rather ordinary haunting phenomena (i.e. the eerie face at the window, the imitation of the cook's dancing, the raps on the walls) and transformed them into a force of malicious evil.

EERIE FOOTSTEPS IN THE ATTIC

The Personal Experience of Karen

The townhouse that Karen and her husband bought in July 1992, was only eleven years old and in good condition. Shortly after they moved in, she began hearing someone walking in the upstairs hallway. At first she thought it was her son sneaking out of bed—and sometimes it was. But other times when she went to investigate, he was in bed, fast asleep. Karen never said anything about the footsteps to her husband, assuming that the sounds were the result of the house settling or that she was imagining them.

"My husband is disabled, so he is home all day. Soon he began telling me that he kept hearing someone walking upstairs when nobody else was home but him. He said that he heard the sounds frequently, so I told him that I was also hearing things at night. Then our four-year-old son started telling us about the 'mice' that were in his room at night. I went into his room and laid down with him one night. I heard so many scratching noises on the floor and sounds like children running around the room that I scooped him up and got out of there. I put him in bed with us, and then we heard the walking sounds in the hallway.

"The next night, while my husband and I were in bed, we heard someone walking in our bedroom. The sounds started on my side of the bed, moved around the bed, then went out of the room, down the hallway and down the stairs.

Karen clearly heard footsteps up in her family home attic, but when she investigated she saw no one there.

"One night, my son came running out of his room into our bedroom, wide-eyed and out of breath, and said that there was a big dog in his room—and he wouldn't go back in there. He was awake until almost dawn before he fell asleep again.

"In the first month after we moved into the townhouse, we went through at least a hundred light bulbs. We couldn't keep them burning. The ceiling fixtures and the lights in the bathroom, hallway, and kitchen blew out constantly—and within hours of each other.

"The previous owners had left several boxes and an old lead mirror in a plain wooden frame in the attic. I brought the mirror down from the attic and decided to hang at the end of the hallway, opposite our son's bedroom door. There weren't any noises until after I hung it. And most of the noises were in that hallway or in our bedrooms off of that hallway. My mother told me to get rid of the mirror, and the noises stopped after I carried it out and set it with the trash."

GHOSTLY RAPPINGS IN A MOBILE HOME

The Personal Experience of Earl

The following account came from a man we'll call Earl, who said that the eerie events that occurred within the thin metal walls of his family's trailer home when he was a child had affected his life forever.

Prior to his parents' divorce, Earl stated, the shower in the mobile home would turn itself on.

"My father always blamed it on my two brothers or me," he stated, "but we knew we were innocent. After the divorce, Father no longer wanted to sleep in the bedroom that he had shared with our mother, so he began sleeping on the couch.

"One night while he was sleeping, there came a loud rapping at our front door. Angrily he went to answer it, but there was nobody in sight."

About that same time, Earl wrote in his account of the haunting, the three boys and their father would wake up during the night dripping sweat. "Father would discover the furnace had been turned up full blast. Since it wasn't winter, no one would have gone near the furnace."

Earl said that on many nights he would see the door to his older brother's room open by itself. "I would hear footsteps walk down the hall, enter the bathroom, flush the toilet, then walk into the room I shared with my younger brother," he said. "I would sit up in my bed, unable to sleep because I could feel a dark presence as the invisible spirit paced through our room. As a child, this experience intensified my fear of engulfing darkness."

One night as Earl and his family sat watching television in the living room, the hall light began to flicker on and off. "Father asked one of my brothers to turn it off," Earl said. "As soon as he would turn it

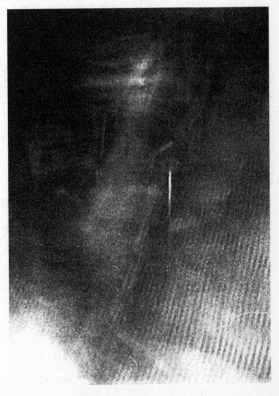

Investigator Terry Gambill took several pictures in a home that had been suffering from paranormal activity. While the majority of photographs he took turned out completely normal, he could not explain this particular frame, in which an entity is clearly visible.

off, it would turn itself back on. My brother turned it off once more before he came back into the living room. Just as he sat down, the light came on again and violently flickered off and on, as if in spite."

The family didn't want to move, so Earl said that his father brought a minister into the trailer and "to pray the spirit away" from their home. "A local preacher, Bible in hand, went into the middle bedroom where we all felt the spirit most often," Earl said. "While my brothers and I stayed in the kitchen to watch over a pot of pasta for the night's supper, we saw the dark shadow of a child form between the kitchen and the hallway. Father said that when the preacher walked into the bedroom with the Bible and began to pray, the entire room filled up with some kind of fog. The preacher thought the spirit left when the fog drifted out of the room."

Later that night, the family found out that it wasn't so easy to get the haunting spirit to leave. "There was such a pounding on the outside of the trailer that we ran outside to see whatever could be the source of the racket," Earl said. "Whatever it was, it could not be seen, and the pounding just kept hammering away, circling and circling the trailer until it finally quieted down."

After spending over a year with this restless spirit, the family gave up and finally moved out. "Later, we found out from a friend that the trailer burned down after we left," Earl said in conclusion. "Almost twelve years later, we drove through the trailer park and discovered that our old lot was still vacant. The story had spread about the ghost that had haunted our home, and no one had ever wanted to set their trailer down on that spot."

⊸⊸⊸ıııı⅏ıⅉıⅉıⅉⅉⅉ⊸

GHOSTS IN RIVERHEAD, NEW YORK
Personal Experiences of Lee Moorhead

Since the early 1970s, Lee Moorhead has been known as The Psychic of the Hamptons. (See her website www.stargaze.com for more information about her work.) In the following stories, Ms. Moorhead shares some of her experiences in the region of Riverhead, New York.

"About fifteen years ago, two ladies who owned the huge mansion on Long Island's northern coast (sometimes called the Gold Coast) invited me to dinner on my birthday. I barely knew them, but they knew of me and were acquainted with the two friends who accompanied me. After cocktails and light chatter, we went into the dining room to have dinner, and my seat near the end of the table was facing the entryway.

"During the conversation, I happened to look toward the entry and saw an elderly lady dressed in a black coat and hat and carrying a large bag. I assumed it was either the housekeeper on her way out or possibly someone they had hired to cook the dinner, so I interrupted the conversation to tell one of my hostesses that the lady was waiting to see them. One of the women asked, 'What lady?'

I said, 'The lady in the hall. She looks like she is ready to leave.'

"They told me that there was no one else in the house, and when I looked again, the lady was gone. They did tell me that they had learned that the house was haunted, but they had never known for certain.

Later in the evening, they took me to the west wing. When I was taken into one of the rooms, I found it very cold, and I told them that a man had committed suicide in that room. Furthermore, I said that his spirit was still there, and the room would never warm up. I suggested they get holy water and sprinkle it in that room.

"They learned a few months later that a man had shot himself in the house, but the persons to whom they had spoken had no idea which room he was in at the time.

"Before I purchased a home in Riverhead, I rented a big old house in Aquebogue on the north shore of Long Island and gave my middle daughter what seemed like a very nice room upstairs. She would come downstairs crying every night that the lady in the white gown kept chasing her out of the room.

"I learned from the owner's grandsons that their grandmother, who was not totally sane, had lived in that room and never came downstairs. Her meals were brought up to her when she became old, and she ended up dying there in that house. I changed that room into the playroom and made a bedroom for my daughter out of the former playroom.

"I am very aware of spirit, and I know there is one who visits me in the home I bought this past April. Once in a while there is a knock on my bedroom door even though no one is here at home, and a few times the water turns on in the tub until I get up to walk in there—then it turns off. However, the water is there—and the faucet is wet."

⌐⟋⟍⌐

THE FACE ON THE TINTYPE

The Personal Experience of Richard Aiello

The old barn on our property was built in June 1863, and it is still intact and solid as a battleship. We had been installing some four-by-four posts in the barn to build stalls for our two Belgian mules. Now the holes that we dug for these posts had to be deep, because the mules the stalls would contain are big and powerful. At the depth of about three feet, I spotted something shiny in one of the holes. All three of us working in the barn saw the object fall out of the posthole digger when it dumped the dirt. I picked it up and looked at it in amazement. It was an old tintype portrait of a bearded man.

When I sent an image of the tintype plate to Eastman Kodak for analysis, they said that judging by the color of the picture and the clothing style of the subject, the portrait would be dated around 1845–1860. Amazingly, the tintype had been under the earth for more than one hundred and forty years and the frame had not rusted away nor had the image disintegrated.

But here is the kicker: When we first moved into this house, we often saw the image of a man looking in our large (four-foot by eight-foot) window. We still saw it when we had the lights on bright and the room was well lit. The image was so detailed that sometimes I thought I was seeing my own reflection.

The image on that old tintype is the same man that we would see looking in at us. And here is another eerie thing to contemplate: When we first unearthed the old tintype, its emulsion covering was clear. Now it has started to fog over and over the man's left shoulder there is another image superimposed on the picture. You can see the glint in its eye and the mustache, too. And it appears that other images are beginning to form. Look for yourself.

The tintype found by Richard Aiello. Analysis showed that the portrait was taken c. 1845–1860.

From the Files of Ghost Hunter

By Richard Senate

Richard Leonard Senate has investigated well over two hundred haunted houses, mostly in the western states. Senate holds a degree in history from California State University at Long Beach and currently works as the historian for the city of Ventura, a position he has held for the past fifteen years.

It was during the summer of 1972 that Senate encountered a ghostly image of a monk while he was working as part of an archeological dig at the old Spanish Mission San Antonio de Padua (near King City, California). Because he had to begin his research with little training in ghost hunting, Senate set up his first investigations along the lines of an archaeological dig. In his opinion, such a model has proved successful over the years, because the same systems used to unravel the mystery of an ancient culture can be used to unravel the reasons why ghosts haunt a place.

Senate believes that the main focus of any psychic investigator is to collect and save data on paranormal events and then attempt to organize the information into a theory as to why a place is haunted (if it really is) and to name the identity of the ghost.

He openly admits that he doesn't know the exact nature of ghosts. "I still don't know what they are after all these years," he says. "But, I know that something beyond our present knowledge is going on. Too many people have seen too many things over too many decades. They cannot all have been

Paranormal investigator Richard Senate.

drunk or crazy. I have seen ghosts, and there is a great deal of truth to the old saying—seeing is believing. I also know that no two haunted houses are alike."

Senate is the author of eight published books on the paranormal. His most recent are *The Ghost Stalker's Guide to Haunted California*, *The Ghosts of the Ojai Valley*, *The Haunted Southland*, and *Ghosts of the Haunted Coast*. In 1995, he became the first ghost hunter on the Internet with the website www.ghost-stalker.com.

"I believe the study of ghosts is currently in its infancy," Senate said. "We are at the same level as the study of electricity was in the time of Ben Franklin. I sometimes feel like I am out there in the storm with my kite and my key. Sure, I might get knocked on my butt, but I will find answers! Do I get scared sometimes? You would be a fool if you didn't. We are dealing with the unknown—adventures in a new country. Psychic research is the greatest exploration of them all!"

A Ghost Hunt with Richard Senate at a Most Haunted House

The sun was setting when we drove up to a house in the Oxnard area of California. *Strange*, I thought, *it doesn't look haunted.*

But then, as I reflected, the worst ones never do.

Debbie Christenson Senate was with me on this investigation, and I watched her closely, knowing that with her psychic gifts, she might pick up some impressions of the house even as we rolled to a stop in the wide driveway. She was silent, but a look of concentration was fixed on her face, and her eyes were glued to the window on the second floor. I felt certain that she would begin receiving some feelings regarding the place, because this house was perhaps the most active I had investigated in the last five years.

I had received the call two weeks before. The family was terrorized by pounding footsteps in the night, moving shadows, and bizarre happenings, such as the curtains billowing out at odd times even with the windows closed.

> They learned that a young man had taken his own life in the house a decade ago....

One night the poundings in the house and the boot-like footfalls grew so menacing that the wife believed that the house was being invaded and called the police. The law enforcement officers arrived quickly to search the premises, but even with their dogs to sniff out any intruders, they found no one. The police then informed the residents that the house was haunted. The family had guessed as much, and after the police confirmed their suspicions, they began to collect information about the history of the building.

They learned that a young man had taken his own life in the house a decade ago and that the present home had been built on the site where a large farmhouse had burned to the ground, taking six lives.

The phenomena were persistent enough for me to organize an investigation.

As always, Debbie was told as little as possible about the site. We do not wish prior information to taint her psychic impressions. She refused even to know the address or anything about the case until we were about to leave for the house. We picked up two other researchers, who, in prior investigations, had managed to record strange, unaccountable, voices on tape recorders. I hoped that they might find some useful EVP (electronic voice phenomena) in our walk through the house. I also brought a camera along to document the ghost hunt.

As we drove up to the house, the family came out to greet us and ushered us into the large, tastefully furnished home. I had warned them not to say anything about the psychic events in the house until Debbie had a chance to look the place over. A sudden chill raced though her and she crossed into a hallway.

"There is something here," she said, looking down toward the door and bathroom off the hall.

I could feel a coldness creeping over my legs. Was it just an overactive imagination or were the forces in the house reaching out to us?

The others in the team were feeling it, too—that cold that comes from no place, yet everywhere. Debbie, now shaken, moved to the bathroom. "This is where he is," she said. "There is a young man, a boy, and a woman."

Debbie didn't know that the hallway was the center of the disturbances in the house and that a witness had seen a roll of toilet paper move by itself in that room. The wife had also reported the feeling of being watched while she showered in that room. Such feelings of being observed by an unseen presence had continued up the stairs and even to the master bedroom—where a shadowy arm had materialized, only to vanish.

Debbie found other locations in the large home that seemed haunted; then we retired into the front room, the living room, to discuss the events in the house and our findings. Almost every night the doors in the house would rattle violently, and there was running, as if by children, besides the footsteps that seemed to be made by a large man wearing heavy work boots.

Debbie felt that the haunting events were somehow linked to the house that had burned before the present home had been built. The rattling doors and footsteps were a reenactment of the last terrible moments when the house had caught fire, trapping the hapless residents inside. The fear and panic, Debbie believed, had left a psychic scar upon the location that had somehow been regenerated by the new family with young children.

> [T]he psychic events began to slow down and to occur less and less frequently—almost as if the spirits had become aware that it was their time to move on.

We all agreed that the house was indeed haunted and that there were prescribed things to do. One was to log the times when the events took place. It was determined that many of the events seemed to take place in the wee hours of the morning, and Debbie felt this could be explained by the fact that the previous house had caught fire in the early morning.

For a short time, our visit to the house seemed to make things worse for the family, but the psychic events began to slow down and to occur less and less frequently—almost as if the spirits had become aware that it was their time to move on. When we listened to the tape recordings, a number of odd manifestations were discovered. There were gaps in the tape, odd clicks, and a voice, the voice of a woman, who said, in a whispered tone, "I've got mine."

The meaning of these words remains unknown. The house is a mysterious place and events continue—but the worst appears to be over.

<hr />

HAUNTINGS FROM THE FILES OF STEPHEN WAGNER

Stephen Wagner has been the editor of the website About.com Guide to Paranormal Phenomena since 1998 (http://paranormal.about.com). Wagner writes a feature article for the site each week. He also edits the paranormal news and reviews readers' true stories and photographs. "My view on ghosts and hauntings, specifically, is that there is overwhelming evidence that the phenomena are quite real," Wagner said. "What they are exactly and how and why they manifest in our reality is, of course, the mystery."

Here are three interesting ghost stories culled from the many that Wagner has received from people who visit his website:

A Little Peeking Ghost

The Personal Experience of Marge

When she was about sixteen, Marge and her two sisters shared a small apartment upstairs in their parents' home. The three girls slept in the bedroom that connected to the living room via a doorway with no door. Her sister Evelyne slept on the top of a bunk with their eight-year-old sister on the bottom. On this particular night, Marge was laying in bed on her right side, facing the doorway, having a conversation with Evelyne, who was in Marge's line of sight.

"We were not talking scary stories or anything like that—just boys, school, and so forth. As we were speaking, I saw a cloud form past the foot of her bunk, gathering like a white mist. Evelyne's bunk had a footboard that came up about eighteen inches, so it obstructed her view, but I could see the cloud take shape like a small person. It then put its hands on the top edge of the footboard and pulled itself up by its hands, peeking at my sister for a moment, then lowering itself, holding on, and peeking again at Evelyne from the side of the footboard. Then it was gone.

"I had stopped talking and just watched the thing for about a minute.
"Evelyne asked, 'Marge, did you just see something?'
I answered that I had and asked what she had seen.
'I thought I saw something looking at me,' she said. 'Something small.'

"I asked Evelyne if it had scared her. She answered, no, because it seemed like a young person, maybe a child. I agreed and that was that. The apartment always seemed haunted, and there were many instances of odd happenings, but this one I remember clearly."

An Encounter with a Hugging Ghost

The Personal Experience of Darnell

Darnell and her husband ran a small construction business and had been contracted to do a job in an older section of a nearby town. They had been hired to gut the inside of a home that was built in the early part of the 1900s, and hang new drywall, put in new flooring, paint, and so forth.

"One day I was in the kitchen, nailing down the plywood flooring. My children were with me and were busy playing in the yard by the back door and inside on the first floor—all of them nearby so I knew what they were up to. I was working at a steady pace, on my hands and knees working my way backward toward the stairs leading to the second floor off the back of the kitchen. I was tired and had stopped for a moment to catch my breath.

"I straightened up at the base of the stairs, still on my knees. I was suddenly hugged from behind by a small child. It was such a loving hug and gave me such a wonderful feeling that I turned around, expecting to see one of my children and planning to give a hug in return. There was no one there.

"I immediately got a cold, eerie feeling and jumped to my feet. I called out to the kids. They were in my pickup truck parked a few feet from the back door, coloring in their coloring books.

"I packed up my things and left. I told my husband what had happened and the reason that I did not finish my work. He was astonished. He then told me that in the 1930s a small boy had been playing with his brother who was emotionally disturbed, and had been accidentally pushed down the stairs and had died.

> I turned around, expecting to see one of my children and planning to give a hug in return. There was no one there.

"When we returned the next day, the owner accused us of going upstairs in the bedrooms and unrolling rolls of wallpaper and pulling down the window shades and generally making a mess. While we worked in the days that followed, we could hear feet running back and forth upstairs. Tools were missing, and the owner kept accusing us of going upstairs where their personal belongings were and messing them up. We never went upstairs at all. We were told not to. We did not invade their personal space.

"We finally left the job unfinished because of these strange happenings. I could not seem to stay in the kitchen. I would get gooseflesh and feel strange sensations of happiness, loneliness, and love."

Ghostly Bells and Boots in a Lumberjacks' Bunkhouse
The Personal Experience of Dennis M.

Dennis M. stated that his father was born in 1907 in Nova Scotia and had once worked in the woods as both a lumberjack and a cook. One night during the winter of 1935, just after the men had retired for the night, they were awakened by the sounds of a sleigh coming to the door.

"They heard the bells on the horse, the sleigh runners squeaking on the snow, and the driver holler, 'Whoa!' Of course everyone got up and rushed to the door to meet the visitor. However, there was no visitor, no sleigh marks, no hoof prints from the horses—nothing.

"The event that finally chased everyone out of the bunkhouse was when the ghost drove the sleigh up to the door, got off the sleigh, opened the door and walked in. Dad said that you could hear the boots walking across the floor, clip-clop, clip-clop. It horrified everyone. Lumberjacks began throwing their boots and whatever else at the ghost. Dad said he finally got a lantern lit—and just like before, there was no evidence of anyone or anything being there."

STRANGE ATTRACTION
By Bret Oldham, Halo Paranormal Investigations

The house sat up on a hill, and on stormy nights when the moon was full and the lightning did its evil dance around it, the house did have an eerie vibe to it. Most of the time, though, the two-story brick home looked rather unassuming. No different than any of the other houses sitting in subdivisions throughout suburban America.

When I moved into the house on the hill, everything seemed quite normal for the first few weeks. I had met my new neighbors who all were very pleasant and friendly folks. I had asked my neighbors some questions about the area and the neighborhood and had learned that there had been some settlers in the area back in the 1800s because of the proximity of a rather large creek that ran behind the homes on my street. The houses in the subdivision were less than ten years old and no one mentioned anything about any of them being haunted or experiencing any kind of paranormal activity. As a history buff, I thought it was cool that settlers had once been on the land and thought no more about it.

After a few weeks, a series of odd things began to take place in the house—all of which seemed to center around me. It started out with things that I tried to justify with logical reasoning.

A light would be on that wasn't supposed to be on. "Oh, I must have forgotten to turn off the light when I left that room," I would say, trying to find a rational explanation.

A door would close, and I would blame it on the air conditioner kicking on.

Things like that.

Then the activity increased substantially. I knew I could no longer dismiss the odd occurrences as I had done in the past. I started to see a trend.

Whenever anyone was around me, especially a female, there would be a paranormal occurrence.

Light bulbs would blow on a frequent basis when I was in a room with anyone. One time while standing in the kitchen talking to guests who were visiting, two baking pans came flying off the shelf and landed seven or eight feet away on the kitchen floor. Two of the people I was talking to were female and happened to be standing next to me. Another time I was sitting down eating a chocolate chip cookie and had a second one sitting on a small saucer in front of me. Everything was fine until my female friend came into the room. As soon as she sat down, the saucer with the cookie on it went flying off the side of the table as if someone had swiped it away with their hand or arm. I saw the connection. I knew that for some unknown reason there was a jealous ghost in the house. It wanted me all to itself! "Hey, don't do that!" I yelled. These incidents were getting more frequent. I knew I had to start to take control.

After a few weeks, a series of odd things began to take place in the house—all of which seemed to center around me.

A couple of days later I was alone in the house and I heard an upstairs door shut by itself. It was time to face the music. I went upstairs to check the door. The vibe had changed dramatically. The air felt thick. I could feel the hair on my arms standing up. I wasn't alone.

"Where are you?," I asked. "What do you want "?

I was standing in the upstairs hallway when I heard a loud thump coming from one of the dormer closets in a room at the end of the hall. Then it thumped two times in succession. I wondered if it wanted me to come into that room. Or was this its way of communicating?

The thumping started in an almost rhythmic pattern. Boom, boom, boom, boom....

I decided to go to it and started walking down the hall toward the room from which the sounds were originating. I only took three steps and the thumping abruptly stopped.

I stood there for a moment to see what was going to happen next. Nothing did, so I turned around and start back in the opposite direction. As soon as I started walking away the thumping started up again. Boom, boom, boom.... Every time I started to walk toward the sound, it would stop. If I would walk away it would start up again. This ghost was playing with me.

I took a deep breath and gathered my nerves. I was going to go open the dormer closet—thumping or not!

The room was silent as I entered. I jerked open the dormer closet. Nothing. I went to the next one and did the same. Nothing! It was gone. Whatever or whoever was in there was gone.

But not for long. It wasn't long after that that this restless spirit made it presence known again. This time it would show me who it was.

I was in bed one night. No one else was in the house. At least no one living. I was peacefully sleeping when something woke me up.

I heard shuffling noises in the hall outside my bedroom. My bedroom door was shut. I opened my eyes, but pretended to be asleep. I thought someone had broken into the house, and I was getting robbed. I thought it was best to pretend to be asleep until I could figure out what to do.

My heart started pounding. My mind was racing. I thought my life could be in danger if the intruders were armed.

> **B**oom, boom, boom.... Every time I started to walk toward the sound, it would stop.

Then my bedroom door slowly opened. I could hear someone, but I couldn't see them because I was facing the opposite direction. I closed my eyes and lay as still as I could.

I heard them walk across the room by the foot of my bed and then back again and then back and forth once again. This person seemed to be pacing. I was lying there wondering if they were trying to decide whether or not to kill me—and wishing I had not left my gun in the closet. "A lot of good it is doing me there, I thought.

I heard the pacing stop. Oh, my God! What now?

I wasn't going to just lie there and let someone do me in, but I knew I had to wait for the right time to make my move. I heard the footsteps walk to the side of the bed. "Wait, wait. Not yet," I told myself.

I had my back to the intruders, so I no idea when they were going to make their move.

Then I felt someone sit on the edge of the bed beside me! That was it! I wasn't waiting any longer. I opened my eyes and swung my left arm around to grab the person.

It all happened in a flash, but as I swung around I could see a woman sitting there with her back to me. She wore a long dress with a high, tight collar. She had what looked like red or auburn hair pulled back in a bun. She never turned her head to look at me. My arm went right through her.

The ghostly presence quickly dissipated! I almost fell out of bed from the momentum of my outstretched arm. I was both relieved and shocked. Relieved to know I wasn't getting robbed and shocked to finally see my visitor from the other side. Needless to say I didn't sleep much the rest of the night.

After that, the paranormal activity subsided, and I thought that was the last I would ever see of this mysterious ethereal stranger. I was wrong!

A few weeks later, a very similar manifestation occurred. This time it was almost dawn. Again I was awakened by movement in my bedroom. This time I suspected the redheaded stranger and not burglars. I opened my eyes and lay still.

I was facing the other direction this time, looking out toward the edge of my bed. I saw her. She was dressed the same as before. She was standing over me and, ever so slightly, I closed my eyes a bit so she would think I was still sleeping. She leaned over me and began to straighten and tighten the covers up around me.

Why was she doing this? I silently wondered. I thought about attempting to speak to her. I was curious. I wanted to know who she was, why she was there.

Then she sat down beside me again. I could feel the bed move as she did.

It then occurred to me that she may be trying to attach herself to me. This was getting to be too much! I opened my eyes and cried out with authority as I sat up in bed: "In the name of Jesus, God, and all things holy, I command you to leave me! Leave me now and never return! You are not welcome here."

The ghostly figure calmly stood up and turned toward me. She looked down at me and smiled as she disappeared. I will never forget her face. After seeing the way she looked at me, I felt an odd sense of regret for treating her so harshly. After all, she did appear to be concerned for my well being. That was the last I ever saw of her. Nothing else ever happened in that house.

I suppose in the end there was nothing else that I could have done. Many times I've wondered who she was. What was her attraction to me? Had she mistaken me for her long-lost husband or relative? Had she cared for someone who looked like me when she was in this world? Was she one of the settlers who had lived on the land around my house and perhaps died an untimely death?

So many questions and the answers can only be found through that thin veil that separates the world of the living and the world of the dead. Only there will I find the real reason for her strange attraction.

⋙ ⋘

JOIN ME IN THE CRAWL SPACE!

The Personal Experience of Anonymous from the files of The Ghost to Ghost website at http://www.ghosttoghost.com.

One day I was working with a friend in a brand new home in Ogden, Utah. We were doing the heating and air conditioning. My friend was checking the furnace and discovered it had a bad transformer, so he left to go get a new one.

While he was gone I continued installing the ductwork. I got an eerie feeling and looked over my shoulder and saw an old woman at the base of the stairs. I figured she was the homeowner. I said "hi" and asked her if she needed anything. She just shook her head "no" and smiled. I went about my business.

Then I felt the same eerie feeling. I looked over my shoulder and, there she was, about five feet from me. I got off my ladder and said, "Can I help you?"

She smiled and, once again, shook her head.

Just then I heard my partner pulling into the driveway. I turned to see where the woman was and she was already by the base of the stairs, about fifty feet away. I said, "Are you sure you don't need anything?"

She just looked at me and motioned with her finger for me to come with her. Of course, I said, "No way!"

Then I heard my friend enter the home on the first floor. The old woman again motioned for me to follow her. She was backing toward a crawl space just under the stairs.

I took my eyes off her for a second to try and figure out where my friend was and when I looked back, I saw the most horrifying old woman motioning to me with a bony, leathery finger. This time she spoke: "Get over here!"

I watched her disappear into the crawl space. That was it. I got out of there fast. Finally my friend joined me and I told him the story. He just laughed and told me to stay outside if it would make me feel better. And that's exactly what I did.

I did some research on that area and learned that most of the land had been used as a Native American tribal burial ground. To this day I haven't returned to that site!

━━∙∙∙━━

A Most Peculiar Barking Ghost

The Personal Experience of Patrick

In 1990, shortly after Debbie, her three-year-old daughter, and I moved into our apartment, strange things began to happen. There seemed to be something else in the place with us. All these years later, I'm still asking myself what it was.

Within the first week of moving in, I was awakened around five o'clock in the morning by what sounded for all the world like a small child barking like a dog. I sat up in bed. Debbie woke a few seconds later and listened to the sounds with me. It came from the hallway, so we assumed that her daughter had gotten up in the wee hours and was pretending to be a puppy—not all that unusual for a three-year-old.

I got up to put her back to bed, but as I opened the bedroom door, the sound moved down the hallway and into the living room. I followed, and it kept moving and barking at a distance of what I'd estimate was about six feet in front of me. As I got to the living room, the barking moved on into the next room, the kitchen.

I stood in the living room and tried to figure out what was happening. The lights from outside the building were spilling into the room, and it slowly occurred to me that if the baby had been playing, I would surely have seen her cross the room between the hall and the kitchen. I listened to the "puppy" bark in the next room, and a chill went down my spine. I now had no idea what I was dealing with. The barking faded within the next moment, and I backed down the hall, ducking into the little girl's room and, of course, found her sound asleep. I roused her and asked her if she'd been pretending to be a puppy. "No-o-o …" came the expected, groggy response.

> The drip-sound itself changed in pitch—and the thing actually played a tune.

I carried her back to our room and put her between us in the bed. I stayed awake until it was time to get up for work, making certain the "puppy" didn't return, but debating what I'd do if it did. We never heard it again.

A few months later, I was up in the middle of the night, using the bathroom. I was in total darkness. No windows in the room, no light, just darkness. Suddenly, from the area to my left, which would have been the bathtub, I heard something sharp and loud enough to make me jump. It was a voice, very clearly shouting, "belly ache!"

The voice was that of a child, but there was something rough, almost gruff, about it, as if the child in question was trying to "do" a voice. Of course, I flipped on the light. Nothing. Not that I was totally surprised.

Less dramatic incidents became frequent enough so that Deb and I began to half-joke about the apartment being haunted. Deb said that she had often seen the figure of a child moving up and down the hall past our bedroom door during the night. I remember her describing a little boy, enveloped in a soft, blue glow. She also admitted this could have been a series of waking dreams.

The last incident that I'll relate happened shortly before we moved out. Again, it was late at night. Our kitchen faucet leaked and dripped fairly noisily on occasion. I was lying in bed, listening to the drip. It had developed a steady rhythm, as drips will. Suddenly, the rhythm changed. The drip-sound itself changed in pitch—and the thing actually played a tune. Now, I could write this off as a dream, but at that point, after a few bars, Debbie had groaned in disbelief next to me and asked, "Was that Funeral March of the Marionettes [the theme music of the Alfred Hitchcock television series]?" "Yeah," I answered, nodding in the dark. "That's what I heard." We both sighed deeply and held each other close the rest of the night.

While none of these incidents may fall under the classification of "terrifying," they were certainly disturbing. I was glad that we moved when we did. Whatever was in that apartment seemed to have a consciousness. It seemed aware of us.

THE "STRANGER" IN THE APARTMENT BUILDING

By Tim R. Swartz

In the summer of 1999, I was doing some freelance work for an apartment complex in Indianapolis, Indiana. They had recently constructed a new swimming pool, and I was taking some advertising photos for them. The apartment manager was making some last-minute adjustments to the pool area, and I had my camera on a tripod ready to start shooting.

The pool was located behind the complex. From where I was standing, I could see the rear portions of two apartment buildings. A wide green space separated these buildings and a sidewalk led to the pool. From where I stood, I could clearly see most of the parking lot in front of these buildings.

As I adjusted my camera, my attention was drawn to a man walking slowly across the parking lot, heading toward the building to my right. He was no more than fifty feet away from me, so I could see him clearly in the bright, summer sun.

He looked to be in his early twenties, thin, and with dark hair. In each hand he carried a plastic grocery bag. His clothes were what really caught my attention. He was wearing a brightly colored, Hawaiian-style shirt, along with shorts that had vertical blue stripes. He also wore a large, floppy sunhat and bright red rain boots. His gait was slow and he walked with a noticeable limp as he went out of sight toward the front door of the apartment building.

I glanced down at my camera and looked back up to see the same man once again walking across the parking lot. It was as if I was watching a video that had been rewound and replayed. The young man repeated his trek across the lot toward the building. But it would have been impossible for him to run out of the building and back across the parking lot in the brief period of time that I had looked away.

The most frustrating thing about this incident was the fact that I had a camera on a tripod ready to go. But instead of taking a picture, I just stood there with my mouth open and did nothing.

The apartment manager walked up and asked me a question. In the moment it took me to look at her and then turn my head back toward the parking lot, the strange figure had disappeared.

The manager became concerned when I told her about the strange man going into the building. It turned out that building was empty and undergoing renovation. Security guards did a compete search, but no one was found inside.

A few months later, the manager called and told me that a former manager was certain that my description fit a mentally challenged man who had once lived in that building. She said that every day he would cut across the parking lot and walk to a local store. Sadly, this man had been injured by a car while coming back from the store and was placed in a long-term care facility.

[I]t would have been impossible for him to run out of the building and back across the parking lot in the brief period of time that I had looked away.

Unfortunately, I was never able to uncover any more information about where this person had been sent, or whether or not he was still alive. Like so many other cases, my encounter did not have a satisfying conclusion. Not only did I miss a perfect opportunity to take a photograph of this possible apparition, but I also failed to find any useful information about this person, or his ultimate fate.

LIVELY GHOSTS IN A WISCONSIN HOME

Brad Steiger's Investigation of a Haunted House.

In 1970, I was among a number of researchers who accompanied the well-known psychic-sensitive and spirit medium Irene Hughes to a very large home in Wisconsin that was afflicted by a wide range of haunting phenomena. From early reports, it seemed as though everything from dolls to dishes might instantly transform into ghostly guided missiles and pelt the occupants of the home, but never seriously injure anyone.

When we arrived on a Saturday in October, we were impressed at once by the size of the sprawling home. According to some sketchy information that we had been given, the mansion had once belonged to an old lumber baron who had a rather dark reputation.

Medium Irene Hughes.

We had only been on the premises for a few minutes and had just begun to interview the lady of the house when I excused myself to use the restroom. Interestingly enough, on the way to the bathroom I ran into an obvious cold spot—a center of ghostly energy that is always many degrees cooler than the temperature in the rest of the house—but the significance of that soon diminished in comparison with a subsequent development.

While I was in the restroom, I could clearly hear the sound of what I thought was a young girl playing with her doll. She was singing a kind of semi-tuneless little song, the kind of melodic chant that appears to be universal with children at play—especially, it seems, with little girls. From time to time, she would interrupt her humming sing-song to speak lovingly to her doll and then she would call rather loudly for her mother. Then, when there was no response from her mother, she would return to her playing and her singing.

At the time, my two daughters were quite young and I could easily fashion a mental image of a little girl dressing her doll, combing its hair, creating her own world of imagination. I could clearly determine that the sound was coming from upstairs, almost directly above me.

When I rejoined the group, I excused myself for interrupting the conversation in progress, announced with some excitement that I had found a cold spot, then, I asked the homeowner how many children there were in the house at that time.

She replied that she had three children: a son in his late teens, who was often too frightened to come home and sometimes stayed with a friend; a teenage daughter in high school; and a six-year-old girl, her daughter by her second, and present, husband.

When I asked to meet any children who might be home on that Saturday afternoon, the woman said that she had sent her two daughters over to a friend's home. "I thought that you would rather work without the interruption or the presence of children," she said.

Irene Hughes told her she had done the right thing, that our investigation could proceed more smoothly without the presence of the children.

By now I was really puzzled. If our hostess had thoughtfully sent her children to a friend's home, who was the little girl I heard playing upstairs?

The woman blanched slightly and shifted uneasily in her chair after I had asked this question.

"My little girl is at a friend's house," she said firmly.

"Then you'd better go upstairs and have a chat with her," I said. "She has apparently returned home. I clearly heard her in a room upstairs."

"Up-upstairs?" the woman echoed. Her hand clasped the arm of a friend she had asked to be present. "You heard a little girl upstairs?"

I was by now becoming quite aware that this was a family who had a great deal of difficulty with their upstairs and that the woman sincerely believed her daughter to be at a friend's home. But I couldn't help being persistent because I had heard so very clearly the sounds of a little girl's sing-song voice. It was hard to believe that I had heard anything out of the ordinary. Surely nothing supernatural.

"A little girl I assume to be your daughter is upstairs," I said. "I heard her playing and singing."

"My little girl could … could not be upstairs," the woman answered softly. It was obvious that she was struggling to maintain control of her fear, trying not to permit her dread of the unknown to warp the sound of her voice. "She is afraid to go upstairs alone. She would never go upstairs. Upstairs is where…."

She seemed unable to complete her sentence and her trembling hands brought a coffee cup to her lips.

"Upstairs is where most of the weird things happen in this house," her friend said, taking up the thread of the statement. "About the little girl. Did you hear it calling for its mother?"

I acknowledged that I had. From time to time, she would pause in her play and call for her mother.

The woman continued to explain. "My friend and her husband often wake up in the middle of the night or in the morning and hear a little girl calling for her mother. But whenever they check on their kids, they find them all sound asleep."

Although the story was eerie and related in the most convincing manner, I still could not be persuaded that there wasn't an actual, physical, real-life little girl somewhere in the home until I carried out my own exploration of the upstairs, the attic, the basement, and the yard. Once I had thoroughly searched the house, I conceded as gracefully as I could that our hostess was indeed telling the truth—her little daughter was nowhere on the premises. If I truly heard what I believe I heard in that Wisconsin home, then it was either the sound of some lost and confused spirit-child, eternally singing and occasionally calling for its mother, or some ethereal kind of phonograph record, endlessly reproducing the sounds of a little girl who had once lived in that house.

However one might theorize about a haunting, the manifestations in that home constituted a persistent living nightmare for its occupants. The woman appeared to be suffering a type of psychic battle fatigue from her constant confrontation with the paranormal incidents in her home, and she would not walk in any area of the house other than the kitchen and the living room without someone at her side.

We did a careful search of the entire home. We explored the basement, where the homeowner had so often heard heavy footsteps, thudding, and scraping. We visited each of the upstairs rooms and discovered two additional cold spots. ventured up to the attic because the family had so often heard the sound of heavy objects being dragged across the dusty floor of that space. As we opened the door, we caught sight of a wispy something retreating to a darkened corner of the cluttered storage area. However, none of our investigating party could swear with certainty that what we had seen was a ghost or an ectoplasmic spirit, and not simply a floating bit of cobweb reflecting the sunlight.

Irene Hughes offered many psychic impressions as we walked from room to room. The woman of the house gave immediate feedback to the medium, and in nearly all cases, Mrs. Hughes had made correct "hits."

As we walked through the house, an occasional object would fly at us without any apparent reason for levitation. These were small objects, mostly children's toys: an alphabet block, a plastic dish, a little doll that had been made from a stocking, etc.

However, this particular haunting turned out to be even more complex than we had anticipated. We began to realize that there might be factors working within the homeowner's own psyche that may have been feeding the phenomena psychically.

The teenage daughter of the family would often find her room in disarray when she returned home from school, and she noted that this would occur most often after a morning when she had taken careful pains to straighten her room before leaving home. On the other hand, if she left her room a mess, she would find that some invisible helping hands had set the bedroom in order—putting the last curler and comb in its proper place.

The phenomena seemed to be centered in the second floor and the attic, and the family reported that they often heard the sounds of something heavy being dragged across the floor. Although the house was quite large, the family used very little of the space. The father, mother and three children, aged nineteen to six, slept in two rooms downstairs. No one slept upstairs.

On occasion, the mother told us, their teenage daughter would adamantly announce that she was not going to be driven from her room, and she would sleep alone upstairs for a stretch of two or three weeks. Then she would hear the sound of mumbled half-words close to her ears and the feel invisible fingers stroking her cheeks and hair, and she would flee back downstairs to join the rest of the family in the relative quiet of the two back bedrooms on the first floor.

The other center of the haunting appeared to be located in the basement, with knocking, thumping, and the sound of footsteps running down the stairs and shuffling across the floor.

Certainly the most dramatic incident was the materialization of four skeletons in one of the upstairs bedrooms. After appearing in startling blood-red color, the skeletal figures would slowly morph into what appeared to be solid, three-dimensional representations of a man, two women, and a little girl. Each of the images appeared in period dress of the 1890s.

Once they had fully materialized, the figures would engage in a bizarre ethereal drama. As the ghost of a lovely, long-haired blonde girl sat playing idly with her dolls, the man would strangle one of the women while the other stood by with a pleased expression of immense satisfaction.

> [S]he would hear the sound of mumbled half-words close to her ears and the feel invisible fingers stroking her cheeks and hair....

Over the years, prior inhabitants of the house and other individuals who had witnessed the grim spirit portrayal had assumed that the haunting might very well have been set into motion by a tragic and deadly triangle. The ghastly reenactment seemed to say that at some time in the past the man of the house had strangled his wife to please his mistress.

Some cursory historical research and an examination of local folklore revealed a scandal regarding previous owners of this home: the lady of the house had disappeared without a trace and her husband had remarried after an extremely brief period of grieving. Local legend had it that the wife had been murdered by her husband and her body dumped in the nearby Mississippi River so that he might marry his mistress.

Although we were denied the dramatic reenactment during our visit to the home, the present occupants claimed to have witnessed the horrid pageant play in the master bedroom immediately after they had moved into the mansion. Since that awful night, they had relocated their sleeping quarters downstairs.

The afternoon and evening of our first visit to the home, no immediate exorcism was accomplished, but after an in-depth counseling session between the family and Mrs. Hughes and a number of return visits to the place, the psychic storm that had swirled throughout the household finally diminished. Later, however, we learned that the family eventually decided to relinquish the house to its very lively ghost inhabitants. The last time that I checked on the mansion in 1976, it remained unoccupied.

HOW WE RID OUR HOME OF GHOSTS

The Personal Experience of Frank Joseph, author of Edgar Cayce's Atlantis & Lemuria *and* The Destruction of Atlantis.

In spring 2000, my wife, Laura, and I moved with our kitty Sally into a rented house overlooking the Wisconsin side of the Mississippi River. It was a small place, just the right size for the three of us, and out in the country, about a two hour drive from Minneapolis-St. Paul.

Not even our landlord could determine the age of the original structure. A local man told us he saw it often as a boy, in the early 1950s, whenever he canoed past our neck of the river. In the mid–1990s, the house was purchased by a retired couple from Arizona. They worked hard turning it into a sweet summer home, planting evergreen trees and a variety of flowers nearby. The exterior was remodeled in attractive redwood siding, while a new room with floor-to-ceiling glass panels provided a 180-degree view of the Mississippi.

But winters in this part of the world can be brutal. Before the century was up, the pair returned to the milder climate of Arizona. Their dream vacation home was sold to a realtor, who put it up for rent. We moved in just seven months after our wedding, and could not believe our good fortune in finding such a wonderful little place.

That first summer, I was walking with Sally in the backyard, when a van pulled up into the driveway. An overweight man in his late sixties hauled his six-foot-plus frame out from the driver's side, while a cheerful little blond lady of approximately the same age emerged from the passenger's door. The big man did not look entirely pleased to see me, and pointedly asked what I was doing here.

After I explained that I was a renter, he forced a gruff smile, while introducing himself and his wife as owners in the previous decade. His wife was obviously a genuinely nice lady and smiled to see that the perennials that she had planted so many years before were still in bloom.

I had encountered her husband's type before. He led me on a private tour of the house he rebuilt, grandly boasting of this improvement or that addition, emphasizing the labor and expense that everything had demanded of him. I dutifully expressed appreciation at polite intervals. There was less sentimentality than ego in his presentation. He was obviously proud of having fixed up the old place, but I also sensed something akin to regret in his voice and choice of words. Perhaps Arizona wasn't all it was cracked up to be. When he learned the amount of money we were paying (an impertinent question, in any case), he expressed dismay, and promised to inform our landlord that we were being charged far too little each month for the privilege of staying at "his" house. I was glad when this oversized trouble-maker climbed back into his van and disappeared in the direction of the American Southwest before carrying out his threat. I hoped never to see him again.

My hope came true. Two years thereafter I learned from someone in town who had known him during the brief period of his residence here that he had died recently in Arizona. In any case, I had by that time pretty well put him out of my thoughts.

About the same time, however, a number of peculiar incidents at home began to convince Laura and me that we were being visited by a discarnate entity. There had been no previous indication that we were being haunted. But now we caught fleeting glimpses of a fast-moving shadow from time to time when we least expected to see such a thing. We did not mention these encounters to each other at first, dismissing them as some kind of trivial optical illusion.

It was only after the smells began that we spoke openly of the shadow. At first rarely, then more frequently, Laura and I might be at other ends of the house when we would be overtaken by a very pleasant scent. To me, it smelled like delicate perfume. Laura thought it was closer to a man's cologne.

Sometimes we encountered the scent together, but in every instance it came and drifted away after only a few minutes. "If we have to be haunted," Laura said, "it might as well be by a pleasant ghost." Although the perfume or whatever was invariably associated with a feeling of presence, neither of us were ever afraid.

After about a month of such unpredictable visits, however, the quality of these redolent visitations began to deteriorate. I was working at my computer in the "river room," three rooms away from Laura, who was sitting up in bed reading when an unspeakably foul odor surrounded me. The stench was comparable to the most nauseating animal excrement one might encounter. It startled me, but I could not imagine its source. Then, almost as quickly as it manifested itself, the poisonous vapors were gone.

Until then, Laura had been unaware of any foul stink in our home, but over the next few days and weeks, she, too, was sometimes overtaken by the repulsive smell of fecal matter which seemed to come and go on a nonexistent breeze. Interestingly, the stench never pervaded the whole house, nor even an entire room, but always confined itself to our immediate vicinity.

Once, when Laura was outside tending the flowers growing under our front windows, she was suddenly enveloped in an invisible puff of strong cigar smoke. This incident confirmed our suspicions that we were being haunted by the recently deceased former owner, who had been a confirmed cigar-smoker. Apparently, he was still annoyed that we were living in the house to which he had been so attached in life, and he wanted to stink us out.

> **T**his is our house! We're here now, and you can't stay! No dead people allowed!

To fumigate our house of this unwanted bore, we tried several suggested de-haunting methods—all very nicey-nice appeals to his higher self to "see the light," while expressing understanding for his sense of loss, and so forth—smudging all the corners with burning sage and lighting candles for the departed. The evil smells continued unabated. In fact, things began to escalate.

One night, while trying to fall asleep, I sensed a large, dark presence in the bedroom. It glided over to me and seemed to hover just over my head, and I received a telepathic command: "I want to know your thoughts!"

At this point in our ghostly relationship, I was more annoyed than frightened, and I told our redolent houseguest: "You can do whatever you want. I'm going to sleep." With that, the disappointed shadow-man vanished. But only temporarily.

Both Laura and I experienced horrific nightmares—psycho-dramas that seemed to have nothing to do with our identity, as though they had been injected into our vulnerable subconscious minds. Still, we continued our feel-good New Age remedies—all without effect. Instead, we now began to hear the sounds of terrific crashes, as though something huge had fallen over somewhere in the house, causing terrible damage. Once I thought the water heater had exploded. Every time, upon investigation, nothing was found amiss.

After the good part of a year, our patience had run out. One evening, while sitting down to dinner, the stench abruptly covered us like a putrescent cloud. We sprang to our feet, and as if with one voice, we shouted in the direction of the stink: "Get out of here! You're not welcome here! You don't live here—or anywhere—anymore! This is our house! We're here now, and you can't stay! No dead people allowed! Out, out, out! We don't care where you go, but you're not staying here! No free-loaders allowed! Get it straight: You're dead! You're dead! You're dead! Get out and never come back!"

Since then, ours is the sweetest-smelling little home you could ever know.

⟨⟩

STEP-BY-STEP GUIDE
TO INVESTIGATING GHOSTS AND HAUNTING PHENOMENA

Dale Kaczmarek, President of the Ghost Research Society, Oak Lawn, Illinois (http://www.ghostresearch.org),has been actively investigating haunting and paranormal phenomena since 1975. He has conducted on-site investigations of ghost lights, haunted houses, cemeteries, Native American burial grounds, murder sites, churches, and sacred sites. He appears regularly on numerous radio and television programs, and information about his research has been featured in more than twenty-five books. Kaczmarek is the editor of *Ghost Trackers Newsletter* and the author of *Windy City Ghosts*, *Windy City Ghosts 2*, *A Field Guide to Spirit Photography*, *Glossary of Occult Terms*, *The Greater Chicagoland and Northwest Indiana Psychic Directory*, and many other books.

Through the research, study, and investigation that he has completed and through continuing analysis of those investigations, Kaczmarek hopes to prove the existence of ghosts and life after death. "Whether I am investigating ghosts, hauntings, poltergeists or any other form of the paranormal or supernatural, I always will follow the same guidelines and procedures to lead me to the end result or conclusion of an investigation," Kaczmarek said.

Listed below are the steps to be followed in the investigation of ghosts and haunting phenomena. They have been listed in the only logical order in which Dale Kaczmarek believes they can be arranged. Using these methods, he has had a great amount of success, and he recommends that all investigators use these or similar steps:

1. When a case or person is called to my attention, the first step is to interview that person over the telephone and try to get all the relevant information concerning the case. We use a regular form that is filled out, and no questions are asked of the individual which might lead them to stretch the story out of proportion. Only general questions are asked at the conclusion of the telephone conversation or those questions which are meant to clarify certain information already given.

2. Once that information is compiled, I personally sit down with professional psychics or clairvoyants with whom I frequently work to go over the information and the telephone interview bit by bit to try to make some sort of determination of what might be going on prior to our arrival on the scene. This is how we are able to screen our cases, and such a procedure also gives the psychic that I have chosen the opportunity to ask questions of

his/her own which I later pose to the client. We are careful not to form any conclusions at this point, but we do make additional notes about areas of the case that we want to keep in focus.

3. The next step is to call the client and tell him/her what we feel may be going on and to set up a time when we might visit the house. I then tell the client to keep a diary of any strange or unusual events which may happen before our arrival date. It is important for the following data to be included in that diary: Date, time, which room, type of event, who was present or witness to the phenomena, the duration of the event, and a description of the event with as much detail as they can remember.

4. One of things that we would be looking for in the above-mentioned diary are patterns that might begin to form. Over the years, we have discovered that most hauntings do have some kind of pattern or string of events.

Prior to arriving at the location, I pack the necessary equipment which I feel is instrumental in solving the mystery of the event. This might include, but not be limited to, 35MM SLR cameras on tripods with cable releases. These cameras would be loaded with two different kinds of film: one would have black-and-white infrared film pushed to 400 ASA; other would have black-and-white high-speed print film to be used as a control film. If possible, simultaneous pictures are taken and later compared for possible anomalies. Other equipment includes portable voice-activated tape recorders, video cameras, cathode-ray magnetometers, spectrographs, microwave detection devices, negative ion detectors, infrared viewing devices, gauss meters, and Geiger counters, as well as Instamatic SX-70 cameras.

5. Upon our arrival at the location, we first check the diary our client has been keeping and make further entries into the casebook. Then we take a slow walk around the location with the psychic or clairvoyant and with various forms of electronic equipment to see exactly what can be picked up. Pictures are taken randomly or at places where the psychic designates as advantageous. Photographs are taken with both cameras, and the tape recorder is constantly going, recording the psychic's impressions and/or feelings.

6. If any spirit or entity is contacted through the psychic, either telepathically or clairvoyantly, communication is attempted in an effort to determine why the spirit remains earthbound. The spirit is then convinced to move on of its own accord or with the help of the psychic. Since most spirits do not realize that

they have passed over, that's usually all that is required to get the spirit to leave. We do not employ the use of Ouija boards, automatic writing, séances, or exorcisms since we feel that these are almost always unnecessary and are extremely dangerous if not done properly.

7. After the film arrives from the laboratory, it is compared side by side with the infrared film. Many times strange images are seen, including strange shadows, anomalous lights, energy balls or streaks—and even faces, forms, and figures. If it is a natural image, then it should show up on both films. If, however, the image only appears on the infrared film, we can assume that it is a supernatural event and invisible to the naked eye. Infrared film is sensitive to a narrow band between 700 to 1200 nanometers (one nanometer = one billionth of a meter).

8. Besides the scientific and psychic investigations, additional research is done on the house and area in which it is built to determine the past history in general and various specifics: details about the location, the former owners, and any previous unusual or traumatic events or deaths. In this way an overall view can be put together, and a profile can be drawn up and documented. We do not normally charge for the investigation, however certain travel charges and cost of film and development are usually requested to help defray costs and to keep this valuable service going.

9. Additional follow-up calls and/or visits are made if necessary to assure maximum efficiency and eventual resolution of the problem. While most events can be alleviated within a weekend, some hauntings have been known to go on for years. We absolutely guarantee the anonymity and confidentiality of all of our clients. The only people allowed to release such information are the clients themselves.

SOME THOUGHTFUL OBSERVATIONS ABOUT "GHOST HUNTING"

By Tim R. Swartz

Hunting for ghosts has become popular … very popular. It seems as if every cable network has at least one show dealing with various methods of paranormal investigation. Ghost-hunting clubs have opened in cities, towns, and villages across the nation, ready to spring into action at the first sign of a disembodied voice or a whole family of spectral apparitions.

I have to admit that I am somewhat envious about the way society has come to accept the idea that ghosts may exist. It is now possible for ghost hunters to be successful gathering paranormal evidence. This is why I sometimes feel the slight pang of jealousy when I see another new paranormal-based show come on. Thanks to reality television, ghost hunting has become cool.

However, this sort of easy acceptance of the world of the supernatural wasn't always the norm. I was a ghost hunter when ghost hunting wasn't cool.

Searching for ghosts is certainly nothing new. Ancient societies had individuals whose sole purpose was to seek out spirits, either to ask for favors or to make sure the restless dead wouldn't harm the living. There was no question whether spirits were real and their influence was felt in every aspect of everyday life.

As time passed, science became the new religion. Science swept away the old ideas of the supernatural and life after death. The idea of having a soul was old fashioned. People were complex biological machines and once you were dead, you were dead. Ghosts and spirits had no place in the age of science and technology.

Yet, despite all the so-called scientific proof against the paranormal, ghosts and hauntings never really disappeared. People continued to be touched by the unexplained. However, the societal understanding and acceptance of the supernatural and the world of spirits was gone. Those who had ghostly encounters were frightened, confused, and afraid to tell anyone for fear of ridicule.

This was what it was like when I chased those elusive spooks. In those days there was interest in the paranormal, but it was considered an extremely fringe subject, right up there with wireless telephones and computers that wouldn't fill an entire room.

I became fascinated with the subject of ghosts and the afterlife when, as a kid, I discovered a little paperback book called *Voices from the Beyond* by Brad Steiger. Nevertheless, it did not occur to me that I could actively pursue ghost investigations until my first experience with the unexplained shortly after I had graduated from college. I am still not sure how to classify my experience, or if it can even be classified. Was it a meaningful coincidence, or a voice from beyond? Whatever the case, it had a major impact on my life.

<hr/>

A THOUGHT NOT MY OWN:
TIM SWARTZ'S EARLY PARANORMAL EXPERIENCE

We all like to think that we have control over our lives and that we are able to mold and shape our destinies. The Bible even insists that God gave us "free will" along with the ability to know the difference between right and wrong. It is all very simple, with free will, we create our lives for better or worse with the decisions we make.

At times it seems as if there is a structure of sorts underlying our reality, a template of our lives that needs to be followed. Think of it as a path through the woods. In order to get out of the woods you have to follow the path. Along the path there are deviations that can take you miles out of your way. Interesting though these deviations may be, you eventually have to make your way back to the original path in order to get out of the woods. In other words, the universe has already chosen a path for you to follow. You can use your free will to follow this path, or, like most of us, you can choose to blunder blindly here and there until the universe steps in and forces you back onto the correct path.

Tim Swartz.

I have often pondered whether synchronicity is one of the ways the universe uses to try to keep us on our intended path. Possibly because we are trapped in linear time and a three-dimensional reality, we are unable to view the "big picture" that may show us the intricate spider web of connections that make synchronicity work. I think that this is why synchronicity can make such a huge impression on us when it occurs, yet at the same time, leave us baffled about the meaning of the event.

My first encounter with the unknown happened in 1978 during my first year in college. Shortly after the Christmas holiday season, my best friend, James, who was a year younger and still attending high school, committed suicide. For me, the shock was devastating. On top of my sorrow, I felt guilty for not noticing the pain that my friend must have been going through. We had spent a lot of time together during my holiday time off from school, but if James had dropped any hints about what he was planning, I did not see them.

Because I was already back in school, which was a considerable distance from my hometown, I was not able to attend his funeral. I sealed myself away from everyone to privately deal with my pain and guilt as best as I could. Because of the circumstances, I had no idea where James was buried. I only knew that he had been laid to rest in a small cemetery outside of town. At the

Tim almost didn't notice the small countryside cemetery, but then he was overwhelmed with the sudden feeling of certainty that this was where his friend James was buried.

time, I did not want to know where he was. This sort of knowledge only increased the pain that I was working so hard to avoid.

The years passed, and the pain slowly faded. The summer after I graduated from college I moved back home to help care for my sick mother. I would take care of her during the day when no one else was at home, but I had the evenings to myself. Small Midwest towns don't offer much entertainment. Mostly I would drive around, listening to music and enjoying the quiet, country air.

One early evening started out like the rest. I was out in the country, driving the back roads and not thinking about anything in particular. I was about ten miles outside of town in an area where I had never been before. As I was driving along, I came upon a small, unfamiliar country cemetery. In this rural area, there are dozens of small cemeteries, so it was not surprising that I had never seen this particular one before.

I barely noticed the graveyard as I drove past. Suddenly, completely out of the blue, as if I was hearing someone else's thought, "This is where James is buried," popped into my head.

Rationally, I knew that this was complete and utter nonsense. I had no clue where my friend's gravesite was. I didn't want to know. I had never asked, and no one had ever volunteered to tell me.

Yet, this thought persisted to the point where it was no longer simply a stray thought. It entwined itself into my brain to the point that it had become knowledge. I was now positive that this little, unassuming cemetery contained the mortal remains of my friend.

What choice did I have? I had to find out what was going on. I turned my car around and pulled through the wrought-iron gate. I turned the engine off and got out.

I didn't know where to start, so I walked a few steps into the cemetery and looked down. There, at my feet, was a familiar name carved upon the headstone. With no deviations, I had walked directly to the grave of my friend. I had not been consciously looking for him, yet, somehow, after all this time, I had finally been reunited with my best friend.

I can offer no good explanation for my unusual experience; to me, it was more than just a meaningless coincidence. It left me with a lasting impression that I have carried with me all of these years. It left me with a certainty that there is more to our lives than chance events, that there is meaning and significance to everything in our lives.

Before my own experience, ghosts, hauntings and other paranormal events were things I only read about in books. They happened to other people, but not to me. However, once that I had been given a glimpse of this strange reality, I wanted to learn more; I wanted to experience more.

Fortunately, my career path helped make this possible. I started working in the news departments of several television stations and this opened doors of opportunity that led to some fascinating paranormal investigations.

I have concluded that everyone, at least one time in their lives, has had a paranormal experience. Most will simply shrug off their experience saying, "That was weird," or, "I didn't really see that," and quickly forget about it. Others, like me, become intrigued and start paying closer attention to the little details that make up our daily lives.

I once had a friend who believed she had psychic abilities. She had grown up always knowing ahead of time things such as when a relative was going to die or who was coming over for an unexpected visit. Lori was eager to try out her special senses on a ghost investigation. She really wanted to communicate with discarnate entities to find out what was keeping them earthbound.

Our first investigation together was at an old movie theater in Terre Haute, Indiana. Along with the theater manager, Lori and I sat in the auditorium of the theater talking about the resident ghost, a mysterious "lady in white." Both the staff and patrons had reported seeing this ghostly figure walking up and down the aisles, or sitting in one of the empty seats.

As we were talking, Lori suddenly flinched and said to me, "that seat just came down." I looked over, and sure enough, the seat next to her was down as if someone were sitting in it.

We watched the seat go up and down several times as if an invisible "something" was standing up and sitting back down again. The manager laughed and said, "Oh that happens all the time. I guess the lady in white wants to know what we are saying about her."

Lori, however, did not think it was very funny and burst into tears.

Our investigation came to a halt, and I had to take Lori home where she spent the rest of the evening crying. That was her first and last time as a ghost hunter. I guess the moral of this story is: Don't go looking for ghosts if you are not prepared to find one.

What often puzzles me are the little spontaneous weird things that happen from time to time with no apparent rhyme or reason. The human brain seeks to find meaning and significance in what goes on around us, so when something truly unexplainable happens, it makes my brain hurt trying to figure out why.

[O]n the counter right next to me, a decorative can that once held candy suddenly started to rattle.

A good example of this happened to me in 2010. One morning I had taken my daughter to the home of her babysitter. I was in the kitchen talking with the sitter when, on the counter right next to me, a decorative can that once held candy suddenly started to rattle. I looked down at it and the can visibly shook as if something alive was trying to get out. The can stopped shaking, but then it quickly scooted about six inches across the counter and stopped.

The babysitter said, "Did that can just move?"

I picked it up and opened the plastic lid, expecting to find a toy or something inside that had made it move. But the can was completely empty. I was absolutely bemused by this little demonstration. The can was one of several sitting in a group on the counter, but none of the others had moved, only this one. The counter was level and dry, so it hadn't slid on water. No one was jumping around in the house, no big trucks outside, no earthquakes, and no easy explanations.

Maybe someday we will have a better understanding of all this, but I doubt it. If I have learned anything from my experiences, I have learned that ghosts, hauntings, and other strange events can happen at any time and at any place. My advice to any paranormal investigator is to throw out any preconceived notions you may have, and always keep your eyes and mind open to what is going on around you. Because you never know when something is going to pop up out of the dark and completely change the world as you know it.

2
ENCOUNTERS WITH GLOWING ENTITIES AND GHOST LIGHTS

OLD BRIT BAILEY'S LIGHT

Brit Bailey's dying request was to be buried standing up. He proclaimed that he had spent his whole life stomping over the Texas prairies, and he didn't aim to stop when he died. They buried old Brit in 1833, but residents in the area of Bailey's Prairie, five miles west of Angleton, Texas, in Brazoria County, claim that the early settler has kept his vow to keep stomping around on the prairies.

The Thomases, who moved into old Bailey's place after he had been planted erect in the sod, were the first to bear witness that the ghost of the old-timer did not wait long to start prowling around. In her diary, Ann Rainey Thomas made a record of her sighting of old Brit—his ghostly face looking in the window at her one night. Her servant girl Melinda reported that the ghost chased the hired hands away from the cows at evening milking time. All members of the household swore they heard old Brit's shuffling footsteps moving around in the house after dark. Once when Mr. Thomas lay ill, he claimed that he clearly saw Brit Bailey in the room with him.

It was not until about the early 1850s that Bailey's glowing, ghostly image began to be seen on the prairies. Colonel Mordello Munson and several of his guests saw an eerily glowing ball of light drift slowly past his home early one evening. Saddling their horses, the colonel and his male guests gave the strange globe of glowing light a hardy pursuit, but were unable to capture it or clearly identify it. From that night on, "Brit Bailey's Light" has drifted across the Texas prairies that the old settler was so reluctant to relinquish.

THE MYSTERY LIGHTS OF BROWN MOUNTAIN

Nestled far from the nearest city of Hickory, North Carolina, the Brown Mountain region has been the dwelling place of mysterious glowing lights for over two hundred years. From sunset until dawn, globes of various colored lights, ranging in size from mere points to twenty-five feet in diameter, can be seen rising above the tall trees and flickering off again, as they fall to the mountain passes below.

Although the Brown Mountain spook lights were first documented in 1771 by Gerard Will de Brahm, a German engineer, they did not truly receive national attention until an account of the southern Appalachian phenomenon appeared in the works of Charles Fort, who described how the lights would chase early settlers along the various trails that lead to the sparsely placed cities.

One of many legends that have sprung up about the origin of the lights is that they are caused by the spirits of Cherokee and Catawba braves who search the valley for the maiden lovers they left behind when they were slain in a big battle hundreds of years ago. Some area residents believe the battle still rages between spirits of the two tribes, for the lights seem to be fighting, butting into each other, and bouncing around like extra-large basketballs.

In 1913, the U.S. Geological Survey tried to explain the lights away by attributing them to reflections caused by the headlights of locomotives or cars running through the nearby Catawba Valley. However, during the spring of 1916 when all bridges were knocked out by a flood, and the roads became too muddy for cars to travel, the Brown Mountain lights were seen in greater numbers than ever before. Besides, residents argued, the lights have haunted the region for hundreds of years, long before automobiles were invented.

Since the early 1900s, people have attempted to come up with scientific explanations for the Brown Mountain Lights. Among these are St. Elmo's Fire (electrical discharges which sometimes occur during thunderstorms), fox fire (phosphorescent illumination issuing from decaying matter), or simply moonlight shining on ground fog. But during all the years that some individuals have tried to dismiss the lights, thousands of men and women have witnessed, photographed, and had bizarre encounters with the mystery orbs. In more recent years, certain researchers have attributed the eerie lights to entities from UFOs.

According to many who have seen the Brown Mountain Lights, they are most often visible on partly cloudy nights when the moon is low. The prime viewing time is between 9:30 and 10:00 P.M. Although the sightings occur during all seasons, some who have experienced the lights state that the best time to see them is on a crisp autumn night after a rain.

Bob Downing, writing in the *Beacon Journal* (September 15, 2002), suggested the following viewing spots for those who wish to search out the Brown Mountain Lights for themselves: "The Lost Cove Cliffs Overlook on the Blue Ridge Parkway, … The Thunder Hill Overlook at Mile Post 290, … Wisemans View south of Linville Falls, … an overlook on Jonas Ridge off state Route 181."

THE GHOST LIGHT OF CHINATI MOUNTAIN

Since pioneer days, night travelers in the area of Chinati Mountain in the Cienega Mountains of southwestern Texas have seen a peculiar glowing orb about the size of a basketball. It materializes, moves about, splits into twin spheres, reforms, and ranges in intensity from a mere twinkle to a blinding glare. According to area residents, the best spot for observing the ghost light is along Highway 90 between Marfa and Alpine.

Local legend attributes the source of the spook light to the spirit of the Apache chief, Alsate, who was tricked into offending a tribal manitou (spirit) after he had been betrayed by some Mexican soldiers. As his eternal punishment, according to the old story, Alsate was condemned to wander the Big Bend Country of Texas, and it is the chief's glowing spirit that people see when they witness a manifestation of the spook light of Chinati Mountain.

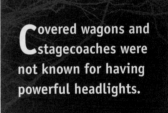

Covered wagons and stagecoaches were not known for having powerful headlights.

Some observers of the ghost light have attributed the source of the eerie illumination to the reflection of the moonlight on deposits of mica in the cliffs and crags of the mountain. However, this theory does not explain the appearance of the brightly glowing ball on nights when the moon is hidden behind thick cloud banks.

Some residents maintain that the spook light is seen under only two conditions: either just before or just after a rain. But others argue that they have seen the light dozens of times when the country was bone dry.

For those demanding a rational explanation for the manifestation, some clever individuals came up with the theory that the mystery light was caused by the reflection of automobile headlights coming down Paisana Pass. But others countered that hypothesis with a question: How could the spook light maintain a steady glow for several hours if it had to depend on the headlights of an occasional motor vehicle speeding quickly by? And then there is the troublesome fact that the earliest settlers and travelers in southwestern Texas mentioned seeing the ghost light. Covered wagons and stagecoaches were not known for having powerful headlights.

Whether the enigmatic light of Chinati Mountain is caused by certain unique climatic conditions working on mineral deposits peculiar to that area or whether observers really are seeing the glowing spirit of Chief Alsate, one indisputable fact remains—the spook light is there.

GHOST LIGHTS OF SILVER CLIFF

In the little town of Silver Cliff, in the Wet Mountain Valley of Colorado, ghost lights have been seen in the local cemetery since 1880. The lights can never be approached for a close look. As soon as anyone comes near them, the lights disappear, only to pop up again in another section of the cemetery.

Local folklore has it that the lights were first seen by a group of miners passing by the cemetery. When they saw the flickering blue lights over the gravestones, they left the vicinity in a hurry. Since then, the lights have been observed by generations of residents of Custer County. According to the old stories, the cemetery was the final resting place for many miners who lost their lives while digging for precious ores. They say the flickering lights of the graveyard resemble the little lights worn on the miners' caps, and they belong to the restless souls of the miners, who still search for the silver they never found.

> **[T]he lights have been observed by generations of residents of Custer County.**

In 1880, Silver Cliff boasted a population of 5,087; today it has only a couple hundred inhabitants and has almost become a ghost town.

The story of the ghost lights of Silver Cliff first reached public attention in the spring of 1956 when an article on the mystery appeared in the *Wet Mountain Tribune*. Over a decade later, on August 20, 1967, the *New York Times* carried a story on the phenomenon.

When some observers of the spook lights noted that the bluish-colored illumination could not be seen as clearly on the sandstone markers, many spectators became convinced that the lights were only a reflection of house-lights in the valley. However, as County Judge August Menzel recounted for the *New York Times*, one night everyone in Silver Cliff and nearby Westcliff shut off their lights. Even the streetlights were turned off, "but the graveyard lights still danced."

Other rational thinkers have believed the Silver Cliff ghost lights to be reflections from the stars. Yet the lights are just as clear on starless, moonless nights. Some have tried to prove that the lights are caused by phosphorescing ore and glowing wood, but the darker the night, the brighter the lights. It was suggested that radioactive ores were causing the flickering lights. But Geiger counters were employed to cover the entire area, and no radioactivity was discovered. Each logical explanation has been disproven.

———

SPOOKSVILLE GHOST LIGHT

One of the most famous of all ghost lights is located in the tri-state corner of Missouri, Arkansas, and Oklahoma. Spooksville's ghostly light is even advertised as a tourist attraction.

In appearance, the ghost light resembles a bright lantern. Often it dims before the spectators, then bounces back over the mountains in a brilliant blaze of light. Hundreds of firsthand encounters with the mysterious ghost light are on record. These accounts demonstrate actual experiences with the unknown—sometimes frightening, but always interesting.

During World War II, the U.S. Corps of Engineers scoured the entire area, using the latest scientific equipment. For weeks

An orb or spook light seen between Joplin and Seneca, Missouri.

they tested caves, mineral deposits, and highway routes, exhausting every possible explanation for the origin of the mystery lights. They finally left, confounded.

Louise G. reported coming home on a school bus from a school carnival at Quapaw, Oklahoma. A ghost light perched on the rear window of the bus as though attempting to enter. Everyone in the bus was thoroughly frightened, and several of the women were screaming. In *Ghost Lights*, a pamphlet written by Bob Loftin, Louise said that the light was so bright that it temporarily blinded the bus driver and he had to stop the bus. Just as the driver stopped, the light went away.

Chester M., a farmer near Quapaw, said that when the weather got intolerably hot, he liked to do his plowing in the evening. Chester recounted the night that the ghost light "felt real neighborly" and hovered over the field where he was plowing. Chester was enjoying the experience until the light suddenly darted directly at him. He said that he "absolutely froze stiff" on the tractor until the light sailed out of sight.

Theo Paijmans.

FIERY SPECTERS AND BURNING GHOSTS IN THE NETHERLANDS

By Theo Paijmans

In a not-too-distant past, much of the Dutch countryside was filled with an atmosphere of mystery. There were no rows of street lights, no maze of highways and busy traffic, only little villages and hamlets sprinkled on the land and along the many waterways. It was advisable to stay indoors at night, since at that time the fields were host to ghostly creatures, an encounter with which could be fatal. Some of the ghostly apparitions that manifested themselves regularly were the terrible and mysterious creatures known as the "firemen."

The Netherlands is rich in stories of glowing, fiery specters and spirits. The explanation for the existence of the firemen was that these fiery ghosts had acquired an awful curse during their lifetimes. They were in essence the spirits of corrupt land surveyors or farmers who illegally moved their poles or stones with which they marked the boundaries of their fields. Others told how these burning specters were the haunted souls of those who had committed gruesome murder.

In the Achterhoek, a rural area in Overijssel, residents of the farming communities shudderingly named these specters *gleunigen*. In the province of Drenthe they were known as *glènde kerels*. It was said that a strange object that looked like a burning bush of straw on the road from Nunspeet to Harderwijk was the ghost of an innkeeper, burning for eternity as divine retribution for killing a man from Münster.

Similar stories abound: it was common knowledge that a fiery spirit seen in Kootwijk was one Klaas Jonkers. He had to burn, since he, too, had committed a murder. At Heelsum a sheep herdsman burned "like a piece of roof (dakschoof)" because he set fire to a sheep shed. At one of the old inlets of the river the IJssel, a glowing man appeared in front of a number of skippers. One time at the Lonnekerberg, three glowing ghosts were seen walking. At Enschede three *gleunigen* also appeared. Tradition further has it that at the side of the river Maas between Roosteren, Echt, and Stevensweert, each night a fireman passes along. If you whistle to him, he will come for you. At the Springhei near Galder below Ginneken, a fireman appears; it was a foreman who once had buried gold on the heath (heide) that was enthrusted to him.

The fiery land surveyors dragging their glowing surveyors' chains as punishment for their corrupt surveying practices were seen at places such as Oosterhesselen, Peize, Zeegse, and at Donderen in the province of Drenthe and Wezepe in the province of Overijssel. In the city of Soest a fiery surveyor was seen in an apparition that began as a small light and increased in size until it was bigger than a burning bushel of straw. In Twente these fiery spirits confuse the hapless travelers who are unlucky enough to have an encounter, playing with their sense of direction so that they wander aimlessly until the break of dawn. Old lore emphatically states that it is very unwise to try to speak to these firemen; once their attention is drawn to you, they are likely to come after you. This was what happened to a farmhand in the city of Venlo. He managed to reach the barn just in time, but in the morning a black handprint was etched into the door.

In the Netherlands, there are stories of the firemen, burning ghosts who are being punished for misdeeds such as murder perpetrated during their lifetimes.

A very puzzling manifestation happened in Tjerkwerd, a small Frisian village at Wonseradeel, half an hour southwest of Bolsward. The recollection of the event was published in 1843. Local lore had it that one could occasionally see glowing witches' globes falling out of the sky. In the year 1827, Lieuwe Klaassens (still alive when his story saw print fifteen years later) was a local innkeeper of the Blue House. Together with the clergyman of Tjerkwerd—who had since passed away—Klaassens saw this very type of fireball descending to the ground. To the amazement of the two men, it took the shape of a human and walked toward a small hill. Once it got there, the mysterious fiery man rolled himself up into a ball like a hedgehog and floated into the air on some mysterious aerial journey.

On the island of Terschelling a burning man was often seen. And at the Betuwe sometimes the ghostly apparition of a knight in full armor was seen, while blue flames danced on the place where a castle once stood.

In the Netherlands, the earliest recorded spook light manifestation dates from the sixteenthth century. In an old manuscript of that time the tale of the Riepsterlicht was told: "on autumn evenings, when the wind howled and the trees swayed the villagers saw behind their hamlet a brilliant ghost light." Legend recounted the origin of these lights was the early middle ages. But local teacher Kuipers testified that around 1861 the light was still seen. This light had the dimensions of a part of a straw roof. The dreaded light was not a fiery surveyor, nor a false lantern or a wandering light orhiplicht as the Dutch call it, but a stationary light that was seen at the same place at a path called the Woldweg. At times it shone very clear, at times it was almost unnoticable.

There are also many tales involving "wandering lights," comparable to the spook lights, will-'o-the-wisps, and ignis fatuus traditions. However, while sometimes a logical explanation points to natural causes, other observations of Dutch ghost and spook lights cannot be so readily dismissed. Take these strange events occuring as recently as 1935: "A short time ago a painter in Drachten strolled in the neighborhood of his house and saw a strange luminous apparition that floated through the woods: 'even through the trees', and he went for his wife so that she could see it too. She became so frightened of the apparition that she urged her man to return home directly and not to meddle with it any further. One of the members of the Drentsche society for the research and investigation into wandering lights told us that from a marsh a green light ascended, it flew higher and in the direction of an old German burial hill. Once it had arrived there, over the hill a second light appeared suddenly, this time yellow in colour, and both lights sunk into the ground there.

"Another time red lights appeared and one of them turned, like the light of a car, in a circle. It also seemed as if the lights sent 'signals' to each other when people approached, and then disappeared. Through binoculars one saw the lights as triangular-shaped forms, with the point downwards and the center was like the swarming of glimmering worms or glistening crystals. They will attempt to observe them with enhancing binoculars or to photograph them. Prof. Schrijnen speaks in his *Volkskunde* about the wandering lights as the souls that appear as flames on graves or in the vicinity thereof, according to folk belief.

"In connection with the theory that in the old times the corpses were not buried (excepting those of social status), but were laid under stones in a morass or river, one could also see the sightings of wandering lights over marshes as belonging to the same folk belief. In the neighborhood of Den Haag (The Hague) wandering lights were observed as well: between Monster and Ter Heyde."

In the cemetery at the Rode Laan of the city Voorburg in January 1950 at about four o'clock in the afternoon, several inhabitants saw a fireball that floated toward the ground. The fiery globe divided itself into two parts, one part expiring in just a few seconds, the other sinking straight down and touching the grassy reclaimed land behind the cemetery. A smoke plume was seen thereafter for some time, a Dutch newspaper reported.

This account is reminiscent of an incident in 1884. As some Dutch newspapers reported that year: "The captain of one of the boats of the steamboat company De Volharding that travel from Leiden to Gouda has seen Friday evening at around 7 hours 15 between Boskoop and Waddingsveen a fireball of oval shape, that moved in East-Northeast direction to the West-Southwest and in the vicinity of the boat fell down without blowing into pieces, and remained there visible for some time. At the same time in the small room where the sideboard was placed and of which the window was not completely closed, a terrible blow was heard, by which the passengers in the cabin jumped up in fright. During an investigation it became apparent that the lamp that was placed in the sideboard was extinguished and two karafs, as well as the petroleum device, were thrown over. As there had been no one in the small room, the opinion was that one was allowed to seek a connection between what had happened there and the floating past fireball."

In Dutch folklore, when lijkenvlammetjes, or corpse flames, would strike they foretold death to the witness or someone close by. Odd lights also manifested themselves around the dying. There is a very strange case mentioned in an old Dutch collection of ghost lore accounts. It relates how, in the night of October 25, 1725 at a place called Hernhoff, people witnessed how the corpse of a thief hanging at the gallows was enveloped in such a quantity of light that it appeared as if he was burning fiercely. The same was witnessed in March the next year on several nights.

> A boy ... saw big glowing orbs looming up and disappearing in front of him.

Many combinations of ghostly phenomena are possible, as the members of two families living at the Dutch village of Axel experienced in 1927. One family heard strange noises which seemed to be the start of a bizarre chain of events. A boy from that household, returning home late one evening, suddenly saw big glowing orbs looming up and disappearing in front of him. Then, members of the family began to see a ghostlike figure. It even materialised at the bed of the wife one morning. At that same time, a second family began to encounter weird events. They experienced poltergeistlike phenomena, such as a hobby horse rocking by itself, and their doors kicked open by invisible powers. People who visited the families also witnessed these ghostly phenomena. As the Dutch newspapers reported: "People have already kept vigils and searched through the place, without having obtained a single clue as to this dark case."

The Netherlands is also rich in accounts of unexplainable poltergeist phenomena, some going back centuries. One was mentioned by Balthasar Bekker, a Frisian clergyman who wrote his famous book *De Betoverde Weereld* ("The Enchanted World"), published in 1691. Bekker relates how a learned man once told him that ghosts in his home had moved the glasses on his table without the interference of a human hand. Directed against superstition in general and a belief in the devil, Bekker's book became a bestseller and was instrumental in ending the witchcraft persecutions craze. Bekker suffered from prosecution from the church during his life. A month after he had passed away, Bekker was appointed a member of the Royal Society.

An Encounter with a Benevolent Ghost Light

In the June, 1968 issue of *Fate* magazine, Arlene O. Meyers tells the story of her mother Laura Jeanette's encounter with a benevolent ghost light in the Willamette Valley of Oregon in the early 1900s.

Several times a year Laura and her husband loaded up the wagon, hitched up the horses, and made the two-and-a-half-mile trip into town. There they traded farm products for staples.

On this particular occasion their usual autumn trip had been delayed because Laura's husband had taken ill, and it was already winter when they set out.

When they had finished their trading in town, they stopped off for supper with some relatives. During the course of the meal Laura's husband became violently ill.

The relatives insisted that he stay for the night, and Laura agreed that that would be a good plan. But she could not think of remaining with him and leaving the five children home alone. Telling everyone she would send her two oldest boys the following morning to get their father, Laura began the two-and-a-half-mile trek home by herself.

When she got out onto the road, however, she discovered it was pitch-black. She began to fear she would not be able to see at all, and her thoughts strayed to the reports of a wild cougar that had been molesting cattle in the area. To forestall her fears, she began to pray.

A safe and peaceful feeling began to spread over her and suddenly a light appeared in front of the horses, illuminating the road ahead. Laura breathed a sigh of relief. Now she need not fear the darkness.

The benevolent light preceded her all the way home, illuminating every step of the way. When she arrived at the farm she woke up one of her sons and he helped her unhitch the horses.

The following morning the son came downstairs, expecting to find the stranger who had held the light. But there was no stranger present. Laura never wavered in her belief that it was an angel sent by God who had held the light.

A Jack-o'-Lantern Followed Her Home

The Personal Experience of Beverly K.

The following eerie encounter with a mysterious globe of light occurred in 1916 when Beverly K. was teaching at a rural school near Wellsburg, Iowa, and boarding with a farm family.

"I was going with a young man in Wellsburg and very much in love," Beverly said, "but he had been acting differently toward me lately, and I was worried. It was in late May, near the end of the school year, and on this particular night I was restless and couldn't sleep. So even though the hour was very late, around eleven, I got up, dressed, crept silently down the stairs, walked out the door, and went for a stroll."

Beverly recalled that it was a beautiful night, and a full moon was riding high in the sky. "It had been an unusually warm spring," she said, "and it was almost like summer. I felt quite exhilarated and not at all afraid. All the farmers in the neighborhood were fast asleep, so there was little chance of meeting anyone on the little-traveled dirt road."

Beverly was enjoying the walk and her solitude so much that she didn't notice how far she had gone. "It must have been two or three miles," she continued. "As I realized that I must start back, the sky became overcast, covering the full moon and making the night darker and darker. My mood changed to an eerie sort of fear, and I kept walking faster and faster. Soon it was so dark that my fear almost became panic, for I could hardly see the road anymore."

At last she reached the crossroads near the farmhouse where she was staying. Suddenly she turned her head and looked over her shoulder. "There, just a few yards behind me, floating about three feet above the ground, was an orange-red ball or disc, following me at the same pace as I was walking. It glowed dully, but shed no light around it or on the ground. Almost as soon as I had seen it, it veered off to the side of the road, rose a bit, then sailed over the barbed-wire fence and disappeared in some shrubbery on the other side. It was with great relief that I got into the house and went back to bed."

Beverly didn't tell her landlady about the strange encounter for a day or two, because she did not want her to know about her midnight walk. "But finally my curiosity got the better of me and I did tell her about what I had seen," Beverly said. "My landlady merely nodded and said, 'We call them jack-o'-lanterns.' From her response it was obvious that lots of other folks had seen them, but I sensed that she didn't care to talk more about the subject so I dropped it.

"I'd heard of such things as the will-o'-the-wisp, but I always picture that as a rather formless white light, and this had been an orange-red globe.

Orbs, fairy lights, spook lights, or will-o'-the-wisps have been seen for centuries. This illustration, from the 1845 edition of Thomas Milner's *Gallery of Nature*, depicts a will-o'-the-wisp.

There were no swamps or marshes around, so it couldn't have been swamp gas. This strange ball of reddish light behaved as if it were intelligent, for it had been following me in a straight line. But as soon as it was discovered, it swerved aside and went into the bushes, as if in hiding. And hadn't there been something unnatural about the sudden darkness? This experience remains among my unsolved mysteries."

GHOST LIGHT ON A COUNTRY ROAD

The Personal Experience of Brad Steiger

Just before sunset one evening in the summer of 1953, I was finishing chores on our farm in Iowa when I heard screams coming from the country road at the end of our lane. There was still enough light for me to see three teenage girls peddling their bikes as fast as they could manage on the loose gravel.

Before I could get to my car and drive down to investigate whatever it might have been that had so frightened them, they were nearly out of sight.

Although we had a long lane and I couldn't see them very clearly, our rural community was small enough for me to figure out who the girls were, so the next time I went into town, I located one of them and asked her what had caused them to scream as if their very lives were in danger.

According to Sandy, the three friends had decided to go on a twilight bike ride in the country. Just as they passed our lane, a large ball of glowing greenish-white light rose up out of the ditch and began to bob about near them, as if checking out each one of them individually. They screamed and turned their bicycles around and headed back toward town, but the ball followed them for about a quarter of a mile before it turned around and left them.

I listened with polite interest to the spooky story. I was seventeen, a high school graduate of two months, so I felt superior enough to indulge the wild imaginations of three fifteen-year-olds. I was quite certain the girls had been frightened by a cluster of lightning bugs that had risen up out of the ditch.

However, a couple of nights later as I was driving home in my 1948 maroon Ford coupe, I was startled to see a greenish-white glowing orb of light bobbing ahead of me in the middle of the road. It appeared to be about the size of a volleyball.

I didn't have time to slam on the brakes to avoid hitting the thing, and I had no idea if it would explode if I struck it or if it would smash in the front end of my car. To my everlasting surprise, the strange illuminated orb passed through the windshield of my Ford, remained a few moments right at the level of my chest directly in front of the steering wheel, then moved around me to pass out the rear window.

Although it had appeared to be a solid ball of some luminous substance, it had passed through the windshield and back window of the car without causing the slightest bit of damage. And whether it just thought it was fun to scare the bejabbers out of me or if it was on some mysterious mission, the ball of light waited for me near the same clump of trees on the next two evenings. On those occasions, it merely raced beside the driver's side of the Ford, accompanied me to our lane, then sped on its way off into the distance.

Although I did not see the mysterious glowing orb again near our farm lane, I did have a similar encounter with such an object in 1985 while driving late at night in the desert country of Arizona. On this occasion, the ghost light shot in front of my car, then angled at great speed off the road and disappeared among the sage and cactus. Interestingly, in 2001, I received an email from the daughter-in-law of one of my high school buddies. She told me that the greenish ball of light still manifested from time to time along the country roads of my hometown.

THE GLOWING GHOST OF THE SINCLAIR MANSION

An Investigation by Brad Steiger

In July of 1970, medium Irene Hughes and I brought a group of researchers to a university city in the Midwest. There we encountered a glowing spirit entity that so impressed itself on the psyches of certain members of our investigative group that for years afterward they reported awakening from nightmares, fearful that the ghost was forming again right in their bedrooms. Because the mansion that was home to the ghost has since been torn down and a new house built on the estate, I have changed the name of the previous owners and omitted the identity of the city in which the mansion was located.

> After one of the sisters passed on and the other was taken to a nursing home, the ghost light continued to make its appearance.

My friend and associate Glenn had received a lead on this particular house from some police officers. Before the house had been vacated, two elderly sisters had lived there alone. According to a number of police officers, who had themselves witnessed the appearance of the ghost, nearly every night a glowing something would manifest in the nearby lane, walk to the house, enter it, and converse with the sisters.

On several occasions, the police had received calls from frightened neighbors who thought the police should do something about the spook light, but the officers who responded to the call really didn't know quite how to handle a ghost. They would just sit in their squad cars outside the house and watch the two elderly ladies converse with the glowing ghost. After one of the sisters passed on and the other was taken to a nursing home, the ghost light continued to make its appearance.

On the first night we arrived in the city, our host suggested that we drive out to take a look at the mansion. It was midnight by then. Glenn was driving my station wagon, and he edged it cautiously into the lane of the once elaborate and well-maintained estate.

The headlights picked up the image of a wooden gate bearing an warning to any trespassers to keep out or to risk being prosecuted.

Glenn said that he had arranged for the caretaker to meet us at the estate on the next day. To make sure we were not mistaken for vandals, Glenn also asked the police to send an officer to accompany us.

Irene complained that it appeared as though we were entering a jungle. There was a heavy overgrowth of weeds and bushes. Thick, drooping branches of untrimmed trees formed a low canopy over the narrow lane. Glenn said that from our present position we wouldn't be able to see more than the edge of what had once been one of the city's loveliest estates.

"What's that?"

I don't remember who first saw it, but no one had to point out the sudden glowing intruder upon the dark and quiet scene. There appeared to be a very large orb of light moving in front of us down the lane.

The moon was covered by clouds that night. The nearest streetlight was a vapor-light, completely cut off from the old estate by the thick wall of trees. We were in total darkness, and when Glenn turned off the headlights, the strange orb glowed brightly.

As we watched, the orb of light moved toward the old house. Everyone turned to look at Irene Hughes, who was seated in the middle of the backseat. In the dim glow of the dashboard lights, I noticed a rather strange expression on her face, and it had occurred to me that she had been extremely quiet during our excitement over sighting the ghostly figure.

"Shall we go right now and investigate the whatever-it-is?" someone said.

"No," Irene answered firmly, breaking her silence. "Not tonight. I have a very bad feeling that it would not be good for us to walk down that lane right now."

There was a certainty to her voice that told us she meant exactly what she said. Her psychic impression was telling her that the time was not right to approach the shimmering orb, which now seemed to be moving toward the deserted house.

"Let's leave ... now!" Irene said suddenly.

No one argued with her.

It was nearly midnight again on the second night when we approached the eerie mansion. Earlier that day, in the company of the caretaker, we had walked around the house and allowed Irene to pick up psychic impressions about its past inhabitants. At first the caretaker had been very skeptical of the idea of a psychic tromping about the grounds of the Sinclair estate, seeking to pick up impressions about the past inhabitants. He had been quite reluctant to take time for such foolishness, and it had required a good measure of Glenn's persuasive abilities to convince the caretaker that he should bother with us at all.

It was very interesting to watch the caretaker change his attitude during his exchange with Irene Hughes, as they delved deeper and deeper into a mysterious territory whose boundaries he had never before dreamed of transgressing. He knew that it was impossible that Mrs. Hughes could have gained any information about the house and its inhabitants. All Glenn knew about the house was that some police officers had seen strange lights moving around inside. None of us had researched the Sinclair house in any manner whatsoever, and it is doubtful that even the most exhaustive search of public records would have turned up the personal minutiae that Irene Hughes had siphoned from the psychic atmosphere of the old house.

When I asked the caretaker afterward how he would rate the accuracy of Irene Hughes' insights, he grinned, and his answer came quickly and easily. "I'd have to give her a ninety percent," he admitted, "and it would probably be higher if there was some way to check out every name she gave. Just about everything she said fit in. I don't know how, but she really knew."

When we visited the Sinclair estate on that second night, we had the caretaker and a policeman with us in the station wagon. We opened the gate and drove cautiously down the lane. When we were adjacent to the old house, Glenn stopped the car.

> **There was a glowing, mist-like substance forming directly in front of the hood of the station wagon.**

"Let us just sit quietly for a few moments, and permit me to gain some psychic impressions of the house by night," Irene requested.

As our medium sat in meditation, I glanced absently out the windshield. Then I blinked my eyes rapidly. There was a glowing, mist-like substance forming directly in front of the hood of the station wagon. The ghost was beginning take shape right before my eyes.

"What is that?" asked the police officer sitting beside me in the front seat.

Previously, we had been accompanied by an open-minded police officer who had witnessed the glowing entity in the lane on other occasions. This fellow had joined us earlier that evening and had been openly skeptical of our investigation, sometimes mocking our efforts. Because he had announced himself a staunch disbeliever, I could not resist having a bit of fun with him.

"What is what?" I asked blandly. "I don't see anything."

"There," he said in a harsh whisper. "Right there in front of the car! What in hell is that?"

I started to deny seeing anything one more time, but decided to stop teasing him when I saw that he was nervously brushing the strap that held his service revolver in its holster. It was clear to me that this man was now dealing with something that was not covered in the police manual and he was struggling with the extremely difficult idea of reconciling this materializing entity with the worldview that he had only moments before held so sacrosanct.

Apparently Glenn had heard our conversation from his post in the backseat because at that moment he whispered over our shoulders: "I've been watching it for a couple of minutes now. At first it was just a wispy tendril that seemed to come from that clump of bushes over there. Then it stopped directly in front of the car and began to take form."

By now everyone in our research group was watching the glowing, mist-like thing, and we all sat in silence for a few moments, observing the orb grow larger and denser and begin to assume a humanlike form. We decided to get out of the car for a closer inspection.

It was a very warm evening, but as I extended my hand into the midst of the glowing mist, I felt its very cold interior. Such a bold act may have been considered very rude by the entity, for suddenly the glowing image vanished.

Before we could speculate on the ghost's rapid disappearance, Irene whispered loudly from the other side of the station wagon: "There are some people coming through the bushes by the house!"

I did not hear the sounds of footsteps and crackling brush myself, but others in the group swore later that they heard the approach of two or more people coming toward us.

Then the footsteps stopped, and someone in our group pointed out the reappearance of glowing images between two trees. But before any of us could approach, the lights winked out, as rapidly as if they had been extinguished candle flames.

At this point, Irene began to get sensations and perceptions that the rest of us were not able to perceive. It seemed her greater sensitivity enabled her to see images where the rest of us could only see glowing mist and orbs. "I swear the ghosts looked real to me, more than spirit," Irene said later.

Then Irene suddenly put her hands to her ears and said that she heard the terrible sound of a woman screaming. "There! There in the bushes," she said. "Can you see her head?" But all Glenn and I could see was a glowing orb. Apparently we were not sensitive enough to tune into the vibrations on the estate and see distinctive features on the entities.

"Well, there are plenty of vibrations around here to tune in to," Irene remarked. "This place is just drenched with psychic vibrations."

The rest of us were unable to confront any of the glowing lights and observe them transform themselves into clear images of men and women. But it appeared as though the sound portion of the ethereal broadcast had been well received, however, as most of the members of our midnight expedition insisted that they had heard the sounds of footsteps and brush being parted.

Except for Irene, with her super-sensitive receiving set, the video portion of the program had been blurred for us. Every member of our party, including the police officer and the caretaker, had seen the ghostly glowing orbs, but only Irene Hughes had been able to adjust the fine tune mechanism within her psyche clearly enough to pick up distinct images of the forms that had been preternaturally recorded on the grounds of the old estate.

There are a couple of eerie postscripts to this case. The first occurred approximately one year after our visit to this home when Glenn and I were conducting some follow-up research on the old Sinclair mansion. We pulled into the lane about midnight in the company of three investigators, only one of whom had visited the place on a prior occasion.

We took particular notice of a wire stretched across the lane. Someone, undoubtedly the caretaker, had strung a number of white and red strips of cloth from the line. We switched out the headlights, got out of the vehicle, and prepared to await the ghost—which had been sighted by Glenn and a university professor just a few nights before.

We did not have long to wait before a column of light about the size of a human being of average height appeared off to the right of the automobile and made its traditional trek down the lane toward the old mansion.

We viewed the glowing orb until it disappeared inside the house, then, satisfied that the phenomenon continued unabated, we turned to walk back to the car. As we were approaching the automobile, we were startled to see that a three-tined pitchfork had been shoved into the ground just a few feet in front of the vehicle.

We all knew that the pitchfork had not been there before we had switched off the headlights and began to walk down the lane. The pitchfork had been driven into the ground just in back of the white and red stripes of cloth on the wire that stretched across the driveway entrance. We had taken such careful notice of the colorful decorated wire when we had arrived; we were certain we would have never overlooked such an obtrusive element as a pitchfork piercing the ground nearby.

If that shimmering column of light had truly planted that pitchfork before us, then I must admit that I was becoming concerned that we may have worn out our welcome at the haunted estate.

Three years later on Halloween, Glenn learned that the old Sinclair mansion was about to be torn down and replaced by a new home. We drove out to the estate for a farewell viewing, and on that particular occasion, even though it was Halloween, we saw nothing out of the ordinary. We decided that the glowing entity must have learned of the imminent destruction of the mansion and had at last moved on to a higher spiritual plateau.

Later that evening, we were invited to stop by a Halloween party in which a number of police officers were in attendance. Egged on by one of the officers who had experienced the haunting at the Sinclair mansion on many different occasions, Glenn and I began to regale the party-goers with some spooky Halloween stories about our encounters with the glowing ghost.

The next day, before I left the city to return home, Glenn and one of the police officers stopped by the motel where I was staying to share the perfect capper to the haunting at Sinclair mansion. It seems that a couple of the police officers who had attended the Halloween party the night before had been highly skeptical of our accounts of the glowing ghost. Since they had to go on duty after the party, they decided to take the squad car out to the estate to see for themselves.

Amidst howls of laughter, Glenn told me that the two officers had sat drinking coffee in the squad car, commenting derisively about our abilities as ghost researchers. Then, to their utter astonishment, the glowing entity materialized directly in front of their squad car. Begrudgingly admitting their terror, the two men confessed to their fellow officer that they had burned rubber getting out of the lane. From cynics to believers in a matter of seconds.

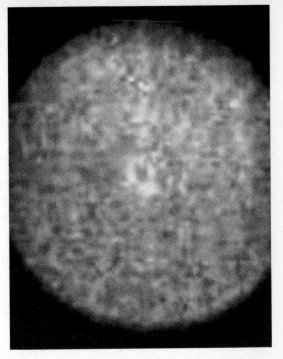

Close-up photograph of an orb seen by Gregory Avery.

ARE ORBS INTERDIMENSIONAL VEHICLES FOR THE SOUL?

In his e-book *Colors of the Soul & Colors of the Web*, author George Michael states that when people come into contact with true orbs, they are viewing real, interdimensional vehicles, known to the Egyptians as "sun boats" and referred to in the Bible as Merkabah. In the Kabbalah and in certain schools of Jewish mysticism, the Merkabah (Merkavah) is the Divine Throne Chariot described by the prophet Ezekiel and associated with the heavenly realms. In George Michael's view the orb or Merkabah is the vehicle for the soul in the earthly dimension after its physical, material, life has ended.

Real orbs, Michael says, can be sensed or heard. The sound they make is a super-high tone, chiefly heard inside the head, beyond normal hearing. Many individuals who have encountered true orbs have experienced the orb speaking telepathically to them.

According to Michael, orbs have many appearances—including globes, globules, balls of light, and hovering round balls—and they range in degrees of illumination from bright and glowing to faded and barely visible. There is great diversity among the erratic, fast-moving objects, Michael states, because there are many different types of orb phenomena. Some may even be separate life forms or nature spirits.

The human spirit or ghost type of orb, he says, is usually seen at an elevation between eye-level and ceiling height and is often found in graveyards and haunted locations. The human spirit type may appear larger than some of the other types of orbs.

But he believes that another type of orb is used in conjunction with electromagnetic vehicles, offering a shield for the interdimensional beings inside and serving as a means of propulsion. Although on occasion these orbs are seen at eye-level, they are primarily seen in the sky as they exist at a higher dimension than human spirit orbs.

In addition, Michael maintains that, just as the human spirit orbs reflect a certain aspect of the inhabitants of Earth, there is a type of orb that may be considered a spiritual aspect of extraterrestrial beings. Such orbs often have a more detailed and complex appearance, which may at times contain figures or faces. Although these orbs are rarely caught on film, photographic evidence of them does exist.

⊸⊸⊸〽⊸⊸⊸

PHOTOGRAPHING THE MYSTERIOUS ORBS

The Research and Photography of Gregory Avery

Glowing balls of light of various hues have appeared mysteriously on the photographs taken inside homes during festive occasions, such as birthday and engagement parties; in churches during solemn gatherings, such as funerals and memorial services; and at cemeteries, haunted houses, and sacred places. These unknown objects have come to be called "orbs," and they are seldom seen by either photographers or others present; mysteriously, the orbs appear only when the film is developed. While some ghost researchers are quick to claim that these orbs are evidence of spirit entities, the skeptics are just as quick to dismiss them as particles of dust, droplets of water, or natural electrical emissions rising from the ground.

Gregory Avery, who has generously contributed a number of his photographs of orbs to this book, says that while orbs may be imaged by any camera, from the cheapest disposable flash camera to the highest end mega-pixel digital cameras, most of the images that he has captured were made with the digital technology so he could study the images easily on a computer. At the present time, Gregory says that he uses the Sony Digital Cybershot, which records a mega-pixel image of fourteen megabytes in size.

Orbs are very often seen in graveyards. While orbs are notoriously difficult to photograph, this picture by Gregory Avery is one of the clearest photographs taken of an orb in a graveyard.

"Flash seems to be required to image the orbs whether film or digital techniques are used," he said. "I know of one exception to this and that is a high-end multiple CCD [charged coupled device] digital video camera that recorded an orb flying through a researcher's backyard in daylight—and no flash, strobe, or additional lighting was applied."

REAL GHOSTS, RESTLESS SPIRITS, AND HAUNTED PLACES

Gregory has taken photographs as an amateur and a professional since 1969; since 1998, he has captured thousands of orb images.

To make sure that the orb images aren't simply dust, moisture, raindrops, or the result of some other natural cause, Gregory recommends taking several flash pictures back to back. If the orbs are the result of natural elements, the first photo will often reveal many apparently unexplained objects floating in the air, but there will be fewer in the second, and quite likely none in the third.

"True orbs, for whatever reason, dart away during the flash," Gregory said. "The flash either overcharges them or reveals them or affects them in other ways that remain unclear—but they will move out, in different directions at high speeds, considering the speed of a flash."

Gregory states that he always cleans the lens of his camera between images to guard against the effects of rain, fog, or other materials affecting the photograph in any way. He has conducted numerous tests to determine whether or not an orb is a genuine anomaly rather than a photographic, atmospheric, or optical artifact effect.

"Dust was thrown in the air," he explained. "Water was sprayed into the air. We acquired an artificial fog machine and photographed the plume. My fiancée Christine even blew bubbles into the air. All of these tests, and more, were conducted in order to reproduce the appearance, color, and geometry of the true orbs. But we have failed to duplicate the orb appearance or capture the astounding geometrical precision of the genuine orbs."

⋙∫⋘

GHOST LIGHTS ARE EVERYWHERE

If peculiar manifestations like these glowing balls of light are as intelligent as their actions seem to indicate, we begin to question: what are they and what is their purpose? We have a folklore at least two thousand years old that equates these mysterious globes of light with spirits of the dead and with those beings we label nature spirits, Devas, elves, and fairies.

It also appears that angelic beings and spirit guides employ glowing balls of light as a means of transportation. Indeed, the globes of light may be the form these benevolent beings assume before fully materializing in our dimension. I have even conjectured that these orbs are themselves an intelligence, manifesting a physical appearance that corresponds to the level of understanding of a particular witness.

And these glowing ghosts may be able to manifest even in space. Shortly after his epic solo orbit of Earth, Lieutenant Colonel John Glenn commented in *Life* magazine (March 9, 1962) that the strangest sight that he had experienced during his flight occurred when he was crossing the Pacific toward the United States. He was checking the instrument panel, and when he looked back out the window he thought for a minute that he must have tumbled upside-down and was looking up at a new field of stars. He checked his instruments to be certain that he was right-side up, then he looked again. "There, spread out as far as I could see, were literally thousands of tiny luminous objects that glowed in the black sky like fireflies," Glenn said. "I was riding slowly through them, and the sensation was like walking backwards through a pasture where someone had waved a wand and made all the fireflies stop right where they were and glow steadily. They were greenish yellow in color, and they appeared to be about six to ten feet apart…. They were all around me, and those nearest the capsule would occasionally move across the window as if I had slightly interrupted their flow. On the next pass I turned the capsule around so that I was looking right into the flow, and though I could see far fewer of them in the light of the rising sun, they were still there. Watching them come toward me, I felt certain they were not caused by anything emanating from the capsule…. As far as I know, the true identity of these particles is still a mystery."

> I have even conjectured that these orbs are themselves an intelligence, manifesting a physical appearance….

Were the glowing, greenish "fireflies" Lt. Colonel Glenn saw actually spirit entities? And do the strange greenish-yellow lights that one of our most respected astronauts sighted in space have anything in common with Spooksville's ghost light? Or the "jack-o'-lantern that followed Beverly home? Or the glowing entity walking across the Sinclair estate?

Various questions remain: Are we dealing with separate phenomena in the different fields of religious, scientific, and psychic thought? Or are we dealing with the same phenomena, but simply expressed in the specific nomenclature of these various disciplines? And will we ever be able to strip aside our preconditioned ways of looking at things to discover what these phenomena truly represent?

3
POLTERGEISTS: UNWELCOME HOUSE GUESTS

Most people think of ghosts as shadowy or invisible beings that throw dinner plates and pieces of furniture around the room, occasionally materialize as fearsome entities, and sometimes levitate people for good measure. As we shall see throughout this book, there is actually a very wide range of phenomena we can popularly and collectively called ghosts. The ghosts that throw things and create rather dramatic household disturbances are known as poltergeists, German for "noisy ghost."

Many contemporary researchers argue that such invisible housebreakers are really not messy and rude ghosts, but berserk bundles of uncontrolled psychokinetic energy, the direct action of mind on matter. These investigators also attribute the often violent disturbances to the sexual changes and adjustments which accompany puberty, the early stages of a marital union, or feelings of inadequacy or frustration accentuated by some traumatic experience.

There may be many instances in which the outbreak of poltergeist phenomena might be associated with puberty and the dramatic changes to a child's psyche brought on by the onset of adolescence. However, many of the classic cases of noisy and disruptive ghosts occurred where no adolescent was in the household. In general, if the extrasensory ability of psychokinesis, or mind over matter, can somehow cause an individual to become an unaware participant in haunting phenomena, then we may have to expand our theory of the poltergeist. Perhaps we need to include those instances in which the human mind, under stress, fatigue, sleep deprivation, and so forth, may release uncontrolled spontaneous energy that has the power to activate and to interact with dormant spirit forces.

THE THROWING GHOST OF SLAWENSIK CASTLE

On October 28, 1806, after the Prussian armies had been mauled at the battle of Jena by zealous French soldiers under the leadership of Napoleon,

Prince Friedrich Hohenlohe was declared a prisoner of war. He was to be taken to France until Napoleon decided to ransom him or to set him free. One of the most trusted members of Friedrich's council, August Hahn, won a parole from the French. The Prince asked Hahn to oversee his castle at Slawensik in Upper Silesia (today one of the most industrialized regions of Poland) until Napoleon saw fit to release him.

Although he was eager to return to his own home, August Hahn admired the Prince and he decided to accept the responsibility. He had never visited this particular castle before, not unusual as the Prince had numerous estates. Hahn would be in the company of several others at the castle: his personal servant, Johannes; two of the Prince's coachmen; and Frau Knittel, the caretaker, who lived on the grounds with her son. In addition to the servants, however, Hahn wanted some intellectual fellowship. So he entreated his boyhood friend, Karl Kern, who had been at Jena as a member of a Hussar regiment, to join him at the castle for the duration of his stay. Kern consented to become a member of the group of self-imposed exiles, and the entourage arrived at Castle Slawensik on November 19, 1806.

It was about nine o'clock on the third evening after their arrival at Slawensik when the two men were pelted with fragments of lime and other debris as they sat reading in the corner room they occupied on the first floor. In those days, lime was commonly used as an ingredient in plaster, mortar, and cement; thinking the old castle ceiling was crumbling, Kern jumped to his feet, and cursed the medieval structure.

Hahn glanced warily toward the ceiling and noticed there were no cracks at all. How could lime and debris fall on them from a perfectly sound ceiling?

The two friends stood up on chairs so that they might better inspect the ceiling. They were unable to detect one single sign of damage, but as they searched the area above them, another shower of lime rained down on them.

Kern picked up a number of pieces and commented that they felt very cold to the touch, as if they had somehow loosened themselves from an outside wall.

Hahn continued to study the ceiling for some kind of opening through which the lime might have dropped. First thing in the morning, he said, they would have to put the servants to work to fix any problems before the winter set in.

The next morning, the men were greatly disturbed to find the room carpeted by the mysterious lime. Kern groused that the ceiling could have fallen in on them while they slept, but Hahn continued to be perplexed. There were no huge, gaping cracks—why was so much lime falling?

That evening, the fourth night of their stay at the castle, the bits of lime did more than fall from an invisible crack. They began to fly about the room and pelt the two men. As they retreated to their beds, the sound of loud knocking began to reverberate eerily down the ancient halls of the castle.

Kern became convinced that Hahn was somehow responsible for the flying bits of lime and the rapping sounds and for some reason was trying to frighten him. But this was disproven by a loud series of knocks that shook the room at a time when both of Hahn's hands were in full view of his nervous and angry companion.

Since the loud raps on the wall made sleep virtually impossible, August Hahn brought out his notebook and began a journal of the haunting phenomena. As an attorney, Hahn was used to analyzing facts—not a man who could be easily deceived or taken in by the work of a prankster.

> They began to fly about the room and pelt the two men.

When the manifestations began on the fifth night, Hahn and Kern were ready with the keys to the rooms overhead. While Hahn remained below, Kern and the son of the caretaker went to search the apartments above their rooms. All the rooms were empty.

Later that night, Kern and Hahn were awakened by the sound of someone wearing slippers moving across the room. A lighted candle showed the room to be empty. Afterwards, the invisible slippers had been joined by what sounded like someone bouncing a walking stick on one end.

By the time another night had passed, the two friends and the servants stopped trying to explain the disturbances in terms of natural causes. It had now become very apparent that the castle was haunted by a very active ghost. Candlesticks flew from one corner of a room to another. When the household sat down to dinner, knives, forks, plates, and foodstuffs became animated and airborne. Anything movable seemed to be possessed with the ability to levitate about the room.

After three weeks of enduring sleepless nights due to knockings on the walls and ceiling of their room on the first floor, Hahn and Kern gave the servants orders to have their things moved into the corner room overhead. Hahn had not slept long when he was awakened by the sound of his friend whimpering.

Hahn rolled out of bed and saw Kern staring into a mirror as though he were transfixed. He was extremely pale and trembling as if suffering from a fever. After taking several moments to compose himself, Kern managed to say that while looking in the mirror, he had seen, clearly reflected, a feminine figure swathed in white. At first he thought it was his imagination, he could see his own reflection behind the ghostly woman.

When the phantasm's eyes met his own, Kern perceived that the face was of an old woman. Her features appeared quite tranquil and not at all distressed, but he could not help being filled with some sort of nameless dread.

Hahn stepped to the mirror and demanded that the shade show itself to him. He stared into the mirror for fifteen minutes before he finally abandoned his attempts to summon the ghost of the old woman.

By now it was nearly dawn, and the two friends forgot about sleep for another night. As soon as they heard the servants stirring, Hahn decided to have their things brought back down to the first floor.

After Hahn and Kern had spent a month at Slawensik castle, the weird tales of unearthly happenings were spread abroad. Two Bavarian officers, Captain Cornet and Lieutenant Nagerle, both hard-nosed skeptics, decided to come out to the castle and see what all the ghost business was about. Lieutenant Nagerle, the most vocal in his skepticism, offered to spend a night in the haunted corner room.

The men had not left the Bavarian officer for more than a few minutes when they heard the lieutenant cursing loudly. The usual noises of the disturbance were punctuated by the sounds of the officer hacking away at table and chairs with his saber.

When they opened the door to the room that the ghost had claimed for its own, they were shocked to see Lieutenant Nagerle chopping at the air with his saber. It was difficult to believe that the officer, who moments before had been so cynical and brave, was now reduced to a frightened man who ran about an empty room, slashing at an invisible enemy.

At the sight of his companions, Lieutenant Nagerle seemed to shake off his fear and replace it with anger. As soon as the others had left him alone, he explained, the accursed thing had begun to pelt him. He had looked everywhere, but could see nothing. At last his anger got the best of him, and he drew his saber.

Once again in control of his faculties, the lieutenant began to suggest that he had been tricked by August Hahn and Karl Kern. The two friends sat down with the officers and earnestly tried to convince them that this was no prank. Captain Cornet also assured his fellow officer that he had not allowed Hahn and Kern out of his sight.

Then, while the four men sat talking around a table, a series of inexplicable things happened: candlesticks rose in mid-air and fell to the floor; a lead ball struck Hahn on the chest, but did not harm him. The sound of footsteps were heard about the room, and a drinking glass jumped off a stand to shatter itself against the floor. Although the Bavarian officers protested that these things were impossible, neither of them accused Hahn or Kern of being responsible for the manifestations.

The phenomena at Slawensik castle continued to increase in strength and ingenuity. Once, after August Hahn had carefully prepared some water for shaving and had heated it to just the temperature that he desired, the

In 1887 the Fowler family suffered from poltergeist activity in their home, depicted here for the 1945 edition of Harry Price's *Poltergeist over England*.

water was sucked out of the basin and disappeared before he was able to moisten his razor.

Herr Doerfel, a local bookseller, had his hat hidden from him as he was preparing to leave the castle. After the household had looked for several minutes in vain, the hat floated teasingly in front of its owner. As the frustrated and frightened bookseller reached for his head piece, the hat jerked out of his grasp. Then the hat led its owner a merry chase before it finally dropped at his feet.

Hahn, who was exhausted from sleep deprivation, announced firmly to the ghost one night that he did not want to feel a single object thrown at him while he attempted to rest on his bed. It seemed for a little while as though the entity was going to cooperate with him. Hahn had just drifted off into a deep sleep when he was rudely awakened by a large quantity of water being dumped in his face.

But one of the most eerie phenomena occurred during the absence of Hahn, who had left the castle for a few days to journey to Breslau. Kern, who was nervous throughout the disturbances, refused to sleep alone in the haunted room, but was just stubborn enough to refuse to move his bed to another location. At last, he persuaded Johannes, Hahn's personal servant, to spend the night with him in the afflicted bedroom.

So after they settled down for the night, they saw a jug of beer rise slowly from a table and begin to pour its beverage into a tumbler. Then, before their unbelieving eyes, the glass was lifted and slowly emptied, just as if someone were drinking from it.

The glass was replaced on the table, and the men walked quickly to the place where the beer had been consumed. There was not a drop of beer to be found on the floor. The men were terrified that the invisible thing could actually swallow liquid.

The disturbances seemed to culminate with the beer-drinking episode. One night, as Hahn was returning home to the castle, he began to hear the footpads of a dog behind him. Thinking it was their greyhound, Flora, the attorney turned and called the dog by name. But there was nothing behind him. Hahn continued walking, still hearing the sound of a dog following close behind. Even when he ascended the stairs leading to the front door of the castle, he could still hear the dog panting at his heels.

Kern met him at the door, taking the doorknob from his friend's hand and calling Flora's name. When Hahn asked if Kern had seen a dog walking behind him up the stairs, Kern answered that of course he had. He had seen Flora behind Hahn and that had been the reason that he had taken hold of the knob. Since it appeared that Hahn did not see the dog, Kern was concerned that Hahn might shut the door on her.

Hahn explained to Kern about the mysterious footfalls of the invisible dog that had been following him in the dark, and the two friends immediately began a search for the greyhound. If one of them had heard a dog, and the other had seen one, surely Flora must now be scampering about in the woods.

They found Flora locked up in the stables. The coachmen assured them that the dog had not been set free at anytime during the day.

After this strange incident, the manifestations at Slawensik came to a halt. Hahn remained at the old castle for another six months until Prince Hohenlohe was released from imprisonment in France. Hahn concluded his journal on November 19, 1808—two years to the day that they had first arrived at Slawensik castle—with these words: "I have described these events exactly as I heard and saw them; from beginning to end I observed them with the most entire self-possession … yet the whole thing remains to me perfectly inexplicable."

Hahn did not seek to publish his bizarre journal until twenty years had ~~passed. He submitted~~ the manuscript to Dr. Andreas Justinus Kerner, the lyric poet, physician, chemist, and pioneer psychical researcher. When Kerner published the journal, it created an immediate sensation in Germany.

The only key to the mystery of the pounding, pelting ghost was discovered in 1830 when Slawensik was destroyed by a fire caused by the direct strike of a lightning bolt. In the ruins, workmen discovered the skeleton of a man who had been walled up in a secret enclosure. His skull had been split and a sword was laying by his side.

The Stone-Throwing Devil of New Hampshire

In 1662, George Walton, an ambitious New Hampshire farmer who lusted for more land, eyed the few acres that bordered his farm with ever-growing greed. The bit of land was owned by an elderly widow, who lived in a small cabin on the acreage. Walton knew that she had neither money nor influential friends, so he had her charged with witchcraft. Then, either through greasing the palms of the officials or some other chicanery, the greedy farmer obtained the widow's land, which had been confiscated by the authorities after her arrest.

"You'll never quietly enjoy that ground," the widow cursed him.

Walton merely laughed at the old woman's malediction, but he did have the decency to drop his charges of witchcraft against the poor, now homeless, widow.

On a Sunday night shortly after Walton had moved his family into the widow's house stones were bombarded against the roof and doors.

Fearing an attack by warriors from a nearby tribe, Walton shouted an alarm and reached for his musket. The occupants of the house cautiously looked out into moonlit fields and saw nothing. No one.

Then, as they blinked in disbelief, the front gate was wrenched from its hinges by invisible hands and tossed high into the air. Walton ventured out to investigate, his musket clenched firmly in his hands. A volley of stones was suddenly hurled at him, and he fled back into the cabin. He slammed the front door and barred it, as his family shuttered the windows. But the shutters were totally ineffective. In the stones came—through the shutters, through the glass windowpanes, rolling down the chimney, smashing against the door.

Objects in the room began to hurl themselves at George Walton. Candles were blown out. The bars on the doors began to bend under the fierce blows of an invisible hammer. A cheese-press smashed itself against a wall.

Somehow, the Waltons managed to survive that night of horror. However, the stone-throwing devil did not vanish with the coming of dawn.

Throughout that day, haystacks in the fields were broken up, and the hay tossed into the high branches of trees. As Walton attempted to go about his farm labors, the stones pursued him.

Richard Chamberlayne, secretary to the Governor of New Hampshire, who later wrote a pamphlet on the "Diabolick Inventions of the Devil," lived with the Waltons for a period of time during the three-month span of the violent disturbances. Chamberlayne tried desperately to trace the source of the pelting stones, and at first suggested that the activity might be the work of "naughty little boys." Chamberlayne had no sooner spoken these words of accusation, than one of the boys, who had been helping the farmhands put up hay, was struck so hard on the back that he began to cry.

The Waltons' devil never spoke a word, but it was quite proficient at snorting and whistling. And while it kept up a steady barrage of stones, it also managed to wreak havoc by smashing pottery and slamming furniture about the house.

Even if one feels that the greedy Walton deserved to have a "devil" set on him after he had displaced the poor widow and taken her land, one has to admire the perseverance of the man, who kept right at his farm work in spite of the vicious attacks of the invisible stone-thrower.

Chamberlayne declared that Walton often received more than forty "shrewd, hurtful blows" in a single day. Several rows of corn were uprooted as if by a sharp tool. Walton's farmhands had sickles knocked out of their hands and the blades broken by the stones of the invisible demon. Chamberlayne himself received a "smart blow on the leg during his stay."

After about three months, the bombardment of stones ceased. Because this occurred in 1662, as one might suppose, the entire disturbance was immediately attributed to the curse of a witch. To have thought otherwise would have been heresy—the ultimate lesson that twenty-four men and women learned when they were executed, or died in prison as a result of the Salem witchcraft trials in 1692.

A Two-Week Bombardment of Stones from Nowhere

The Oakland, California police had been frankly skeptical when they received a frantic call from Mrs. Irene Fellows on August 17, 1943. Mrs. Fellows claimed that someone was pelting her stucco home on 89th Avenue with stones. For two weeks, she claimed, she and her granddaughters Donna Lee Wade, five, and Audrey, nine, had been bruised by stones that seemed to fall from nowhere.

In 1973 a Brazilian family was plagued by a poltergeist that would slash their furniture.

When two bemused patrolmen arrived to investigate the complaint, they were quick to notice that the walls and roof of the cottage were unmistakably pockmarked. Their amusement quickly turned to professional concern as they examined the indentations. Then, as they questioned the frightened woman, a stone fall occurred, hammering the roof with violent intensity. "It has been like this since dawn," Mrs. Fellows insisted.

The police officers looked around outside, and despite their skepticism, they could not ignore the many piles of worn rocks littering the lawn.

An official vigil began on August 18th. The police officers interviewed the neighbors—with special emphasis on the children—and exonerated all of them. Whatever was responsible for hurling the rocks seemed to react against the interference of the police by launching even more malicious attacks on Mrs. Fellows and her grandchildren. Several witnesses saw the inhabitants of the stucco cottage barraged by stones that struck and bruised their bodies. Irene Fellows was dealt a solid blow on the shoulder even as she talked with Sergeant Austin Page.

Sightseers began to arrive, and some of them boldly invaded the lawn to collect the "bewitched" stones as curios. Someone suggested that Mrs. Fellows open a museum to display her "stones from the blue." One so-called psychic investigator said that it was her considered opinion that the family was being dive-bombed by sea gulls carrying rocks they had obtained from the beach.

Scientists from the nearby University of California investigated Oakland's mystery house and acknowledged these brief facts: Whenever Mrs. Fellows and her grandchildren left their home, stones from a cloudless sky struck one or more of them. Other stones fell on the cottage. No stones were visible until they hit. The stones made no sound in flight. They came from all directions and fell with sufficient force to mark the house or bruise the bodies of Mrs. Fellows, Donna Lee, and Audrey.

At noon, September 1, Mrs. Fellows, exhausted from lack of sleep, was talking with Special Officers Johnston and Nordendahl, in her garden. The stones had been falling day and night for two weeks, and the elderly woman was on the brink of collapse. As the three of them were discussing the phenomenon, a huge stone suddenly crashed down at their feet. It was the last of the mysterious stones to strike the stucco cottage on 89th Avenue.

Ivan T. Sanderson, world-famous zoologist, natural historian, and investigator of the unusual, once told me when I visited him at his estate in New Jersey that one should not use the term "throwing" when speaking of the poltergeist's manipulation of stones. "The stones are not thrown; they are dropped or lobbed or just drift around," Sanderson insisted.

Sanderson went on to declare that such cases are actually within the realm of physics rather than psychical research. Stone-dropping, he said, is a purely physical phenomena and will, in time, be completely explained through physical principles—though not necessarily those proposed by Newton or Einstein, or other conventions of our particular space-time continuum.

Sanderson told me that he "played catch" with flying rocks in Sumatra. "If somebody would measure their speed of fall on arrival," he maintained, "it might be demonstrated that they are obeying some law or, at least, following some pattern that is not entirely random. They might be obeying some other so-called 'law' of dynamics. If we could establish this, we would have at least two principles of dynamics in our space-time continuum."

A FIERY GHOST CALLED LARRY

The Stringer finally had to call the ghost "Larry," because their four-year-old son kept asking about the column of vibrating light. The boy's father, Graham Stringer explained to a reporter for United Press International that they didn't want to frighten him with a lot of ghost talk.

Larry would be benign most of the year, but each Easter season beginning in 1958 the strange entity brought mysterious fires to their home on Trafalgar Avenue in the Peckham district of London.

It was on Good Friday of 1958 that the Stringers first saw the ghost. It was a milky, fluorescent column of vibrating light about as tall as a man. Shortly after seeing the apparition, the Stringers smelled smoke coming from the baby's room. There they found that something had burned a hole through the center of a pile of the baby's clothes. It looked just as though a blowtorch had ignited the clothes. Curiously, though, a pair of highly inflammable nylon stockings on the bottom of the pile was untouched.

In 1959, the Easter season once again brought Larry, instead of the Easter Bunny, to the Stringers' home. When Graham Stringer had a pair of shoes yanked out of his hands, he decided that it was time to call in the experts.

A team of investigators from the College of Psychic Science did not come to a firm conclusion after analyzing the disturbances, but they definitely identified the phenomenon as being poltergeistic in nature. Asking some psyche-probing questions, they established that Mrs. Stringer had experienced the visitation of a poltergeist during her adolescence. Mr. Stringer also recalled similar phenomena during their honeymoon, although they had barely noticed it at the time.

Although the Stringers were prepared for Larry the fiery ghost when he returned in 1960, they were powerless to prevent the murky column of light from burning up another pile of clothes. Clocks were still moving about on the mantelpiece, and objects were still floating around the apartment for several days after Easter Sunday. Stringer, a freelance photographer, reported being enveloped in a gray, fluorescent cloud while working in his darkroom. "The room just lit up," he told reporters. "And there was Larry vibrating and glowing at my side."

In 1961, the Stringers attempted an exorcism, asking a Catholic priest to administer the rites shortly before their annual visitor was due. It seemed to have worked, but their rejoicing over the ecclesiastical triumph was short-lived. Larry had simply taken a year's sabbatical. He returned with a vengeance in 1962, when the Stringers' living room furniture burst into flames. The fire erupted spontaneously, destroying several pieces of furniture, their carpet, and their son's bed.

On April 21, 1962, a spirit medium disclosed that Larry was in reality Mrs. Stringer's brother, Charles, who had died from burns twenty years earlier at the age of eighteen months. Now that the spirit had made his identity known, the medium promised, he would leave the family in peace.

Whether Larry the ghost actually was Charles' spirit or whether the phenomenon was due to some long-repressed, subconsciously nurtured guilt on the part of Mrs. Stringer, who may have considered herself in some way responsible for her brother's death, the Easter poltergeist of Peckham did not return to the Stringer household.

A MESSY UNINVITED GUEST IN BALTIMORE

When the poltergeist is at its peak, the host family may be beleaguered to the psychological breaking point. Psychoanalyst Dr. Nandor Fodor maintains that the poltergeist is unquestionably sadistic. Dr. Fodor theorizes that such projected aggression through unknown biological factors is the one way in which an adolescent can release hostility against his parents and other figures of authority and still maintain his conscious innocence.

Between January 14 and February 8, 1960, the Edgar C. Jones family in Baltimore, Ohio, were the unhappy hosts to an uninvited guest that proved to be very messy. The poltergeist activity began when a row of Mrs. Jones' prized ceramic pitchers exploded one by one. Then, while the startled family watched in bewilderment, a flowerpot lifted itself from a shelf and smashed through a nearby windowpane. A sugar bowl floated up to the chandelier and scattered its contents in the candleholders. Pictures were tossed off the walls, and a brass incense burner became airborne and sailed six feet off a bookshelf.

Once when Mrs. Jones and her married daughter, Mrs. Pauls, were preparing a meal, several glasses danced off the shelf in the cabinet and shattered on the floor. No sooner had the women cleaned up the shards of glass when two dirty ashtrays flew into the kitchen and dumped their contents on the floor. A suddenly animated table on a stairway landing came bounding down the steps to splinter itself at the foot of stairs.

The home-wrecking poltergeist did not ignore the basement in its domination of the Jones household. A case of soda bottles popped open, their caps flying off in a series of explosions that sounded like a string of firecrackers on the Fourth of July. A neatly-stacked pile of firewood erupted in violent bursts of energy that sent bits of bark and pulp flying across the floor.

No one received any substantial physical harm (it is seldom that anyone ever does during a poltergeist attack), but Mr. Jones was struck on the head by a falling can of sauerkraut as he stooped to pick up a can of corn that the invisible, rambunctious ghost had thrown. The can of sauerkraut barely bruised him, but Jones felt true anguish when he saw some of his most valued pieces of furniture rudely destroyed by their violent and unbidden guest. In fact, although none of the Jones household—Mr. and Mrs. Jones, their daughter, Mrs. Pauls, and their seventeen-year-old grandson, Ted—were injured in any appreciable way, they all suffered terrible mental and emotional pain during the three-week siege of the poltergeist.

Many researchers have noted that, sadistic attacks are often directed toward people of authority (parents, older siblings, police officers, clergymen). But the psychic "eye of the storm,"—the individual who serves as the energy center for the poltergeist—may receive attacks as well: stigmata on the flesh, painful puffing up of the body, or the appearance of writing on walls or various personal objects relating vile and obscene threats. Whether such abuse is due to unconscious feelings of guilt is difficult to assess. It would seem that, in at least some cases, the agent of the poltergeist is subconsciously aware that he or she is responsible for the psychic storm which has been unleashed in the home.

In 1967 a lawyer's office in Germany was invaded by a poltergeist. This photograph reveals the poltergeist's favorite method of making its presence known: forcing chandeliers to swing aggressively.

Dr. Fodor was able personally to investigate the Jones case in Baltimore. He learned that the crime laboratory of the police department found no trace of volatile substances in any of the moving or exploding objects. The city engineers had been there to test for earth tremors with a seismograph, but they found nothing. A radio repairman had arrived with a theory that high-frequency radio waves had been responsible for the weird occurrences, but his sophisticated equipment could find nothing to substantiate his thesis. A local plumber claimed the ghost was nothing but suction coming from the hot-air furnace, but none of his tinkering did anything to hinder the activities of the noisy demon in the Jones house. Newspaper reporters, television crews, press photographers, and radio interviewers stomped through every inch of the home and photographed the phenomena from every conceivable angle. Kooks, cranks, and cultists had plagued the Joneses, each with his own time-tested method of ridding a home of an unwanted ghost.

But Dr. Fodor felt that he had discovered the poltergeist with little effort at all. Seventeen-year-old Ted was a shy, brooding youth, who had left school at the legal age because he said that his classes bored him. He liked to sit alone in his room and read. He confessed to the psychoanalyst that what he wanted most to do was to write short stories. Dr. Fodor put the ghost to rest by encouraging the teenager to do what he most desired, write fiction. A very simple exorcism, indeed, but it worked. When the youth realized that he had found a sympathetic audience for his opinions and someone who would listen to a recitation of his ambitions and goals, the poltergeist activity ceased.

Dr. Fodor had come to alter an earlier opinion that poltergeist phenomena only occurred in prepubescent children. The psychoanalyst believed that the mechanics of poltergeist activity were accomplished by what he termed "psychic dissociation." Dr. Fodor theorized that the human body is capable of releasing energy in a manner similar to atomic bombardments. Through such psychic bombardments, for example, a projected energy force was apparently able to enter soda bottles and burst them open from within.

Noted British author and art critic Sacheverell Sitwell also expresses the opinion that the poltergeist most often finds its energy center in the psyche of an adolescent, who performs the ghostly effects, both consciously and unconsciously, " … being gifted for the time being with something approaching criminal cunning. The particular direction of this power is always towards the secret or concealed weaknesses of the spirit … the obscene or erotic recesses of the soul. The mysteries of puberty, that trance or dozing of the psyche before it awakes into adult life, is a favorite playground for the poltergeist."

Perhaps Dr. Fodor said it simplest when he told the press during his investigation of the Jones case that a ghost haunts a house and a poltergeist haunts a person. In his opinion, the psychoanalyst said, the poltergeist was very often not really a ghost, "but a bundle of projected repressions."

POPPING BOTTLES ON LONG ISLAND

When the two Herrmann children, twelve-year-old James, Jr. and thirteen-year-old Lucille, walked through their front door after school at 3:30 P.M. on February 3, 1958, they received a most bizarre "five-gun salute." The caps of bottles located in various rooms of the suburban Long Island home began to pop like champagne corks.

Scurrying from room to room, Mrs. Herrmann and the children found that a bottle of bleaching fluid had blown its top in the basement. In the kitchen, they located an uncapped bottle of liquid starch. The bathroom yielded both an uncapped bottle of shampoo and a topless bottle of liquid medicine. Mrs. Herrmann also discovered that a bottle of holy water had been spilled in the master bedroom.

Mrs. Hermann called her husband, who was a representative for Air France in New York City, and told him about the strange "popping" sounds and capless bottles throughout the house. Herrmann was puzzled, but since no one had been hurt by the peculiar event, he decided that he not to come home immediately.

By the time he got home that evening, James Herrmann already had a solution fixed in his mind. Some chemical reaction in the formulas of the various products had caused the bottles to erupt. The fact that they had all popped at once was undoubtedly due to some weird coincidence and probably the result of excessive humidity in the house, or some other atmospheric oddity. He was a bit baffled, however, when he found out that each of the bottles had screw caps, requiring several turns before they could be removed. If the bottles had had the crimped caps commonly used on soda pop bottles at that time, his theory would have seemed much more valid. It seemed quite impossible that a chemical reaction could have blown off the screw caps without damaging the necks of the bottles. He was relieved that his family had calmed down because he had no comforting explanation to offer them.

There were no further disturbances in the Herrmann household until two days later. Then it was a repeat performance of the poltergeist's debut. The children walked in the front door from school and the fireworks began. A bottle of nail polish popped open, and so did a bottle of rubbing alcohol, a bottle of bleach, starch, detergent, and, once again, the holy water. And all the bottles had screw-on caps.

When the bottles began to pop on the next night as well, James Herrmann began to suspect that his science-fiction loving son had somehow hatched a little plot to have some fun at the expense of his family. Herrmann conjectured that James, Jr. had dropped some type of carbonate capsule into the bottles and loosened their lids in the morning before he left for school. He had probably succeeded in timing the explosions so he could be present to witness the startled expression on the face of his mother and sister.

Herrmann spent most of that weekend surreptitiously observing his son. He was determined to catch the boy in some action that would give him away as the agent behind the mysterious poppings. No one, therefore, was more surprised than Herrmann when, on Sunday morning, several bottle caps popped off, and their containers began to jiggle on the shelves. He had kept an eye on the boy day and night. How could James, Jr. have slipped anything into the bottles? Herrmann began to question the boy, who stood at the bathroom sink brushing his teeth and vigorously proclaiming his innocence. In the middle of the interrogation, James Herrmann was startled to see a medicine bottle move across the sink top and smash itself to the floor. Within seconds, it was joined by a bottle of shampoo.

REAL GHOSTS, RESTLESS SPIRITS, AND HAUNTED PLACES

He called the police, begging the officer who answered to take him seriously. Herrmann told the officer he knew it sounded unbelievable, but his family was being bothered by bottles that popped their caps and flew about the room. The officer accused Herrmann of drinking, but he agreed to send a policeman to investigate the disturbances. James Herrmann had a good reputation in the community. It wasn't like him to annoy the police with wild stories.

Patrolman James Hughes had only been in the house a few minutes when several bottles in the bathroom fired a barrage at him. He rapidly concluded that the Herrmanns were not imagining this—they did, indeed, have a very peculiar problem. Detective Joseph Tozzi listened to Patrolman Hughes' report with professional interest, then concluded that if bottles were acting up at the Herrmanns, they were doing it with human help.

Detective Tozzi began his vigil on February 11. On that day, an atomizer in Lucille's bedroom tipped over when no one was in the room. Or, Detective Tozzi noted skeptically, at least no one would admit to having been in the bedroom. For the next few days, the disturbances were confined to the parents' bedroom, where the bottle of holy water was upset repeatedly. On the evening of February 15, however, the manifestations became much more impressive. As the family sat watching television, a porcelain figurine lifted itself from a coffee table and began to float through the air.

After this demonstration of prowess on the part of their uninvited guest, the Herrmanns decided to call upon a priest to aid the baffled Detective Tozzi in his investigations. Father William McLeod of the Church of Saint William the Abbott answered their plea for clerical help and administered a blessing to the home by sprinkling holy water liberally in six rooms. But the priest was too late. "Popper," as the strange force in the Herrmann house had come to be called, had grown too strong to have its spark of psychic life extinguished by holy water.

Much worse than the antics of Popper, the Herrmanns soon discovered, was the invasion of privacy they endured when the news media began to give their strange house a great deal of publicity. Letters scrawled with barely intelligible messages arrived, either condemning them for fraud or encouraging them to take heart and fight against the evil tricks of Satan.

On February 19, a porcelain figurine flew off a table and traveled over twelve feet in the air before it smashed against a desk. On February 20, another figurine became airborne, a bottle of ink unscrewed its cap and splashed its contents against a wall, and a sugar bowl took its leave of the dining table. Seventeen days after its arrival, Popper was steadily acquiring the strength to perform more dramatic and more spectacular demonstrations.

The Herrmanns, who had remained remarkably calm and patient throughout the phenomena, decided that they needed to get away from the

In 1952 the Glynn family of Runcorn, Chesire, United Kingdom, suffered the exploits of a
nasty poltergeist that would wreck entire rooms. The police even attempted to set traps
around the home to prevent further abuse, but the attacks continued. In this photograph,
John Glynn surveys his wrecked bedroom.

house before their nerves gave out. While they spent the night of February 21
with relatives, Detective Tozzi maintained his vigil in the house that Popper
had taken over with its infantile pranks. Although Tozzi's attitude toward
paranormal manifestations had altered considerably from the first night that
he had spent with the Herrmanns, it didn't bother him in the slightest to
remain alone in the "haunted house." The night was quiet and without incident. There were no poppings, no moving of furniture, no flying figurines. But
the truce at the Herrmann house was ended as soon as the family returned.
Once again the sugar bowl became so animated that it shot off the table and
crashed to the floor.

On February 24, Detective Tozzi investigated a loud thud that had
come from James, Jr.'s room. The officer was certain that no one had been in
the room or near it, but upon entering the bedroom, he found that a heavy
bureau had been tipped facedown on the floor. The next night, the boy's

A still taken from the classic movie *Poltergeist*.

phonograph orbited itself around the room while he was doing his homework. In the master bedroom, a statuette of the Virgin Mary flew over twelve feet to strike the frame of a mirror across the room. A bookcase full of bulky encyclopedias was upended. A globe of the world shot down a hallway, narrowly missing Detective Tozzi. A photographer saw his own flashbulbs raise themselves from a table, float across the room, and bounce against a wall. For the first time, Popper began to knock on the wall, but no attempt at any sort of communication was attempted.

Detective Tozzi was worried about the sudden flurry of violent activity on the part of Popper. Previously, he had had the house checked by electricians and physicists; he even enlisted the help of the Air Force to determine whether or not jet flight patterns might somehow be causing supersonic vibrations. He had taken the advice of occultists, self-styled preachers, and anonymous letter writers. Any plan that seemed remotely plausible, he had tried to apply to the Herrmann household. But nothing worked. The manifestations seemed to be growing in strength and were becoming increasingly violent in their demonstrations.

Just as the detective was about to recommend that the family move to avoid personal harm, Popper appeared to use up its last reserves of energy. The poltergeist said its farewell at ten o'clock on the evening of March 2. It sent a dish shattering in the dining room, a night table falling in James Jr.'s bedroom, and a bookcase tumbling in the basement. With this parting gesture, Popper left the Herrmanns, never to return.

⸺⚬⚮⚬⸺

THE SPRINGFIELD POLTERGEIST

By Tim R. Swartz

Tim R. Swartz is an Indiana native, an Emmy-Award winning television producer/videographer, and the author of a number of popular books. As a photojournalist, Swartz has traveled extensively and investigated paranormal phenomena and other unusual mysteries from such diverse locations as the Great Pyramid in Egypt and the Great Wall in China. He has worked with television networks such as PBS, ABC, NBC, CBS, CNN, ESPN, Thames-TV, and the BBC.

When you are working in a television newsroom you are often the first to hear about strange events such as hauntings. Most assignment editors would take these leads and throw them away, but, because of my interest in the subject, I often managed to rescue them from the trash pile to conduct my own investigations.

Most people who are experiencing a haunting are not interested in publicity. Instead, they are looking for help, answers, and reassurance that they are not alone. They usually first seek help from their church or local police and only turn to the media as a last resort.

One such case involved an elderly couple who lived in a rural area near Springfield, Ohio. This happened in 1983 when I was working as a videographer at a station in nearby Dayton. I received word that this couple was experiencing unusual activity in their house; they were bewildered and frightened. I quickly called the Huberts (not their real name) who told me that they were not interested in being on television; they just wanted help to put an end to the haunting. They told me that they were hearing strange sounds, loud knocks on the walls, voices talking in empty rooms. Furniture moved around. Bottles, ashtrays, and other small items would suddenly jump off a table and fly across the room as if thrown by an invisible hand. The telephone would ring incessantly, but there would be no one on the line. Electric lights would turn on and off repeatedly and the bulbs would suddenly shatter with a loud bang. Small animals would unexpectedly appear in the middle of the room, dart across the floor, and vanish through a closed door.

I reassured the couple that I was not going to put their story on television and set a date to come out to their house. Today, paranormal investigators have access to all sorts of electronic devices like electromagnetic field detectors and full-spectrum cameras. Even though these types of instruments were not available to me at that time, I was fortunate to have a broadcast-quality portable video camera and a 3/4 inch recorder to take with me. Rounding out my ghost-hunting gear was a mini-cassette recorder, and two cameras: a 35mm and a Polaroid.

The Huberts' house bore no resemblance to the stereotypical haunted house. There were no broken windows, peeling paint or fluttering bats. Instead, I found a very normal 1950s-style ranch home with a well-manicured front lawn. The place was surrounded by cornfields and somewhat isolated. Their nearest neighbor was almost half a mile away.

Once I was inside, Mrs. Hubert provided me with a large iced tea and I sat down with the entire family for an friendly chat. The family consisted of Mr. and Mrs. Hubert and their two grandchildren: a twelve-year-old girl and a nine-year-old boy. The grandchildren had recently moved in because legal circumstances had forced them to be separated from their parents. I also found out that the paranormal activity began shortly after the children moved in.

The Huberts said that when the activity first started, they would hear what sounded like heavy footsteps on a wooden floor coming from the vicinity of the attic. The problem with this was the attic had no floor and was covered with insulation. After that came strange knocks and raps on the walls. Sometimes the raps were so soft you could barely hear them. Other times they said it sounded as if someone was beating the walls with a baseball bat.

Mr. Hubert said that one day he was alone in the house and had gone out to collect the mail. He was gone no more than a few minutes, but when he came back, he found the backdoor blocked by the refrigerator. Another time Mrs. Hubert walked into the bathroom and was shocked to see a geyser of water shooting out of the toilet. The force of the water was so strong that it struck the ceiling and soaked the entire bathroom. The two children told me that whenever they were outside, rocks started pelting them, but since the rocks were coming at them from different directions, they could never see who or what was throwing the stones. The children became so frightened that they refused to go outside.

During our discussion, it became clear to me that the children were extremely unhappy about being forced to move in with their grandparents. In many so-called poltergeist cases, unhappy children are responsible for causing the disturbances. This can be a way of venting frustrations, or getting some much-needed attention. Children have been caught throwing things when they think no one is looking. Then again, truly mystifying paranormal activity by poltergeists has been observed. Extreme care is the key to investigating these types of events, and one should never let personal bias get in the way of arriving at the true cause of the occurrences.

> I... found out that the paranormal activity began shortly after the children moved in.

After getting to know everyone, I hooked up my camera and started to take some video of the interior of the house. In less than a minute, the low battery lights on both the camera and the recording deck started flashing and everything shut off. This was surprising because both sets of high capacity batteries had been fully charged and should have lasted at least several hours. But the unexpected draining of the batteries of my electronic equipment was something that had become all too familiar to me. In other investigations, in fact, this often turned out to be a good clue that sometime soon, paranormal activity was going to commence.

I started to pack away my gear when a loud bang emanated from somewhere near the ceiling. Mr. Hubert said, "It's starting."

I could see everyone from where I was standing; their eyes were focused on the ceiling. I heard a sharp click on the wooden floor in the center of the room. I looked down and saw a small, white rock on the floor. Then another dropped down next to it. Looking up, I saw other rocks dropping down from the ceiling. The room was well lit and I could clearly see that the rocks were actually dropping from a space in the air about an inch below the ceiling. It was as if they were coming from an invisible hole hanging in the air. I tried to capture this event with both my 35mm and Polaroid cameras (both continued to work, by the way), but the photographs didn't come out because the rocks were falling too quickly.

I gathered up the eight rocks and examined them closely. They felt warm and they were about the size of a nickel. They looked no different from the crushed limestone rocks that were in the Huberts front driveway. On an impulse, I grabbed a marker and drew an X on each rock. Saying out loud, "Let's see if they come back." I opened the backdoor and threw them into the cornfield behind the house. Almost immediately, rocks reappeared from the same spot above us and dropped to floor. Each rock was marked with an X.

After this, the tense atmosphere in the room seemed to lift and everyone started talking and even laughing at the strange event we had all just witnessed. I examined the ceiling closely but couldn't find any hole that the rocks could have fallen from.

> John searched for a logical explanation; however, logic seemed to vanish as he came face to face with the unknown.

Since I was the only one there, outside of the Huberts, it occurred to me that there was the possibility that someone was trying to pull a fast one on me. However, I have no idea why. The Huberts were not seeking attention; they just wanted to know what was going on and how to make it stop.

I revisited the Huberts a few more times after that. But after my first visit, the energy seemed to have been dissipated and the unusual activity vanished as quickly as it began. I don't know if additional electronic gear that ghost hunters now use would have been helpful. I only know what I saw with my own eyes. To this day, I still marvel at my experience and consider myself lucky to have been a witness to the unknown.

◆◆◆

THE WHITEHALL POLTERGEIST: NIGHTMARE IN THE NORTHEAST

By Paul B. Bartholomew

The word poltergeist is of German origin and means noisy or mischievous spirit. It usually involves an unseen force inhabiting a home or structure, which moves or throws various objects around. It often generates fear and bewilderment. It is nothing new. Cases documenting poltergeist activity can be traced back centuries.

In his book *Poltergeist*, Colin Wilson describes an incident from 858 B.C.E. that took place near Bingen, Germany. What was perceived as an "evil spirit" was apparently responsible for throwing stones and shaking walls at a farmhouse. In his classic *The Poltergeist*, William G. Roll also mentions the appearance in 1682 of the "Stone-Throwing Devil" of Great Island, New Hampshire. And there are numerous other examples to help illustrate the rich history of this unexplained phenomenon. Therefore, it should come as no surprise to learn of a modern poltergeist afflicting a home in the upstate town of Whitehall, New York.

"John" is an elderly man who lived alone in an apartment building in that small community. Certain details have been left out to help ensure his anonymity. "I don't want people to think I'm crazy," he said.

John would not be classified as a believer. Before this incident he had never encountered the unknown and regarded it with only a passing interest. That attitude began to change on November 23, 1988. It started with a bang. At about eleven o'clock in the morning, John heard a loud noise coming from inside his apartment. Thinking someone must have broken in, he systematically searched every room. No one was there.

"I figured it must have been my cat, but I knew it really wasn't," explained John, "there wasn't anything knocked over."

At about one o'clock in the afternoon, a repeat performance. This time a search produced the source of the noise—a small ashtray was resting in the center of the living room floor, far away from the table where it had previously rested. Unable to explain how the ashtray had moved, John went into his bedroom and laid down to rest. He tried not to think about it, but the questions still nagged away at him. At about 2 P.M., after a brief nap, John was awakened by the sound of his name being called. "They were like whisperings, but I couldn't find where they were coming from," he said.

Thinking someone must be at the door, he arose to answer it. No one was there. This really spooked John, who would find it impossible to sleep for the remainder of that day or evening. "I knew I wasn't crazy," explained John, "because the cat got up and looked around for somebody too."

At 4:30 P.M., John was startled to hear "footsteps" walking across the attic floor. Reasoning that it must be an intruder, he grabbed a flashlight and ascended into the dark, dusty attic. Again he found nothing. In fact, the attic had been sealed up from the inside and there were no signs that anyone had been there recently. Within a half hour, a drum-shaped table, weighing approximately thirty pounds, inexplicably toppled over in his bedroom. John searched for a logical explanation; however, logic seemed to vanish as he came face to face with the unknown.

At 10:15 P.M., John was seated at his kitchen table enjoying a hot cup of coffee. He slowly sipped from the cup while effortlessly glancing across the room. Suddenly, his eyes fixed in amazement on an ashtray as it moved from the kitchen counter to the floor, coming to rest quite a distance from the counter. Unable to explain it and unwilling to remain, John grabbed his jacket and immediately left for work. He didn't mind at all that he left a half hour early.

The events of that date only marked the beginning of a long line of poltergeist outbreaks. On December 1, a bookend which had always rested firmly on a three-foot-high shelf, was found smashed to pieces on the floor between the living room and the kitchen. John's neighbor began hearing strange noises coming from inside the apartment when John wasn't there. On one occasion she thought she heard someone calling his name. While John, to say the least, was not thrilled about these noises, he was reassured by his neighbor's comments—at least they confirmed what he had been experiencing. "I know I'm not imagining this because they heard the noises too. It's like someone rapping at the door all the time … and I've gone down a couple of times [to answer the door] but no one is ever there," explained John.

The mystery deepened when on December 19, John received a visit from his twelve-year-old granddaughter. John was sitting at the kitchen table, while she was watching television in the living room. Soon after, she walked into the kitchen with a puzzled look on her face and asked, "Who is that woman in the green dress walking around (in the living room)?" John quickly glanced into the room, but saw no one. Realizing that they were the only people in the apartment, and fearing he might frighten the young girl if he pressed her for details, John quickly changed the subject. The question went unanswered. "I didn't want to scare her," John said, "I didn't want her to be afraid to visit."

Two days after Christmas, John was awakened by a series of knockings at about 12:30 P.M. He checked the door but wasn't surprised to find nobody there. Since he was already up, he went into the kitchen to make a cup of coffee. As he panned the room he glimpsed something moving in the living room. "I saw movement, like out of the corner of my eye," he said.

Curiosity got the better of him as he cautiously walked into the living room to investigate. Carefully examining the room, he was satisfied everything looked normal. He turned around and headed back into the kitchen. It was then that an ashtray struck him in the back, just above the belt. "It didn't hurt, but it scared the hell out of me!" he exclaimed.

The phenomena subsided for several days. As 1989 quietly rolled in, John had hoped his poltergeist had run its course. It hadn't

On January 15, between 9 and 10 P.M., "slow knockings" were heard coming from inside the home. The exact origin of the sounds could not be located. Also, John noted a growing anxiety as if "something was building up" in his home. This feeling of uneasiness would last a week before any physical effects would be noticed.

January 22 was Super Bowl Sunday. Like millions of football fans worldwide, John was watching the big game on his living room television set. Again, he heard "short knockings" coming from somewhere inside the home. Conducting a room-by-room search turned up nothing. Upon returning to the living room he found a box of drink coasters, which had been resting on the table, were now lying on the floor, spread out like a deck of cards. The incident seemed harmless enough, but served as an annoying reminder that he wasn't alone.

On February 13 and 14, John's second granddaughter was visiting. She said she heard low-volume screaming and "voices" she couldn't understand. The pair both heard the now-common footsteps coming from the attic floor. Since this granddaughter had no prior knowledge of the poltergeist activity, these incidents helped to confirm that the phenomena seemed to be connected with the house, not just the owner. It also helped to reassure John of his own sanity.

On February 23, at about 8:30 P.M., a mirror which hung securely above the stereo inexplicably fell to the floor. Fortunately, it didn't break.

Glimpses of dark shadowy figures barely visible, footsteps and knockings which originate from nowhere, and small objects tossed about became the norm. John now expected to find these things. So on February 27, he wasn't surprised to find his living room wastebasket knocked over. It should be noted that John's cat had been locked out and could not have caused this.

> The incident seemed harmless enough, but served as an annoying reminder that he wasn't alone.

On March 11, at about 8 P.M., a large heavy almanac, resting on the desk in the kitchen, suddenly fell to the floor. He heard the loud noise, saw what had happened and was "spooked" by it. He decided it would be a good time to take a walk. Four days later, between 9 and 10 A.M., a pencil, and then an ashtray, fell from the same desk to the floor. All this happened while John's cat was asleep on his lap.

The mysterious visitor became more and more insistent, almost as if it was trying to intimidate John—or perhaps communicate with him. On March 27, at about 8 P.M., he was asleep on his bed when he was jolted awake by what he thought was something pulling on his leg. He saw nothing unusual and cautiously went back to sleep. Then on April 8, between 7 and 7:30 P.M., he was grabbed again. Wide awake and very shaken, John found this a terrifying experience. "No way that was any dream. I could feel it and it had a firm grip on my leg. I was so nervous, I got up on the edge of the bed and smoked a cigarette," exclaimed John. The uneasy stress created by the poltergeist was taking its toll. More objects fell to the ground—a cup dispenser fell in the bathroom, a writing tablet and two pens were scattered across the kitchen floor. John was at his wits end. "Let me tell you, I'm about ready to fly out of the house … to be honest about it. I would say that I was scared. I felt an urge to get the hell out of there."

August brought more trouble. A battery-operated clock fell off the kitchen wall. "I just picked it up and didn't bother to put it back up," said John. On August 26, a stack of "eight or nine books piled in two piles" and "about fifteen magazines" in one pile, were resting on the living room coffee table. After hearing a loud noise, John entered to find "the coffee table wasn't moved, but all the books and magazines were spread out across the floor."

In just under a year, over fifty instances of a possible parapsychological nature were noted.

September and most of October saw nothing unusual. John was relieved. He began feeling more at ease in his own home. Hoping the poltergeist was gone, he tried to put the subject behind him. He should have stayed on guard. Apparently, the phenomenon that was invading his residence was just building and would climax in a terrifying manifestation.

On October 28, sometime between 4 and 5 A.M., John was awakened from a sound sleep to the sight of a ghostly image appearing to be staring at him.

> All attempts to record the mysterious whispers or film the activity ... were unsuccessful.

"Something woke me up. The top of it was at the ceiling, so it had to be at least seven feet tall. It wasn't just a quick look ... it was several seconds because, I'm going to be honest with you, I was beginning to get terrified. I'm not kidding you, I was. It seemed like an hour, but it was probably really a half minute, anyhow," an excited John explained.

The apparition was of a "dark mass" which had a blurry white face in the upper part. He received no impression of a particular gender and said it made no harmful actions toward him. John was frozen to the bed as the hovering apparition seemed to block the doorway, as if intentionally preventing him from leaving the room.

"It was the most terrified I've ever been in my life," said John, "time seemed to stand still." Finally, the apparition simply faded away and John leaped out of his bed and headed for the kitchen. He turned on lights, made himself a cup of coffee, then sat down and gathered his thoughts.

Twice, John tried unsuccessfully to move from the residence. Finally in the late 1990s he found another home. Minor poltergeist activity was reported through 1990 and 1991, but paranormal activity became less frequent. The phenomena seemed to peak that October evening. The only significant reports from then on were of a rocking chair that rocked by itself and a lamp that occasionally tumbled over. All attempts to record the mysterious whispers or film the activity as it happened were unsuccessful.

Unlike Hollywood movies, there are no clear-cut answers. Theories range from demonology to classic haunting.

Some would suggest that this man was a victim of a demonic attack. They would say that ancient diabolical evil inhabited the home and unleashed this attack to continually feed off of the negative energies produced by John during his terrifying ordeal. They may suggest that an exorcism be performed to get rid of the evil. (It should be noted that no exorcisms or religious rite was ever conducted in the home.)

REAL GHOSTS, RESTLESS SPIRITS, AND HAUNTED PLACES

Probably most parapsychologists would argue that this is a classic poltergeist case—that some sort of unknown energy manifested itself in the home and caused the objects to move about. They would argue the energy did not intend to scare John, but simply ran its natural course.

As for John, he felt the outbreak had something to do with the death of his ex-wife, who died in December "a few years before the first incident." Although his ex-wife didn't pass away in the home, he remembers she was buried in a green dress. He feels "the woman in the green dress" seen by his granddaughter may actually have been her ghost.

John did some research into the home, but it produced only one documentation of a death taking place there. In the mid–1960s, a man died of a heart attack while climbing the stairway. But, if this was the source of the haunting, why didn't anything of note happen until more than twenty years later?

While none of these theories can adequately explain the enigma completely, perhaps the answer lies in a combination of several factors. One thing seems certain. An unknown energy seemed to build up and release itself into various manifestations that plagued this man intensely for a year. Although the true nature of this phenomenon is unknown, the details are consistent with poltergeist outbreaks and haunting experiences.

On January 12, 2001, the mystery disappeared into smoke as the apartment building burst into flames. An investigation suggested the fire which leveled the structure "was accidental and may have started on the second floor." ("Cause of Whitehall apartment fire still unknown," *Post-Star* [Glens Falls, New York], January 16, 2001.)

REVISITING THE SALEM WITCH HYSTERIA AS POLTERGEIST ACTIVITY

Because of the accusations of a small circle of prepubescent girls who had frightened themselves into a hysteric response to real or imagined phenomena, an entire community in the Massachusetts Bay Colony of 1692 became crazed, caught up in the fear that many of their neighbors were secretly serving Satan.

A strong case might be made for the argument that the famous Salem witchcraft hysteria of the late seventeenth century is really an example of the trickery of poltergeists. The young girls, who claimed to have been bewitched by invisible spirits controlled by various elderly women in the village, complained of being pinched, having their hair pulled, and being stuck with pins.

A "witch trials" memorial statue at the Salem Wax Museum of Witches and Seafarers in Salem, Massachusetts.

All these classic symptoms of a witch's wickedness we now recognize as familiar manifestations of the poltergeist.

Pursuing this thesis just a bit further, we might observe that throughout the centuries people have believed that witches have the power to command invisible agents to hurl stones at their victims and to torment people by the production of eerie night noises and destructive fires. All of these powers of the prototypical witch coincide with the attributes of the poltergeist. Perhaps an accomplished witch in the classic, rather than the religious definition of the name, is simply one who has somehow retained that strange psychokinetic fragmentation of the psyche which sometimes occurs during pubertal change and who has learned how to control it.

The madness at Salem began innocently enough in the home of the Reverend Samuel Parris when his slave Tituba began telling stories of voodoo and restless spirits to his nine-year-old daughter Betty and her eleven-year-old cousin Abigail Williams. Soon the exciting story-telling sessions in the Parris household were attracting older girls, such as sixteen-year-old Mary Walcott and eighteen-year-old Susannah Sheldon, who wanted Tituba to tell their fortunes and predict their future husbands as well. Although Reverend Parris and the other preachers fulminated from the pulpits about the dangers of seeking occult knowledge from spirits, the girls of Salem ignored such warnings in favor of a thrilling pastime that could help them through a long, cold winter.

Perhaps the psychic energies grew stronger when Ann Putnam, a fragile, highly strung twelve-year-old, joined the circle in the company of the Putnams' maid, nineteen-year-old Mercy Lewis. Ann had a quick wit, a high intelligence, and a lively imagination, and she soon became Tituba's most avid and apt pupil. Perhaps while a part of Ann's psyche was thrilled with the forbidden knowledge that Tituba was sharing with them, another more conservatively religious aspect was racked with guilt that they were flirting with devilish enchantment. Undoubtedly this conflict with conscience and the fear of discovery also affected the other girls.

This engraving of poltergeist activity in a French home appeared in Leo Taxil's book *Les Mystre de la Franc-maconnerie*, 1860.

I couldn't really tell where the sounds were originating. Les came back down from checking the roof and said that he could find nothing up there that could possibly make such noises. I told him to call Officers B. and L. to come and help us go through the apartment house. I thought right away that maybe son, especially a female, can serve as the center for these kings of weird disturbances, and I wonder if Mrs. C. and her daughter had been experiencing an emotional conflict of greater duration than an argument about school over dinner that night. Officer Les H. stepped into a number of apartments around and below the C's apartment, and neither he nor any of the occupants could detect any unusual sounds—certainly not the terrible pounding that we had experienced. Officer L. pointed out that there was a large cemetery across the street, and he admitted that he thought that he had seen and felt spirit presences in the C's apartment. Later, I learned that Mrs. C. and her daughter had moved out, because Sophie refused to return to the apartment. I think they also moved out of the city soon afterward."

⚛

A WEEKEND ENCOUNTER WITH A POLTERGEIST
The Personal Experience of Stacie Freeland

I had heard about the movie *Poltergeist*, but I didn't expect to spend an evening with such a rambunctious entity. The event in question took place at the family home of a friend, in Vista, New York. There were six "professional" adults present for a weekend gathering, and all of us had driven up from New York City earlier that morning.

It was a typical blustery, fall day, and the iridescent leaves that were falling when the wind tore them from their summer homes showered the ground with flashes of yellows, reds, and oranges, making perfect highlights to the all-gray backdrop. The converted barn which was to be our home for the weekend was situated on a lake and completely surrounded by forest. There were plenty of last-minute activities to keep us all busy—firewood to be collected, beds to be made, food shopping, and other errands to run.

After all the details had been attended to, we split up. Some of us went hiking in the woods, one person settled down to read a book, and others went for a joyride in the convertible that was at our disposal. I'd opted for the hike in the woods with Maura, our hostess, and the only other female present that weekend.

By the end of the day, the weather had grown threatening, and the wind became aggressive and unpredictable. It was clear to all of us that it was time to go inside. We had left the windows and doors open all afternoon, and after closing the building up tight, we built a fire and removed the first course of the evening meal from the fridge and set it on the stovetop. We were having homemade summer squash and red bell pepper soup. I'd been given the responsibility of choosing the music, and when Maura walked by me and asked me to keep an eye on the soup for a minute, I responded with a "sure."

Maura had just shut the bathroom door when I heard a very strange sound coming from the kitchen. Before I could get up from my cross-legged position on the floor, Maura, who had also heard the noise, came rushing out of the bathroom. Basically, we arrived on the scene together.

Somehow, the soup had violently exploded, spewing a third of its contents into an area three feet in every direction. I picked up the pan, thinking that the temperature change must have caused rapidly-formed air bubbles to erupt. But when I felt the bottom of the saucepan, it wasn't even warm. "That's really odd," I said to Maura. We called the rest of the crew into the kitchen to find out if anyone had tampered with the soup. Everyone claimed to be as confused as we were.

We began the task of cleaning up the mess, and Maura became concerned that there might not be enough soup to go around. The clean-up efforts took twenty minutes because we kept finding other places where the soup had splashed. The fan grate and light just above the stove was the hardest hit, and we used a lot of paper towels trying to wipe the infiltrated areas clean. Maura and I were still in the kitchen when Gordon, one of the houseguests, decided that he wanted a glass of wine. He had just opened the bottle and was in the process of pouring from it when the wineglass he held in his hand flew in a perfect upward arch and then came straight down to the floor. I saw with my own eyes the very deliberate movement the glass had taken and the lack of control that Gordon had over the glass. It was as if an invisible hand had knocked it out of his grasp on purpose.

We stood there, mouths slightly open, until Gordon asked, more as a joke than a serious question, "Is there a ghost in the house?"

"No, there are no ghosts," Maura said emphatically.

We all marveled at the fact that the wine glass had broken by the stem and not the delicate rim as we would have expected. "Strange," was Gordon's response.

Maura was in the middle of handing out what was left of the homemade soup when, without warning, all of the lights in the house went out. We all became motionless as if our bodies had become pillars of salt. After a moment of silence, everyone started speaking at once.

I heard someone blame Maura's husband, Ed, for this most recent occurrence. I called out quietly for Maura, and when she answered, I took a step closer to the sound of her voice. Then suddenly the lights came back on. Ed was visibly agitated, and he picked up the phone in order to call the electric company to find out whether or not the pending storm was causing power outages. His face went ashen.

"What's wrong?" Maura demanded.

"Well … the phone is dead," was his reply.

Again, everyone began to offer possible causes all at once. A few well-chosen swear words hit the air and, once again, the house lost all power, plunging us into darkness.

Ed went to the window to see if the streetlights were off as well, because the power to the house was connected to the lines that fed the lights lining the old country road. Those lights were on, so we thought our predicament must be the cause of a blown fuse. But the fuse box was in the basement, and no one offered to go down and check it out. It's funny how logic and rational thought disappear when there's an overload in the imagination. "It's the storm," someone said.

By now Maura had lit some candles, and we at least had the glow of the tiny flames to guide our steps. We made our way to the dinner table in almost complete

Stacie Freeland.

darkness and sat down just in time for the lights to come back on, returning all foreign shadows to their proper places. "That's no blown fuse!" Ed declared. This is going to be an interesting dinner, I thought to myself.

A warm fire was burning behind us, and the conversation around the table soon became centered on the odd occurrences that had taken place in the house. Suddenly Gordon, who was seated opposite me, stopped with his spoon halfway to his mouth. The manner in which his shoulders climbed up to his ears and his head jerked ever so slightly to the right made me stop what I was doing and turn my attention in the same direction as his gaze. I heard myself gasp.

Within the indoor atrium, which had become sanctuary to a collection of antique weather vanes, a single weather vane, which hung from the ceiling by a chain, was swinging violently in a 180-degree angle! No other object was moving, not even a single fern frond swayed! Nothing! The pace with which the lone weather vane was swinging was purposeful, and exact. The violence with which it swung was very disturbing.

Everyone was watching, unable to fully comprehend the event we were all witnessing. My husband, Erik, stood up from his chair and took a candle from the center of the table over to the atrium to search for a possible draft of some kind. None was found.

All the while, the weather vane continued its mad antics, swinging closer and closer to the wall. There was an orb in the center of the weather vane made of some type of non-opaque glass, and if it were to hit the wall, it would shatter—and we would have a lot of explaining to do to Maura's father, who owned the place. I asked Erik, who was still standing, if he could stop the antique vane from swinging. Ed dramatically bellowed out, "Don't touch it!" But Erik reached out and manually stopped the object from swinging. However, just as he did so, our friend Ed immediately started to have trouble breathing. Ed was hyperventilating and had to go outside into the cold night air to recover and catch his breath.

> **E**rik and I were standing in the middle of the room, staring at each other, when the lights slowly dimmed....

The wine was beginning to take effect and that seemed to help our ability to deal with the events of the evening. The dishwasher had been loaded and the table cleared. Nobody really seemed to want to talk about the incidents—perhaps because there was no way to agree upon an explanation. Soon, however, we couldn't help ourselves and the discussion turned to what might be going on in the house. Ed was accused by one of the guests of having rigged the whole affair, but I really doubted that was the case.

Our host decided he wanted to play a game on the antique roulette wheel that stood in the hallway, probably thinking this would quiet the unrest we were all feeling. On route to the hallway that housed the weathered roulette wheel, Ed stopped dead in his tracks. In the corner of the room that he was facing there was a fine cloud of cold air visible to the naked eye. It was so cold we could see Ed's breath as he exhaled. Nowhere else in the house was it this cold. Everyone placed a body part in the cold spot to feel for themselves, and sure enough, the area was much colder than the thermometer outside which read an even forty degrees. "This is really weird," Ed said in a disbelieving tone.

Ed then led everyone over to the roulette wheel. I held back, but everyone else joined in the game of calling out a number to see if the wheel would stop on it. There were some failed attempts, but when it was Ed's turn, he said something like, "let's see if that old ghost wants to play with me!" He called out a number while challenging the specter to play, and I kid you not, during the next three turns, even before the wheel could come to a stop naturally, it stopped abruptly on the number Ed called. Not once, not twice, but three times!

I wasn't amused and directed my displeasure at the unseen player. "Get out of here," I said to the invisible guest. "We're bored with your silly antics. Go find someplace else to camp out!"

By now it was really late. Maura was the first to announce that she was off to bed and asked Ed to lock up the house. Ed chose me to go around the house and help him secure the locks on all the windows and doors. Together, we systematically locked up the entire house.

The front door was the last on our rounds. This was an original door belonging to the barn from which the house had been converted. It was over-sized, old, and very heavy. The door had a large black rusty bolt on it that acted as the knob, and it made a lot of noise when it was slid aside. I watched Ed as he used the weight of his body to aid him in shutting the wooden door tightly. Once finished, he gave me a peck on the cheek and took himself up to bed.

The four of us who were still up moved into the den area and set about discussing the fashions and music of the twenties and thirties. We had chosen to ignore the night's events, and we spent a pleasant half-hour talking about purely material things.

Then I suddenly felt a cold blast of air. The chill was directly followed by a noise that was an almost inaudible creaking sound. I looked at the three men who sat opposite me and shook my head. "No, no way!" I said adamantly. I got up from the chair and in one step climbed up the three short stairs to peek around the corner. And I saw just what I expected. The front door stood wide open—just hanging on its hinges, laying flat up against the wall. I couldn't believe it! The poltergeist was back!

The door hadn't made the normal hideously loud noise it usually made when it moved across the threshold and that was what gave me the creeps! I asked Erik to please close the door, and this prompted everyone to call it a night.

The other guests disappeared into their allotted bedrooms. Erik and I were to sleep in the den. For the first time that evening, I wondered if I could muster up enough energy to drive back to the city. Then I took stock of the hour and the amount that I'd had to drink. "All right," I said to the uninvited guest, "if you are spending the night, then please go to bed now!"

The lights in the den were on a dimmer switch. Directly following my tired, yet motherly, command to go to bed, the lights turned themselves up to full brightness. Erik and I were standing in the middle of the room, staring at each other, when the lights slowly dimmed—then climbed up again to the highest level of brightness. Finally, they stayed off.

That capped off the spooky events for that weekend. But the following weekend, just after midnight, I picked up the telephone receiver and was greeted by a very excited voice, saying, "It's happening again!" I thought it was a prank caller and almost hung up. Then I realized it was Ed, and I sat upright in bed, very alert.

"What's happening again?" I asked him. Ed then proceeded to tell me that he and Maura had driven up to the house in Vista from Kennedy Airport after picking up some friends of theirs who had just arrived from Europe. They had told their friends the story from the weekend before and were met with disbelief and no small amount of chiding.

Upon entering the country house, the two couples made their way to the atrium so that Ed could show the faithless just what he had been talking about. Ed turned on the light so that all could see—and much to the surprise of everyone, the weather vane was again swinging violently! Without interfering with the lightening-rod-gone-mad, Ed immediately phoned me. Why? Good question! I was five hours away in Pennsylvania. It was past midnight, and there was really nothing I could do over the phone, anyway! I told him to calm down and to tell the poltergeist to get the hell out of the house, NOW!

There were no more phone calls and no further incidents. Ed's friends did walk away from the weekend with a bit more of an open mind—but Maura's father still doesn't believe our story.

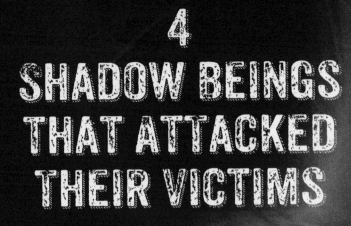

4
SHADOW BEINGS THAT ATTACKED THEIR VICTIMS

As we saw in Chapter 3, poltergeist cases often involve mischievous physical attention toward a particular member of a family. In this chapter, as we continue to identify certain kinds of ghosts and hauntings, we'll examine those cases in which the intelligence that directed the phenomena appeared to be motivated more by malice than by mischief. And sometimes, for reasons that may never be adequately explained, ghosts violently attack an individual, physically torturing and tormenting them.

THE BELL WITCH: THE QUINTESSENTIAL AMERICAN HAUNTING

Hollywood finally discovered the Bell Witch in *An American Haunting* (2005), starring Donald Sutherland and Sissy Spacek. While this film is quite accurate and effective, an independent production entitled *The Bell Witch Haunting* (2004) is even more detailed.

The story begins in 1817. One night, the John Bell family was disturbed by mysterious rapping on the windows of their cabin near Clarksville, Tennessee. Later that evening, twelve-year-old Elizabeth "Betsy" Bell began to complain that there was an invisible rat gnawing on her bedpost. At midnight, the entire family—John and Lucy (Luce) and their children Betsy, John, Drewry, Joel, and Richard—were disturbed by having their covers jerked off their beds in a rough manner. And everyone in the Bell family heard a strange sucking noise, an eerie smacking of lips, as if an invisible baby was nursing.

Several investigators of ghost phenomena have noted these same peculiar sounds of psychic "nursing." Some researchers have noted that these eerie signal noises often occur shortly before an evening of particularly violent disturbances. It is as if the entity beginning to manifest is a kind of obscene infant being born in some dimension of reality that borders our own. Sacheverell Sitwell, a distinguished British poet and writer of art criticism, wrote that such a being might be "an embryonic phantasm" that comes into existence on "the borderlands, upon one frontier or the other, of human life.... It is in all things unholy, unhallowed, and not human."

When the Bell family arose the next morning, stones littered the floor of the front room and furniture had been overturned. The children were wide-eyed and spoke of ghosts and goblins. John Bell lectured his family severely. They would keep the problem to themselves. They didn't want their family to become the subject of common gossip.

That night, Richard was awakened by something pulling his hair so hard his head lifted right off the pillow. Joel began screaming at his brother's invisible attacker, and from her room, Elizabeth began howling that the gnawing rat was pulling her hair, too.

Most of the family awakened the next day with sore scalps from having their hair yanked and tugged during the night, and John Bell reversed his decision. They needed help. That day he would confide in James Johnson, their nearest neighbor and closest friend. Johnson accompanied his friend to the Bell cabin that evening. The tale that Bell told was a strange one, but Johnson knew that John Bell was neither a drinker nor a liar. While he watched at Elizabeth's bedside that night, Johnson saw the young girl receive several blows on the cheeks from an invisible attacker.

"Stop in the name of the Lord Jesus Christ!" Johnson adjured the phantom assailant. There was no activity from the ghost for several minutes, then something yanked little Betsy's hair with such force that she screamed in pain. Again Johnson admonished the evil spirit, and it released it's grip

After witnessing this, Johnson made two conclusions: the invisible spirit understood the English language, and, for some reason, twelve-year-old Betsy was the center of the haunting. The next day Johnson met with other neighbors, and they agreed to help the family as best they could. A committee was selected to keep watch at the Bell house all night to try to keep the evil spirit from molesting Betsy. But this well-intentioned effort provoked an especially vicious onslaught on the unfortunate girl. A number of neighbors volunteered to have their daughters sleep with Betsy, but they were terrorized as well. Betsy was taken out of the cabin and into the home of neighbors, but the nasty, hair-pulling entity simply followed her there and upset the other households.

By now the haunting had achieved wide notoriety, and the disturbances were thought to be the work of the ghost of old Kate Batts, an accused witch, who, for some unknown reason, had returned to work evil upon the Bell family. Each night the house was filled with those who sat up trying to get the ghost to communicate with them.

There seems little doubt that somehow the ghost was able to "feed" itself upon the energy of the psyches of the true believers who gathered nearly every evening in the Bell home. Soon, the spirit entity was powerful enough to venture outside the cabin and away from Betsy, its previous center of energy. Neighbors reported seeing lights like candles or lamps moving through the fields, and farmers became the victims of stone-throwing attacks from the Bell Witch.

But the pelting seemed to be more in the nature of mischief than some of the other manifestations of the Bell Witch. Young boys in the area often played catch with the Witch if she happened to throw something at them on their way home from school. Once an observer witnessed several boys who were suddenly pelted with sticks that flew from a nearby thicket. He noted

The Bell children were frightened and told their parents they saw goblins and ghosts.

that the sticks did not strike the boys with much force, and, with a great deal of merriment, the boys gathered up the sticks and tossed them back into the thicket. Once again, the sticks came flying out. This time the observer cut notches in several of the sticks before the boys returned fire. He testified that he was able to identify his markings when the Bell Witch once again threw the sticks from the thicket.

But the Witch was not at all playful with any scoffers who came to the Bell home to expose the phenomena as trickery. Those who stayed the night had the covers jerked from their beds, and some were slapped soundly on the face. These blows were heard distinctly by the Bell family. Like the open palm of a heavy hand striking flesh, one of them noted in a diary.

Spiritualists, clergymen, reporters, and curiosity seekers trooped to the Bell farm and tried to get the Witch to declare herself and her intentions. Their efforts were finally rewarded when one day the ghost began to speak.

At first the Witch's voice was an indistinct babble, then it became a louder, a kind of husky whisper issuing forth from shadowy corners of the cabin.

REAL GHOSTS, RESTLESS SPIRITS, AND HAUNTED PLACES　　　**111**

After a few more attempts, the ghost spoke in a full-toned voice that spoke to people not only in the darkness, but in lighted rooms and in daytime hours.

When Betsy was accused of trickery or ventriloquism, John, Jr. brought in a doctor to examine her. He placed his hand over Betsy's mouth and listened at her throat while the voice of the ghost chatted noisily from a far corner of the room. The doctor stated firmly that young Betsy was definitely not making the sounds.

Twelve-year-old Betsy Bell began to suffer from seizures and fainting spells, similar to those which spirit mediums undergo when in a trance. Observers noted that the spells came on at regular hours, just before the Witch put in an appearance. The ghost was always silent when the girl lay prostrate upon her bed; then after Betsy recovered, the Witch would begin her haunting once again.

From the very beginning, the Witch had been outspoken in its hatred of John Bell, Betsy's father. "I'll keep after him until the end of his days!" the ghost often swore to visitors in the Bell home. "Old Jack Bell's days are numbered."

Even before earliest incidents of rapping on the windows and hair-pulling, John Bell had complained of a strange pain in his throat. He had described it as feeling like "a stick stuck crosswise," punching each side of his jaws. As the visits of the ghost became more aggressive, Bell was often plagued by a swelling of the tongue that lasted for ten to fifteen hours, leaving him unable to talk or eat.

Some researchers have suggested that the onset of John Bell's physical afflictions and his daughter's psychic persecution was no coincidence. Hungarian psychologist and psychic researcher Dr. Nandor Fodor, writing of the Bell Witch, made the observation that the swelling of Bell's tongue suggests that he may have been keeping a dreadful secret that sought physical release. Dr. Fodor also speculated that Betsy, approaching puberty, may have undergone a shocking sexual experience for which her father was responsible. "It was probably to save her reason," Dr. Fodor wrote, "that a fragment of her mind was split off and became the Bell Witch."

Dr. Fodor's theory about the Bell Witch as manifestation of poltergeist phenomena may account for the remarkable range and power of the Witch. However, the Bell Witch could also have been a negative entity that was attracted to the psychic energies that had been produced by sexual shock, pubertal change, and a father's guilt.

Once a visitor asked the entity about identity, to which the Witch replied: "I am a spirit who was once very happy, but who has been disturbed and made unhappy. I will remain in this house and worry old Jack Bell until I kill him."

Later, the Witch declared itself to be the spirit of a Native American, and it sent the family on a wild "bone chase" to gather up all of its skeletal remains. "If my bones are all put back together, I'll be able to rest in peace," the entity said deceitfully. When the Bell family admitted that they had been unable to find any of the bones of the old warrior, the Witch cackled and informed them that she was really the ghost of old Kate Batts. Interestingly, Kate Batts was not dead at the time of the haunting and was not actually a witch. She was a rather eccentric woman who was quite shrewd in her dealings with the citizens of Clarksville and may have been given the title of witch from certain irate townspeople. John Bell had run afoul of Kate in the matter of some territorial disagreements and there was likely bad blood between them.

The spirit of the Witch was attracted to the psychic energies that had been produced by sexual shock, pubertal change, and a father's guilt.

The Bell home became even more crowded when members of the Witch's ghost family moved in with her. Four nasty entities named Blackdog, Mathematics, Cypocryphy, and Jerusalem—each speaking in a distinctive voice of its own— soon made every night a maddening, raucous party. The sounds of riotous laughter rattled the shingles of the Bell home, and witnesses noted the strong scent of whiskey that permeated every room in the house.

The Bell Witch was adept at producing odd objects out of thin air. At one of Mrs. Bell's Bible study groups, the ladies were showered with fresh fruit. Betsy's friends were treated to bananas at one of her birthday parties. "Those came from the West Indies," the Witch told the delighted girls. "I picked them myself."

Although John Bell was the butt of malicious pranks and cruel blows, his wife, Luce Bell, was looked after solicitously by the Witch. Once when Mrs. Bell was ill, the Witch was heard telling Luce to hold out her hands. When she did, a large quantity of hazelnuts dropped into her palms. "Eat them, poor Luce," the Witch instructed her. "They will do you good. When Luce Bell weakly protested that she did not have the strength to crack the nuts, the Witch volunteered to perform the act on her behalf. Family members and neighbors watched in wide-eyed awe as the nuts cracked open and the meats were sorted from the shells.

The Witch was also adept at producing pins and needles. Luce Bell was provided with enough pins to supply the entire county, but sometimes the Witch would impishly hide them in the bedclothes or in chair cushions, where they would jab an unsuspecting victim.

John, Jr., Betsy's favorite brother, was the only other member of the family who received decent treatment from the Witch. He could even talk back to the Witch and get away with his sass. On the other hand, Joel and Richard were often whipped unmercifully by the ghost, and Drewry was so frightened of the Witch that he never married, fearing that the entity might someday return and single out his wife and children.

Elizabeth and her father by far received the brunt of the Witch's ill nature. The cruelest act perpetrated on Betsy was causing the dissolution of her engagement to Joshua Gardner (spelled Gardiner in some sources). The entity protested violently when the engagement was announced and begged John Jr. to help sever the relationship; according to the Witch, Betsy would never know a day of happiness if she married Joshua.

The Witch screamed at Joshua whenever he entered the Bell home and embarrassed both young people by shouting obscenities about them in front of their friends. Richard Bell noted in his diary that the "vile devil" never ceased to torment Betsy, insulting her modesty, sticking pins in her body, pinching and bruising her flesh, slapping her cheeks, disheveling and tangling her hair.

When Frank Miles, a close friend of the Bell family, learned of the Witch's objection to Betsy's engagement he vowed to stand up to the evil spirit on her behalf. As an elderly woman in her eighties, Elizabeth still remembered how the dear man Miles had "fairly shook the house, stamping on the floor, swearing terribly." According to the family members who witnessed the duel, Miles challenged the Witch to take any form it desired and he would fight it. He made motions in the air as if warming up for a wrestling or a boxing match. "Just let me get a hold of you, and we'll soon send you packing," Miles roared. "I'm not afraid of an invisible windbag." Suddenly Miles' head jerked backwards as if a solid slap had stung his cheeks. He put up his forearms to block a series of facial blows, leaving himself vulnerable to a vicious punch in the stomach. He slumped against a wall, desperately shaking his head to recover his senses. "Begone!" the Bell family heard the Witch warn their courageous friend. "Or I'll knock your block off!" Reluctantly, Frank Miles picked up his hat and coat. A man couldn't fight an enemy he couldn't see.

Although the valiant Miles had been pummeled into submission by the Witch, word reached an old friend of John Bell. It was none other than General Andrew Jackson, Old Hickory himself, who heard that a malignant spirit was interfering in the course of true love between Betsy and Joshua. At the urging of his wife, Jackson set out for the Bell farm in the company of several servants and a professional "witch layer." Along the way, the party picked up a number of other rugged individuals who swore that they could handle the Bell Witch. As the Jackson party neared the Bell farm, Jackson's driver was startled when the wheels of the general's coach suddenly froze and would not budge. Jackson ordered the men to put their backs to the coach, but when the combined strength of men and horses could not make the wheels budge an inch, the General began to suspect supernatural forces at work.

Cackling laughter from a nearby bush alerted the ghost hunters to the presence of the Bell Witch. The entity welcomed the party, then uttered a command that unfroze the wheels of the coach. The General and his men had lost the element of surprise. Somehow, the Witch had known they were coming.

That night, in spite of their previous boasts of an easy conquest, the witch-layer and then the ghost-layers fled in terror when the Witch attacked them. According to the accounts of the incident, General Jackson told John Bell that fighting the Witch was tougher than facing the British at the Battle of New Orleans. Although Jackson had planned to stay until the ghost had been vanquished, because his little army of ghost chasers had admitted defeat, he decided to leave with his men. With the decisive rout of her champions, Betsy had no choice but to give into the Witch's demands and break her engagement with Joshua Gardner. On the night that Betsy returned the ring the Witch's laughter could be heard ringing triumphantly from every room in the house.

> The entity protested violently when the engagement was announced and begged John Jr. to help sever the relationship....

With Betsy's marriage plans terminated, the ghost began again to concentrate its energy on the destruction of John Bell. Richard was walking with his father when John Bell collapsed into a spasmodically convulsing heap. Young Richard was terrified by the agonies that beset his wretched father, and he wrote later that his facial contortions were so hideous that they seemed to transform him into "a very demon to swallow me up." John Bell was brought home to his bed where he laid for several days in a very weakened condition. Even during the man's illness, the cruel entity would not leave him in peace, but continued to torment him by slapping his face and throwing his legs into the air.

On the morning of December 19, 1820, John Bell lapsed into a stupor. John, Jr. went quickly to the medicine cabinet to obtain his father's prescription and found instead "a smoky looking vial, which was about one-third full of dark-colored liquid." The Witch cackled that it was no use to try to revive Old Jack. She had him at last. When John, Jr. demanded to know where the vial came from, the Witch answered smugly that it had placed the vial in the medicine cabinet that night. "I gave Old Jack a big dose of it while he was asleep. I fixed him!" the entity laughed. John, Jr. sent for the doctor. When the physician arrived, he asked one of the boys to fetch a cat from the barn. While John, Jr. held the cat, the doctor dipped a straw into the dark vial and wiped it on the animal's tongue. The cat jumped into the air, whirled about the floor, and died "very quick." And, sure enough, John Bell passed away, never rousing from his unconscious state.

The Witch sang bawdy songs all during John Bell's funeral and annoyed the assembled mourners with the sounds of crude celebration during the last rites.

The Witch behaved much better toward Betsy after the death of her father. It never again inflicted pain upon the young woman and even began to address her in terms of endearment. The psychic energy which had nurtured the ghost appeared to be waning. During the rest of the winter and on into the spring months, the manifestations decreased steadily. Then, one night after the evening meal, a large smoke ball appeared to roll out of the chimney of the fireplace and into the room. As it exploded, a voice told the family: "I'm going now. I will be gone for seven years." True to its promise, the Witch returned to the Bell homestead in 1828. Betsy had entered into a successful marriage with another man; John, Jr. had married and now farmed land of his own. Only Mrs. Bell, Joel, and Richard remained at the family home. But the disturbances during the ghost's second appearance consisted of its most elementary pranks—rapping, scratching, and pulling the covers off the bed. The members of the Bell family still living in the cabin agreed to ignore the unwanted guest. Their psychology worked, and the Witch left them after two weeks of pestering them for attention. But before it did, the entity sought out John, Jr. and told him that it would return to one of his descendants in "one hundred years and seven."

Dr. Charles Bailey Bell should have been the recipient of the Witch's unwelcome return visit, but Dr. Bell and his family survived the year 1935 without hearing the slightest unexplained scratch or rapping. Dr. Bell wrote the official record of the mystifying disturbances endured by his ancestors in *A Mysterious Spirit: The Bell Witch of Tennessee*. Dr. Bell made note of the precognitive powers of the Witch, who revealed a series of "wonderful things" and prophecies to his grandfather, John Bell, Jr. According to Dr. Bell, the Witch predicted the Civil War, the emancipation of the slaves, the acceleration of the United States as a world power, the two world wars (the date for World War II was off by only four years), and destruction of our civilization by "rapidly expanding heat, followed by a mighty explosion." The date of the prediction of the end of the world was not given.

Today, the land where the abandoned cabin of the John Bell family stood is owned by a private trust and visitors are not allowed to explore the property. The only site associated with the Bell Witch that remains open to the public is the nearby Bell Witch Cave.

THE NASTY GHOSTS OF AMHERST

One night in September 1878, eighteen-year-old Esther Cox awakened her twenty-two-year-old sister Jane and asked if she felt something in bed with them.

The home where the young ladies lived with their married sister, Olive Teed, and her husband, Daniel, was a two-story cottage on Princess Street in Amherst, Nova Scotia. Although it was kept clean and neat, the possibility of a mouse invading the sisters' bed was not impossible. The two girls jumped out of bed with a scream and began to search their mattress. Jane noticed the straw of the mattress was moving about and concluded that the rodent must be trying to make a nest. The two sisters set to beating the mattress vigorously in an attempt to drive the tiny intruder out of their bed, but no mouse retreated from the straw of the mattress. The girls watched the mattress for a bit, detected no further movement, and concluded that the mouse must have escaped without detection.

> They lit a lamp to investigate, and a large cardboard box filled with patchwork jumped out from under the bed.

Esther and Jane decided they had better get back to sleep, worried they might have awakened the rest of the household. Not only did the young women reside with their sister, but the Teeds had two sons, Willie, five, and George, thirteen months. In addition, the household included Daniel's brother, John Teed and William Cox, the brother of Olive, Jane, and Esther. All the men of the household worked in the Amherst Shoe Factory. The next morning, the girls decided to make no mention of the mouse in their bed, thinking it would only result in laughter and teasing from John and William.

The next night, however, Esther and Jane heard a loud scratching from under their bed. They lit a lamp to investigate, and a large cardboard box filled with patchwork jumped out from under the bed. When Jane put it back in its place, it once again leaped into the air. The girls had had enough of trying to deal with the energetic "mouse" and began to call for help. Daniel Teed groggily slipped on a pair of trousers, entered the girls' bedroom, and kicked the box back under the bed—where it stayed. Grumpily, he cautioned them about repeating their little joke.

The girls were quite indignant, when, at breakfast the next morning, they were heartily teased by the whole family. The young women were insulted that, at their age, they would be considered empty-headed tricksters by the others.

That night, the disturbances were much more dramatic and could no longer be considered a joke by the Teed residents. Esther awakened in the night, gasping to Jane that she was dying. Jane lit a lamp, then nearly dropped it in horror as she took in the ghastly appearance of her sister. Esther's complexion had become bright scarlet, and her eyes bulged from her skull. Her hair seemed to be standing on end, and her flesh was extremely hot to the touch. Her entire body seemed to be swelling, as if she was being inflated with a pump. Then, while Jane watched in horror, loud thuds and rumbles, like that of thunder, began to sound from the walls of their room.

> Incredulously, they watched as an ominous message formed on the plaster.

Daniel and Olive appeared at the door to the room. They had been awakened by the loud noises and wondered what on earth could be their cause. They were shocked at Esther's inflated appearance, then puzzled, when after a particularly violent report, her body began deflating. Soon her flesh had returned to normal, and Esther was sleeping peacefully. Perplexed, the family resolved not to say anything of the mysterious disturbances to anyone outside of the household.

But secrecy would soon become impossible. That night, the bedclothes flew off the girls and landed in a heap in a far corner of the room. Esther once again began to swell, and when John Teed came to investigate, a pillow shot from the bed and struck him full in the face. The young man could not be coaxed to re-enter the room, but the other members of the household sat on the edge of the bed, struggling to keep the blankets covering the swollen Esther in place. While they fought with the bedclothes, a series of sharp explosions began to sound about the room. Then, in the middle of the crash and bang of the mysterious eruptions, Esther began to deflate just as she had done the night before.

Daniel Teed resolved to be ready on the next night, so he asked their family physician, Dr. Caritte, to join the vigil. The doctor examined Esther, and, while he felt her pulse, stated that the girl seemed to be suffering from some kind of nervous shock. The doctor's words seemed to be the signal to the phenomena; Esther's pillow straightened out as if it was a balloon, suddenly filled with air.

Although he had been frightened from the room on the night before, an emboldened John Teed re-entered the bizarre fray and grasped for the pillow. As if intimidated by his courage and his lunge toward it, the pillow deflated itself. But then, in a way that seemed to mock its opponent, the pillow re-inflated and wrenched itself from John Teed's closed fists as if it were alive.

Dr. Caritte and the assembled household heard the sounds of scratching on the wall above Esther's bed. Incredulously, they watched as an ominous message formed on the plaster. "Esther Cox," wrote the invisible hand, "you are mine to kill."

The doctor returned the next evening with a powerful sedative for the supernaturally afflicted young woman. He admitted that the phenomena was beyond his medical knowledge, but he concluded that as Esther seemed to experience the symptoms of nervous excitement, the only thing that he could prescribe would be sedation. But the bromide that he brought had a completely opposite effect than the one he had expected. As soon as the drug had eased Esther into a deep slumber, the noises began, louder than they had ever been. It sounded as though someone was up on the roof, attempting to pound its way into the house by means of a heavy sledgehammer. The doctor retreated shortly after midnight, and as he walked away down the street, he could still hear the powerful blows shaking the Teed home.

The disturbances continued in this manner for three weeks, with Dr. Caritte attending Esther three times a day in vain attempts to help her. Then, one night, the girl fell into a trance and spewed out the whole story of how she had escaped an attempted assault on her honor.

Bob McNeal, a man who worked with Daniel and John Teed and William Cox at the shoe factory, had arrived at the Teed home one evening and requested the pleasure of Esther's company on buggy ride. He had only laughed when she had expressed her reluctance at going for a ride when the sky looked so black. They had not ridden far when Bob pulled into a wooded area outside of Amherst. He had wanted her to get down from the buggy and go with him into the woods. She had refused. Suddenly, Bob leaped out of the buggy, jerked a pistol from his coat pocket and leveled it at her breast. He threatened her: either she came with him into the woods—or he would kill her. Esther told him not to be a fool. Her honor could not be broken by the sight of a madman waving a pistol at her.

Bob cursed her with a foul stream of profanity. He cocked the hammer of the pistol, and for an awful moment, she wondered if he might not make good on his threat. Then there was the sound of wagon wheels creaking toward them. Another couple was seeking out the cover of the woods. Bob thrust the pistol back into a pocket and climbed back into the driver's seat. Sullenly he stared at her, his eyes revealing terrible embarrassment and violent anger. He cracked the reins and they sped back toward the village. On the way home, it began to rain, but as if to punish Esther for not appeasing his lust, Bob refused to put the hood of the buggy over them. He delivered her, soaking wet, to the Teed household at ten that night.

The family had known nothing of Esther's secret until that moment. When Esther regained consciousness, Jane told her what she had said, and Esther confessed that it was all true.

Interestingly, the family members realized that Bob McNeal had not been seen since the night that he had tried to seduce Esther. He had not reported for work at the shoe factory that next morning, and his landlady said that he had paid for his lodging and left. Evidently shame for what he had tried to do to Esther and fear of the consequences if she told her brother-in-law, Daniel (who was his foreman at the shoe factory) had driven Bob McNeal out of Amherst. He could not have known that Esther had told no one. She had kept the memory of that terrible night tightly repressed and bottled up inside her.

"Could it be," Olive wondered, "that Bob McNeal was killed or took his own life and has come back to haunt Esther?" As if on cue, three loud knocks sounded on the room wall. Jane was slightly conversant with Spiritualism and spirit mediums and suggested that whatever it was that had been bothering her sister might be trying to establish contact with them. This comment, too, was met by three raps.

Dr. Caritte quickly devised a simple code. One rap was to represent "no," two raps would signify "no answer" or "doubtful," and three raps would stand for "yes." The ghost immediately used the code to answer elementary questions put forth by the household, but it ignored all attempts on the part of Dr. Caritte to establish a pattern of clues to determine its existence.

By now, the secret of the phenomena could no longer be confined to the walls of the Teed home. For one thing, neighbors and passersby had heard strange sounds and had inquired as to their cause. Village clergymen started to fulminate against Esther from their pulpits or to defend her. The Teeds' minister, Reverend R. A. Temple of the Wesleyan Methodist Church, had himself witnessed a pail of cold water suddenly begin to boil in Esther's presence.

Daniel Teed had just applied for police protection to keep the gawkers from turning his home into a public curiosity, when Esther contracted diphtheria and all manifestations ceased for a period of two weeks. Upon her recovery, she was sent to recuperate from her illness at the home of Mrs. Snowden, another married sister, who lived at Sackville, New Brunswick. There was no return of the phenomena throughout the duration of her stay.

When she returned to the Teed home in Amherst, everyone hoped that Esther was cured of whatever it was that ailed her. Daniel Teed had never been very sympathetic to Esther during the onslaught of the mysterious phenomena and had seemed more concerned about "what the neighbors would say" than he had been about her health. As an additional measure to help guard against a return of the unwelcome phenomena, the Teeds gave Esther and Jane a new room to help Esther get a fresh start.

On the first night of Esther's return to the Teed residence, lighted matches began to fall from the ceiling. All of the tiny flames were extinguished, but the incendiary activity was by no means over. Rapping began to shake the walls, and by using the code that Dr. Caritte had developed, the family learned that the entity intended to set their house on fire. As if to signal that it meant business, a dress jumped from its place on a nail and burst into flames as it slid under Esther's bed. For three days, the entire household kept vigil against the ghost's threat of destroying their home.

On the fourth day, just when they were beginning to think that the entity's threat might have been an idle one after all, Olive smelled smoke coming from the cellar. Grabbing one of the buckets of water that they kept at the ready, she and Esther hurried toward the smoke and found a pile of wood shavings blazing in a corner. The water seemed to have little effect on the flames. The sisters fled from the house, screaming for help, and ran into a passing stranger, who fortunately had enough presence of mind to beat the fire out with a doormat.

Rapping was one thing, Daniel Teed decreed that night at dinner, but fires were something else. If their house had caught fire and the wind had been right, half of the town of Amherst would have gone up in smoke. Teed said that he was sorry, but he just couldn't allow Esther to stay with them any longer. Olive may have been dismayed by her husband's decision, but there was little that she could say. He had, after all, been remarkably patient with his sister-in-law.

> By now, the secret of the phenomena could no longer be confined to the walls of the Teed home.

John W. White offered to employ Esther in his restaurant and provide lodging for her, but the well-intentioned gentleman soon regretted his decision to come to Esther's aid. The heavy door of his large kitchen stove refused to stay closed, even when braced by an axe handle. Metal objects clung to Esther's body as if she were a living magnet. Metal utensils, which came into contact with her flesh, became too hot for customers to hold. The furniture shifted about wherever she walked, and a fifty-pound box once shot fifteen feet into the air. White soon appealed to Daniel Teed to take Esther back because she was ruining his business.

A Captain James Beck invited Esther to come to stay for awhile with him and his wife at St. John, New Brunswick. He had read of the Amherst Mystery and wished to study the alleged agent of the phenomena at leisure in his own home. However, Esther proved to be a big disappointment to Captain Beck and the groups of medical men and scientists who had gathered to examine her. For three weeks, the girl did nothing other than tell wild tales of three ghosts, "Peter Cox," "Maggie Fisher," and "Bob Nickle," who appeared regularly to threaten her with fires and stabbings.

Upon her return to Amherst, Esther spent another quiet sojourn at the farm of a Mr. and Mrs. Van Ambergh. At last it was deemed that all traces of the phenomena had left her, and Esther was once again welcomed back into the home of Daniel Teed. Unfortunately, she had barely unpacked her things when the disturbances began with renewed vigor.

Teed was desperate enough to accept the proposition of a magician named Walter Hubbell, who offered to attempt an exorcism of the ghost that afflicted Esther and pay rent if he might stay in the house and observe the disturbances firsthand.

The day that Hubbell, as star boarder, moved into Teeds' home marked a particularly violent onset of the phenomena. His umbrella was jerked out of his hand and tossed into the air. A large butcher knife appeared and menacingly flew in his direction. Whenever he entered a room, all the chairs would fall over or dance about noisily. "The ghosts don't like you," Esther said finally. It was certainly an understatement.

But Hubbell was undaunted, even pleased, that the manifestations had become so robust since his arrival. Throughout his stay of six weeks, Hubbell witnessed a potpourri of haunting phenomena: whistling and drumming to the tune of "Yankee Doodle," the extremely active behavior of the furniture, the blasting of an invisible trumpet, and the subsequent materialization of a very tangible trumpet made of German silver.

However, his stay in the Teed home was not without its dangers. Several knives were thrown at him, a large glass paperweight narrowly missed his head, and he sustained a variety of bruises on his limbs because of the boisterous activity of the dancing furniture. Esther, too, seemed to suffer more personal attacks after the paying observer had arrived in the house. Once, thirty pins materialized out of the air and drove themselves into different parts of her body. On another occasion, after returning from church, her head was cut open by an old bone that had been laying in the yard.

> For three weeks, the girl did nothing other than tell wild tales of three ghosts....

Hubbell had not been completely honest with the Teeds when he told them that be wished only to observe the disturbances caused by the ghosts. As an accomplished stage magician, the man had found himself completely awed by the girl's ability to produce genuine spirit phenomena. It wasn't long before he was envisioning Esther on tour, with himself as her manager. At the same time, he was taking copious notes for a book which he intended to write on the Amherst mystery. It didn't take Hubbell more than a few hours to convince Daniel Teed that he should be permitted to make all the arrangements necessary to put his sister-in-law on the stage. Olive and Jane objected to placing their sister on public display, but Teed squelched all arguments by pointing out that their home was in a shambles. Esther had caused all the destruction they witnessed around them by setting her ghosts loose on them, Teed complained. It seemed only right and proper that she should pay them back in some way for all the grief that she had caused the family.

during the crucifixion. But there were no special holy days in the Philippines during the month of May.

Clarita spent the rest of the night on a bench in the front office of the police station, closely attended by an officer who had been assigned the undesirable task of keeping watch for the monster. The next morning, the girl was brought to court to face charges of vagrancy that had been levied against her. There, before the incredulous eyes of the entire court, Clarita endured another attack by her invisible monster. Reporters rushed to stand beside her for a closer look. Dr. Mariana Lara took the girl in his arms as she swooned from the excruciating pain of unseen jaws that had attached themselves to her flesh. "This girl is definitely not having an epileptic fit," Dr. Lara told the reporters. "These teeth prints are real—and they are most certainly not self-inflicted."

But there was no need to attest to the reality of the teeth marks to the reporters. They were startled witnesses to the cruel indentations that were appearing on the girl's arms, shoulders, palms, and neck. Dr. Lara told a police officer to send for the Mayor and the Archbishop at once. "This is outside my realm of physiology and medicine," he said. "Perhaps a clergyman will be of more value in this case than a doctor."

By the time Mayor Lacson arrived, the unfortunate girl had become a veritable mass of deeply embedded teeth prints and swollen and bruised flesh. "You poor girl," the Mayor commiserated, taking one of Clarita's hands into his own. Then, while he held her hand, deep teeth marks appeared on opposite sides of her index finger, as if a hungry fiend were trying to chew the digit off.

Dr. Lara called for an ambulance, and he and Mayor Lacson rode with Clarita to the hospital. The driver thought that Clarita was a victim of some horrible beating until the teeth began to attack her in the vehicle. He wheeled the ambulance through the streets of Manila, one eye on the traffic signals and the other on the tortured girl in the back. Throughout the fifteen-minute ride to the hospital, Clarita shouted that this time there were two creatures attacking her, each of them with large, buglike eyes and awful teeth. As the doctor and mayor watched in horror, teeth marks appeared on both sides of the girl's throat and on the hands that Mayor Lacson still held, trying to comfort her.

For some unexplainable reason, the attacks ceased when Clarita entered the hospital. When she was released six weeks later, she had nearly recovered the health that had deteriorated under the merciless fangs of the bug-eyed monster. Clarita Villanueva never again suffered from the terrible invisible jaws that had torn at her flesh, but her body would forever bear the scars of those vicious attacks by her invisible assailant.

"What happened to Clarita Villanueva is a complete mystery, something that simply defies rational explanation," Dr. Lara commented. "I don't mind saying that I was scared out of my wits."

DEVIL VOICES AND VICIOUS DARK, SWIRLING ENTITIES
The Experiences of Randy

In this one house where we lived for a while, we were troubled by entities that seemed set against us by Black Magic. From time to time, we would see a hooded figure moving about the house. Once my daughter Cindy saw the figure with its cowl down around its shoulders, and it appeared to be the image of an older man with thinning white hair on the sides of a bald head. Cindy said that on one occasion she saw the hooded figure with some kind of animal that was a catlike creature about three feet tall with pointed ears and a long tail. He stopped and looked at her, then moved on and disappeared.

One night in her room, Cindy heard several voices whispering, but she couldn't figure out what they were saying. They were all tumbled together. Another time when she was in the kitchen, someone said her name right in her ear. Recently, she heard a voice that she described as the perfect demon voice—throaty, hoarse, and very mean. It said to her, "Cindy, show yourself to me!" She could pinpoint the exact location from where the voice had come. It unnerved her so much that she fled her room and wouldn't sleep until the sun came up. That was the last encounter that she had.

Cindy heard a voice that she described as the perfect demon voice—throaty, hoarse, and very mean. It said to her, "Cindy, show yourself to me!"

I saw the hooded figure only once. The creature that bothered me appeared to be a black, floating, swirling mass about four feet high and three feet wide that could change it's shape. I only saw it about four times, but I would wake up sometimes and feel it sitting on my chest, choking me. I actually felt it when I would grab it and throw it off of me. When I got out of bed to confront it, it would disappear into a wall.

One night about two in the morning, something hit the wall with such force that it knocked all the pictures off the dresser and cracked the dresser mirror. It looked like there had been an earthquake in that one particular spot. Even the pictures hanging on the wall were knocked on the floor.

Sometimes I felt the thing behind me, watching me. It always attacked at the most vulnerable times. But I always confronted it. I wasn't afraid of it. Still, we decided to move after a month or so to keep all of our furniture from being smashed to pieces by the thing.

AN ENTITY SAVED HIS BABY SISTER, BUT TORMENTS FRIENDS
A Report from Will

My father's side of the family, beginning with my great-grandparents, have a good-sized farm in North Carolina with a large house. Around 1986, when my sister was learning to walk, she managed to crawl up the long set of steps going to the third story of the house. She was going to attempt to walk down, and as Mom and Grandma stood, helpless, at the bottom of the steps, my sister began tilting as if she was going to fall. However, something appeared to grab the collar of her shirt, and she was pulled backwards to safety. No apparition was seen, but the collar of her shirt clearly was pulled back by something invisible.

We often hear strange noises in the home, and we have occasionally seen eerie shadows. However, the most disturbing events occurred around 1994 when my friend, Matt, went to the farm with us to celebrate my twelfth birthday. Matt was thirteen or fourteen, and because of the spooky stories that we had told him, he was visibly scared once he saw the old farmhouse.

We drew pictures of airplanes the first night he stayed there, and before we went to bed upstairs, we placed them in a neat pile. We also turned off the light in the living room, which was the room in which we had been drawing and where we kept the pictures. After we had been in our upstairs bedroom for a while, Matt said he needed to use the bathroom. I walked downstairs with him to make sure "nothing got him." We walked into the living room, and to our shock we found our drawings strewn about and the light on.

Matt was very shaken, and he insisted that we sleep in the same bed in case something should attack him. The next morning, he said that he had heard something come up the steps in the middle of the night. He heard it go through the room in which my older sister was sleeping, then enter the center room of the third story where my parents were sleeping. Matt and I were in the bed just across the room from them.

Matt said that the ghost walked up to the foot of the bed, then pressed down hard on him, making it impossible for him to yell. He said that although he managed to nudge me, I sleepily responded by mumbling, thinking that my younger sister was bothering me. Matt was relieved because nothing further happened to him the rest of the trip, or on following visits to the farm.

However, one of my other friends once came with us to the farm, and became so frightened upon entering an upstairs room that he shook visibly for hours on end and was unable to sleep. He wouldn't even let us turn out the lights until 1:00 A.M. As before, though, everything was normal on the second night of the visit.

5
SPIRIT PARASITES THAT POSSESSED THEIR VICTIMS

After a careful consideration of nasty entities that attack people, such as those presented in chapter 4, perhaps we are now ready to face the grim possibility that there are some spirit beings that have become agents of evil and wish to possess the bodies of the living.

Many men and women who were granted the blessing of seeing the ghostly image of their loved ones pass to the Other Side, or who later received messages of comfort from them, have told us that those souls were often met by angelic beings and more advanced spirits who assisted them in evolving to higher planes of awareness (See especially chapters 6, 7, 8, and 9). As these souls progressed, all of their prior physical concerns faded into irrelevance. Sensual memories of their previous material existence were forgotten.

But, on occasion, it seems that something goes wrong during a soul's evolution into the Light. If certain individuals have spent their entire lives on Earth in pursuit of sensual pleasures, their psychic soul personalities may experience the same hedonistic drives after death. They may attempt to return to all of their old, pleasurable places, and they may undergo traumatic shocks when they slowly realize that they no longer have physical bodies. And if there are additional negative factors, such as a bitter dispute left unsettled, an old score left unpaid, an argument left unresolved, then these restless spirits might hunger to return to the physical world in order to obtain revenge.

Such hedonistic or vengeful discarnate spirits refuse to allow the natural order of spiritual progression into the higher levels of awareness to ease their desires, pain, and anger. They wish only to return to the world of the living. These disembodied entities will seek out vulnerable humans and attach themselves to these victims.

Humans are very susceptible to invasion when they are fatigued and exhausted; when they have undergone a period of severe emotional stress; when they are emotionally upset or very angry; and when they are under the influence of drugs, alcohol, or any other mind-altering substances.

Because of their unfettered imaginations and undisciplined lives, young people can be very susceptible to possession, especially if they are excited, even titillated, by the lure of exploring the unknown through such devices as the Ouija board. Venturing into the sometimes dark areas of spirit communication and the occult becomes especially dangerous when attempted by those who have not taken the time to study the arcane or who have not acquired the discipline necessary to exercise the minimal amount of caution necessary for safe exploration into the world of shadows. It is especially dangerous if such undisciplined, untutored young people should be under the influence of drugs or alcohol at the same time that they are trying to make contact with the spirit world. The result may be temporary or long-term possession by a spirit entity who enthusiastically takes advantage of the psychic doorway that has been unknowingly opened by the unprepared.

In addition to spirits of the dead who take over the minds of people who are emotionally or physically weakened and leech upon their physical bodies, there also appear to be discarnate entities that have never been human, but strongly desire the chance to feel the emotions and sensual expressions that are unique to the human experience. These beings very often identify themselves as agents of evil. Traditionally, they have been called demons. I chose to label them as spirit parasites—nonphysical beings from other dimensions of reality that have the ability to seize the controlling mechanism of its host body and undermine the victim's will. Such enslaved humans are then forced to perform harmful acts against themselves and others.

POSSESSED BY SPIRITS FOR TWENTY-SIX YEARS

Shortly before the two priests were to begin an exorcism in the convent, Father Theophilus Riesinger, the exorcist, complimented Father Joseph Steiger for having the bravery to allow him to perform the rites in his parish. "The devil does not deal softly with those who attempt to interfere in his work," Fr. Riesinger said solemnly.

The two men had been friends for many years, and since the woman afflicted with demon possession lived near Fr. Steiger's parish, Fr. Riesinger had prevailed on him to allow the convent in Earling, Iowa, to be used as the place in which to conduct the exorcism. According to Fr. Riesinger, Anna, the woman who lay quietly in a room awaiting the holy rites, had been the victim of violent and loathsome demonic attentions since she was fourteen years old. On several occasions, she had tried to commit suicide in order to rid herself of the terrible voices that screamed in her ears. Now the poor creature was forty years old. Marriage hadn't helped her; dozens of doctors hadn't helped her; someone had to help her.

Despite the benevolent motives behind their actions, Fr. Steiger had admit to his friend that it seemed strange to him that two priests were about to

The untrained novice should avoid use of items like the ouija board, which will often attract lesser entities.

begin the rites of exorcism in an attempt to cast out a devil in Earling, Iowa, on September 1, 1928. Although he believed the case to be genuine and he had deep faith that Fr. Riesinger would in some manner be able to give the poor woman some peace, he still couldn't help thinking that the whole process seemed extremely medieval.

But what else could be done? Here was a woman who could not take the sacraments because of taunting voices that mocked her. Here was a once-pious young girl who could not even go to confession without attempting to strangle the confessor. Here was a woman who never got past the eighth grade who could give a literal translation of Latin prayers and correct her priest when he mispronounced a word. The bishop had been studying this case for twenty-six years, so no one could accuse him of having made a hasty decision when he declared Anna's affliction to be unmistakably that of diabolic possession.

That was why Fr. Riesinger had been sent to Iowa to conduct a rite almost forgotten by the clergy and the laity alike, a rite which could not be

Cardinal Jorge Medina Estevez of Chile holds the book *De Exorcismis et Supplicationibus Quibusdam* (Of all kinds of Exorcisms and Supplications), comprising the Vatican's new guidelines on exorcism. The new guidelines, presented in 1999, are the first updates to rules that have been in place since 1614.

conducted without the full approval of church superiors. Fr. Riesinger was a cleric who was convinced that the world was very different from what most people believed, and he felt certain that the modern age had not succeeded in altering the basic truths of the scriptural texts. In his view of reality, the struggle of good versus evil was still very much a part of the contemporary scene. With God's good help, they would rid the woman of demonic possession.

Fr. Steiger stepped aside to allow the exorcist to enter room at the end of the hall where the nuns had given Anna a bed. Although he was nearly sixty years old, Father Riesinger was still a strong, muscular man, with a body that had been kept in good physical condition by a regimen of disciplined monastic living. He wore the robes of his Capuchin order, a long white beard, and an oversized crucifix, which rested in the cincture of his robe like a broadsword at the ready for the diabolic battle.

A special Mass had been said that morning, and the Mother Superior and a number of sisters flanked the bed of the possessed woman. The Capuchin priest made the Sign of the Cross, and everyone present joined in the opening prayer of exorcism, the Litany of All Saints. Anna began to tremble, then a dreadful growl filled the room. Father Steiger was amazed to note that in spite of the rising chorus of animal howls that were ostensibly coming from Anna, neither her tongue nor her lips moved. If Father Riesinger noticed such a phenomenon, he was apparently unconcerned.

The exorcist raised his voice in an invocation, but he had only uttered a few words when an incredible phenomenon occurred. Before the nuns who surrounded Anna could intervene, the trembling woman on the bed was suddenly carried through the air until she landed just above the doorway of the high-ceilinged room. There, as if she had been filled with helium, the bedeviled woman remained fixed. The sisters screamed in horror and amazement.

"Bring her down!" Fr. Riesinger said in a voice that was loud and steady. "Help me," he said to Fr. Steiger. "We must not let hysteria take control here or we are beaten before we begin." Fr. Steiger helped the Capuchin calm the nuns, then, with effort, they brought the tormented woman down from the ceiling. "She's lapsed into a coma," Fr. Riesinger told the others. "That may mean the devils have taken full possession and are about to speak."

The exorcist intoned his litany. The unconscious woman's body jerked about and a violent moaning and yelping sounded from her closed lips as Fr. Riesinger recited certain holy names. Undeterred, the priest continued the rites of exorcism.

By late afternoon Fr. Steiger had to excuse himself to disperse the crowd that had gathered outside. People had heard the terrible howling coming from the convent and had come to determine its cause. To quell rumors that a nun was being murdered, Fr. Steiger was forced to tell the people that a rite of exorcism was in progress. Before he left the astonished crowd, he beseeched the faithful to remember the tormented woman in their prayers.

When he returned to the room, he found the Sisters in a state of profound anxiety. Anna's body had become bloated beyond recognition. Fr Steiger felt his stomach jolt as he looked at the grotesquely distorted woman writhing on the bed. How could they be certain that they were not killing her?

In a soft but firm voice, the exorcist told them that Satan would use every device within his power to make them quit the rites and leave the poor woman in his embrace. He advised the nuns to take turns getting outside and walking around a bit to get some fresh air. He also recommended that Mother Superior draw up a schedule so the nuns might take turns keeping vigil. It would be wise if there were always a fresh group ready when Anna needed them most. "That's right, old man," came a voice from within the possessed woman, "those screaming brides of Jesus are going to need all of their strength!"

At last the howling and growling had formed itself into a voice. Fr. Steiger stared in wonderment as the mocking entity spoke from the woman's tormented body without utilizing either her lips or her tongue. Fr. Riesinger moved in on his adversary without a moment's hesitation. He demanded to know how many devils inhabited the body of the woman. The guttural voice declared that there were many of them, far too many for the exorcist to handle.

The gauntlet had been tossed. Now the battle would begin in earnest.

As if to strike an immediate blow at Fr. Steiger's sensitive stomach, the woman began to vomit foul excrement. Some of the obnoxious matter resembled vomited macaroni, or chewed and sliced tobacco leaves. Nausea would seize the woman as many as twenty times a day, and some of the substances found within her vile outpourings were things that were not likely to be found in a human body. The retching continued at a prodigious rate, in spite of the fact that the woman was conscious each day for only a little while in the morning and took only very light nourishment before the rites of exorcism were renewed. Fr. Steiger worried that Anna would waste away from dehydration, but the exorcist advised him that Satan would not go so far as to kill her. They must not weaken.

Fr. Riesinger determined that the woman had been possessed by two types of demons, those from the realm of fallen angels and those that had once been humans living on earth. He had also singled out their leader, Beelzebub. Beelzebub told Father Riesinger that although the priest fought a hard battle, he would not win the woman away from the demons that had possessed her. Anna had been theirs since her fourteenth year. According to the demon, her own father had cursed them into her. Lucifer had been happy to oblige the curse and had commanded the demons to enter her.

Beelzebub conversed with the exorcist in German and Latin as well as in English. The demon's command of each language was so perfect that he took great delight in correcting Fr. Riesinger whenever he mispronounced a word. But the priest was not interested in playing word games. He wanted to learn why a girl's own father would bring down the hordes of hell upon her. "Ask him yourself!" Beelzebub snapped one day when the exorcist had been probing since early morning. "You mean," Fr. Riesinger asked incredulously, "that he is one of the devils within her now?" Beelzebub laughed and said that the spirit of Anna's father Jacob had been within her since the moment of his damnation.

When the exorcist commanded the spirit of the father to come forth, he stirred up a demon unlike the others. A bass voice thundered the room with such vehemence that Fr. Steiger excused himself from the room. The new speaker claimed to be Judas Iscariot, the betrayer of Jesus. The spirit of Judas told Fr. Riesinger that it was his demonic mission to make Anna commit suicide—preferably by hanging herself, as he had.

At this point Anna's face contorted grotesquely and a terrible stench filled the room. Her emaciated body inflated like a balloon, and the stench become so overwhelming that the sisters were forced to flee the room for fresh air. Only the exorcist stood his ground.

The entity that now spoke from Anna's body claimed to be that of the Prince of Darkness himself. Fr. Riesinger challenged Satan, telling him he was fighting a losing battles—the exorcist had the love of Christ on his side. Satan responded by saying that whether his work was useless or not depended upon one's point of view. "Such things are beyond your understanding," the voice told the priest. "But this whole issue began before time itself and in accordance with a set of strict laws."

Fr. Theophilus Riesinger advanced on Satan with a large cross that a Sister had left in the room for him. Satan laughed and told the exorcist to put aside a silly toy made of papier-mâché.

Fr. Riesinger looked down at the cross and saw that it had indeed been made of papier-mâché. Momentarily flustered, the exorcist left himself vulnerable to two uninterrupted hours of maniacal laughter.

When the terrible laughter had subsided, Fr. Steiger again joined his fellow priest—only to receive a verbal assault from the demon. "So there's the sniveling pup who brought this whole thing about is it?" Satan snarled at the parish priest. "I'll attend to you, Joseph Steiger. I'll set the entire parish against you. Such hatred will be built up against you that your parishioners will demand your removal!"

That night at dinner, while Sisters watched over the entranced woman, Fr. Steiger spoke earnestly to the Capuchin exorcist. He was beginning to become concerned what people in the parish were thinking about the whole affair. The exorcism had continued for days with the endless screaming, cursing, growling. Fr. Steiger had even overheard some parishioners saying that those who are able to conjure up Satan must themselves be in his power. With a deep, weary sigh, Fr. Riesinger told his fellow priest that he had begun to fall right into Satan's plan. It was part of the demon's strategy to sow seeds of doubt in his soul. What a victory it would be for Satan if he could turn two old friends against one another.

Fr. Steiger left the dinner table for a place where he could be alone in quiet prayer and meditation. Later, when he rejoined Fr. Riesinger in Anna's room, he felt buoyed up and confident, grateful that he had not fallen into Satan's snare. The demon seemed surprised to see Fr. Steiger rejoining the spiritual combat, and in a voice that was low and filled with menace, he threatened the priest. He had had better priests murdered on their own altars! He'd had priests butchered alive. He'd had them skinned, baked, boiled, and burned. He had even hung Jesus on a cross and had Peter crucified upside down. After a series of rambling threats, the demon vowed that he would personally attack Fr. Steiger on the coming Friday.

That Friday, Fr. Steiger received an emergency call from one of his parishioners who lived in the country. As he approached a bridge near Earling in the new car which had been a gift from his parish, a "black cloud" obscured his vision. The new car was totaled, but Fr. Steiger escaped with some external scrapes, but felt extremely nervous. When he returned to the room in which Fr. Riesinger held perpetual debate with Satan, the entity laughed at Fr. Steiger's appearance and asked how the priest liked the car crash for "openers." Then the demon promised the priest a lot more fun.

The "fun" came that night in Fr. Steiger's room. Eerie, ratlike noises were heard scuttling across his floor until dawn. Doors opened and slammed shut. Sudden, jolting movements of his bed kept him on edge all night long.

After two weeks of harassment against the priests and the nuns involved in the exorcism, Satan took leave of Anna's body and left the battle

RICARDO PUSTANIO 2012

After two weeks of harassment against the priests and the nuns involved in the exorcism, Satan took leave of Anna's body and left the battle to his demonic underlings.

to his demonic underlings. A few nights later, during the litany of exorcism, a voice revealed its presence. It was the voice of Jacob, the woman's father. To show contempt for the exorcist, a torrent of filth gushed forth from Anna's mouth.

Father Riesinger was forced to change his robes four times that next day. After one terrible vomiting session, the voice of Mina, the mistress of Jacob, came forward to admit that she, too, dwelled within the body of the tormented Anna. Mina laughed that Jacob may have cursed his daughter, but she had murdered four of her children.

Fr. Riesinger had been in the throes of the rites of exorcism for twenty days, a period which was without precedence in the Roman Catholic Church. Although he was growing physically weak, he refused to slow his pace. He could sense that the demons, too, were losing strength; they had begun to plead not to be dispossessed. The exorcist resolved to stay with Anna from dawn to dawn without ceasing—until either he dropped from exhaustion or the devils had quit the body of the possessed. For seventy-two hours straight, Fr. Riesinger pressed the exorcism. The entities began to cry and to plead for mercy. They agreed to quit Anna's body, but they begged to be directed into another mortal dwelling of flesh and blood. The exorcist was not about to enter into such a hellish bargain. With prayers for strength and guidance, he stepped up the pace.

At last the devils had had enough. Fr. Theophilus Riesinger had sustained the rites of exorcism for twenty-three days. At 9:00 P.M. on September 23, 1928, Anna stiffened upright in her bed, with only her heels touching the edge of the covers. The sisters gasped. Was she about to spring again for the ceiling? Fr. Riesinger motioned for them to remain calm, and he drew his large crucifix from his robe. He warned the devils that he would bide no deception. He did not want a single one of them going back on their word and remaining within the woman. As they left, he commanded each of them to call out its name. A terrible moan filled the room, a moan that came from many throats. Then: "Beelzebub! Judas! Jacob! Mina!"

The entities departed, and as if from a great distance, the priests and nuns could hear the echoes of tormented wails chanting over and over again: "Hell! Beelzebub! Hell! Judas! Hell! Jacob! Hell! Mina! Hell … hell … hell."

On the bed, Anna lay, freed of her bondage. The ordeal had been extremely hard on her, as well as on the exorcist, and her features were gaunt and haggard. Anna tried to form her lips into a smile. "God bless you, Father," she said in a hoarse whisper.

Suddenly a vile odor filled the room, and a nun screamed that the demons had returned. Fr Riesinger calmly told them to open the windows, air out the convent. It was just their parting shot. "Be assured," he told them. "It is ended."

Anna went home to a new life, free for the first time since that terrible day when, as a fourteen-year-old girl, she had been cursed by a "loathsomely unchaste" father.

The Roman Catholic Church decreed the case to be an authentic instance of diabolic possession. The exorcism, which took place in Earling, Iowa, remains the only instance in which even a semi-detailed account of an exorcism has been released by the church body. On July 23, 1935, the Most Reverend Joseph F. Busch, Bishop of St. Cloud, Minnesota, placed the Imprimatur on a clerically approved summary of the case which had been prepared by the Reverend Celestine Kapsner, O.S.B., of St. John's Abbey, Collegeville, Minnesota. Father Kapsner's account was based on an earlier record of the case by the Reverend Carl Bogl, who had written the account in German. It is recorded that by 1935 the Capuchin Fr. Theophilus Riesinger had performed nineteen successful exorcisms.

⚬⚬⚬

DR. WILSON VAN DUSEN ON THE HIERARCHY OF SPIRITS

Although Dr. Wilson Van Dusen, PhD considers himself a scientist, he studies multi-leveled mysticism with the perspective of an empiricist, which one might observe in such works as *The Presence of Other Worlds* (1994), *Testimony to the Invisible: Essays on Swedenborg* (1995), and *Beauty, Wonder, and The Mystical World* (1999). For anyone who is interested in examining the phenomena of ghosts and spirits from a broad perspective, the work conducted by Dr. Van Dusen while he was chief psychologist at Mendocino State Hospital in California offers an interesting area for additional research. First it must be noted that Dr. Van Dusen is fascinated by the life of the intellectual colossus Emanuel Swedenborg (1688–1772), who may have been the last of the Renaissance men. Swedenborg wrote 150 books in seventeen sciences. He was also an expert in numerous crafts, an accomplished musician, a politician, a prolific inventor, and fluent in nine languages. Those who recognize his name today usually think of Swedenborg as a Swedish mystic who claimed daily communication with angels, demons, and other inhabitants of the unseen world and whose manifestations of remarkable psychic phenomena were well documented.

Through the course of his study and research, Dr. Van Dusen found what he believed to be the confirmation of one of Swedenborg's most unusual doctrines—that the life of human beings depend on their relationship to a hierarchy of spirits. In his position as a clinical psychologist in a state mental hospital, Dr. Van Dusen set out to describe his patients' hallucinations as faithfully as possible. Although he noticed consistency between the descriptions given by his mental patients and Swedenborg's discussions of the relationships of humans to spirits, it was not until three years after Dr. Van Dusen had collected all his major findings that he discovered the striking similarities between what his twentieth-century patients had told him and what the eighteenth-century Swedenborg described in his accounts. In Van Dusen's opinion, Swedenborg's system was an almost perfect fit with his patients' experiences. But, even more impressively, it accounted for otherwise quite puzzling aspects of hallucinations.

After dealing with hundreds of patients who hallucinated—chronic schizophrenics, alcoholics, the brain-damaged and senile—Dr. Van Dusen discovered that he was able to speak directly to their hallucinations. He began to look for patients who were able to distinguish between their own thoughts and the products of their hallucinations. He told them that he wished to gain as accurate a description of their experiences as possible. He promised no special reward and offered no hope for recovery. Some patients, he learned, were embarrassed by what they heard or saw. In other instances the hallucinations were frightened of the psychologist. Once he had reassured the patient and his hallucination, Dr. Van Dusen attempted to establish a relationship with both his seen and unseen interviewees.

The psychologist would question these other persons or entities directly, and he instructed the patient to give a word-for-word account of what the voices answered or what was seen. In this way, the psychologist could hold long dialogues with a patient's hallucinations and record both his questions and their answers. Dr. Van Dusen's method was that of phenomenology. His only purpose was to come to as accurate a description as possible of the patient's experiences. He treated the hallucinations as realities because that was what they were to the patient.

On numerous occasions Dr. Van Dusen found that he was engaged in dialogues with hallucinations that were quite far above the patient's ordinary comprehension. He found this to be especially true when he contacted the higher order of hallucinations, which he discovered to be of a symbolical depth beyond the patient's normal understanding. The psychologist also learned that in most cases the hallucinations had come upon the patients very suddenly.

Van Dusen consistently found that the patients believed that they had somehow established contact with another world, dimension, or order of beings.

Very soon, the psychologist learned that all of his patients objected to the term hallucination. Each had coined his own term such as The Other Order, the Eavesdroppers, and so forth. The voices had the qualities of real voices, and on occasion could assume the voice of a specific person to deceive the patient. Such pranks and the shouting of vile and obscene messages and threats were the work of the "lower order" of entities. Members of the lower order also suggested lewd acts and encouraged the patient to indulge in them—then they would scold the patient for considering such thoughts. These beings sought to find a weak point of conscience and work on it interminably. According to Dr. Van Dusen, "They invade every nook and cranny of privacy, work on every weakness and credibility, claim awesome powers, lie, make promises and then undermine the patients' will. They never have a personal identity though they accept most names or identities given them." Van Dusen found the lower order consistently anti-religious, and some actively obstructed the patient's religious practices. Occasionally they would refer to themselves as demons and speak of hell.

> These beings sought to find a weak point of conscience and work on it interminably.

The higher order of hallucinations stood in direct contrast to such demonic manifestations, but Dr. Van Dusen found that they made up only a fifth or less of the experiences he documented. The higher order respects the patient's freedom and does not work against his or her will. While the lower order prattles on endlessly, the higher order seldom speaks. Dr. Van Dusen also discovered that the higher order is much more likely to be symbolic, religious, supportive, genuinely instructive, and communicate directly with the inner feelings of the patient. In general the higher order is richer than the patient's normal experience. The psychologist likened the higher order to Carl Jung's archetypes, whereas he compared the lower order to Sigmund Freud's id. "In contrast to the lower order, the higher order thinks in something like universal ideas in ways that are richer and more complex than the patient's own mode of thought," Dr. Van Dusen said. The communications from the higher order can be very powerful emotionally and carry an almost inexpressible ring of truth. "The higher order tends to enlarge a patient's values, something like a very wise and considerate instructor," he commented.

After intensive study, Dr. Van Dusen concluded that there were a number of points which make the similarity between Swedenborg's description of a spiritual hierarchy and the psychologist's own findings impressive. Van Dusen's patients acted independently of each other and yet gave similar accounts. "They also agree on every particular I could find with Swedenborg's account," he said. "My own findings were established years before I really examined Swedenborg's position in this matter." In Van Dusen's opinion, it seemed remarkable that, "over two centuries of time, men of very different cultures working under entirely different circumstances on quite different people could come to such similar findings.... Because of this I am inclined to speculate that we are looking at a process which transcends cultures and remains stable over time."

Dr. Van Dusen also wondered whether the hallucinations of his patients—described by the vast majority of his colleagues and the psychological literature as being "detached pieces of the unconscious"—and the phenomenon of spiritual possession "might not simply be two ways of describing the same process. Are they really spirits or pieces of one's own unconscious?"

Van Dusen reflected that, "as Swedenborg has indicated, our lives may be the little free space at the confluence of giant higher and lower spiritual hierarchies." The psychologist perceived some kind of lesson in such a view of the unseen world. As humans who contend that we have free will, we may, in actuality, be "freely poised between good and evil," under the influence of cosmic forces most of us don't even believe exist. Men and women, thinking they make free choices, "may be the resultant of other forces."

Most people find the thought that they might be at the mercy of unseen forces to be very discomforting, and they will argue quite forcefully that they have free will to choose their own destiny. Others who have come face to face with the unknown are less certain and are willing to ponder the possibility that entities from some other dimension of reality may seek to influence, disrupt, or control our lives. As Michael came to conclude after the experience he relates in the following account, some people may not really want to know about what's really out there.

⊷⦿⊶

ENCOUNTERING SHADOW BEINGS AND
SPIRIT POSSESSION DURING WINTER BREAK

The Personal Experience of Michael

I have spent the last thirteen years trying my best to forget the events that took place that week in 1989, but it sticks in my memory as if it happened yesterday.

It was winter break at college, and I was bracing for a week alone on campus as my school was in Tennessee and my home was in New Hampshire. My friend Jim invited me to spend the week with him and his family in Ann Arbor, Michigan, and I accepted.

On the trip to Michigan Jim told me that his younger brother Mark was doing a favor for someone who was out of town—feeding their dog and hanging around their place once in a while so the house looked lived in. We arrived at Jim's house in Ann Arbor on a cold and rainy night. I met his parents, his sister, his brother Mark, and the youngest brother Chucky, who was about thirteen.

Jim, Chucky, and I rode along with Mark when he went to check on the house he was watching, and on the way over, he told us about some strange things that had happened to him while he was there. Mark said that late one night around 2:00 A.M. when he was sitting alone upstairs watching television he heard voices downstairs. At first he was afraid that someone may have broken in. All the lights downstairs were out, and when Mark turned the volume down on the television set the voices became louder. He went out into the hall and looked out over the thin metal railing by the stairs. (The master bedroom was farther up the hall from the room he was in; a fact that will be important later.) He heard loud whispers at the bottom of the stairs, but he couldn't make out what they were say-ing. Then he saw a large, dark shadow of a woman coming up the stairs, and as it approached the whispers became louder and seemed to be emanating from the shadowy figure. Mark could even hear the footsteps as the entity came up the stairs.

> Mark felt a cold wind pass by him, and the curtains billowed as the shadowy being went out the window....

At this point, Mark said that he was really scared. He ran back into the side room at the top of the stairs, sat in his chair, and turned the television to a Christian channel where a minister was preaching. Mark grabbed a Bible and held on for dear life. He sat there with the volume up and his Bible in hands, but the dark shadow kept coming. The footsteps and the voices kept growing louder. The shadow of the woman stopped at the opening to the door of the side room wherein Mark was praying hard. Then it disappeared. Mark felt a cold wind pass by him, and the curtains billowed as the shadowy being went out the window that he had opened earlier to get some fresh air.

By the time we turned up the road to the house, Mark had finished his story. We prayed and tried to prepare for anything. The house was large, dark brown or black, and situated next to a cemetery, which was separated from the side yard by a metal fence. It may have appeared to be a normal house by day, but at night it looked like something right out of a horror movie. We pulled into the driveway which went up the side of the house and extended into the backyard. Now I don't know who lived there even to this day, but one wonders how they couldn't have known their house was possessed by dark spirits.

When we got out of the car, Mark pointed up to the top floor and indi-cated the window of the master bedroom where he occasionally watched tele-vision. As I looked up to the window, I saw a bluish, flickering light, and I asked Mark if he were absolutely certain that he had turned off the television the last time he had used it. He replied that he was sure.

As we reached the back sliding glass door, we found the dog scratching wildly against the window. When we opened the door, the dog shot out into the yard like a bullet out of a gun and kept looking back, cowering, and keeping its distance from the house. As we entered the house, it seemed as though we could cut the atmosphere with a knife. This was the first time I actually sensed the presence of a spirit. Mark went about his promised duties as a house sitter, and for the first few minutes there were no problems. Mark just had to check phone messages, make a call or two, take the mail inside, and so forth.

> Then we began to hear the same kind of whispers that Mark had talked about, as if many voices were speaking at once in an unintelligible murmur.

I was convinced that in spite of what he had said Mark had left the television on in the master bedroom, so Jim and I were preparing to go upstairs and turn it off—but suddenly we all had the spooky feeling that we were being closely watched. I looked around and Chucky was gone. As I expected, he had gone outside, and when I glanced upward, I was shocked to see that it was totally dark in the master bedroom.

By now we knew something weird was going on, but we were staying calm. We told Mark to complete his business in the place, and we would get out in about fifteen minutes with no problems. But as we were waiting for Mark, we began to hear footsteps coming from the upstairs hallway. Then we began to hear the same kind of whispers that Mark had talked about, as if many voices were speaking at once in an unintelligible murmur. They were coming from upstairs and getting louder with every footstep. By now we were all more than ready to leave, so we prayed for protection and tried to hurry Mark along.

I stood at the bottom of the stairs, and I could hear that the footsteps and voices were now becoming louder and moving down the stairs. I called Jim over, and he heard and sensed the same thing. The voices and footsteps were getting closer to where we were stood at the bottom of the steps. Finally Mark was finished with his chores, and we were getting ready to lock up. Jim dragged the dog into the house against the frightened animal's whimpering protests. Chucky wandered outside again, and I found him once again staring up at the window of the master bedroom. He stood as if in a daze, but he broke out of it when the flickering, bluish lights came back. I told Chucky to stay where he was, and I went back inside.

The voices and footsteps were not quite as loud, but just as we were ready to leave something began moving toward us from out of a dark side room located off the downstairs hall. At that time, we were Pentecostal Christians. Believing ourselves to be in the presence of devils, we began to rebuke the creature in the name of Jesus, as we had been taught to do in such situations. The spirit, entity (or whatever it was) did not go away, but it stopped moving toward us. By now the voices and footsteps were just about at the bottom of the stairs, so we ran out, slammed the sliding glass door shut, locked it, grabbed Chucky, got in the car and drove away.

I felt guilty leaving that poor dog in there. I saw part of that spirit downstairs, but Jim and Mark got a better look as they were in front of me, blocking my line of sight. Jim described it as being small and hairy with a hideous face.

We assumed that would be the end of it because Mark didn't have to go back, at least not while Jim and I were there. But we were wrong. The night before Jim and I were to go back to school, we were told to sleep in the bunk bed in the attic. Jim and I were studying to be preachers, so we believed in faith and spiritual warfare. I could not sleep that night. I had the same sensation of being watched closely. This unnerved me: why was it happening in Jim's house? I took a blanket, went downstairs, and just hung out and read. Chucky came downstairs and wanted to talk. We decided to try and get some sleep, after saying a prayer together. Chucky wanted to receive what Pentecostals called the baptism in the Holy Ghost as evidenced by speaking in other tongues. We knelt by the couch to pray on our knees, and Chucky sounded like he was speaking in tongues—but then something really strange happened. Chucky went from kneeling with his head bowed to a posture where his head suddenly flew back with his eyes rolling into the back of his head—and he was on the floor, lying unconscious on his back. At first I misinterpreted what happened as another Pentecostal experience called being "slain in the spirit," when God lays you out like a light and communes with you. But it didn't take long for me to figure out that this was not the work of God. Chucky was writhing on the floor and speaking in weird tongues that I had never heard before, and his eyes looked totally glazed. By now, I knew he was possessed. At that time in my Pentecostal faith, I believed Chucky was possessed by the Devil or a devil, but now I believe it was an evil entity or spirit that had followed us from the house. That was why I couldn't sleep. I had been aware of its presence on some level of consciousness.

I was just about to get Jim and Mark when Chucky stopped writhing and sat straight upright, stiff as a board, and spoke in a deep voice completely different from his own naturally high-pitched tone. He spoke in an unearthly voice deeper than I had ever heard. He pointed at me and said in a dark, evil tone, "YOU!" To this day I don't know what that was all about. In my youth and pious pride, I thought the devil was aware of who I was because I was such a good Christian. I ran upstairs and got Jim, Mark, and their parents. By now it was around 3:30 A.M. Jim, Mark, and I got our Bibles, and for the next hour and a half we tried to rebuke the evil spirit that had entered Chucky. He sat up and spewed forth the "YOU!" again, once to me and once to Jim. The more we rebuked and prayed and quoted Bible verses, the harder Chucky writhed and the deep, dark evil voice within him shouted many foul things at us.

All these years later, I can't believe that there was any way this kid with a high-pitched voice could have faked that deep, otherworldly sounding voice. We were grasping at straws, but we were unwilling to give up on Chucky. I finally had an idea, and the next time when Chucky started writhing and spewing his dark tongues, we all rebuked the devil in the name of Jesus and placed our King James Bibles on his chest at the same time. Chucky shook violently—and he was back. Whatever had possessed him had fled. He was back to his high-pitched voice. By now it was 5:30 A.M., and we just had time to eat some breakfast before Jim and I headed back to school in Tennessee. I was quite ready to go back to college. Weeks later, Jim invited me back to Michigan with him, but I respectfully declined.

Even now I get chills writing this. Chucky described what it was like when the evil spirit possessed him. He said that gruesome creatures were holding him in a zone that was all white in color. He had no idea what was going on outside his body. As I said, back then I believed in devils. I do not now, but I do believe there was something evil in that house. I am reluctant to tell this story, for I have found that most people just don't want to know the truth about what's out there.

THE MINOTAUR OF CLEARWATER, FLORIDA

By Azhran

On the outskirts of Clearwater, Florida there is an area long since converted into a county park that I have for many years called "The Land of the Minotaur" because of a spectral entity/shape-shifter that makes an occasional appearance there. In my studies I haven't come across anything quite like this creature. Although it functions in a similar fashion to a Norse mythological creature called a "Wight," which is similar to a Wraith, it seems content to feed off the souls of the sleeping dead; possibly, it guards gateways between realms of living and of the dead.

The park is split in two distinct halves, separated by a small river that is almost more of a creek. A metal bridge spans the two banks, and often on foggy nights you can stand on the bridge and know what it is like to stand in isolation among the stars and space, or feel a very heightened assault on your perceptions at the very least.

The two halves of the land split by the river also radiate very different energies. I don't like to use the terms "good" and "evil," for I believe ultimately there is only energy, its application and formation, and it is this intention that defines benefit or threat. In the natural world where ultimately all life is food (in one way or another), there cannot conceivably be good and evil as theology dictates, there can only be motive and agenda—but that is best left for other discussions and ponderings, for there truly isn't anything more complicated than perspective.

Across the bridge there are energies that are both very enticing and heavy, lingering with the essence of damnation. It is here that this Minotaur reigns. When you return from that side of the river, you are aware of overwhelming calm; in essence, without realizing it, you feel "safe" again, even though consciously (most times) you never felt like you were in danger to begin with.

It is this unique blend of harmonic disharmonies that has kept me returning to this place. Nevertheless, I will never again completely cross the bridge on the nights of the eerie fog because of what happened on the night that I took five friends who were intrigued by my descriptions and wanted to explore. Occasionally, I still awaken screaming out of terror and guilt. This was one of the very few times that I ever felt pure horror in my life, yet it wasn't immediately recognized at the time.

> In my studies I haven't come across anything quite like this creature.

Years before, legend had it, there was a cemetery in the area beyond the bridge. I have found no records of it, but when I was a child, I did find a half-buried cedar coffin lid. It wasn't attached to anything, it was just a lid, admittedly a peculiar find. But that was when they were converting the area to the county park and many such odds and ends were turning up.

The night my friends and I went to the park happened to be an evening of the heavy, eerie fog. Once we spanned the bridge we could see the sidewalk and how it curved around in all sorts of ways—an eerie labyrinthine yellow brick road so to speak. Close to the ground was the eerie fog, a kind not seen too often in the humid climate of the summer in Florida. Around a bend in the sidewalk there was one of the strangest-looking trees I have ever encountered. And we all saw a man hanging from a branch at the top. We froze. The fog moved away from the tree as several spirits emerged and surrounded the tree—and then from behind it the Minotaur emerged. The spirits were herded into a strange quasi-circle as they moved around the tree and behind this creature. I hadn't encountered a thing like this before. This was uncharted territory for me, and I was bothered because I had friends with me. I felt responsible for their safety, and I wasn't sure what to do.

A passing train blew its horn, which snapped us out of it, and we screamed and bolted down the sidewalk. The only destination we had in mind was "away." Except for my friend Jack, who for whatever reason charged the Minotaur.

The scene faded. We stopped once we realized what had happened. Jack wound up hitting the tree. He laughed at us for being scared, and we started to hear the breath of a bull we couldn't see. At the sound, Jack's laughter ended, and he joined us in running farther down the sidewalk. Now it was our mission to reach the end of the path. Oddly, the path has two endings—the first end of the path is at a very small bridge overlooking a creek and a small little pond/whirlpool, but the ultimate end is at a huge overpass of a major highway. We stopped at the bridge for that was all the adventure we had left in us.

We rested a bit and discussed what we had seen. After recovering, it was time to get out of there and go home.

As we headed back, the fog returned. Some of us saw red eyes. Some heard the breath of the bull. None saw it, but we all knew where it was, and we ran full tilt toward the main bridge to the other side. After what seemed like an hour of running, we arrived at the small bridge. We tried to figure out what had happened. This was a strange evening. We figured in our panic that we had just managed to back track without realizing it.

> The energy of peace and calm at last descended on us, and the fright of just minutes ago faded into imagination.

As we neared a darker area of the journey, I started to feel something, a presence of a different sort. "One of you must return, for the rest of you to escape." At first I thought I heard this audibly, but as time went on, I am sure it was in my head. Nobody else indicated that they had heard anything. For the first time I knew that the fog on the ground meant it was some kind of feeding time. Something had chosen one of us to stay. A bush to the right cracked and bounced heavily as something crashed through it—yet the wind was still. We screamed and ran once again.

Instead of risking getting turned around again, when we got to the creek I knew what we had to do. We swam to the other side, bypassing the rest of the path, the tree, the lingering dead, and the Minotaur. In comparison, facing the alligators that live in and around the lakes somehow seemed safer.

We made it to the bank on the peaceful side, climbing up and out. We were soaked, but apparently unharmed. We stood there dripping wet and looking at a sight that, to this day, doesn't completely register with me. I saw my friend Jack standing over on the shore of the other side, yet his hand was on my shoulder. "I'll hand this to ya Az, you were right about this place." Jack said with his usual ironic tone. I looked at the rest of the gang: Annie was pale as a ghost. I knew then that she saw what I saw, and she realized it meant something that hadn't sunk in with me. She had a tear in her eye. (She and I had shared many adventures like this, but this was the first time I saw her so terrified.)

I couldn't speak. I still saw Jack in both places. I didn't know what it meant then, but I would have an answer all too soon. Annie refused to talk about it. She was afraid of making it happen by speaking of it. She hated leaving me in the dark, but the only thing she would tell me was this: "Az, just remember this when the time comes, it wasn't your fault. You saved more than you know by getting us to swim instead of staying on the path."

I was so confused at that moment that I wasn't certain what reality was for a short while. All of us were acting strangely. The energy of peace and calm at last descended on us, and the fright of just minutes ago faded into imagination. I looked across the lake. All of it had faded. Jack was now only with us on our side of the shore.

We came to the bridge as we exited the park, and I saw one of the elders that I see from time to time. With the wisdom of the ancients, he leaned heavily on a staff, and I could swear I saw a tear in his steely grey-blue eye as well, but he seemed to show no emotion. I blinked my eyes and rubbed them a bit. I was cold from the water, and the elder was gone. Usually I get some message or insight from him/them whenever they appear, quite often at the foot of that initial bridge, but not this night. Somehow I felt had failed him. Yet I don't know why I felt that way.

The night came to an end, and we parted our ways. It would be a few days before I could talk with Annie, but she still wouldn't talk about our experience. By this time I had already begun to convince myself it was mostly imagination, a fun night with live action "Campfire Ghost Stories." I couldn't have been more wrong.

Three weeks later, I got a frantic call from Laura who was with us that night, and who was also Jack's roommate. Within minutes I would be in the emergency room with my friends. Jack's lungs were collapsing. He couldn't breathe, a genetic problem he had dealt with since birth. Unfortunately this time it triggered heart palpitations and it sent him into cardiac arrest. His family flew him to his native home in Connecticut where two days later I got the call telling me that Jack had crossed over. He died at the age of twenty-three surrounded by his family.

Instantly that night came back to me with full force. I fled to the land of the Minotaur; the bridge was foggy, completely covered. I raced to the bridge, and Annie's words finally came back to me. Although they provided little comfort right then, I am all but certain they kept me from losing my mind.

I've never mentioned that night in the land of the Minotaur in connection with Jack, mostly out of survivor's guilt. I will never return to that portion of the land when the fog hugs close to the ground. It was also the last time I tempted fate with creatures that I don't fully comprehend. Annie also knew that night that I would blame myself, and I do. I hold it deep in my heart to this day.

POSSESSED BY A SPIRIT PARASITE

If someone you know has demonstrated a dramatic alteration in their behavior and you are certain that he or she does not abuse drugs and has no previous history of mental problems, that person may have been invaded by a spirit parasite. Consult with a physician, a psychologist, or a psychiatrist and consider possession by a spirit parasite as one of many possible diagnoses. Those who suffer from invasion by an uninvited entity may begin to manifest changes in personality or personal behavior as listed below.:

- They may begin to hear voices directing them to perform acts they never before even considered.

- They may frequently see the image of the spirit parasite as it existed in its physical life as a human—or, in the case of a non-human entity, as it truly appears in its demonic countenance.

- In the weeks and months that follow, the spirit-possessed may fall into states of blacked-out consciousness, and later have absolutely no memory of that time.

- On occasions, sometimes even in the midst of conversations, their conscious minds may be blocked and a trancelike state will come over them.

- They may be observed walking differently, speaking in a different tone and manner, and acting in strange, irrational ways.

- They may begin doing things that they have never done before. Friends and family will remark that they are behaving like totally different people.

- In the very worst cases, the parasite being will consume its victim's life. The evil spell climax with the possessed committing murder, suicide, or some violent antisocial act.

Remember that spirit parasites cannot achieve power over anyone unless they are somehow invited into that person's private space or unless they are attracted to an individual by his or her negative thoughts and actions. A person will become especially vulnerable to such spirit invasion if he or she abuses alcohol or drugs or exploits someone mentally, physically, or emotionally.

Evil or negativity is an imbalanced, chaotic, destructive energy, the opposite of growth and productivity. When an individual is negative, depressed, and discordant, he or she opens the psyche to an invasion from a parasite from the lower frequencies of the spirit world.

One should be wary of an indiscriminate exploration of the occult or of "ghost hunting" in haunted houses or places. Without the proper discipline, study, and discernment, the ill-prepared will be liable to interact only with those entities who will seek to deceive and entrap them.

Experienced psychical researchers understand that the physical world is closer to the realm of the lower, more negative, spiritual frequencies of the spirit world than it is to the dimension of higher beings. Because we exist in a material world, our psyches will always contain more aspects that are similar to those of the lower vibratory realm than the higher spiritual planes.

If you should have an encounter with a negative being from the more chaotic regions of the spirit world, you will quite likely experience a prickling sensation that will seem to crawl over your entire body. You will instantly be filled with an awareness that you have entered into a very dangerous liaison. If you continue the contact, you will experience a mounting sense of terror or a distinct sensation of unease, depending upon the strength of the discordant vibrations emanating from the spirit parasite. If it seems you have found yourself locked into such an encounter, utter prayers of love and harmony and ask that angelic or higher spiritual guidance be manifested around you.

Experienced ghost researchers have become aware that troubled spirits will continue their contentious ways beyond physical death....

Those who have accumulated many years of experience researching and exploring the unseen world have come to understand that the spirit world is populated by all manner of discordant entities as well as more benevolent and benign beings. Experienced ghost researchers have become aware that troubled spirits will continue their contentious ways beyond physical death, and they will often attempt to influence the minds, and therefore the lives, of those who will receive them.

Psychic investigators who have spent many years perfecting their knowledge of the unseen world have also become aware that many of the inhabitants of other dimensions have never been human. While some of these disincarnated envy human flesh and their human experiences, other such beings hold the human species in the greatest contempt and will seek devious ways to humiliate and destroy their victims. The best way to avoid a negative encounter with a spirit parasite is to seek always to elevate one's thoughts, works, and deeds to the highest levels.

6
SPIRITS SEEN
AT DEATH BEDS
AND FUNERALS

Dr. Carla Wills-Brandon, PhD has spent over two decades investigating the mystical experiences of the dying and those who were at their bedside. According to Wills-Brandon, who has collected nearly two thousand modern-day deathbed vision accounts: "Deathbed visions come in all shapes and sizes. As physical death draws near, some people receive visitations from deceased relatives while others encounter angels or other religious figures."

Many of the accounts collected by Wills-Brandon mention seeing a wisp of "something" leaving the physical body of a friend or relative at the moment of passing. "Those who are about to leave will often talk about seeing beautiful landscapes on the other side and then state with conviction that this is where they will be after they pass," she said.

A licensed marriage and family therapist who has been in private practice for twenty years with Michael Brandon, Ph.D., her husband of over thirty years, PhD Wills-Brandon is the author of *One Last Hug Before I Go: The Mystery and Meaning of Deathbed Visions* and *A Glimpse of Heaven: Spiritually Transformative Mystical Experiences of Everyday People*. Her extensive research has convinced her that deathbed visions bring comfort not only to the dying, but also to those who love them. "In most cases, once one has had such a vision, death is no longer something to fear," she said. "This phenomenon is nothing new. It has been described over and over again, across all cultures and religions, for as long as time can remember."

As Wills-Braden reminds us, deathbed visions of the soul leaving the body have been experienced by humans in all cultures and religions; in fact, the existence of the soul is one of the few things upon which the major religions agree. In Judaism, Christianity, and Islam the soul or spirit is the very

Angels are one of the most common forms that individuals see during out-of-body projections, near death experiences, after death has occurred, and during times of emotional turmoil.

essence of the individual, more important to his or her identity than the physical body, which is only a temporary possession that will turn to dust.

"The body is the sheath of the soul." The Talmud (Judaism).

"Then the Lord God formed man out of the dust of the ground, and breathed into his nostrils the breath of life; and man became a living being." Genesis, 2:7 (Judaism/Christianity).

"And He originated the creation of man out of clay, then He fashioned his progeny of an extraction of mean water, then He shaped him, and breathed His spirit in him." The Qur'an, 32: 8–9 (Islam).

In Hinduism, the soul is a fragment of the Divine Self, the Atman. "Now my breath and spirit goes to the Immortal, and this body ends in ashes; OM, O Mind! Remember the deeds. Remember the actions." Isha Upanishad 17.

The great Hindu work the Bhagavad Gita contains the oft-quoted lines which tell us that the spirit within is unborn, eternal, immutable, indestructible, immemorial, and unchanging: "As a man abandons his worn-out clothes and acquires new ones, so when the body is worn out a new one is acquired by the Self, who lives within … The Self, cannot be pierced or burned, made wet or dry. It is everlasting and infinite, standing on the motionless foundation of eternity. The Self is unmanifested, beyond all thought, beyond all change." Bhagavad Gita 2: 19-25.

Buddhism perceives the spirit as the end-product of a life of conditions and causes. "Behold this beautiful body, a mass of sores, a heaped up lump, diseased … in which nothing lasts, nothing persists. Thoroughly worn out is this body….Truly, life ends in death….Of bones is this house made, plastered with flesh and blood. Herein are stored decay, death, conceit, and hypocrisy. Even ornamental chariots wear out. So too the body reaches old age…." Dhammapada 147–151.

The teachings of Seicho-no-Ie, a new religion becoming popular in Japan, state that the nature of human beings is primarily a spiritual life "which weaves its threads of mind to build a cocoon of flesh, encloses its own soul in the cocoon, and for the first time, the spirit becomes flesh. But understand this clearly: The cocoon is not the silkworm; in the same way, the physical body is not man but merely man's cocoon. Just as the silkworm will break out of its cocoon and fly free, so, too, will man break out of his body-cocoon and ascend to the spiritual world when his time is come." Nectarean Shower of Holy Doctrines.

[P] rehistoric people believed that death was not the end and that there was some part of the deceased that still required nourishment, clothing, and protection....

We cannot state dogmatically when the earliest members of our species, *Homo sapiens* (c. 30,000 B.C.E.), conducted burial rituals of a nature that would qualify them as believers in an afterlife, but we do know that they buried their dead with care and consideration and included food, weapons, and various personal belongings with the body. Even the earlier Neanderthal species (c. 100,000 B.C.E.) placed food, stone implements, and decorative shells and bones in the graves with the bodies of their deceased, which they often covered with a red pigment. Because of the placement of such funerary objects in the graves, it seems that even these prehistoric people believed that death was not the end and that there was some part of the deceased that still required nourishment, clothing, and protection in order to journey safely in another kind of existence beyond the grave. The graphic paintings found in the European caves of the Paleolithic Age (c. 50,000 B.C.E.) clearly seem to indicate that early humans sought by supernatural means to placate the spirits of the animals they killed for food, to dispel the restless spirits of the humans they had slain in territorial disputes, and to bring peace to the spirits of their deceased tribal kin. Therefore, it seems quite likely that for fifty thousand years, human beings have believed that one of the most common places to witness the spirits of the deceased would be around deathbeds and funerals.

The Spirit of a Beautiful Woman Came for Mary

The Personal Experience of Dr. E. Hanner

Dr. E. Hanner, a retired general practitioner from Michigan, said that he would never forget the time back in 1939 when he was visiting a sick child who had been slowly dying from the ravages of typhoid fever.

"This girl that I was tending was the youngest child of the Reddings, a family of hardworking German Catholics," Dr. Hanner said. "I was a staunch Baptist, and in those days in some of the more remote rural regions of the state, there were certain prejudices that were strongly maintained between Catholic and Protestant. But when one of the children in any of the Catholic families was sick, it didn't matter to them if I worshipped crows or trees. I was the only doctor in town, and they wanted me there looking after their kids."

Late one afternoon in August, just after Dr. Hanner had finished examining the seven-year-old girl, he heard a rustling sound off to his right side. "I assumed that I was hearing the sound of the mother's dress, so without turning around, I expressed my sad regret that I didn't think there was anything more that I could do for little Mary. Her condition had not improved, and it seemed to be quickly worsening. I suggested that they call their priest for last rites. My pills and powders could not help her any longer."

When there was no response, Dr. Hanner turned to see a beautiful young woman he guessed to be in her late teens standing just a few inches from his right shoulder. "She had dark brown shoulder-length hair, and she was dressed completely in white," he recalled. "I knew that she was not any member of the family, for the oldest of the Redding children was only thirteen. She seemed not to pay any attention to me, and she brushed by me to approach the girl in her bed."

Dr. Hanner was astonished when the lovely young woman bent over the child, then lifted the spirit form of the little girl into her arms. "I was so stunned by the action that I thought my knees would buckle. I was witnessing a sight that few mortals are privileged to see," he continued. "Little Mary's spirit was identical to her physical body, except it was translucent and it no longer bore the ravages of the terrible illness that she had suffered for over a month."

And what Dr. Hanner beheld next was even more startling. The beautiful lady in white passed right through the wall with the child's spirit in her arms. He sat quietly in a chair for several minutes, attempting to recover his mental balance. When he felt that his wits had returned and he could examine the girl, he verified what he already knew. Little Mary had died at the very moment when the beautiful woman in white had lifted her soul from her body.

A few minutes later, Dr. Hanner walked down the stairs of the farmhouse to give the weeping parents the sad announcement that their youngest child had died. Hoping to somehow alleviate their grief, but stumbling for the proper words, he offered his sincere conviction that he had seen an angel take Mary's soul to heaven.

"I stayed with the family, offering what little comfort I could," Dr. Hanner said. "A while later, as we sat in the parlor drinking coffee and discussing funeral plans, I saw a picture of a beautiful young woman amidst a number of other photographs on a shelf near the upright piano. When I involuntarily gasped and said that I was seeing before me a photograph of the angel who had lifted Mary's soul from her body, Mrs. Redding told me that the portrait was that of her sister Rose Ann.... The portrait was Rose Ann's high school graduation picture ... taken shortly before she was killed in an automobile accident," Dr. Hanner said. "Rose Ann had just turned eighteen, and she had died in 1930, nine years prior."

Dr. Hanner said that when he swore that was the lovely young woman who had ascended with Mary's spirit in her hands, the Redding family seemed to receive great comfort from his words. "They knew me as a man who was a bit hard-nosed and not given to exaggeration or flights of imagination," he said, concluding his account. "And what I saw that afternoon in that Michigan farm home provided me with all the proof that anyone could ever ask that there is life after death."

Grandfather Accompanied Catherine to the Other Side

Lisa Shellenberg of New Hampshire has written that she saw the spirit of her grandfather James Hedrick in the sickroom of her thirty-year-old daughter Catherine ten hours before Catherine's death. It was her grandfather's spirit, she has testified, who later called Catherine's soul body out of her physical form.

Mrs. Shellenberg has stated that she also lost consciousness at the time of her daughter's death, and together with Catherine's spirit she was taken out of her body by her grandfather. For several hours she was with her daughter in the spirit world. Here, Mrs. Shellenberg says, she saw many angels and spirit beings. Finally, Grandfather Hedrick told her that she must return to her body. She bade Catherine farewell, and she was soon in her flesh form once again.

"I had always had a special connection with Grandpa James," Lisa Shellenberg says. "It really didn't surprise me that our connection would extend after death and that he would grant me that last journey with Catherine as she passed away."

The Kiss of a Stranger Foreshadowed Death

Beth Domke of Omaha, Nebraska, said that her fifteen-year-old daughter Stacy was caring for the infant child of neighbor when a strange man approached them and stopped before the park bench on which they were sitting. At first Stacy became very nervous, fearing that the man might have malicious intentions toward the baby. Her mother had cautioned her so often about child molesters and abductors. But, as she told her mother later, there was such a feeling of peace and love issuing from the man that she relaxed and smiled up at him. Not only did he seem kind and friendly, but there was something about him that seemed so familiar to her.

Stacy was startled, however, when, without saying a word, the man suddenly leaned forward, kissed the baby on the forehead, and walked briskly away. Stacy said that he walked so fast that it seemed as though he just disappeared.

Confused and experiencing vague feelings of guilt, Stacy stopped by their apartment before she returned the baby to its mother and told her own mother about the incident.

"Stacy said the man appeared to be in his fifties or so, tall, silver-haired, very distinguished in his appearance," Beth Domke said in her account of the incident. "Stacy kept saying over and over that the stranger had seemed so nice, so loving." Mrs. Domke assured her daughter that she had not done anything wrong. No harm had been done. But she should be more cautious regarding strangers in the future.

That night, according to the baby's parents, a knocking was heard at their front door. When they answered the knock, they found no one there. In a few minutes, the sound was heard again. On an impulse, the mother went into the room where her baby was sleeping. To her great sorrow, she found that the child was dead. Later, an autopsy revealed that she had died from sudden infant death syndrome.

> At first she thought that he must be the Angel of Death, but then she saw a photograph of a man and woman on the mantelpiece.

That next day when the Domkes visited the bereaved family and expressed sorrow over their loss, Stacy became nearly hysterical. Assuming that her sensitive daughter was reacting strongly to the death of the baby, Beth got Stacy out of there as quickly as she could. "On the way home," Beth wrote, "Stacy told me that she had freaked out because she had seen a ghostly image of the man who had kissed the baby in the park standing directly behind the grieving mother, resting a hand on her shoulder, as if comforting her. At first she thought that he must be the Angel of Death, but then she saw a photograph of a man and woman on the mantelpiece.

"That was when Stacy realized why the man had seemed so familiar to her. She remembered the first time that she baby-sat for the family and the mother had showed her a photograph of her parents. She said that her mother was still alive, but that her father, whom she had loved so very much, had died several years ago. Stacy insisted that the man in the park was the spirit of the woman's father."

In her account of her daughter's remarkable experience, Beth Domke stated that she believed Stacy's story, and she further believed that the spirit of the woman's father had come to escort the soul of his infant granddaughter to the afterlife. Mrs. Domke reasoned that the family had heard the spirit knocking at the front door as it came for the soul of the child, then rapping again as it left.

An Angel Came to Get Mommy

Richard Riggs' wife and nine-year-old daughter were killed in an automobile accident and his six-year-old daughter Robin was severely injured. Riggs entered little Robin's hospital room and steeled himself for the awful task of informing her about the death of her mother and sister.

But before he could break the sad news to Robin, she told him that she already knew about the deaths. "While I was lying hurt on the ground," she began, "I saw an angel come to get Mommy. The angel started to go back up into the sky, but it stopped, came back for Becky, and took both of them into heaven."

An Angel Tapped at the Window

Pastor Raymond Tigge had known for several months that his child, Samuel, would not recover from his lengthy illness. One warm July night, the whole family decided to sleep in the one room that was somewhat cooler than the others. Pastor Tigge said that he and his wife were both awakened by a soft tapping at the window near their bed. They then saw an angel come through the window, walk over to the sleeping boy, kiss him, and leave.

A few days later, in an effort to divert the boy's mind from his illness, a friend asked Samuel what he wanted for Christmas. The boy shook his head soberly and replied that he would be in heaven. He wouldn't need any toys there.

Within a week, Samuel Tigge died.

His Friend's Soul Left during the Funeral

Dr. D. P. Kayser said that while attending the funeral of Dr. A.N Costello, a colleague he had known for over thirty years, he perceived his friend's soul leaving the body. "There was no question in my mind that Angelo was truly clinically dead before the funeral," Dr. Kayser stated, "but I had once heard it said that 'real death' is not accomplished until the soul actually leaves the body."

Dr. Kayser knew that his friend's life had been one of kindness and service. "Angelo had always been a sincere, practicing Catholic, but even so I was quite startled when I saw the spirits of a group of white-robed children materialize with what seemed to be flowers woven of mingled sunbeams and roses. Assembled near the coffin were white-robed spirits, some of whom I recognized as deceased friends, relatives, and patients of Dr. Costello's."

As the funeral service progressed, Dr. Kayser was somehow able to observe the process of death. "I saw a vapor or mist gradually rise from the body in the casket. When the transition had been completed, the mist gradually took on the image of Dr. Costello.

"Almost at that very moment, a very beautiful angel, robed in the purest white, approached the newly liberated spirit. In its hands, the angel bore a lovely wreath, the center of which supported a large white flower. With this floral diadem, the angel crowned the spirit body of Dr. Angelo Costello.

"When the spirit form was completely separated from the physical body, the image of my friend, together with the angels and the attending spirits appeared to float away."

⟿⟍⟋⟼

ANGELS OR SPIRITS?

One could engage in a ceaseless and tiresome debate about whether people are really seeing angels at the deathbeds of their loved ones or if spirits pose as heavenly messengers to soothe the fears of the dying and their family members. And then one could easily argue that angels assume the image of beloved deceased family members in order to help the dying make the transition between life and death.

Contrary to the popular culture of the past one thousand years or so, humans do not become angels when they die. At least that's according to the monotheistic traditions of Judaism, Christianity, and Islam. According to the scriptures of these faiths, angels were created as an order of spiritual beings prior to the creation of humans and thus remain as entities separate from humans. Angels serve as God's messengers, intermediaries between humankind and the divine, and as guardians and guides for men and women while they live on Earth.

To the dismay of traditional theologians in the United States, Canada, Great Britain, and Europe, the spirituality of the contemporary generation is becoming increasingly defined by angel-belief. Although books on angels became popular in the mid–1990s and encouraged the proliferation of numerous stores specializing in angel merchandise—from a vast array of statues of the heavenly creatures to a variety of scents designed to attract them to one's home—the number of believers spiked dramatically after the attack on the World Trade Center on September 11, 2001. Clergy members of organized religions claim large numbers of young adults and teenagers who have grown up with no organized religious instruction have turned to a belief in angelic beings. These individuals consider the faiths of their fathers tarnished and marginalized and no longer able to offer any practical rules for life or insight into its myriad mysteries.

The December 24, 2002, issue of the Toronto *Globe and Mail*, featured an interview between religion and ethics reporter Michael Valpy (Toronto *Globe and Mail*) and Thomas Beaudoin, a theology professor at Jesuit Boston College and the author of *Virtual Faith: The Irreverent Spiritual Quest of Generation X*. Beaudoin verified that the angel phenomenon was extant wherever he encountered young Christians, Jews, or Muslims. Angels were nearly always spoken about in personal terms and, Beaudoin maintained, this reflected the need among young people for mentors and role models in an age when heroes and heroines are in short supply. In addition, Beaudoin said that a belief in angels reflects the desire of young people to be connected with the dead and shows their conviction that human existence is too profound to terminate with physical death.

This engraving by William Blake depicts the author's vision of death.

Other theologians, such as David Reed of University of Toronto's Anglican Wycliffe College, have stated that angels are extremely believable and accessible as spirit guides. Leonard Primiano, a teacher of religion and folklore at Pennsylvania's Cabrini College, said that young North Americans are interested in everything that is supernatural—UFOs and ghosts, as well as angels.

Perhaps the majority of young people believe that angels are the spirits of people who have passed on, and that the heavenly beings are proof of life after death. To have a faith in angels is to have faith that the human soul lives on after the grave.

> To have a faith in angels is to have faith that the human soul lives on after the grave.

In chapter 11, we shall explore in greater detail the concept of spirit guides communicating through mediums, but it is worth noting here that the popularity of a growing number of "channelers," who claim to contact angels illustrates the manner in which angels and spirits of the dead have blended in contemporary times. Just as there are mediums who claim to be able to contact the spirits of the deceased and obtain guidance and wisdom for the living, there are angel mediums or channelers who claim to be able to establish communication with angels and relay information that will help their clients solve financial problems and difficulties in human relationships.

In December 1999, Emma Heathcote, a researcher at Birmingham University (UK) who was working on her doctorate appeared on a program on the BBC and appealed for reports from Britons who had encounters with angels. By November 2000, she stated that she had heard from eight hundred Britons—Christians, Jews, Muslims, agnostics, and atheists—who claimed to have interacted with angels. The respondents stated that the angels had appeared to convey a message, to provide comfort, and in some instances intervened to prevent serious accidents.

In January 2001, The Allensbach Institute, a surveyor of public opinion in Germany, released their poll findings which indicated that 30 percent of the German population believed in angels and one-fifth of that group claimed to have seen an angelic being.

On December 20, 2001, Scripps Howard News Service and Ohio University published findings that belief in angels cuts across almost all ranges of education, income, and lifestyle. Women and young people were slightly more likely to believe in angels, but a majority of almost every demographic group in the United States had faith in these supernatural beings. According to their survey, 77 percent of adults answered "yes" to the question: "Do you believe angels, that is, some kind of heavenly beings who visit Earth, in fact exist?"

The fact that angels and spirit beings visiting Earth from some heavenly realm are synonymous in the minds of the great majority of men and women does little to affect the research of those who pursue the matter of ghosts and the great mystery of life after death. Whether these entities are separate beings who work together to bring peace and comfort to the dying and their families or facets of the same benevolent intelligence manifesting in ways most acceptable to the dying and those at their bedside, the testimonies of thousands of individuals for thousands of years proclaim that these comforters and guides do exist.

A Dream of His Sister's Death
The Personal Experience of Charles Downey

Charles Downey had a dream that provided him with the information that his sister Jean was dying. Since he had experienced similar dreams before the deaths of other members of his family, he was inclined to pay heed to the nocturnal revelation.

"Either it's a dark Irish curse or a blessing," Downey said, "I had experienced a similar dream before the death of our mother, our cousin Paul, and a close school friend. Because of such a sorrowful track record, I knew that I had better pay attention to this sad dream about Jean." When a telephone call from Jean's husband, David, confirmed her approaching death, Charles and his wife, Marcy, left immediately to be at her bedside.

Jean's eyes did not open, but she seemed somehow to know who was present in her room and even to know where they were standing. As Charles bent to kiss her cheek, Jean spoke in a voice barely audible: "Don't worry, Charlie, they've come for me. Mom, Da, Paul, Uncle Sean, they're all here, waiting for me, just outside the window. And there's a lovely angel with them. She'll escort us to our heavenly home."

David was standing by the window when Jean asked him to step aside so the angel and the others might enter to take her home. Confused, David moved back from the window, and all those present in the room were startled when a whiff of sudden wind stirred the curtains at the same time that the breath of life left Jean's body.

Charles Downey wrote that his sister's face bore a lovely and restful smile as her soul left with members of her family and her angel guide.

An Angel Appeared with Her Parents to Take Her Home
The Personal Witness of Steve Preteroti

I saw three separate clouds float through the doorway into the room where Rochelle lay dying. The clouds enveloped the bed.

As I gazed through the mist, I saw what at first appeared to be the form of a woman take shape. It was transparent and had a golden sheen. It was a figure so glorious in appearance that no words can describe it. The beautiful entity was dressed in a long Grecian robe, and there was a brilliant tiara on her head. It had to be an angel. The majestic figure remained motionless with its hands uplifted over the form of my wife, seemingly engaged in prayer. Then I noticed two other figures kneeling by Rochelle's bedside. I recognized them at once as the forms of her deceased parents. They had come in the company of an angel to guide my beloved Rochelle to heaven.

In a few moments there appeared a spirit duplicate of my wife's body lying horizontally above her physical body. It seemed to be connected to Rochelle's body by a cord.

The whole experience lasted for five hours. As soon as my dear wife had taken her last breath, the glorious angel, the spirits of Rochelle's beloved parents, and the spirit form of my wife vanished.

The Manifestation of an Angelic Comforter

Reverend Maurice Elliott and Irene H. Elliott state that they were present at the bedside of a dying woman when an angel-comforter appeared to stand near her and say, "I have come to take you home."

According to the minister and his wife, three other angels and the images of many of the dying woman's deceased friends and relatives were then seen to join the angel-comforter. A white, hazy mist rose above the woman, hovered there for a few moments, and eventually congealed to take on perfect human form.

After the soul-body had been released from its physical shell, the woman's spirit left in the company of the angels and those dear ones who had already become residents of a higher dimension.

An Angel Severed the Cord

Don P. said that directly above his dying brother Nick he saw a shadowy form floating in a horizontal position. The form became more definite until it became an exact counterpart of Nick's physical body.

"Then I clearly saw an angel materialize and sever a cord which appeared to have connected Nick's spirit form with his physical body," Don stated. "Once the cord had been separated, Nick's spirit form and the angel disappeared together."

DEATHBED RESEARCH OF REVEREND W. BENNETT PALMER

During the course of his extended research into reports of deathbed visions, Reverend W. Bennett Palmer has commented on various consistencies.

Typically, a bedside witness will claim they have seen a mist or a cloudlike vapor emerging from the mouth or head of the dying man or woman. The vaporous substance soon takes on a human form, which is generally a duplicate of the living person—only in most cases any present deformities or injuries are partially or wholly absent. Angels or spirits of deceased loved ones are often reported standing ready to assist the newly freed spirit form to move to higher dimensions of light.

In numerous reports, the immediate process of death is not witnessed, but the deceased is seen leaving the earth plane for the higher world, most often accompanied by angelic beings. Frequently, such spirit and angel leave-taking is in an upward direction, but this seems to be a mode of disappearance, rather than an indication that heaven is in any particular spatial area.

"A fact often noted in connection with deathbed visions is that they are quite different from a patient's delirium and are coherent, rational, and, on reflection, apparently real," Reverend Palmer has said. "It has also been observed that visions of the dying are different from visions of those who only think themselves to be dying, such as those undergoing a near-death experience. However, visions of the dying are similar to those who claim to have been out-of-the-body during altered states of consciousness.

"Revelations concerning the nature of the future life which are received in deathbed visions seem to be regarded with favor by all churches, and no stigma attaches itself to the deathbed visionary experience," Reverend Palmer continues. "Persons having deathbed visions often claim to have seen the dead—or what is so regarded—and to have had them reveal knowledge of events which could not be known in any normal way. Frequently, the person having a deathbed vision claims to see a person in spirit who is not known to be dead. Later, investigation proves that the person was deceased at the time of the visitation.

"Another aspect of deathbed visions," Reverend Palmer concludes, "involves visions of angels and other Holy Figures seen by other persons in the presence of the dying."

Bill W. told Reverend Palmer that he saw the spirit of his brother as it was disengaging itself from the dying body. The cloudlike vapor took on human shape, clapped its hands for joy, then passed upward through the ceiling in the company of an angel.

Jerry C. of Denver, Colorado, said that at the time of death of his ten-year-old son, he saw the child's spirit leaving the body as a luminous cloud and rise upward toward the ceiling.

In Reverend Palmer's church in New Port Richey, Florida, two members of the congregation, Mr. and Mrs. S., who were very ill, had been placed in separate rooms in their home to insure periods of peace and uninterrupted sleep for both of them. One afternoon, as Mr. S. lay back against the pillows of his bed, he saw the form of his wife pass through the wall of his room, wave her hand in farewell, and rise upward in the company of an angel. In two or three minutes, the nurse came into his room and informed him that Mrs. S. had passed away. "I know," he said, blinking back the tears. "She had enough of this desperate struggle to maintain life. She came to say good-bye and to ask me to join her with the angels." Mr. S. died two days later.

> [A]s Mr. S. lay back against the pillows of his bed, he saw the form of his wife pass through the wall....

When Mrs. Ernestine Tamayo entered the sickroom to bring her husband his newspaper, she saw a large, oval light emerging from his head. The illuminated oval floated toward the window, hovered a moment, then was met by a lovely angelic figure. Within seconds, both the oval of light and the angel had vanished. "I knew that Miles was dead even before I reached my husband's bedside," she told Reverend Palmer. "I had seen his angel guide come to take him home."

His many years of research have led Reverend Palmer to record that people who are about to transcend the physical shell often mention a final boundary. After the dying persons have passed that line of demarcation, they cannot return to their physical bodies. In fact, they are sometimes turned back before they can reach it again. The environment and the scenery described in deathbed visions may be said to be much like the scenery of Earth, only more beautiful as the spirit progresses. Eventually, the environment becomes ineffable, incapable of description in human terms or in earthly comprehension.

In instances where it appears that one has achieved a glimpse into heaven, the forms of deceased relatives and friends, as well those of esteemed or saintly figures, are often seen. Angels are frequently described in the company of deceased loved ones. The angels may come to sing heavenly music, to summon the soul from the dying body, or to accompany the newly released spirit to the other world. Most of the men and women who have perceived spiritual deathbed comforters are able to describe the beings in great detail, including their eyes, hair, apparel, and other attributes and accouterments.

⚬⟨⟩⚬

A SURVEY OF DOCTORS AND NURSES ON DEATHBED VISITATIONS

For thousands of years now, many individuals have received personal proof of survival in an afterlife by observing their loved ones at the moment of death. Reports of deathbed experiences have long intrigued investigators of psychic phenomena, and today we have the work of such researchers as Dr. Elisabeth Kubler-Ross, Dr. Raymond Moody, Dr. Kenneth Ring, Dr. P.M.H. Atwater, and Dr. Carla Wills-Braden to add to our knowledge of this most personal, and final, of all human phenomena.

Interestingly, however, a systematic investigation of deathbed reports was not attempted until the early 1960s when the pilot study of Dr. Karlis Osis sought to analyze the experiences of dying persons in a search for patterns (*Deathbed Observations by Physicians and Nurses*, Parapsychology Foundation, Inc., New York, 1961).

Chosen because of their specialized training, their ability to make accurate medical assessments, and their proximity to dying patients, Dr. Osis selected 640 doctors and nurses as informants. Each of the respondents to Dr. Osis's questionnaire had observed an average of fifty to sixty deathbed patients, totaling a remarkable sum of over thirty-five thousand cases. The initial survey was followed up with telephone calls, additional questionnaires, and personal correspondence.

A total of 385 of the medically trained respondents reported 1,318 cases in which deathbed patients reported seeing apparitions of previously deceased loved ones or ghosts of individuals who were known to them. Visions of heaven or scenes of wondrous beauty and brilliant color were reported by 248 respondents in 884 instances.

The physicians and nurses stated that the experience left nearly all of the patients in a state of peace or exaltation. In about half of the cases, the spirits of loved ones or religious figures seemed to manifest to guide the dying patient through the transition from death to the afterlife. Those who had visions of the other side seemed serene and elevated in mood. One distinct observation gleaned from Dr. Osis's study was that few patients appeared to die in a state of fear.

Interestingly enough, the more highly educated patients evidenced more deathbed phenomena than those who were less educated, thus contradicting the allegation that more superstitious people are the only ones to have such experiences.

Those with strong religious beliefs most often identified a saintly figure or previewed heaven, but holy or angelic figures were often reported even by those patients with no religious affiliation.

Another interesting finding of the study was that deathbed visions, spirits of deceased loved ones and mood elevations are reported more often in cases where the dying patients are fully conscious and appear to be in complete control of their senses. Sedation, high fever, and painkilling drugs seem to decrease, rather than to increase, the ability to experience these deathbed phenomena. At the same time, cases of brain damage or brain disease were found to be unrelated to the kind of deathbed experiences that were relevant to Dr. Osis's survey.

The study also discovered cases in which there was collective viewing of the apparitions by those who had gathered around the deathbed. There were numerous instances of a telepathic or clairvoyant interaction between patients and their attending physicians and nurses, and there was also a good number of cases in which a physician or nurse had a change in personal philosophy after having witnessed the experience of a dying person.

7
GHOSTS THAT RETURNED TO BID FAREWELL

⟨⟨⟨⟨⟨⟩⟩⟩⟩⟩

THE PILOT KEPT HIS PROMISE

Captain Eldred Bowyer-Bowyer was shot down in his plane over France on March 19, 1917, the same day that he was to be named the godfather of his half-sister's baby. Mrs. Spearman, who was staying in a hotel in Calcutta, India, was fussing with her baby when she suddenly turned around and saw her half-brother standing behind her. Delighted to think that Captain Bowyer-Bowyer had been transferred to India—and just in time to attend the baptismal service—Mrs. Spearman turned back to the bed so that she might set the baby down and embrace her brother. When she once again faced the spot where her brother had been standing, she found that he had vanished.

Captain Bowyer-Bowyer had appeared so natural and so lifelike that Mrs. Spearman thought at first that he must be playing a trick on her. She called for him and searched everywhere, then, puzzled, she continued on her way to the church. It was not until two weeks later that she read in a newspaper that her half-brother had been shot down on the very day that he had appeared in her hotel room.

On the same day, March 19, Captain Bowyer-Bowyer was also seen by a young niece back in England. At about 9:15 A.M., the girl ran up to her mother, who was still in bed, and excitedly informed her that "Uncle Alley Boy" is downstairs! Her mother smiled and reminded the girl that her uncle was in France, but the excited girl insisted that she had seen "Uncle Alley Boy" downstairs.

A less dramatic, but equally important incident occurred concerning Mrs. Watson, an elderly friend of the airman's mother. On March 19, she wrote Mrs. Bowyer-Bowyer—to whom she had not written for eighteen months—expressing great feelings of anxiety about Eldred.

Author's Commentary:

A downed aircraft in France, a hotel room in Calcutta, a favorite niece in England, a family friend in yet another locale—time and space mean nothing to the phenomena of the ghosts who come to bid farewell. Two common features of such phenomena are apparent in the case of Captain Eldred Bowyer-Bowyer.

One is that the ghost appears so lifelike and so much like the human being it represents that it is almost always mistaken for the living person. The other is that such ghosts materialize when people least expect them. They suddenly pop up completely disassociated with prior feelings of distress or anxiety about the person, and they usually manifest while the percipients are engaged in their normal duties or while they are preparing for sleep.

The Reverend Arthur Bellamy told the highly respected psychical researcher Frederic W. H. Myers about the lady he saw one night sitting by the side of the bed where his wife was sound asleep. He stared at the strange woman for several minutes until she vanished, all the while noting the elegant styling of her hair.

When Mrs. Bellamy awakened, her husband described the mysterious visitor. He was startled to learn that he was describing his wife's friend from her school days. The two girls had once made a pact that the one of them who died first would appear to the survivor.

The astonished Reverend Bellamy asked if there was anything outstanding about her friend so that they might be certain. "Her hair," his wife replied without hesitation. "We girls used to tease her at school for devoting so much time to the arrangement of her hair." Later, when the clergyman saw a photograph of his wife's friend, he was able to verify that it was her ghost that had appeared at their bedside.

It would appear, judging by such cases as the ones that we will encounter in this chapter, that at the moment of physical death, the soul, the essential self in all persons, is emancipated from the confines of the body. It is able to soar free of time and space—and in some instances make a last, fleeting contact with a loved one. These projections at the moment of death betoken that something nonphysical exists within the human body and that it is capable of making a mockery of accepted physical laws. Even more importantly, it is capable of surviving physical death.

THE PHONE WAS OUT OF ORDER
SO HER SPIRIT CAME TO SAY GOODBYE

In the summer of 1913, Stella (Libby) Rife moved away from Bernice Moore, her best friend and "double cousin"—Bernice's father was Stella's mother's brother, and her mother was Stella's father's sister. The two girls had been fast companions and confidantes until the Libbys moved from Lansing, Michigan to Jackson, Michigan.

Three years later, on the evening of December 19, 1916, Stella and a girlfriend were home alone getting ready for an evening out with some other young women. Stella was leaving her room and descending the brightly lighted stairway when she suddenly froze. "Standing in the bright illumination stood my cousin Bernice," she recalled in "My Proof of Survival," *Fate* magazine, February, 1968: "She looked terrified. I saw her clearly, yet I knew she could not be there."

Stella ran hurriedly down the stairs, brushing past the apparition and out the front door. She did not stop until she was a block away from the house. When her girlfriend caught up with her, Stella tried her best to explain what had startled her and made her run away.

When they met their friends later that evening, one of the young women, who worked as an operator for the telephone company, seemed troubled. Even before they had greeted one another, she asked Stella if she was aware that her phone was out of order. Lansing, Michigan, had been trying to call them, the operator said, and when the message could not get through, she volunteered to deliver the message personally since she would be seeing Stella soon.

On November 16, 1968, Robert A. Ferguson addressed a spiritualist convention in Los Angeles, California. Several Polaroid photographs were taken during his speech; this one allegedly shows Ferguson's brother, Walter (who died in action in 1944, during World War II), standing next to him.

The message was that Bernice Moore had died suddenly that evening. When the telephone could not perform its function of relaying vital information, the spirit of her cousin traversed time and space and manifested before Stella to say a last farewell.

A WHITE FORM, GLIDING AWAY, STRUCK THE DOCTOR

Mrs. Margaret Sargent, a certified nurse, was caring for a young woman in Augusta, Georgia, when, about eleven o'clock one evening, the patient took a dramatic turn for the worse. The physician decided not to wake the patient's mother, for fear of adding to her emotional distress. As related in Sylvan Muldoon and Hereward Carrington's *The Phenomena of Astral Projection*, Mrs. Sargent later recalled that although they knew that the patient ardently desired the presence of her mother, "since she had become unconscious, we did not think it necessary to satisfy that desire."

The doctor and nurse recognized the final symptoms setting in, and they stood by the bedside solemnly anticipating the moment of the young woman's death. Mrs. Sargent was sitting at the foot of the bed when she glanced up and saw "a white form advancing, a robed form." She was unable to see the robed figure's face because it was turned away from her, but she was clearly able to observe the form because it remained for a moment by the inert body of the young female patient. "Then [it] passed swiftly past the doctor and glided toward me, but always turning its face in the opposite direction," she said.

Just before the apparition passed through the wall to the room in which the patient's mother lay sleeping, it paused to strike the doctor on the shoulder. Startled, the physician turned around, saw nothing, and remarked perplexedly to his nurse that something had struck him on the shoulder. Mrs. Sargent managed to overcome her awe and tell him that the woman who had just passed him was the one responsible for the blow. "What woman?" the doctor asked. "There is no woman in this room but that poor dying young lady on the bed. But someone struck me. What does this mean?"

Before either of them could speculate further, the patient began to mumble in a feeble voice. To their complete astonishment, the woman had regained her senses. She remained conscious for another twenty-four hours before she died with her head resting on her mother's arm.

⬤═⬤

A BIZARRE FAREWELL FROM BEYOND THE GRAVE

A Personal Recollection with Commentary by Dr. Franklin R. Ruehl, Ph.D.

After the dead have passed over, are they able to muster up enough strength to make contact with the living? Or is all communication between individuals terminated when quietus enters the scenario for one of them?

My mother, Florence Ruehl, had a dramatic experience some years ago that offers persuasive evidence for the first possibility. Back in 1955, we were living in a second-floor apartment in Glendale, California. On the evening of Tuesday, April 5, my father, a bookkeeper, was at the office preparing tax forms, which always piled up right before the dreaded deadline of April 15; I was in my room doing homework. My mother was in the living room, dancing to music playing on the phonograph.

Suddenly, at approximately 8:10 P.M., she saw a small human form materialize in the room a few feet away from her. It was a dwarf-sized man, about three feet tall, attired in a colorful cowboy outfit, complete with a ten-gallon hat and leather boots. After about a minute, this entity, which simply stood staring at her with a smirk but saying nothing, slowly faded away into nothingness.

Mother was shaken and called to me. Describing the incident, she asserted that the homunculus she saw was, without a doubt, her father, and she was certain he had just visited her from beyond the grave—despite the fact that, as far as she knew, he was in good health at age sixty-four and living back in Pittsburgh.

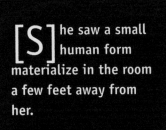

[S]he saw a small human form materialize in the room a few feet away from her.

Now, it should be stressed that in life he was of ordinary stature, about five feet, eight inches tall. And, to her knowledge, he had never expressed any interest whatsoever in the Wild West, being a lifelong Easterner. Moreover, he was always very loquacious, unlike the taciturn entity. But, in spite of all of these contradictions, she had absolutely no doubt that it was his spirit who had called upon her.

While the shade smirked at her, she did not feel it was menacing. However, on the other hand, she did not feel it was friendly, either—but this was fitting because she and her father had been more or less estranged for several years running and rarely communicated.

Her apprehensions were confirmed the very next morning when a telegram arrived about 10 A.M., informing her of her dad's demise from a heart attack the previous evening shortly after 11 P.M. EST, corresponding precisely to the time he had materialized before her.

My mother Florence often thinks about her brief encounter with the paranormal, stating: "I recall that night as vividly now as when it first transpired. There is absolutely no doubt in my mind that the spirit of my father appeared before me!"

As to the small stature of the being and his cowboy attire, she hypothesizes: "Perhaps he longed to be a child once more, and conceivably, he harbored a secret wish to play at being a cowboy, even if only for a brief instant in time."

Contacts between the Living and the Newly Dead

Transitory contacts between the living and the newly dead are well chronicled in parapsychological literature. As just one intriguing example, there is the case of prolific horror/sci-fi director Reginald Le Borg, who helmed such films as *Voodoo Island*, *The Mummy's Curse*, *The Black Sleep*, and *Diary of a Madman*, starring such luminaries as Boris Karloff, Bela Lugosi, Vincent Price, Basil Rathbone, John Carradine, George Zucco, and Lon Chaney, Jr.

While living in Los Angeles in 1938, Le Borg was awakened by an unsettling dream one warm night at 2:15 A.M. In Le Borg's dream his father shouted, "Stay here! Don't say no!" The admonition referred to a long-standing quarrel between them; Le Borg's father objected to his son's plans to come to America and pursue a career in Tinseltown. Le Borg immediately felt a presentiment of death concerning his father. In the morning a telegram arrived, informing him that his dad had indeed just passed away. He later learned that the precise time of death corresponded to the moment he had awakened, and that the last utterances from his lips as he lay dying were, "Stay here! Don't say no!"

> **At the far end of the hall, she saw her husband clutching at the wall, trying to stand up.**

Such cases offer powerful testimony to the theory that the human spirit persists after death, often attempting with its last scintilla of strength to make final contact in some way with a loved one, especially an estranged loved one, whether by a brief materialization in person or through an appearance in a dream, irrespective of the physical distance separating them. The dark corridor of death does indeed appear to allow for at least a temporary exit.

"Don't Touch Me. I Must Return."

When Larry Exline finally got a two-week vacation with pay in August 1954, his wife, Juliette, was overjoyed. As she has recalled the event in *Fate* magazine, July 1969, Larry had been working so hard without relaxation; she felt this vacation would give him an opportunity to relax while fishing in Nevada with a friend.

On the evening of the fourth day of her husband's absence, August 29, Mrs. Exline awakened in a cold sweat. She was certain that she heard Larry's voice calling her. The voice was faint, as if it were coming from a great distance away, as if it were in pain, and suffering, but it was Larry's voice.

Mrs. Exline fought back the fingers of icy terror, slid out of bed, turned on a nightlight, and stepped into the hallway. At the far end of the hall, she saw her husband clutching at the wall, trying to stand up. His clothes were drenched with blood. She screamed and rushed toward him. "Don't touch me," he warned her with a sob. "I must return."

She begged him to explain: where must he return and why? She told him to wait, that she would call a doctor. At that instant, the telephone rang. It was a sheriff from Ely, Nevada, calling to inform Mrs. Exline that her husband had been killed instantly in an automobile accident.

"Oh, no," she said. "'My husband's here!" She hurried back into the hall, "But Larry wasn't there. He indeed had 'gone back.'"

"I'M ALL RIGHT NOW"

The Personal Experience of Colette Bransen

When Colette Bransen awakened one chilly November morning in 1983, she arose with an acute sensation that something was very wrong. As she prepared breakfast, she carefully examined her thirteen-year-old daughter Melissa and her seven-year-old son Tim. Since they seemed well and happy, Colette knew that it had to be her husband, Jeff, who was institutionalized in the big veterans' hospital nearly two hundred miles away.

Jeff, a Vietnam veteran, suffered from a progressive disease that he had contracted while in the service. He had dealt courageously with his illness, but in the spring of 1981, the stresses of rearing a family, adjusting to society, and combating a debilitating disease had brought about a nervous breakdown. Tragically, Jeff had succumbed to a more complex mental illness after he had nearly recovered from the shattering of his nerves.

Colette went to work that November morning feeling extremely distracted and ill at ease. "I was lucky my boss didn't fire me," she said. "I was continually drifting off into thoughts of great concern for Jeff." That evening when she returned home, she was no longer able to contain herself. She knew that it was always difficult to get through to someone of authority in the hospital, but she also knew that she had to try.

At last she managed to contact an exceedingly authoritative and cool-mannered doctor who informed her that her husband's condition remained unchanged. Furthermore, the doctor grumbled, Jeff's condition was not likely to change for several months, perhaps years. She would just have to content herself with the knowledge that he was being well cared for and that the medical staff was doing the best that they could under the circumstances.

The doctor's brusque assurances that Jeff's condition was the best that it could be "under the circumstances" did nothing to calm Colette's concern. In fact, the words so professionally designed to pacify her had achieved the opposite effect. She felt all the more convinced that something was wrong with her husband.

"After the kids were in bed, I retreated to my own private altar that I had constructed in a corner of my bedroom," she said. "I read from the Psalms, the New Testament, then lighted some candles and incense and began to pray. After a period of intense meditation, I soaked in a warm tub and went to bed." Colette was awakened from a sound sleep by the voice of her husband calling her by his pet nickname for her: "Hey, Bright Eyes, wake up!" The sound of Jeff's voice brought a choked cry of joy. "Perhaps I was in that in-between space between wakefulness and sleep, for I felt there was nothing strange about Jeff's standing firm and solid at my bedside," Colette said. "As I reached out to touch him, I asked with an inner knowing,'You're all right now, aren't you, Jeff?'"

Colette's fingertips touched the firm flesh of Jeff's hand, and he closed his own fingers tightly around them. "Yes, Bright Eyes," he replied. "Everything is all right now. Always remember that I loved you so very much. Kiss the kids good-bye."

And then he disappeared. Colette's hand now clutched only a memory. She turned on the light and took careful note of the time on her clock radio. It was 2:08 A.M.

"I had no doubt that the visitation that I had just experienced was the result of my husband's death," Colette said. "I knew that Jeff had come to say good-bye."

She had just finished making the children's breakfast when the official call came from the veterans' hospital at 7:30 A.M. A more sympathetic sounding doctor expressed his condolences, then informed her that Jeff had died at about two o'clock that morning. Metastatic melanoma to the brain had snuffed out his life.

"He died at 2:08, to be precise," Colette said aloud, not really knowing why it felt so important to correct the doctor. There was a moment of awkward silence, and then the doctor asked if someone—an unauthorized someone—had called her earlier with the news of her husband's death.

"None of your staff disobeyed your orders not to call me until 7:30," Colette said. "I'll be ready to drive to the hospital in an hour or so. I'll explain it to you when I see you." It was on that long two-hundred-mile journey to the veterans' hospital that Colette once again heard Jeff's voice. "He told me that he was now free, free of pain, free of confusion," she said. "And he told me that we would always be together on some level of awareness. I know that ever since his death, his spirit has always looked after our children's welfare from his dimension of being, and I have felt his loving presence in my own life on many occasions."

⟨⟨⟨≺∿≻⟩⟩⟩

A MOTHER'S KISS FROM BEYOND THE GRAVE

The Personal Experience of Ken Lehmann

Feeling sad and depressed, Ken Lehmann had left the bedside of his mother, who was dying of cancer. The ordeal had been a long and painful one for his poor mother, and an emotionally exhausting one for him. Ken's father had passed away four years before, and his mother had been in ill health since that time.

"Please go home and get some rest, Kenny," his mother had told him. "You must not stay here another night worrying over me. Go home and see to Audrey and the children." Ken said that he would go home and look in on his wife and kids, but then he would come back to the hospital in a few hours to be at her side.

When he arrived at home, he saw that the kids were already tucked in their beds, so he sat and talked with Audrey and told her that he was certain that Mom was soon to pass. "I really didn't want to leave her alone," he said softly, trying to hold back the tears. Audrey urged him to get a little rest before he returned to his vigil at the hospital. She told him that she had a sales presentation to finish before she went to bed, so she would be up if the phone rang.

Ken checked his watch and decided that he would nap for a bit before he returned to his mother's bedside. "I couldn't have slept more than thirty minutes when I felt what I knew to be the touch of my mother's lips on my cheek," Ken said. "It was a kiss of such sweetness and love that it could only have come from my mother.

"I opened my eyes and sat up. I had left a small lamp on in the room, and there, in the dim light, I could distinguish a kind of mist that had assumed human shape. Although I could not make out any distinct features, I knew that it was Mom. I felt the strongest emanations of pure love flowing to me from that vaporous form. Then it floated out of sight through the ceiling."

When Ken called the hospital a few moments later, he was not surprised to learn that his mother had just died. The night nurse said that she had been about to call him.

"The kind nurse spoke a few words to console me," Ken said. "But I had just received the greatest sort of consolation from my mother, who had come to show me that there is life beyond physical death. And no one will ever be able to convince me that it was not my mother who gave me that wonderful good-bye kiss!"

⊶⊷

"I WILL NEVER LEAVE YOUR SIDE"
The Personal Experience of Gretchen

Gretchen had always been very close to her maternal grandmother, Deborah K. In point of fact, Grandma Deborah had raised Gretchen since her mother's death when the girl was four years old. "My mother and I had been living with Grandma when Mom became terribly ill with cancer," Gretchen said. "My father had been killed in Vietnam, and Mom and I had gone to live with Grandma in 1970. If it were not for the photo album and pictures of Mom to keep an image of her alive, I would actually have very little memory of her. I remember that she was sick a lot. And I dimly recall her telling me that she would not be coming home from the hospital, that she was going away to be with Daddy and that Grandma would take good care of me."

When she was twenty-eight, Gretchen was living in Spokane, Washington, separated by many miles from Grandma Deborah, who resided in a nursing home in Rochester, New York. Gretchen was filled with regret when her mother's brother, Uncle Ted, had placed Grandma a nursing home. She knew that Grandma was seventy-seven years old and had been quite ill, but Gretchen was expecting her first child. And, as she told her husband, Larry, she really wished Grandma Deborah could with her when the baby came. But Gretchen knew that her grandma wouldn't be able to make the trip to Spokane by herself, even if they could afford to fly her there.

On October 17, 1992, two nights before her due date, Gretchen experienced a very difficult night. She was extremely nervous and uncomfortable. When she did slip into brief periods of fitful sleep, she would dream of terrible things happening to the baby during the delivery. She looked at the alarm clock for what seemed like the thousandth time that night, saw that it was 2:15 A.M., then tossed off the covers on her side of their king-size bed and began to weep.

"That was when I saw Grandma standing by the side of the bed," Gretchen said. "I know I was not dreaming, for I was having some kind of anxiety attack, and I had just moved back the covers and sat up in bed, wide awake and irritable."

Gretchen remembered clearly that Grandma just stood quietly for a few moments before she said soothingly: "Everything is going to be all right, honey. You just stop your crying and fussing now. Be brave and be Grandma's big girl. I'm going to be with you every minute of the delivery. I will never leave your side. Everything will be fine. Now, blow Grandma a big kiss, and remember that I will always love you!" Gretchen found herself blowing a kiss toward Grandma's smiling face—and then the image of her beloved grandmother disappeared. Gretchen cried out her grandmother's name and awakened Larry, who sat up rubbing his eyes, wondering if she was in labor.

"I told him about my vision of Grandma and about how good it had made me feel," Gretchen said. "I always knew that Grandma and I were in telepathic contact, so, in one sense, her image appearing to me in a vision did not really surprise me that much. Anyway, I knew that now I would be able to get some sleep." Later, when Gretchen awakened him with loud and painful moans at 5:47 A.M., Larry knew that this time what she was experiencing was not a vision or a false alarm. This time it was the real thing: labor pains!

At 1:27 P.M., Deborah Esther was born, named after Gretchen's grandmother and Larry's mother.

This picture was taken immediately after two-year-old Greg said "Nanna's here."

Truthful and dependable as Gretchen's grandmother had always been throughout her lifetime, the vision of her had accurately predicted a safe delivery. And to Gretchen, it did seem as though she could feel the loving presence of her grandmother supporting her throughout the entire painful process.

That evening, after Gretchen had rested, Larry sadly presented her with a telegram from the nursing home in Rochester. With tears blurring her vision, Gretchen read that Grandma Deborah had died in her sleep. Larry pointed out the time that Grandma had passed: "Honey, according to the people in the nursing home, your grandmother died this morning at about 5:15. Allowing for the difference in time zones, that would be about 2:15 our time, just when you said that you had a vision of your grandmother telling you that everything was going to be all right."

"Grandma was with me in spirit to watch over the birth of little Deborah Esther and to see that she safely made her entrance into the world," Gretchen said, concluding her account. "Maybe it is like that song says, when one of us dies there will be another child born to take our place and to carry on."

<hr />

"Remember Me with Kindness"

The Personal Experience of Stanley

While he was stationed in Germany in 1972, Stanley enjoyed a wonderful relationship with a beautiful girl named Karla. They were both in their early twenties and they discussed marriage many times. Even though he had decided upon a career in the navy, there were times when he thought of leaving it all for the good life with Karla in Germany. Once Stanley went so far as to buy an engagement ring, but he never showed it to Karla. Somehow, the time just didn't seem right to make such a commitment.

When it came time for Stanley to return to the States, the two lovers were faced with the moment of truth. They spent a last weekend together in a lovely old hotel, and they spoke again of marriage as they were finishing what they knew might be their last meal together. As they were slowly sipping cool glasses of Rhine wine, Karla said that she couldn't see herself marrying anyone but Stanley. Stanley admitted that he felt the same way about her.

"Perhaps, then, we should see how we feel after you return to the States," Karla suggested. "Let us correspond. Let us see how we deal with the absence of one another. Let us test our love and see if we should be married."

They touched wineglasses and toasted Karla's plan.

After Stanley's return to the United States, the two lovers began a passionate correspondence. Six months later, however, Stanley began concentrating more intensely on his navy career. He had opportunities for advancement and that meant putting his spare energy into preparing for exams, not writing love letters. His correspondence to Karla slowed from a letter a day, to one a week, to one a month. Karla's letters continued at a more steady pace for a few months, then she began to match his once or twice a month schedule.

About that time, Stanley met Darcy, a navy brat, whose father was a career man. Darcy really understood his love and commitment for the sea. Shortly after his engagement to Darcy, Stanley wrote to Karla and told her the news about his approaching marriage to another woman. "I never received an answer to my letter," Stanley said. "I felt bad. I wondered how I would have felt if Karla had been the one to have sent me such a letter. But I couldn't help feeling that I had done the best thing for both of us."

After his marriage, Stanley reported to duty aboard a destroyer based at the Virginia Beach, Virginia, shipyards. Darcy remained in Massachusetts while the ship was deployed to the Middle East and then passed into dry dock. It was Stanley's intention to move Darcy to Virginia Beach as soon as the overhaul of the destroyer was completed.

> To Stanley's complete and total amazement, he beheld the image of Karla, standing in the doorway....

Late on the evening of June 15, 1975, Stanley was working in his disbursement office, preparing for payday only a few days away. He sat at his desk, typing up the pay roster until about 12:20 A.M. He had just leaned back in his chair to doze for a few minutes when he was awakened by a soft tapping at his office door. Assuming it was the security watch, he rather grumpily opened the door. To Stanley's complete and total amazement, he beheld the image of Karla, standing in the doorway, in what appeared to be a diaphanous white nightgown. "Karla looked just the way that she had the day that we said good-bye in Germany," Stanley said. "And it hurt me to see that she had been crying."

Stanley was nonplussed, speechless. At last he managed to ask her how she knew where he was and how she had been able to get aboard the destroyer without security stopping her. She ignored Stanley's questions, but spoke directly of other matters. "Stan, I am here to tell you that I understand about Darcy—and I forgive you."

Stanley began to speak, but Karla held up her hand for silence so that she might continue. "I knew that you were right in doing what you did," she said in a soft voice. "So I accepted another's proposal of marriage not long after I received your letter." Karla blinked back tears, then asked Stanley to promise to remember her always with kindness.

Stanley nodded, choked with emotion. "With great kindness, Karla," he managed to whisper. "And with love." Karla smiled, turned to leave, then looked over her shoulder and added, "And please be happy in your life with

Darcy." Then she stepped away from the doorway and walked quietly and quickly down the passageway until she was out of sight.

Stanley cannot estimate how long he sat quietly in reverie after Karla left him. He does remember being roused by the security watch, who had come to check on him.

"Did you happen to see a pretty blonde woman in the passageway a few minutes ago?" he asked the security watch. "Yeah, right," the man laughed. "I thought you were supposed to working in here, not dreaming. Are you all right?" Stanley mumbled something that somehow satisfied the watch, then went back to work on the pay roster.

> Stanley was certain that he was fully awake when he saw Karla.

But whatever had occurred in those incredible few moments had completely disoriented him. There was no way that he could remove the incident from his mind. He tried desperately to sell himself on the concept that he had dozed off and had a vivid dream, perhaps partially inspired by the guilt that he still felt about his breakup with Karla. But such a rationalization was out of the question. Stanley was certain that he was fully awake when he saw Karla.

He set aside his paperwork and wrote a letter to Karla, detailing his remarkable experience and asking her to let him know if she was all right. "I wanted to know if she might be ill, or if she might have been thinking intently of me at the time that her image had appeared in my office aboard the destroyer," he said.

A few weeks later, Stanley received a reply from Karla's mother, who informed him that Karla had died instantly in a head-on automobile crash early in the morning of June 16. The time of Karla's death was equivalent to about 12:20 A.M. June 15 in Virginia Beach. "Mrs. G. told me that she had been looking for my address to inform me of her daughter's death just as my letter arrived," Stanley said. "Only days before Karla's fatal accident, she had spoken of me and said how sorry she was that she had not answered my letter about my marriage to Darcy. Mrs. G. also verified that Karla was engaged to be married at the time of her death. The bond of love that we had once shared had somehow enabled her to bid me a tender and forgiving farewell."

THE GOBLET

From the Files of Professor Ian Currie

Professor Ian Currie, a former lecturer in anthropology and sociology at Guelph University in Ontario, Canada, and author of the book, *You Cannot Die*, shared the following cases:

Early one morning a U.S. serviceman who was stationed in Germany showed up quite unexpectedly at his family home in a Detroit suburb. His mother, who was startled in the act of preparing breakfast, was overjoyed to set another plate for her son. "Sorry, Mom," he said, declining the meal with a gentle smile. "I can't stay for breakfast. I just wanted to say good-bye."

The young soldier waved farewell and walked out the door. His heartbroken mother ran after him, shouting for him to return and stay longer—but she saw that he had completely disappeared.

A few hours later, an officer appeared at their door to inform the family that their beloved son had been killed in a training accident six thousand miles away in Germany—just a half an hour before his mysterious visit.

In another case from Professor Currie's files, it seems that two friends went into partnership in a Boston clothing store, but one later skipped town with all of their money. In spite of the one partner's treachery, the business went on to prosper.

Half a dozen or so years later, the owner of the clothing store was stunned when his old friend and former partner walked in the door. The prodigal partner waved aside all amenities and immediately got to the point of his visit. He said that he had come back to apologize or what he had done. The successful businessman embraced his old friend and said that he forgave him. The long-lost friend's face brightened at once. "Thank you," he said, then quickly left the store.

It was several days before the businessman learned that his ex-partner had died the morning of his sudden visit—just three hours before he walked into the store to ask forgiveness.

"SORRY FOR ALL THE TROUBLE I'VE CAUSED YOU"

An Experience of Brad Steiger

Some years ago I was appearing on a radio show at station CKTB, St. Catherine, Ontario, when a young woman called in to relate an experience that had provided her with her own proof of survival. She had been sleeping one night for just a few hours when she was awakened by the form of her brother standing at the foot of her bed. "I'm sorry, sis, for all the trouble that I may have caused you. I love you," he told her.

Her husband was awakened, too, but by the time that he was fully conscious, the image of his brother-in-law had disappeared.

His wife insisted that she had truly seen her brother standing in their bedroom, and she described in detail what he had been wearing. She had particularly noticed that he was wearing a plaid shirt that she had never seen before. No sooner had she completed her description of the apparition when the telephone rang, and she received the tragic news that her brother had been killed in an automobile accident.

Later, when they visited the morgue to identify the body, both of them were startled to see the corpse attired in a plaid shirt like the one she had described.

<hr />

THEY SAID FAREWELL THROUGH MUSIC ON THE RADIO
The Personal Experiences of Patrick

In some instances, rather than manifesting at the moment of physical death, the spirit of the deceased may wait until some other appropriate time to say a final farewell. Some witnesses report receiving a last goodbye days, weeks, or months after their friend or family member died. In other accounts, the spirit may deliver a remembrance of the loved one years later, as a kind of ethereal reminder of a dear one's memory and place in the heart of the witness.

My mother died from brain cancer in 1981. A few weeks after her funeral, I had the radio on as I was going through things in my parents' room. The radio was tuned to the station that my mother had always enjoyed, and country music filled the room. Suddenly, without an intro from the DJ, a song called "Softly as I Leave You" by Elvis Presley began to play. I was familiar with the song, but had never, ever, heard it before on the air. The song is about a man who is dying in the hospital and awakens to feel that he is slipping away. He sees his wife sleeping in a chair next to his bed, and rather than wake her, he writes a note in which he says that he will leave her softly, long before she will miss him, long before her arms can beg him to stay for another hour or another day.

I felt emotion well inside me, and I sat and listened to the song, almost in tears. My mother had died before we could say good-bye. She had been staying at my sister's home, and on the morning of her death, I'd gone home to sleep. She had, in fact, died "long before I missed her." I got the very real impression that my mother was somehow using the medium of the radio to say good-bye. Elvis had been her absolute favorite performer in life. No reason he wouldn't still be her favorite in death.

In 1986, my father passed. On the first night of his visitation at the funeral home, I rode with my brother and his family in their car. I had gone out to warm up the engine, and when I turned on the radio, Roy Orbison's song "For the Good Times" immediately came across the speakers. The lines about not looking so sad that things are over, that life goes on and that we should be glad that we had some time to spend together, made me cry and I turned the radio off. After my mother died, my father and I had shared the house. We'd never been close, but in the five years since Mom's passing, we'd grown to appreciate each other. And, yes, I was very, very glad that Dad and I had had some "time to spend together." That piece of song couldn't have summed up my feelings that night any better if I'd written it.

> [I]t seemed that something on a spiritual level was preparing me for a last farewell shortly before the actual death occurred.

The final significant time I've had anything like this happen was a year later. In this instance, it seemed that something on a spiritual level was preparing me for a last farewell shortly before the actual death occurred.

A close friend of mine was diagnosed with a life-threatening illness. He'd made me promise not to tell anyone else in our circle; only one other mutual acquaintance knew the situation. The evening I found out about my friend's illness, I had picked up another friend and was en route somewhere when he asked me what was wrong. I replied that there was nothing wrong, but he persisted, pointing out that I was acting like something was bothering me. I reached over and turned on the radio. The chorus of Billy Joel's "Only the Good Die Young" blared through the car. I turned off the radio. Again, coincidence? I really don't think so. Not three times, not so specific.

<hr />

JOE CAME TO SAY A LAST GOOD-BYE

The Personal Experience of Rick Aiello

Eight years ago, I was about to close on our new house in the picturesque Finger Lakes region of New York, and I wanted to take another look at the rural property. Anita, the seller, thought it would be appropriate for my wife and me to meet our closest neighbor. We went up the road and found Joe working on his tractor. He was introduced to us as "the hardest working man in the county."

Joe was a family man who, regardless of the fact that he had two jobs, was always there for someone in need. As a displaced city dweller, I felt unprepared for work involved in maintaining my new rural property. I now had three acres of lawn and many more acres of brush and weeds to keep in check. Because Joe did landscaping as his second job, he had all the necessary equipment. He made it clear that he would help out with the mowing and bush hogging.

Joe had a great love of animals. No matter how tired he was or how late he might be for dinner, he would always take the time to come to the aid of an animal. He'd pick up a kitten that had been dumped on one of our rural roads by some town dweller who thought the animal "would be better off in the country." When he rumbled up our long driveway, we never knew what Joe would have in his truck until he stopped and opened the door of his cab.

In the summer Joe would take a week off his regular jobs and rent a bulldozer. He would move earth and build ponds and have an all around good time. Joe built two ponds for me in the eight years I knew him. Every time I see my geese paddling around, I thank Joe.

> **I reached the bottom step and looked out the patio door, still hearing the truck. The moment my eyes met an empty driveway, the sound stopped.**

Joe would also take care of my snowplowing, showing up at four o'clock in the morning, the time he usually started his day. It was always a reassuring sound, hearing Joe rumble through the snow, plowing a clear path up to my house. When he would make his first pass up to the house, I would bolt out of bed and run downstairs to greet him. While the big diesel dump truck idled, I would jump into my boots and run outside to join him in the warm cab of his truck. We'd talk about the deer he had just seen saw or the fox that had been chasing his chickens. We would chat as he was finishing my driveway, then he would be gone for the rest of the day.

In November 2001, Joe had a sudden and unexpected heart attack at the age of forty-four. We were all devastated. Joe had been such a big part of so many lives. After his death, there were many stories exchanged of all the self-less deeds he had done for so many people.

Joe was a good and caring man, and he would never be so inconsiderate as to leave without saying good-bye. As in life, he did not let me down in death. One month after his death, my wife and I were awakened by the sound of a diesel truck. I instantly woke up, as I had for the past eight years whenever I heard that big noisy vehicle. I bolted out of bed, took a few steps—then realized I could not be possibly hearing Joe's truck. I must be dreaming!

But there I was, standing up, wide awake now, listening to this truck idling up next to the house. I rushed downstairs, fully expecting to see Joe's big truck sitting there, with him waving for me to join him in the cab. I reached the bottom step and looked out the patio door, still hearing the truck. The moment my eyes met an empty driveway, the sound stopped.

I instantly felt depressed, confused, and cheated. But when I went back upstairs and discussed it with my wife, she confirmed that she, too, had heard the truck. I then realized that Joe had come to say goodbye in a way that I would understand, for I had never missed running down to greet him whenever I heard his truck. I didn't feel cheated anymore. I felt blessed and honored that he remembered me. It seems like only yesterday when my good friend pulled up to say his last goodbye.

A cautionary note: As we discovered in chapters 4 and 5, there are shadow beings and spirit parasites from the unseen boundaries that lie at the edge of our material world and who take delight in assuming control over humans or even in entering a physical body and taking possession.

The two accounts shared in this segment indicate that caution must be taken even when one is led to believe that one is interacting with a departed family member or a dear friend. As I have emphasized repeatedly throughout this text, I have no intention of being dogmatic or of demeaning anyone's personal religious faith. But I believe in the reality of the spiritual dimension and the unfortunate truth that therein lies entities who will masquerade as something or someone they are not for the sole purpose of deceiving us and of wreaking havoc in our lives.

The following was written by a woman who contacted me about unsettling visits from her "father."

"SHOULDN'T DADDY BE RESTING IN PEACE?"
The Personal Experience of Cindy

You talk a lot about the paranormal on the radio. You really seem to know your stuff. There is something I need to ask you. I've been having periodic paranormal experiences since my father's passing back in August 1998. The first three years after his death, they were especially frequent.

What would you say if I told you I had actual physical contact with my late father? I know it's my father, because I've seen him briefly. Also, when he makes physical contact with me when I'm lying down to sleep and he enters my body, it feels like a "blob" of electrical energy that paralyzes me from my mouth to my toes. But not my brain! In fact, when I force myself to say, "Daddy," he immediately leaves my body. Then I remain quiet and still. It's one hell of an experience.

When he enters my bedroom on other visits, you can feel the energy, as if someone is in my room. I work the midnight shift at my job, and I've had experiences there as well. They're all from my old man. Sometimes, it is a little scary because of his sudden entrances. It still takes a little getting used to.

I must clarify that these experiences happen while I'm fully awake—only one or two times after I was asleep. I'm under the impression that he is checking up on me, to see if everything is ok. He has also used other methods to contact me, to let me know he is with me.

I've told my brother about my experiences, and I found out that he, too, has had a few experiences, but nothing—and I mean nothing—compared with what I experience. My brother is still not fully sure whether he is willing to accept the contact. He has doubts. I seem to be the stronger one—or the most receptive.

What's your opinion? Shouldn't my father be resting in peace by now? Or can he find a way to come back and forth from his dimension to ours? I'm into sci-fi, paranormal activities, and so forth, and very open-minded to the possibility of such phenomena—so to have such events actually happen to me makes me a true believer. I've not told my mother of these visits from Dad because of her Christian beliefs. I also don't want to scare her.

And neither did I wish to scare Cindy, but I advised her that her love of her father and her open-mindedness to the paranormal may have made her susceptible to the deceit of an astral masquerader who was taking pleasure in entering her body from time to time under the guise of being the spirit of her deceased father. Maintaining contact with the spiritual essence of a departed loved one is something quite different from permitting that alleged nonmaterial spirit to possess one's material body. In this author's opinion, one should always resist the advances of any spirit being who attempts to occupy one's body—whether its alleged identity is known or unknown. Nor should one ever allow any spirit entity to engage one in acts of physical intimacy.

⚜

DISCERNING THE SPIRITS

The Personal Experience of Jack, a member of Alcoholics Anonymous

I am a member of Alcoholics Anonymous, and at their meetings, I became friends with a lady I will call Mary, who was ten years older than I and who had been twenty-nine years sober. She had once been a speaker in AA, traveling around the country, speaking at meetings and AA conventions. She had curtailed many of these activities after she had fallen ill with Hepatitis C. Before Mary died from the disease, we had become very close friends.

The night of Mary's death, I was awakened by the sense of a presence in the room. I felt it draw near and envelope me. It felt like electricity, but without the pain. It was like nothing I had ever felt before or since. It surrounded me like a hug, and I felt a kiss on my cheek. Then it was gone.

I sat up in my bed and said out loud, "Good-bye, Mary." I knew she had come to say farewell.

The next night I felt another presence in my room, but this was not Mary. It felt darker. It would make itself known by pressing down on the side of my bed as I tried to sleep. I would turn to see who was there and see nothing. A couple of nights later, I heard something rattle in the bathroom. It was the sound of someone shaking a jar of vitamins that I kept there. When I got up to investigate, the jar was right where I had left it.

I thought at first that the sounds might be caused by mice, so I set out traps. But there were no mice to catch. A few days passed, and one night I was nearly overcome by the smell of rotting flesh. I got out of bed and checked the pantry, refrigerator, and trash. But the smell had not come from there. Angrily I shouted out to whoever or whatever it was that it was not welcome.

The next night I was listening to *The Jeff Rense Show*. Brad Steiger was the guest. I decided to call, and after telling him the story, he suggested that I perform a cleansing ritual and prayer. I did this and it worked! The apartment became silent.

For readers' interest, here is the above-mentioned cleansing ritual:

Visualize yourself being surround by a violet light and ask that your spirit protector or guardian angel connect you to the highest vibration of your concept of God, the Great Mystery, the Source of All That Is. Visualize and feel the violet light moving over you in a wave of warmth. See and feel it touching every part of your body (and the bodies of any others who are present). Feel it interacting with your spirit (and the spirits of all others who are present). Then say aloud to your spirit protector/guardian:

"Assist me in calling upon the highest of energies from the Great Mystery, the Source of All That Is. Summon the law of harmony, for I (and any others with me) have found myself (ourselves) in a dark place of shadows that resist the Light. Permit the violet light of transformation and cleansing to move around and through this dwelling place. Allow this cleansing energy to purify and to elevate all negative energies, all improper memories, all entities of evil purpose, all spirits who delight in wrongdoing, all lower vibrations that encourage impure desires. Allow the transforming energy to replace all darkness with light. Remove all chaotic energies and replace them with the purest of energies, the power of love, and the glory of all good and benevolent spirits. Bless us with the light, so that I (we) may go forth on this new day (night) of cleansing rejuvenated with perfect physical and mental health, perfect joy, perfect illumination, and perfect wisdom. Amen and so let it be!"

THE STORY OF MR. JENKINS

By Emma Pullis

The spirit of Mr. Jenkins, although not particularly pleasant and thoughtful in life, returned in spirit to let his neighbors know that some part of him still survived in the neighborhood.

Emma Pullis is known in the paranormal community of YouTube as "Jelliclesforever." She uses her channel to tell of her personal paranormal experiences and those of her family. She has had a life-long interest in the paranormal, stemming from many childhood experiences with ghosts, and she has been researching all aspects of the paranormal for more than fifteen years. Emma lives in Sussex County, New Jersey, with her husband, son, and three dogs.

Having grown up in a haunted house, I've always had experiences with the paranormal. My husband, on the other hand, was much more skeptical about ghosts until this one day last fall. It was the day of the big snowstorm in October 2011. The entire east coast was bracing for the first snow of the season, and widespread power outages were predicted as a result of such a storm in early fall. My husband and I were preparing for a trip we were about to take for a week to celebrate our second wedding anniversary. Knowing that we were running against the clock trying to beat the very likely loss of power, we wanted to have everything ready.

A blanket of very heavy wet snow had already begun to pile up in the backyard and, we knew this would be an issue when our three dogs needed to go outside. My husband went out to shovel a path for the dogs while I kept busy in the house doing laundry and packing for our trip.

When he came back in from his task, he said casually to me, "Jenkins isn't dead. I just saw him out there in his backyard." To which I responded with a shrug and "ok, whatever."

Mr. Jenkins is our next-door neighbor, the grumpiest old man in the world. We weren't even certain of his actual name, so we just called him, "Mr. Jenkins." At the time my husband spotted Mr. Jenkins walking around his backyard, we hadn't seen the old man in over a year. Nobody knew what happened to him … one day he just stopped coming out of his house.

Usually he would be seen coming out of his house to get his mail, or in his backyard when I went to check to see what my dogs were barking at, only to see they were barking at the old man yelling at them to "stay over there, don't you dare come over here!" If we had family over and they needed to park on the street anywhere near his house, he would appear by at his door and yell "You can park there but don't come any closer!" He was not the nicest of old men that was for sure, and I'm almost positive if he had a cane he would spend his day at that door shaking it at every person that happened by.

I clearly remember the last time I saw Mr. Jenkins, I was outside getting my mail and the frail old man was coming out of his house to get his mail. I remember it was a beautiful, hot September day. I also remember thinking that it was very odd that Mr. Jenkins was wearing a wool winter hat, in such warm weather. Was he getting sick?

After that day I never saw Mr. Jenkins again. We kept seeing his son or daughter in law come to get his mail and stop in his house for a half hour or so, and we just assumed that he had fallen ill and was either bedridden or living with one of his adult children. Every night the light in his living room was burning.

About two weeks after my husband saw Mr. Jenkins in his backyard I was at the eighteenth birthday party of my eldest niece. My husband was still at our house; that early season snowstorm really did a number on some big trees in our yard, and he was cleaning up the mess with his father and planning on joining at the party later on.

Out of the blue my youngest niece—who lives in my neighborhood and has fallen victim to many of Jenkins' "get off my grass" scoldings along with her siblings—came up to me and said, "Your old man neighbor died." After a moment what she said to me sunk in and I giggled a bit and said "No, he didn't. Your Uncle Justin just saw him two weeks ago … the day of that big snowstorm." My niece went on to tell me that her mother had spoken to a friend who knew Jenkins' son personally, and the friend indeed told her mother that he had passed on.

> [M]y neighborhood … came up to me and said, "Your old man neighbor died." After a moment what she said to me sunk in and I giggled a bit and said "No, he didn't. Your Uncle Justin just saw him two weeks ago.…"

Taken aback, but wanting to stay rational, I immediately thought that maybe he died within the two-week period that my husband saw him before the party. I had my niece send her mother a text message asking her if her friend told her when Jenkins had died and her mother's response was "I think about a year ago."

Unsure of Jenkins' real name, but determined to get to the bottom of the mystery of when he died, I went online and looked up the tax records for his address. As soon as I saw the name associated with the property I knew that our "Mr. Jenkins" was indeed dead because the tax records had the suffix "estate," indicating that his estate was now handling his property.

Now that we had his actual name—and I was almost positive he had passed—I decided to do one last thing to prove to my niece that Mr. Jenkins was among the very recently deceased … after all how else could you explain how my husband saw him?

We googled the name on the tax records and in the first search results I saw that the date of death was "November 8" before I clicked on the full article. "See," I told my niece, "he just died four days ago."

The words came out of my mouth just as I clicked the article for Jenkins obituary, and my jaw hit the floor as I read the true date of death, November 8, 2010, nearly one year before my husband saw him.

I immediately called my husband and told him to tell me exactly what he had seen. Here's how he described it: "I went to shovel a path for the dogs and just happened to look up and see Jenkins standing in the snow in his backyard. He didn't look at me. He just sort of looked around at the snow and then stared at the sky for awhile until I went back inside."

I made him promise me that he had really seen him walking out in his yard and that he was sure it was him. Hearing the urgency in my voice, my husband said, "Why would I make that up?" Then I told him that Mr. Jenkins died in November of 2010. My husband's reaction to seeing his first full-bodied apparition was one of amazement! "That's so cool," is what he said to me.

Now whenever I let my dogs out into my backyard I have a hard time looking in the direction of Jenkins' backyard. I know what my husband saw was very rare, and very special, but I am not so sure I want to encounter the spirit of Mr. Jenkins. I just can't help but wonder if he's as mean in death as he was in life.

GHOSTS THAT WARNED OF APPROACHING DANGER OR DEATH

SAVED FROM A NAZI TORPEDO BY HIS MOTHER'S GHOST

The Personal Experience of Victor L.

During World War II, I had the misfortune to be on a freighter that had temporarily gotten stranded in the middle of the Atlantic Ocean. Our engine had broken down about seven days out of port, and even though we were part of a convoy headed for Italy, the crucial war schedule demanded that the rest of the ships leave us behind while they went on ahead.

In the period from 1942 to 1943 the waters of the Atlantic were thick with Nazi submarines, and they all had commanders eager to sink a ship for der Führer. We were all tense and nervous, expecting at any minute to see two or three of those terrible metal "fish" streaking toward our helpless vessel.

By the third day of bobbing in the water like a sitting duck during hunting season, the crew was becoming really jumpy and tense. We had a few guns on deck, but we all knew that they would be of little use against submarines unless the U-boat surfaced. And it was hardly likely that any Nazi commander, no matter how fanatical, was going to waste all that time and effort to surface in order to engage us in an old-fashioned sea battle when launching a couple of torpedoes at our ship from the safety of Neptune's domain would do the trick.

In late afternoon of the third day, I was on my bunk, trying to get some rest before my next watch. I was completely alone in the quarters. I was awakened by the sensation that a warm hand was nudging my shoulder. I grunted and tried to shrug off the annoyance that was interfering with my sleep. But then, strangely enough, there seemed something very familiar about that particular style of nudging.

I opened his eyes to see the image of my mother standing next to my bunk. She was still pushing at my shoulder, and when my eyes widened in astonishment at her presence, she smiled at me. "Vic, honey," she told me in her usual softly pleasant voice, "you had better get up now. It is time to get up." Before I could respond in any manner whatsoever, the form of my mother disappeared.

Mom had been dead for eight years. I thought for a minute or so that maybe I had been dreaming, perhaps reliving a day in my childhood when my mother had been waking me to get ready to go to school. But the more I thought about the apparition, the more I began to feel so damn uneasy that I wanted to get dressed and get out of the bunk room as quickly as I could.

> [T]here would have been one fatality if the ghost of my mother had not awakened me when she did.

Since I did not wish to be alone after that strange experience and I still had a couple of hours before I was to report to my watch, I decided to go down to the engine room and kibitz with the engineers who were working on the repairs. I had no more than nodded hello at one of the firemen who was a good buddy of mine when a tremendous explosion shook the entire freighter and knocked us all off kilter. I went down on one knee, and a couple of the men fell flat on their backsides.

No one had to tell us that we had been hit by a Nazi torpedo. One of Hitler's mighty U-boat commanders couldn't resist slamming one into a helpless freighter that was sitting dead in the water. Within a matter of minutes all of the crew members were crowded into lifeboats and rowing away from the sinking ship. Fortunately there were no casualties.

But as I looked back at the slowly sinking freighter, I saw clearly that there would have been one fatality if the ghost of my mother had not awakened me when she did. From my position in the lifeboat I could see a massive hole that had been blasted in the starboard side where the torpedo had slammed us midship. Directly above that scorched and tangled mass of steel was the exact spot where I had been sleeping only moments before the torpedo had struck. My mother had somehow managed to go on recess from heaven so that she would be able to wake me up just in time.

THE SPIRIT OF THEIR MOM WAVED THEM BACK FROM DANGER

The Personal Experience of Susan

We lost our mother when I was just a young girl of twelve and we were living in Yreka, California. I was terribly despondent over the loss of Mom, and Dad and my siblings were taking her death just as hard as I was. There were four of us kids: I was second oldest, Debra was fourteen, Paula was eight, and Douglas was six. We all cried ourselves to sleep every night for weeks after Mom's funeral in March 1973. We could hear Dad crying in his room, too. We all just missed Mom so much.

Daddy stuck it out in Yreka until school was dismissed for the summer. Then he decided that it would be best for the entire family if we moved to another town and made a fresh start. There were just too many memories of Mom in Yreka, he told us. It would be easier for all of us to get on with our lives if we weren't thinking about Mom all of the time.

Dad decided that we should try a whole new and different lifestyle while we were at it. Through one of his cousins, he had heard about this old farmhouse outside a small town in Oregon, and he thought that we should check it out. On June 16, when we stepped out of our station wagon, we kids took one look at the ramshackle house and started to pray that Dad wouldn't like it out in the country.

The house was big enough. It had six bedrooms, a large country kitchen, and a neat living room with window boxes. The problem was, it was really run-down and needed a lot of fixing up. Debra and I knew that Mom's illness had cost Dad a lot of money. And then, of course, there had been the funeral expenses. While the low asking price of the big old house might appeal to Dad's busted budget, we hoped that he would realize how much money we would have to spend to fix the place up to make it really livable. Paula and little Doug were excited about the large barn and the various outbuildings and animal sheds. They began immediately to dream about having horses to ride.

While Dad discussed terms with the landlord, the four of us kids set off on a tour of inspection of the sprawling house. We had already decided which one of us got which room, and we had even climbed the dusty steps to the walk-up attic and found some potential treasure chests of old clothes and hats that some family had left behind. They would be just great for playing dress-up.

Finally, only the basement remained for us to explore. Paula protested that she didn't like basements because they were dark and smelly and spooky. Little Douglas was certain that monsters were living under the stairs, and his large blue eyes grew even wider at the thought of braving the dank unknown. I teased them not to be little sissies, and I promised that we would find some neat things that someone had left down there. However, Paula was adamant that she and Dougie would stay upstairs while Debra and I explored the underworld.

"If we're going to live here," Big Sister Debra told them, "you can't be afraid to go down in the cellar." Paula could not suppress an involuntary shudder. "Oh, I hope we don't have to live in this creepy old place."

"That's for Dad to decide," Debra reminded her. "Come on, now, I'll take Dougie's hand, and Paula, you take Susan's hand, and we will all run down the basement stairs together. You can't be afraid if we are all together." Reluctantly Paula and Douglas did as they were told, and we were about halfway down the stairs when we all came to a sudden stop. There at the bottom of the stairs was Mom!

[W]e all came to a sudden stop. There at the bottom of the stairs was Mom!

All of us clearly saw an image of our deceased mother, and each of us later described her in the same way. She had on this really pretty sundress with big flowers on it that all of us kids had loved so much. Her long blond hair was braided, like she often fixed it in the warm weather. But most of all, we all saw her beautiful smile. She was smiling up at us so lovingly. I will never forget the image of the way that I saw Mom that day in that old basement. We all probably would have run into the arms of our lovely, smiling mother if she had not begun to make motions that we should go back up the stairs, that we should not continue our descent into the basement. When Paula moved down a couple more steps toward Mom, she frowned and made a motion that Paula should stop. I know that we were all crying and calling out to her and saying that we wanted to hug and kiss her, but she kept waving her arms and motioning us to go back. Just when we were probably all that the point where we might have ignored Mom's gestures and run down the steps toward her, the image of our mother disappeared.

We ran upstairs to get Dad and tell him that we had seen Mom at the bottom of the basement stairs. Since we were all crying and talking at the same time, he could hardly ignore us or argue that we were all seeing things. When the landlord, an elderly man in his mid-eighties, finally understood that we were talking excitedly about something in the cellar, he became very agitated. "No, no, you mustn't let those kids go down in the basement!" he said, extra loud because of his partial deafness. "There's an old cistern down there right at the bottom of the stairs. The boards have rotted away, and I'll have to fix it before anyone goes down there."

Dad was shocked that the landlord hadn't mentioned such a potential danger spot immediately, but it was easy to see that the elderly gentleman had trouble keeping his mind on more than one thing at a time. And he had quite obviously forgotten long ago how young children will want to explore old houses when given the opportunity.

When Dad went to investigate, he found things exactly as the old man had described them. The cistern, an uncovered well about eight feet deep with about a three feet of water at the bottom, was right in the shadows at the bottom of the basement stairs. The way that we kids were running hand in hand down those stairs, we all would have fallen into the well and certainly been severely injured, perhaps even killed.

Dad decided on the spot against renting the old farmhouse and he never once doubted us when we told him that our beautiful mother had returned with her loving smile to save our lives. "Because she was the one who gave you life in the first place," Dad said, "it surely does stand to reason that she would do her best to protect your lives even from beyond the grave."

Then Dad got tears in his eyes and added, "Now you kids know for certain that love never dies."

<hr/>

THE VOICE OF HER DECEASED HUSBAND CALLED HER NAME
The Personal Experience of Kristin F.

Kristin F. was seventy-one in March 1992 when she wrote a detailed letter describing how she had been sleeping soundly in her comfortable two-bedroom cabin on the shore of a northern Minnesota lake when she distinctly heard the voice of her late husband, David, calling her name.

I sat up in bed and fumbled for the light, glancing wildly about the dark room as I did so. I knew with every fiber of my being that I had not been mistaken about the source of the voice. I would forever recognize the sound of my beloved David's voice, even though he had been taken from me by a heart attack five years before.

I finally managed to locate the light switch, and I got out of bed, sliding my feet into warm slippers and pulling on my robe. It was a chilly night in late November, and I knew the floorboards would be cold.

"Kristin." The voice spoke again, seemingly just over my right shoulder. "Look sharp, girl," I heard David say. "Something is burning! You are in danger, my beloved. Look sharp, now!" I spun around, hoping to catch at least a fleeting glimpse of my husband's spirit. I saw nothing. But the voice was so distinctly David's. Years ago, after we had been amused by a British movie in which a military man had always prefaced his commands with a snappy "look sharp," we had used the phrase teasingly whenever we wanted the other to get right at a domestic chore.

The furnace in the cabin was run by electricity, and I had adjusted the thermostat before retiring. I knew that I had not left any electrical appliance plugged in. David had been almost phobic about the idea of our house burning. His maternal aunt's house had caught fire when he was just a boy. The lovely old house had burned to the ground, but even worse, David's favorite cousin, Kathy, had been horribly burned and left badly scarred.

Once, three or four years after we were married in 1943, David had awakened in the night and found some trash smoldering in the kitchen wastebasket. He was mortified when he discovered that he had carelessly dumped an ashtray with a live butt into the trash, and he was horrified when he considered that he could have been responsible for setting our house on fire. He had become even more fearful of fire, and he quit smoking, cold turkey, that very night.

As I made my way into the living room to investigate further, I pondered these things and began to consider quite strongly that my mind might have played back a kind of mental tape of David's voice. I heard a noise in the backyard and looked out a window to see a graceful family of deer moving down toward the lake. An owl hooted mournfully from somewhere deep in the forest. All was peaceful and as it should be.

> Through a tiny crack between the fireplace mantel and the wall, I could see raging flames.

I had just about convinced myself that I had only awakened from a strangely vivid dream, when, as if in answer to my mental debate and its rational conclusion, I heard David's voice once again. This time the message was brief and forceful: "The cabin is on fire!" Becoming even more confused and perhaps a little frightened, I walked from room to room in the ranch-style cabin. Nothing! I could find no sign of any threatening flames.

Earlier, when I had taken my nightcap of warm cocoa, I had built a nice, crackling wood fire in the fireplace. The fire had burned out hours ago. There were only a few still-glowing embers visible behind the fire screen.

"Fire!" David's voice was insistent, demanding. I began to cry in frustration. "Where?" I asked. "Please tell me where!" I leaned back against the wall next to the brick chimney in a state of near collapse—and, then, suddenly, I felt that the wall was hot. When I turned to place my open palm against the wall, I was horrified to find that it was extremely hot to the touch. Through a tiny crack between the fireplace mantel and the wall, I could see raging flames. The house was on fire!

I forced myself to remain as calm as possible and to head for the telephone in the kitchen to dial 911. Although the village was small, it had an excellent volunteer fire department. I knew that they would get to me as quickly as possible.

After I cradled the receiver, it seemed as though I had at last become truly wide awake. I could now hear quite clearly the terrible, crackling sound of the fire spreading toward the roof. Tendrils of dark smoke were moving across the living room like greedy fingers of the fire seeking objects for consumption.

I decided it would be safer to await the fire department in the yard, and even as I was pulling on a heavy coat to wear over my robe, I could hear the eerie wail of a siren shrilling a summons to the volunteer firemen.

"Thank you, David," I said to the stars. "Thank you, my darling, for saving my life."

The prompt action of the local firefighters prevented the complete destruction of our cabin, but the estimated cost of the repairs played a major factor in my decision to move into an apartment in a nearby larger city. I miss the solitude of our cabin by the lake, but I sense strongly that David's spirit feels better now that I am nearer our friends and family and not so lonely.

⚊⚊⚊

THE GHOST OF A NEIGHBOR SAVED THEM FROM A DEADLY FIRE

The Personal Experience of Maybelle Johnson

In September 1994 the ghost of their dead neighbor saved Maybelle Johnson and her family from a possible death by fire or smoke inhalation.

At the time of the fire I lived with my husband, Lamar, and our three kids in a fourplex apartment in a suburb of Charlotte, North Carolina. That winter our neighbor, Jeanette, a sickly young woman in her early twenties, began suffering from advanced stages of leukemia. Jeanette had been such a cheerful, hardworking lady that it was hard on all of us who were her friends to see her so ill and in so much pain.

When Jeanette's steady boyfriend stopped coming around to see her, I tried to take more time from my busy schedule with my job and my family to visit with her. It was hard to get away from my own duties, what with three little kids and all, but Jeanette had always been there to help me with baby-sitting and other things whenever she could, so I wanted to offer some kind of support for her in her hour of need. I usually had to wait until Lamar was home from work because I didn't want any of our babies saying anything hurtful to Jeanette. You know, like why did she look so awful and stuff like that.

Jeanette died in April. She was courageous and cheerful to the very end. I so admired her spirit, and all of us in the fourplex considered it a real tragedy that such a good person had to die so young.

One night, about a month after Jeanette's passing, I was in bed with my husband, just starting to drift off to sleep. I had been feeling kind of restless with worry about bills and stuff. As I was finally falling asleep, I rolled over on my side, and there, solid as life, standing right by my side of the bed, was

Jeanette. I wasn't scared of her being a ghost and all, but I admit that I was startled to see her there. I blinked my eyes and shook my head. When the image of Jeanette remained at my bedside, I giggled and said out loud, "I always thought that if I ever saw a ghost, I would be scared silly. But I'm not at all afraid of you, Jeanette." Jeanette's spirit form smiled at me, but her features immediately became very serious in appearance. "Girl," she said, "if you don't get up and get your family out of here, you're gonna be a ghost just like me!"

With that warning pronounced, Jeanette's image vanished, but she surely had my complete attention. I wasn't ready to be a ghost yet. I had three little kids to raise. I elbowed my husband into wakefulness and told him that I had just seen Jeanette's ghost, and she said that we had to get out of the house.

Lamar rubbed his eyes and grumbled at me. "It's two o'clock. What are you doing waking me up at this hour? You know I've got to be at work by six. I need my sleep." I told Lamar again that Jeanette's ghost had come to me and told me to get up and out of there fast, but he just grumbled some more and said that I only had a dream about her and I should let him get back to sleep.

After a few more minutes of arguing about the reality of Jeanette's ghost and the urgency of her warning, I finally convinced Lamar to get out of bed and at least look around our apartment. Lamar had no sooner shoved his feet into his slippers at the side of the bed when he said that he smelled smoke. Suddenly wide awake, he ran to the door of our apartment and opened it to find the hallway beginning to fill with thin clouds of smoke. "Oh, my God," he shouted back to me, "the place must be on fire! You get the kids up and dial 911, and I'll wake the others in the building!"

Within minutes we had vacated our apartment and spread the alarm that saved the other lives in the fourplex. Because of the early detection of the fire, the firemen were able to keep damage to a minimum. It was later revealed that the new occupant in Jeanette's old apartment, a heavy cigarette smoker, had accidentally dropped a live butt in the cushions of an easy chair before he had gone out to shop at an all-night supermarket.

In the days that followed, I was not at all shy about letting everyone know that they all owed their continued existence on the planet to the warning message of Jeanette's ghost.

⊷⊶⊷

HER HUSBAND'S SPIRIT WATCHES OVER THEM

The experience of Margaret G. retold by Brad Steiger

In 1992, after one of our seminars in San Diego, Margaret G. told my wife, Sherry, and me this inspirational account of her deceased husband's continued interest in his family.

"**I** was half asleep one night, reading the newspaper in my reclining chair in the front room, when I thought I heard Cissy, my three-year-old daughter, whimpering in her bedroom," Margaret said. "About the same time I heard the trash can in back of the house go clattering into the alley. Cautiously I peeped out a window in the kitchen and caught a glimpse of a man standing in the shadows beside the garage."

Margaret did her best to quiet the trembling fear that seized her. Taking a deep breath to center herself, she walked purposefully back into the front room and called the police. "I sat in my easy chair, using all of my willpower to retain control, praying earnestly that a police car would pull up in the alley before I could count to ten.

"Then I heard my little girl whimpering once again. Suddenly a new terror seized me and sent my heart pounding: What if there was already an intruder inside the house?" Margaret opened the door to Cissy's bedroom and was unable to suppress the cry of horror that escaped her lips when she saw a man leaning over her daughter's bed. Her brain struggled with a hundred different fears. She was alone. The police were nowhere in sight. Did the intruder mean to hurt her child?

> **S**uddenly a new terror seized me and sent my heart pounding: What if there was already an intruder inside the house?

But then, to her complete amazement, she heard the man singing softly to Cissy. Within another moment or two she was able to focus her senses sharply enough to recognize the tune of a song from the sixties that had been a favorite of her husband's.

"Who … who are you?" Margaret asked the man. He had drawn the hood of a sweatshirt over his face so she could not distinguish any of his features in the dim light of the child's bedroom. "Who are you?" she repeated, trying to control all inflections of fear in her voice. As the man raised his head and turned, Margaret was startled to see the face of her husband, William. In the next instant the image vanished.

"I was about to collapse, but that's when the police officer knocked on the front door," Margaret said. "He was just checking to see if everything was all right, and he told me that they had picked up a man just leaving the alley in back of the house. They immediately recognized him as a known burglar. According to the officer, the man had a rap sheet of prior offenses as long as his arm."

Margaret thanked the officer for the quick work in apprehending a criminal who had quite obviously scheduled her house as one of his targets for the night. "Glad to be of service, ma'am," the police officer said, "but you are extremely lucky that your husband was at home with you tonight."

"My husband?" Margaret echoed hollowly. "Yes," the officer went on. "You see, most burglars just like to slip in and out of a house without even being seen, but this man is different. He's got a real sadistic streak. If he should happen to see a woman home alone, he doesn't mind breaking in and hurting her while he loots the place. And if there should happen to be a youngster around, he doesn't hesitate at all to beat up the kid, too."

Margaret had to ask for confirmation of what she herself had witnessed in Cissy's bedroom just before the officer had knocked on the door: "Are you saying that the burglar saw my husband in the house?" The police officer nodded. "Yeah, the guy said that he kept peeping in your windows, but he always saw this big man standing right beside your chair. A couple of times he went around to try to enter through the child's bedroom, but then he saw your husband in there, bending over your daughter's bed, singing to her. He said your husband had on a hooded sweatshirt like he had been working out or running or something. So it's a good thing he had come home and was in the house."

The officer frowned quizzically, glanced around the front room. "Where is your husband now? Did he go to bed or something?" "Officer," Margaret answered, "my husband, William, died nearly two years ago. He and a couple of his buddies were out jogging on the beach when he decided to add some hurdles to the run by running and jumping over the tops of some large rocks that were still exposed by high tide. He slipped and fell when a large wave suddenly crashed into the rocks. He was pulled out to sea immediately. The heavy, hooded sweatshirt that he was wearing quickly absorbed water and probably was a great factor in his death by drowning. His body was washed up on shore the next morning."

The officer became very quiet, excused himself, said goodnight, and left.

"I don't know if he believed me or not," Margaret said. "I really didn't care. I knew that William's great love for us had drawn him back to protect us on the night when we were threatened by a man who would have stolen our valuables and harmed us physically. And I will never forget the glimpse that I received of him in Cissy's room or the beautiful sound of him singing over our daughter's sleeping form. In addition to saving us from pain and theft, William gave us the greatest gift imaginable: proof that there is life and love beyond the grave."

⊸⊸⊸⊸

A Ghost Saved Her from Attack by a Rapist

The Personal Experience of Dorothy

My experience with a benevolent ghost took place just a few months after I married David in 1970. We didn't have much money in those days, and we lived in a pretty rough section of Kansas City. We moved into the third house in a run-down string of five, all identical, built sometime around the turn of the century, and we kept telling ourselves that one day we would have it better.

I usually got home from my job as a waitress about two hours before David came home from the factory where he worked. David said that it was humiliating that I had to do such menial work. In his family tradition, the man of the family had always supported his wife. Although he agreed to let me work to help us achieve a better life faster, he insisted that because of the rough neighborhood we lived in, I must be home before dark. To make matters even worse, the young women in our section of Kansas City had been the target of a rapist-slasher who had already killed one unfortunate victim and cut and raped at least a half-dozen others.

> I was suddenly stopped dead in my tracks by some invisible force that prevented me from passing through the doorway.

Three nights a week David went right to night school after work, so I had to keep his dinner warm until after ten o'clock. It was tough on both of us, but we hoped that those business courses that David was taking would eventually prove to be our ticket to better times.

It was on a chilly October night that the incident occurred. David was still at school, and I was keeping his dinner warm in the kitchen. I was relaxing in the living room by putting my bare feet up on a footstool and reading a new book. I didn't expect David for at least another hour, and it felt so good after being on my feet all day just to sit and take it easy for a while. At about ten minutes to nine, though, I thought it was time to check David's meal to be certain it didn't dry out. When I reached the door between the living room and the kitchen, I was suddenly stopped dead in my tracks by some invisible force that prevented me from passing through the doorway. Some unseen, solid barrier that I could actually feel pressing against my chest and arms was holding me back.

Stunned, doubting my own senses, I lunged toward the doorway with all of my strength. I was thrown back with such force that I lost my balance and dropped to one knee. I have always been a tall woman, standing just over five-feet-ten. I was just twenty-two at the time of the occurrence, very athletic, solidly built, weighing about one hundred and forty pounds. I had grown up on a Missouri farm doing a man's work, and I was completely shaken by the experience of being knocked to my knees by something I couldn't see.

I slumped against the side of the sofa and studied the open doorway. I don't really remember how long I sat there trying to figure out what it was that had prevented me from entering the kitchen. I thought for a few minutes that maybe I had been working too hard, not getting enough sleep, and I was having some kind of breakdown.

The doorway was clear. I could see absolutely nothing that could have blocked my path to the kitchen, so I got back up and rushed the doorway once again. This time I experienced the flash of brilliant blue light as I struck the impenetrable invisible barrier, and I felt a fairly powerful electric type of shock that knocked me back on my posterior.

I shook my head to clear it of fear and confusion. When I looked up once again to confront the open doorway, I saw a blue light shimmering there. For just a few seconds the light took the shape of a tall, powerfully built man, and then it faded away.

> "He's got a big butcher knife in his hand, and it is plain to see that he has been waiting for you to come back into the kitchen."

I was completely awestruck. There was a ghost in our house that wouldn't let me enter the kitchen. A shiver went up and down my spine and centered in my solar plexus. David and I had no idea the place was haunted. Slowly I got to my feet and approached the doorway. This time I gingerly poked a finger in the air and saw the blue light manifest again. As incredible as it may seem, I saw my fingertip rest lightly against the dimly defined upraised palm of a big man composed entirely of shimmering blue light. When I tried to pass through the doorway, the spirit's palm moved from my fingertip to my chest, and once again I felt it push me back into the living room.

When the telephone on the end table began to ring, I was so startled that I felt as though I jumped to the ceiling. It probably rang three or four times before I had the presence of mind to answer it. It was my next-door neighbor, Pearl. In a hoarse whisper, she told me to be quiet and just listen carefully to what she was about to say. "You know that these five houses in a row are all built just exactly alike," she said, "so I know just where your telephone is. You just sit there and talk to me and don't move away from the sofa."

My head was swimming. First a ghost made of blue light blocked my path to the kitchen and now my next-door neighbor was telling me not to move from the telephone. Pearl kept her voice low, but her words were beginning to gain powerful meaning. "Now, don't you be afraid, but I can see a man standing right outside your kitchen door. He's got a big butcher knife in his hand, and it is plain to see that he has been waiting for you to come back into the kitchen." I could not suppress a gasp of horror. I felt a cold sweat break out over my entire body.

"Now don't you go screaming or being afraid," Pearl said sternly. "He can't see you there on your sofa when you talk on the telephone, so you just stay there!" "But he has a knife?" I whispered into the receiver. "Do you think … that he …?"

"I think he might be the rapist-slasher, all right," Pearl said matter-of-factly, "so you just sit tight. I called the police the second I spotted him walking up our back alley, so they should be here any minute now." Just then, in answer to my unspoken prayer, I heard the sound of police sirens. "Praise the Lord," Pearl said, "I can hear the police cars coming right now! You just sit tight, honey, until they come into your house."

I remained frozen in place until, almost simultaneous with the knocking on our front door, I heard the sound of scuffling and shouts outside the kitchen. Poor David came home just in time to see the police lead the rapist away in handcuffs. The way David came bursting into the house all trembling and shaking with tears in his eyes told me far more than words could say that he really loved me.

A police officer told us that the rapist was a small, slight man, who had apparently been attracted to me by my size and had thought that I would make a great conquest. But the little monster was also a physical coward, who was also intimidated by my height. Apparently that was why he had waited in the kitchen to attack me by surprise rather than approach me in the living room where I had been sitting reading. When I told David about my incredible experience with the ghost that would not permit me to enter the kitchen, we both knew that my life had been saved because of its actions. David said that it had to have been my guardian angel protecting me, and I had to agree.

9
INSPIRATIONAL MESSAGES FROM THE OTHER SIDE

A STRANGE SPIRIT MANIFESTED AT HER SICKBED

Between her twelfth and thirteenth year in November of 1839, young Mary Jobson began to suffer from a strange illness that would afflict her frail body for nearly eleven weeks. While they attended their sick daughter, John Jobson and his wife were concerned about the sound of mysterious rapping coming from the area around Mary's bed. At first, they had thought that the child was pounding at the bedstead while in the delirium of her fever, but they had been in the room and had heard the knocking while her hands were plainly in view.

The rapping proved to be but the beginning of the phenomena that were soon to manifest themselves in the Jobson home. A strange, whispering voice that seemed to come from nowhere in particular began to predict events in the Jobson family circle—events which later proved to be accurate. The knocking matured into violent explosions and such loud rumblings that the tenant below Mary's room often yelled up that he feared the ceiling was about to crash down on him. Footsteps stomped loudly about Mary's bed, closet doors opened of their own accord, water seemed to fall from the ceiling, and strangest of all, an invisible organ began to play sweet and ethereal music.

Their family doctor remained skeptical about the phenomena, as did John Jobson, but the spirit manifestations, especially the "heavenly" voice, began to attract wide attention. The voice declared that it issued from a benevolent spirit and was able to administer good advice to those who came to hear it. The voice told the distraught parents that their child had been temporarily "possessed" by a good spirit. The Jobsons were told that though Mary appeared to suffer, she did not. She did not know where her body was. Her own spirit had left the physical body, and the good spirit had entered it.

The skeptical father demanded physical proof and a large quantity of water was dumped at his feet. Jobson called for more water, and a deluge was forthcoming. He called and again and again—until he had commanded the appearance of water twenty times and the bedroom was drenched.

Mary's teacher, Elizabeth Gauntlett, was summoned by the voice while she was doing housework in her own home. "Elizabeth Gauntlett, one of your scholars, a certain Miss Mary Jobson, is ill," the voice said. "Go and see her; it will be good for you." Miss Gauntlett obeyed the voice, inquired as to the address of her pupil, and received "many marvelous signs" at the bedside of the young girl.

> The celestial music that attended the manifestation of this spirit is most intriguing.

Mary's bedroom became a sort of shrine as her body became a "speaking-trumpet" for the voices of departed friends and loved ones and the revelations of the good spirit. "Look up, and you shall see the sun and moon on the ceiling," the voice once said. Before the bewildered eyes of a roomful of witnesses, a beautiful representation of the celestial orbs appeared in lively colors of yellow and orange.

John Jobson immediately set about whitewashing the figures, but he soon learned that the voice had intended that its artwork be permanent. He put his brushes away when he discovered that, after several coats of whitewash, the figures still remained visible.

The celestial music that attended the manifestation of this spirit is most intriguing. Not only did the sound of a melodious organ continually fill the room with the sound of hymns, but on several occasions lovely voices of an invisible choir sang to its accompaniment.

In spite of the voice's assurances that Mary Jobson was not really suffering, her young body continued to give every evidence of an extremely long convalescence. At last, the voice announced that Mary would be the recipient of a miracle which would be wrought on June 22. Their doctor advised the Jobsons that the miracle could come none too soon. Mary was as ill as ever, and, if the strange, undefined disease continued its peculiar course, death would be imminent.

When the appointed day arrived, Mary's strength seemed to be rapidly diminishing. Her fever had risen, and the doctor was not optimistic about the young girl's chances of seeing another day. At five o'clock, the voice instructed Mrs. Jobson to lay out some clothes for Mary. Too dazed by grief and worry to refuse, the woman did as she had been told. After this was done, the voice ordered everyone from the bedroom with the exception of Mary's two-year-old brother. The Jobsons and the doctor spent an anxious fifteen minutes outside the door of Mary's room before they heard the voice cry: "Come in!" When they entered the room, Mary sat smiling in a chair, completely dressed, bouncing her baby brother on her knee. From that moment on, she seldom suffered from any illness and never received another visitation from the "good spirit." She matured into a very well-educated and highly respected young woman. In spite of the "undetermined disease of the brain" which lasted for seven months, Mary Jobson apparently suffered no psychic scars from the possession by a most unusual ghost.

She Visited the Other Side before Her Death

The *Journal of the American Society for Psychical Research* for 1918 contains the remarkable account of a ten-year-old girl named Daisy Dryden who, during the last three days of her life in October 1864, experienced numerous out-of-body visits to the other side.

Daisy, the daughter of David Anderson Dryden, a Methodist minister, encountered the spirit of her little brother Allie, who had died seven months before, and conversed with him as well as with many other spirit beings. The detailed record of the visions and heavenly scenes witnessed by the child were related by her mother shortly after Daisy's death.

Although the doctors had assured the Dryden family that their daughter would soon recover from her bout with typhoid fever, Daisy told them that Allie had informed her that she would soon be joining him in the spirit world. Then, expressing a kind of clairvoyance in which she appeared to be aware of both the material and the nonmaterial worlds, Daisy wondered aloud if she would still be able to visit the loved ones that she would leave behind on the Earth plane.

"I'll ask Allie if it will be possible," she said to those friends and family members gathered around her bed. After a brief pause she relayed her brother's answer: "He says that it is quite possible and that I shall return sometimes, but you will be unaware of my presence. Nevertheless, I shall be able to talk to you."

Two days before she died, Daisy's Sunday school teacher came to see her, and before she left, the well-intentioned lady said to the child: "My dear little Daisy, you are about to pass over the dark river." When she had gone, Daisy asked her father what her teacher had meant by the dark river. Reverend Dryden did his best to explain the metaphor of a river to represent the dividing curtain between life and death.

"What nonsense!" his daughter exclaimed with a burst of derisive laughter. "There is no river here at all. There is no dividing curtain. There is not even a line between this world and the next." Stretching out her little hand as if to indicate a clear pathway, she continued her description of the world beyond. "What is here is there. I know it is so, because I can see you all here, and I can see the others over there at the same time."

When Daisy's mother asked her to explain what she meant by her reference to "over there," the child said, "It is impossible for me to explain to you— it is so different from our world that I can't make you understand what I mean." Her mother moved to her bedside and held her hand. "Dear Mama, I wish you could see Allie." Daisy smiled. "He is quite close to you."

Instinctively, Mrs. Dryden turned around, but Daisy continued: "He told me that you would not be able to see him, because your spiritual eyes are shut. I can see him, because my spirit is now tied to my body by a very fine thread of life."

The next day when her Sunday school teacher returned, Daisy informed the woman that her two children were present. The teacher's children had gone to the other side many years before, and if they had lived, they would have been young adults. All of the people present that day were quite certain that Daisy had never heard anyone speak of the woman's children, so she would have known nothing whatever about them before seeing them in the spirit world. When her teacher asked Daisy to describe the children, she could not relate to the girl's descriptions of them as greatly matured individuals. "You are describing grown-ups, the teacher protested. "They were just little children when they passed on."

Allie explained through Daisy that children did not stay children when they crossed to the other side. "They grow up, just as they do in this life."

The Sunday school teacher shook her head in wonder. "But my little daughter Mary fell and was so injured that she could not stand up straight." Daisy smiled and assured her that her daughter was all right now: "She is straight and beautiful; and your son is looking so noble and happy."

In her report of Daisy's final days, Mrs. Dryden wrote that another family friend who came to pay her respects was informed that her daughter, who had died some years before, was also now an adult on the other side. The mother could not recognize her from the description given until Daisy said, "She used to have a mole on the left side of her neck, but she does not have it now." With this added bit of information, Mrs. Dryden declared, the woman was convinced.

Mrs. Dryden asked her daughter how she was able to converse with Allie. "I don't hear you speak, nor do you move your lips." Daisy smiled and replied: "We speak with our thoughts." Mrs. Dryden wished to know in what form Allie appeared to her. "He is not dressed as we are," Daisy explained. "His body is clothed in something dazzlingly white. It is wonderfully bright. Oh, Mama, you should see how fine, light, and splendid his robe is—and how very white!"

Reverend Dryden cited the psalmist of the Old Testament who declared, "He is clothed with light." "Oh, yes, father," she agreed. "That is very true."

Daisy loved to hear her sister Loulou sing some of her favorite hymns. In one particular stanza, when Loulou was singing about the wings of angels, Daisy began to giggle. "Oh, Loulou, it is so funny. We were always told that angels had wings. But it is not so. It is a mistake. Angels do not have any wings at all." Loulou found such an assertion difficult to accept. "But they must have wings, dear Daisy. Or else how could they fly down from heaven?" Daisy explained further: "They don't fly. They just come. Do you know, the very moment that I think of our brother Allie, he is here at once."

> "**I** possess a spiritual body, which shall replace my old one. I have already got it on me...."

Mrs. Dryden, who had been listening to the conversation between her daughters, wanted to know how it was that Daisy managed to see the angels. Daisy was quick to admit that she did not always see them. "But when I do, the walls seem to vanish and I can see ever so far away—and I see crowds and crowds of spirits. Those spirits who come close to me are those whom I knew in my life, but others I have never seen before."

On the day of her death, Daisy asked her mother for a hand mirror. Mrs. Dryden hesitated, fearing that the child might be horrified by her pinched and haggard features. But after calmly considering her reflection in the looking glass for several minutes, Daisy said, "My poor body is used up, like one of Mama's old dresses that she hangs up in the wardrobe and never wears again. But I possess a spiritual body, which shall replace my old one. I have already got it on me, and it is with my spiritual eyes that I see the spirit world—even though my earthly body is still attached to the spiritual one. You will place my body in the grave, because I shall have no further use for it, but I shall be clothed in another body much more beautiful than this one—one just like Allie's! Mama, darling, don't cry, for if I have to go away, it is for my benefit. God knows what is best."

The child asked that her mother open the window, and Mrs. Dryden complied with her request. "I want to have a last look at the beautiful world," Daisy said, "for after the sunrise tomorrow, I shall be no more." Daisy asked her father to raise her up a little. "Good-bye, good-bye, my pretty world. I still love you, but, nevertheless, I don't wish to remain here any longer."

Mrs. Dryden's journal recorded that it was a quarter to eleven that night when Daisy called out to her father: "Papa, lift me up. Allie has come to look for me." When the child had been placed as she wished, she asked that someone sing a hymn.

"Go and get Loulou," one of the adults in attendance at Daisy's bedside said. "She's the singer in the family." "No," Daisy said in a soft voice. "Please don't disturb her. She's asleep."

Then, just as the hands of the clock pointed at eleven, Daisy lifted up her hands and said," I am coming, Allie!" It was at that moment, Mrs. Dryden stated, that her daughter ceased to breathe.

The heavenly visions of Daisy Dryden made quite an impression upon psychical researchers of the day. Professor James H. Hyslop of Columbia University, author of *Science and a Future Life* (1905) and *Borderlands of Psychical Research* (1906), conducted a full investigation of the case and reported that he could confirm every detail. Professor Ernesto Bozzano quoted the case in his *Phénomènes psychiques au moment de la mort* (1923), as did George Lindsay Johnson in his *Does Man Survive?* (1936).

In his summation of the Daisy Dryden case, Johnson affirms that in his opinion:

> This case affords one of the most convincing proofs of the continuation of life after death and of the survival of all our faculties that it is possible to obtain…. [Daisy's] artless patter is of infinitely more value—and far nearer the actual truth—than all the learned philosophy and disquisitions of scientists and divines. As Jesus exclaimed, "I thank thee, Father, Lord of the wise and the learned, Thou hast revealed them to the childlike."

⊶⊷

SPIRIT MESSAGES TO LOVED ONES LEFT BEHIND

These excerpts relate messages from loved ones on the other side. They are responses to our Steiger Questionnaire of Psychic and Mystical Experiences gathered since we began distributing the questionnaire in 1968:

Heaven Is the Summation of Perfect Harmony and Love

"From what the spirit of my husband, Sam, has told me," Bridget C. said, "Heaven seems to be the summation of perfect Harmony and Love. He says that it is a person's inner life that makes for righteousness and happiness."

Ann H. said that her mother's spirit informed her that the entities in heaven were always busy with pleasant activities. "It seems as though the spirits in the next world are always learning and continually engaged in meaningful pursuits and recreations."

"In heaven," said Marion Palmer, "Love is the great guiding star. Love fills the spirit entities with the highest joy. The spirit of my sister Jackie has told me that the souls of all those in heaven are filled with unimagined happiness. She said that the divine energy of living, being, and becoming permeate their essences with an intensity of which we on Earth can have no conception."

His New Spiritual Sight Detected the Malignant Lump in Her Breast

The personal account of S.A.

The spirit of my husband, Philip, appeared to me and told me to go at once to my physician to have a lump in my left breast examined. A biopsy determined that the pea-sized lump was malignant, but because of Phil's early warning, the surgery was effective and the cancer was removed with very little trauma.

Phil had been able to see inside my body, and he explained that a spirit's sense of color is vastly superior to ours. Their range of sight extends far beyond our small share of the spectrum. Their sight moves beyond even what we know as the ultraviolet range. He said that everything that was around me in my environment appeared totally different to him—and different from the way that he had remembered it.

Phil surprised me when he said that there was no sunlight in heaven, but that everything was intensely bright, nonetheless. I guess that was why my physical body was more or less transparent to his spiritual eyes. His sight could penetrate between the molecules of my body, just like X rays do.

After Forty-six Years, She Still Feels the Spiritual Presence of Her Husband

The Personal Account of M.K.R.

Our children were all under six years of age when my husband, Larry, was killed in the Korean conflict in 1952. But even today, forty-six years later, I still feel the guiding and protecting influence, as well as the spiritual presence, of my husband.

I have come to understand that when the spirits in heaven develop spiritually, they pass to a higher sphere. Those spirits who graduate to that higher plane eventually lose all their interest in the mundane, the earthly, the material. The higher the spirits evolve, the less often they will be concerned with earthly considerations. In fact, the highly progressed entities will rarely come to anyone on Earth—unless there is such a strong bond of affection between the spirit and those left behind that the spirit frequently returns to monitor loved ones until the loved ones join him or her in heaven. I know that Larry's spirit remains concerned about us and that he awaits us on the other side."

DR. GEORGE LINDSAY JOHNSON'S ANALYSIS
OF THOUSANDS OF SPIRIT MESSAGES

Among Dr. George Lindsay Johnson's conclusions after evaluating thousands of spirit communications was that whatever creed or religion one might adhere to in this world, on the other side such belief constructs are purely a matter of indifference.

"Whether we believe in one God or three Gods or no God at all—whether we are Christians, Mohammedans, Jews, Buddhists, or Free-thinkers without any religion except that of nature—will count for nothing on the other side; nor will our beliefs affect our happiness at all, except indirectly," Dr. Johnson wrote. "Our religion or nonreligion is merely an accident of our birth and bringing up, and we are in nowise responsible for it."

Dr. Johnson also learned that many spirits, especially if they had lived extremely materialistic lives on Earth, are unaware that they have passed over to the other side. "Such a state must be the exception rather than the rule," he said, "and I believe that it never takes place if the person who passes over has accustomed himself before his departure to higher objects in life than mere selfish gratification." Thus Dr. Johnson maintained that the more spiritually minded a person is on Earth, the more his or her thoughts would be centered on new goals and aims on the other side.

Even after his extensive firsthand study of spirit communications and his analysis of the investigations of dozens of other psychical researchers, Dr. Johnson expressed no reluctance in admitting that we are "lamentably ignorant" concerning conditions on the other side. At the same time, he insisted that certain well-established facts were worth recording and, if the reader could grasp the following passage, he or she would be in a better position to comprehend conditions in the next world:

The Universe is a vast exhibition of intense activity, movement and intelligence—a becoming through perpetual evolution. This consists of two systems—the natural or the physical, and the psychic or spiritual world, and each of them is governed by its own laws, which are entirely different in their action. These two-world systems are perpetually acting and reacting on each other; the physical world being subservient to the spiritual world and controlled by it. Furthermore, the inhabitants of the spirit world are merely human beings freed from the limitations imposed upon them by their physical bodies.

Achieving Spirit Communication

Those men and women who have been blessed with messages from their loved ones in heaven have received them in many different ways—through dreams, visions, direct spirit communication and materialization, mediums, séances, automatic writing, and so on. Whether one should deliberately seek spirit communication is an age-old question which is certain to spark debate in many homes.

Surely, it is best if spirit contact and communication should be spontaneous—a true blessing beyond all human understanding which grants a temporary reprieve from the final sentence of death in order for loved ones to share a last farewell.

Hell and Belief Constructs

Taking a consensus of the spiritual communications related to us by respondents, we have found that hell appears to be the negation of all virtues and pleasures. Rather than a specific place, it seems to be a condition or state of being which embodies the summation of all misdirected energies, such as those of greed, lust, malice, hate, and jealousy.

At the moment of physical death, the spirits newly freed from the confines of flesh are profoundly influenced by the belief constructs which they maintained while on Earth. A good Roman Catholic, therefore, will often perceive a saint or the Virgin Mary waiting to welcome them to the next world. A practicing Jew may envision Moses or Father Abraham stretching forth a hand of greeting. A Protestant may perceive Jesus or an angel waiting to open the gates of heaven. After the spirit has adjusted to existence in the afterlife, however, once strongly held religious concepts seem to fade and become a matter of little or no importance.

Paradise

According to numerous reports of spirit communication, a person does not go directly to heaven after he or she dies. What the newly deceased has described is commonly referred to as "paradise."

"Georgia said that it is a kind of gathering place for all newly arrived spirits," Douglas J. said, referring to the communication that he had received from his wife, who is in the next world. "She said that the place has nothing to do with whether or not you lived a good life or a bad life. Everyone goes there, regardless. It is something like a kind of resting place before the spirit moves on."

Johnson stated that he had looked up the word paradise in a dictionary and discovered that it is a Persian word for a park or a garden. "From what I can ascertain," he continued, "it is after the spirit entity has been deceased for awhile that it begins to grow weary of the familiar scenes of life on Earth. I am certain that it all depends upon the individual entity and the personal circumstances of his or her passing, but it seems that the spirits must be willing to set aside their material interests before they are ready to progress more completely into the Light of higher awareness."

The Wonder of the Afterlife

Peggy Ann L. said that she sometimes felt as though the communicating spirit of her husband, Patrick, found it impossible to convey the beauty and the brilliance of the next world in mere mortal words. "I am not certain if Patrick is simply unable to describe the wonder of the afterlife or if my finite mind is simply unable to grasp it all. Patrick told me that at first everything in the next world was so marvelously different from existence on Earth that he found it impossible to grasp. Now, I fear that Patrick has given up the task of teaching me to perceive the glory of the afterlife. He said that I will just have to wait and see it all for myself."

Remaining Unaware of the Transition of Physical Death

An aspect of the afterlife that has been confirmed many times in spirit communications throughout history is that many entities, especially if they lived exceedingly material lives on earth, may remain unaware that they have passed over for many days, months, or even years.

The spirit entity of Camille A. who made her transition in September 1987, told her sister Louise that many spirits remain oblivious to the death of their bodies because they may be in a kind of dreamlike state immediately upon their transition. According to Camille, "This kind of spirit dreaming is different from earth dreaming in that the dreamer will never again awaken to physical realities. When the spirit does awaken, it will do so in a world of new realities which are unknown to it. It will only be some time later that such materialistic entities will emerge from their stupor and gradually become convinced that they are no longer living in the physical world."

Meeting Friends and Relatives

As a general rule, it seems that the moment that people die, regardless of the kind of life that they have led, a spirit entity, usually a friend or a relative, comes to meet the newly deceased. For those who have recently died this entity becomes a kind of guide—greeting them, comforting them, and showing them around. Without such guides, the recent arrivals would feel desperately lonely and confused the moment they woke up to their new life.

"My wife, Ramona, told me that she was met by her grandparents and by her best friend Carmen, who had been killed in a car accident two years ago," said Joaquin S. "I had been so sad, so frightened, until the spirit form of my wife told me that she was not alone on the other side. It brought me great peace, just knowing that she had someone with her."

Spirit Duplicates

Many of those who have received spirit communications have been repeatedly assured that all the objects of the earth plane have their spiritual counterparts on the other side. "We have our spirit form duplicates of everything that you can see around you," Edward B. heard the spirit voice of his wife, Donna, tell him. "We have trees, flowers, animals, mountains, rivers, and seas."

The inquisitive Edward insisted on receiving a more complete description of the environment of the next world. "We have clouds and rainy days, storms and lightning," the spirit entity continued. "We have the thousand and one forms that make Mother Nature so beautiful. We have houses and books and clothes. Everything on Earth has its mental duplicate or counterparts in the spirit world."

On the Other Side, the Living Are the "Spooks"

In an interesting twist, Kathy B. said that her sister Barbara communicated from spirit that those of us who dwell on the physical plane are deemed "spooks" by the entities in the next world. "Life is intensely pleasurable here," Barbara said from the other side. "Although you think of us over here as ghosts, to us it is the other way around. We look upon you as spooks and shadowy beings, because you are transparent to our mental vision. From our perspective, it is we who are the real thing. We appear to one another as perfectly solid."

There Is No Pain in the Next World

The spirit being of Frank M. appeared to his wife, Teresa, and told her that since spirits have no physical bodies, they have no nerves, and therefore cannot feel pain. "Life cannot help being more virtuous here," he said. "Spirit entities do not harm or kill one another, because our bodies cannot be harmed or murdered. There is not the slightest temptation to steal, because there would be nothing to steal that we cannot form mentally with our own minds. It is pointless to tell lies, for the obvious reason that we can read one another's thoughts. We do not eat and drink, therefore drunkenness and gluttony cannot exist.

"Although we keep a concept of sexual identity, we do not marry. And because we have no physical bodies there can be no such things as adultery, lust, or jealousy. The concept of possessiveness of one another has completely disappeared. We are no longer attracted to the promise of the physical delights of the body, but to the prowess of one's mental strength and the beauty of one's soul."

Beyond the Fourth Dimension

Sherrana P. had been deceased for nearly three years before her spirit entity appeared to her husband, Ronald. "Darling, if you can grasp the concept that thoughts are things," the spirit told him, "you will be in a marvelous position to understand many of the essential mysteries of the universe—including life after death. Because of my more rapid ethereal vibration, I can appear before you in your more physically dense world. Likewise, I can easily walk through your doors and walls, because they are objects of the third dimension. I now exist beyond the fourth dimension."

Warnings about Spirit Entities in the Lower Vibrations

"If you should encounter spirit entities who appear interested in matters of the flesh and who are selfish and exploitative," warned the spirit entity of Jack K., "you have met beings from the lower and less spiritual planes of existence. On planes of higher spiritual vibration, love is the chief emotion."

Kris C.'s spirit essence communicated to her mother that like-minded souls are attracted to one another. "Here, the happiness of the soul depends upon its own resources. We do not work to earn money for the pleasures of existence. We are free to utilize our individual talents as we prefer. Because our thoughts and our characters are completely open and naked for all to see, there is no attempt at pretense. Spirits of similar vibrational frequencies just naturally move toward one another.

"Those souls who for whatever reason are slow to adjust to the next world may stay on the lower planes for years. Some exist for quite some time in a kind of mental darkness. That is quite sad, for the heavenly life is one of growth in wisdom, insight, and love."

The Realms of Spiritual Expression

The spiritual essence of Floyd A. materialized to his wife, Lillian, to explain three distinct realms or dimensions of spiritual expression.

"In the afterlife," he said, "there is the Etheric, the Mental, and the Spiritual. Your plane, my dear one, is the world of Matter, wherein you have a physical body that is controlled by your mind. On the other side, however, we manifest a mentally formed etheric body that is controlled by our spirituality. The key to all of this is to interpret the physical in terms of the mental—and to control the whole by means of the spiritual."

Al M. had been confined to a wheelchair for eleven years before he passed on in September 1988. "Time and space do not have the same meaning over here," his spirit told his wife, Terry. "I can travel from one spot on the earth to another, simply by thinking it to be so. I'm not confined to that darn wheelchair any longer, darling, and I'm traveling all over the place now."

Spirits Communicate by Telepathy

According to Goldie C., her father's spirit form told her that telepathy was the normal means of intercommunication among spirits and between spirit beings and humans. "Telepathy dispenses with the clumsiness of language and renders sound superfluous," the spirit said. "It is this mechanism that permits spirit entities to communicate with the living in whatever country they may exist. It is also such a mechanism that allows spirits from ancient times to be able to be understood by men and women in the twentieth century."

The Next World Is One of Thought Forms

When Tiffany J. received communication from the spirit essence of her husband, Norman, he told her that the principal difference between life on Earth and that of the other side lies in the fact that we living humans exist in a material world wherein everything is governed by physical laws. "In the next world," Tiffany stated, "the spirit beings live on a mental plane and thought replaces physical action and crude matter. In the world of thought, the limitations of time and space do not exist.

"Another main difference," she added, "is that over there, love is the principal energy that controls every thought, every deed, every vibration."

Ghosts Are Merely Humans Freed of Their Physical Limitations

In his quest to solve the enigma of life after death, scientist George Lindsay Johnson thoughtfully observed what he believed to be an axiomatic truth: "The Universe is a vast exhibition of intense activity, movement, and intelligence—a becoming through perpetual evolution. This consists of two systems—the natural or physical, and the psychic or spiritual world—and each of them is governed by its own laws, which are entirely different in their action. These two world-systems are perpetually acting and reacting on each other; the physical world being subservient to the spiritual world, and controlled by it. Furthermore, the inhabitants of the spirit world are merely human beings freed from the limitations imposed upon them by their physical bodies."

10
GHOSTS THAT GAVE PROOF OF THEIR EXISTENCE

THE SCRATCH ON HIS SISTER'S CHEEK

In 1876, Mr. F. G., a traveling salesman, was sitting in a hotel room in St. Joseph, Missouri. It was high noon and Mr. F. G. was smoking a cigar and writing out orders. Suddenly conscious of someone sitting on his left with one arm resting on the table, the salesman was startled to look up into the face of his dead sister, a young lady of eighteen who had died of cholera in 1867.

"So sure was I that it was she," he wrote later in an account to the American Society for Psychical Research (*Proceedings*, S.P.R., VI, 17), that I sprang forward in delight, calling her by name."

As he did so, the image of his sister vanished. Mr. F. G. resumed his seat, stunned by the experience. The cigar was still in his mouth, the pen was still in his hand, the ink was still moist on his order blank. He was satisfied that he had not been dreaming, but was wide awake.

"I was near enough to touch her, had it been a physical possibility, and noted her features, expression, and details of dress .... She appeared as if alive. Her eyes looked kindly and perfectly naturally into mine. Her skin was so life-like that I could see the glow or moisture on its surface, and, on the whole, there was no, change in her appearance ...".

Mr. F. G. was so impressed by the experience that he took the next train home to tell his parents about the remarkable visitation. His mother nearly fainted when he told them of " ... a bright red line, or scratch on the right-hand side" of his sister's face.

With tears streaming down her cheeks, F. G.'s mother told him that he had indeed seen his sister. Unbeknownst to anyone else, his mother had accidentally made a scratch on his sister's face while doing some little act of kindness after the girl's death She had carefully tried to obliterate all traces of the slight scratch with the aid of powder—"and this she had never mentioned to a human being from that day to this."

It seems a bit more than coincidence when the narrator adds: "A few weeks later my mother died, happy in her belief she would rejoin her favorite daughter in a better world."

In discussing this case, the noted psychic researcher Frederic W. H. Myers, author of the classic work *Human Personality and Its Survival of Bodily Death* (coauthored with Edmund Gurney and Frank Podmore, publishing posthumously in 1903) wrote that, in his opinion, the spirit of the daughter had perceived the approaching death of her mother and had appeared to the brother to force him into the role of message bearer. Also, by prompting F. G. to return home unexpectedly at that time, the spirit enabled him to have a final visit with his mother.

Myers is further intrigued by the fact that the spirit figure appeared not as a corpse, but as a girl full of health and happiness, with the symbolic red mark worn simply as a test of identity. Myers discounted the theory that the spirit figure could have been a projection from the mother's mind. Myers, one of the original group, together with Henry Sidgwick and Edmund Gurney, that founded the British Society for Psychical Research in 1882, concluded the following regarding the famous "scratch on the cheek" case:

"As to the spirit's own knowledge of the fate of the body after death, other reported cases show that this specific form of post-mortem perception is not unusual. However explained, this case is one of the best attested, and in itself one of the most remarkable, that we possess .... [It] certainly seems probable that recognition was intelligently [intended]."

RAYMOND'S LAST PHOTOGRAPH

The noted British physicist, Oliver Lodge, was knighted in 1902 while he was serving as the president of the British Society for Psychical Research. In 1913, Sir Oliver was elected president of the British Association for the Advancement of Science, his brilliant work with electricity and the early forms of radio more than compensating for his fascination with the spirit world in the eyes of his more conservative scientific colleagues. In August 1915, Sir Oliver received what he considered absolute proof of survival after death when

In the 1999 movie *The Sixth Sense,* actor Haley Joel Osment (left) plays a young boy who is able to see ghosts. The young boy realizes that the ghosts come to him for help in resolving issues from their lives. Shown at right is Bruce Willis.

Leonora Piper, the famous spirit medium from Boston, relayed what he believed to be convincing messages from the spirits of two close friends and associates, Fredric W. H. Myers, who died in 1901, and Edmund Gurney, who died in 1888.

Regardless of Sir Oliver's and Lady Lodge's acceptance of the reality of life after death, we may assume that they grieved the death of their son, Raymond, who was killed on September 14, 1915 while serving as a medical officer of the Second South Lancers. On September 25, Lady Lodge sat with the medium Gladys Osborne Leonard who described a photograph that had been taken of Raymond with a group of fellow officers. The Lodges had numerous portraits of their son in uniform that had been taken in the early months of World War I, but they did not possess a single photograph depicting a group the medical officers. Intrigued by Mrs. Leonard's insistence that such a photograph existed, a puzzled Lady Lodge could only shake her head in puzzlement, for she knew of no such photograph. "He is insistent that I should tell you of this," Mrs. Leonard told Lady Lodge. "He stands with his fellow medical officers, his walking stick under his arm."

Sir Oliver was impressed with the emphasis that the medium had placed upon Raymond's particular message concerning the photograph. Then, according to Sir Oliver's report on the case (*Proceedings*, S.P.R. Vol. XXIX), on November 29, a letter was received from a Mrs. Cheves, a stranger to them, but the mother of a friend of Raymond's. Mrs. Cheves informed the Lodges that she had half a dozen photographs of the group of medical officers including Raymond and her son. Would the Lodges, inquired Mrs. Cheves, like a copy of the photograph?

Although Sir Oliver and his wife responded immediately, the photograph did not arrive until the afternoon of December 7. In the meantime, Lady Lodge had gone through Raymond's diary, which had been returned from the front, and had found an entry dated August 24 which mentioned that a group photo had been taken.

"The exposure was only made twenty-one days before his death," Sir Oliver wrote in his report, "and some days may have elapsed before he saw a print, if he ever saw one. He certainly never mentioned it in his letters. We were therefore in complete ignorance of it."

While the Lodges were waiting for the photograph from Mrs. Cheves, they visited another medium whose guide contacted the spirit of Raymond and gave them additional details concerning the group picture. "Raymond is doubtful about the stick," the spirit control said through the physical agency of the medium, "but he says there is a considerable number of men in the photograph; that the front row is sitting, and that there is a back row, or some of the people grouped and set up at the back; also that there are a dozen or more people in the photograph, and that some of them he hardly knew."

Through the spirit control, Raymond named two friends who were prominently featured and said that he himself was sitting down with officers behind him, one of whom had annoyed him by leaning on his shoulder.

When the photograph was delivered to the Lodge home on the afternoon of December 7, Sir Oliver and Lady Lodge noted at once that the picture offered a poor likeness of Raymond, but excellent evidence that their son had communicated to them from beyond the grave. The walking stick was there, though not under Raymond's arm, as Mrs. Leonard had said. The fellow officers whom Raymond had named through the second medium were in the photograph, and the general arrangement of the men followed the mediums' description.

"But by far the most striking piece of evidence is the fact that someone sitting behind Raymond is leaning or resting a hand on his shoulder," Sir Oliver said. "The photograph fortunately shows the actual occurrence, and almost indicates that Raymond was rather annoyed with it; for his face is a little screwed up, and his head has been slightly bent to one side out of the way of the man's arm. It is the only case in the photograph where one man is leaning or resting his hand on the shoulder of another."

Sir Oliver once again contacted Mrs. Cheves and learned where he might obtain prints of other photographs which had been taken at the same time. Upon examination of all accessible prints, Sir Oliver found that the basic group pose had been repeated with only slight variations for three different photographs. The Lodges felt the evidential value of the communication had been greatly enhanced by the fact that one medium had made a reference to the existence of Raymond's previously unknown last photograph and another medium, independent of the first, had supplied the details of the photograph in response to Sir Oliver's direct question.

In his *My Philosophy* (1933), Sir Oliver Lodge wrote: "I am absolutely convinced not only of survival, but of demonstrated survival, demonstrated by occasional interaction with matter in such a way as to produce physical results."

❦

James Chaffin's Other Will

On September 7, 1921, James Chaffin, a farmer in Davie County, North Carolina, died as the result of a fall. Although Chaffin was survived by his widow and four sons, his will, which had been duly attested by two witnesses on November 16, 1905, left all of his property to the third son, Marshall.

One night in the latter part of June 1925, four years after James Chaffin's death, James Pinkney Chaffin, the farmer's second son, saw the spirit figure of the deceased standing at his bedside and speaking about another will. According to the son, his father had appeared dressed as he often had in life. "You will find the will in my overcoat pocket," the spirit figure said, taking hold of an image of the familiar garment and pulling back the lapels.

The next morning James Pinkney Chaffin arose, convinced that he had truly seen and heard the spirit of his father and that the spirit had visited him for the purpose of correcting some error. His father's black overcoat had been passed on to the oldest son, John Chaffin, so James traveled to Yadkin County to examine the pocket referred to by the spirit. The two brothers found that the lining of the inside pocket had been sewn together, and when they cut the stitches, they found a roll of paper which bore the message: "Read the 27th chapter of Genesis in my daddies Old Bible."

James P. Chaffin was then convinced that the spirit had spoken truthfully, and he brought witnesses with him to the home of his mother where, after some search, they located the dilapidated old Bible in the top drawer of a dresser in an upstairs room. One of the witnesses found the will in a pocket which had been formed by folding two of the Bible's pages together.

The new will had been made by James Chaffin on January 16, 1919, fourteen years after the first will. In this testament, the farmer stated that he desired his property to be divided equally among his four sons with the admonition that they provide for their mother as long as she lived.

Although the second will had not been attested, it would, under North Carolina law, be considers valid because it had been written in James Chaffin's own handwriting. All that remained was to present sufficient evidence that the hand that had written the second will was, without doubt, that of the deceased.

Marshall Chaffin, the sole beneficiary under the conditions of the old will, had passed away within a year of his father, nearly four years before the spirit of James Chaffin had appeared to his second son, James Pinkney Chaffin. Marshall's widow and son prepared to contest the validity of the second will, and the residents of the county looked forward to a long and bitter court battle between members of the Chaffin family.

The scandalmongers were immensely disappointed when ten witnesses arrived in the courtroom prepared to give evidence that the second will was in James Chaffin's handwriting. After seeing the will, Marshall Chaffin's wife and son immediately withdrew their opposition. It seemed evident that they, too, believed the will had been written in the hand of the testator.

James Pinkney Chaffin later told an investigator for the *Journal of the Society for Psychical Research* that his father had appeared to him before the trial and told him that the lawsuit would be terminated in such a manner. "Many of my friends do not believe it is possible for the living to hold communication with the dead," James P. Chaffin said, "but I am convinced that my father actually appeared to me on these several occasions, and I shall believe it to the day of my death."

It does seem strange that James Chaffin should have kept the second will secret, especially in view of the subsequent claim that his disturbed spirit came back from beyond the grave to right the wrong that had been done to his widow and three disinherited sons. Perhaps the farmer had intended some sort of deathbed revelation and these plans went unrealized when his life was cut short by accident.

Society for Psychic Research investigators were unable to establish any kind of case for a subconscious knowledge of the will in the old Bible or of the message in the coat pocket. Fraud must be ruled out because of the ease in which ten reliable witnesses, well-acquainted with James Chaffin's handwriting, could be summoned to testify to the authenticity of the handwriting in the will. Charges of a fake will would seem to be further negated by the immediate withdrawal from the contest by Marshall Chaffin's widow and son once they were allowed to examine the document. Evidently they, too, recognized the handwriting of the elder Chaffin.

The *Journal's* summation of the strange case of James Chaffin's will emphasized the difficulty in attempting to explain the case on normal lines. "If a supernormal explanation be accepted, it is to be noted that the present case is of a comparatively infrequent type, in which more than one of the percipient's senses is affected by the phantasm. Mr. J. P. Chaffin both 'saw' his father and 'heard' him speak. The auditory impression was not strictly accurate: what was in the overcoat pocket was not the second will, but a clue to its whereabouts, but the practical result was the same."

GRANDDAD CAME TO SAY GOOD-BYE

On the night of June 11, 1923, Mrs. Gladys Watson had been asleep for three or four hours when she was awakened by someone calling her name. As she sat up in bed, she was able to discern the form of her beloved grandfather leaning toward her. "Don't be frightened, it's only me. I have just died," the image told her.

Mrs. Watson started to cry and reached across the bed to awaken her husband. "This is how they will bury me," Granddad Parker said, indicating his suit and black bow tie. "Just wanted to tell you I've been waiting to go ever since Mother was taken."

The Watson's house was next door to the Lilly Laboratories in Indianapolis. The bedroom was dimly illuminated with lights from the laboratory, so Granddad Parker was clearly and solidly seen by Mrs. Watson. But before she could awaken her husband, Granddad Parker had disappeared.

Mr. Watson insisted that she had had a nightmare. "Your grandfather is alive, and well back in Wilmington," he told her.

Mrs. Watson was firm in her conviction that she knew that she had seen Granddad Parker and that it had been no dream. He had come to bid her farewell.

It was 4:05 A.M. when Watson called his wife's parents in Wilmington, Delaware, to prove that the experience had been a dream. Mrs. Parker was surprised to receive the call. She had been up most of the night with her father-in-law and had been waiting for morning before she would let the Watsons know that Granddad had passed away at 4:00 A.M.

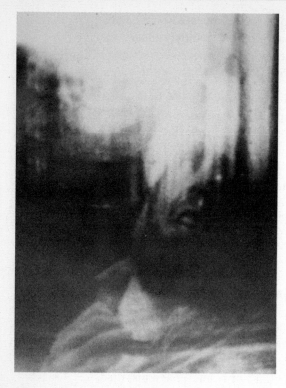

Materialization of a spirit entity.

Mrs. Watson had been awakened by the fully externalized apparition of her grandfather at approximately 3:30 A.M. Indianapolis time. Her husband had got out of bed and made the telephone call at about 4:05 A.M. Granddad Parker had died at 4:00 A.M. Eastern Time—half an hour before Gladys Watson saw him.

Mrs. Watson wrote an account of her experience for the *Journal of the American Society for Psychical Research* (Vol. LXV, No. 3) in which she mentioned that both she and her husband were children of Methodist ministers "schooled against superstition from the time of their birth."

When Mrs. Watson was asked by an investigator for the A.S.P.R. whether the experience of hearing her grandfather speak could be compared to hearing someone in the flesh or to hearing with one's "inner ear," she answered that it had been as if Granddad Parker had been there in the flesh, speaking in a soft, yet determined voice.

Mrs. Watson's father, Reverend Walter E. Parker, Sr., corroborated his daughter's story in a letter to the A.S.P.R. in which he wrote, in part: "Gladys had always been my father's favorite grandchild and we had promised to let her know if and when he became seriously ill. (He made his home with us.) He took sick the day before. We called the doctor and thought he was going to be all right. The end came suddenly around four o'clock in the morning. We were going to wait until later in the morning to get in touch with Gladys. I believe sincerely in the truth of this experience as my daughter writes it."

A DEBT REMAINED TO BE PAID

In his *The Dead Have Never Died*, Edward C. Randall wrote about twenty years of experiments conducted with the medium Mrs. Emily S. French. Mrs. French was an extremely frail woman who was hard of hearing, and Randall felt that her partial deafness provided an excellent self-imposed test condition. Because of her deafness, Randall said, Mrs. French would often fail to hear the spirit voices that would sound about her, and would go on speaking, unmindful of entities she might be interrupting. No mediumistic trick could enable one to speak in three or four different voices at the same time, each voice discussing some topic completely unrelated to the others. Randall admits that such conditions often made for confusion, but in his estimation, greatly increased the validity of the more than seven hundred sittings he held with Mrs. French.

On May 26, 1896, the Brown Building in Buffalo, New York, collapsed while undergoing repairs. The city was filled with rumors about the number of people who had lost their lives in the tragedy. At a sitting with Mrs. French that evening, four voices identified themselves as victims of the accident and gave their names and addresses. Randall writes that these were verified when the bodies were discovered some days later.

At another sitting, Randall, a lawyer, said that the voice of his father was heard. The senior Randall told his son that one small item in the settlement of his estate had been overlooked. Randall spoke a bit harshly to the voice, chiding the spirit because his father's mind had always been very concerned with amassing money.

"The estate has already been divided," Randall told the spirit voice. "Why bother me with this now?" The spirit of Randall's father replied that he had worked too hard for his money to allow an asset to remain undiscovered. When Randall indicated that he was paying attention, the voice proceeded to tell of a small sum of money lent to an individual in Erie, Pennsylvania. Before the note had matured, the deceased had filed it with the prothonotary in Erie. Although there would be no record of the loan in his books, the voice told Randall, he could find the judgment of the note on record in the prothonotary's office. "I want you to correct it," the voice concluded.

The lawyer was surprised when he received a transcript of such a judgment entered on October 21, 1896, and with such evidence, he obtained payment of the note, with interest. Randall questioned all of his father's employees to determine if anyone had had knowledge of the debt. He could find no one who had known of the loan. It would certainly have been impossible for the medium Mrs. French to have known the undisclosed dealings of a man she had never met.

"My father's voice was clearly recognizable on that occasion, as it has been on hundreds of others," Edward Randall wrote. "I cite this instance for the benefit of those who measure everything from an evidential standpoint."

THE SPIRIT REMEMBERED A FORGOTTEN KINDNESS

Arthur Findlay, a stockbroker and accountant in Glasgow, Scotland, began to investigate psychic phenomena in 1918. Although early in his studies

Findlay had been completely skeptical and had hoped to expose the medium John C. Sloan, he soon found himself becoming increasingly convinced of the authenticity of the messages Sloan conveyed.

After more than fifty sittings with Sloan, Findlay became convinced not only of the medium's integrity, but of human survival after death. In his book *On the Edge of the Etheric*, Findlay relates the following case as one he considers completely free of any suggestion of fraud or alternative theories of telepathic or clairvoyant interaction.

It was in 1919 when Findlay took his brother John to a séance with Sloan that a voice calling itself "Eric Saunders" manifested itself and claimed acquaintanceship with John. John Findlay denied ever having known a man of that name, but the voice persisted that they had known each other in the army. "Where might that have been?" John asked. "Among other places, I served at Aldershot, Bisley, France."

As John Findlay recited a number of locations which had figured prominently in various British campaigns, he deliberately omitted naming Lowestoft, where he had actually spent most of his army life training machine gunners. "I knew you at none of those places you have listed," the voice of Eric Saunders said. "We knew each other near Lowestoft."

John managed to repress his surprise and excitement and countered with the question: "Why did you say near Lowestoft?" "Because we were not actually in Lowestoft but in the village of Kessingland, which is located near the larger city," the voice replied.

John Findlay admitted that this was correct. Then, piqued by his inability to remember the man and still suspicious of some kind of fraud, he continued his questioning. "Who was our company commander?" The voice replied that the name had been MacNamara—and scored another hit. Then, to test the voice further, John Findlay said, "You must have been one of my Lewis gunners." "No," the voice answered, evading the trap, "you instructed us in the use of the Hotchkiss, not the Lewis."

The disembodied voice of Eric Saunders continued to answer all questions correctly. The spirit said that he had been killed in France when he had crossed the channel in the big draft in August 1917.

John Findlay asked the voice what it meant by the "big draft." "Don't you remember?" the spirit of the machine gunner wondered a bit incredulously. "There was an extra large draft of men to France that month and even the colonel came out on the parade ground to make a speech to us."

Findlay commented that this was correct. It was, in fact, the only occasion that he could remember in which the colonel had personally said goodbye to the men. Now that the identity of Eric Saunders seemed to have been

Ken Webster of Dodleston, Chester, United Kingdom, lived in a home that had often suffered from paranormal activity. In May 1985 he started to receive messages on his computer, and then written by hand on his floors, from one "Tomas Harden" living in the sixteenth century, who said Katherine Parr was his queen. This photograph shows messages left on the floor of Webster's house.

established, John Findlay asked the next logical question. Why had the machine gunner returned to speak to him? "Because," the voice said with some emotion, "I have never forgotten that good turn that you did for me."

"Eric Saunders" seemed to fade away before further explanation could be delivered identifying the good deed that had been done. After the séance, John told his brother that he could vaguely remember securing leave for one of his gunners under rather unusual circumstances, but he could not honestly remember if Saunders had been that trooper's name. It was not until six months later that John Findlay was able to meet with the man who had been his corporal. The corporal could not remember an Eric Saunders, but he had brought a notebook with him in which he had entered the names of all the men who had served under him.

In the records for the company for 1917, they found the name of Eric Saunders with the notation "August 1917." A red line had been drawn through the name and the words that followed it. The ex-corporal had always drawn a line through the men's names when they were shipped overseas into combat.

John Findlay left to marvel at the proof of survival which had been brought to him by an anonymous machine gunner, who had remembered a long forgotten act of kindness.

⊷⊷⊷

A Mysterious Visit from the Spirit of a Priest

The Personal Experience of Anita Stapleton

Is life after death only a matter of religious beliefs? Is it just wishful thinking? Comfort for the bereaved? Or has it ever been proved?

These questions pass, at one time or another, through the minds of most people. There have been many stories about visions and apparitions, verbal and written messages from "beyond." Are they genuine, or are they caused by imagination, hallucination, self-hypnosis, mental telepathy, or any other form of brainpower? As a person with an inquisitive mind, I have reflected upon these questions many times, until one day I received an answer most unexpectedly.

That day in 1989 had been a normal one for me in my home in Labrador, Queensland, Australia. I had gone about my daily chores, watched television in the evening, and finally went to bed, while my husband was still watching the late movie on TV.

The bedroom was not dark, because the bright light of a full moon fell through the window. I had just lain down, ready to go to sleep, when I suddenly noticed that I was not alone. Right in front of the wardrobe, and looking directly at me was a middle-aged man, dressed like a Catholic priest. I rubbed

In April 2000 a family in northern Wales had strange figures appear on the walls of their home. Crosses, circles, Welsh words, and figures of monks were all visible.

my eyes and pinched my arms to make sure I was fully awake. Yes, I most certainly was. Was I having hallucinations?

The priest was still standing there, looking at me. He was rather a frail man with hollow cheeks. His face showed traces of a hard life and illness. If he had any hair at all, it was covered by his hat. He looked so real, not like a ghost. I was not a bit scared, because he radiated vibrations of utter peace and tranquility. There seemed to be nothing to be afraid of, so I decided to talk to him, keeping my voice as low as possible. "Hello, Father," I said. "God bless you."

"And God bless you, my child," came the priest's prompt reply. He was well spoken, his voice soft. His English accent was not hard to distinguish. After giving me a few personal messages and stressing the point that there is survival after death, he told me who he was. He was Frederick William Faber, and he had lived in England from 1814 to 1863.

When I remarked that at the time of his passing he was only forty-nine years old, he confirmed this and added that he had died of a kidney disease.

After quietly talking about religious matters for a few more minutes, he bade me farewell and disappeared.

This boggled my mind. As late as it was, it was impossible to think of sleep. I wrote down my unearthly visitor's name and other details. Then I told my husband what had happened.

Naturally, his first reaction was disbelief and the assertion that I had been asleep and dreaming. Of course, I knew I had been fully awake.

The whole thing, however, seemed so incredible that doubts came into my mind. The name Faber seemed a bit unusual for an Englishman. Being of German descent, I know quite a few Germans by that name. I recalled a girl, Hildegard Faber, who had gone to school with me. Was this some trickery by my subconscious mind? The incident troubled me for days. How could I ever find out the truth?

Then my husband reminded me of Somerset House in London, where a record of every person born and deceased in Britain is kept. However, he did not know how far back these records went. Father Faber, if indeed he had existed, had been dead for over one hundred years.

Should I write to Somerset House? I hesitated. I did not want to make a fool of myself in case the whole thing was just a hallucination. A few days later, however, I took the plunge and wrote to Somerset House, requesting a search. I was sent a form to fill in, giving details of the required person, and I was asked to include a small search fee. This I did immediately.

Now I waited for a reply from Somerset House. This suspense drama would soon reach its climax. Either I would be told that there was no record of this person or … I did not dare finish this thought.

Two weeks later an airmail letter from London arrived. The sender was Somerset House. My hands were shaky. I trembled like a leaf. I was barely able to open the letter. Then I almost fainted.

The letter contained a certified copy of a death certificate. It stated that Fredrick Will Faber's death had occurred on September 26, 1863 and that he had been forty-nine at the time of his death and had been a doctor of divinity, in Brompton, County of Middlesex. The cause of death was stated as kidney disease. In other words, the official document in my hands confirmed what the apparition had told me.

If this is not a genuine case of a visit from beyond the grave, what is it? An authority like Somerset House would not send a fictitious document halfway around the world to back up someone's fantasy or hallucination. To the best of my knowledge Father Faber had not been a well-known personality, so books would not have been written about him which I might have read and forgotten about. Nobody alive today is old enough to remember him.

While it is true that I have been in England, I did not visit any cemeteries there, which rules out the possibility that I may have seen his name on a tombstone. I am absolutely positive that I had never before heard of Father Faber. As much as I rack my brain, I cannot find a logical explanation, but I now know for sure that there is life after death. To me it has been proved beyond the shadow of a doubt.

> *Author's note: Various Roman Catholic references stated that Father Frederick William Faber was a man of great charm and an eloquent preacher. Fr. Faber is most well known as a writer of hymns, such as "The Shadow of the Rock," The Eternal Father," and "Sweet Savior, bless us ere we go." While Fr. Faber might be known to certain theologians, we are likely to concede Anita Stapleton's contention that he would not be well-known to a layperson. The mystery is why Fr. Faber's spirit should appear to a housewife in Australia and offer her proof of survival after death. As Anita writes, she considers the visitation a great blessing.*

THE RED-HEADED MAN IN THE CLOSET

From the Ghost to Ghost Website: The Personal Experience of Tom

In the mid-80s we bought a two-hundred-year-old farmhouse. Some records came with the house, so we had an idea of some of the changes and remodeling done over time.

The oak pantry door had once been the main entrance to the house through a doorway that had been covered at the turn of the century. This door latched with a three-inch iron thumb latch, but we often found it open when we came in from being outside or when we got up in the mornings. I would blame my wife for not shutting the pantry door, and she would blame me. Finally, it got so annoying that we put a chair against it to keep it closed. That worked for a couple of weeks.

One night, preparing for company, I was mopping the floor in an unused room that had another old main doorway. This door was never used and was bolted from the inside. Yet I found muddy boot prints coming from the door and crossing the room. In the kitchen a bit later I told my wife about the boot prints. She joked that they must have been made by the guy who kept coming in the pantry door and we had locked him out. Looking toward the pantry she said, "It's OK, if you prefer this door, go ahead and use it."

Immediately the latch clicked and the door swung open, pushing the chair aside. Needless to say cold chills ran through both of us. We never worried about the pantry being open again and never saw anything else.

But apparently our three-year-old son did. Sometime later after the incident when the door swung open at my wife's invitation, our son came downstairs and told us that he'd been talking about farming with the red-headed man in his closet. Many kids have an imaginary friend, so we gave it little thought. However, he continued to talk about the red-headed man who told him about farming and wagon making, and warned him to be careful around the river. When we asked about the farmer, our son described him as short, with a red beard, and stooped over with a limp.

A couple of years later, while doing research to register the home with the National Register of Historic Places, I discovered that the man who had lived in the home before the turn of the century was short, bearded, red-haired, and built buckboards for a living. He had also walked with a limp due to an accident. Immediately after his death his son did the remodeling involving the pantry door and turned what had been a sleeping room facing south into the upstairs closet. As for the warning to our son about the river, I learned that the red-headed farmer had had two children drown in the river about a mile away from the house.

A GHOST FIXED HIS PLUMBING

By Mark Stewart

(An earlier version appeared in "Your True Tales" section of paranor mal.about.com.)

I have never forgotten the event that I'm going to describe, because it's such an odd tale. Not scary or startling, but much more subtle. So much so that I didn't even realize anything unusual had happened to me until after the fact.

Here is my experience as I recorded it in 2004:

I live in an older apartment complex, and the plumbing is always breaking down. Recently, I turned on the bathroom sink only to have a growing gush of water pouring out around the handle. It was quite a mess. I sighed, went downstairs, turned off the water flow to the apartment and called the manager's office to report the problem. They said they'd send someone over right away. I was surprised when almost immediately there was a knock at the door and a blond-haired man in a bright red sweatshirt told me he was here to look at the plumbing.

I showed him upstairs; he looked it over, then left to get some tools, since he didn't bring any with him. When he returned, I stayed with him while he worked, offering him a soda and chatting with him. We talked about the usual things—weather, what was wrong with the sink, etc. He fixed it in about ten minutes, I thanked him, and he left. Though I'd never seen him before during one of my previous plumbing problems, he was a friendly guy and I enjoyed talking to him.

It was not long after the plumber left that two more maintenance guys came to the door, and told me they were there to fix the plumbing. I was naturally surprised, and I told them that someone had already been over to fix it. They seemed confused by this, so I described the blond-haired man with the red sweatshirt to them. When I saw that their faces remained blank even after I described the man, who I remembered in great detail, I was a little flabbergasted since the man had been in my apartment working for ten minutes, but the maintenance department had no idea who he was. They wanted to check the sink anyway, so I let them in and they looked it over thoroughly and then asked me about it again.

I told them what the problem had been and what the blond man had told me about it. Still looking a little confused, they said it was completely repaired and that there was nothing they needed to do. Later that day the apartment manager called me on the phone to ask about the plumbing. I told her about the blond man fixing it for me and about the two other maintenance men coming by later and checking it over. She asked me to describe the blond man, which I did in detail, and then she flat out asked me if I myself had fixed the plumbing problem. I know next to nothing about plumbing and told her so. I was starting to suspect she was just as confused as the two maintenance workers had been, so I asked her for a straight answer: Did she know who this blond man was who came to my apartment?

Finally, a little dismayed, she admitted that she had no idea who I was talking about and neither did the maintenance department. They had no employees who matched that description and the work order for my apartment had only been given to the two men who showed up after the blond man had already fixed the problem. When she told me this, I remembered how the blond plumber had arrived almost instantly to fix the problem, but strangely had arrived with no tools and had to leave to get them. I asked her about this, but she had no answer as to how he could have arrived so quickly after I had called the office. After that, I've always looked around when I see maintenance people working here and there on the property, but I have never seen the blond man again.

11
SPEAKING TO SPIRITS: THE MYSTERY OF MEDIUMSHIP

꧁꧂

MEDIUMS, SHAMANS, AND SPIRIT CONTACT

The idea that we survive physical death, that some part of our being is immortal, profoundly affects the lives of those who harbor such a belief. While Christianity, Islam, Judaism, and many other religions promise their followers some form of a life after death, throughout all of human history many thousands of men and women feel that they have received proof of a life beyond the grave based on the evidence of survival that manifests through spirit mediums.

I first began investigating and researching spirit mediums in 1957 and subsequently had "sittings" with dozens of men and women throughout the United States and Canada who believed that they had become qualified in some special way to form a link between the living and the dead and to relay messages of comfort, support, and personal information from the next world. While some mediums gain impressions from the spirits in a fully conscious state, others place themselves into a trance, which is often accompanied by manifestations that appear to defy known physical laws, such as the movement of objects without anyone touching them, the levitation of the mediums' own body, and the materialization of spirit forms of the deceased. Perhaps the essential attribute that qualifies one to be a medium is an extreme or abnormal sensitivity which seemingly allows the spirits to access the individual's psyche more easily. For this reason, mediums are often referred to as "sensitives."

After over fifty years of research into various aspects of spirit communication and related phenomena, I have reached the opinion that those with mediu-

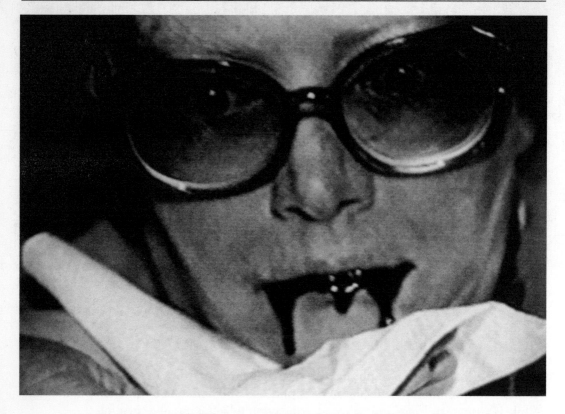

During a séance, blood begins to exude from the mouth of a medium. Seventeenth-century alchemist and freemason Prince Raimundo de Sangro de Sansevero was reported to be manifesting through this medium.

mistic abilities are individuals whose psyches preserve certain of the ancient qualities and requirements of shamanism. A shaman is one who serves his people by acting as an intermediary to the spirit world. Originally, the term "shaman" was applied to the spirit doctors and exorcists of the Tungus of Siberia, but in recent years the title has been applied to the medicine men and women of the various North American tribes. These shamans serve their people as mediums, healers, and visionaries. Many tribal traditionalists still revere the wisdom that is shared by those men and women who maintain the shamanic traditions and who travel to the other side in the company of their spirit helper.

Anthropologist Ivar Lissner, who spent a great deal of time among the Tungus of Siberia, as well as native peoples in North America, defines a shaman as one "who knows how to deal with spirits and influence them....The essential characteristic of the shaman is his excitement, his ecstasy and trance-like condition.... [The elements which constitute this ecstasy are] a form of self-severance from mundane existence, a state of heightened sensibility, and spiritual awareness. The shaman loses outward consciousness and becomes inspired or enraptured. While in this state of enthusiasm, he sees dreamlike apparitions, hears voices, and receives visions of truth. More than that, his soul sometimes leaves his body to go wandering."

During séances, spirit mediums, very often working in a trance state, claim to be under the direction of a spirit control or spirit guide that serves as an intermediary between themselves and the spirits of deceased men and women. Once contact has been made with particular spirits in the other world, the guide speaks through the medium and relays messages to the sitters, those men and women who have assembled in the séance room for the opportunity of hearing words of comfort or guidance from their departed loved ones.

In the shamanic tradition, the spirit guide or spirit helper is usually received by those who choose to participate in a vision quest. Before initiates embark upon this ordeal, tribal elders and shamans tutor them for many weeks on what to expect and what is expected of them. In many shamanic traditions, the spirit helper serves as an ambassador from the world of spirits to the world of humans and often manifests in animal form to serve as a kind of chaperone during visits to other dimensions of reality.

For the more contemporary spirit mediums, who often prefer to call themselves "channels," the guide may represent itself as a being who once lived as a human on Earth or as a light being, an extraterrestrial, or even an angel. Regardless of the semantics involved, in my opinion, today's mediums and channels follow the basic procedures of ancient shamanic traditions.

MEDIUMS AND THEIR SPIRIT GUIDES

In the Western world, the concept of a spirit guide goes back to antiquity. The great philosopher Socrates furnishes us with the most notable example in ancient times of an individual who freely referred to a guiding voice as his daemon (not to be confused with "demon," a fallen angel or a negative, possessing entity). Daemon is better translated as guardian angel or muse, and the philosopher believed that his guardian spirit kept vigil and warned him of approaching danger.

Spirit mediums believe that while they are in an entranced state of consciousness, they fall under the control of a particular spirit that has become their special guide and who speaks through them and works all manner of mysterious phenomena on their behalf. Although this spirit was once a living person, it has, since its time in the spirit world, become greatly elevated in spiritual awareness.

While some psychical researchers maintain that the only difference between those individuals who proclaim themselves to be psychic and those who call themselves spirit mediums is that psychics attribute their talents to some manifestation of extrasensory perception—that is, clairvoyance, precognition, telepathy—while mediums attribute their powers to an interaction with unseen spirit intelligences. Other researchers have theorized that the spirit guide may be an as yet little-known power of the mind which enables the medium's subjective level of consciousness to dramatize another personality, complete with a full range of personal characteristics

Of course, mediums perceive the spirit guide in a very different manner. While many of them may admit that the action of the subjective mind is not entirely eliminated during trance and the arrival of the guide, they will insist that their subconscious mind is taken over and controlled by a spirit entity of great compassion and wisdom.

In his autobiography written in collaboration with Marguerite Harmon Bro, the highly respected medium Arthur Augustus Ford (1897–1971), an ordained minister of the Disciples of Christ Church, explained the working relationship that he enjoyed with his spirit guide, Fletcher. According to Ford, Fletcher had been a boyhood friend who had been killed in action in Europe during World War I.

When Ford wished to enter trance, he would lie down on a couch or lean back in a comfortable chair and breathe slowly and rhythmically until he felt an in-drawing of energy at the solar plexus. Then he focused his attention on Fletcher's face, as he had come to know it, until gradually he felt as if his guide's face had pressed into his own at which instant he experienced a "a sense of shock," as if he were fainting or "passing out." At this point, Ford said, he lost consciousness—and when he awakened at the completion of a séance, it was as if he had had a "good nap."

Olof Jonsson, one of the greatest physical mediums of the twentieth century, once told me that while he accessed the Universal Mind through meditation, he was aware of spirit beings on other planes of existence. Olof, who was the psychic-sensitive who participated in astronaut Edgar Mitchell's Apollo 14 ESP experiment between Earth and the moon in February 1971, said that we humans might interpret these intelligences in any way that would be most compatible with our own psyches. "One person might perceive such an entity as an Indian," he said, "another as an old wise man, yet someone else as a holy figure. But all these seemingly separate beings are bodiless forms of benign intelligence. These intelligences cloak themselves as Tibetans or cosmic teachers because the human brain will more readily accept an entity that looks like a human being, rather than a shapeless, shimmering intelligence."

Olof went on to say that he believed that these spirit beings have the ability to absorb our actions and our thoughts so that they may know better how to direct us toward cosmic harmony. "These beings avoid language and work with us on an unconscious level," he said. "Telepathy affords us proof that language means nothing to the unconscious. We do not think in words, but in ideas and feelings. What language does God speak? The feelings and the harmony communicated between the unconscious levels of self comprise the one 'language' that all people understand."

Bertie Catchings, a remarkable psychic-sensitive and spirit medium from Texas, once remarked that when a person dies, the soul becomes more alive than it was in the flesh. She was able to relay messages from the deceased to their loved ones because, in her view, "The spirit wishes to communicate with loved ones and let them know that they are alive and that they are well-off in another dimension." Bertie said that many spirits feel surprised and elated when they truly find out what has happened to them. "They usually have so many friends and family members on the other side that they enjoy quite a reunion, quite a wonderful occasion."

Regarding her spirit guides, Bertie said that sometimes she would be awakened in the middle of the night by a pleasant voice speaking to her. "I am told things that are going to happen or things that I must do," she explained. "I am used to these things. They don't bother me."

In a controlled experiment, Deon Frey, an exceptionally powerful medium, sent her spirit guide Dr. Richard Speidel from Chicago to London, England, to move a large mirror that hung above the heads of the witnesses. Deon had her first spirit visitation on the night her father died. "I was fifteen," she told me. "Eternal life was proved to me that night. The spirit of my father, who had never been a churchgoer or a believer in the afterlife, appeared at my bedside and said, 'If I live after death, then everyone lives.'" According to Deon, Dr. Richard Speidel first appeared to her in 1942. He was of sober appearance, dressed formally in a black coat with a black bow tie. "I have been sent to be your guide and your teacher," he told her.

I conducted many séances with Deon as the medium, and she believed as I do that all those who apply themselves to serious study, discipline, and discernment could develop mediumistic or shamanistic abilities. "The creative God-force works through us at all times," she said. "The more we use it, the more we are able to grow within ourselves. You must learn to experience the light, let it flow through you, giving it force so that others may feel a portion of it through you. Become a channel for the light, and you will leave a portion of it with whomever you meet."

Popular Chicago psychic sensitive Irene F. Hughes, who served as the medium in investigations presented in chapters 1 and 2, explained how she can tell when her spirit guide wishes to bring forth a message from a discarnate entity on the other side. "I am quiet, completely relaxed, deep in meditation," she said. "I may be alone at home or among friends in a prayer circle. A tingling sensation, similar to a chill, begins on my right ankle, then on my left. Slowly the tingling spreads to cover my entire body. It is as though a soft silken skin has been pulled over me, glove-tight—even over my face, changing its features—yet comfortable and protective. At this point I am on the way to that golden flow of consciousness that we earthlings term the spirit plane. I am in semi-trance. Were I in full trance, I could not recall a single detail."

As her involvement with the spirit plane progresses, Ms. Hughes says that her body becomes as "icy cold as death itself," yet a delightful warmth engulfs her inner self. Soon, Kaygee, her spirit teacher, appears, smiles, bows to her as a trusted friend, indicating approval of her incursion into the spirit world. By a slight waving of his hand, he ushers in those of the spirit plane who wish to speak through her. "I am bound to my spirit teacher by ties that are ethereal, yet mighty as a coaxial cable," she said. "Every thought that flashes through his consciousness becomes crystal clear also in my consciousness."

MEDIUMS, CHANNELS, AND ESP

Certain psychic researchers maintain that the principal difference between a psychic sensitive and a trance medium is that psychics or intuitives attribute their talents to some manifestations of extrasensory ability, such as clairvoyance, precognition, or telepathy, whereas spirit mediums credit their abilities to their interaction with spirits. Some researchers have observed that the intelligence exhibited by the alleged spirits seems always on a level with that of the individual through whom they manifest. These psychic investigators may admit that on occasion the information relayed often rises above the medium's known objective knowledge, but they point out that the limits of the subjective mind are not yet ultimately defined.

Skeptics point out that the spirits can often be controlled by the power of suggestion and can be made to respond to questions that have no basis in reality. These critical investigators state that they have been able to establish communication with an imaginary person as readily as a real one.

Some mediums have found themselves the object of ridicule or exposure when they have relayed a "spirit message" from a fictitious individual whose identity was supplied by a skeptical researcher or when they have relayed profound ghostly advice from a person who is actually still alive.

In the 1970s, after the publication of Jane Roberts' books *The Seth Material* and *Seth Speaks* "channeling" became a more popular name for mediumship, and it remains so to the present day. Jane made spirit contact with an entity named Seth after undergoing a trance state while Robert Butts, her husband, recorded the thought, ideas, and concepts communicated by the ethereal being in notebooks. The material dictated by Seth was of very high quality and extremely provocative, well-suited to a generation of maturing sixties' flower children and baby boomers. It wasn't long before Seth discussion groups around the nation were reciting such concepts as "we each create our own reality," "our point of power lies in the present," and "we are all gods couched in our own creaturehood." Nor was it long before "channelers" were emerging in such large numbers throughout the land that for a time it seemed as though every strip mall boasted the office of a professional spirit communicator. Often, these individuals were "instant mediums," suggestible men and women who had attended a new age workshop or read *Seth Speaks* and became convinced that a spirit guide was speaking freely through them. Most of these gullible and self-styled channelers soon vanished and returned to their day jobs. On the other hand, there were more talented and con-

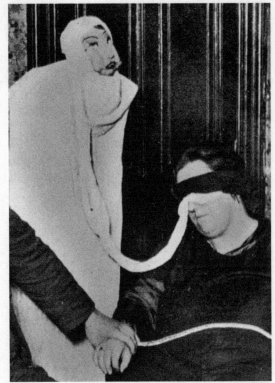

During a séance held in the 1930s, medium Helen Duncan helps an ectoplasmic spirit materialize.

vincing individuals who attained large audiences of devoted followers and achieved international celebrity status. In the mid–1980s, it was standing-room only when Jach Pursel channeled "Lazaris," Kevin Ryerson hosted "McPherson" and other spirit entities, and J.Z. Knight strutted across the stage and boomed forth teachings for "Ramtha," a thirty-five-thousand-year-old warrior from the lost continent of Lemuria.

Whether it was in the minds of their audiences or in the minds of the channelers, the designation of "mediums" apparently seemed to conjure up images of the traditional, darkened séance parlors of an earlier time that seemed distasteful and outdated in an age of technology. In the twenty-first century, spirit communicators very often relay messages from guides and master teachers in the full light of a platform setting or a television studio.

Whatever title is preferred by those who claim to relay messages from the spirits, the process of communication remains the same; spirit entities occupy the physical bodies of the "channelers" or the "mediums" and speak through them. And the interest in after-death communication has never been stronger. Such individuals as Sylvia Browne, James Van Praagh, and John

Scene from a séance.

Edward have moved into the national spotlight with their own syndicated television programs and a seemingly endless number of media appearances.

Beginning in the latter decades of the nineteenth century, spirit mediums began to contend with an increasingly materialistic and mechanistic science that did a great deal to obliterate the idea of a soul and the duality of mind and body. The concept of an eternal soul was being steadily eroded by an emphasis on brain cells, conditioned responses, and memory patterns that could exist only while the body remained alive.

Sometime in the 1940s, Dr. J. B. Rhine summarized the research on survival evidence provided by spirit mediums in the laboratory to be inconclusive.

However, in March, 2001, scientists involved in a unique study of spirit mediums at the University of Arizona announced that their findings were so extraordinary that they raised fundamental questions about the survival of human consciousness after death. Professor Gary Schwartz, who led the team of researchers, concluded that there were highly skilled spirit mediums who were able to deal directly with the dead, rather than merely manipulate the minds of the sitters. In the opinion of the scientists, all the data that they gathered was "consistently in accord with survival of consciousness after death." Based on all their data to date, Professor Schwartz said, "The most parsimonious explanation is that the mediums are in direct communication with the deceased."

SUBJECTING A SPIRIT GUIDE TO RIGOROUS TESTING PROCEDURES

Eileen Garrett was a gifted medium who throughout her long career never ceased to study the phenomena of her mediumship in a manner that was remarkably detached. As a child she was ill a great deal, and at a very early age she began to experience visions and to see "people" who were not there.

She did not realize that she was developing as a trance medium until she was a good deal older and accidentally fell asleep at a public meeting. When she awakened, she learned that the voices of deceased relatives of many of the people gathered that night had spoken through her. One gentleman present explained to Eileen what had happened to her and informed her that he had communicated with an Oriental spirit named Uvani, who would thereafter be her spirit guide and work with her to prove the validity of the survival of the spirit after physical death.

Eileen Garrett was so horrified at the prospect of an Oriental spirit sharing her mind and body that for weeks she slept with the light burning in her room to ward off the advances of Uvani. Later, someone at a London spiritualist society did his best to explain away her misgivings about sharing her psyche with a spirit guide. He assured her that Uvani would not be at all interested in her daily and private life and that the spirit guide's entire purpose would be based on a sincere wish to be of service to humanity.

During the years in which she perfected her communication skills with Uvani, Eileen Garrett often expressed doubts about her spirit guide's psychic independence, and she frequently voiced her suspicions that he might only be a segment of her own subconscious mind. The respected psychical researcher Hereward Carrington administered an extensive battery of personality tests to both the medium and her spirit guide so that researchers might compare the two sets of responses. Eileen Garrett and Uvani sat through sessions of the Bernreuter Personality Inventory, the Thurstone Attitude Scale, the Woodworth Neurotic Inventory, the Rorschach Test of inkblots, and a seemingly endless number of word association tests.

Carrington concluded that in cases of genuine mediumship, such as that expressed by Eileen Garrett, the spirit guide succeeded in bringing through a vast mass of supernormal information which could not be obtained

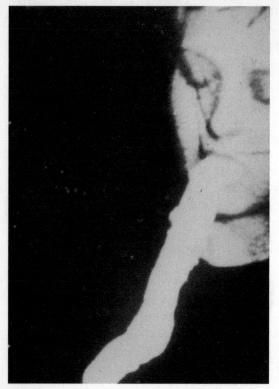

This medium reportedly materialized ectoplasm, or spirit essence, which is spewing from her mouth.

through normal sensory means. The spirit guide, he theorized, appeared to act as some sort of "psychic catalyzer."

The psychical researcher went on to explain that the function of a spirit guide seems to be that of an intermediary; and whether the entity is truly a spirit or a personification of the medium's subconscious, it is only through the cooperation of the guide that veridical messages are obtained. The essential and significant difference between the ordinary secondary personality as observed in pathological cases and the personality of the spirit guide in mediumistic expression is that the spirit entity brings forth supernormal information.

"In the pathological cases," Carrington theorized, "we seem to have a mere splitting of the mind, while in the mediumistic cases we have to deal with a ... personality which is ... in touch or contact, in some mysterious way, with another (spiritual) world, from which it derives information and through which genuine messages often come."

During the course of extensive testing, Uvani emphasized the fact that although he controlled Eileen Garrett's underconsciousness, he had absolutely no control over her conscious mind—nor would he consider such control to be right. The spirit guide also clarified that he had no interest in the medium's normal thinking processes or in the activities of her conscious mind. The trance state was the only time when Uvani and other spirit entities could utilize Eileen Garrett's underconsciousness as a vehicle for their communication with humans.

When Carrington asked how Uvani would know when Eileen was ready for him to manifest, the spirit guide replied that he would receive a "telegraphed impression" that the mediumistic instrument was ready. "The moment that the conscious mind becomes very low, then the soul-body becomes more vibrant," Uvani explained.

During the course of the experiments, Carrington also asked a question which we are certain has occurred to every psychic investigator who has every sat with a medium: Why is that spirit entities who claim foreign origins, such as Uvani who claimed to be from the Orient, are able to speak fluent English through their mediums?

Uvani immediately replied that he did not speak English: "It is my instrument [Eileen Garrett] who speaks. I impress my thought upon her, on that 'figment' on which I must work upon, but no word of mine actually comes to you. The Instrument is impressed by my personal contact." Thoughts, Uvani went on to elaborate, are impressed and expressed automatically.

"I Am Your Control, Your Teacher, Your Friend"

It was on June 13, 1961, that Irene Hughes' spirit teacher first appeared to her. She was recovering from surgery, and when the turbaned Oriental materialized in her bedroom, she did not know at first if she was suffering from hallucinations or if she had died in surgery without realizing it.

The spirit entity permitted Irene to test it, and promised to fulfill three desires of her choosing. When the being, who called himself "Kaygee" had granted her wishes, he led Irene back through a dramatic past-life recall of a prior existence in Egypt—and he predicted in what manner she would soon meet the other principals from her Egyptian life experience. "I am your control, your teacher, and your friend," Kaygee told her. "You will learn many things unknown to others. You now have the key to all of life. Use it well, and it will grow. I will always be there to help you."

As their spiritual relationship progressed, Irene could see that the entity that she had at first assumed to be a turbaned Indian was quite obviously a Japanese gentleman.

Once he held out a hand of friendship, and when Irene accepted it, she was startled to find it solid, warm, filled with life—although the air about Kaygee was chilled. Kaygee explained that it had been necessary for him to leave the earth plane before Irene was about to fully achieve total development. "I had to go before you could come," he said.

On another occasion, Kaygee told her that he would teach her that love is truly the whole law of life, that "love is the mightiest power in the universe. You will learn this and teach this and lecture to people about this eternal truth. You will be given the power to see beyond the thin veil of the earth plane."

Irene Hughes wanted to know who Kaygee had been on the earth plane. In response, the spirit teacher provided the name of his daughter, who, at that time, was in the United States, studying at Cornell University. "Write to her," he bade Irene. "She shall verify who I was on the earth plane." Irene wrote down the name and address of the woman Kaygee claimed was his daughter. She decided that she had nothing to lose by writing such a letter of inquiry—although she felt that the envelope was likely to be returned marked "addressee unknown."

In five days, Irene received a reply from the woman, verifying that she was indeed Kaygee's daughter. She went on to declare that her father had been one of the greatest Japanese Christians who had ever lived and that he had died in April of that year, 1961.

> "I had to accept the fact that his spirit was coming to work through me."

"The fact that the name and the address were correct seemed to me to be most evidential of Kaygee's survival after death," Irene said. "I had to accept the fact that his spirit was coming to work through me. He had lived a life of poverty, and he had given his life to help others. Perhaps he felt that I was so physically, emotionally, and psychically constructed that he could work through me. I considered myself honored that he had chosen me as a channel by which he might continue certain facets of his work."

Shortly after the initial appearance of Kaygee, Irene Hughes had confided in two highly respectable members of the prestigious Spiritual Frontiers Fellowship and had relayed her experiences with the spirit entity. After she received verification from his daughter, she allowed them to read both the letter that she had written to Kaygee's daughter and the letter that she had received in reply from the young woman, confirming the evidence of survival which the spirit being had channeled through her mediumship.

Irene recalled the time when Kaygee spoke to her of his life and how he had fought for the living truth in the slums and along the highways. He had met with continued opposition in life, but now he was at peace. "I know my work will go on through you and others like you," Kaygee said. "You, Irene, are a prophet, so filled with the knowledge of love and life that you are my vibratory equal. I have chosen you to work through, as you will see."

<hr />

THE APPEARANCE OF A SPIRIT GUIDE TRANSFORMED HER LIFE
The experience of T.K.H.

I was going through a lot of emotional trauma, raising four sons alone, becoming desperate about my finances, beginning a new relationship that seemed uncertain. I was at the point where I was beginning to think that if there really was a God, he sure had a grudge against me for some reason.

Then one spring night in 1991, just as I was drifting off to sleep, something made me open my eyes—and there he was! I can still see him standing there in his drab robe, the hood closely draped around his darkly-shadowed face, a rope loosely knotted around his waist. He was about five-feet-eight, of slim to average build; and, by the look of his hand in the moonlight, he had an olive complexion.

After an initial feeling of fear, I immediately became calm. He said nothing, but, very slowly, brought his hand close to mine so that the backs of our hands nearly touched. I think that our auras must have mingled somehow and that was the means of communication.

I have a hard time finding words to describe all of this, but at that moment I was filled with a feeling of total and complete unconditional love. If there had been a gauge to measure my heart and spirit, it would have shown maximum capacity. The forgiveness and the absolute divine lovingness that he was conveying brought tears to my eyes—and I had the feeling that this was but one molecule of one grain of sand in an entire universe of love. I felt that if he were to turn up his love energy to full power, there could be no way in which my mind would ever be able to handle it. Then I fell asleep.

This visitation brought me back to my senses spiritually, and it seemed to have been a turning point in my life. In essence, I think that I was being told to "let go, and let God." I wish I could have seen his face!

<hr />

MATERIALIZATION: THE ULTIMATE MEDIUMISTIC MANIFESTATION

Perhaps the ultimate in séance phenomena is the materialization of a spirit form that is in some way recognizable to one or more of the sitters. In Spiritualist churches and camps, such phenomena are often accomplished through the utilization of a cabinet from which the materialized spirit emerges and communicates with those gathered around the medium. Spirit cabinets may be elaborate wooden structures or they may simply be blankets strung across wires in order to give the medium some privacy while in trance.

"The miracle of materialization," Maurice Barbanell writes in *This Is Spiritualism*, "is that in a few minutes there is reproduced in the séance room the birth which normally takes nine months in the mother's womb." Numerous psychic researchers have claimed to have seen a nearly invisible cord which links the materialized spirit figure to the medium and all have made the obvious comparison to an umbilical cord. The name that Spiritualists give to the substance which comprises the spirit image is "ectoplasm," and they contend that it is drawn from the medium's body.

Barbanell, through information given to him by his spirit guide, Silver Birch, claimed that ectoplasm is ideoplastic by nature and may be molded by the psychic "womb" of the medium into a representation of the human body.

Spirit beings compound ectoplasm until it assumes a human form that "breathes, walks, and talks, and is apparently complete even to fingernails."

French researcher Dr. Charles Richet christened ectoplasm in the 1920s, but Baron A. von Schrenck-Notzing, a German investigator of the paranormal, gained a medium's permission to "amputate" some of the material and to analyze it. He found it to be colorless, odorless, slightly alkaline, fluid with traces of skin discs, minute particles of flesh, sputum, and granulates of the mucous membrane.

I have witnessed what I would consider authentic ectoplasm issuing from a spirit medium on only about half a dozen occasions. There remain very few contemporary mediums who even attempt to produce ectoplasmic materializations in the séance room. Today, the vast majority of séances conducted by professional mediums fit into the categories of

1. "direct-voice" communication, during which the spirit guide speaks directly to the sitters through a medium who appears in a deep state of trance;

2. "twilight" communication, during which the medium in a very light altered state of consciousness relays messages from the guide in a conversational exchange with the sitters; or

3. a "reading," in which the medium in a fully conscious state presents a series of images and messages that are "shown" or "told" by spirits who have some personal connection to the sitters.

A MESSAGE TO MOTHER FROM BEYOND THE GRAVE

On February 10, 1933, Maurice Barbanell (1902–1981), the founder and editor of *Psychic News*, sat in a darkened séance room with medium Estelle Roberts (1899–1970) and heard the spirit voice of a young girl begin to speak in a hesitant manner through the spirit trumpet. Barbanell, who was himself an accomplished medium, encouraged the disembodied voice. "Come along. Come and talk to me."

"I am Bessy Manning and I want you to send a message to my mother," the voice told him. "Mother has been reading some of your articles about direct-voice séances in *Psychic News*. Please tell her you spoke to me." Barbanell assured the spirit voice that he would send a message the next morning.

Pleased with his response, Bessy continued: "Tell Mother I still have my long braids. I am twenty-two and have blue eyes. I died with tuberculosis last Easter. I have brought along my brother Tommy who was killed by a motorcar accident nine years ago. Could you bring Mother here?"

Although Barbanell was sympathetic to the request, he needed more essential information to fulfill the spirit's request. "I must know where your mother lives," he told her. The reply came without hesitation: "14 Canterbury Street, Blackburn."

The next day Barbanell sent a telegram to Bessy Manning's mother telling her that Red Cloud, Estelle Roberts' spirit control, had brought her daughter to a séance the night before. The address which the spirit had given Barbanell proved to be correct. Within a few days, Barbanell had received a letter that told of the Mannings' "glorious happiness" at the contact which Red Cloud's spirit circle had achieved with Bessy.

Mrs. Manning substantiated the information which the spirit had given Barbanell during the direct-voice séance. Bessy had passed on the preceding Easter, and her brother had been killed in an automobile accident nine years before.

> "I regard Bessy Manning's return as flawless evidence for the afterlife,"

"I regard Bessy Manning's return as flawless evidence for the afterlife," Barbanell stated in his books *The Trumpet Shall Sound* (1933) and *This Is Spiritualism* (1959). "No theories of telepathy or the subconscious mind can explain it away. No suggestion of collusion or any other kind of fraud can be entertained. Mrs. Manning had never met Estelle Roberts, or corresponded with her or any member of her family. Neither had she written to me or anyone who attended these direct-voice séances. Yet her daughter's full name and address had been given, accompanied by a complete message which was accurate in every detail."

Barbanell later arranged for Mrs. Manning to travel to London so that she might speak to the voice of Bessy and judge for herself whether or not her daughter had survived the grave. "I heard my own daughter speak to me, in the same old loving way, and with the same peculiarities of speech," Mrs. Manning wrote to Barbanell. "She spoke of incidents that I know for a positive fact no other person could know. I, her mother, am the best judge, and I swear before Almighty God it was Bessy.... I have no fear of so-called death. I am looking forward to the glorious meeting with my loved ones."

<hr />

ARTHUR FORD'S TELEVISED SÉANCE WITH BISHOP JAMES PIKE

In February 1966, at the age of twenty-two, Episcopal Bishop James A. Pike's son committed suicide. On several occasions shortly after his son's death, Bishop Pike found straight pins paired together, simulating clock hands indicating the time of James, Jr.'s suicide.

On September 3, 1967, through the mediumship of the Reverend Arthur Ford, an ordained minister of the Disciples of Christ Church, Bishop Pike heard spirit messages which he believed to be from his deceased son. The séance, which took place in Toronto, Ontario, Canada, was unique in that it was not limited to a drape-darkened room, but was taped and broadcast on CTV, the private Canadian television network. Allen Spraggett, the man who arranged the televised séance, was a former pastor of the United Church of Canada, and at the time of the spirit sitting was religion editor of the *Toronto Star*.

On September 17 the program was televised and it precipitated a great furor in the field of psychic research. The controversial bishop, frequently spotlighted in the news for his dispute with the church over interpretation of certain traditional doctrines, stood his ground as firmly on the matter of communication with the dead as he had on other emotion-charged religious issues. Later, he would tell media representatives, that he firmly believed that he had spoken directly with his son, James A. Pike, Jr., through the medium, without the intermediary aid of Ford's customary spirit control, Fletcher. However, Spraggett told me later when we discussed the séance that it had been Fletcher who had initially brought forth the bishop's son and other communicating personalities and continued to serve as a control.

Just prior to beginning the séance, Reverend Ford explained that he would go into a trance or a sleep. He placed a dark handkerchief over his eyes, commenting that it was easier to go to sleep if one did not have light, and the bright lights of the television studio would make the acquisition of the trance state that much more difficult.

"So many people associate spirit contact with dark rooms," Reverend Ford said, "so I'll leave you [Bishop Pike and other observers] in the light. Any [genuine phenomenon] that takes place in the dark can usually take place in the light."

Once Reverend Ford had attained the trance state, Fletcher soon made an appearance. Fletcher said that he had two people eager to speak with others who were waiting. The first communicating entity was that of a young man who had been mentally disturbed and confused before he departed. The young man revealed himself as James A. Pike, Jr. He spoke of how happy he was to be able to talk to his father.

Next Fletcher introduced George Zobrisky, a lawyer who had taught history at Virginia Theological Seminary. Zobrisky said that he had "more or less shaped" Bishop Pike's thinking, a point which the clergyman readily conceded. The spirit of Louis Pitt then sent greetings to the Bishop; Pitt was acting chaplain at Columbia University before Pike became chairman of the Department of Religion.

Fletcher next described an older gentleman whose lectures Bishop Pike had often attend. The man had a Scottish name, and in life had had two cats,

At a séance held on December 25, 1919, Polish medium Franek Kluski reportedly materialized a spirit (center).

which had formerly belonged to James, Jr. "And there is something about Corpus Christi." Bishop Pike said that there was a college at Cambridge by that name. Spraggett asked Fletcher if he could not provide a name. The spirit control stated that the name sounded something like "McKenny, McKennon, Donald McKennon." Donald McKennon, Bishop Pike confirmed, had been the principal influence on his thinking at Cambridge.

The last spirit to come forward told Fletcher that he had called himself an "ecclesiastical panhandler" in life. Bishop Pike seemed to know at once who had carried such an appellation. Spraggett again asked Fletcher for a name. "Oh," said the spirit control, "like Black or something. Carl. Black. Block."

"Carl Block," Bishop Pike agreed, "the fourth bishop of California, my predecessor. I admired and respected you, and yet I hoped you weren't feeling too badly about some changes." Speaking through Fletcher, Bishop Block told his successor that he had done a magnificent job, and that he had magnificent work yet to do. Bishop Pike told the Associated Press that he did not see how any research done by Reverend Ford could have developed such intimate

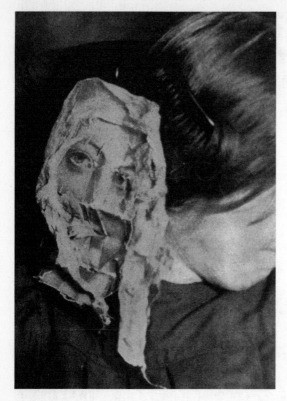

An ectoplasmic face materializes on the neck of famous medium Eva C.

details about his life and such facts about the roles that certain individuals had played in shaping his thinking. The clergyman felt that the details had been quite cumulative. They were not just bits and pieces or an assortment of facts. "They added together," he said. "They made a pattern. Also, the persons who communicated had one thing in common—they were in varying ways connected with the development of my thought. They knew me at particularly significant times in my life, turning points."

The Controversy Begins

Allen Spraggett told the Associated Press that he while he accepted the possibility that true spirit contact had been achieved by Revered Ford, he was certain that during the séance there had been strong evidence for some sort of communication or extrasensory perception at the least.

Martin Ebon, formerly administrative secretary of the Parapsychology Foundation in New York, responded to a request for comment by saying that Bishop Pike represented "the kind of searching individual and researcher who has found subjective proof in an area where many scientists … hold that objective proof cannot be found with current investigative methods." Ebon speculated that while the séance may not offer conclusive proof of survival, it demonstrated a "high and specialized form of E.S.P. The medium could have picked Pike's memory."

Parapsychologists, ever mindful of the scientific method, were careful to qualify their remarks; they emphasized the fact that they had not been present, so they could not evaluate with certainty and stressed that one really could not determine very much from a single séance.

Dr. Karlis Osis, director of research for the American Society of Psychical Research, said that there were some facts discovered in parapsychological research which suggested the possibility of survival. Dr. J. B. Rhine of the Foundation for Research on the Nature of Man stated that it has been established there is a nonphysical capacity of the human mind, but stressed the point that he could offer no conclusion in regard to the validity of the communication which Bishop Pike had received.

Arthur Ford and the Houdini Code

Arthur Ford was no stranger to controversy resulting from his abilities as a spirit medium. In 1929, he received a message that he believed he had obtained from the spirit of the late master magician Houdini (1874–1926) and conveyed it to Mrs. Houdini. Immediately a storm of fierce arguments erupted in the media. It was well known that before his death Houdini had left a coded message with his wife, telling her he would send that particular message to her from beyond the grave to prove life after death. Some feature writers championed the authenticity of Ford's relayed after-death communication from Houdini, while others quoted his widow as saying that the message was not correct.

On February 9, 1929, however, according to Ford's supporters, Beatrice (Bess) Houdini wrote the medium to state with finality: "Regardless of any statement made to the contrary: I wish to declare that the message, in its entirety, and in the agreed upon sequence, given to me by Arthur Ford, is the correct message prearranged between Mr. Houdini and myself."

Harry Houdini.

Eventually it came to be widely known that the various words in the Houdini code spelled out the secret message: "Rosabelle, believe." Ford's detractors argued that there was nothing paranormal involved in the medium's ability to provide the secret message to Mrs. Houdini. Rather, it was divulged, Ford had carefully studied an interview that Bess Houdini had given in 1928 in which she had inadvertently revealed the code to several reporters when she explained that the message her late husband would pass on from the world beyond was based on their old vaudeville mind reading routine that used a secret spelling code.

Bishop Pike Continued to Explore the Other Side

Even before the séance in which his son communicated with him, Bishop Pike had expressed belief in the possibility of contacting the dead. Before the séance, in answer to a direct question on the subject, Bishop Pike had said that he firmly believed in life after death. He also held the belief that on occasion there could be communication with those beyond with the living.

REAL GHOSTS, RESTLESS SPIRITS, AND HAUNTED PLACES

In 1967, Bishop Pike wrote *The Other Side: An Account of My Experiences with Psychic Phenomena* with his wife, Diane Kennedy Pike. In 1968, he renounced the church to form the Center for Religious Transition. James Albert Pike died on the expedition that he and Diane undertook to the Judean desert in 1969. In 1970, Diane Kennedy Pike published *The Search*, which chronicled those last days of her husband's great spiritual quest.

In 1972, while I was speaking with Diane Kennedy Pike regarding spiritual matters, she said that she thought it was important to make a distinction between messages that came through from the spirit world and a higher dimension of awareness. "If Higher Beings choose to relate something to humans," she said, "I think they do so in a very selective fashion. I am sure that there is always some distortion that goes on when [messages] are brought in from other states of consciousness into expression on this plane. Many times people seem to get into mental things that are really out of their own idea realm. They think they are communicating with Higher Intelligences, but really they are not. Of course, the trick becomes, how do you know the difference?"

Diane said that her personal feeling was that the test that Jesus of Nazareth gave concerning spiritual manifestations is really the safest one: By their works, you shall know them." In her opinion, those who have received a revelation from the higher realm will manifest noble characteristics or qualities in their life and understanding. There will emerge in them a deeper sense of peace as a result of their communication and a deeper sense of wholeness.

"I think a person who is on his own mental trip will manifest what we call ego qualities, which is a kind of deceptiveness, self-assertiveness, pride and so forth, which are not really characteristics of highly developed spiritual people," she said. Diane added that any spirit communication or alleged revelation from a higher realm that is fear-oriented, "is obviously not of the higher spiritual realm." In her opinion, such a "so-called revelation that indicates that you should fear something coming to you from somewhere else or that incites fear in other people when you tell them about it" should be immediately disregarded by the percipient.

In 1981, Diane assumed the name "Marianne Paulus" in order to express her commitment to writing a series of books carefully designed to present the ancient wisdom teachings in a manner acceptable to contemporary men and women. She currently resides in Scottsdale, Arizona, where she has established the Teleos Institute with her colleague, Arleen Lorrance.

⊸≡⫯⬯∫⫯⊸

THE MATERIALIZATION OF ROSALIE

Through an interesting chain of circumstances in the early 1970s, I was granted the privilege of receiving, and personally examining a great many of

Harry Price's original notes and manuscripts, including his account of the famous Rosalie materialization. To personally examine Price's own account of the experience, one of the most controversial in psychical research, was to be touched by the investigator's excitement of discovery and to be moved by the deeply felt emotion of Mrs. Z and her circle. No additional disclosures were revealed in Price's notes—such as the actual identity of Mrs. Z or the individual members of the spirit circle—and there was no supplementary data that would offer absolute proof to stun the skeptic into silence. So, it remains for each of us to decide the truth of the account for ourselves.

The spirit of Katie King materialized during séances held by Florence Cook. This photograph of "Katie" was taken in 1873.

Price had just concluded a radio broadcast concerning psychic phenomena on December 8, 1937, when a listener contacted him and informed him that they conducted a family séance every Wednesday evening at which they materialized the spirit of a child. Price was invited to attend on the condition that he never reveal the location of the séance circle or the identity of the members. In addition, he had to promise not to touch the spirit without the permission of those in the circle. If he would agree to those terms, the family would permit the researcher to attend the séance and to exercise any controls or to conduct any examination that he wished.

Price readily agreed to the family's stipulations and made arrangements to attend a séance on December 15. When he arrived at the home, Price was given some background information on the spirit child. Rosalie was the daughter of one of the sitters whom Price called "Mrs. Z" in his notes. The girl had died of diphtheria in 1920.

One night in 1925, Mrs. Z had sensed the etheric presence of her daughter and heard the child's voice calling to her. Before dawn, Rosalie had materialized and had become sufficiently solid for her mother to clasp her hand. When members of Mrs. Z's family and certain close friends of hers learned of Rosalie's remarkable return, they offered to donate their time on one night each week for the purpose of establishing a systematic schedule, hoping that would encourage the spirit to visit her mother on a regular basis.

The séances had proved to be most successful, and by the time they invited Harry Price to join them, the circle had been meeting weekly for twelve years.

Price subjected the room to a thorough examination before the sitting. He removed all ornaments, the clock, and any small items of furniture so the séance room might be as bare as possible. He locked the door and slipped the key into his own pocket. The door and windows were sealed with adhesive tape. The fireplace was covered with sheets of paper. Every drawer was emptied; every cushion examined; and every inch of the floorboards sounded. With apologies to his hostess, Price sprinkled liberal coatings of powdered starch around all the movable objects that remained in the room and in front of the door and fireplace.

When Price had completed these extensive preparations, he indicated that the séance might begin. It was just a few minutes after 10:00 P.M. when Mrs. Z told the others that she sensed the presence of Rosalie, according to Price's notes. The mother began to weep softly, and she cautioned the other members of the circle not to speak. The room was by no means dark. A small lamp gave enough light for Price to distinguish clearly the shape of a small girl materializing beside him. "May I touch Rosalie?" Price asked when it seemed that the materialization had been completed. The researcher was given permission to put out his hand to touch the spirit child.

He found her flesh to be somewhat cooler than that of a living human. His fingers moved up to test the soft, silken quality of Rosalie's hair. Then, with the mother's permission, Price lifted the spirit girl to his knee, just as he might any living child. To his astonishment, he was able to hear a heart beating when he placed his ear to Rosalie's chest. Her pulse rate was ninety beats a minute. Price turned her face toward the lamp and later wrote that Rosalie's classical features would have "graced any nursery in the land."

With Mrs. Z's indulgence, Price queried the girl about conditions in the spirit world. Interestingly, Rosalie responded to none of these questions, but when the investigator asked her if she loved her mother, the spirit child responded rapidly in the affirmative. At this point, Mrs. Z could no longer contain herself, and she went to Price's chair and took the spirit child from his lap. Price noted later that all the women in the circle were weeping and that he also was deeply affected by the emotional scene.

After Rosalie had been with the circle for a total of about five minutes, she slowly began to fade back into her ethereal state. Within a few moments, the spirit child had completely disappeared. Price called for the lights to be switched back on and conducted an immediate inspection of his seals and coatings of powder. He found all of the tapes intact and discovered no tracks of any kind in the powdered starch that he had dusted about the room.

When Price made public certain details of the remarkable return of Rosalie, many other investigators were greatly intrigued by his account and

On February 12, 1897, a spirit entity named Y-Ay-Ali appeared to medium Mme. D'Esperance.

wished to learn more about the incredible materialization of a spirit child. Price remained true to his word and never disclosed the names of those individuals who met in the circle that summoned Rosalie back from the grave each Wednesday night.

Already a controversial figure in psychical research, Price damaged his reputation further by refusing to reveal the actual names of the alleged spirit circle, thereby denying other researchers the opportunity to violate the sanctity of Mrs. Z's home so they might conduct experiments of their own to corroborate his account. While my review of Price's actual notes of the encounter did not reveal any objective proof that might convince the skeptic of Rosalie's materialization, the sincerity expressed in the manuscripts do offer a testimony to the strength of a mother's love—love that may even be able to summon the spirit of a deceased child to revisit Earth for a limited period of time.

CLARISA BERNHARDT: SEERESS, INTUITIVE, MEDIUM

I first met Clarisa Bernhardt, a Swedish-American/Cherokee psychic sensitive in her native Oklahoma in 1973. Over the years, Clarisa has gained an international reputation as the "Earthquake Lady," for her accuracy in predicting seismic rumbles. She has served as a medium for entities who wish to communicate from the other side, and has become known as one of the most accurate psychic-sensitives in the world. She has also become a dear friend to my wife, Sherry, and me.

While Clarisa accepts the designation of spirit medium, she does not have a single spirit guide on whom she relies. Rather, she feels receptive to guidance from angels or other higher intelligences from what she terms our great "cosmic family." Clarisa prefers her term "interdimensional communication" to describe her contacts with spirit beings.

And she has certainly met a good number of ghosts during her work as a psychic-sensitive. "Some of the my ghostly encounters were startling," she said. "Some were scary, and some were very helpful to myself or to others." We shall meet Clarisa again in chapter 15 when she describes her work with the "Cross Over Club" and her sittings with Hollywood celebrities, but below she describes how her psychic mechanism works. She requires neither a spirit control nor a trance state to pick up details from those who have passed to the next world.

Clarisa Shares a Ghostly Encounter

On one occasion when I was visiting in North Texas, I was requested to come to the home of a Mrs. Wilma S., whose loss of her mother had been hard for her and all her family, for everyone was extremely fond of "Granny."

Medium Clarisa Bernhardt.

When I arrived at the S. home with an associate from the local newspaper who brought me there at the request of Wilma, I was told by the family that they had felt the late woman's presence in the home very strongly for the past week. When I walked into the hallway I could see an energy field which was frantically moving about. It suddenly moved quickly toward me—and just as quickly I tried to move out of its path. It stopped and then moved back to a door near the end of the hall, flitting back and forth. I felt an overwhelming vibration of anxiety in the atmosphere of the home, so I asked everyone to please be quiet so that I could concentrate on what was happening. I then went alone back into the hall area and walked toward the door where the energy seemed to concentrate its activity.

Then I froze, for I saw this image of a woman, and she was throwing herself at this door. I could hear a crash as she would hit it. And then I was overcome with the message that there was great danger for her family.

After the spirit in the hallway had demonstrated such an incredible explosion of energy, it was suddenly gone.

I went back to the front area of the home and asked what was behind that door at the end of the hallway. Wilma said, "Oh, there's a stairway that goes down to the basement and into the cellar." I inquired when they had last gone down there, and Wilma responded that it had been about a year, for there were lots of things that were stored there. I advised them of the message her mother had given me about the danger that was in the cellar and that it should be checked immediately. Wilma said that she would have it looked into.

When we walked out of the house, I was given a quick tour of the grounds of the house. As we approached the garage which supported an apartment on the second floor, I once again heard the spirit of Wilma's mother telling me that she had buried some money in the area. She also said something about some old silver spurs that were worn on cowboy boots. I mentioned both of these comments to the S. family and to my friend who was an

During an 1873 séance, several photographs were taken as medium John Beattie attempted to contact the spirit realm. This photograph reveals that something was in the room with Beattie during the séance.

associate of the area newspaper. We said goodbye, and I left, hoping that the S. family would follow my advice.

A couple of months later when I was in Sedona, Arizona, for the winter I received a phone call from Doug, a nephew of Wilma's, who told me that

I should know that his aunt had followed through on my spirit message from his grandmother. When Wilma opened the basement door, it had immediately become obvious that there was a gas leak. By making such a discovery—thanks to the message from the ghost of Wilma's mother which had come through clearly to me—a tragedy was avoided. Doug also advised me that a pair of silver cowboy spurs had been found buried near the fence when some post work was being done. They also uncovered several canning jars filled with fifty dollar bills—a very specific and certainly helpful communication for Wilma and her family.

12
GHOSTS THAT CAME BACK TO LIFE

◄═══◙◘═══►

OUT-OF-BODY PROJECTIONS

Throughout all of human existence, men and women have testified to the existence of another kind of ghost, one that is an extension of the living rather than the dead. While in the ecstasy of meditation or the illumination of the semiconscious state of physical pain and suffering, people through the ages have testified to having left their physical body to briefly travel through other dimensions of reality in their spirit bodies before they returned to the material plane. Thousands of people have claimed to have seen the spiritlike image of a friend or a relative appear before them while the living counterpart of the apparition was known to be residing thousands of miles away. Numerous individuals have claimed to have had an out-of-body experience during sleep, and have maintained that they witnessed activities during their strange "dreams" that were later verified. Some even argue that they have received or conveyed messages of great personal importance during astral flight.

Based on my research and personal experiences, I have found that out-of-body projections seem to fit into one of seven general categories:

1) The projection of the soul while the subject is asleep.

2) Projection while the subject undergoes surgery, childbirth, tooth extraction, etc.

3) Projection during an accident, when a subject receives a terrible physical jolt and his/her spirit seems literally thrown from the physical body.

4) Projection during intense physical pain.

5) Projection during a high fever or severe illness.

6) Projection during pseudo-death (the near-death experience), wherein the subject "dies" for several minutes and may appear to a living percipient with whom they have an emotional link, or may travel to other dimensions of existence before being subsequently revived and restored to life.

7) The conscious out-of-body projection in which the subject deliberately seeks to free his/her spirit from the material body.

In December 2001 an article in the British medical journal *Lancet* reported on a study that examined 344 patients from 10 hospitals in the Netherlands who had been successfully resuscitated after suffering cardiac arrest. Researchers spoke to these survivors within the week after they had suffered clinical death and been restored to life, and found that 18 percent of the patients recalled some portion of what happened to them when they were clinically dead. Another 8–12 percent remembered having near-death experiences, such as seeing lights at the end of tunnels or being able to speak to deceased friends or relatives.

> Somewhere in their out-of-body travels to the world beyond death, these disembodied souls are told that their time is not yet completed on Earth.

In the past three decades a great deal of attention has been paid to the near-death experience (NDE), both by medical doctors and individuals claiming to have experienced the phenomenon. Among the stellar researchers drawn to study NDEs have been Dr. Elisabeth Kubler-Ross, Dr. Raymond Moody, Dr. Kenneth Ring, Dr. Karlis Osis, Robert Crookall, and Dr. P. M. H. Atwater. Dozens of books have been published that generally describe the phenomenon as occurring when someone appears to have died and is then returned to life, complete with a story of having been drawn down a tunnel toward a light in the company of angels or relatives. Somewhere in their out-of-body travels to the world beyond death, these disembodied souls are told that their time is not yet completed on Earth. They must return to life, often with instructions to complete a particular mission.

The well-known psychical researcher Harry Price put forth the view that the whole point of our life on Earth might very well be to provide us with a stockpile of memories out of which we might construct a meaningful image-world at the time of our death. Such a world would be a psychological world and not a physical one, even though it seems to be quite physical to those who would experience it. Price conjectured that the other world would be the manifestation of the memories and desires of its inhabitants, including their repressed or unconscious memories and desires. It might be every bit as detailed, vivid, and complex as this present perceptible world that we experience now. We may note that it might well contain a vivid and persistent image of one's own body.

According to Price's concept of survival, the surviving personality is actually an immaterial entity: "But if one habitually *thinks* of oneself as embodied (as one well might, at least for a considerable time), an image of one's own body might be, as it were, the persistent center of one's image world, much as the perceived physical body is the persistent center of one's perceptible world in this present life."

Although this is a book about real ghosts, I include a chapter about these "ghosts" that came back to life because of the testimony they provide, which demonstrates not only the existence of a soul and life after death, but that ghosts are real. And, as the reader shall see, the serious study of the near-death experience is nothing new.

⎯⎯◦⊙⎯⎯

GHOSTS OF THE LIVING

Soaring Above His Body

Richard Evans of St. Louis, Missouri, was crossing a busy intersection when a car roared around the corner and was on top of him before he could jump back to the curb. He wrote that in an eternal moment before impact, his true "soul body" seemed to jump out of his physical self. The *real* Evans seemed to soar high above the street, and he could see the automobile about to hit his physical body. "I had a stunned deer-in-the-headlights look on my face," Evans wrote, "but there was a lady watching from the curb who seemed about ready to go into hysterics. I knew the car was going to hit me, but it seemed as though my real consciousness was not terribly concerned."

Richard Evans then saw his body go sailing through the air like someone had drop-kicked a football. He did not feel any pain in his physical body, and he seemed to have a strange feeling of indifference to the man he saw flying through the air. He had no sense of consciousness connected with the body that had just been struck by the speeding automobile. He was the dispassionate observer.

A crowd began to gather around Evans's crumpled body. Evans, still floating somewhere above the street, wanted to leave the scene, to soar free in space, but something held him to the pitiful scene below him. A wail of sirens directed his attention to a rapidly approaching police car, then to an ambulance following closely behind. A doctor leapt out of the vehicle and knelt beside the body. Evans saw the doctor fill a syringe from a small bottle, then shoot the liquid into his arm.

The substance that was injected into his body from the syringe was like a magnet and pulled Evans back into his body. He described the sensation as feeling like he was "one of those balls on a rubber string that had been thrown as far as the string would stretch and was now being pulled back." The next thing Evans knew, he was back in his physical body, blinking his eyes. Everything was blurred. And, most of all, he was conscious of the terrible pain. He devoutly wished he were back soaring above the street, away from the agony of his injuries.

Visited by Her Injured Mother

It was 2:00 a.m. on July 17, 1957, when Patricia Mann opened her eyes and glimpsed a shadowy form that resembled her mother. "Come, I need your help," the apparition said to her. Her mother lived 10 miles away from her, but Patricia was convinced that the ghostly form was truly her mother. She picked up the telephone and dialed her mother's number. She could only get a busy signal. A call to the telephone company produced the information that the line was out of order.

Somehow Patricia Mann knew that she could not wait until morning to find out if her mother needed her help. She dressed hurriedly and drove to her mother's house. When she arrived, she found all the lights on, and she could hear the television set blaring at full blast. She pounded on the door and called her mother's name, but received no response. Finally she found an unlocked window and crawled through. She found her mother lying in a pool of blood, clutching the telephone receiver in her hand. Patricia called an ambulance.

After her mother's forehead had been stitched up in the hospital's emergency room, she told Patricia what had happened. Patricia later summarized the strange experience: "[Mother] had fallen, and from the gushing blood she knew she had sustained a deep cut. She was trying to phone me when she blacked out, but she remembered calling my name. She also knew that it had been about 2:00 a.m. when she fell" (Patricia Mann, "True Mystic Experiences," *Fate*, February 1967).

Her Spirit Gave Her Body a Rest

One night Sara Norris arose sleepily from her bed and reluctantly left the hollow of warmth next to her husband. It was 3:00 a.m. and time to feed the baby. As she wrote in her response to the Steiger Questionnaire of Mystical and Paranormal Phenomena, she walked into the kitchen and turned up the gas flame beneath the old pan in which she warmed the baby's bottle. While she waited for the water to heat, Sara looked out over their moonlit farmyard and listened to the night noises.

She had felt exhausted when she had gone to bed that evening. She had carried the heavy load of her pregnancy through an exceptionally hot summer. The delivery had been long and difficult, but Sara had left her hospital bed to come back to the farm and help with the harvest. She had not been able to get caught up on her sleep. There were the late meals that had to be made for all of the extra help that had been brought in for the harvest, and they could not afford to hire someone to assist her with the housework. Then, while her husband slept, she had to get up during the night to see to the baby. She would have given nearly anything to be able to sleep one night through. Just one night of sleep without interruption.

The bottle was ready. She tested it on her arm, walked into the baby's room, and slid the nipple between the baby's lips almost before he was able to cry. Sara did not want to awaken her husband or the two other children who slept in the next room. Nor did she wish a piercing scream to shatter the blissful dreamlike state she moved in.

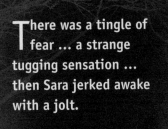

There was a tingle of fear ... a strange tugging sensation ... then Sara jerked awake with a jolt.

It was as she returned to bed that Sara was startled to see her own sleeping form lying next to her husband. The form was unmistakably her own body: hair in disarray, mouth slightly open, one forearm resting across her brow. But how could she be in two places at once? There was a tingle of fear ... a strange tugging sensation ... then Sara jerked awake with a jolt. A dream. It had all been a bizarre dream.

But the baby was in bed, content with his bottle, working the rubber nipple in his tiny mouth. It would seem that Sara's soul, her nonphysical true self, separated itself from her sleeping body so that the bone-tired shell of her physical self could rest undisturbed. Her spirit saw to the baby. Not only had she freed the spiritual essence from within her physical body, Sara was able to see her own ghost.

A Doctor Becomes a Spirit and Returns to His Body

When Dr. Wiltse of Skiddy, Kansas, believed that he was dying, he called to his family and friends to bid them farewell. His attending physician, Dr. Raynes, later testified (*St. Louis Medical and Surgical Journal*, 1889; reprinted in *Proceedings*, vol. VII, Society for Psychical Research, 1892) that for the duration of four hours, Wiltse lay without pulse or perceptible heartbeat. Raynes did state, however, that he may have witnessed very slight gasps occasionally emitted by his patient.

During this lengthy period of clinical death, Wiltse found himself in what he later termed a state of "conscious existence" that bore no relationship to his physical body. He began to rock back and forth, trying to break the tenuous bond of tissues and fibers within his physical form. He began to feel and hear "the snappings of innumerable small cords," as his spirit began to retreat from his feet and collect in his head like "a rubber cord shortens." Shortly after that, the doctor felt that his true self had gathered in the area of his head, and he began to emerge through his skull. In his report he stated that he distinctly remembered resembling "something like a jellyfish as regards to color and form." [Author's note: *Many men and women who project from the Earth plane in their near-death experiences often discard concepts of body image and report perceiving themselves as a "shiny cloud," a "bright balloon," an "egg yolk," or "something like a jellyfish."*]

> Then the doctor found himself soaring high above the neighborhood, enjoying the aerial view that his unique situation afforded him.

As his true self emerged from his skull, Wiltse experienced the floating sensation so common to near-death projections. He felt himself bobbing gently up and down until his exertions landed him squarely on the floor. At that point, he gradually arose and expanded himself to the full stature of his regular physical body. "I seemed to be translucent, of a bluish cast, and perfectly naked," he said. The doctor cast a glance at his woeful physical body on the sickbed and decided that he had no further use for it. Without further ado, he headed for the front door.

As he reached the door, Wiltse observed that he was suddenly fully clothed. At the same time, he noted that two of his friends were standing by the door and that they were completely unaware of his presence. With a great deal of surprise and amusement, Wiltse discovered that he could pass directly through his friends; he did so and continued on out through the door. He never saw the street more distinctly than he saw it then, he stated. Glancing around, he noticed that he was still attached to his body in the house by means of a small cord, like a spider's web. Then the doctor found himself soaring high above the neighborhood, enjoying the aerial view that his unique situation afforded him. However, just as he was relaxing into his newly achieved emancipation from the confines of bodily flesh, Wiltse found himself on a road with steep rocks blocking his path. He attempted to climb around them, but as he was doing so, a black cloud surrounded him and he found himself back in his bedroom, once again confined to an ill body.

Witse's experience raises many mundane questions: for instance, why is it that those who undergo near-death experiences usually see themselves clothed, rather than naked, as Wiltse first saw his body? I believe that since near-death experiences involve the essential stuff of human personality, the projected mind may—if it wishes to do so—"create" its clothing by exercising the same kind of mental machinery that is utilized in dreams. Wiltse's case provides us with a very good look at some of the mechanics of the near-death experience. When he first projects his true self from the skull, he perceives himself as "something like a jellyfish as regards color and form." Then, because his mind had been conditioned on the temporal plane to think in terms of physical body concepts, the "jellyfish" expands into the full stature of a naked human male. When Wiltse confronts his sober-faced friends at the door, he suddenly finds himself clothed. Even though he is certain that they cannot see him in his spiritual body, a lifetime on the Earth plane living in a conservative culture had conditioned him not to go about in the nude. It may well be this same psycho-spiritual mechanism that explains why we never perceive naked ghosts.

It is worth noting that Wiltse's near-death experience terminated when he was confronted by steep rocks that blocked his journey. Generally speaking, there seem to be two types of environments in near-death experiences:

1) The environment of this planet Earth, in which the projected personality observes the actions of people in faraway places and sees actual occurrences at great distances that can later be substantiated.

2) The environment of other planes of existence or dimensions of reality, in which the projected personality may encounter entities that he perceives as angels, masters, guides, saints, or the spirits of loved ones who have previously passed away. The geography of these spiritual planes seems to be quite similar to that of Earth, and the individual's religious views often determine whether the plane is interpreted as heaven, paradise, or a place of eternal bliss.

The "rocks" that halted Wiltse's advance may indeed have been rocks on another plane of existence, or they may have been formed by his own mental machinery as a symbol that he was not meant to venture farther but was instead supposed to return to his physical body.

Aloft in the Spirit Body

Dr. Robert Crookall, author of such classic works as *The Study and Practice of Astral Projection*, has reported on a case of near-death experience that was first published in the *Moscow Journal* in 1916. The subject of the NDE was a Russian who had rejected the idea that the spirit survives in any kind of afterlife.

The subject remembered feeling dizzy during a stay in a hospital. He called for a doctor, then became aware of a "certain state of division" within himself. He was conscious of his physical self, yet at the same time, he had a feeling of indifference toward his material body. It seemed as if he was actually two beings—one, the main part of him, was concealed somewhere deep within; the other, his physical body, was external and less significant. He felt the "main part" of himself being drawn *somewhere* with irresistible force. He felt like something he had been allowed to use for a brief period of time was being recalled and pulled back to its source. At the same time, he was filled with the conviction that his essential self would not disappear.

The entire medical staff seemed to be crowded about his bed. The "main part" of him moved forward, and he saw his physical husk lying there on the bed. He tried to grasp the hand of his material body, but his spirit hand went through it. Struck by the strangeness of the situation, he wanted someone to help him understand what was happening. He called to the doctor, but the air did not seem to transmit the sound waves of his voice. He tried everything he could think of to make his presence known, but none of the medical staff seemed aware of his "real" self. Had he died? He found this inconceivable, for death meant the cessation of being, and he had not lost consciousness for even one moment. He was as aware of himself as ever. He could see, hear, move, touch, think. Even when the doctor declared that it was all over for him, the perplexed Russian refused to accept the idea of his death. A nurse turned to a religious icon and asked for a blessing on the man's soul. The words had scarcely been uttered when two angels appeared at his side. They picked him up by his arms, carried him right through the wall into the street, and began to ascend quickly.

Although it was evening and dark, he saw everything clearly. He was able to perceive a much greater expanse than he would have had with his ordinary vision. On the ascent, they were suddenly surrounded by "a throng of hideous beings, evil spirits" that tried to snatch him away from the angels. The man, who had proclaimed himself an atheist during his life, found himself praying for deliverance, and to his astonishment there suddenly appeared a "white mist which concealed the ugly spirits." The ascent upward was halted when an intense light appeared before them and a voice thundered: "Not ready!" At once, the angels began to descend with him.

At first, he did not understand the meaning of the thunderous words from the light, but soon the outlines of a city became visible. He saw the hospital, and then he was being carried into a room completely unknown to him. In this room there stood a row of tables, and on one of them, covered partially with a sheet, he saw his dead body. His guardian angel pointed to his body and told him to enter it. At first the Russian felt as though something was pressing against him; the sensation was unpleasantly cold. An awareness of ever-increasing tightness continued, and just before he lost consciousness, he felt very sad, as though he had lost something.

When he became aware of his surroundings the head physician sat at his bedside, astounded by the medical miracle that he had witnessed. The subject had no doubt that his soul had temporarily left his body and then returned to it.

Report to the Royal Medical Society, 1937

When the Royal Medical Society of Edinburgh met on February 26, 1937, Sir Auckland Geddes, a medical doctor and professor of anatomy, read a most unusual paper before the august body of medical professionals. A colleague who wished to remain anonymous had experienced what we today would call a near-death experience, which he wanted to bring to the attention of his fellow professionals. When the anonymous physician had been near death, he realized that his "being" had separated from his physical body. Upon recovery, he immediately began to dictate his amazing experience to his secretary.

> It was at that point that he realized that he appeared to have two levels of consciousness, one of which was separate from the other.

According to his account, one evening shortly after midnight, the doctor was stricken with gastroenteritis so severe that by ten o'clock the following morning he was too ill to even ring for assistance. However, though the doctor's body was in terrible agony, his mental faculties remained quite clear, and he began to review his financial affairs, firmly convinced that his death was imminent. It was at that point that he realized that he appeared to have two levels of consciousness, one of which was separate from the other. Later, while dictating the experience to his secretary, he labeled these two states of consciousness "A" and "B." His ego—the true spiritual self—was the "A" state of consciousness. The "B" consciousness remained with the physical body.

The physician observed that as his physical health continued to deteriorate, the "B" personality began to fade, while the "A" personality began to embody his complete self. As the process continued, the "A" personality vacated the physical body entirely, and he was able to observe his body lying inert in the bed. As his awareness increased, he realized that he could also see his entire house and garden. Testing his new range of existence, he discovered that he could instantly travel to any earthly place that occurred to him.

He became aware of the presence of a guide or mentor who explained to him that he was in another time dimension of space, a fourth dimension in which *now* was equivalent to *here*. This fourth dimension corresponded in its makeup to everything that existed in three-dimensional space. Moreover, everything in the third dimension also existed in the fourth. The doctor's guide pointed out that in the fourth dimension, he appeared as a blue-colored cloud. In his report to the medical society, the physician apologized for the lack of words to describe his extraordinary experience. No words adequately put forth his actual feelings and sensations. He stated that his spirit mentor had impressed on him that "all our brains are just end-organs projecting as it were from the three-dimensional universe into the psychic stream ... and flowing with it into the fourth and the fifth dimensions."

Many more mysteries were revealed to the physician when one of his servants entered his bedroom and discovered his employer's dying body. He watched his servant rush to the telephone and place a hasty call to one of the physician's colleagues; at the same time, he saw that physician take leave of his patients because of the emergency. When his colleague arrived, the doctor's "A" consciousness could hear the man think, "He is nearly gone!" He was able to hear the man speaking to him, but he was unable to respond. He was no longer in the "B" consciousness that resided in his physical body.

The visiting doctor pulled a syringe out of his medical bag. The "A" consciousness of the physician saw this act and became very angry, as it did not wish to return to the "B" consciousness. As the injection flowed into the doctor's body, however, the "A" consciousness once again began to take notice of his heartbeat and gradually allowed itself to be pulled back into the physical body. Finally, the doctor became fully aware of his complete self once again and realized he was lying on his bed. He felt intensely annoyed, because he had just begun to understand where he was and what he was seeing. He was angry at having been pulled back into his body. "And once back, all the clarity of the vision of everything disappeared, and I was again possessed of a glimmer of consciousness which was suffused with pain."

In his concluding remarks, Geddes told the members of the society that their colleague's experience had helped him define "the idea of a psychic continuum in which we all exist."

The Day I Became a Ghost, by Brad Steiger

On my parents' wedding anniversary, August 23, 1947, when I was a boy of 11, I had a near-death experience as a result of a terrible accident on our family farm in Iowa. My body lay crushed and bleeding, sprawled where the mangling, metallic blades of the farm machinery had dropped it. Almost at once my essential self left my body and distanced itself from the tragic scene.

Although I could clearly perceive the events taking place below me, I felt only dimly associated with the dying farmboy who lay bleeding in the hay stubble. I felt the concern and panic of my seven-year-old sister who was running for help, but I had no connection to the emotions she felt. I had become an orange-colored spheroid, intent only on soaring toward an incredibly beautiful and brilliant light above me. I felt blissfully euphoric, and I began to revel in the glory of a marvelous sense of oneness with the power and intelligence of All-That-Is.

Then I discovered that bilocation was a facet of my spirit body. I could be in two places at once. I could exist physically in my father's arms as he carried my terribly injured body from the field; and at the same time, I could be above us, watching the whole scene as if I were a detached observer. When I became concerned about my mother's reaction to my dreadful accident, I made an even more incredible discovery: the "real me" could be *anywhere* that I wished to be. My spirit, my soul, was free of the physical limitations that we humans incorporate into our definitions of time and space. I only had to think of my mother, and there I was beside her.

I put the newly found freedom to other tests. I thought of my friends—one at a time—and I was instantly beside each of them as they worked with their fathers on their own farms. I was a ghost, a spirit. I was able to pass through walls, soar through the clouds, and be wherever I wished. It was wonderful. From time to time I would feel a fleeting pinch of regret over having left my family and my friends, but whenever the sorrow of earthly separation impinged on my newly extended consciousness, I was shown something that I can only describe as a series of brilliant geometric designs. It was as if these colorful patterns were somehow a part of the great tapestry of life; my ability to perceive these figures illustrated the order and the rightness of existence. To view this cosmic panorama was to peek into God's notebook and see that there truly is an underlying meaning to existence on Earth. Suddenly it became obvious that there is, indeed, a divine plan; life on Earth is not simply the result of some cosmic accident. Yes, I was dying, but that was not really the end of me. Nor was it the end of the world. Life on Earth would be able to continue without me.

> As I drifted closer to the brilliant light, I had a sudden sense of longing for my simple and pastoral life on the farm with my parents and sister.

Viewing these geometric designs completely removed my fear of death and allowed my spirit essence to move closer to the light. At the same time, the light appeared to be intelligent and to manifest a kind of benevolent presence that brought me immense peace and tranquility. As I drifted closer to the brilliant light, I had a sudden sense of longing for my simple and pastoral life on the farm with my parents and sister. At that instant, a geometric mobile manifested before me, and it seemed that in a flash I was shown the great secret of all existence. How I wish that I could have retained that knowledge, but I was left with "the peace that passes all understanding."

I was in and out of my body during the desperate 140-mile run to a hospital in Des Moines. Whenever the real me would enter the body of the dying 11-year-old boy, it seemed to reject the choice and return to the dimension of spirit where there was no pain. Rather inconveniently, I returned to my physical body just as the surgeons were preparing to operate. I returned with such force that I sat up, shouted, and pushed an intern off balance. It took the calming and caring tones of love from a Roman Catholic nun to pacify me until the anesthesia could take effect.

I began to sense a kind of intelligence or personality within the light itself, and I asked it if I might leave the operating room. I was just bobbing around above my body, and I really didn't want to watch the surgery. The accident had given me numerous skull fractures and had essentially scalped me. In answer to my prayer, I remember being taken to what appeared to be a kind of ideal little village, complete with a bandstand, ice cream vendors, and friendly people walking about.

During the two weeks of my hospital stay, the nuns seemed to have sensed that I had been "somewhere" and had seen "something." They asked me again and again about my experience as a spirit being, traveling between the two worlds. A mystery had been pierced, they told me. I would never again have to ask the troubling question about whether we humans survive the experience of physical death. I would be able to testify that there truly was an existence that transcended the material realm. Because of what could well have been a fatal accident, I was given the ability to understand that we do survive physical death in our spiritual essence, our souls. I knew with an unshakable certainty that we are spiritual beings. Regardless of the technology that may surround us, the physical environment that may complement or discourage us, political or cultural boundaries, we are spirits inhabiting a physical body—the things of the spirit world are the most lasting.

I have never felt chosen or special because of my near-death experience and the cosmic geometric designs I was given the opportunity to see. But I believe I was blessed with the chance to *know* what so many others accept on the basis of faith. Having received proof of existence in the afterlife, I became convinced that I am to here to testify that the human spirit is eternal, and that benevolent spiritual beings of light exist to help us and to guide us in our spiritual evolution.

For many years after my near-death episode, I assumed that my viewing of the geometric designs had to be classified as an ineffable experience, impossible to translate into physical expression. Whenever I attempted to articulate the cosmic panorama and describe the geometric patterns for others, my mind would literally blank-out due to the lack of an appropriate vocabulary. From time to time, I would meet other individuals who'd had a near-death experience and had seen geometric visions similar to mine, and they would agree that these awesome messages from All-That-Is are beyond words.

In 1988 my wife, Sherry, began conducting healing seminars utilizing computer derived images of fractal geometry, and in these sessions I finally saw images that were close approximations of what I had been shown during my NDE. I was struck with a powerful shock of recognition when she projected these brilliant images during her seminar. Interestingly, the effect on the audience was profound, and many individuals claimed healing experiences after viewing the images.

LEARNING TO CONTROL AND PROJECT THE GHOST WITHIN

The cases presented thus far in the chapter have dealt with the inadvertent projection of the "astral" self, but a great many people have exer-

cised this function of the transcendent self to the extent that they can project their "ghosts" at will. The pioneer psychical research Frederic W. H. Myers wrote that cases of astral projection present "the most extraordinary achievement of the human will. What can lie further outside any known capacity than the power to cause a semblance of oneself to appear at a distance? What can be a more central action—more manifestly the outcome of whatsoever is deepest and most unitary in man's whole being? Of all vital phenomena, I say, this is the most significant; this self-projection is the one definite act which it seems as though a man might perform equally well before and after bodily death."

Sylvan J. Muldoon was one of the earliest practitioners to claim that the process of instigating an out-of-body experience can be learned, developed, and mastered by a serious student. In his two books, *The Projection of the Astral Body* (1929) and *The Case for Astral Projection* (1936), Muldoon offers a detailed record of many experiments he has personally conducted and provides a systematic method of inducing the conditions necessary for astral projection. According to Muldoon, it is possible to leave the body at will and retain full consciousness in the "astral self." Muldoon is also cognizant of the "silver cord" mentioned by many individuals who have had a near-death experience as the link that connects the spirit and physical bodies. This cord, says Muldoon, is extremely elastic and permits a journey of considerable distance. Muldoon claims that while he was out of his body, he was able to move objects and gain information that he could not have acquired via any of the normal sensory channels.

> According to Muldoon, it is possible to leave the body at will and retain full consciousness in the "astral self."

Muldoon is generous in providing the reader with copious descriptions of the mechanics involved in astral projection so that the truly interested student can follow the procedures and experiment on his or her own. The fundamental law of projection, according to, Muldoon, is expressed in these words: "When the subconscious will becomes possessed of the idea to move the body, and the physical body is incapacitated, the subconscious will moves the astral body out of the physical body."

The Projections of S. H. Beard

In his groundbreaking book *Phantasms of the Living* (1886), Edmund Gurney wrote of the remarkable experiments conducted by S. H. Beard. Beard began his experiments with astral projection on a Sunday evening in November 1881, after he had read philosophical material about the great power that the human will is capable of exercising. Beard exerted the whole force of his being on the thought that he would make his spirit-form manifest before his

Author Theodore Dreiser.

fiancée, Miss L. S. Verity, on the second floor of her home at 22 Hogarth Road, Kensington, London, England; his experiment was a success.

Three days later, when Beard called upon Verity, she excitedly told him that both she and her 11-year-old sister had nearly been frightened out of their wits by an apparition that had looked just like him. When Verity's sister confirmed the appearance of such a phantom, Beard, who had not revealed the part he had played in the mysterious visitation or broached the topic with his fiancée, felt quite pleased with his experiment.

Verity later told Gurney that she had seen Beard in her room at about one o'clock. She stated that she was perfectly awake and "much terrified." She had awakened her sister with her screaming, and the 11-year-old girl also saw the apparition. Neither Verity nor her sister had ever experienced hallucinations of any sort on any prior occasion. Beard had not yet disclosed his actions to his fiancée because he was by no means finished with his research.

For his second experiment, he willed his presence before Verity's married sister, whom he had met only briefly once before. Beard walked up to the bed on which the woman lay, took her long hair into his hand, and then lifted her hand.

When Gurney learned of Beard's second successful projection, he wrote him a note urging Beard to let him know when he planned to conduct his next experiment. Beard complied, and in a letter dated March 22, 1884, he simply told Gurney, "This is it." This message was explained in his next letter, which was received on April 3. A statement from Verity was enclosed: "On Saturday night, March 22nd ... at about midnight, I had a distinct impression that Mr. S. H. B. was present in my room, and I distinctly saw him whilst I was wide awake. He came towards me and stroked my hair.... The appearance in my room was most vivid and quite unmistakable." Verity testified that she had voluntarily given Beard the information without any prompting on his part. Beard concluded his experiments after this episode, for Verity's nerves "had been much shaken, and she had been obliged to send for a doctor in the morning."

A Famous Writer Turns Himself into a Ghost

The American novelist Theodore Dreiser often told the story of the night that he entertained the English writer John Cowper Powys. On that particular night, the Englishman had to leave rather early, and both men expressed regret that their evening had been so short. Seeing that Dreiser's disappointment was genuine, Powys told him, "I'll appear before you, right here, later this evening. You'll see me."

"Will you turn yourself into a ghost?" Dreiser asked, chuckling at the Englishman's peculiar sense of humor.

"I'm not certain yet," Powys told him. "I may return as a spirit or in some other astral form."

Several hours later, as Dreiser sat reading in his easy chair, he glanced up and was startled to see Powys standing before him, looking exactly as he had earlier that evening. When the writer moved toward the apparition and spoke to it, Powys's astral projection disappeared.

SEEING YOUR OWN GHOST

Another phenomenon that must be closely related to the projection of the astral self is that of the appearance of one's own double. This phenomenon is called "autoscopic hallucination" and appears to serve no particular purpose, such as providing a warning or disclosing valuable information. In fact the only service it appears to provide is to allow an individual the opportunity to see his/her own body image without having to use a mirror. The April 1966 issue of Fate *contained an article entitled "Have You Seen Your Double?" in which Dr. Edward Podolsky wrote of a number of cases where people had reported seeing their own ghosts. According to Podolsky, there are two main theories that discuss possible causes of autoscopy. One is due to "the result of some irritating process in the brain, particularly of the parietotemporal-occipital area (the visual area)." The other, a psychological theory, sees autoscopy as a projection of memory pictures "that may be projected outside the body as very real images" when conditions of stress or other unusual psychological situations arise.*

The Experience of Harold C. from Chicago

In March 1958 Harold C. returned home after a hard day at the office with a splitting migraine. As he sat down to dinner, he saw, sitting opposite him, an exact replica of himself. This astonishing double repeated every movement he made during the entire course of the meal. Since that time, Mr. C. has seen his double on a number of occasions, each time after he has suffered from a migraine.

The Experience of Samuel V.

Samuel V. of Kansas City, Missouri, was startled to see an exact double of himself mirror his every movement as he went about his gardening chores. The double was visible for about two hours.

The Frightening Case of Jeanie P.

The case of Jeanie P. is the most frightening of those recounted by Podolsky. As she was applying her makeup, she saw an exact duplicate of herself that was touching up *her* features. Jeanie reached out to touch the double, and the image reached out to touch her. Jeanie actually felt her face being touched by her mysterious double.

⊸⫘⫘⊸

THE VARDOGR

Neither of Podolsky's theories regarding autoscopic hallucinations explains the Scandinavian phenomenon known as the *Vardogr*. Wiers Jensen, editor of the *Norwegian Journal of Psychical Research*, wrote a series of articles on the Vardogr as early as 1917. The individual that possesses a Vardogr unconsciously employs it as a type of spiritual forerunner to announce his or her physical arrival.

"The Vardogr reports are all alike," wrote Jensen. "With little variation, the same type of happening occurs: The ... Vardogr *announces* his arrival. His steps are heard on the staircase. He is heard to unlock the outside door, kick off his overshoes, put his walking stick in place, etc. The listening percipients—if they are not so accustomed to the prelude of the Vardogr that they remain sitting quietly—open the door and find the entry empty. The Vardogr has, as usual, played a trick on them. [A few] minutes later, the whole performance is repeated—but now the reality and the man arrive."

Based on the research he conducted *c.* 1917, Jensen theorized that only Scandinavians and the Scots experienced the phenomenon of the Vardogr. I have learned that this bizarre spiritual forerunner is not limited to these ethnic groups, but being of Norwegian and Danish descent, I can attest to the reality of the Vardogr, a unique manifestation of a living ghost.

The first really dramatic encounter with a Vardogr that I can recall occurred one Saturday night when I was about 16. I had arrived home before my parents, and I went upstairs to my room to lie down on my bed and thumb through a new magazine I had purchased that evening. I had not been there long when I clearly heard noises downstairs. As I have stated elsewhere in this book, my childhood home was a center for a lot of ghostly phenomena, such as doors opening and closing, the footsteps of unseen guests, and the occasional manifestation of spectral beings. But the sounds I heard that night were not the "spooky" sounds; what I heard downstairs sounded like my parents and sister entering the house. First there was the opening of the front screen door, then the squeaking of the inside door. Next, the sound of feet walking up the three steps to the inner hallway, followed by the subsequent sounds of footsteps moving about various rooms as they prepared for bed. "Goodnight!" I called downstairs after a few minutes. Both my parents and sister had bedrooms on the first floor, so they would not be coming upstairs to retire.

> The ... Vardogr announces his arrival. His steps are heard on the staircase.

There was no answer. I flipped through a few more pages of the magazine, thinking that my parents and sister had not heard me as they prepared for bed. "Goodnight down there!" I shouted after a few moments, a bit louder that time. Again no answer. By that time it had become very silent downstairs. Too silent for those footsteps to have belonged to my family. My mind was instantly flooded with a variety of startling images. Maybe intruders had thought my house was deserted and had decided to enter the house. Had my shouts alerted them to the presence of a lone occupant? What would their next move be?

Just as the icy fingers of fear had begun to trace a slow, deliberate path up the length of my spine, I once again heard the familiar sounds of my parents and sister arriving home. The noises were precisely as they had been before, only this time when I shouted my goodnight, the voices of my parents and sister quickly responded.

The next time I experienced my parents' Vardogr was no less eerie, and neither were any of its subsequent arrivals. Each time it tricked me as thoroughly as it had before. My sister fell victim to its spooky pranks as often as I did. One night my parents arrived home to find her in a state of near panic. She had been sitting in a chair with her back to the door. She had heard the door open and close and the sound of footsteps enter the house and approach to the spot directly behind her chair. As she was engrossed in the book she was reading, she had not bothered to turn around at the sound of the opening door. After a few moments had passed, she began to wonder why her mother and father preferred to stand behind her chair in complete silence. Imagine her horror when she turned around and saw no one was there.

Weirs Jensen notes that as a general rule, the Vardogr announces itself only by imitating the sounds made by inanimate objects, such as "the sound of the key in the lock, the placing of overshoes in their proper spots, the stamping of shoes on the floor. The jingle of horsebells and the cracking of whips may also be heard."

It is interesting that in his early research, Jensen singled out Scandinavians and Scots as the primary progenitors of the Vardogr. Some years ago, I shared an office suite with two friends who were both of Scottish descent. The combination must have produced a powerful Vardogr, for on many occasions, Glenn or Dave would enter my office to confer with me, only to find that I had not yet arrived. They would later swear that they heard me arrive, move my chair into position in front of my trusty 1923 Underwood typewriter, and begin tapping out words on the keys. When I would arrive at my office, I would often find my two puzzled friends standing in my office, wondering what joke I would try playing that morning. They soon learned about the reality of the Vardogr. Their spiritual forerunners fooled me from time to time as well.

Since my wife, Sherry, is also of Scandinavian descent, our two Vardogrs have played tricks on us on innumerable occasions. In some instances, the pranksters have almost precipitated arguments when one of us wants to know why the other came home and then left again, only to return a few minutes later. Then, laughingly, we realize a Vardogr has tricked us again. Our particular combination of personalities has strengthened our Vardogrs to such a level that they have been able to duplicate our voices, which can prove really perplexing and somewhat disturbing.

Not long ago, I received a letter from Mr. K. L. H. regarding his son's Vardogr: "I came across one of the archived shows on the *Jeff Rense Program* where you mentioned a phenomenon called the Vardogr. This immediately gave me cause to ponder some recent events in our home. I have a small office-studio in our basement where I have my computer, my musical instruments, and some recording equipment. My son's room is immediately above this office. He is 13.

"Every weekday he arrives home from school at about 3:30. When I hear him come home, I always go upstairs to ask about his day, but sometimes I find that he is not actually home yet, in spite of hearing the sounds you would normally expect to hear from a teenager coming home. Before hearing the program, I just brushed it off as normal house noises, or the cat, or whatever; but after I heard the show, I decided to try an experiment.

"The first day, I made sure the cat was not in my son's room, and I closed his door. I was certain that all TVs, radios, and so forth were turned off. Then I went back downstairs and listened.

"Sure enough, at about 2:30, I started hearing sounds from upstairs, just like he was arriving home from school. I heard footsteps, doors opening, and so forth. I was so sure that these were actual sounds that I figured the experiment was a bust on the first try. But after going upstairs, I discovered to my surprise that no one was home!

"The second day was an almost exact duplicate of the first. The next day I decided to place a tape recorder in his room, and I was able to actually record the sounds!"

13
APPARITIONS OF RELIGIOUS FIGURES

Early in 1967 the *Irish Independent* of Dublin carried the account of a miracle healing that had restored a dying nun to a healthy normal life after Pope John appeared and spoke to her.

Sister Caterina Capitani, a nun of the Sisters of Charity of St. Vincent de Paul, suffered from varicose veins of the esophagus, a condition thought to be incurable and inoperable. However, because the unfortunate sister endured continual hemorrhages, physicians decided to attempt an operation at Medical Missionaries of Mary of the Clinica Mediterranea in Naples, Italy. Two surgeries were performed, but they were unsuccessful; soon after, the incision on her stomach opened, and Sister Caterina's condition steadily worsened to the point where she collapsed. Desperate to attempt any new therapy, her doctors sent the nun south for a change of air, but she was soon returned to Naples when it was obvious that she was dying. The Medical Missionaries had no bed immediately available when she arrived, so Sister Caterina was taken to a nearby hospital.

The next day, when they had suitable accommodations for the nun, the Medical Missionaries were advised that it would be useless to move Sister Caterina, as she was dying and had only a very brief time to live.

Later, Sister Caterina recalled that she had been turned on her side and left alone. Then she felt somebody place a hand on her stomach. Summoning all her strength, she turned to see Pope John standing beside her bed. Although he did manifest in his papal robes, Sister Caterina said that she had recognized him easily.

In a quiet yet authoritative voice, the ethereal image of Pope John XXIII, who had died four years earlier on June 3, 1963, spoke words of great

Pope John XXIII lying in state inside St. Peter's Basilica on June 6, 1963.

comfort: "Sister, you have called to me so many times, as have so many of the Sisters of Charity of St. Vincent de Paul, that you have torn out of my heart this miracle. But now do not fear. You are healed!"

The spirit of Pope John then told Sister Caterina to call in the sisters and the doctors so that a test could be made. But first he assured her once again that no trace of her illness would remain. Just before he vanished, he told Sister Caterina to come to Rome and pray at his tomb. The moment the spirit of the deceased Pope disappeared, Sister Caterina rose from her bed and was elated that she felt no pain. When she summoned the sisters and doctors into her room, they were amazed to find that the scar on her abdomen, which had been open and bleeding, was now completely healed. There was, in fact, no longer any scar or any other physical sign to indicate that just moments before there had been a gaping wound. Sister Caterina was not expected to survive the day, yet that evening she was up and eating her supper with the community.

According to the *Irish Independent*, the miracle healing of Sister Caterina by the ghost of Pope John XXIII occurred in May 1966. "Ever since," the account reads, "[she] has lived a healthy life. This is a phenomenon that cannot be explained in a human way."

Psychic News, the well-known British Spiritualist weekly, agreed that the miraculous healing of Sister Caterina was a splendid event that could not be "explained in a human way," but it could not resist musing that when such an intervention of spirit entities occurred among conventional Christians, the act was often deemed a miracle. But whenever similar phenomena occurred among members of Spiritualist groups, the orthodox clergy would be likely to denounce the "miracle" as the work of the devil.

The observation made by *Psychic News* seems a fair one. While the healing of Sister Caterina may well be attributed to a nonphysical being, was it truly the spirit manifestation of Pope John XXIII or some other benevolent being who chose a form acceptable to the nun to better accomplish the miracle? And is the reported healing by an intervening ghost or spirit entity any less valid than such a miraculous act accomplished by a saint or a religious figure?

It has been repeatedly emphasized in this book that the author has no intention of undermining or criticizing any reader's personal religious faith. The author freely acknowledges that miracles do occur and that appearances of religious figures are commonly reported expressions of the individual mystical experience. This chapter does not seek to challenge any belief system that regards certain manifestations of religious figures as authentic. The transient materialization of benevolent spiritual beings is a universal phenomenon reported by members of all religious faiths. However, the entities who represent themselves as a particular figure may not always reveal their true identities. Indeed, they may reveal themselves in an image that may be more easily recognized by the percipient to be an agent of help and healing. It will be for each individual reader to decide if the accounts that follow were truly manifestations of the holy figures that witnesses believed them to be, or if they were guardians and benefactors from the spirit world who materialized in a certain guise to offer guidance and healing.

The most common religious figure seen in the Western world is that of the Madonna, Mother Mary, who appears to Protestants and Jews as well as Roman Catholics. For some reason, many individuals confuse the devotion that many Roman Catholics have for the Virgin they believe to be the mother of Jesus Christ with ownership of the Blessed Mother. This is far from the truth, although it cannot be denied that the most well-know apparitions of the Madonna have been to Roman Catholics in countries where that denomination is particularly high.

Those who give the appearances of the beautiful mother image a more universal interpretation believe that these manifestations may be that of the Magna Mater, the Great Mother, a personification of Gaia, the planetary feminine intelligence, herself, come to warn her many human children to take better care of their environment and the creatures that inhabit it. Others theorize that the apparitions of the Madonna may be that of benevolent nature spirits, who choose to appear as beautiful young women to appear less threatening to the visionaries who receive their messages of love and admonition. Indeed, perhaps the majority of individuals respond better to the gentle scoldings of a loving mother than the angry growls of a stern father.

Appearances of Jesus

With all the protestations of evangelical Christians who proclaim what a friend they have in Jesus, it seems strange that there are virtually no apparitions of Christ who have manifested to large groups of believers in a manner similar to the Blessed Mother, who has appeared to audiences of thousands of the devout and the penitent. At the same time, it may be the Christian tenet that Jesus is a personal savior that is dramatized by the Christian mystics and repentant sinners alike who claim a one-on-one spiritual interaction with a powerful being they believe to be Jesus Christ.

In an addendum to his response to the Steiger Questionnaire of Mystical and Paranormal Experiences, an Episcopalian priest wrote that he was awakened one night by the image of Jesus, who placed a kind of "burning coal" on his lips: "I began to speak. My wife woke up and she heard me speaking in what she later said was the strangest, most beautiful language that she had ever heard."

The next day, during his meeting with the bishop, he eloquently expressed his congregation's needs and won his superior's support for greater financial aid. "I know that without the appearance of Jesus and his help, I would have been intimidated, tongue tied, and argued ineffectually with the bishop for my cause," the priest said.

* * *

A young salesman wrote to testify how he had been mired in the despair of drug addiction and alcoholism. He had been reduced to a shaking skeleton that weighed barely a hundred pounds. What transforming influence and power had redeemed him from a miserable and ignoble death?

He had walked into a dirty, dingy motel room with a bottle and his usual bad attitude. Someone had left a Gideon Bible open on the bed. As he bent down to move it aside, the book flipped open and certain words in the text seemed to be glowing a bright red: Lo, I am with you always, even to the end of the world. The salesman mumbled sarcastic words to the effect that Jesus certainly had never been with him—and then there was a brilliant flash of light and an image of a bearded man in a robe stood there before him.

"He reached out to touch me, and it was like electricity going through me," the salesman said. "I felt pure, loving energy moving through every cell of

E. Debat-Ponsan's rendition of Christ appearing to soldiers on a battlefield.

my body. I know that it was Jesus who appeared in my room that night. He was gone in the next blink of an eye—but he took all my addictions, all my pain, and all my weaknesses with him. I have not taken any drugs or alcohol since that day eleven years ago."

APPEARANCES OF MOTHER MARY

It should be acknowledged that most claims of miracles and reported appearances of religious figures are not sanctioned or authenticated with unquestioning acceptance by the clergy of any organized religion. Although there are regular reports of visitations of Mother Mary from around the world, the Roman Catholic hierarchy officially recognizes only seven appearances of Mary.

- Guadalupe, Mexico: In 1531, an Indian named Juan Diego saw Mother Mary four times and was given a miraculously created

At the old castle in Hohenbaden, Germany, a vision of Virgin Mary was seen. The Virgin promised to stop the plague that had been raging in the surrounding area.

Nineteenth-century print of the Virgin Mary appearing to Melanie Mathieu and Maximin Giraud at La Salette, France, on September 19, 1846.

serape as evidence of her heavenly visitation. Currently, there is a petition to have Juan Diego canonized and made a saint, but a vocal minority of priests and church historians oppose the movement on the grounds that there is no convincing proof that Juan Diego ever existed. Some historians argue that he was probably fabricated by the Spanish conquerors as a device to convert the native tribes to Catholicism.

- Paris, France: The Holy Mother appeared to a nun in 1830 and asked her to fashion a medal to commemorate the immaculate conception.

- La Salette, France: A weeping, sorrowful Mary manifested to two peasant children on September 19, 1846, and instructed them to do penance for their sins.

- Lourdes, France: Identifying herself as the Immaculate Conception, Mary appeared eighteen times to fourteen-year-old Bernadette Soubirous between February 11 and July 16, 1858.

The waters of the miraculous spring that appeared according to Mary's promise are world famous for their healing powers.

- Fatima, Portugal: Mother Mary appeared to three children near Fatima, instructing them to say their rosary frequently. During her six visits between May 13 and October 13, 1917, Mary issued a number of prophecies, one of which is still said to be held secret by the Vatican.

- Beaurahng, Belgium: Between November 29,1932, and January 3, 1933, five children at a convent school experienced three remarkable encounters with Mother Mary in the school garden.

- Banneaux, Belgium: Mother Mary appeared to an eleven-year-old girl eight times between January 15 and March 2, 1933, in the garden of her parents' humble cottage.

Since 1981 the Virgin Mary has appeared and spoken to children in Medjugorje, Bosnia-Herzegovina.

There are a number of other visions of Mary that have been highly publicized and may be better known than many of those on the approved list:

- Garabandal, Spain: A series of two thousand ecstatic visions of Mother Mary began for four children one Sunday after Mass in 1961. The visitations continued until 1965 and produced numerous prophecies and astonishing miracles.

- Zeitoun, Egypt: As many as a million witnesses may have glimpsed the figure of the glowing Madonna standing, kneeling, or praying beside a cross on the roof of St. Mary's Coptic Church. Miraculous cures manifested among the pilgrims from 1968 to 1971.

- Medjugorje, Yugoslavia: In 1981, six children saw Mother Mary holding the infant Jesus near the village. The holy figure appeared on an almost daily basis for five months, leaving behind a continuing legacy of miraculous hearings.

- Bayside, New York: From 1970 until her death on August 3, 1995, the "Bayside Seeress," Veronica Lueken, issued pronouncements from Mother Mary against the spiritual abuses of contemporary society.

⸻◦⸻

THE DANCING SUN AT FATIMA

When two bursts of lightning flashed across the sky on that cloudless day of May 13, 1917, the three shepherd children tending the flocks of Antonio dos Santos outside the village of Fatima immediately stopped what they were doing and looked quizzically at one another. Lightning did not come out of a clear sky.

In the next few moments ten-year-old Lucia dos Santos and her cousins seven-year-old Francisco and nine-year-old Jacinta Marto had their attention drawn to the leaves of an old oak tree in a high plateau that was called Cova da Iria. There, to their astonishment, they saw a strange globe of light emanating a kind of iridescent radiance.

The children were frozen with fright as they saw an aura develop in the center of the globe of light. Then the image of lovely young woman who appeared to be about eighteen years old manifested within the illuminated ball. As they stared wide-eyed in awe, she told them not to be afraid. Lucia was the only one who could actually hear the words of the beautiful woman and she related the message to the others.

The children wanted to know who she was. Again, Lucia repeated what the vision said: "If you return to this very spot on the thirteenth of every month until October, I will tell you then who I am."

"For now," the lady said, "you must keep my appearance a secret. You must tell no one that you have seen me. And you must say your rosary every day!" And then the ghost, the spirit, whatever it was, vanished almost as suddenly as she had appeared.

Lucia, Jacinta, and Francisco did say their rosary every day, but the lady had asked too much of three children to expect them to remain silent about the wondrous vision that had manifested before them while they tended sheep. When they did try to tell their families, however, all three of the children received the same reaction. They were scolded for lying. Within a few days, the parish priest stopped by their homes to express his intense displeasure with children who made up silly ghost stories—and then ended up believing them. Of course, the story of the mysterious lady spread throughout the villages, and on June 13 the children were accompanied by nearly sixty of their neighbors when they went to the high plateau where the spirit had said she would appear again. Try as they might, the assembled townsfolk saw nothing,

Every year thousands of worshipers gather at the Fatima Sanctuary in Portugal.

but Lucia claimed to see a flash of lightning—and soon the crowd could clearly hear Lucia asking the unseen visitor a number of questions. Francisco and Jacinta testified that they, too, could hear the lady.

Although visitation did not last long, the message from the beautiful lady was both sorrowful and startling. Francisco and Jacinta would soon be completing their earthly mission and returning to heaven, and Lucia would remain to spread her message.

Although the village of Fatima was populated by only a few hundred inhabitants, the word of the miraculous manifestations traveled quickly throughout all of Portugal. By the time July 13 arrived, five thousand pilgrims joined the three children at the foot of the oak tree. During her third visit, the lady identified herself as the Immaculate Heart of Mother Mary, and Lucia repeated her words announcing that World War I would soon end. There was a proviso, however: humanity must cease offending God or another and more terrible war would begin.

After word of the third visitation of the Lady had been widely circulated, Lucia, Jacinta, and Francisco were arrested and placed in jail. At that time the civil authorities were seeking to control and to minimize the influence of the Roman Catholic Church. Although Portugal had always been known as the "Land of Mary," its traditional monarchy had been replaced by a revolutionary republican government. The new regime had already sought to abolish the Catholic sacraments, and they boasted that in two generations they would completely eliminate the Roman Catholic Church in all of Portugal.

And now there were these three peasant children from the hills of Fatima who were about to foment a religious revolution. The only hope the state had was to expose the children as liars—or intimidate them into making full retractions of their statements about their supposed visions. But the three little visionaries remained steadfast. Even the prospect of being tossed into boiling oil did not deter them from testifying to the validity of their experiences.

On August 13, the day of the next visitation of the Lady, fifteen thousand pilgrims gathered at Cova da Iria. When they learned that the three children had been placed in jail, they were outraged. The authorities soon discovered that they had stirred up more unrest among the population than they had estimated. A staggering number of people believed in the visions that the children reported. A decision was quickly made to release Lucia, Jacinta, and Francisco before thousands marched on the jail and the police found themselves attempting to quell a riot. A few days later, the children kept their fourth appointment with the lady—and although they were a bit late, she did appear.

By September 13, the time for the fifth visitation, the children found themselves nearly crushed by the vast crowd that had appeared. Among the pilgrims in the great assemblage were those begging for healing and for the forgiveness of their sins. The blind, the crippled, the maimed, the deaf, the terribly ill had all come to Fatima to pray for a personal miracle.

When the three children at last managed to arrive at the oak tree, they began to say the rosary. After only a little while there appeared the flash of light that prefaced the beautiful lady's arrival, and then she manifested before them. She told Lucia that she would heal some of those who had come expecting miraculous cures, but in October she would perform a miracle so that all would believe. At that time, she promised, a number of other holy figures would accompany her.

It is well known that the Roman Catholic Church has a number of committees and ecclesiastical authorities who examine all matters pertaining to claimed miracles or visitations from holy figures. The Reverend Doctor Manuel Nunes Formigao was assigned to investigate the occurrences taking place near the tiny village of Fatima, and he was immediately struck by certain similarities between the progression of the Fatima visitations with those that had occurred in La Salette, France, in 1846. At that time two shepherd children had seen Mother Mary in a vision and had been told to warn others that great calamities would come to France if its citizenry did not cease offending God. Lucia admitted that she had heard of the visitation of Our Lady at La Salette, but she said that the story had never crossed her mind until the priest reminded her of it.

Although Fr. Formigao was impressed by the sincerity of the children, he remained quite uncertain whether some—or all—of what they said was simply their own flights of fantasy. He told his superiors that he must wait until the appointed day of October 13 and appraise those events before he could make any kind of objective judgment.

By early morning on October 13, 1917, all roads to Fatima were clogged with people who had come from Portugal and much of Europe to see Mother Mary's promised miracle for themselves. They came hobbling on crutches, carrying the children who were too ill to walk, hoisting others on stretchers. Some had walked all night, the rich and poor alike, all hoping for a cure, a revelation, an absolution. An estimated seventy thousand people managed to gather on the Cova da Iria by noon. To add to the discomfort, confusion, and impatience of the vast crowd, it began to rain.

At noon, Lucia stood beside her cousins Francisco and Jacinta at the oak tree and commanded the vast crowd to close their umbrellas. After several minutes of standing unprotected in the downpour, the crowd began to get restless. It was a chilly day in October. Everyone was soaked, and they were afraid they would all be catching colds or coming down with pneumonia. Suddenly, Lucia cried out that everyone should kneel down. Thousands of eyes and ears strained to see and hear what the ten-year-old girl was perceiving, but even the most devout among them were not able to behold Mother Mary; just Lucia and her two cousins could see the vision.

Lucia repeated the Lady's words that she wished a chapel to be built in honor of the Lady of the Rosary. Lucia asked the Lady about the healing of sick persons and the conversion of sinners. The Lady replied that certain of those who had gathered on the high plateau that day would be healed, but all must amend their lives and ask forgiveness for their sins. The rain stopped abruptly, and the clouds parted to allow the sun to appear in a patch of bright blue sky. Lucia, Jacinta, and Francisco watched the Lady ascend into the sky, and then, alongside the sun, they beheld St. Joseph with the Child Jesus and Our Lady robed in white with a blue mantle.

While no other members of the multitude assembled that day saw the holy figures described by Lucia dos Santos, they beheld a sight equally as astonishing. According to thousands of observers, the sun began to spin, extending fiery fingers across the blue sky. As the sun danced and spun, Earth itself appeared to change colors. At first the terrain seemed cast in a kind of red shadow, which altered color to shades of orange, yellow, green, blue, indigo, and violet.

According to witnesses, this eerie phenomenon repeated itself three times. Then to the complete horror of the assembled pilgrims, the sun began to plunge toward Earth. As if with one voice, thousands of men and women screamed at the terrible sight. Thousands fell to their knees in terror, pleading with God to have mercy. Others silently stared upward, too frightened even to pray.

Most of the seventy thousand who gathered outside Fatima that day believed that it was the end of the world. The dramatic demonstration of supernatural power continued for ten minutes. Finally, as if in answer to the crowd's collective prayer for mercy, the sun ceased its devastating plunge to Earth and began to climb back toward its position in the heavens.

Avelino de Almeida, editor of the newspaper, *Seculo*, had joined the crowd that day as a skeptical journalist who was also very much opposed to the beliefs of the Roman Catholic Church. But on October 13, 1917, he admitted that his cynicism toward religion and his doubts concerning miracles had been severely shaken. Writing in *0 Seculo*, he stated: "Certainly beyond all cosmic laws were the sudden tremblings and movements of the sun, dancing as it were … before the astonished multitude who gazed in awe. It remains for the competent to pronounce on the dance macabre of the sun, which today at Fatima has made hosannas burst from the breasts of the faithful and naturally has impressed … even freethinkers and other persons not at all interested in religious matters. To this unbeliever, it was a spectacle unique and incredible if I had not been a witness to it. I can still see the immense crowd turn toward the

This photograph was taken in Karascond Church, Hungary, in 1989. The vision of the Virgin Mary and Jesus was not seen by the photographer through his lens as the picture was taken, but it was seen by Karoly Ligeti, an art restoration specialist who was working on the scaffolding above.

sun, which reveals itself free of the clouds, and I hear the nearest spectators crying, 'Miracle, miracle!'"

After the day of the dancing sun at Fatima, Lucia, Francisco, and Jacinta were elevated to celebrity status and became the darlings of the secular press. Wherever the children went, crowds gathered to ask them weighty questions about the meaning of life and the world beyond death. Reporters were never far from their sides, and every word that any of the three children uttered was dutifully recorded and published. Photographers declared anywhere the children walked as a golden photo opportunity.

Although Jacinta and Francisco Marto had been told by the Lady that they would die soon, they remained untroubled. In fact, they told anyone who asked about the brief duration of their earthly mission that they were looking forward to returning home to Heaven.

However, Jacinta had always been a very sensitive, somewhat intense child, and she was greatly disturbed by what she considered to be the "worship" that the masses directed at them. As she became increasingly withdrawn, Jacinta began to experience prophetic visions of her own. Most of these glimpses into the future were quite violent and ghastly in nature, and she revealed that she had been shown terrible bombings in France and Holland. London and Frankfurt, she said, would be nearly in ruins as the result of bombs that would rain death from the skies. All these awful things, she foretold, would take place in twenty-five years (that would be in 1942, when the destruction wrought by World War II would be devastating Europe and Great Britain).

Early in 1919, Francisco became ill with influenza. On the morning of April 3, the eleven-year-old boy received his first Communion. On April 4, at ten o'clock in the morning, he died. Jacinta became a victim of influenza a few months after her brother's passing. Medical specialists recommended a complicated chest surgery, and she was brought to the Hospital of Dona Stefania in Lisbon. Before she was transported to the city, the nine-year-old girl told Lucia that The Holy Mother had told her that she would die alone in Lisbon.

There are many stories concerning the appearances of the Holy Mother to the little girl as Jacinta lay struggling for life in the hospital so far from her village. She repeated a good number of Mary's prophetic visions, and she uttered personal predictions for those around her that astounded many. In one instance, one of the doctors who was treating her asked Jacinta to pray for him before she went to heaven. Jacinta sighed and tearfully informed the physician that he and his daughter would enter the heavenly gates before she did. The startled doctor left Jacinta's room shaking his head in disbelief, but it was not long before he and his daughter were killed in a tragic accident. On the afternoon of February 20, 1920, her attending nurse found Jacinta Marto dead, a beatific smile upon her lips, as if welcoming the Lady who had come to take her home.

Shortly after the deaths of Jacinta and Francisco Marto, Lucia dos Santos entered a convent school and took the name of Sister Maria das Dores, "Sister Mary of Sorrows." The young girl proved that she had seriously assumed the responsibility given to her by the Lady, and she spent her life perpetuating the message, the mystery, and the wonder of Fatima.

The astonishing collapse of the Soviet empire in 1991 no doubt came as less of a surprise to those who had faith in the predictions that the Lady made to the three children outside the Portuguese village in 1917. Millions of men and women throughout the world believe that the dissolution of the Communist superpower was the work of the Holy Mother and was intended by her to be the fulfillment of a promise that she had made seventy-four years before to Jacinta, Francisco, and Lucia. The children were given three prophecies, the first of which forecast the end of World War I (which was still raging at the time of the visitations) and the terri-

Karoly Ligeti holds a photograph of the vision he saw in Karascond Church, Hungary.

ble destruction wrought by an even greater war if humankind failed to repent of its sins. The second prediction foretold the advent of the Russian Revolution and the subsequent rise of Communism, which would spread atheism throughout the world. However, Mother Mary promised that if the Pope, in concert with all the world's bishops, consecrated Russia to her holy name, the nation would eventually be converted. In 1984, Pope John Paul II consecrated Russia to the Virgin Mary at St. Peter's in Rome. Seven years later, the Soviet Union was shattered.

Lucia kept Mary's third prophecy a secret, but she was said to have entrusted its contents to Pope John XXIII in 1960. The prediction remains the source of much controversy and speculation. It was said to have been made public at the request of Pope John Paul II on June 26, 2000, and revealed that a "bishop dressed in white" would be shot during a widespread persecution of the Church. Pope John Paul interpreted the prediction as referring to an assassination attempt that wounded him in 1981. After the third secret had been made public, Pope John Paul proclaimed its message an invitation for all believers to pray for peace in the world. In January 2002, Sister Lucia, who at that time still lived in a Carmelite convent in Coimbra, Portugal, denied rumors that she had received new revelations from Mother Mary.

━━⟪∫⟫━━

AN ANGEL AND A BEAUTIFUL LADY APPEAR AT GARABANDAL

On June 18, 1961, four young girls were playing on the outskirts of the small village of San Sebastian de Garabandal, Spain, when they heard what they believed to be a loud clap of thunder, which heralded the appearance of a bright figure that they knew at once must be an angel. The magnificent being confirmed their first impression by identifying himself as the Archangel Michael.

Conchita Gonzalez, Maria Dolores Mazon, Jacinta Gonzalez, and Maria Cruz Gonzalez had come to the area to play, not to have a mystical experience. Maria Cruz was only eleven; the other three girls were twelve. They were all from very poor families, and in spite of the common Gonzalez surname, none of the girls were related.

That single remarkable experience would probably have lasted the village girls for life, but Michael appeared to them many times throughout the month of June. Finally he promised them that on July 2 they would be able to meet the Blessed Mother herself.

Located in the northern part of Spain in a rugged area of the Picos de Europa Mountains, the population of the tiny town of Garabandal was only about three hundred. There was no doctor in the village, nor was there a resident priest. But there were dozens of the devout and the curious who vowed that they would accompany the four girls to the spot where Archangel Michael had predicted Mother Mary would appear.

At six in the evening, the girls walked to the area to keep their important appointment. In a short time, according to the young revelators, the Holy Mother appeared in the company of two angels, one of whom was Archangel Michael. The girls went into ecstatic states, and witnesses declared that their faces reflected the light that they claimed to behold around the Blessed Mother. They described her as dressed in a white robe with a blue mantle and a crown of golden stars. They said that her hands were slender. Her hair, deep nut brown, was parted in the middle. Her mouth was very pretty, and she had a fine nose. To their eyes, she appeared to be a young woman of about eighteen, rather tall. And the girls excitedly agreed that there was no voice in the world like hers. Mother Mary had manifested herself, the girls said, as Our Lady of Carmel.

During 1961 and 1962, the Lady appeared to the girls a number of times every week. Whenever the visitations occurred, villagers and pilgrims alike could clearly see the girls entering into ecstatic, or deep trance, states that could last from a few minutes to many hours. Numerous eyewitnesses said that the faces of the visionaries revealed an extraordinary sweetness when they were enraptured by the Blessed Mother. It was as if they were transformed by an inner light and their beautiful faces were reflecting a holy glow from a divine spark within.

It was observed by many that the girls seemed transported to a dimension of reality where time did not matter. They never gave the slightest sign of fatigue or discomfort, in spite of the fact that they might be kneeling on rocks with their heads violently thrown backward. On cold days the children came barefoot in the snow to listen for hours to the messages of Mother Mary.

At first there were thoughtless, insensitive skeptics who, during the children's period of ecstasy, would hit them, burn them with matches, or stick them with needles. None of these cruel stimuli elicited the slightest physical response from any of the four girls. On one occasion an inconsiderate photographer flashed powerful beams of light in the revelators' eyes that under normal circumstances would have burned their retinas and perhaps even caused blindness. Their eyes remained wide open and joyful, and none of the girls even blinked.

On May 2, 1962, the angel told Conchita that God would perform a miracle and allow the Sacred Host to be seen on her tongue as she received the wafer during an angelic communion service. The date for this miracle, the heavenly being said, would be July 18. At the appointed place and the designated moment, Conchita dropped to her knees, opened her mouth, and put out her tongue to receive the sacred host. As excited pilgrims drew near with lanterns and flashlights, photographer Don Alejandro Daminas who was standing only three feet from Conchita, was able to get clear pictures of the wafer materializing on the twelve-year-old revelator's tongue. Those who witnessed the miracle stressed the point that Conchita's arms were at her side the entire time. Never did she raise her hands to her mouth to "palm" a communion wafer on her tongue.

Over a period of nineteen months, the Blessed Mother and Archangel Michael appeared to Conchita or to one or more of the other three girls some two thousand times. Witnesses observed the girls being levitated in their ecstasy, rising as if to kiss or embrace the holy figures. Sometimes they were seen to be lowered slowly backward to the ground, their backs ramrod stiff and straight. Once a large crowd even saw them walking in the air.

One of the strangest of the phenomena associated with the manifestations at Garabandal occurred when a young Jesuit priest named Luis Andreu begged the girls and the Blessed Mother to be granted the ability to behold the wondrous sights that the blessed little ones were permitted to see. At last Father Andreu's request was acknowledged, and he was given permission to participate in a holy visitation. Although the thousands who assembled that day to watch the simple farm girls in their ecstasy, conversing with the unseen holy personages, were unable to see an angel or the Holy Mother, Father Andreu became the single exception, permitted to gaze upon the celestial beings as clearly as Conchita and her friends.

> **W**ithin thirty-six hours of his remarkable interaction with the supernatural, Fr. Luis Andreu died....

The healthy, robust young priest left Garabandal fervently proclaiming his great, ineffable joy. Within thirty-six hours of his remarkable interaction with the supernatural, Fr. Luis Andreu died in the midst of exclaiming to a friend that he had just experienced the happiest day of his life. Doctors at the clinic who examined the young priest's body stated that they could find no discernible causes for the healthy man's sudden demise. His fellow priests simply stated that Luis had died of joy.

Conchita Gonzalez received her final visitation from Mother Mary on November 13, 1965. Conchita said that she was shown a preview of the awful chastisement that would be humankind's fate if the warnings of Mary were ignored, and she urged everyone to repent quickly.

⸺᚜ᛟ᚛⸻

Twenty-four Similarities in Appearances of Ghosts and Holy Figures

Reverend B. W. Palmer, a retired Methodist clergyman from Haines City, Florida, spent many years collecting documentation on hundreds of contemporary visions of religious figures from around the world. His exhaustive research on the subject, which he kindly shared with me, indicated that there were at least twenty-four methods that these religious figures utilized to manifest their images. Without stressing the point, the reader can easily determine that such a list of the revelation of religious figures might also apply to the materialization of ghosts and spirit entities.

1. The skies appear to open up, and the religious figure appears to descend to Earth.

2. In the presence of a human witness, the religious figure appears to descend in a shaft of light.

3. The holy being appears or disappears through a solid object, such as a door or a wall.

4. Witnesses may hear footsteps outside the house. When they hear a knock at the door, they open it to behold the religious figure.

5. The figure appears as though he or she is a picture on the wall.

6. Witnesses may awaken because they feel a spiritual presence in the room or they may feel someone's touch. When they open their eyes, they see the religious figure bending over them.

7. An angel may first appear to the witnesses and lead them to the materialization of the holy figure of Mother Mary, Jesus, Moses, and so forth.

8. A witness may see the face of the religious figure appear above a person who is desperately in need of help.

9. Witnesses may hear a voice that tells them to go to a certain place and to do a certain thing. When they comply, they encounter the Holy Mother, Jesus, or other figures.

10. The image of Mother Mary or another religious figure may appear in the sky, greatly magnified.

11. Witnesses may be awakened by what they at first suppose is the light of a very bright moon. In the next few moments they see the image of the religious personage.

12. The Virgin Mary has often been seen appearing out of a cloud and moving toward witnesses. She has also often used clouds to make her departure.

13. A cloud or a heavy mist may materialize in a witness's room. Out of that mist, an image of the religious figure will appear.

14. During the Fatima miracle, the Holy Mother appeared to the three children in exactly the same way. As often as they were interrogated, all three consistently gave the same description of what they had seen. In many cases, however, Mother Mary or another religious figure appears to several witnesses at the same time and is seen in different ways by the individual percipients. To one witness at the scene, the figure may appear as a ball of light; to another, a flash of lightning; to yet another as a disembodied voice.

15. On some occasions, the being may appear in a room occupied by many people and yet is seen by only one or two witnesses.

16. The image of the holy figure may appear in the dreams of witnesses. Many times such a manifestation will bring about a healing.

17. After the figure has manifested, it may vanish suddenly, or it may fade away slowly, moving into a cloud or through the ceiling, doors, or the floor. The figure may also walk away

In 1968 crowds of people would gather outside the Coptic Orthodox Church of St. Mary in Zeitoun, Egypt, to witness the visions of the Virgin Mary, which were often visible for hours at a time.

from the witnesses, fading from view as it moves farther and farther away from them.

18. In most manifestations of holy figures, only the witnesses singled out for communications may see or hear them, even though there may be thousands of people present; this was the case when Mother Mary appeared at Fatima.

19. The religious figure often manifests in a strange light that illumines both it and the witnesses.

20. In a number of visionary appearances, the witnesses said that they did not see the holy figure, but they were aware of its presence through the manifestation of a supernatural light or through a voice that came to them.

21. Numerous men and women have experienced out-of-body phenomena in which they claimed to have seen the holy figure looking after them.

22. In other out-of-body experiences, people claimed to have seen the holy figure together with deceased friends or relatives.

23. In still other out-of-body experiences, witnesses have said to have perceived the lower-spirit worlds where good spirits attempt to assist lower-level entities and where the holy figure and attending angels seek to give solace and comfort.

24. During near-death experiences, men and women have returned to consciousness stating they journeyed to heaven, where they saw the holy figure together with deceased friends or relatives and attending hosts of angels.

MYSTERIOUS LIGHTS ATOP ST. MARY'S IN ZEITOUN, EGYPT

On April 2, 1968, two mechanics working in a city garage across the street from St. Mary's Church of Zeitoun, Egypt, were startled to see what appeared to be a nun dressed in white standing on top of the large dome at the center of the roof. The two men decided not to waste a single moment in fearful speculation. One of them ran into the church to get a priest; the other telephoned for a police emergency squad. When the priest ran from the church to look up at the dome in the center of the roof, he was the first to recognize the remarkable event for what it truly was, a manifestation of Mother Mary. The now glowing white image of the Blessed Mother remained in full view of the priest, the two mechanics, and a growing crowd of excited witnesses for several minutes, then disappeared.

> Amazingly, the appearances of the glowing Lady manifested sporadically atop the dome of St. Mary's Church at Zeitoun for three years.

The news of the Holy Mother's visitation spread rapidly from the residents of Zeitoun, a suburb of Cairo, to the greater metropolitan population of over six million. While it is true that the religious makeup of Cairo is largely Muslim, there exists a fairly large Coptic Catholic minority. Thousands began to gather around the majestic church of Zeitoun at Tomanbey Street and Khalil Lane to see for themselves the Queen of Heaven come to Earth.

When the mysterious image came again to rest upon the dome of the church on April 3, a large crowd of men and women were there to greet her with awed shouts of jubilation and whispered prayers of supplication. As if responding to such a devout and enthusiastic reception, she returned to the church on April 9.

Amazingly, the appearances of the glowing Lady manifested sporadically atop the dome of St. Mary's Church at Zeitoun for three years. Millions witnessed the visitations, and numerous photographs of the spiritual phenomenon are in existence.

The apparitions were most often heralded by mysterious lights, which were said to flash somewhat in the manner of sheet lighting. These unusual displays of illumination would continue for about fifteen minutes before the image would appear in a brilliant burst of light. According to witnesses, these peculiar lightning-like flashes would manifest sometimes above the church and at other times in the strange clouds that occasionally formed over St. Mary's. It was frequently reported that these formations of clouds would take shape over the dome from a sky that only a brief time before had been clear and completely free of even a wisp of a cloud.

On one occasion Bishop Gregorius declared that the clouds were formed of incense, admittedly of such a quantity that millions of censers could not produce their equal. The perfumed clouds descended from atop the dome and settled over the multitudes encircling the church, who also bore testimony to the scented blessing.

Another aspect of the phenomenon reported by witnesses was the mysterious appearance of glowing, birdlike creatures, which would often materialize both before and after the apparition of Mother Mary. According to numerous journalists who traveled from all over the world to record the miraculous series of phenomena in Zeitoun, the entities resembled glowing white doves. Other observers argued that the airborne beings were larger than doves, more the size of pigeons. They could not be any kind of ordinary bird, stated one account of the mysterious, illuminated birds because, first of all, they flew too rapidly—and without ever moving their wings. They were spotless, emitting white light, and they appeared to glide before, into, and around the image of Mother Mary. The mysterious birds materialized, appeared, and disappeared without any sound at all.

In his book *Our Lady Returns to Egypt*, Reverend J. Palmer documents the various attitudes of the Blessed Mother as she manifested atop St. Mary's dome: "At first she appeared above the dome in traditional form, wearing the veil and long robes associated with other appearances, such as at Lourdes and Fatima….Mary does not stand motionless, but is seen bowing and greeting the people in silence. She bends from the waist, moves her arms in … blessing and sometimes holds out an olive branch to the people."

Reverend Palmer, an American priest who traveled to Cairo to witness the miracle for himself, stated that Mary was seen to appear "between the trees in the courtyard in front of the church; she has appeared under each of the four small domes, through the windows of the larger dome, and has often walked on the flat church roof so as to be seen by those standing on all sides of the church."

The visions of the Blessed Mother continued to manifest at the church at Zeitoun from 1968 through 1971. The duration of her visits varied greatly, from a few minutes to several hours. One evening in June 1968, she was viewed from 9:00 P.M. to 4:30 A.M.

Strangely enough, Mary chose to remain silent from her majestic and commanding pulpit atop the church in Cairo. Although thousands of people claimed miraculous cures as they looked upward at the glowing figure of the Holy Mother, no one announced any special messages from Mary. There were no warnings of impending Earth changes, no admonitions to repent or to cease sinning. Neither were there any predictions, secret or otherwise.

GHOSTLY ENCOUNTERS WITH FAMOUS MEN AND WOMEN

THE LITTLE RED GHOST OF FRANCE

France has a ghost whose history is so well-established that it is mentioned in scores of books, official records, and even Napoleon's diaries. According to legend, the ghost known as "the little red man," appeared to some of the nation's most notable personalities for more than 260 years, garnering a reputation as a harbinger of tragedy. The ghost seemed to center its activity in Paris, at the Louvre and Tuileries palaces.

Catherine de Medici is said to have been the first person to have confronted the apparition. In was in 1564, during the construction of the Tuileries, that de Medici came face to face with a gnome-like creature dressed completely in scarlet. It soon became apparent to haughty Catherine that her unannounced companion was not a man of flesh and blood, and she interpreted the strange visit as an omen of bad luck. As Catherine had already begun to foment trouble between Roman Catholics and Protestants in France, and she induced the king to order the terrible St. Bartholomew's Day massacre of the Huguenots, scarlet was an appropriate color for the ghost to have worn.

The little red man appeared to Henry IV just before the monarch was assassinated by an insane schoolteacher in 1610. In 1792 startled chambermaids discovered the scarlet-clad gnome in the bed of Louis XVI when the threatened king was making a futile attempt to escape the machinations of the French revolutionaries. A few months later, guards claimed to have seen the little red ghost in the prison where Louis and Marie Antoinette awaited their turn with the guillotine.

Napoleon Bonaparte, by Paul Delaroche.

The red-hued entity first appeared to Napoleon in 1798, during the military leader's Egyptian campaign. The spirit is said to have materialized before Napoleon and to have made a bargain with the ambitious officer. According to the terms of the contract, Napoleon was to enjoy victory and triumph on the battlefields of Europe for a decade. The strange visitor said that he had advised the rulers of France in the past and declared that he had appeared to Napoleon in order to counsel him as well. The ghostly advisor told the military genius that he had been at his side since he had been a schoolboy. "I know you better than you know yourself," the spirit chided him. The entity told Napoleon that his orders to the French fleet had not been obeyed. While the Egyptian campaign had begun on a note of triumph with the Pyramids, the ghost told him that the enterprise would fail; Napoleon would return to France and find her closed in by England, Russia, Turkey, and an allied Europe.

As the scarlet ghost predicted, the Egyptian campaign failed. In 1809, after the Battle of Wagram, Napoleon made his headquarters at Schonbrunn, and his mysterious advisor once again appeared to him. Napoleon had conducted 10 years of successful campaigning, and he asked his supernatural advisor for five more years of guaranteed triumph. The ghost granted his request with the admonition that the greedy conqueror should not launch a campaign that would take him on Russian soil. Napoleon ignored the warning and met with a disaster that proved to be more significant than the physical defeat he suffered at Waterloo.

The red ghost made his third and final appearance before Napoleon on the morning of January 1, 1814, shortly before the emperor was forced to abdicate. The gnome first appeared to Counsellor of State Molé and demanded that he be allowed to see the emperor on matters of urgent importance. Molé had been given strict orders that the emperor was not to be disturbed, but when he told Napoleon that a red man wanted to speak with him, the emperor asked for the mysterious stranger to be granted immediate entrance.

It is said that Napoleon beseeched the ghost for time to complete the execution of certain proposals, but the prophetic messenger gave him only three months to achieve general peace or it would all be over for him. Rather than attempting to bring peace to Europe, Napoleon desperately tried to launch a new eastern campaign. Such a move left Paris to fall into the hands of the allies; and on April 1, three months after the red man's final visit to the emperor, Talleyrand and the senate called for Napoleon's abdication.

The ghost's last reported appearance occurred in 1824, when Louis XVIII lay dying in Tuileries Palace. The mysterious, gnome-like apparition has, however, earned itself a strange but secure position in French history.

KING CHARLES XII OF SWEDEN MEETS THE LITTLE GRAY MAN

Interestingly, King Charles XII of Sweden sought the counsel of a little gray man with a ruddy complexion, who gave Charles a ring that vanished on the day of the ruler's death. As he cut a mighty swath across Europe, Russia, and Turkey, the young King Charles became known as the "Alexander of the North." As his bravery and feats in battle became legendary, Charles resisted his mysterious counselor's entreaties to make peace. In 1718, as the Swedes were besieging Fredrikshald, one of Charles's officers noticed that the ring the king had worn throughout his reign was no longer on his finger. Moments later, Charles fell dead from a head wound.

A Prophetic Spirit Appeared to George Washington

In 1880, 81 years after George Washington's death, the *National Tribune* ran a story that had often been told by Anthony Sherman, a man who had been a close friend to Washington. The story related Washington's encounters with a prophetic visitor from the spirit world. According to Sherman, in the winter of 1777 a despairing General George Washington was studying maps and making military plans in his cabin at Valley Forge when he saw a rising, curling vapor filling the room. An astonished Washington watched a dark-haired, long-robed entity materialize before him. At first the general thought it was the ghost of a Native American taking form, but then he heard three loud blasts from a trumpet and a deep, commanding voice say, "Son of the Republic, look and learn."

The vapor that surrounded the ghost glowed with surging life as it formed an image of the globe. The entity dipped water onto the forms of Europe, Asia, and Africa, and Washington was horrified when thick black clouds began to arise from each continent. The odious clouds merged into one dark mass that began to move toward North America. Within the black cloud, Washington saw hordes of armed men land and begin to devastate cities that had sprung up only moments before. Washington's ears rang with the roars of the cannons, the shouts and cries of millions who had become locked in mortal combat. Above the sounds of strife, the mysterious voice once again admonished him to "look and learn." Then the shadowy figure sprinkled water upon North America, and the invading armies were swept away.

Washington told his friend Sherman that when the invading armies were swept away, he was once again able to see villages, towns, and cities springing up. In a loud voice the spirit cried out, "While the stars remain, and the heavens send down dew upon the earth, so long shall the Union last." As the vivid scene faded, Washington once again became aware of the mysterious figure in the shadows of his rude cabin at Valley Forge. "Son of the Republic," the figure said, "what you have seen is thus interpreted. Three great perils will come upon the Republic. The most fearful for her is the third. But the whole world united shall not prevail against her. Let every child of the Republic learn to live for his God, his land, and his Union." With those words, Washington told Sherman, the spirit being vanished. Revitalized in body, mind, and spirit, Washington rose from his chair convinced that he had seen a vision that had presented him the birth, progress, and destiny of the union. He was filled with a renewed conviction that the revolution would not fail. As miserable and depressing as the conditions were during that terrible winter in Valley Forge, the ragged, freezing, starving soldiers would not be defeated, and the goals of freedom and independence would be won.

THE GHOST OF WASHINGTON HALTED ROBERT E. LEE

It was September 1862, and the inexperienced Union troops had been shattered in battle after battle by the sharp-shooting, determined Confederate forces. President Lincoln had called on General George B. McClellan to take charge of the chaos and whip the Union troops into shape.

A 1795 oil painting of President George Washington by Rembrandt Peale.

McClellan slumped wearily over the desk in his tent. Before him lay campaign maps, battle reports, and a large scale map on which all known Confederate positions had been marked. His eyelids drooped, and he fell asleep on his desk.

His slumber did not last long. A booming voice suddenly filled his campaign tent. "General McClellan, do you sleep at your post? Rouse yourself, or before you can prevent it, the foe will be in Washington!" Wondering if some bold messenger had arrived with news of an impending confederate attack, McClellan snapped to attention. When he opened his eyes, he beheld a luminous apparition of George Washington. General McClellan later told the Portland, Maine *Evening Courier* that the spirit of Washington wasted no time in delivering his message: "If God had not willed it otherwise, before tomorrow's sun had set, the Confederate flag would have waved above the Capitol and your own grave! Note what you see. Your time to act is short!"

After Washington's ghost made a gesture, a living map detailing the most current Confederate troop positions appeared in front of McClellan. He grabbed a quill from his desk and began to jot down all that he could see. He was very much aware that if the Confederate armies took Washington, D.C., they would break the spirit of the entire union. The living tableau changed, allowing McClellan to see maneuvers the Confederates planned in the future. He furiously marked the positions that the map revealed to him on his own campaign maps. "You have been warned in time, General McClellan," the spirit of Washington said softly. With those words, the image of George Washington began to fade and McClellan once again found himself alone in his tent.

At first he thought the experience had merely been a vivid dream, but then he saw the markings and the symbols of Confederate maneuvers he'd made on his campaign maps. He would give the orders to move out at once.

Because of the knowledge that McClellan gained during his unusual paranormal experience, the Union troops were able to halt the Confederate invasion of Washington at Antietam and pursue General Robert E. Lee by anticipating several of his subsequent campaigns. McClellan later wrote of the ghostly manifestation in these words, "Our beloved, glorious Washington shall rest … until … he may once more become a Messenger of Succor and Peace from the Great Ruler, who has all nations in his keeping."

LINCOLN, THE PRESIDENT WHO CONSULTED "SPOOKS"

During his lifetime, Abraham Lincoln—one of the most revered presidents in the history of the United States—was constantly chided for his consultations with the spirit world. Shortly after he was elected president, the Cleveland *Plain Dealer* lashed out at him for "consulting spooks." The president-elect's candid reply was, "The only falsehood in the statement is that the half of it has not been told. The article does not begin to tell the wonderful things I have witnessed."

Lincoln openly admitted having consulted the mediums and spiritualists of his day. Reared in an atmosphere where people sought advice from the spirit world, Lincoln was never a skeptic. Historians and biographers have made little fuss about recording that he inherited a strong spiritual heritage from his mother and her family. His consultations varied from those received from backwoods "granny women" when he was in his youth, to sittings with the most famous mediums of the day during his tenure as president.

In times of great crisis, the president's wife, Mary Todd Lincoln, would arrange séances to calm her husband. Some of the gatherings took place in the White House itself. One of Lincoln's favorite mediums, Nettie Colburn, and other spiritualist channels would relay information from the spirit world that the thoughtful president would consider with all the intensity of his serious

President Abraham Lincoln sitting with his son Tad on February 9, 1864.

nature. Other participants in these séances were Colonel S. P. Kase, Major Vanvorhees, and Daniel E. Somes. Lincoln admitted that the messages he received from the spirit world enabled him to come through crisis after crisis. His influence extended to other figures of the time—even hard-nosed Union general and future president Ulysses S. Grant later turned to spiritualism.

REAL GHOSTS, RESTLESS SPIRITS, AND HAUNTED PLACES

LINCOLN'S GHOST STILL WALKS WHITE HOUSE HALLS

While Lincoln consulted the spirits in life, after his assassination in 1865 his ghost has been seen by many witnesses. President Calvin Coolidge's wife claimed to have seen Lincoln's ghost in the Oval Office; his hands were clasped behind his back as he looked out a window toward the Potomac River.

Perhaps because Franklin Roosevelt's years in the White House were full of strife due to World War II and his spirit was often troubled, Lincoln's ghost appears to have been most active during Roosevelt's 13-year occupancy of the White House. A clerk in the White House claimed to have seen Lincoln's ghost sitting on the edge of a bed and pulling off his boots. In a famous incident, Queen Wilhelmina of the Netherlands, a guest at the White House, was awakened late at night by a knock on her bedroom door. When she opened the door, she saw Lincoln looking at her from the hallway.

First Lady Eleanor Roosevelt used the Lincoln bedroom as a study. Although the first lady never claimed to have seen his spirit, she stated her belief that Lincoln watched over her as she worked in the room.

One would expect Lincoln's spirit to be courteous and always knock before entering a room. Presidents Theodore Roosevelt, Herbert Hoover, and Harry Truman all claimed to have heard what they believed was Abe Lincoln's spirit walking through the hallways of the White House and stopping to knock at their doors.

Ronald Reagan was certain that when his dog Rex began to bark, the canine had sensed the ghosts of Lincoln, Dolly Madison, Andrew Jackson, and Abigail Adams, whose spirits have all been sighted in various rooms of the White House. It is said that Regan's daughter Maureen, who slept in the Lincoln bedroom during visits, saw Lincoln's ghost on several occasions.

VALENTINO'S SPIRIT REMAINED IN FALCON LAIR

Shortly after Rudolph Valentino's untimely death in August 1926, stories began to circulate that the great Latin lover's ghost haunted his favorite places. Falcon Lair, the dream home he had built on Bella Drive for his bride Natacha Rambova, became the most commonly reported site for ectoplasmic manifestations of the departed Valentino.

Fans whose worship of the great lover approached idolatry began to haunt the grounds in hopes of catching a glimpse of Valentino's ghost. The more important and persistent of the faithful somehow managed to wrangle invitations to spend a night in the glamorous mansion. A chosen few were fortunate enough to stay in Valentino's own bedroom.

Like children awaiting a visit from Santa Claus, the excited and expectant fans would lie in his room, ready to receive and transcribe any messages Rudy might choose to deliver from beyond the grave. All of Valentino's faithful knew that he firmly believed in the afterlife and that he had often spoken of his spirit guide, Meselope. If his ghost did not manifest during a visitor's stay in Falcon Lair, they concluded that the fault lay either with themselves or with adverse spiritual conditions in the atmosphere.

One story about the appearance of Valentino's ghost involved a caretaker who ran down the canyon in the middle of the night, screaming at the top of his lungs that he had seen Rudy. Another popular legend told of the stableman who left the grounds without collecting his belongings after he had seen his master's ghost petting his favorite horse. The myth makers made a

Actor Rudolph Valentino.

great deal over the fact that the New York jeweler who had won the bid for Falcon Lair later backed out of the transaction. Those who supposedly knew the details claimed that the restless spirit of Rudolph Valentino had not wished to be usurped by the physical presence of one who dealt with materialistic items such as jewelry. In another story, a woman from Seattle visited the caretakers of Falcon Lair and later claimed that when she had been alone in the mansion she heard muffled footsteps and saw doors open and close. She had been completely alone in the house except for Rudy and Brownie, Valentino's two favorite watchdogs who were trained to bark or snap at everyone except their master. Strangely, the dogs didn't bark, they only whimpered at what may have been their master's ghostly footsteps.

FIERY GHOSTS IN THE HOME OF JOAN CRAWFORD

Over a period of 20 years in her extensive film career, Joan Crawford transformed herself from the embodiment of the devil-may-care flapper, a symbol of America's "flaming youth," in *Our Dancing Daughters* (1928) to the heroine of America's favorite melodramas in films such as *Rain* (1932) and her Academy Award–winning performance in *Mildred Pierce* (1945). Many considered Joan Crawford the quintessential glamorous Hollywood movie star, as well as a leading lady whose strength and charisma were a match for any of the top-billed actors of her day, including Douglas Fairbanks, Jr., Franchot Tone, and Phillip Terry. These men were, perhaps without coincidence, also three of her four husbands. The fourth was Alfred Steele, chairman of the board of Pepsi-Cola Company.

In 1978 Christina Crawford, Joan's adopted daughter, released her book *Mommie Dearest* and shocked moviegoers around the world with her heart-wrenching revelation that growing up with one of Hollywood's most famous leading ladies was not full of sweetness and light like fan magazines had portrayed. *Mommie Dearest* was on the *New York Times* best-seller list for 42 weeks and was made into a 1981 film starring Faye Dunaway.

In 1989 my wife and I heard rumors of haunting manifestations in Joan Crawford's former home on Bristol Avenue, and Christina Crawford seemed genuinely surprised that we were aware of the manifestations. When we interviewed her for *Hollywood and the Supernatural* (1990), Christina said, "Not many people know that the house I grew up in may be haunted. It's not in print anywhere." When asked if she remembered unexplained phenomena occurring in the home when she lived there as a child, Christina admitted that she had vivid memories of some strange things. "When you are severely abused as a child, you tend to block out some things," she said. "But I'm positive that there were manifestations occurring when I was little…. I saw them! There were places in the house that were always so cold that nobody ever wanted to go in them. As a child, *I saw things in the house!* There was, of course, no context or framework in which to put what I saw and felt. I had nobody to speak to about the occurrences."

Christina recalled that any time she would become extremely frightened and would get out of her bed to try and find somebody to comfort her, she was always treated as though she were being a "bad child" who didn't want to go to sleep. "I used to have terrible nightmares and that kind of thing," Christina recalled, "but a lot of it had to do with the fact that I saw *things* in the night; so the solution to that finally was just to leave the lights on everywhere. One of the things I saw seemed like an apparition of a child … or children."

Christina told us that she had not been back to the house since she had left for college at the age of 17, back in 1956. When we interviewed her in 1989, she had just learned that the new owners of the house had called in the Reverend Rosalyn Bruyere of the Healing Light Center to work with the house. Reverend Bruyere told her that she had discovered many spirits in the house and that there had been signs of ritual abuse in one of the rooms. Christina told us that other people had heard children's cries coming from within the walls.

Publicity shot of Joan Crawford.

"Every single owner has had trouble," she said. "The *first* one was Crawford herself. She built the majority of the house. It was a small cottage when she bought it. Every single family that has lived in that house has had horrible things happen … illnesses, alcoholism, addictions, relationship problems, and now, evidently with the current owner, the walls are breaking out in flames! I've heard that in particular it's the wall that was behind Crawford's bed."

Christina Crawford.

Christina said that it would not have surprised her in the least if the "haunting" spirit in the house was Joan Crawford. "She was capable of real evil," she told us. "My brother and I were absolutely terrified of her. In fact, there is a passage in *Mommie Dearest* that describes 'the look' on her face when she tried to kill me when I was 13. My brother and I talked about it extensively. It was not of an ordinary human being!"

Christina said that Joan Crawford sold the place to Donald O'Connor, who sold it to the Anthony Newleys. They sold it, she thought, to the new owners, who were friends of the Reverend Rosalyn Bruyere, and they asked her to heal the house.

When we were able to contact Reverend Bruyere, she confirmed that the former Crawford house was afflicted with spontaneous fires, primarily in the wall behind where Joan Crawford's bed used to be. Reverend Bruyere expressed her opinion that the house had been supernaturally poisoned in some way, even before Crawford had moved into the place, but that the evil in the house had added to Joan's neuroses. The noted healer, who in this case served as an exorcist to clear the home, said that she found the haunting existing in levels. "It was a place of conspicuous negativity. I called it an 'astral central,' a gathering of spirits that were attracted to the negative vibrations. I picked up on gangland figures, corrupt politicians. There is an area in the house where a child [not Christina] had been tortured and molested. Terrible things went on in that house."

Reverend Bruyere felt that ghosts were trying to burn the house down. "Once the Beverly Hills Fire Department spent four days there attempting to solve the mystery of the spontaneous fires that would break out on the walls. I feel the spirits were trying to burn the house down to protect some horrible secret. There is something hidden there. I am certain that there are bodies buried in that basement. The house had become an astral dumping ground, but it seems clean now."

In 1992 the family that occupied Joan Crawford's former home graciously allowed my wife and I to film a segment for a Halloween television special in areas of the house that had seemed to be the most haunted. To their immense relief, spontaneous fires were no longer breaking out on the walls.

The appearance of apparitions throughout the house and grounds had not ceased. They reported seeing ghostly images in a number of locations, especially the pool house, where they believed they had seen an image of Joan Crawford and an unidentified man playing billiards. They also reported hearing the clicking sounds of the billiard balls coming from the house when they knew no one was there. Another interesting manifestation sometimes seen in the large front room was what appeared to the ghost of a Native American shepherd.

Our hosts also allowed us to film in their basement wine cellar, where Reverend Bruyere had psychically detected the presence of buried bodies and a "terrible secret." Sherry and I immediately sensed that the atmosphere was very powerful, but the basement provided us with nothing other than eerie shots for our program. The only spirits we saw were in the bottles racked along the walls.

<hr/>

THE LITTLE BOY GHOST IN RICHARD HARRIS'S LONDON HOME

Irish actor Richard Harris (1930–2002), who starred in films such as *This Sporting Life* (1963), *Camelot* (1967), *A Man Called Horse* (1970), and *Cromwell* (1970), lived in a haunted English mansion for a time. The actor described the place as glorious. The home had a dining room with stained-glass windows decorated with signs of the Zodiac, a library with carved biblical figures, and a frieze of strange wild plants designed to appear as though one were in the sea looking at the sky with stars in the background. Harris said that he discovered the home when he was 24 years old. One morning, he woke up in the garden of the London house. He had no idea how he had gotten there, but he knew that he had to own that beautiful house.

Fourteen years later, Harris learned that the owners were interested in selling the house to a developer. The actor would not disclose exactly how he managed to close the deal in his favor. He simply said that it was a mystical thing that was meant to be. Harris said that right before he moved into the house, he had a burglar friend check out the mansion. He wanted to see just how burglar-proof the house was, and he thought that no one could offer a better evaluation of a house's security than one who made his living invading them.

The man managed an easy entrance, then just as he was preparing to leave, he heard the sound of a child crying. Since he knew the house was empty, the burglar was puzzled and stood still for a few moments, attempting to determine the direction the sound was coming from. When he heard the cry again, the man knew that he had made no mistake. A distressed child was sobbing somewhere within the dark old mansion. The burglar reasoned that a child must have somehow managed to enter the house during the day and had become lost in one of its many rooms.

Actor Richard Harris, 1965.

The burglar tracked the sound to an upstairs room. The child cried quite vigorously as he reached the room. The man pushed open the door to the room and found himself in a room completely devoid of any other living human. Moonlight passing through a large window bathed the room in sufficient light to permit an immediate evaluation. As an eerie silence fell upon the old mansion, the burglar realized he was quite alone. The man reported back to his friend Harris and provided him with the necessary details on how to make the old mansion a bit more burglar-proof. Then he added, "But that's a strange house you've got there, mate."

Harris said the ghost that roamed the house was that of an eight-year-old boy. He knew the ghost's age because old records revealed that an eight-year-old boy had been buried in the house's tower. The restless spirit became an intriguing part of the actor's life. He even had the ghost perform for friends. But Harris also confessed to having had some terrific rows with the spectral lad. The ghost would often awaken him at two in the morning, banging closet doors and running up the tower stairs. Harris explained to the ghost that it had better be good, because an actor needed his sleep. If the ghost wouldn't quiet down, Harris threatened to have it exorcised. Finally, Harris built the ghost a nursery, complete with toys, at the top of the stairs. After he made that concession, the ghost behaved a bit better.

THE BEATLES CONTACTED THEIR DECEASED MANAGER

Brian Epstein, former manager of the Beatles, died in London on August 27, 1967, following an overdose of sleeping pills. In the wake of this tragedy, the Beatles—George Harrison, Paul McCartney, Ringo Starr, and John Lennon—found themselves adrift in a sea of intense soul searching and developed a strong interest in the hereafter. McCartney remarked that since the earliest days of the Beatles, Epstein had been their guiding light. He had showed them everything and taught them all they knew. Epstein had always known the best thing to do for the Beatles. Without him, they would not have enjoyed the level of success they had.

The Beatles' search for the meanings of life and death led them down many paths. They tried the way of transcendental meditation but became disillusioned with their teacher and began to look elsewhere for knowledge. In 1968 Harrison felt that he received Epstein's first message from the other side. Harrison told the others that the message had not come in words, but in a compelling feeling that had come to him while he had been relaxing in his home. The band had always believed that Epstein's spirit would be with them. They had never been able to accept the fact that death would mean that they would never be able to speak to him again. All four felt certain that if Epstein had found the bliss he had been seeking, he would try to let them know. In order to encourage Epstein's messages from the other side, a séance was arranged.

The first attempt to communicate with Epstein was an amateurish affair, with the four musicians sitting quietly for 90 minutes with their hands spread on a round table. When the session broke up, the Beatles expressed their determination to have another go at it with a professional medium.

After a careful selection process, the Beatles found an elderly gentleman who came highly recommended, a medium of the finest reputation. During their initial séance with the medium, the Beatles heard a voice coming out of the darkness that they definitely thought was Epstein's. The spirit voice told them that he was happy in the afterlife and that he was pleased that they had sought to communicate with him. Epstein gave other brief messages then faded back into silence.

Encouraged by their success, the Beatles arranged for two more séances. They later said that Epstein came through again, but that he did not add a great deal to the messages from their first sitting. The Beatles were convinced that they had spoken with their departed friend. Each identified the particular inflections and voice patterns of Epstein's voice. They had great respect for the abilities of the medium who brought their friend back to them, but they refused to divulge his name. Whether the spirit of Epstein predicted the breakup of the Beatles was not known, but the four young musicians stated that they had never felt more together as a group than they did during those evenings around the séance table.

THE SPIRIT MESSAGE THAT ENCOURAGED BARBRA STREISAND TO FILM *YENTL*

Barbra Streisand, the famous singer, actor, and director, told Claudia Dreifus (*The New York Times*, November 11, 1997) of the indecision she felt about directing the 1983 film Yentl. As she was internally debating the matter, she went to visit her father's grave for the first time. She admitted that she had not

Barbra Streisand, 1993.

done so earlier because she was angry "that he died on me." Later that same day, she invited a medium, "a nice Jewish woman who had a spiritual guide," to her older brother's home.

During the séance, the table began to move and Streisand later confessed that she became so frightened that she ran into the bathroom. After she had regrouped her courage and rejoined the séance, she observed the leg of the table raise and lower itself to the floor and spell out "M-A-N-N-Y," which was her father Emanuel's nickname. Then she received the messages, "S-O-R-R-Y" and "S-I-N-G-P-R-O-U-D." Streisand said that the messages she received from the medium's guide were a definite signal to her that she should direct the movie. She has said that of all the films she has made, she is most proud of *Yentl*, because it was dedicated to her father.

HE FACED GHOSTS IN FRONT OF THE CAMERA AND LIVELY SPIRITS IN HIS HOME

In his later films, British actor Donald Pleasance (1919–1995) epitomized the very essence of the eerie. Pleasance carved out a niche for himself in horror films with the release of the cult classic *Halloween* (1978) and its four subsequent sequels, and he also appeared in numerous other movies that featured hauntings and apparitions.

In the early 1970s Pleasance and his wife, Meira, bought a seventeenth-century home in Strand-on-the-Green, England. The large home had been divided into two separate houses, and as both were up for sale, they decided to buy both. And that was when the fun began.

Shortly after moving in, the Pleasance family began hearing strange thumping sounds. Although they checked throughout the house, they could not find the source of the mysterious noises. Pleasance admitted that at first he was frightened to death. But the family gradually came to realize that the sounds were distinctly like those of children running, and they had an insight. They knocked down the walls that separated the home into two houses, and allowed the ghosts of children once again to run through the house, as they had probably done many years before when they were alive and it had all been one big house.

Once the Pleasance family had determined the origin of the thumps and bumps, they had no problem with the concept of sharing their home with the ghosts. The sounds, Pleasance observed, were sounds of joy. They could feel that the children seemed happy to once again have a free run of the place after all those centuries.

SHARON STONE SAID THE ONTARIO SET WAS HAUNTED

When Sharon Stone was filming the movie *Cold Creek Manor* (also called *The Devil's Throat*) in the North Dumfries, Ontario, mansion used in the motion picture, she said that the entire crew experi-

Actress Sharon Stone, 1998.

enced "incredibly spooky stuff." Stone thrilled reporters at a Milan, Italy, fashion show by telling them about the frightened crew members who reported seeing the ghost of a little girl who wandered around the 150-year mansion where doors would open and close of their own volition.

Joan Chaplin, one of the owners of the mansion, told Jeff Pappone of the *Ottawa Citizen* (January 14, 2003) that the members of the movie crew were not the first people to report seeing a ghost in the home. A visitor had once told her that he had seen a woman sewing at a sewing table in a bathroom. Research indicated that a former owner, Margaret Keefer, had used the room on the west side of the house as her sewing room; it had since been converted into a bathroom. Chaplin said that she had not seen any ghosts in the mansion. The atmosphere of the home gave her a "really nice feeling."

Cambridge archivist Jim Quantrell said that the ghost of the little girl that was seen by the film crew might have been one of the daughters of Matthew Wilks, who purchased the mansion in 1858. The girl died at about the age of 15, but no one had previously reported seeing her ghost wandering throughout the house.

JULIANNA MARGULIES CONTACTED SPIRITS AS A CHILD

In the motion picture *Ghost Ship* (2002), Julianna Margulies, a former star of the television series *ER*, portrays a member of a salvage crew that discovers a lost ship and decides to tow it back to port. When they board the vessel, they discover that it is full of fiendish phantoms that they must vanquish if they are to survive.

Margulies confessed to reporter Rachel Blackburn that when she was a little girl, her family lived in an old barn that was built in 1348 and had been converted into a house. She and her sisters sensed something in the old place, but they weren't afraid. When she was about 13, she and her sisters made their own Ouija board to try to communicate with any spirits that might be near them. Apparently contact was made, for Margulies recalled that they all asked "Are you here?" and then what they were doing felt "freaky and wrong," leaving Juliana in tears. Although she no longer works the Ouija board, she said that she definitely believes in ghosts.

THE GHOST OF SUPERMAN

Mystery still surrounds the death of television's "Man of Steel," George Reeves (1914–1959), who starred in the television series *Superman* (1950–1957). Numerous witnesses claimed to have seen his restless spirit in the home on Benedict Canyon Drive where his body was found. Although Reeves's death on June 16, 1959, was ruled a suicide, friends, relatives, and thousands of fans still insist that it was murder. Singer Don McLean wrote the song "Superman's Ghost" in tribute to the anguish experienced by those who still mourn the actor.

People have reported seeing Reeves's ghost wearing a bathrobe, quite likely the one he was wearing the night of his death. One couple, ignorant of the history of the home on Benedict Canyon Drive, moved out after confronting his spirit. Others claim to have seen his ghost dressed in his full Superman costume, cape blowing in some nonexistent breeze.

THE NIGHT MARILYN MONROE RETURNED

During the summer of 1946, Bob Slatzer met Norma Jean Baker in the lobby of Twentieth Century–Fox Studios. He was a correspondent for an eastern newspaper, and she was a young model trying to get work by making the rounds.

They struck up a conversation and made a date for later that evening. Thus began a long relationship that led to their brief marriage in 1952. Even after Norma Jean had been transformed into the Hollywood love goddess known as Marilyn Monroe, they remained close friends until her death in 1962. Since her passing, many strange things have manifested in Bob's life that have convinced him that her spirit is still with him. In 1973 he participated in an experiment that actually caused Marilyn Monroe's spirit form to materialize.

Slatzer had known Anton La Vey, the author of *The Satanic Bible*, for about two years when he learned that La Vey was fascinated with Marilyn Monroe. One night La Vey contacted him and told him an astrological "dark moon" would occur on Saturday, August 4, just as it had 11 years earlier when Marilyn had died. La Vey needed someone who knew Marilyn very well to help him manifest her spirit. Bob agreed to participate in La Vey's plan, and later that night they went to Marilyn's former home on Helena Drive. La Vey had received permission from the then-current owner to be at the house. Although she closed the gate that led up to the home, she allowed them to sit in the cul-de-sac that led to the property. They positioned their car against the gates, looking out, and there was no one else around.

Slatzer sat in the front passenger's seat, next to Anton. Mrs. La Vey was in the backseat. La Vey had a tape recorder with songs from Marilyn's pictures, and about 11:45 p.m., he turned it on at a low volume. He also had a small penlight he used to read something he had written. Slatzer remembered that it was sort of like La Vey was speaking in tongues or chanting. "About 12:15 a.m., the night was still," Slatzer told us when we interviewed him about the extraordinary encounter for *Hollywood and the Supernatural*. "Not one single blade of grass was moving. The leaves on the eucalyptus tree by the corner of the house were still. All of a sudden, a terrific wind came up. The tree looked as if it were in a hurricane for three or four minutes—yet nothing else on either side of the road was moving. Then from out of nowhere—I didn't even turn my head or blink, and I have 20-20 vision—this woman appeared! It was as if somebody suddenly set her there. She had on white slacks with a little black-and-white, splash-pattern top, little white loafers, and I could see a shock of blond hair. She started walking toward the car. I had goose bumps all over!"

After recovering from his shock, Slatzer began to think like a journalist. He wondered if the whole thing was a setup by La Vey, a kind of publicity stunt, but he didn't think that La Vey would do anything like that. He seemed too intense and serious about his work. As the figure of the woman began walking slowly toward the car, Slatzer asked La Vey, who was sweating profusely, if he wanted to turn a light on. La Vey indicated that they should remain silent. "The figure came slowly toward us and stopped about 30 feet in front of the car," Slatzer said. "Anton had dimmed the music a little and finished his chant when she was about halfway to us. All of a sudden, she veered off to our left. There used to be a big tree there, and she just stood there, almost as if she were made of cardboard, with kind of a wooden look, but the figure was highly recognizable as Marilyn Monroe!"

Slatzer told us that at that moment he truly became a believer in the paranormal, in life after death. "Marilyn was so real!" he recalled. "Mrs. La Vey had practically turned white and looked almost petrified! Anton … well, his breath was taken away, I can tell you that!" The image of Marilyn Monroe hesitated for a minute, her hands clasped. It appeared that she was looking past their car rather than directly at them. Slatzer thought it seemed as if she was looking past the gates, as if she wanted to enter the gates and go in but didn't want to pass the car. Then she turned to her left and slowly started to walk down the middle of the boulevard.

When the ghost of Marilyn Monroe was about three-fourths of the way down the street, Slatzer decided to get out and walk after her. As he approached her, the ghostly image turned, walked to the middle of the street, and *vanished* into thin air! "I saw this happen with my own eyes," Slatzer said. He had walked hurriedly through a small drainage ditch about two and a half feet wide in his attempt to catch up with Marilyn's ghost. He noticed his wet shoes had left an imprint on the road. The apparition of Marilyn had been taking short, small, measured footsteps, and had also walked through the ditch, but it left no footprints.

Slatzer told us that he had repeated the story to only two people: psychic-sensitive Clarisa Bernhardt and Norman Mailer, who had written a book about Marilyn Monroe. "When I got through telling it to him, he said, 'I do not disbelieve it. I do believe these things—and that is quite a strange experience.'"

CLARISA BERNHARDT AND THE CROSSOVER CLUB

"The astral plane hangs heavy over Hollywood," our good friend and psychic-sensitive Clarisa Bernhardt observed. "There are too many people there who were unprepared to make their transition to a higher dimension. Part of my work with the spiritual Crossover Club is to encourage these confused entities to move on, to leave the Earth plane, and to walk into the light."

In 1982, two years after the death of Mae West, Bernhardt was asked to serve as the medium at a séance held in the lounge of Hollywood's Ravenwood Apartments on Rossmore Avenue, where Mae had lived for nearly 50 years. "Immediately I could feel a sense of joy coming from Mae's spiritual vibration," Bernhardt said. "She was extremely psychic herself when she was alive, and she doesn't like the term 'séance.' She prefers 'interdimensional communication.' I think the most important thing that came out of the meeting was Mae telling us about the Crossover Club, a group of spirits who help new entities adjust to life in that new dimension. She told us that she would soon be qualified to assist and to greet some of those who will be coming to the other side."

The information about the Crossover Club was of great benefit to a medium like Bernhardt, but the participants in the séance were more interested in receiving specific references about Mae West's life to convince them that they were, in fact, communicating with the late actress's spirit. Several of West's closest friends were there, and Bernhardt was able to channel information that convinced them that her spirit essence was truly present.

"I received a communication about a problem with Mae's leg," Bernhardt said. "She had broken an ankle back in the 1940s, but no one else had known about it. Her spirit also referred to some inspirational writings of hers that she now felt might be helpful to others. She said that she had writ-

Actress and "sensitive" Mae West.

ten 10–15 sheets of onion-skin paper and placed them in a thin brown cover. A friend of hers confirmed that such papers did exist." When Bernhardt told the sitters in the spirit circle that West expressed concern about a ring that had been lost, a friend of the actress immediately recognized the incident to which the spirit referred to. He stated that only West and he knew about the lost ring.

Since that session in 1982, Bernhardt has assisted many spirits as they attempted to adjust to the other side. "It is so important that we all keep our spiritual house in order," she said.

Bernhardt has told me of an experience that she had shared with Dotty Knight, the widow of the late actor Ted Knight, well known for his portrayal of the egocentric Ted Baxter on *The Mary Tyler Moore Show* (1970–1977).

"I first met Ted Knight when he was appearing in a stage presentation of *You Know I Can't Hear You when the Water's Running*, produced by Rita Streamer at her Santa Monica Theatre Playhouse in West Hollywood," Bernhardt said. "My late husband Russ was doing some public relations for Ted on that project through his Russ Bernhardt Enterprises. Russ and Ted had been friends a long time, and Russ did special publicity assignments for Ted. As a result I got to know and become friends with Ted and his wife Dotty. They were both aware of my strong intuitive ability, which seemed always to produce accurate and unexpected information for them. My talent was particularly interesting to Ted.

"I recall that once I dreamed that Ted was possibly going on a boat ride, and the message was clear that he should not go. I called him and relayed the message. He listened and was very quiet. And then he said to me in a manner very much like his television personality 'Ted Baxter' that he didn't even know a close friend with a boat. I felt a bit uncomfortable, but that was the information that spirit had given me, so we said goodbye.

"[Less than an hour later] my phone rang. It was Ted, and he [told] me that a close friend had just called and invited him to go for a ride on a new boat he had just bought. Ted said he thought it was incredible that I had told him about that unexpected invitation in advance, and I was delighted that my dream information for him was correct. Ted said that he declined the invitation, and although he later learned that nothing occurred when the others went in the boat, the message that I received had been specifically for him, and he told me he truly felt that if he had gone perhaps he would have fallen overboard or something.

"Ted passed away in 1986, and Dotty and I have remained good friends. After Ted's passing, it was no real surprise to me that he began to appear to me in dream-visions. Sometimes he gave simple messages. Other times he expresses his concern for Dotty or other members of his family.

"The message that truly got Dotty's attention [was] when I gave her a telephone call after not having spoken to her for some time and told her that I had just received a rather strange message from Ted. Dotty was immediately interested to hear his message. So I told her that Ted had said to tell her that it was okay to sell the house, but [not to] sell the silverware. And that was the message. Dotty responded with an outburst of joyous laughter, and she confirmed to me that she was in the process of selling the house and a lot of things associated with the past, but she said to me, 'Clarisa, I won't sell the silverware.'

"Just recently, when Dotty and I were visiting by telephone, as we sometimes do, she asked, 'Do you recall when you told me about the message from Ted that I was not to sell the silverware? Well, I made a point not to sell it, because silverware was very important to Ted. He collected it. I just wanted to be certain to tell you that I truly believe you really did hear from him.'"

⌁⌁⌁

THE GHOST OF HEATH LEDGER
IS SORRY HE CAN'T BE A HELPFUL FATHER

Michelle Williams, nominated for an Academy Award in 2011 for her role as Marilyn Monroe in the motion picture *My Week with Marilyn*, said that she saw the ghost of Heath Ledger on two occasions. Ledger, critically and popularly acknowledged as one of the most promising actors of his generation (*Brokeback Mountain*, *The Dark Knight*), died in January 2008 of an accidental overdose of sleeping pills.

Williams, his ex-fiancée and the mother of his child, stated that on the first occasion of Ledger's ghostly visit, she was awakened by strange noises and the sight of furniture being moved around in her bedroom. In addition to the physical movement of objects, she said that she saw a shadowy figure, which frightened her. On the second manifestation, the apparition of Ledger was quite vivid, and he told Williams that he was sorry for not being there to be a helpful father in rearing their daughter.

ELVIS, FROM HEALING ANGEL TO GRACELAND GHOST

Long after his death in August 1977 of a heart attack, people were claiming to have sighted a very much alive Elvis Presley attempting to lead a hidden life in various cities around the world. So powerful was Presley's fame and the devotion of his fans that millions of individuals could not concede that he might really have died. Eventually, however, even the most devoted fan had to accept the cruel reality of The King's death.

It was comforting for some to recall that Elvis had been a spiritual seeker throughout his life. The belief that Elvis had many psychic abilities, some fans said, allowed his spirit essence to appear to many as an angelic figure. His glowing image, so it was claimed, accomplished miraculous healings of the sick and dramatic rescues of those involved in what could have been deadly accidents. Years later, after the immediate psychic hysteria caused by his death had begun to subside, Presley's ghost began to be sighted in Graceland in Memphis, the recording studio in Nashville, and at the Las Vegas Hilton, where he had performed so often in his later years.

ORSON WELLES REMAINS LARGER THAN LIFE, EVEN IN DEATH

The imposing ghost of Orson Welles in his trademark black cape and wide-brimmed hat has been sighted puffing on a cigar at Lady Jane's, his favorite Los Angeles's restaurant. Welles died of a heart attack in 1985 at his Hollywood home at the age of seventy. Many fans of the late actor and director, hailed as one of the most brilliant, innovative, and creative figures in theater, radio, and film, state that the ghost of such a larger than life and dynamic fig-

Orson Welles.

ure almost had an obligation to manifest in one of his most frequented spots. After all, there is not a Halloween that arrives without a rebroadcast of his 1938 Mercury Theater production of H. G. Wells' *War of the Worlds*, which convinced its terrified listening audience that they were being invaded by aliens. Welles's *Citizen Kane* (1941) is still regarded by many critics to be one of the greatest Hollywood films ever made.

THE GHOST OF ANNA NICOLE SMITH WANDERS THE HALLS OF HARD ROCK HOTEL

Anna Nicole Smith, who sought to become the next Marilyn Monroe by posing for *Playboy* and by emphasizing her full-figured, blonde beauty, became famous mostly for marrying an elderly oil tycoon and fighting with his children for his money after his death. Tragically, like Marilyn, she died too young of a drug overdose, not in Hollywood, California, but in February 2007, while staying at the Seminole Hard Rock Hotel in Hollywood, Florida. Since that time, guests and employees at the hotel have claimed to have encountered her ghost wandering through the halls, seemingly in a confused state.

OZZIE NELSON'S ADVENTURES CONTINUE AFTER DEATH

Those who have occupied the former home of Harriet and Ozzie Nelson on Camino Palermo Street in Los Angeles have stated that they have seen the ghost of Ozzie on numerous occasions in various parts of the house. *The Adventures of Ozzie and Harriet* was a very popular television sitcom that ran from 1952 to 1966 and starred real-life dad and mom Ozzie and Harriet, and their real-life sons, David and Ricky. Ozzie died of liver cancer in 1975, and residents of the home who have lived there after the family moved out have, in addition to reporting sighting Ozzie's ghost, reported hearing the sound of footsteps, doors opening and closing, and faucets turning themselves off and on.

LUCILLE BALL STILL HAUNTS THE OLD DESILU STUDIOS

Although Lucille Ball died in April 1989, she remains one of the most influential of American comediennes. Reruns of *I Love Lucy*, *The Lucy-Desi Comedy Hour*, *The Lucy Show*, and *Here's Lucy* are still being telecast throughout the United States and the world. While she might have made her reputation as a ditzy, wacky redhead always getting herself into outrageous situations, Lucille Ball was known to her friends and associates as a wise and clever businesswoman who was never reluctant to express her point of view. Residents of her former home on Roxbury Drive in Beverly Hills have reported hearing loud voices coming from the attic and witnessing furniture being moved about in different rooms of the house. Night watchmen at the old building that once served as DesiLu Studios on the Paramount lot also claim to have encountered a familiar female ghost on the upper floor.

LADY GAGA WANTS NO GHOST ATTENDING HER MONSTER BALL

Stefani Joanne Angelina Germanetta, better known as Lady Gaga, claims that a very annoying ghost named Ryan has been following her everywhere she tours across the world. The *Born This Way* super recording star admitted to Britain's *Daily Star* newspaper that at times she is actually terrified by the pesky spook that just won't leave her alone. It is not that he has done anything to particularly frighten her, she explained, but his continual presence just "freaks" her out.

The singer was brought up Roman Catholic, and she has continued to follow a spiritual path that generally puts her in tune with the spirit world, but Ryan is just "a step too far." Although she believes in paranormal phenomena, she doesn't wish to have an unwanted ghost risking her very best performances while on the road. Fearing that she had somehow picked up a bad omen, it was alleged that she spent thousands of dollars on "ghostbusters" and nearly $50,000 on state-of-the-art electromagnetic field meters designed to detect spirits.

When Lady Gaga, twenty-five, was on her *Monster Ball* tour in Ireland, she reportedly contacted a spirit medium and organized a séance to find out what Ryan wanted. She wanted to find the reason why he had been following her everywhere, and she hoped to convince him to leave her alone.

15
ANIMAL GHOSTS—
DOMESTICATED
AND WILD

Do Pets Go to Heaven?

My wife and I write a column called "Frequently Asked Questions" for the Internet magazine *Beliefnet* (<www.beliefnet.com>). In June 2001 we gave our answers to the questions, "Do pets go to Heaven?" and "Can pets be reunited with their owners in the afterlife?" To briefly summarize, we stated that 45 years of research have convinced us that just as there is life after death for humans, animals also have some form of existence on the other side. Just as our beloved pets are our loving companions in the material world, we believe that our spiritual essences remain connected somehow beyond the grave.

We quoted Janice Gray Kolb, author of *Compassion for All Creatures*, who expressed her conviction that the breath of God "breathed into man was the same breath breathed into the animals, birds, and other creatures. Genesis 1:21–22 (New American Catholic Bible) says, 'God saw how good it was and God blessed them.'" In her opinion, God's blessing of the animals is further proof that all creatures have a soul. "Blessed," she explains, "means 'to make holy,' 'sanctify,' 'to invoke divine favor upon.' God blessed his creation of man and woman and thereby granted them a soul. Why else would God have blessed the animals if it were not to bestow a soul upon them?"

Tulsa, Oklahoma, attorney M. Jean Holmes is convinced that any distinction between humans and animals that may allegedly be found in scripture is the result of a translator's "philosophical construction." In her book *Do Dogs Go to Heaven?*, Holmes argues that an examination of the original Hebrew texts for concepts such as the "soul" and "spirit" reveals that the authors of

In 1926 Lady Hehir and her Irish wolfhound Tara were photographed by a friend. The developed photograph showed the head of a small dog right above the rear of the wolfhound. Lady Hehir immediately recognized the small dog to be her cairn terrier Kathal, which had died six weeks before this photograph was taken. The two dogs had been inseperable friends, and the spot where this photograph had been taken was a favorite of theirs.

various books of the Bible believed that animals have souls and spirits, just as humans do.

Most pet owners will agree that their pets will be numbered among their best friends in heaven, as they are on Earth. In conjunction with our column in *Beliefnet*, the editors decided to run a poll of their readers to gain a clearer picture of how many pet owners believed that they would be reunited with their pets in the afterlife. An astonishing 85 percent said that they did believe that their pet had a soul and that they would see them again one day on the other side. However, when ABC News picked up the item for a telecast, they expanded the base of the poll beyond the readers of our column to include the general public, and then only 43 percent of pet owners surveyed answered "yes" to animal companionship in the beyond.

We still maintain that those pet owners who have taken a good look into the eyes of their beloved animal friend will not deny that the same breath that God breathed into humans was also breathed into animals, birds, and other creatures.

⊰⊱

SNOOPY CAME BACK TO SHOW THAT HIS SPIRIT WAS OKAY

The Personal Experience of Patrick

"[In 1971, when I was 10,] I had a dog I absolutely loved that was killed (as many dogs were before leash-laws were commonplace) when he was struck by a car. It was the first time I'd ever experienced the loss of something I'd loved so dearly and I was devastated. I grieved for what seemed to be weeks.

"The dog's name was Snoopy, he was a little black and white mongrel, marked very distinctly, with a black mask over his eyes and a black spot on his back. He didn't look like any dog I'd ever seen before or since. Snoopy was killed in October of 1971. Late one afternoon in the summer of [1972], every kid in the neighborhood was involved in a giant game of hide-and-seek and I was 'it.' Most of the game was taking place in our field, which consisted of about two acres of wild wheat, roughly waist-high to a 10-year-old. I counted to whatever number I was supposed to before I ran off into the field to find my hidden friends. It was near dusk, and we were trying to get as much playtime in as we could before our parents started calling us in.

"I headed into the wheat … and nearly tripped over my dog, Snoopy. Snoopy was less than five feet in front of me. It was Snoopy. There was no mistaking the markings, and he still had his winter coat. He looked at me and wagged his tail. He was happy. A few seconds later, he turned and trotted away. The wheat didn't move as the ghost of the dog traveled deeper into the field. I followed but quickly lost sight of him. A moment later, I came upon a concrete block that was against the fence. It was what we had used for the headstone when we'd buried the dog. The letters that my mother had written on the block with a permanent marker on the block had almost faded away: *Snoopy, October 28, 1971.*

"I stood and stared at the stone for a moment, realizing what had just happened. Snoopy had wanted to see me again, and he had wanted me to see him again … and we did … and he was okay … and he was happy. A 10-year-old boy who'd lost his best friend slept a little better that summer's night knowing that his friend was still around and that he just might be with him again someday."

⚡〰⚡

BROWNIE, THE GHOST DOG OF DAYTONA BEACH

A Personal Investigation by Dusty Smith, Founder of the Daytona Beach Psychical Research Group (http://www.dbprginc.org)

"At one time the most popular resident of the Daytona Beach downtown business area did not come in the form of a human. The most popular ambassador Daytona Beach has ever had was a dog that came to be called 'Brownie.'

"[Somehow] this weary, yet wise, canine traveler made his way to Daytona Beach. Like many before him, and many more after him, Brownie explored the sidewalks and storefronts of Beach Street for several days before staking a claim. Brownie's first, and best, friend was Ed Budgen, Sr., the owner of the Daytona Cab Company, located on the corner of Orange Avenue and Beach Street. When Brownie met Ed, he offered Brownie part of his lunch. Being the smart and resourceful dog the he was, Brownie gladly accepted the free meal. Brownie quickly learned how to capitalize on this gracious human trait. Many of the downtown workers and restaurant owners would feed him scraps on a regular basis.

"Brownie took up residency at the Daytona Cab Company. Brownie's new friend Ed even made him a doghouse from a cardboard box. Eventually Brownie's home became a bit more upscale. It was quite an elaborate home, complete with Brownie's name on it and a collection box. Many people donated to the 'Brownie care fund.' This fund would provide food, veterinary care, and money for Brownie's annual license.

"One local resident remembers that Brownie became a Daytona resident in 1940. At that time downtown shopping was popular. Brownie quickly became know as 'the town dog.' It was customary to greet Brownie on a shopping spree. His reply would always be a wag of his tail.

"Brownie became a trusted companion to many of the local cab drivers. He took it upon himself to accompany the police on their nightly rounds.

Brownie would assist the officers by sniffing at shadows in dark alleys, and he would stand beside officers while they checked on local businesses.

"Brownie's fame grew, but his ego didn't. Even after being written up in national magazines and newspapers as 'Daytona Beach's dog.' As they walked and shopped along Beach Street, many visiting tourists would seek Brownie out in order to have their picture taken with the country's most popular dog. Ed's wife Doris remembers Brownie getting Christmas cards and presents from all over the country. Doris would respond on Brownie's behalf and include a photo of the famous dog.

"Brownie passed of old age in October of 1954. Many fine folks from across the country felt the loss and sent letters and cards of condolence. Brownie's bank account had enough money in it to purchase a headstone and construct a plywood casket. City officials provided a resting place in Riverfront Park, which is directly

One of the few remaining photographs of Brownie.

across from the place that Brownie had spent the best years of his life. There were 75 people in attendance, including four pallbearers, at Brownie's funeral. As Mayor Jack Tamm stated in Brownie's eulogy, 'Brownie was indeed, a good dog.' Many shed a tear.

"Now that I have told you about Brownie's life in this world, let me tell you how I met Brownie in the next world. On one of our little outings, I decided it might be worthwhile to go and visit Brownie's resting place. We arrived at Riverfront Park at about 11:00 p.m. I took off in one direction, and my fellow researchers, Kyle and Tracy, went in the opposite. Normally we would stick together, but we had no idea exactly where Brownie was buried. Riverfront Park is quite large with many fishponds, small footpaths and bridges, and beautiful gardens. I walked to the south [and] they went north. My radar must have been in tune that night because I walked straight to Brownie's grave.

"When I turned around to see where Kyle and Tracy had gotten to, they were completely out of sight. I decided to have a little chat with Brownie and take a few pictures. I introduced myself and explained to him how I had read about how famous and humble he had been. I noticed the shrub to the north of his headstone was supposed to be in the shape of a dog, but was a bit lack-

Grave of Brownie the dog.

ing. Boxwoods can be hard to train some-times, especially when they are so close to a saltwater source. Anyhow, I noticed how wonderful Brownie's headstone was; the mayor's quote that Brownie had been 'a good dog' was inscribed at the bottom.

"As I stood there thinking about what a wonderful impact Brownie had on this town and the folks who were lucky enough to encounter him, I suddenly felt sad. I wondered how many people still remembered this fine animal. Obviously the grass was mowed on a regular basis, but how many even knew of this location? Did some-one still come and talk to Brownie? Did any-one ever bring him flowers or maybe lay a dog biscuit down for him? Did Brownie still recall what it felt like to be petted?

"My belief is that we take these feel-ings and thoughts onto the other side with us. How sad would it be if no one remem-bered to remember us? I realize that in 100 years there [will] be no one around to remember who and how we really were. But couldn't someone make the afterlife a little special for this obviously special dog? Yep, you're right, it would be me! I decided at that moment to take Brownie on as my very own spirit pet. I would visit him as often as I could. Talk to him, offer him biscuits, or as they are known in my house, 'cookies.'

"I noticed a park bench just west of Brownie's place of rest. It seemed to be so inviting. Sitting on a park bench, dog at your side, listening to the wind, and watching the traffic go by. I told Brownie that if he cared to join me, I would be more than happy to sit with him for awhile. After several minutes, I felt warmth at my left leg. Could it have been Brownie? Or just a warm breeze coming in off the inter-coastal waterway? Just then I noticed Kyle and Tracy headed my way. The warmth was gone. I spoke to Brownie again, 'Thank you for taking time to sit with me. I needed to feel a loyal friend tonight. I do hope you will reveal yourself in a picture. You *are* a good dog,' I said.

"I snapped a picture of where I had been sitting with what I felt was my new friend, Brownie, the spirit dog. I looked at the LCD screen on the digital camera and noticed a bright orb in front of the palm tree. When we returned home and viewed the digital photos, I was delighted. Not only had we gotten some decent orb activity, Brownie had made his presence known. I looked at the picture for less than two seconds before realizing it had a face in it. Not an ordinary face though, Brownie's face! It seems to me that this famous ambassador is still doing his job: sitting next to visitors or weary travelers in a cool shady corner of the park; keeping an eye on the passing traffic; walking alongside pets that still reside in this world; maybe even romping through the park to visit with other worldly residents. Whatever the case, Brownie is still doing his job."

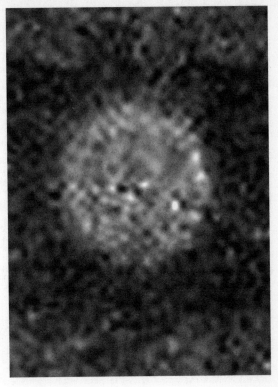

A close-up of Brownie's orb.

HIS CATS WERE GHOST DETECTORS

The Personal Experience of Eric Wilson

"In the late 1990s our family moved into an old two-story house that still had asphalt shingles, real wood flooring, and a genuine dining room complete with a swinging door into the kitchen. We chose the place because of its proximity to my work and its old style interior beauty. I took a small room with French doors as my office. All of our bedrooms were upstairs, so I didn't have to worry about waking anyone up during my late-night activities.

"Shortly after we moved in, I began noticing some noises in the living room when I worked late in the evenings. I chalked it up to one of the cats, who had a tendency to get wild. But as the weeks passed, I kept hearing noises outside of the room and became curious. They seemed to happen around 1:00 a.m. on a regular basis, so I started timing my activities to make sure I was in the living room at that time. At 12:55 a.m., I would go out and relax in the dark living room, hoping to solve the mystery of the sounds. At first nothing happened. Every time I would go out there, no noises. If I stayed in my office, I'd hear them. I had almost decided that my theory of the cats being responsible was correct. Then one night they were all in the office when the noises started.

"Late one Friday night, while I sat in our dark living room, I made careful note of the location of our cats. At 1:00 a.m., I heard someone coming down the stairs. The cats also heard the movement and went to the stairs expectantly. Step by step I heard someone come down the stairs, but no one was there. Then, as the footsteps reached the bottom step, the cats ran toward

In 1974 Alfred Hollidge took a photograph of his cat, Monet. When the picture was developed, he noticed a second cat in the photograph, which Monet seemed to be looking at. The appearance of the second cat has not been explained.

the unseen entity as if their favorite friend had just entered the room. As the sounds of someone walking moved across the living room, they followed. I heard the doorknob rattle as if someone was checking the lock. I think that was the point that the invisible being decided that it was okay to be around our family.

"After the initial display, we had things going on all the time. It was almost as if two families lived in the house. Doors would open; floorboards would creak. One night I woke up to find that every light upstairs had been turned on. I was panicked, thinking that we had a break-in. But there were no physical intruders. My little girl was sick at the time, and I think the spirits were insisting that I check on her. The ghosts even tried helping with the cats. Our cats are spoiled and prefer to drink running water out of the faucet in the bathroom. We'd often turn the water on and let them get a drink. Several weeks after the upstairs lighting incident, I was in my office and heard the water come on in the bathroom sink at full force. After the first time, it wasn't uncommon to hear the water turn on in the downstairs bathroom. It was pretty amazing though, to realize something could actually turn the handle on the cold water from fully off to fully on. We had many paranormal occurrences at that house, and we loved living there."

⋘∿⋙

"I'M A GHOST IN THE FORM OF A WEASEL"

While it would seem that the great majority of accounts of animal spirits tell of benign and loving entities that return to their owners for a final visit, or to provide a reassurance that life goes on beyond physical death, there are tales that speak of more hostile and frightening animal beings.

It was in the fall of 1931 that a mysterious entity manifested in the home of James T. Irving and his family on the Isle of Man. His daughter, Voirrey, saw it first, just seconds before Irving caught a glimpse of it himself. It was as large as a full-grown rat, with a flat snout and a small yellow face. Voirrey suggested that perhaps it had been the creature responsible for the scratching noises they had heard in the parlor on the previous night.

The strange animal was not satisfied with simple pranks and disturbances for very long. It began to mimic the calls and cries of the family's barnyard animals. Irving then made the remarkable discovery that the creature was extraordinarily intelligent. Members of the family only had to call out the name of an animal and the mysterious creature would respond with the correct imitation. The night noises began to increase, and the family was beginning to find them less than pleasant. Their strange visitor would blow, spit, and growl from the dark corners of the bedrooms, keeping the family awake all hours of the night. Once, in an effort to lull herself to sleep, Voirrey began to chant nursery rhymes aloud. She was startled to hear the weird animal begin to repeat the rhymes after she had finished. In an excited voice, she called to her parents to come and share her discovery. The creature had developed the ability to talk! The Irvings stood at the door of their daughter's bedroom and exchanged incredulous stares. The animal's voice, although a full two octaves higher than any human's, was clear and distinct as it sing-songed nursery rhymes.

The mysterious animal quickly put itself on intimate terms with the Irvings, addressing them by their first names, "Jim" and "Maggie." It carried on long conversations with them and announced that it had chosen to make its home with them. The Irvings were not very enthusiastic about having the strange animal become a permanent resident. The family got so little sleep that they were almost to the point of selling the farm and leaving. However, they realized that it would not be easy to sell a farm that was not only quite isolated but also haunted. And their talking rodent was no longer a secret. On January 10, 1932, the Manchester *Daily Dispatch* and the *London Daily Sketch* both ran articles on the mysterious "talking weasel."

"Have I ever heard a weasel speak?" wondered a reporter for the *Daily Dispatch*. "I do not know, but I do know that I heard, today, a voice I never imagined could issue from a human throat." The journalist found the Irving family "sane, honest, and responsible folk not likely to indulge in difficult long-drawn-out practical jokes to make them the talk of the world." As the number of newspapermen wanting information about the ghost increased, James Irving insisted that there were no ghosts on his farm. He explained that it was only a strange animal that had taken up residence on his property.

Since the peculiar animal's arrival, the "talking weasel" had caused ghostly poltergeist phenomena to occur. Strange scratchings and unexplainable sounds were followed by furniture and small objects moving about on their own. But this ghost did something that that no other entity of its ilk has ever done before or since: during the course of its stay with the Irvings, it left the family more than 50 rabbits on the kitchen floor. Each of the rabbits had been strangled. If a true weasel had done the stalking, it surely would have used its teeth on the throat of its prey. As the phenomena increased and the entity became stronger, it claimed to be a mongoose born near Delhi, India, and it often used Indian words and sang Indian folk songs. The creature's claim that it was a mongoose was reinforced by the fact that a farmer in the local village of Doarlish Cashen had once brought a number of the animals from India to kill off the rabbits that had become a threat to his field crops. No one ever received more than a glimpse of the animal that had moved in with the Irvings, but those who did see the strange thing described it in terms that might well have applied to a small mongoose.

James Irving began calling his uninvited guest "Jef." This name met with the approval of the self-proclaimed mongoose, who told Irving that when he was in India, he lived with a tall man who wore a green turban on his head. Jef also informed Irving that he was born on June 7, 1852, which made him 79 years old.

Jef's activities were by no means confined to the Irving cottage. He wandered far afield to stalk rabbits for the family meal, and he took delight in hiding in village garages and in bringing back gossip to share with the Irvings. The weird entity also had a cruel streak that it most often unleashed on the villagers. Once, it harassed a group of men repairing a road by carrying off their lunches. Several of the workmen swore that they had seen their lunch bags being toted off by some invisible force. Another time, Jef was blamed for striking a garage mechanic with a large iron bolt. Irving later said that Jef had boasted of the deed.

The famous psychical researcher Harry Price sent an associate to the Isle of Man to investigate the news stories that he had begun to collect on the Irving family and their unexplained guest. It was a rare stranger who made a favorable impression on Jef, and Price's investigator, a Captain Macdonald,

Arthur Springer, a retired inspector for Scotland Yard, took this photograph in 1916. The dog was not present in the frame when the photograph was taken.

was no exception to the rule. From the safety of his hiding place, Jef screamed that the man was a doubter and demanded that James Irving send him away. When Macdonald tried to coax Jef out of his crack in the wall to pose for a picture, the entity displayed its ill humor by squirting water on the investigator. Later, it hurled a needle at the man, which missed him and struck a tea pot. Irving tried to console the researcher by revealing that Jef often threw things at the family. When the mongoose was seen sitting on a wall in the farmyard, Macdonald pleaded with Voirrey to take his camera and see if she could approach Jef and get a picture of him. The girl began walking toward him, speaking to the entity in a low, pleasant voice. She lifted the camera to take Jef's photo, but he was gone before she could click the shutter. Captain Macdonald received little more than the entity's curses for his troubles, but at least he had heard the mysterious mongoose speak and got a glimpse of it. When Price went out to the island to investigate the disturbances for himself, the temperamental Jef was silent during the entire duration of his stay.

The entity demanded to be served food by the Irvings and was especially fond of bananas and pastries. Although it often seemed genuinely concerned about the family's welfare, the mongoose did not relish any open expression of affection. Once Mrs. Irving put her hand into Jef's hiding place and began to stroke the animal's fur. She instantly withdrew her hand with a sharp cry of pain. Jef had bitten her and had drawn blood. The fact that Mrs. Irving had actually touched the manifestation encouraged Harry Price to suggest that the family attempt to obtain a bit of Jef's fur for laboratory analysis. As if it had read their thoughts, the mongoose awakened the family late one night and promised the Irvings that it was going to present them with a special gift. Jef directed them to a particular bowl on a shelf in the kitchen. The Irvings turned on the lights and hurried quickly downstairs to seek out the appointed bowl. There, in its center, was a tuft of fur. The next morning, James Irving mailed the fur off to Price, who, in turn, relayed it to the London Zoo. Unfortunately, it turned out that the cunning Jef had simply played a prank. The fur was that of a dog, not a mongoose.

Determined to obtain some shred of tangible evidence of the creature's physical existence, Price sent the Irvings four plasticine blocks on which Jef could stamp the impressions of his feet. James Irving set the blocks in Jef's hole in the wall and coaxed his strange house guest to imprint its feet in the doughy material. The next morning, the family awakened to Jef's cursing that making impressions in the plasticine was "hard as hell," but he had done it, and he bade them to go and look. That time it seemed as though the entity had really cooperated with the family's wish to secure a permanent memento of its visitation. Excitedly, James Irving shipped the casts off to Price and anxiously went back to his farm to await the results of analysis and identification.

Mr. R. I. Peacock of the British Natural History Museum's zoological department concluded that one print might have been made by a dog, but the others were of no mammal known to him, unless they belonged to an American raccoon. In Peacock's opinion, he doubted if the casts represented foot tracks at all. He stated that the tracks had most certainly not been made by a mongoose. R. S. Lambert, an associate of Price's, suggested that Jef was voice and nothing more, but witnesses claimed to have seen something scampering about that was decidedly a physical being. Throughout the duration of the phenomena, James Irving wrote in a journal. In the journal he stated: "The mongoose said to my wife, 'I know what I am, but I shan't tell you. I might let you see me, but not to get to know me. I'm a freak.... If you saw me [as I truly exist] you'd be petrified, mummified.... I'm a ghost, in the form of a weasel.'"

Jef continued to live with the Irvings for four years, alternately chatting with them or cursing them. Then, the mysterious talking mongoose simply seemed to fade into nothingness, becoming but another of the Isle of Man's many legends. In 1947 a farmer actually shot a mongoose near the village of Cashen's Cap. There was a great deal of conjecture on the part of the villagers whether or not this animal might have been a descendant of one of the mongooses turned loose in 1914, but the farmer was certain that the creature had not spoken to him before he pulled the trigger.

⚬⚬⚬

GHOST DOGS FROM BACHELOR BOULEY'S HELLHOLE

Russell Madsen said that not far from where he grew up in Missouri there was a long lane that led to an old haunted, burned-out farm known as Bachelor Bouley's Hellhole. There are a number of local legends about Bachelor Bouley. Some say he lived with a pack of hounds he used for hunting; others say he was a bootlegger and that his still blew up his house. There's the legend that Bouley practiced black magic, and one night when his satanic majesty came to collect Bouley's soul, the devil's flaming footprints caught Bouley's house on fire. Still others insist that one night some angry prohibitionists in a frenzy of self-righteousness judged Bouley an old reprobate who sold moonshine to minors, and burned the house to the ground with him and all his howling hounds inside.

Madsen said that there are two consistent elements in the legends about Bouley:

1. He was a cranky old recluse whose only companions were a dozen or more hunting dogs that lived, ate, and slept with him in his ramshackle farm house.

2. The angry spirits of the hounds that were burned alive with their master still protected the place.

According to Madsen, over the years it had become a rite of passage for teenage boys to drive out to Bachelor Bouley's Hellhole and tempt the ghost hounds to chase them. Over the years dozens of people have sworn that something hellish resides on the property, and there have been all kinds of testimonials about ripped clothes, clawed fenders, and scratched faces that were attributed to Bouley's hellhounds.

"When I was 16, my buddies and I heard that a bunch of senior football players had driven out to Bachelor Bouley's and gotten the devil scared out of them," Madsen said. "They said they heard the hounds baying, howling, and jumping around their car. The toughest guy among them got out of the car and swore that something ripped the sleeve of his letter jacket. The others pulled him back in and they burned rubber getting out of there."

Madsen and his friends Don, Todd, and Joe decided to test their manhood against Bouley's hellhounds. Don drove the group out to Bouley's house, because he had managed to get his father's new station wagon by telling him that the gang was going to a drive-in movie. When they pulled up next to the charred ruins of the house, Don shut off the headlights because he said that he wanted to be able to see if the ghost dogs' eyes really glowed in the dark. According to Madsen, they heard noises that sounded very much like a pack of very large dogs surrounding their car. "Within moments we could hear and feel some very solid *things* bumping up against the sides, hood, and rear of the station wagon," he recalled. "Joe wanted to get the hell out of there. Todd just sat there shivering. I pleaded with Don not to get out and investigate as he claimed he was going to do before we left town."

And then the howling started. A high-pitched, mournful howling that Madsen said he would remember for the rest of his life. "Todd clamped his hands over his ears and began to cry," he said. "Joe, sitting in the front seat beside Don, punched him in the shoulder and shouted at him to burn rubber and get us the hell out of there. Don seemed paralyzed, as if he had somehow been placed under a spell by the terrible frequency of the ghost dogs' ear-piercing howls. At last, he managed to shake himself free of the fear or the fascination that had held him immobile, and he tore out of the place as if we were truly escaping from the outer rim of hell."

The following day was a Saturday, and when Madsen went over to Don's house to talk over the incredible events of the night before, he saw that the new station wagon was covered with dozens of scratches that looked like they had been made by the paws of very large dogs. Don's father was angry and demanding to know what kind of drive-in movie would produce effects like that.

Russell Madsen concluded his story by stating that none of his friends ever went back to Bachelor Bouley's Hellhole. "But I hear that teenage boys still have to drive out to Bouley's," he said. "Like I said, it's like some kind of rite of passage for boys in that region."

THE GHOST DOG THAT SMOTHERED A CHILD

One of the most frightening accounts in the annals of the paranormal is this report of a ghostly dog—or an evil entity manifesting in the form of a dog—that suffocated a child.

Although the photographer did not notice anything unusual when this picture was taken, when it was developed strange figures resembling a woman and a dog were noticed in the doorway. This family had just moved into this house, which they later found out had been inhabited by an old woman and her bulldog.

In May 1955 the Pell family moved into their new home on Coxwell Road in Birmingham, England. During their first weekend in the house, they were awakened by the sound of a slamming door. Frank Pell was puzzled because he knew that he had carefully locked all the doors before retiring that evening, so he got out of bed to investigate. As he stood in the kitchen, he heard a scraping sound like the noise of a scrambling animal. After that the house was silent, and Pell returned to bed.

As time passed, the Pells received nightly visits from an array of strange sounds. The greatest concentration of noises occurred around midnight, and no matter how the doors had been secured, they would bang to-and-fro as if they had a will of their own. Eerie whispers and incomprehensible phrases echoed in the air around the family. Both Frank Pell and his wife lay awake at night, listening and wondering, knowing that what was happening in their home could not have a natural explanation. Their dream house had begun transforming itself into a nightmare.

Once while she was cleaning the bedroom, Mrs. Pell felt a cold draft and what she described as "icy, intangible fingers" running over her body. Even though the sense of evil had clearly presented itself to the Pells, both were sure that fear of it would only give it greater power over them. They reasoned that only those who feared supernatural forces could be harmed by them.

Then one hot June morning, the family awakened to find that their baby had suffocated during the night. The child had been in the best of health and no mark of violence appeared on its body. Shortly after the child's burial, one of their sons startled them by asking if the baby had gone with the little white dog. The Pells knew that no dog had ever entered their house, so they asked their son when he had last seen the white dog. "On the night the baby left us," the boy replied. "The dog was sitting on the baby's face." Mrs. Pell became hysterical, and Frank could not calm her. The thought that a supernatural force had suffocated her baby to death horrified her. Although they summoned a priest to exorcise the negative spirits from the house, the bumping and banging continued with even greater regularity.

By early July the feeling of evil in their home had become very strong, and Frank Pell feared for his wife. One day he rushed to the stairs where a frightening scene awaited him. His wife stood on the upstairs landing, transfixed with terror. Her limbs had stiffened and her hands clutched frantically at her side. The veins along her neck had swollen. Her eyes bulged with terror, and her mouth gaped open in a silent scream. When Pell ran up the stairs to help her, he ran directly into an invisible force that would not let him pass. It seemed to shroud him like net. At last he broke through the wall of evil with a powerful lunge. At that instant, his wife's screams filled the house.

Without bothering to pack, the Pells took their children and left the house. Later, friends collected their belongings. They, too, heard the strange whispers and the weird thumpings, and once they finished packing, no inducement could bring them back into the house.

16
RESTORED SCENES
OF THE PAST

On a rainy evening in October 1916, Miss Edith Olivier was driving from Devizes to Swindon in Wiltshire, England. The evening was so dreary that Miss Olivier started searching for a nice, warm inn in which to spend the night. Leaving the main road, she found herself passing along a strange avenue lined by huge gray megaliths. She concluded that she must be approaching Avebury. Although Edith Olivier had never been to Avebury before, she was familiar with pictures of the area and knew that the place had originally been a circular megalithic temple with long stone avenues leading up to it.

When she reached the end of an avenue, she got out of her automobile so that she might better view the odd array of megaliths, leaning in various directions. As she stood on the bank of a large earthwork, she could see a number of cottages standing among the megaliths, and she was surprised to see that, in spite of the rain, there seemed to be a village fair in progress. The laughing villagers were walking about merrily, holding flares and torches, trying their skill at various booths, and applauding lustily for the talented performers of various shows.

Miss Olivier became greatly amused at the carefree manner in which the villagers enjoyed themselves, completely oblivious to the rain. Men, women, and children walked about without any protective outer garments and not a single umbrella could be seen. Wishing she could join the happy villagers at their fair, but growing increasingly uncomfortable in the rain—which was becoming heavier by the minute—Miss Oliver decided that she was not made of hardy stock like these villagers and got back into her automobile to resume her trip.

She did not visit Avebury again until nine years had passed. At that time, she was perplexed to read in the guidebook that, although a village fair had once been an annual occurrence in Avebury, the custom had been abolished in 1850!

When she protested that she had personally witnessed a village fair in Avebury in 1916, Miss Olivier was offered a sound and convincing rebuttal by the guide. Even more astounding, perhaps, was the information she acquired concerning the megaliths. The particular avenue on which she had driven on that rainy night of her first visit had disappeared before 1800.

Can a scene from the past return and assume temporary physical reality once again? Did Miss Olivier drive her automobile on an avenue which was no longer there, or perhaps a solid surface which had once been there and had temporarily returned?

> The conventional idea of time existing as some sort of stream flowing along in one dimension is obviously an inadequate one.

The conventional idea of time existing as some sort of stream flowing along in one dimension is obviously an inadequate one. In this view, the past does not exist; it is gone forever. Neither does the future exist, because it has not yet happened. The only thing that one can rely upon is the nebulous present. But if the past completely ceased to exist, we should have no memory of it. Yet each of us has a large and varied memory bank. The past, therefore, must exist in some sense. Perhaps not as a physical or material reality, but in some sphere or dimension of its own. It may be, as some researchers have theorized, that our subconscious minds—our transcendental selves—do not differentiate between past, present, and future. To the subconscious mind, all the spheres or dimensions of time may exist as part of the "Eternal Now."

A materialized ghost seems as solid as any human. Twentieth-century science no longer regards solids as solids at all, but rather as congealed wave patterns. Psychical researcher James Crenshaw notes that the whole imposing array of subatomic particles—electrons, protons, positrons, neutrinos, mesons—achieve particle-like characteristics in a manner similar to the way that wave patterns in tones and overtones produce characteristic sounds. Crenshaw theorizes that ghosts may be made up of transitory, emergent matter that appears and disappears, "can sometimes be seen and felt before disappearing … behaves like ordinary matter but still has no permanent existence in the framework of our conception of space and time. In fact, after its transitory manifestations, it seems to be absorbed back into another dimension or dimensions."

❦

WITNESSING AN ANCIENT RITE OF ANIMAL SACRIFICE

When the Beckers of Ebenezer, New York, built their new home they knew that the lot they had purchased had originally been part of the Seneca

Reservation. On the night of February 22, 1966, Carolyn Becker took her dog for a walk along the Cazenovia Creek. Suddenly from out of nowhere, she heard the howl of a strange dog. Her dog heard it, too, for his ears pricked and his hackles rose as he froze in his tracks.

Then on the creek bank a tall pole decorated with cloth strips of vivid color appeared and Carolyn said that she watched in astonishment as a buckskin-clad Native American man, wearing a strange headdress, strangled a beautiful white dog. As she stood observing the strange scene, the man wrapped the now limp body of the dog in brightly colored strips of cloth. Next he wound strands of wampum around the dog's broken neck.

Dimly she discerned glowing campfires and throbbing drums, and the smell of tobacco smoke penetrated her senses. The scene soon faded, and the woman and her dog were left standing, shivering, in the snow.

After doing some research on the customs of the Seneca, Carolyn Becker explained that what she had witnessed had been the Seneca's New Year Jubilee ceremony, in which a pure white dog was sacrificed for the tribe's sins. Mrs. Becker searched the old records of the reservation and learned that the ceremony had last been held on those grounds in 1841. She could only deduce from this information that time had somehow turned backward to allow her to witness this ceremony.

⌐═══ ○ ═══¬

A GHOSTLY STREET FIGHT

Francis J. Sibolski said that he has witnessed a phantom street fight take place outside of his home thirteen times in twenty years. From his front window, Sibolski claims that he has seen a 1937 Plymouth taxicab pull up and disgorge two angry men in their mid-twenties. The punching and mauling lasts about three minutes, and then the smaller man jumps into the waiting taxicab and it speeds off. The larger man rummages for a cigarette, shakes the last one out of the pack, throws the crumpled package on the sidewalk, and begins to walk toward the corner. Before the taxi reaches the corner or before the big man has taken more than a few steps, the tableau fades away.

Sibolski has had his wife witness the phantom fighters, and he has researched the incident and has identified the two men [now both deceased, though one was still alive when Sibolski began witnessing the restored scene from the past]. He has also obtained testimonials from those who remember the original altercation. Sibolski claims that the cigarette package exists for several minutes, sometimes even hours, after the tableau has vanished.

Once Sibolski approached the phantom scene and attempted to become a part of the past. When he came within six or seven feet of the fighters, his nostrils and throat suddenly became congested with a taste and smell that recalled his childhood colds. While he was capable of moving, he had no desire to. He retreated to the bottom of his porch steps, watching the act complete itself, feeling very odd—as if he were looking at old clothing in a forgotten attic.

DRIVING DOWN A STREET OUT OF TIME

Not all restored scenes of the past are as dramatic as observing an ancient rite of animal sacrifice or witnessing a phantom street fight. All Alan did was to take the same route home that he had traveled for years. Without deviating from his habitual route, Alan suddenly found himself driving down a street completely unrecognizable to him. Everything seemed quiet—too quiet for his liking—and when he tried to pick up a station on his car radio, all he got was static.

The only other car in sight was an extremely old one, parked in front of a little diner named "Henry's." When Alan reached the intersection, he remembers experiencing a "funny feeling like going through cool water." After that, everything was all right. Alan knew where he was; he came out just where he should have been all along.

> He asked friends if anyone knew of such a diner, but no one had ever heard of a Henry's.

Alan claims to have driven that route a couple of thousand times without ever having seen a diner named Henry's. Even if he had taken a wrong turn, his knowledge of the town would have enabled him to recognize the street. He asked friends if anyone knew of such a diner, but no one had ever heard of a Henry's. Finally, in the city records, he found that a diner with that name had once existed in 1914 on a street that had been destroyed by fire in 1923 and rebuilt in 1926.

SHARING A CAMPGROUND WITH GHOSTS

In August 1941, Leonard Hall and a number of friends took an extended fishing trip, and decided to camp out along the Upper Current River in the Ozarks. Just before sunrise, Hall was awakened by the sound of many voices speaking in a strange language. He opened his eyes and saw to his amazement that another party of campers had moved into the area while he and his friends were sleeping.

Several figures were silhouetted against a roaring fire about a hundred yards from his tent. Hall was further astounded to see that the entire clearing along the riverbank was ringed with campfires. The majority of the figures were recognizable as Native American men, who were dressed only in breech-cloths. They spoke a language unfamiliar to him, but Hall could hear another tongue that sounded like Spanish. When he realized that he was hearing Spanish voices, he rubbed his eyes and pinched himself to convince himself that he was awake, for there, sitting around a campfire in the Ozarks, were men sporting the armor of Spanish conquistadores.

Leonard Hall feared that he was experiencing either an extremely vivid dream or some dreadful mental aberration. He did not awaken his companions to confirm what he was witnessing. Instead, he returned to his sleeping bag and managed to doze off again, somewhat fitfully.

The following morning, with the eerie scenes of the night fresh in his mind, Hall made a careful check of the riverbank, but failed to unearth any evidence that he and his friends had shared the site with other campers. Hall's curiosity was aroused, however, and he decided to do a bit of private research. He did not release his findings until several years later. In the interim he learned that bands of conquistadores under the leadership of Hernando de Soto and Francisco Vasquez de Coronado had been in the area of the Upper Current River in August 1541. In his story, eventually written up in the *St. Louis Post-Dispatch*, Hall wondered if he had viewed adventurers from out of the past-exactly four hundred years later when he chanced to camp on the same stretch of ground they had chosen.

⊸⊸⊸⊸⊸

THE WORLD WAR II CANTEEN IN NORTH PLATTE THAT COMES AND GOES

By Dale Bacon

Following is the account of my experience in North Platte, Nebraska, both in 1997 and 2003. I've gone over this incident in my head many times, and have put it down on paper on more than one occasion.

On September 18, 1997, I had been returning from a visit to South Dakota's Black Hills. I had been driving from the Pine Ridge to Lincoln, Nebraska, most of the day and arrived at North Platte in the late afternoon. I was tired, but still wanted to see some of the local sights that might be open. I had remembered the stories of the North Platte Canteen, an historic landmark from World War II, and thought it might be interesting to visit.

I recall how easy it was to find, across from the railroad tracks, looking very much like it did in the photos I had seen. It even still had the sign hanging on the front façade. I thought that seemed a bit hokey, but whatever brings in the tourist trade, I figured.

The details of my visit are short and sweet. As I entered the front door I recall a reception counter to my right, a visitor's log on the counter, and a woman behind the counter. Gathered in a small circle were six or seven elderly women who just seemed to be chatting. Everyone was very friendly to me, and I took a quick look around. The interior was open, with very minimal decorations or exhibits. I thought it odd the place wasn't full of World War II regalia and artifacts based on the history of the canteen.

I couldn't have been inside the place more than five minutes before I had seen the whole thing, and then left to find a motel. In essence, I turned on my heels and started back to the door. One of the ladies spoke to me, saying that she and her friends used to work at the canteen as girls and they would sometimes gather to talk about the old days and share their stories with any interested parties.

In true small-town fashion, all the other ladies chimed in with the first speaker. Within about a minute I had been told how many eggs were used each day to prepare the cakes, how many gallons of milk were used, how much flour and sugar was needed, and how hard it sometimes was to get deliveries. However, the people of North Platte and the surrounding communities were patriotic above reproach and helped without (much) complaint. One of the canteen's claims to fame was recognizing any soldier, sailor, or marine who was celebrating a birthday when they passed through the canteen during the war years by giving them a cake. Thousands of cakes had been passed out.

I listened and smiled politely, but excused myself after a few minutes. I recall opening the cover of the guest register, and I might have even signed the book. I'm just not sure about that detail anymore. Regardless, I left and didn't look back.

Now we move forward in time to May 23, 2003. I took a trip into the Panhandle region of Nebraska along with my good friend, Linda Keith. This particular trip had been planned according to several mysterious and macabre accounts appearing in newspaper articles and eyewitness reports from my file collection of Paranormal Nebraska. Our intention was to capture certain historical locations on film, which could later be used in my capacity as storyteller specializing in ghost tales. I wanted to present original stories with updated information, connecting everything through digital imagery. One of our first stops was North Platte.

We arrived there around 1:30 in the afternoon and proceeded to the railroad tracks in our quest for the historic canteen. I had asked Linda if she wanted to see this piece of Cornhusker State history, and I wanted to see it again with fresh eyes. Since it had been so easy to find six years prior I was surprised to not find it on the first sweep of the tracks. There were some buildings, but nothing looked familiar. We drove around looking for any structure with similar features to the canteen, but found nothing.

We sought assistance at a local gas station, but the best we could get were directions to a restaurant called "The Canteen" near Interstate 80. A second gas station provided us with the same information.

I remembered that we had driven past the town library earlier in our pursuit, and I suggested we go there for directions. Upon arrival we learned that the library closed at 2:00 P.M. and we only had ten minutes to spare. We determined this to be a moment of synchronicity.

The three ladies in the library were more than anxious to help us. We were given the location by the tracks and easiest way to drive there. But we were greatly encouraged to visit the Lincoln County Historical Society Museum and see the canteen exhibit. It was the only place where any of the original artifacts could still be seen.

Just as in 1997, I thought it odd that the museum wasn't actually located within the original building. As I recalled, the canteen appeared structurally sound, unless there was something I didn't know regarding the building. When I asked the ladies about this I mentioned my visit six years prior and how I had enjoyed my brief stay.

> "**No, that building isn't there anymore. It was torn down in 1973.**" I recall feeling the blood drain from my face as I heard this casual comment.

The three librarians looked confused for a moment, and one of them said, "No, that building isn't there anymore. It was torn down in 1973." I recall feeling the blood drain from my face as I heard this casual comment. The only thing at the original site today is a marker and mini-park.

Linda and I drove to the location given by the librarians and found it immediately. We had driven past it several times not realizing what it was. We also drove to the Lincoln County Historical Society Museum to see the exhibit. I thought for a moment that I might have actually gone there in 1997 and somehow confused the two in my memory. While the museum was a very nice place to visit, I quickly ascertained it was not the same place I visited six years prior.

In retrospect, it was one hell of a way to kick off our vacation of paranormal hotspots within the state.

I've talked with a few residents of North Platte, and I have not been shy about my experience. In these conversations I've learned that I'm not the first person to have had this experience involving the canteen. But as you well know, it's one thing to read about someone having an experience and another to actually have the experience yourself.

⋘⊶⦿⊷⋙

HE WAS TRYING TO GET TO HIS WEDDING ON TIME

In his *Orbits of the Unknown*, John Macklin relates the experience of Father Litvinov, who just before midnight one evening in 1933, opened the church door to admit a young man in ornate knee breeches who had a look of horror on his face. Once the priest managed to calm his strange, hysterical visitor, he heard a most incredible story.

The young man said his name was Dmitri Girshkov, and he claimed that he was supposed to be married that day. On his way to the church, he had stopped by the cemetery to visit the grave of a boyhood friend. As he had stood there paying his respects, he was startled to see an image of his friend, who had been dead for over a year. The next thing he knew it was evening, and as he made his way back to the village, he was frightened to find nearly everything had changed in the small Siberian town.

> [T]wo other priests and a schoolmaster had seen the boy who stepped out of the past....

Dmitri ran from the church, shouting in anguish that he must find his family, his friends, his bride. Father Litvinov became aware of a strange light and a gray mist. In the blink of an eye, the curiously dressed young man had vanished.

Greatly intrigued by the provocative and eerie experience, the priest went back through old parish records. He discovered that, within the last two centuries, two other priests and a schoolmaster had seen the boy who stepped out of the past (or who stepped into the future, depending upon one's point of view).

At last he found the name of Dmitri Girshkov. It had been recorded that, on his wedding day in 1746, the young man had stopped to visit the grave of a friend and then disappeared.

TRAGEDY AT BOX CANYON

By Richard Senate

I got this story from a firefighter friend of mine. While fighting a fire in Box Canyon, California, he and the crew were exhausted, resting in the shade, when he swears he saw figures moving in the shadows—figures of men and women wearing white robes, bare footed, some with water skins like one would see in Biblical times. He wondered if these were ghosts from Atlantis? This was a perfect example of the reason ghost hunters need to understand local history. Instantly, I knew what he had seen, and it had nothing to do with Atlantis.

On the night of December 10, 1958, the tranquility of Box Canyon, south of Simi Valley, was broken by a powerful explosion. The blast occurred at the headquarters of a religious cult called the Fountain of the World, blowing apart their stone headquarters building. When the police arrived they found the trees filled with clothing, laundry that had been blasted from the clotheslines where it had been hanging. Nearly a hundred cultists survived the explosion and were found wandering the grounds in a confused state of shock. A simple investigation revealed that ten members of the cult were missing, including the cult leader and self-proclaimed messiah and cult founder, Krishna Venta

Krishna Venta's real name was Francis Pencovic, born in 1911 in San Francisco. His criminal record stretched back to 1941 when he was arrested for sending threatening letters to President Franklin D. Roosevelt. He was questioned by the FBI and released as a "harmless crank." In the years that followed, Pencovic was in and out of jail for such crimes as burglary and larceny. For a time he was a patient at the California state mental hospital at Camarillo. Between stays in jail he held a variety of colorful jobs—perhaps his most successful that of a door-to-door Bible salesman. He was a gifted speaker with a natural charisma. He began to drift toward religion. In 1949 he founded his own religious cult. In it he blended Christian and Hindu philosophies into a new harmonious religion. It was based on this motto: "Be positive, creative and constructive in all you think, all you say, and all you do."

He grew his beard long and changed his name to Krisna Venta and claimed that he wasn't of this world but from a distant planet called "Neophates" (this was the era of UFOs). He also claimed that he was incredibly old, some 244,000 years in age! He moved back to California from Denver where he started his new religion and managed to receive enough support from his wealthy converts to establish his commune in Box Canyon. It was with success that problems began to surface with the cult. Locals hated the newcomers with their strange white robes and arrogant leader. On several occasions they tried to evict them without success. The cultist won some support by helping with the fight against brushfires and providing water and food to firefighters. Once, when a plane went down in the remote backcountry, a member of the Fountain of the World brought the fourteen survivors of the crash to safety.

Within the cult some of the new converts began to question the authority of "The Master." They liked his religion but didn't care for some of the things he was doing—most especially seeking sexual favors from the female members of the cult, some of them wives of other members! When two men spoke out, they were expelled from the commune.

After the blast, the police found an abandoned blue pickup truck. Inside was a new tape recorder with a reel-to-reel tape. When the tape was played, it was found to be from the two members who were cast out. They listed what they were going to do. They would compel Krisna Venta to step down as the day-to-day leader of the cult and become instead a figurehead spiritual leader. The two vowed to take twenty sticks of dynamite to threaten Venta. The tape ended with a terse message: "If we don't return, people will know what has happened." The police found fingerprints of the two men in the ruins of the headquarters as well as a thumb that was identified as that of one of the two men. Clearly, Venta had called their bluff.

Perhaps the spirits of the cultists still haunt Box Canyon, still trying to practice their unique faith and help firefighters when Simi Valley is in danger. Maybe the penitent ghost of Krisna Venta himself still walks the valley; perhaps he is trying to expunge his many sins before he can move on. Who can say?

GHOSTS OF THE PAST

Psychoanalyst Dr. Nandor Fodor theorized that genuinely haunted houses were those that had soaked up emotional unpleasantness from former occupants. Years, or even centuries, later, the emotional energy may become reactivated when later occupants of the house undergo a similar emotional disturbance.

The haunting—mysterious knocks and rapping, opening and slamming doors, cold drafts, appearance of ghostly figures—is produced, in Dr. Fodor's hypothesis, by the merging of the two energies, one from the past, the other from the present.

In Dr. Fodor's theory, the reservoir of absorbed emotions, which lie dormant in a haunted house, can only be activated when emotional instability is present. Those homes which have a history of happy occupants, the psychoanalyst believed, are in little danger of becoming haunted.

There is another kind of paranormal phenomenon in which an entire section of landscape seems to be haunted. In most cases of this particular type of haunting, a tragic scene from the past is recreated in precise detail, as if some cosmic photographer had committed the vast panorama to ethereal film footage. Battles are waged, trains are wrecked, ships are sunk, the screams of earthquake victims echo through the night—all as it actually took place months or years before.

Thomas A. Edison theorized that energy, like matter, is indestructible. He became intrigued by the idea of developing a radio that would be sensitive enough to pick up the sounds of times past—sounds which were no longer audible to any ears but those of the psychically sensitive. Edison hypothesized that the vibrations of every word ever uttered still echoed in the ether. If this theory ever should be established, it would explain such phenomena as the restoration of scenes from the past. Just as the emotions of certain individuals permeate a certain room and cause a ghost to be seen by those possessing similar telepathic affinity, so might it be that emotionally charged scenes of the past may become imprinted upon the psychic ether of an entire landscape.

An alternate theory maintains that surviving minds, emotionally held to the area, may telepathically invade the mind of a sensitive person and enable him or her to see the scene as "they" once saw it.

It cannot be denied that some locales definitely have built up their own atmospheres over the years and that such auras often give sensitive people feelings of uneasiness, fear, and discomfort. Whether this may be caused by surviving minds, a psychic residue, or an impression of the actual event in the psychic ether is a question that remains unsolved at the present stage of parapsychological research.

THE STRANGE ADVENTURE OF PETIT TRIANON

When Eleanor Jourdain and Anne Moberly took the train from Paris to Versailles on August 10, 1901, they did not expect to meet Marie Antoinette. Neither did they expect to find people dressed in the costume of her era, speaking in a French dialect that dated from the late eighteenth century. These and other mysterious circumstances transformed a tourist's visit to the palace grounds, especially those of the Petit Trianon, the "little chateau" that Louis XVI of France built for his Mistress Marie, into a journey into the past.

Like all proper tourists, the two academics, Anne Moberly and Eleanor Jourdain, principal and vice-principal of St. Hugh's College Oxford, began their promenade with a visit to the long rooms and galleries of the palace. It was a pleasant afternoon. The French late summer had been hot, but on this day a protective curtain of gray cloud had been drawn across the sun, and a cool breeze enticed the travelers to visit the Petit Trianon.

The two friends started out on the path that would take them to the pavilion where Marie Antoinette and her friends had diverted themselves by playing at peasant life, a pastime that enjoyed great vogue among the French aristocracy at that time. They made their way down the great steps of the palace and past the fountains. They walked along the central avenue until they reached the fountainhead of the pond, then they turned right, as indicated in their guidebook.

The mood of the day seemed to change as they passed the Grand Trianon and turned off the paved walkway onto a broad, grassy drive. In their haste, they missed the path that would have taken them directly to the Petit Trianon. Instead, they crossed it and walked up a lane leading in the other direction.

As they proceeded along this route, Anne Moberley saw a woman lean out of the window of a nearby building to shake a dust cloth. It would not be until later, when they compared notes, that they learned that Eleanor Jourdain

The Palace at Versailles.

had not seen the woman and that Anne had not perceived a number of figures Eleanor had clearly seen.

The travelers found that the path they were following had suddenly branched into three. Confused, and believing they had somehow gotten off the main path, they decided they would ask the two men they supposed were gardeners who were walking just ahead of them with a wheelbarrow. Strangely dressed in long, grayish-green garments of the finest cloth and wearing three-cornered hats of black velvet, they answered Eleanor Jourdain's question by directing the two women to walk straight ahead.

The path that they were traveling ended abruptly in another, which ran across the other at an angle, like a ribbon across the edge of a package. Beyond this they saw a woodland. As if the new path was a dividing line between sections of a patchwork quilt, it chopped off the blue-green lawn from a stretch of ground covered with tufts of wild grass and dead leaves. The environment in which Eleanor Jordain and Anne Moberly now found themselves began to take on an eerie, unnatural look; and though it was still afternoon, the light was diminished. Although the wind still moved around them, no branches waved, no leaves stirred. The trees almost appeared to be part of a woven tapestry and they cast no shadows.

Beside the bandstand a man, dressed in the same manner as the others, sat with his back turned to the women. As Anne and Eleanor approached, he turned and the women almost gasped from the sight of his face. His countenance was dark, and his pockmarked face, with its mouth that drooped like a Greek mask of tragedy and staring, sightless eyes, gave the appearance of decay and evil.

Anne and Eleanor were so stricken by this sight that they did not see another man who approached until he called to them. The two frightened women spun around to face the newcomer, then became composed enough to ask him for directions. He pointed the way, but he spoke in an accent which neither of the two teachers could comprehend. They thanked him, nevertheless. At once the man ran off and disappeared into the woods. And, although they could no longer see him, the pair still heard the sound of his running footsteps.

Eleanor and Anne started off in the direction their mysterious guide had indicated. Hurrying along a narrow path nearly roofed by overgrown trees, the women soon found themselves at last before the Petit Trianon. Rough grass, such as one might expect to find growing around the cottage of a French peasant in the days of Louis XVI covered the terrace around the north and west sides of the house. Unmindful of their presence, a woman sat holding a pad at arm's length, busily sketching the scene. Eleanor could not help remarking that the woman was dressed like a picture she remembered seeing of Marie Antoinette, complete with full skirt and wide white hat. There must be some kind of historical pageant in progress.

As the two women walked up the steps to the top of the terrace, the strange atmosphere of the place hung over the scene like a musty blanket. When they reached the top, they looked back at the woman with the sketch pad. She glanced up to meet their gaze, and they saw that her face was old and ugly.

A door slammed, and a young man dressed for kitchen work stood before them on the terrace. He carried a broom and seemed to have stepped out to shake the dust from it. He seemed as surprised by their presence as they were by his. He asked if they were lost.

Anne and Eleanor politely refused his offer to show them the way, and once inside the Petit Trianon, they found a wedding in progress—not one from the time of Marie Antoinette, but one which was unmistakably an event of 1901. Standing in the midst of the cheerful celebrants, Eleanor Jourdain and Anne Moberly felt the cloud of depression that had followed them to the Petit Trianon lift. Later, they took a carriage back to Versailles.

A week passed, and still the two did not speak of the strange afternoon at the Petit Trianon. And then one day, Anne and Eleanor concluded that the place was haunted and that they had somehow either walked into scenes

Queen Marie Antoinette.

from the past or they had encountered a number of ghosts during their afternoon tour of the estate.

Eleanor Jourdain and Anne Moberley returned to Versailles, separately and together. Eleanor's second visit to the haunted grounds was on January 2, 1902. In contrast to the late summer day on which the two had made their first visit to Versailles, the day of her return was cold and raining. She did not walk to the Petit Trianon this time, but traveled in a carriage. As she moved along the drive, she tried to mark each incident as it occurred when she and Anne Moberley make their memorable trip on foot. Once again she saw the darkness deepen. The same depression she had felt the first time descended upon her with the cold rain.

She puzzled over the activity of men who were out in the rain filling a cart with sticks. She glanced away for an instant, and when she looked back the laborers and their cart were gone and the landscape was barren as far as she could see. She hastened out of the village and found herself lost in a maze of crisscrossing, diagonal paths that all seemed to end in other paths.

A man in the same costume as the one who had given them directions the time before came slipping through the dripping woods. Suddenly, Eleanor Jourdain felt herself being jostled, as if by a passing crowd, and heard the whispers of silks brushing the tall grass. She heard voices speaking French close to her ears. From the distance eerie music drifted in from an unseen group of musicians.

Eleanor looked at her map, quickly selecting a path, thinking only to get out of this other-worldly place as quickly as possible. She started out, only to find herself drawn to another path by a sense of urgency she could not understand. She bolted onto the path she had first chosen and was immediately lost. The clouds seemed to lower, and the rain seemed to thicken. Grayness was everywhere. Even the raindrops had the look of wet clay. The ground itself appeared to dissolve in grayness and ooze over the edges of the paved walk. Fear drew the breath from Eleanor Jourdain's lungs as she desperately sought her way back to the present.

In her haste, she almost ran into a bearded giant of a man who suddenly appeared on the path in front of her. Eleanor was too tired to be frightened. Catching her breath, she simply asked for directions. He told her to follow the path that she was on. The man's directions proved accurate, and soon a badly shaken Eleanor Jourdain was on her way back to Versailles.

Although Miss Jourdain made several trips to Versailles with her classes of students, it was not until July of 1904 that Miss Moberley was able to accompany her again. As Eleanor had told her incredulous friend, things had changed since their first visit. Gates that had been open when the two had first visited the grounds were closed and locked, and the passing years had placed a seal of cobwebs upon them, as they had upon the kitchen door which the jovial youth with the broom had slammed. Only the ghosts that remained at Petit Trianon knew when that door had last been opened. Marie Antoinette had gone to sketch other scenes, and in her place, rose a well-rooted shrub of a size that gave mute testimony to decades of growth.

Had the great wheel of time somehow turned back, bringing the past into the present? Or had the two women somehow managed to summon spirits from an earlier time? Or, as some of their critics believe, had they imagined the whole series of remarkable events?

When they later published a book describing their strange afternoon at Versailles (*An Adventure*, 1911), both wrote under pseudonyms. They were adverse to brash statements that contained more emotion and drama than reason, and they stoutly defended their version of their strange encounter with ghosts of late eighteenth-century France. They were, after all, academics: Eleanor Jourdain held the post of Taylorian lecturer in French at Oxford University, and Anne Moberley was the principal of an Oxford girl's school. Both were daughters of Anglican clergymen. They were both interested in music, not only in listening or playing, but in the theory of harmony itself. Interestingly, both women were psychically sensitive, but each was reluctant to speak of her abilities and spoke of their "horror of many forms of occultism."

Opening a Door to the Past

A more contemporary, but classic case: At approximately 8:50 A.M. on October 3, 1963, Coleen Buterbaugh, secretary to Dean Sam Dahl of Nebraska Wesleyan University in Lincoln, Nebraska, set out to deliver a message from the dean to a professor, opened a door and walked into an office out of the past. As Mrs. Buterbaugh entered the first room of the professor's suite, she suddenly smelled a musty, intensely disagreeable odor. Standing before her was a tall, black-haired woman dressed in a floor-length skirt. The woman was raising her right arm to reach the top right-hand shelves of an old music cabinet. The room was filled with a deathly silence, and the tall woman took no notice of Mrs. Buterbaugh.

The tall woman was not transparent—but she was not real, Mrs. Buterbaugh said, recalling her strange experience. And while the secretary was looking at the woman, she just faded away, her whole body, all at once.

Mrs. Buterbaugh looked out the window. It was then that she received the fright that sent her hurriedly scurrying from the office. There were no modern buildings or streets anywhere in sight. In fact, most of the campus was just an open field. All at once Coleen Buterbaugh realized that she was no longer on the college campus of 1963. Fearing that she had somehow stepped through a door into another time dimension, she quickly fled the room. Once back in the hallway, it was clear that she had returned to the present.

The startled and confused secretary hurried back to her desk in Dean Dahl's office. She tried to work, but the whole bizarre incident was too much for her to keep to herself. When she entered the dean's office, he got to his feet to help the pale and obviously shaken woman to a chair. His listened courteously and without comment to her story, then he asked her to accompany him to the office of Dr. Glenn Callen, chairman of the division of social sciences, who had been on the Wesleyan faculty since 1900. Once again, the secretary was fortunate to have a listener who heard her out and who treated her account with respect.

After a careful quizzing of Mrs. Buterbaugh, together with the aid of a number of old college yearbooks, Dr. Callan theorized that Coleen had somehow walked into the office as it had been circa 1920. Lengthy research managed to produce a photograph of the campus as Mrs. Buterbaugh had seen it. The picture had been taken in 1915. Still more investigation into the college's old yearbooks revealed the picture of a music teacher who fit Coleen Buterbaugh's description of the woman in the office. The teacher's name was Clara Mills, and she had died shortly before 9:00 A.M. one morning in the late 1930s in the office in which Mrs. Buterbaugh had just seen her. The filing cabinet which Mrs. Buterbaugh had seen her opening was found to contain choral arrangements dating back to Clara Mills' tenure at the college (1912 to 1936).

Psychical researchers Gardner Murphy and H. L. Klemme employed hypnotic time regression as a means of eliciting further details of Mrs. Buterbaugh's remarkable paranormal experience. After they had placed the secretary in the hypnotic trance state, they instructed her to relive and to describe the events of that most extraordinary morning.

Once again, the secretary heard the sound of students practicing music. She dodged the students moving from their first-period classes, then entered the first room of the professor's suite. While in the state of hypnotic regression,

The photographer was the only one present when this photo was taken after a 1995 fire at Wem Town Hall in the United Kingdom. In 1677 a fire started by a young girl destroyed the original building.

she was again stopped short by a very musty, disagreeable odor. Raising her eyes, she saw a very tall, black-haired woman extending her right arm to the upper right-hand shelves of an old music cabinet.

Coleen Buterbaugh told the researchers that when she had first walked into the office, everything had seemed quite normal. But after about four steps into the room, the strong odor had hit her. And when she said "strong odor," she emphasized, she meant the kind that stopped a person in his or her tracks and almost choked them.

> That was when she realized that these people were not in her time, but that she was back in their time.

As soon as she was stopped by the odor, she felt as though there was someone in the room with her. It was then that she became aware that there were no noises out in the hall. Everything had become deathly quiet.

She looked up and something seemed to draw her eyes to the cabinet along the wall in the next room, and there was Clara Mills, standing with her back to Coleen, reaching up into one of the shelves of the cabinet with her right hand, standing perfectly still. Coleen Buterbaugh explained that while the woman was not transparent, she knew somehow that "she wasn't real." Then, while the startled secretary was looking at her, she just disappeared.

Until the time that the woman faded away, Mrs. Buterbaugh said that she was not aware of anyone else being in the office suite. But as the one ghost was fading from sight, the startled secretary suddenly felt as though she was not alone. To her left was a desk, and she had a feeling that there was a man sitting there. She turned around and saw no one, but she still felt his presence.

It was then that she looked out the window behind that desk, became terribly frightened, and left the room. There wasn't one modern thing out there. The street was not even there. Neither were the new campus buildings. That was when she realized that these people were not in her time, but that she was back in their time.

Researchers Murphy and Klemme received permission to conduct a thorough search of the university files, and they at last uncovered a photograph dated 1915 that depicted a campus scene similar to the one which Mrs. Buterbaugh had glimpsed out of the window. The two investigators thought it highly unlikely that the secretary could ever have come across the picture, or even one like it, prior to the time of her most unusual experience. They also agreed that the picture of Clara Mills found in old yearbooks fit the description of the tall, dark-haired woman whom Mrs. Buterbaugh had seen in the office, and they established the fact that Miss Mills had died shortly before 9:00 A.M. in the same building in which the secretary had begun her trip into the past at about 8:50 A.M.

In the summer of 1970, I accompanied the Chicago psychic-sensitive Irene Hughes to the campus of Nebraska Wesleyan and the office in the C. C. White building wherein Coleen Buterbaugh had stepped into the past in an effort to test whether a gifted sensitive might elicit the recall of another's psychic experience. Irene Hughes had no idea where we were, other than being on a college campus. "I know that you don't want to tell me anything about the experiment tonight, Brad," she said, "but I am receiving psychically that it has to do with something that happened in one of these classrooms."

Irene walked directly to the back office of the suite. "I have the feeling that the desk was farther over this way," she said, "because I feel like I want my back right to the window. You know," she added, "I am just getting so many different impressions. People … people … so many people have been walking through here."

Then Irene began to receive an impression that made us instantly more attentive: "She came as a young lady. I see her in a long skirt that seems to open in the back. Her hair is bouffant … pompadour … rolled over. I feel her around in here very much. She seems to be a very pleasant and pretty woman. Involved with teaching."

It seemed as though Irene was indeed providing us with a description of Clara Mills.

"When I look outside this window, it does not look the way it did when I was seeing it through her eyes. Those buildings weren't there. There was only a road or a sidewalk," she added. After a few more minutes, Irene said, "I can see a man in this office. He came in and sat down at the desk. Then I see a secretary walking down the hall and entering the office. She walked in and wanted … tried to see him at the desk. Then I see the woman in the office—not the secretary, now, but the woman who belongs in there—I can see her hair, and it is very pretty. She is very tall for a woman, and her hair is dark, but not really black. It is worn in a roll and pushed over. I can see her skirt dark and long. And she has on a white blouse. She has a very pretty smile, and she busies herself around the office."

In the 1915 yearbook, a picture of Clara Mills bore the caption: "A daughter of the gods thou art, divinely tall and most divinely fair." The picture and the description, according to Coleen Buterbaugh, matched the appearance of the tall, dark-haired woman she had seen in the office. It also seemed to match the description which Irene Hughes had divined through her psychic sensitivity.

Irene continued receiving impressions: "I see the secretary walking in and seeing the woman over there (pointing toward the wall where the filing cabinet had been). Then she looked and saw the man sitting at the desk. Then … then she looked out the window. I think maybe she saw him looking out the window and turned to see what he was looking at. And … and things weren't the way they are now."

I found it very interesting that, although the Coleen Buterbaugh had seen the image of Clara Mills rather than the man at the desk, Irene seemed to be saying that it may possibly have been the man who was the stronger entity or vibratory force. We may have a reverse of what seemed to be obvious to the percipient.

In my opinion, and in the opinions of those researchers who accompanied us to Nebraska Wesleyan campus, Irene Hughes accurately described the image of Clara Mills as seen by Coleen Buterbaugh in this classic paranormal case. After speaking with knowledgeable faculty members we discovered that Clara Mills wore that style of dress all of her life, even after the styles had changed, which made it difficult to determine the date of the paranormal scene which Mrs. Buterbaugh had witnessed. Miss Mills joined the faculty in 1912, and it would appear that her spirit has not thought of retiring.

17

HAUNTED CHURCHES, CEMETERIES, AND BURIAL GROUNDS

AN UNINVITED GUEST UPSETS EPWORTH RECTORY

It was on December 1, 1716, that the children and the servants of Reverend Samuel Wesley brought their complaints to him. For several nights they had been hearing eerie groans and mysterious sounds in their rooms at Epworth Rectory, Dorcester, South Yorkshire. In addition to those frightening manifestations, they also said that they had heard the sound of footsteps ascending and descending the stairs at all hours of the night.

Reverend Wesley was skeptical about the allegations that eerie manifestations were occurring in his house; and after a week of careful nocturnal surveillance of the rectory without hearing a single sound, he promised to severely lecture the child or servant who brought him any unsubstantiated story about ghosts prowling the stairs and the bedrooms. One night at dinner, he told his family that he been unable to detect any night noises in the rectory. Any peculiar sounds, Wesley decreed, were undoubtedly caused by the silly young men who came around the rectory in the evenings to court his daughters.

The Wesleys had four grown daughters who had begun to entertain beaus and suitors, and the girls bristled at their father's veiled sarcasm. One of the older daughters wished aloud that the ghost would come knocking at the door to their father's study or bedchamber and give him a fright.

The girls were so peeved with their father that they stubbornly fought down their fright and vowed to ignore the disturbances until they became so loud that even he would have to acknowledge them. They didn't have long to

It's not only the Holy Spirit that one might find in churches; other ghosts have made them-selves known to the faithful as well.

wait. The very next night, nine loud knocks thudded on the walls of Wesley's bedchamber.

Wesley could not deny the reality of the harsh intrusions into his time of rest, but he dismissed the notion of a ghost being responsible for the sounds and concluded that some rogue had managed to get into the rectory unnoticed by the servants and was trying to frighten them. Wesley whispered to his wife that in the morning he would buy a large dog "big enough to gobble up any intruder."

First thing in the morning, the clergyman obtained a huge mastiff and brought it into the rectory. Such a brute would be able to deal with any spook, he decreed.

That night, however, as the knocks began to sound, Wesley was startled to see his canine ghostbuster whimper and cower behind the frightened children. One of the older girls teased that the dog was more frightened than they were.

Two nights later, the sounds in the house seemed so aggressively violent that Wesley and his wife were forced out of bed to investigate. As they walked through the rectory, the unseen noisemakers seemed to follow them. Mysterious crashing sounds echoed in the darkness. Metallic clinks seemed to fall in front of them. Somehow managing to maintain their courage, the Wesleys searched every chamber but found nothing.

After he called a family meeting to pool their knowledge about the invisible intruder, Wesley learned from one of their older daughters that she had observed that the disturbing phenomena usually began at about ten o'clock in the evening and were always preceded by a "signal" noise that sounded something like the winding of a very large clock. The noises also appeared to follow a pattern that seldom altered. They would begin in the kitchen, then suddenly move up to visit one of the children's beds, knocking first at the foot, then the head. This routine seemed to comprise the ghost's stretching exercises. After it had warmed up with these preliminaries, it would indulge any spectral whim that appealed to it.

"Why do you disturb innocent children?" Wesley demanded to know one night as the knockings in the nursery became especially explosive. "If you have something to say, come to me in my study." The ghost ignored the clergyman's invitation and continued to bang about on the bedsteads of the children.

"You deaf and dumb devil, why do you frighten these children that cannot answer for themselves?" he roared in righteous indignation. "Come to me in my study like a man!" As if in answer to Wesley's challenge, a sharp knock sounded on the door of his study with such force that the cleric thought the boards must surely have been splintered.

Although there were no more disturbances that evening, Wesley soon found out that his invitation to come to the study had not been ignored. Once he was pushed heavily against his desk "by an invisible power," and another time he was slammed into the doorjamb of his study just as he was entering the room.

Wesley decided to obtain reinforcements in the struggle against the devil that had invaded his rectory. He sent for Mr. Hoole, the Vicar of Hoxley, and told him the whole story. Mr. Hoole listened patiently to his fellow cleric's story, and told Wesley that he would lead devotions that night. They would see if the thing would dare to manifest itself in his presence.

The ghost was not the least bit awed by the Vicar of Hoxley. It put on such a powerful demonstration of paranormal power that night that the clergyman fled in terror, leaving Wesley to combat the unseen demon as best he could.

The children overcame their initial fear of the invisible entity in a most remarkable way and came to accept its supernatural antics as a welcome relief from the boredom of village life. They began to call their unseen guest "Old Jeffrey," and the ghost achieved something like the status of a pet. Old Jeffery,

When photographer Chris Brackley developed this photograph of the inside of St. Botolph's Church in London, he noticed the strange appearance of a woman in the right upper balcony. Only three people were in the church at the time, none of them upstairs.

it was soon observed, was a bit testy and temperamental. If any visitor slighted him by claiming that the rapping was due to natural causes, such as rats, birds, or wind, the phenomena were quickly intensified so that the doubter stood instantly corrected.

The preternatural disturbances kept up their scheduled arrival time of about ten o'clock in the evening until the day that Mrs. Wesley remembered the ancient remedy for ridding a house of evil spirits. Old texts and perhaps even older folklore recommended that those afflicted by such bothersome entities should obtain a large trumpet "and blow it mightily throughout every room in the house," she told the family. "The sounds of a loud horn are unpleasing to evil spirits."

The eardrum-shattering experiment in primeval exorcism was not only a complete failure, but now the ghost began to come around in the daylight hours as well. Old Jeffery had either resented the charge of being an evil spirit or else it was simply expressing its criticism of the terrible trumpeting by retaliating with increased activity.

The children seemed to welcome the fact that Old Jeffery would be available during their playtime hours as well as being an amusing nighttime nuisance. Several

Close-up of the entity in St. Botolph's Church.

witnesses swore that they had seen a bed levitate itself to a considerable height while a number of the Wesley children squealed merrily from the floating mattress. The only thing that seemed to disturb the children was the eerie sound, like that of a trailing robe, that Old Jeffery had begun to make. One of the girls declared that she had seen the ghost of a man wearing a long, white robe that dragged on the floor. Other children in the Wesley household claimed to have seen an animal, similar in appearance to a badger, scurrying out from under their beds. A number of the servants testified that they had seen the head of a rodent-like creature peering out at them from a crack near the kitchen fireplace.

Then, just as the Wesleys were growing accustomed to Old Jeffrey's antics, the bizarre phenomena ended as abruptly as they had begun. While the entity never returned to harass Epworth Rectory with its mischief, the memory of its disrupting period of occupancy has remained a challenge to scholars of Christian history and the paranormal for more than two centuries. Among the nineteen children of the Reverend Samuel Wesley who witnessed the phenomena were John and Charles, the founders of Methodism and the authors of some of Christendom's best-loved hymns.

BORLEY RECTORY: THE MOST HAUNTED HOUSE IN ENGLAND

It was the well-known psychic researcher Dr. Harry Price who applied the title of the "most haunted house in England" to the Borley Rectory, located about sixty miles northeast of London on the Essex-Suffolk border. Over the years, the claim of "most haunted" has been contested and the case has become controversial, but the old accounts of the occupants and the teams of researchers still make for chilling reading.

According to one of the legends of Borley, shortly after Reverend Guy E. Smith arrived to take over clerical duties at the Rectory in 1928, he opened the cabinet in the library to put away some books and saw a human skull grinning at him from a shelf. Mrs. Smith sucked in her breath as her husband removed the skull from the cabinet and began to examine it. "You don't suppose," she asked with nervous laughter, "that the rectory really is haunted? You don't think that could be the skull of the nun that's supposed to walk through these halls or the skull of one of the poor devils that was buried in the Plague Pit?"

Smith cautioned his wife to calm down or she would have herself believing all the weird tales they had heard about Borley Rectory. Still, it was difficult to deny the fact that no fewer than a dozen clergymen refused to live there before he accepted the call. Nor could he forget the story that a former rector had had a window in the dining room bricked up because he could not stand to see the ghost of a nun continually peering in at him.

Reverend Smith tried to ignore his wife's suggestion that something evil had made its abode in the rectory. He and the sexton gave the skull a solemn burial in the churchyard, and he and his wife fought to stave off the depression that seemed to have enveloped them. It was not many nights, however, before they were given awesome evidence of invisible forces at work.

The haunting phenomena usually began shortly after they had retired for the evening. They would be lying in bed, and they would hear the sound of heavy footsteps walking past their door. On several nights Smith would crouch in the darkness outside of their room with a hockey stick clasped firmly in his hands, lunging at something that passed their door—but he never struck anything tangible.

A female voice began to moan from the center of an arch leading to the chapel. Keys were dislodged from their locks and were found several feet from their doors. Hoarse, inaudible whispers sounded over their heads. Small pebbles appeared from nowhere to pelt them.

When the Smiths reported their supernatural plight to the *London Daily Mirror*, Dr. Harry Price was notified. In the summer of 1929, Price, his secre-

Once known as the "most haunted house in England," Borley Rectory was said to house many different types of phenomena including ghosts and poltergeists. This photograph of the rectory was taken in 1929.

tary, and C. V. Watts, a reporter for the *Mirror*, set out to visit the rectory and to see for themselves if Reverend Smith and his family were truly beset by authentic haunting phenomena.

Before the trio left London, their research revealed that the rectory, though constructed in modern times, stood on the site of a medieval monastery. There had once been a nunnery close at hand, and the ruins were much in evidence. There was a persistent legend about a nun who had been walled up alive in the convent as punishment for eloping with a Benedictine brother, who was later hanged for his indiscretion. Occupants of the rectory, and several villagers, had reported seeing the veiled nun walking through the grounds. About a quarter of a mile away stood a castle where many tragic events had occurred, ending with a siege by Oliver Cromwell. A headless nobleman and a black coach pursued by armed men had also been listed as frequent phenomenon.

The present rectory had been built in 1863 or 1865 by the Reverend Henry Dawson Ellis Bull, who had fathered fourteen children and needed a large home. Bull died in the Blue Room in 1892 and was succeeded in occupancy by his son, Harry, who died at the rectory in 1927. The building was

On the grounds of the church and rectory, a soft voice called out, "Marianne, dear."

vacant for a few months—while a dozen clergymen refused to take up residence there because of the eerie tales which they had heard—until Reverend Guy E. Smith and his family accepted the call in 1928.

After Price, his secretary, and C. V. Watts arrived at the rectory, they had lunch with Reverend Smith and his wife and listened to the couple describe the range of psychic phenomena that they had witnessed. While they spoke, a glass candlestick struck an iron stove near Price's head and showered him with splinters. A mothball came rolling down the stairwell, followed by a number of pebbles.

Price busied himself for the next several days conducting interviews with the surviving daughters of Reverend Henry Bull, the builder of the rectory, and any former servants who had remained in the village. A man who had served as gardener for the Henry Bull family told Price that every night for eight months he and his wife had heard footsteps in their rooms over the stables. Several former maids testified that they had remained in the employ of the Bulls for only one or two days before they were driven away by the strange occurrences.

The eldest of Reverend Bull's three surviving daughters told of seeing the nun appear at a lawn party on a sunny July afternoon in 1900. She had attempted to approach the phantom and engage it in conversation, but it had disappeared as she drew near. The sisters all swore that the entire family had often seen the nun and the phantom coach. It was their father who had bricked up the dining room window so that the family might enjoy dinner without the spectral nun peering in at them.

Mrs. Smith said that she, too, had seen the shadowy figure of a nun walking about the grounds of the rectory. On several occasions, she had attempted to confront the phantom, but it had always disappeared. Before the investigators left the Smiths, Watts wrote in an article for the *Daily Mirror*, that he, too, had seen the phantom nun and heard the sound of the ghostly carriage and horses hooves.

The Smiths left the rectory shortly after the visit of the investigators. They had both begun to suffer the ill-effects of lack of sleep and the enormous mental strain that had been placed on them.

The supernatural phenomena reached new heights of activity when the Reverend Lionel Algernon Foyster, his wife, Marianne, and their four-year-old daughter Adelaide established residence in the rectory on October 16, 1930. Reverend Foyster was a cousin of Caroline Foyster Bull, the wife of Reverend Henry Bull, so he must have had some idea what dreaded things they might face in the rectory after dark. They had lived there only a few days when Mrs. Foyster heard a voice softly calling, "Marianne, dear." Thinking her husband was summoning her, Mrs. Foyster ran upstairs. Foyster told his wife that he had not spoken a word, but he, too, had heard the calling voice.

On one occasion, Marianne Foyster set her wristwatch by her side as she prepared to wash her hands in the bathroom. When she finished washing, she reached for the watch and discovered that the band had been removed. It had disappeared and would never reappear.

When Reverend Foyster realized that the eerie tales that he had heard about Borley Rectory had all been true, he was not frightened, for he believed that he would be protected by his Christian faith. He used a holy relic to quiet the disturbances when they became particularly violent, and he remained calm enough to keep a detailed journal of the phenomena which he and his family witnessed.

For some unknown reason, Marianne Foyster became the brunt of the most cruel and sadistic facets of the haunting. While carrying a candle on the way to their bedroom, she received such a violent blow in the eye that it produced a cut and a black bruise which was visible for several days. On another occasion, she narrowly missed being struck by a flat iron which shattered the chimney of the lamp that she was carrying.

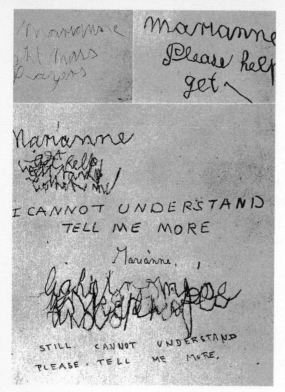

Strange messages were written on the walls of Borley Rectory, reportedly by the spirits that inhabited the house. Investigators tried to communicate with the spirits by writing messages back (seen here in large capital letters). Responses would often appear written in pencil, although they were not always legible.

Strangely enough, while one facet of the haunting persecuted Mrs. Foyster, another seemed desperate to establish contact with her. Messages were found scrawled on the walls: "Marianne … please … get help."

When Reverend Foyster learned that the well-known psychic researcher Dr. Harry Price had once shown an interest in the Borley phenomena, he wrote to London to inform the psychic researcher of renewed activity in the rectory. Upon arrival, Price and his two assistants once again set about examining the house from attic to cellar. While Price was in an upstairs room, an empty wine bottle hurled itself through the air, narrowly missing him. Shortly after that welcoming salvo from the haunting, the investigators were startled to hear the screams of their chauffeur, who had remained behind in the kitchen to enjoy a leisurely cigarette. The frightened man insisted that he had seen a large, black hand crawl across the kitchen floor.

Reverend Foyster showed Dr. Price the entry that he had made in his journal on March 28 when his wife had confronted a grotesque entity while ascending a staircase. She had described it as a monstrosity—black, ugly, apelike. It had reached out and touched her on the shoulder with an "ironlike touch." Price soon learned that others had seen the creature on different occasions.

The Foysters also told Price and his team that the haunting had begun to materialize items they had never seen in their house before. A small tin trunk had appeared in the kitchen when they were eating supper. A powder box that contained a wedding ring manifested in the bathroom, and, after the Foysters had carefully put the ring away in a drawer, it disappeared overnight. In his book, *The Most Haunted House in England*, Price documented more than two thousand incidents of paranormal activity that occurred during the Foysters' residency in the rectory.

The Foysters endured the supernatural harassment for five years before leaving Borley Rectory in October of 1935. After the Foysters left, the Bishop wisely decreed that the place should be put up for sale—and it should have come as no surprise to the parish to discover that there would be no interested parties waiting in line to bid on it.

In May of 1937, Harry Price learned that the rectory was once again vacant and offered to lease the place as a kind of ghost laboratory. His proposed sum was accepted, and the psychic investigator enlisted a crew of forty men who would take turns living in the rectory for a period of one year. Price outfitted the place with special ghost-detecting equipment and prepared a booklet of instructions that told his army of researchers how to correctly observe and record any phenomena.

Shortly after Price's crew began to arrive, strange pencil-like writings began to materialize on the walls. Each time a new marking was discovered, it would be carefully circled and dated. Two Oxford graduates reported actually seeing new writing form while they were busy ringing and dating another. It appeared that the entity missed Marianne Foyster. "Marianne ... Marianne ... M ..." it wrote over and over again. "Marianne ... light ... Mass ... prayers.... Get lights ... Marianne ... please ... help ... get."

Professor C. E. M. Joad, of the Department of Philosophy and Psychology at the University of London was one of those who watched the pencil markings appear on the walls. In the July 1938 issue of *Harper's* magazine, Professor Joad commented on his experience. "Having reflected long and carefully upon that squiggle I did not and do not see how it could have been made by normal means.... The hypothesis that poltergeists materialize lead pencils and fingers to use them seems to be totally incredible.... And the question of 'why' seems hardly less difficult to answer than the question 'how.' As so frequently occurs when one is investigating so-called abnormal phenomena, one finds it equally impossible to withhold credence from the facts or to credit any possible explanation of the facts. Either the facts did not occur, or if they did, the universe must in some respects be totally other than what one is accustomed to suppose."

The investigators soon discovered a "cold spot" in one of the upstairs passages. Although this is a common aspect of haunting phenomena, it had gone unnoticed in previous explorations by the psychic researchers and by any of the rectors who had lived in Borley. Some of Price's investigators noted that they shivered and felt faint whenever they passed through it. Another cold spot was discovered on the landing outside of the Blue Room. Thermometers indicated the temperature of these areas to be fixed at about forty-eight degrees, regardless of the temperature of the rest of the house.

On the last day of Dr. Price's tenancy, the wedding ring that had materialized during the Foysters' occupancy again appeared. To be certain that the ghost would not snatch it away again, the investigator brought it home to London with him.

The ruins of Borley Rectory, photographed on March 28, 1939. The rectory was derelict until 1944, when the property was razed.

In late 1938, the Borley Rectory was purchased by a Captain W. H. Gregson, who renamed it "The Priory." He was not at all intimidated by stories that the place was haunted, but he was upset when his faithful old dog went wild with terror on the day they moved in and ran away, never to be seen again. He was also somewhat concerned with the strange track of unidentified footprints that circled the house in freshly fallen snow. They were not caused by any known animal, the captain swore, nor had any human made them. He followed the tracks for a time until they mysteriously disappeared into nothingness.

At midnight on February 27, 1939, the Borley Rectory was completely destroyed by flames. Captain Gregson testified later that a number of books had flown from their places on the shelves and knocked over a lamp, which had immediately exploded into flame.

In December 2000, a book was published with the challenging title *We Faked the Ghosts of Borley Rectory*. In this exposé, Louis Mayerling, who claimed that Borley Rectory had been a second home to him in his younger days, made the charge that Harry Price, a host of other psychic researchers, and the world at large had been taken in by hoaxers who took special delight in playing ghost. Mayerling stated that he was but a lad in 1918 when he first arrived at Borley Rectory to discover Reverend Harry Bull and his family having great fun perpetuating the local folklore about a phantom nun and other things that went bump in the night. Later, according to the author, the Foysters got in on the spooky pranks, and encouraged Mayerling to don a black cape and stalk the gardens at dusk.

Mayerling revealed how those in on the hoax took great delight in ringing bells, tossing pebbles, and making eerie groans and moans. However, he did admit to one incident that he could not explain, which might indicate that there really was something paranormal occurring at Borley Rectory.

On Easter Sunday in 1935, quite a prestigious group of believers in the haunting phenomena at Borley Rectory joined Mayerling and Marianne Foyster for a séance at the rectory. Among those in attendance were the acclaimed playwright George Bernard Shaw; T. E. Lawrence, the heroic "Lawrence of Arabia" ; Sir Montagu Norman, Governor of the Bank of England; and Bernard Spilsbury, the Home Office criminal forensic scientist. According to Mayerling, all at once the kitchen bells clanged as one and a brilliant silver-blue light seemed to surround them from the walls and the ceilings. From his previous experience as a ghostly imposter making eerie sounds and noises in the rectory, Mayerling knew that it was impossible to cause all the bells to sound at once and he had absolutely no idea what could have caused the brilliant, lightning-like flash. He admitted that he was, in fact, temporarily blinded by the strange phenomenon and eventually recovered sight, but only in one eye. Shaw and Norman refused to stay the night after such a violent display of the supernatural, and Mayerling confessed in his book that the memory of that occurrence still unnerved him.

In spite of Mayerling's confession of participating in the hoaxing of many of the alleged phenomena at Borley Rectory, the authenticity of the haunting remains controversial and a subject of debate among psychic researchers. Although Mayerling may have joined the Bull family in perpetuating the legends of the rectory and later encouraged the Foysters to play along with the hoax, the admitted pranksters were not present during the years of occupancy by Reverend G.E. Smith and his family, the year-long observation of extensive phenomena by Price's team of researchers, or the period of manifestations reported by Gregson after he assumed ownership of Borley Rectory.

THE GENTLE SPIRITS OF MISSION SAN ANTONIO DE PADUA

Monks living at the Mission of San Antonio de Padua, one of North America's oldest Roman Catholic spiritual centers, have seen and heard ghosts

In September 1999 a photographer and one other person were taking photographs inside Sefton Church in Merseyside, United Kingdom. Neither individual saw a ghost or a living individual standing in front of the camera before the photograph was taken. The blurred figure of a man remains unexplained.

and watched strangely colored clouds hover just above the mission on hot, cloudless days. The mission, constructed in 1771, is located in the Santa Lucia mountain range of central California, thirty miles north of Paso Robles. A nearby U.S. Army base is the only other settlement in the area.

Franciscan brother Timothy, historian at the mission, said that even when the first padres came there in 1770 there were mysteries about the area. Local Indians told them of monks just like them who had come before—flying through the air.

On one occasion in the mid–1980s, Brother Timothy recalled being in the refectory with some archaeologists when they all heard someone moving in the attic above them. Everyone heard the footsteps taking a few paces, then stepping over the crossbeams, and the consensus was that there was an intruder in the refectory. Two of the archaeologists went up, one to the door at each end, and searched with flashlights. Nobody was there, and the thick dust was totally undisturbed.

Richard Senate, the well-known psychic researcher, was walking through the courtyard to get a cold drink from the icebox. It was about 12:30 A.M. Through the dense blackness of the night, Senate saw a light on the other side of the courtyard. He finally realized that it was a candle, and he changed his course to see who it was; he knew that the monks were strict about the use of candles because of the fire hazard. Senate was about twelve feet from the figure, and he see clearly that the person was wearing a monk's habit and was less than average height. They were both approaching the door to the chapel—then, just as Senate opened his mouth to speak, the monk vanished right before his eyes.

Senate clicked on his flashlight, but there was nothing there. The monk couldn't have quietly opened the door, because it was heavy and it squeaked. There was only blank wall around.

It was that experience that led the now-famous paranormal researcher to first believe in ghosts. Senate found out later that the timing of the ghost's appearance had been significant. In the past, the padres would get up about 12:30 A.M. and pray in the chapel for an hour and go back to bed. Senate is convinced that he saw a three-dimensional image from the past—the ghost of a long-dead monk going to prayer.

The monks of Mission San Antonio de Padua have often seen a small colored cloud, about three feet square and about eight feet high, above the tile roof over the women's guest quarters. The strange cloud changes colors, going from white to green to blue, then yellow and red.

The monks tell of the day Father John Baptist died and a similar mysterious cloud appeared that seemed to signal the priest's passing. Father John had been working in Atascadero, seventy miles away from the mission, when he died, and the monks had not yet gotten the news.

Brother Timothy remembered that a wispy white cloud floated out of the door of the winter chapel. Father Joe saw it as well, and the two of them watched its eerie movements. The cloud went along the cloister, then turned abruptly along the path. As Brother Timothy and Father Joe watched it, it went out to the fountain at the center of the courtyard, hovered there for a minute or two, then turned again and went along another path, along a cloister, and into the church. The two men ran to follow it, but it had disappeared inside.

The clerics noted that the white cloud had followed the exact route Father John had followed each day on his way to say his noon office. He had always walked the same path, even pausing to feed the goldfish in the fountain. Brother Timothy and Father Joe are convinced that Father John's soul was following his familiar path one last time.

THE THING THAT MOVES AT NIGHT

By Pastor Robin Swope

I was a gravedigger. A lot of people get satisfaction out of having a jacket or shirt that displays those words upon it with casual recklessness, but I was never too proud of the occupation.

It was a very dirty and disturbing occupation. With every worm that I smashed into the ground with our dirt-tamping machine, I could not but think of the human flesh we sent to the nether regions below. The worms were pink, mutilated flesh helplessly smashed into the ground, such as we will all be. When you are in such a disturbing occupation you have no one to turn to but your coworkers, who often relay to you stories of the strange and unusual. Perhaps you do so to find sanctuary, to help you cope, to help you think you are not going insane. Needless to say I was told quite a few stories. For some reason the most startling stories are set in the mausoleums.

The graveyard where I was employed for six years was in Erie County, Pennsylvania. It has a large mausoleum situated on its eighty-acre grounds. The tomb is distinctive because it is the only Protestant mausoleum in all of Erie County. Many well-to-do Protestant families are buried in the simple T-shaped building.

In the late 1990s, one of the gravediggers was placing a body into one of the crypts. To do this you need a casket elevator—a simple device that raises the casket to the crypt level so the coffin can be slid into its niche. Since many crypts are at a high level, the device is an essential tool for any mausoleum.

On any mausoleum crypt, the crude cement container is covered by more expensive stone such as granite or marble. The front piece and the facing are taken off to access the crypt. The superintendent and his helper were on the fourth level, about thirty feet off the ground, putting an elderly woman into a double crypt. One side contained the remains of her deceased husband. The funeral service itself was held inside the mausoleum since the building also doubled as a chapel. When the crowd departed, the funeral director helped place the coffin on the elevator, then left.

The gravediggers placed the elevator in position and raised the casket up. It was then that they noticed that they were not alone. It seemed as though someone had lingered to watch the burial internment itself take place. It was an elderly man in an old suit standing in the middle of the mausoleum. He stared at them intently.

Now this in and of itself was not an unusual happening. Many times the family of the deceased will linger after the service to see their loved one laid into their final resting place. They had not noticed the old man before when only the funeral director was in the building. But they just ignored it and proceeded with the entombment.

They placed the casket into the crypt, put the cement front piece on, and sealed it with caulk. As they lowered the elevator to raise the granite facing for the tomb they noticed the man nodded at them. The supervisor waved back and nodded in response.

Then the old man faded into nothing. He simply disappeared into the wall behind him.

The supervisor and the helper stood there frozen in fear as the elevator came to a screeching halt. The helper asked his boss what they had just beheld, but his boss had no idea. After a quick look around the building they still had no explanation.

So they went back to work. Each taking one end, they placed the heavy granite crypt front onto the elevator and raised it to the open hole that held the dead couple. They set it in place, and as they closed it they had the fright of their lives.

A mausoleum.

The crypt plate had pictures of the husband and wife. The pictures were taken years ago when the couple had first purchased the crypt. The woman they had just buried looked much older than her picture. But the husband looked very familiar. It was the man who had been watching them. There was no mistaking it. He was even in the same suit. It seems that the spirit of the husband wanted to bear witness to their final unity for eternity.

Not all the stories that were related to me by various gravediggers were so touching or heartwarming. Some were right out of horror movies.

In the late 1970s a cemetery near Pittsburgh built a new mausoleum. It had been promised for years, and the salesmen eager to make a lucrative commission had presold crypts long before they were available. So many makeshift cement above-ground crypts were quickly built for those who had purchased mausoleum spaces and had passed on before the tomb was built.

When the mausoleum was finished, it was the job of the gravediggers to disinter the bodies and place them in their new crypts. It was a disgusting and dirty job, for the liquefied remains of the deceased had leaked out of many of the caskets. To make matters worse for the gravediggers, every body had to be physically identified by the mortician who had originally embalmed the victim, and not by clothing or jewelry, to guarantee that the corpse in the casket was the person named on the makeshift crypt.

The supervisor remembered each decaying face, for the experience had been burned into his memory, but one in particular stood out. Most of the bodies had long since dried up and become desiccated. If any flesh was left, it was almost like tanned leather hanging off the bony skeleton. Some looked as if they were made out of Jell-O® as the corpse had decomposed into a liquid goo. But one was odd.

When they opened the coffin of the old man, it was like he had just been laid to rest. Except for one disturbing and obvious fact. He was covered with a furry gray-green fungus. All his flesh had been eaten by the fungus, but it held the shape of his face so well it shocked the superintendent and the undertaker. Except for the odd color and the fleecelike look of his skin, he looked like he might just open his eyes or mouth at any moment.

They quickly got over the initial shock and noted that, yes, he was who he was supposed to be and put the coffin in the second level in the back of the newly constructed mausoleum.

Monday morning when the maintenance crew came to open up the office they noticed the mausoleum door was open. As they drew near the open door they immediately knew something was wrong. Something was smeared on the glass door of the mausoleum, and as they looked inside, they saw that one of the crypts was open. And it was empty.

Fearing they had grave robbers they went to call the police, but as they rounded the corner to head back to the office they passed the old makeshift cement crypts. One was open and it held a casket.

It was the casket of the mold man, right back in the place he had been interned for the last five years. To be sure everything was all right and they did not have a grave robber playing a joke, they opened up the coffin. The body was still there and the jewelry he wore was still on his corpse. They called the police but there was nothing the police could do but file a vandalism report. The body was placed back in the mausoleum.

After they sealed the crypt again, the staff noticed that the smear on the door was the same color as the mold that covered the man. There also seemed to be small pieces of the stuff on the carpet that covered the floor from the crypt to the doorway. The body did not look molested at all, and the casket had shown no visible signs of forced opening, but it was still very disturbing.

Two weeks later it happened again. Everything was the same—the crypt was opened and the casket was found resting in its old spot. Even the smear and pieces of mold scattered here and there. But one thing was different this time. It had recently rained and the ground was soft. A single trail of footprints ran from the mausoleum to the makeshift crypt. And they were almost erased by the tracks left by the dragged coffin. And it was then that they noticed the handles of the coffin were also smeared with the gray green mold. It was if the mold man had somehow came out of the coffin and dragged it back to his original resting place.

But that was physically impossible, wasn't it?

Nevertheless a close look at the corpse and the fallen mold made everyone present shiver. They were definitely the same material.

Once again the body was laid to rest in the mausoleum, and the funeral director brought in a Catholic clergyman to give Last Rites and bless the tomb.

Mold man stayed put this time.

The maintenance crew always gave his crypt special attention. They always feared that one morning they would find it open again, and see the evidence of mold man once again walking the earth.

The interior of a mausoleum can be a spooky place, even when not haunted.

When you work at a cemetery for any length of time and meet others who have lived the life of a gravedigger for years, you hear some strange and unexplainable stories. And you hope that you are not the next one to come in the one morning with fear in your eyes and tell the others, "You are not going to believe this but …".

THE VOICES IN THE WALLS

By Pastor Robin Swope

As I previously stated, I worked at a local cemetery for six years while ministering in a para-church organization.

A lot of odd things happen in cemeteries.

When you work around death day in and day out, you kind of get used to it. But you never get used to the sometimes unexplainable things that happen.

One of the head maintenance men was clearing snow from the sidewalks and offices of the cemetery early in the morning one day in the middle of January. It was still dark, but the freshly fallen snow illuminated the landscape in an eerie glow.

When it was time to shovel the snow around the mausoleum, the maintenance man decided to save gas and walk the quarter mile from the office building to the tomb. Halfway there he saw a figure walking behind the building. From the size of the figure, it looked like a child, but the worker could not be sure.

It was a little odd, but not entirely out of the ordinary, that someone would take an early morning walk around the cemetery for exercise. But it was downright peculiar for someone—especially someone with a child in tow—to do it after a heavy snowstorm. Wearily he surveyed the grounds for any sight of a child or parents who might be getting some brisk morning exercise. But he saw no one as he neared the building.

He circled around to where he swore he saw the figure of the child, but there were no footprints in the snow. As he looked up from the new snow, he saw a face peering from around the corner on the other side of the building just fifty feet away from him. He could not make out features, but he saw the rough shading of eyes, nose, and mouth, on the shadowy figure that was examining him. It was about three feet tall, the size of a young child. "Hey, what are you doing here?" he shouted and started to make his way through the drifts to the curious face.

But as soon as he started to move the head quickly disappeared from the corner. The maintenance man walked faster, but when he arrived at the corner the child was gone. As he looked down to see where the young one had run to, he once again saw no footprints.

Amazed and disturbed, he threw his shovel into the ground and mumbled to himself. He was sure someone was playing a trick on him, but who could it be? As far as he knew he was alone in the seventy-acre cemetery.

Alone except for that small child who could disappear without leaving any tracks in the snow.

He shrugged and made a mental note to drill the other members of the crew when they came in to see if one of them was up to shenanigans. If it was a trick they would probably egg him on a bit, just to get some jollies at his expense. So, trying to push aside the oddness of the event, he went about shoveling the snow. That was when he heard the voices.

At first he thought it might be the wind. The mausoleum was out in an open field, and sometimes the wind whipped around the building fiercely and made all sorts of odd noises. But after awhile he knew it was not the wind. He heard the whispering voices even when the air was still. They were barely audible, but they were clearly distinct and individual voices. It was as if a large group of people had gathered together in the mausoleum and were having a conversation.

He silently moved around the sidewalk to try and locate the voices. They seemed very close, but at varying distances; it was as if many people were having a whispered conversation from a distance. Then one of the voices seemed to be a little closer, and his heart almost stopped when he realized where they were coming from. The voices were coming from inside the crypts in the mausoleum walls.

The old lady saw no distinct features, but from the silhouette in the sunrise she could tell it was a woman with a lithe figure who was standing erect with her head tilted down to the grave she was standing over.

Frozen in fear, the maintenance man thought he was going insane, so he slowly moved closer to the cold marble slab, layered with ice. The icy slabs concealed the cement crypts that made up the inner and outer walls of the building. As he put his ear to the freezing stone, he heard a distinctive whispering voice say, "Shhh. He hears us!"

In an instant he dropped the shovel and ran to the office building. He never heard the voices again, but perhaps that is because that was the last time he shoveled the snow around the mausoleum in the dark.

However, that was not the last story I heard of caretakers and others seeing shadow people in the early morning twilight on the cemetery grounds.

One morning, I had come in early to get ready for a trip to a neighboring cemetery that needed some help because someone had called in sick. The sun was just about to rise and I was sitting at a desk with the supervisor, drinking coffee and discussing current events when an elderly lady came into the office. She seemed quite distressed. She had barely enough strength to get inside and was hanging onto the front door as if it was a lifeline. She must have been in her early eighties and almost collapsed just as my supervisor caught her and helped her to a seat.

She had been visiting her deceased husband's grave to put flowers on it before she went to an early morning breakfast appointment with some friends. She was sitting on a blanket and arranging the flowers in the vase as the morning sun was just rising. Sitting there and taking in the bright sunrise, she saw a figure move to her right. About forty yards away on the other side of the garden in which her husband was buried, she saw a lady dressed in a long black shawl. The old lady saw no distinct features, but from the silhouette in the sunrise she could tell it was a woman with a lithe figure who was standing erect with her head tilted down to the grave she was standing over.

The old lady wondered who the woman in black was, because she had not seen her before when she had walked back and forth from her car to bring the flowers and water to her husband's graveside. In fact, she was sure at that time that she was alone.

She was considering these things as the sun rose over the treetops to the east and the rays of light began to filter into the garden with intensity. The figure seemed to fade a bit. Then it slowly sunk into the ground. It was as if the earth had sucked up the silhouette of the woman.

We calmed the old lady down and gave her some water. I went out to investigate and found her small blanket at the foot of the grave and the fresh flowers arranged in the vase just as she said. But I saw no other person on the grounds. A few minutes later my supervisor came out with the old lady and we asked her where she saw the figure. I walked out to the opposite side where she gestured, but saw nothing out of the ordinary. So I called to her to have me move where she thought she saw the figure vanish into the ground.

When she had finished directing me, I looked down. I was standing over the grave of a young teenage boy who had shot himself earlier that year with his father's gun. He had been an honor student with a bright future. Then a random school drug search found a few ounces of cocaine in his locker. He was kicked out of school and faced serious charges. Instead of facing a bleak future he chose to take his own life. But the family tragedy did not stop there. Within a few months the father had gunned down the boy's mother and a coworker he suspected of having an affair with her. Then he put a bullet into his own head, just as his son had done just a few months before. The graves were side by side. Father, mother, and son slept together for eternity.

According to the startled old lady, something had visited the son's grave early in the morning light. Was it the mother? A figment of the old lady's imagination? An illusion of the diffused light coming through the pine trees?

Or was it a dark entity that had influenced the family to commit such tragic and needlessly violent acts and still lurks at the gravesite?

I have no idea. All I could do was pray that God would have mercy on their souls and grant them peace.

Even though once in a while I did come in early in the morning to help out, I never came into the graveyard at night. I was a bit afraid of what I might see.

⊷∽∿∾⊷

THEY PROVIDED A HOME FOR DISPOSSESSED SPIRITS

In 1971, Donald Page, who had been a medium since he was fifteen, revealed that he and an eminent canon of the Church of England, Canon John D. Pearce-Higgins, had been running a home for wayward ghosts for nearly three years. Page said that he kept a spare bedroom in his London apartment expressly for the purpose of offering shelter and spiritual comfort to the ghosts that he had dispossessed from their old haunts—where their presence had been decidedly unwelcome by the human occupants.

Medium Page said that he and the Church of England cleric had been a ghost-hunting team for more than fifteen years, and he claimed that they had helped hundreds of ghosts find peace. Canon Pearce-Higgins kept a well-documented account of their work for the Church of England's Fellowship for Psychical Research. The cleric stated that their primary aim was to help both the haunters and the haunted. When the two men weren't helping restless spirits to move along to higher realms, Reverend Pearce-Higgins was minister of London's Southwark Cathedral and Page headed a Spiritualist church, the Fellowship and Brotherhood of Paul.

When they received a request from someone who was experiencing an unpleasant haunting, they carefully investigated the disturbances to determine if they were truly being caused by a troubled ghost. If they found a restless spirit or an evil earthbound entity to be the culprit, Page would go into a trance and permit the spirit to possess him. Then his spirit guides would take over, remove the spirit from him, and escort it to their sanctuary—a small guest room, decorated with psychic artwork. Here the displaced spirit was given an opportunity to adjust to life in a transitional state before it moved on to a higher, more spiritual plane of existence.

The medium emphasized the point that one could not simply remove such spirits from the places they haunt and leave them to flounder helplessly in a spiritual twilight zone. Page said that they permitted the ghosts to stay in the sanctuary until they had regained their spiritual equilibrium and were able to move on to the next plane of existence.

As the Reverend K. F. Lord was photographing the interior of his church, located in Newby, North Yorkshire, United Kingdom, he saw nothing unusual in front of him. When the film was developed, he noticed that a translucent hooded figure seems to be standing next to the altar.

The spiritual ministers kept their troubled ghosts in the sanctuary for as long as it took to assist them in the transitional period. During this time of spiritual therapy, the two men, their assistant, Mrs. Edna Taylor, and Page's spirit guides, were able to show the confused ghosts the way to continue their journey on the other side.

Canon Pearce-Higgins, editor/contributor to *Life, Death, and Psychical Research* (1973), admitted that many people might doubt the efficacy and the validity of their work, but all he would say for certain was that when they went into a house and performed their procedure and the phenomena stopped, they assumed it was because of what they had done.

THE MALEVOLENT SPIRIT THAT INVADED ST. PAUL'S

In 1972, Peter Chapman of the Saratoga Springs *Saratogian* and Marty Hughes of the *Journal-Salem Press*, reported that St. Paul's Episcopal Rectory in Greenwich, New York, had received visitations from at least two ghosts. The central figure in the accounts was Reverend William R. Harris, who gave a detailed account of events in the rectory, including a chilling description of a malevolent entity's attempt to possess him.

Late one night he had awakened with a terrible sensation of pressure at the foot of his bed. The pressure increased, a chill swept over him, and he felt as if he were "literally pinioned by an inexpressibly oppressive weight."

Suddenly, a scant foot away from his face, he saw a shroud of whitish grey. In the portion of the shroud which would normally contain a head, he perceived fierce, burning, laser-like eyes that were filled with hatred. Reverend Harris sensed a tortured, demonic, aggressive, and malevolent spirit; and he realized intuitively the possibility of this being an attempt at demonic possession. As a contemporary man of the cloth, he had previously regarded the notion of possession as a superstitious notion, but now he felt the definite need for counteraction. He thrust his right arm through the ghost and shouted loudly for it to leave in the name of Jesus Christ. And the spirit disappeared.

Reverend Harris described the entity as having a long, sharp, aquiline nose, severe cheekbones, a small thin mouth, and pointed features ending in a pointed chin. He also mentioned wisps of grayish beard that hung on its chin like Spanish moss.

Mrs. Harris reported that something invisible attempted to snatch a tea tray she was carrying into the kitchen one morning in 1968. The Harris daughters, Jan, Julie, and Page, also had encounters with the apparitions. Julie and Page once ran to their mother with the startled report that they had seen something white go down the hall, "like an old man dressed in clothes from Jesus' time." Julie reported seeing the same apparition perched on the bannister in the upper hall. As she watched, it went right through the wall.

Reverend Harris' mother encountered a strange visitor in the rectory when she was staying there in the family's absence. She described it as a figure of a woman dressed in Puritan-type garb that passed from the living room, across the entry hall, and into the studio room. Although Mrs. Harris raced into the studio, there was nobody there.

The carefully documented account of the ghost of St. Paul's Rectory was enhanced even more by an amazing drawing of the phantom done by professional artist, Paul Fung. Fung saw the ghost at close range on July 4, 1972, when he returned to the rectory with the Harris family after a circus at the Washington County Fairgrounds. Fung, who used to draw the "Blondie" comic strip, felt the coldness associated with the ghost and got a good look at it. He even returned for a second look.

THE GHOSTLY MONK OF BASILDON

A number of women who do cleaning at night at a factory near Holy Cross Church in Basildon, England have seen a phantom monk on several occasions. They usually finish work about 4:00 A.M., and it is as they are leaving the factory and walking past the old church that they often see the ghost. They agree that the ghost is definitely that of a monk, and it walks across the church road and disappears among the graves in churchyard.

One woman stated that one time she ran right through the spook on her bicycle when she wasn't able to put on her brakes in time. She said that she didn't feel any impact at all, but she described the air as cold and clammy.

Witnesses all mention that the monk wears a red cowl and has a chalk-white face that is set in a kind of grim mask. Some have described the ghostly monk as transparent. Others say that he appears to be floating and observe that his feet don't seem to be touching the ground at all.

An interesting aside might be interjected at this point concerning reports of ghosts that appear to "float" on air. In one interesting case, it was noted that each time the ghost appeared, it seemed to be walking about six inches off the floor. Investigation revealed that the floor of this particular ground-level room had been lowered six inches after the death of the individual whose image the ghost resembled. The same may hold true for the phantom monk of Basildon. The animated ghost of the monk may be several centuries old, and the streets in front of Holy Cross Church may have settled sufficiently in that time to make the ghost appear to float, as it treads the old ground that is no longer where it was a few centuries back.

THE PLAYFUL SPIRIT IN THE OLD CHURCH

The personal experience of Jason M.

When I was sixteen years old, my stepfather helped out at this church built in the 1800s in Hartford, Connecticut. It was a hot, late summer Saturday. My friends Ryan, Joey, and I came to the church to help my stepfather with some yard work for a few extra bucks. While we were in the janitorial room getting supplies, I told Ryan and Joey that the empty church had lots of open space and we could all run around if we could get away from my stepfather.

About one hour later, somewhere in the front of the church, Joey and my stepfather were raking and bagging some lawn clippings, while Ryan and I were grabbing leaves that had gathered in the lower recesses of the ground-

The "Black Abbot" that is said to haunt the churchyard at Prestbury, near Cheltenham, Gloucestershire, United Kingdom. Photographed in 1990.

floor windows. The heat was intense, and we were soaked with sweat. I had what seemed to be a bright idea: Let's sneak into the nursery daycare to cool off; that part of the building is always cooler in the summer! Every door was locked because the church was closed, so the first time we went in the daycare nursery, we had to ask other people working that day to open the door for us.

On our way out, I placed a twig in the lock to the nursery. When the other workers weren't looking, Ryan and I crept off around the wall leading to the door to the nursery.

From the windows overlooking the front lawn, we could see the members of the congregation working in the sun. We sat in very small chairs laughing and joking about how we got out of the hot labor. Suddenly, from the hallway by the windows we heard what seemed to be a small kid, like our friend Joey, running down the hallway toward us. We thought he saw us disappear and decided to sneak in, too.

We were on the other side of the doorway to the hallway, so he couldn't see us. I thought it would make be really funny if we jumped out at him as he came in. The person running down the hallway sounded like he would be there in a few seconds. On the count of three, we would jump out and say BOO!

When the person got to the very edge of the doorway, we could hear his breath. It sounded just like Joey! So we jumped out to say Boo, and when we did ... no one was there! Suddenly, a quick gust of wind blew by. It must have been the spirit of a child sensing our playful intent and wanting to join in on our fun.

—⬤⬤—

THE MYSTERIOUS FORCE IN ARENSBURG CEMETERY

In the summer of 1844, the Ecclesiastical court, which assembled periodically at Arensburg, on the island of Oesel in the Baltic, was stunned by the complaint they received. A number of people attested that a mysterious force from one of the private chapels in the cemetery was killing their horses.

The first complaint had been registered on June 22, 1844, by a peasant woman, who had driven to the cemetery for one of her regular visits to her mother's grave. Her horse was tethered near the Buxhoewden family chapel. The animal allowed her only a few moments at the graveside before it began to shriek in terror. By the time she reached the animal, it had collapsed in a wild-eyed frenzy and was frothing at the mouth. The woman ran for a veterinarian, who managed to save the horse by bleeding it.

On the following Sunday, several people hitched their horses near the Buxhoewden chapel while they attended services in the church. When they returned to their animals after Mass, they were shocked to find their horses trembling in terror. Some people claimed that they could hear weird rumbles and groans coming from within the Buxhoewden chapel.

On the next Sunday, services were interrupted by the loud stampings and snortings of eleven horses that had been tied near the same chapel. As the owners left the church in alarm, they were startled to find several of the animals struggling on the ground in various stages of nervous collapse. Bleeding was immediately prescribed as treatment, but the veterinarian was too late to save four of the horses. Again, several people insisted that they heard eerie moanings issuing from within the Buxhoewden chapel.

The Consistory chose to ignore the complaints of the people for the time being. Perhaps the horses had eaten some noxious plants. Perhaps there was an outbreak of some new disease. The mysterious death of the horses was obviously a matter for a practitioner of veterinary medicine and could not in any way be considered the business of an ecclesiastical court.

The strange happenings in and around the Buxhoewden chapel became impossible to ignore, however, just a few days after the Consistory had dismissed the complaint. During a funeral service in the chapel, the assembled mourners were horrified to hear terrible groans coming from the vault below. After the service was concluded, some of the stouter hearts went down to the vault to prepare for the interment of the latest coffin. They were quite unprepared for the sight that greeted them when they unlocked the heavy vault door and pushed it open. Nearly all of the coffins in the Buxhoewden vault had been removed from their resting places and had been heaped in a disorderly pile.

It seemed impossible to account for such a disrespectful act. No one had the key to the vault but a representative of the Buxhoewden family—the same man who now stood incredulously surveying the havoc that had been done to his family's final resting place.

A representative of the Buxhoewden family protested to Baron de Guldenstubbe, President of the Consistory, that it seemed apparent to them that some enemy of their family had managed to find a way into the vault in order to commit senseless acts of desecration. The Baron pointed out that it would be impossible to enter the vault without a key, and the representative of the Buxhoewden family who stood before him had the key that opened the door to the vault. The Baron added that there might be more to the matter than met the eye. The Baron convinced two members of the Buxhoewden family to accompany him on an inspection of the vault. All three men gasped in shock when they found the coffins once again strewn about the underground vault.

An official committee of investigation was formed consisting of eight members, including Baron de Guldenstubbe, the bishop of the province, two other members of the Consistory, a physician, the burgomaster, one of the syndics, and a secretary. Their first act was to examine the vault thoroughly. They were hardly surprised when they unlocked the vault to find the coffins again in a state of disarray. The Baron de Guldenstubbe gave the order to open two or three of the coffins to determine whether or not robbery had been sufficient enough motive to tempt some despicable fellow into committing this awful act of desecration. The order was carried out, and all rings, jewelry, and other personal effects buried with the corpses were accounted for. Next the Baron speculated that some practitioners of the dark arts of devil worship might have dug a tunnel into the crypt for the sole purpose of terrorizing the village. Workmen took up a section of the floor, the foundations were tested, and the walls sounded, but no evidence of any tunneling could be discovered.

The committee considered itself baffled for the time being. Perhaps whatever had caused the disturbance had passed over and would simply become a topic for a winter evening's storytelling session around a blazing fireplace. But the Baron insisted upon an official test of the phenomenon.

After the coffins had been replaced, fine wood ashes were scattered over the floor of the vault. The committee then sealed the door with both Consistory and municipal seals and scattered ashes over the stairs leading from the vault to the chapel. Armed guards would maintain a twenty-four-hour-a-day watch for three days and nights to prevent any person from even approaching the crypt. The Baron proclaimed that it was now humanly impossible for anyone to gain entrance into the vault.

At the end of the three-day testing period, the committee returned and ordered the guards to open the vault. The seals remained unbroken until the guards swung the huge door on its hinges. The coating of ashes on the stairs leading down to the vault had betrayed no imprint of either human or animal.

The committee could only utter exclamations of frustration and wonder when their sputtering torches revealed the coffins of the Buxhoewdens in an even worse state than before. This time, many of the coffins had been set on end; and one coffin (that of a suicide) had its lid opened. It was as if the strange force responsible for the disturbances had felt compelled to put on an extra exhibition of its abilities for such an illustrious group of gentlemen as the committee from the Consistory.

The Baron de Guldenstubbe made out an official report, and each of the committee members signed as witnesses. To the committee, the curious occurrences in the Buxhoewden chapel were totally inexplicable.

⊶⊷

HOWLING HORROR OF THE OLD CEMETERY

By Chris Holly

I am going to tell you a story that I have been told is true. Since I did not experience it firsthand I am only able to repeat to you what was told to me.

This event took place in the mid 1960s in a small town along the Long Island coast. This little town is built along the banks of a river. The town looks like many small New England towns you may find along the coast of the eastern seaboard of the United States. Many of the houses and buildings in this little town were built long ago when the area was first established. Some date as far back as the 1600s. It is an old area full of lots of history.

One of the houses found in this town dates back at least to the 1750s. It is an old mansion that stands large and tall a few hundred yards behind a little church that was built in front of it about a hundred years later. Alongside the church there is an old graveyard filled with broken headstones and fallen grave markers. The church, graveyard, and old house have stood together in this old town for as long as anyone can remember.

Everyone who lives in this little town knows the house to be haunted, and supposedly many in town have seen a ghost or two wandering about the grounds of the graveyard.

The little church is still used. In fact it has been the Sunday place of worship for most of the townspeople as far back as anyone can remember. The interior of the church was renovated in the mid-1960s. It was at that time that a new pastor took over the congregation. He was young and was determined to bring the church back to its original strength and beauty. I must admit he did a great job—the church is one of the towns most beautiful buildings. The new pastor also had a lovely little cottage built for himself on the grounds.

The old house behind the church has a reputation going back hundreds of years as being a haunted, dangerous place. Everyone in town knew from the time they were small children to stay far away from that house. No one ever went near it other than the people hired to be the caretakers of the property. The caretakers spent very little time there. They would finish their work quickly and leave the place locked tight and alone as it has been for centuries.

Now and then you would hear a story floating around town that someone in town heard screams or saw strange people looking out of the windows of the old mansion. There were stories that once a very crazy doctor and his witchlike wife lived there. Town legend claims the couple practiced monstrous experiments on both animals and humans, murdering many and burying the dead on the property. Claims of seeing ghostly figures of both people and animals wandering the place have been passed along by the townspeople for as long as any of us can recall.

I never thought much of the old house. I stayed away from it, mainly because it had a dark, bleak appearance that really did not entice you to go near it. An interest in this old mansion and the church nearby came to me by way of my cousin who also lived in town.

My cousin was a few years older than I was. She was in her late teens at the time of the incident. It was in October, about a week before Halloween, that the event happened. My cousin and her boyfriend were driving around town with a few other friends when one of them brought up the old mansion and all the ghostly tales that were told about it. They decided it would be fun to take a closer look at the old house and the graveyard on a little ghost hunt of their own. Being young and foolish it never occurred to them that this may be a very dangerous—even deadly—thing to do without the necessary experience or protection. They soon found out that "fun" was far from what they would encounter on this cool October night.

My cousin, her boyfriend, two other girls, and one other boy were all packed into the Ford Mustang that belonged to my cousin's boyfriend. Slowly and silently they entered the dirt driveway of the old mansion that ran along the side of the old graveyard. They parked the car at the corner of the graveyard, in between the house and the cemetery.

The group got out of the car and made their way into the graveyard first to see if they could find a ghost and have a giggle. The five teens walked along under the moonlight reading the old grave markers while the wind blew the fall leaves about their feet. It was a typical fall night in the northeast and perfect for hunting ghosts.

But as they walked along the rows of old gravestones the five teens began to feel uncomfortable and a bit frightened. The two girls in the group started to hear noises behind the group as they walked along. The one girl insisted she could hear someone or something following them. As they became more and more uncomfortable walking among the dead, they decided it may be more fun to venture on to the mansion to have a look around.

The five teens had no idea what a dangerous decision this would prove to be. They walked toward the old mansion, jumping from behind bushes, pushing and shoving each other, trying to frighten one another. They were giggling and acting as kids their age do.

Only one of the girls noticed something in the window of the second-floor window in the front of the house. She stopped dead in her tracks, hushing the others, and telling them to look at the window. As the five kids stood there watching the dark house, my cousin's boyfriend whispered "Did you all just see that?" He too saw something or someone standing at a window on the second floor. The group stood there, watching.

The other boy with them suddenly yelled out "BOO!" which sent the other four kids jumping clear off the ground. The group laughed and continued walking around to look at the side and the back of the strange old house. As they made their way to the rear of the mansion they noticed a broken-down shed in the back corner of the yard. The group walked toward it to see what the little building was used for. The shed was a smaller version of the large main house. The teens thought it may be a elaborate playhouse and wanted to take a closer look.

The small building was about the size of a old-fashioned double garage, not quite as big as a modern double garage. The little house was exactly like the big one including an open front porch. The teenagers wandered onto the porch and tried to look in the windows. The windows were so dirty and the night was so dark, it was impossible to see inside.

One of them twisted the front doorknob, and to the shock of all, the door flew open as if someone had pulled it from the other side. Uncertain what to do for a minute, the teens stood there looking at each other. Then they decided to just take a peek inside. The five of them walked in to find a large open room with walls that were lined with shelves. In the middle of the room was a large table. The place was filled with cobwebs and dirt. The group walked around looking at the shelves, which were lined with bottles of different sizes.

The teens were silent as they carefully looked around. Finally one of the girls picked up a bottle and held it to the moonlight coming through the dirty window. She yelped in disgust and tossed the bottle back on to the shelf. The bottle had what appeared to be a dead animal floating in it. The teens began to look more carefully at the bottles lining the shelves. To their revulsion every jar had what looked to be some type of fetus or a piece of some kind of living creature. The group was stunned and quickly became frightened.

They decided it was time to leave and quickly ran back out into the yard to make their way back to the car. The five teens were so fearful, they started to run around the front of the old house toward the waiting Mustang.

That's when it happened.

The two girls and the other boy were ahead of my cousin and her boyfriend. They were running as fast as they could toward the car. As the group ran across the yard my cousin slipped on the fallen leaves and fell hard to the ground. Her boyfriend stopped running to help pull her to her feet, but the other teens kept running full speed toward the car.

So my cousin and her boyfriend found themselves alone on the side of the dark old house. My cousin's ankle was badly sprained and she could hardly walk, much less run. Her boyfriend lifted her to her feet and half-carried, half-dragged her along toward the front of the house to make their way to the car. Without warning, without any sense that it was coming, my cousin and her boyfriend were hit by a force that sent them both flying into the air. They landed about ten feet apart on their backs on the dark side yard of the house.

Before either could react to what had just struck them my cousin started to scream and fight with an invisible attacker. Her boyfriend watched in horror as my cousin tried to fight off something that he could not see. He ran to her side as she punched and fought with the air. He could not believe his eyes. He tried to pull her up from the ground. But each time he would reach down to pull her up, he would be shoved back to the ground a few feet away from her. He could see her face was bleeding as she continued to scream and fight.

Her boyfriend made a few more attempts to help her to only be thrown in the air away from her. My cousin's face and arms ere covered with blood. He knew he needed help and started to run and scream for the others to help him. But his friends had already heard the struggle and had started back when they saw my cousin's boyfriend being thrown through the air like a rag doll. Thankfully, one of the girls knew immediately that they needed help and took off at a full run for the pastor's cottage to get help. She made it to the pastor's cottage in seconds, and started pounding on his door, yelling for help and crying at the same time.

The young pastor was home and quickly opened the door, stunned to find a hysterical girl at his door. She told him her friends were being attacked by something invisible at the old mansion and needed help. The young pastor did not blink or think twice. He grabbed three things—a bat, a large wooden cross, and a Bible.

When the girl and the pastor arrived at the old house, the scene before them terrified them. My cousin lay on the ground, covered in blood, still fighting against her attacker. The other three teens were trying to stop the attack, only to be thrown all over the yard.

The pastor began to yell prayers even as he ran toward the group of teens and the evil invisible attacker. He ran to the side of my cousin and placed the cross on her chest. Immediately, it was thrown into the air. The pastor yelled for the others to get it, then he placed it back on her body and held it firmly in place with all his strength. He told the boys to help him, and they all pressed the cross to her body. The pastor started to pray while holding the Bible to his heart. The beating by the invisible thing stopped. The pastor cautiously pulled my cousin to her feet.

For a few seconds it seemed as if it was over. The young pastor instructed the group to run toward the church, while he and my cousin's boyfriend followed, dragging the badly beaten girl. The group had almost made it to the edge of the church yard when they all heard and felt it coming.

Behind them they could feel the ground shake as thunderous pounding footsteps charged from behind. The pastor screamed for the group to continue running toward the church. The corner of the old graveyard that belonged to the little church was only a few yards ahead of them when the pounding stopped. The three teens entered the church-owned land first and kept running toward the church as the young pastor had commanded.

The pastor, my cousin, and her boyfriend were right behind them. As they arrived at the church property they no longer felt their attacker behind them. But then they heard it. From the yard of the old house came a howl of rage so horrifying all five teens broke into tears.

The group made it to the church. The pastor brought all five teens inside the little church and prayed over them before doing anything else. He then took them into his little cottage where he called the police. My cousin was taken by ambulance to the local hospital where she was treated for her cuts and bruises and released.

The police wrote this incident up as teenagers assaulting each other. The hospital listed it as my cousin being in a fist fight. The young pastor was ridiculed for playing along with the teens, who had obviously let their fantasies run wild during their trek to the haunted house.

The pastor, my cousin, her boyfriend, and the other three teens all tell a different story. They talk about the night they came face to face with evil, fought it, and won.

I believe my cousin, of course. I know her to be a logical, well-balanced adult who has lived a good, productive life. I will tell you she stayed in contact with that pastor her entire life.

Shortly after this incident, the haunted house was fenced off at the pastor's insistence. The old house was finally demolished about twenty years ago, but up until that time it continued to be known as the haunted house behind the church.

Who knows what evil lurks in dark places? My cousin will tell you only that she knows it does exist.

THE HAUNTED GRAVE DIGGER

The personal experience of Ronnie

I own an excavation company. I build rural water and sewer systems and handle other jobs. One of the things that comes along from time to time is digging graves. I live in a small farming, and ranching town that also has an oil field and I know just about everybody in the surrounding area.

The wife of a lifelong friend passed away and the family asked me to dig the grave. I told them I would be honored to do so. Now, keep in mind her husband had passed away about four and a half years prior, so my helper and I dug the grave for the recently deceased woman alongside her husband's.

Now, like I said, these people were lifelong friends of mine. When we were just about finished—all that was left was to get the measurements right and finish off the bottom of the grave—I stood up and looked down from the

This photograph was taken at Bachelor's Grove Cemetery in Chicago. There was no one seated on the bench when this photograph was taken.

back of my backhoe while my helper was bent over measuring the dimensions of the grave.

As I looked up I saw the deceased woman's husband standing there along with a man he worked with, a person I knew to be dead as well. Frank and his friend Mick were standing there with their hands crossed in front of them, looking up at me with smiles on their faces and nodding their heads in approval.

I looked back down into the open grave and when I looked back up, they were gone.

But the kicker of all this was the way Frank was dressed. He was wearing a blue-and-white bib overall. Mick was wearing the work clothes that he wore each day, right down to the shiny belt buckle he loved so much. I have asked a few people around here if Frank ever wore bibs in his younger years. But none of them could remember. Most of these people were in their eighties when I asked them and, in fact, many of them have passed on in the four years since. So I never did learn the reason Frank was dressed that way.

And, needless to say, I didn't do any more digging that day.

In 1946 or 1947 Mrs. Andrews of Queensland, Australia, took a photograph of her daughter Joyce's grave. Joyce had died at the age of 17 in 1945. When developed, the photo of Joyce's grave revealed the appearance of a small child. Mrs. Andrews was sure that there was no child present at the graveyard when she took the picture; she was also sure that the child in the photo was not her daughter. Researcher Tony Healy visited the graveyard in 1995 and found two graves of young infant girls near Joyce's grave.

THE WARRIOR WANTED HIS HEAD REJOINED TO HIS BODY

In 1964, two young archeologists were assigned by a museum in New Mexico to undertake what had been planned as a very ordinary examination of one of the countless early Pueblo villages dotting the flatlands of the state. No extraordinary finds were expected, but the diggings at the site were overdue. And the work was a good summer opportunity for the two young people to work side by side with the Navajo diggers hired to aid in the project.

Work was proceeding as anticipated when a Navajo workman doing rough excavation on a refuse pit at the edge of the village hurriedly approached the team leaders with news of a curious discovery. While digging, he had uncovered a piece of bone among the rubble deposited there nearly a thousand years ago by the inhabitants of the ancient village. Unwilling to touch the bone for fear that it might be human and bear a curse, the digger alerted the archeologists to the find and stood back at a respectful distance as they took up the digging.

What emerged, to the archeologists' surprise, was the skull of a Native American man whose body had apparently been thrown without ceremony into the garbage pits. It was a strange find, considering the reverence with which the New Mexican tribes were known to bury their dead.

After the two archaeologists had searched for hours without finding the rest of the skeletal remains, they returned their attention to the skull and came up with a gruesome explanation. The man had probably died from a blow to the back of the skull. The shape of the head suggested that it was not a Pueblo tribesman, but probably the skull of one of many Apache invaders who had filtered into the area during a wave of migration in about 900 C.E. And there were marks on a piece of cervical vertebra still clinging to the skull that indicated that someone had hacked through it, using some early weapon similar to an ax.

The aged bones that lay in the refuse heap had belonged to a captive Apache who had been killed and beheaded by the Pueblo, then consigned to the garbage as a further degradation. No more attempts were made to unearth any remaining skeletal bones after the first search of the nearby area had proved fruitless. The bones were of no great archeological importance, and more urgent work in the heart of the old village required all of the hours that they were permitted to spend on the summer dig.

But then strange events began occurring at the old Pueblo ruin. What appeared to be the work of vandals suddenly began causing havoc at the dig site. When the archaeologists and Navajo workmen slept, someone entered the village and smashed unearthed pottery and kicked in carefully excavated trenches. Events took on an even more macabre turn in the week that followed. Frightened workers swore that they saw the glowing head of a man appearing before them in their bunkhouse at night. Utter nonsense, the archeologists laughed, until they slept with the workmen one night and saw the faintly phosphorescent glow of what might have been the head of a man. There was no rational explanation for the sight.

Panic at the diggings reached its peak when the workers became certain they were hearing words carried on the winds of the inky desert nights, in a tribal dialect that they did not understand.

The young archeologists turned to an aged shaman at a nearby Navajo reservation as a last resort to explain what was taking place at the dig and in an effort to restore calm, so the work at the village could progress. The shaman said that the head of the long-dead Apache was seeking his body because he could not enter the spirit world without it. The ghost would haunt the excavation until head and body were joined together in burial. Native superstition, the archaeologists believed, but in order to calm the nerves of the jittery workmen, they decided they would see what could be done about finding the rest of the restless Apache's bones. The search for the missing remains centered on the area of the village where the vandalism had occurred. That, reasoned the Navajo workers, was a sign being given to help guide the diggers.

As digging proceeded in the area over several days, the team could not help observing that the vandalism had stopped. Was it a sign the ghost was pleased?

Then, as workmen softly prodded the earth around an old ceremonial circle in the village, a wall of dirt fell away to reveal bones protruding from the soil. When the bones were laid out, they formed the skeleton of a young male—a headless young male. When the skull that had been discovered earlier was brought out for comparison, the severed vertebrae matched with those of the skeleton. The bones of the doomed Apache brave were finally brought together.

With the aid of the shaman, the young archaeologists gave a reverential burial to the yellowed skeletal remains, and the troubles that had plagued the summer expedition ended at once.

Because they were scientists, when the young archeologists made their final report to the museum about the diggings at the site, they did not include a record of the strange events that had taken place there. But they were willing to share the tale of those experiences with their friends, who puzzled as earnestly as they did over the curious happenings that led them to help a long-dead Apache find peace in the next world. Not a scientific achievement, to be sure. But a very human one—and one of which they were proud.

18
HAUNTED MANSIONS AND PLANTATIONS

Dr. Augustus Jessopp was in high spirits on that chilly autumn night in 1879. Lord Orford had invited him to spend the night at Mannington Hall and had given him permission to examine some very old books in his extensive library. Although Dr. Jessopp enjoyed the animated conversation with the other guests, he could hardly wait until the others went to bed so that he could begin taking notes from the old books in the library. A dentist by profession, Dr. Jessopp was an antiquarian by hobby.

At last, around eleven o'clock, Lord Orford and his other guests had retired for the evening, and Dr. Jessopp was alone in the library with all the treasured volumes. He set to work immediately, taking notes from six small books. He had four large candles on his desk and a crackling fire in the fireplace. The light was excellent. Exhilarated from an evening of stimulating and delightful companionship, he felt as though he could work through the night.

At 1:30 A.M., Dr. Jessopp glimpsed something white about a foot from his left elbow. Upon closer examination, the object proved to be a large, extremely pale hand with dark blue veins across its back. Putting his pen aside, Dr. Jessopp turned and saw that he shared the desk with a tall, solidly built man, who seemed to be intent upon examining both the dentist and the books he had been studying. The strange visitor had a lean, rugged profile and reddish-brown hair, which had been closely cut. He was dressed in a black habit of the type worn by clergymen in the early 1800s, and he sat in a posture of complete relaxation with hands clasped lightly together. After a few moments, Dr. Jessop realized that the man was not staring at him at all; rather, the stranger seemed completely unaware of his presence.

Dr. Jessopp had not for one moment considered his late evening visitor to be anything other than a living person, but he did think it most peculiar that he had not met the clergyman earlier in the evening and a bit strange that the man would enter the room and seat himself so silently at the same desk. It was not until the man vanished before his eyes that Dr. Jessopp realized he had been visited by a ghost.

Dr. Jessopp was a very stolid sort of individual, not easily frightened or easily impressed by anything out of the ordinary. His most pronounced reaction was one of disappointment, because he had not had time to make a sketch of the ghostly clergyman.

He returned to his note taking and was perhaps wondering how he could sensibly relate the story of his spectral visitor to Lord Orford when he once again saw the white hands appear next to his own. The figure sat in precisely the same position as before and the expression on his face had not changed in the slightest. The ghostly clergyman still seemed to sit, hands folded, in an attitude of contemplation or complete relaxation.

Dr. Jessopp turned to give the ghost his full attention. It had occurred to him that he might speak to the specter, and he began to form a sentence in his mind. He wanted it to be just the kind of provocative statement that would prompt a ghost to utter a response. Then, before his lips could form the sentence and give it utterance, he suddenly realized the eeriness of the whole situation. He was filled with a sense of deep dread and fear. In a movement brought on by an unconscious reflex, Dr. Jessopp knocked a book onto the desk, and the ghost vanished instantly at the harsh sound.

The tale of Dr. Jessopp's encounter with a ghost became so exaggerated when others told and retold the story, that the dentist allowed the London Athenaeum to print an authorized account of the incident about two months after the uncanny experience.

Dr. Jessopp emphasized in the article that he was not in the habit of engaging in flights of fancy and did not wish to be regarded as having mediumistic powers, did not regularly receive supernatural visitations, and was not suffering from any problems of the nervous system that would make him susceptible to delusions. The dentist stressed the point that he had been in perfect health on the night of the materialization and had been in no way approaching weariness or fatigue. He also stated that the talk at Mannington Hall that evening had concerned itself with travel and art and had in no way touched upon the supernatural. The ghost, he added, did not appear wispy or cloaked in a traditional sheet. The figure appeared lifelike, natural, and so solid that it had blocked the light from the fireplace. After the aforementioned experience, there was no question in Dr. Jessopp's mind that ghosts do exist.

And where is there a more likely place for ghosts to manifest than at an old mansion like Mannington Hall in England? Or Washington, D.C. for that matter.

THE OCTAGON: THE CAPITAL CITY'S FAVORITE HAUNTED HOUSE

There is a brick mansion on the corner of New York Avenue and 18th Street, Washington, D.C., that harbors a ghost and a legend to go with it. Built in 1800 by Colonel John Taylor, the stately mansion, known as the Octagon, was used temporarily as an executive residence by President James Madison when the British burned the White House during the War of 1812. Today the mansion is the national headquarters of the American Institute of Architects and a historic shrine.

But caretakers and maintenance men have long told eerie tales of moans, groans, and shifting furniture. A gardener told a journalist that he had heard "groans of distress" follow him up the stairs. A former caretaker spoke of the sounds of invisible feet, which he had often heard walking up the stairs.

The "eye" of the haunting seems to be the stairwell. According to legend, one of the young women of the Taylor family either fell or leaped to her death down the elegant stairwell. A maintenance man described how each morning upon opening the mansion, he would find the rug turned back at the foot of the stairway. According to tradition, this was the spot where the young woman had died over 190 years ago.

A hostess at the Octagon has said that, while she has seen no ghosts, she has watched the chandelier in the stairwell sway as if a hand moved it. And she admits that she is at a loss for a rational explanation to explain the swinging chandelier. There is no draft in the house, or any kind of vibration that could set the ornate fixture swaying.

Another maintenance man recalled that, a few years ago, every bell in the mansion would begin to ring at a certain hour every night. That particular disturbance has ceased, but according to some observers, there remains enough activity in the Octagon to qualify the mansion for the title of "the capital's favorite haunted house."

THE HALLOWEEN SURPRISE AT THE ANCHORAGE MANSION IN MARIETTA, OHIO

By Bret and Gina Oldham

Sitting high on a hill on the banks of the Muskingum river is an imposing sandstone Italian villa now known as "The Anchorage." This twenty-two-room Mediterranean-style mansion overlooks the charming town of Marietta, Ohio. The Anchorage was built in 1859 by Douglas Putnam for his wife, Eliza.

Over 200 years old, the Octagon is home to many ghosts.

She had visited friends in New Jersey and was so impressed by their home that she asked her husband, Douglas, to build an exact replica for her in Marietta. The home was completed in 1859, but sadly, Eliza didn't get to enjoy the lovely home she cherished for long. She died of heart disease in 1862 after having lived in her dream house for only three years. It is believed that because Eliza so loved the house, she refused to leave after her death and her ghost still haunts the mansion to this day.

The house has changed hands several times over the years. A number of prominent Marietta citizens have owned the mansion. In 1896 it was bought by the Knoxes, who owned a boat-making business. It was, in fact, the Knox family who gave the mansion the name "The Anchorage." It was last used as a nursing home from 1960 until 1986. The Anchorage is currently being used by the Washington County Historical Society and is in the process of renovation.

On October 30, 2009, we drove up to Akron, Ohio to attend a paranormal conference where a couple of friends of ours were speaking. We had stopped to visit relatives in Ohio on the way home and heard about a Halloween night ghost hunt at The Anchorage. We called and made reservations to attend since it was only about a forty-five-minute drive from where we were.

We are serious paranormal investigators, but we had decided to go on this "ghost hunt" just for fun and to learn about the history of the location. We've been on many ghost investigations and have visited numerous haunted locations with high paranormal activity, but we always go alone or with small groups of other investigators so we weren't taking this one too seriously. One of Bret's relatives had asked us to bring our investigation equipment with us on our trip to Ohio because they had been having some strange things happening in their house which they could not explain and had begun to suspect paranormal activity. As we left for the Halloween event at The Anchorage, we decided to go ahead and bring a digital camera, a digital recorder, a K2 meter and a flashlight with us just in case the opportunity to use them did present itself.

As we pulled into the parking lot down the hill from the house we gazed up at the large, ominous-looking old mansion. Both of us felt a hint of excitement, soon followed by the sobering realization that this wasn't going to be an actual investigation. We savored the thought of doing a full-fledged investigation in this once-majestic old structure. After years of doing ghost investigations, your senses to the energies that are in a location become sharpened, and we both could feel the "vibe" of The Anchorage right away.

We couldn't wait to get inside, but wait we would. As we made our way up the hill to the front entrance we could see a line forming outside the door. At this point, we even discussed turning around and leaving because it looked like quite a little crowd had gathered for the event, perhaps hoping to get a glimpse of a ghost on this chilly Halloween night. Thankfully, we decided to

The Anchorage.

stay and take the tour as it was. By the time they opened the doors, there were about twenty-five or thirty people in attendance.

We stepped inside and marveled at the intricate woodwork, the beautiful designs of the fireplaces, and the many features that reminded us just how awe-inspiring this house had once been. It was comforting to know that renovations were being done even though the mansion was still in quite a state of disrepair.

The guide began the tour and filled us in on the history of the house and told us some of the legends and lore that had been passed down for generations about the place. Of course, these consisted of several ghost stories.

We entered a large second-story bedroom where the tour guide told us of the story of Eliza Putnam. What is believed to be her ghost has been seen by many people over the years. A ghostly figure of a beautiful young woman has been seen on several occasions standing in the bell tower of the house, staring out over the city. Others have reported seeing her ghost in the master bedroom. While the guide was telling the story of Eliza as we were all gathered in her bedroom, Bret noticed a white misty form several feet above the tour guide's head. It was there for a few seconds and then dissipated.

We lagged behind as the group left the room, but didn't see anything else. By this time in the tour both of us felt that there was definite ghost activity in the house.

We continued on with the tour which eventually led to a third- story attic. We entered a very narrow staircase that led up to the attic and entered the almost completely dark attic. We both laughed and figured that at any moment some Halloween actor would jump out of the blackness and scare everyone. We were happy to find out that that kind of silliness wasn't a part of this event.

We listened intently as the tour guide told us of stories over the years about people who had heard the sounds of children playing in the attic. Footsteps, running and jumping, the sounds of the old game of Jacks being played, and sometimes the sounds of children laughing and giggling had all been reported. We figured a lot of that kind of activity was probably residual.

The tour guide then told us the story of a little girl who had been seen in the attic and sometimes in other areas of the house. She appeared to be around the size of a ten- to twelve-year-old child and was always seen wearing a white dress or nightgown. At this point the tour ended and we were told we could explore the house on our own. Quite a few people left right away.

We decided to return back to the bedroom where Bret had seen the misty form. After all, it was Eliza's former bedroom, and there had been several reports of her ghost being seen there. We made our way down the dark narrow staircase from the attic to the second floor. As we entered the large master bedroom, we saw two other ladies sitting on the floor and a third lady standing, who seemed very excited about some video footage she had just captured in the bedroom. "I caught a ghost moving the closet door!" she exclaimed. "Do you want to see it?" she asked. "Sure, let's see what you've got there," we replied.

We took a look at her brief video footage and saw the closet door open a few inches just as she had described. Bret then walked over to the door of the closet and shut it. As he did he noticed that the door was not shutting properly. Right about that time someone else entered the bedroom. When they opened the door to the bedroom, the closet door opened a few inches just as it had done in the woman's video. "We're sorry, but it looks like the closet door is broken. I don't think you captured anything paranormal on your camera," Gina explained to the now somber lady. "Well I still think it's a ghost!" she replied as she scurried out of the room.

Within a few minutes, everyone had left the bedroom except us and the two women who were sitting on the floor. We asked the women if they would mind if we did an EVP (electronic voice phenomenon) session, and they said they wouldn't mind at all. We turned on our digital recorder and began to ask questions. We both felt strongly that the ghost of Eliza was indeed still in the house and quite possibly with us in her former bedroom, so we directed the questions specifically to her.

Our intuition was correct. Within minutes of beginning our EVP session, Gina felt the left side of her open jacket being pulled out eight to ten

It is believed that because Eliza so loved the house, she refused to leave after her death and her ghost still haunts the mansion to this day.

inches from her body and then quickly released. Just to be certain, Gina asked if any of us had pulled on her jacket. No one had; there wasn't anyone within six feet of Gina. We knew then that we weren't alone.

Still believing that we were experiencing contact from the ghost of Eliza, we thanked her for touching Gina and told her that we knew she was here. We then caught an EVP of a woman responding to our statement. "I'm here," the ghostly voice replies.

During the tour, the guide had mentioned that Eliza had always wanted to cut her long hair, but in her day that was considered a very taboo thing to do so she was never able to have short hair. At that time Gina had short hair so Bret, still feeling that it was Eliza in the room, asked, "Did you touch Gina because she has short hair?" Later, when we reviewed the audio, we caught a very clear EVP from a woman who replied to us with a "Yes, it's so fun!"

We continued on with our conversation with the ghost of Eliza. "We'd like to communicate with you Eliza," Bret told her. "Yes," the female voice spoke back, as we heard on the EVP on our recorder.

Everyone in the room then asked Eliza if she would touch one of us again. Bret held out his arm and raised it up about chest high as he was asking for Eliza to touch him. Within a few seconds he felt the soft tingly feeling of someone stroking the back of his hand and up his wrist and arm. He knew it was Eliza and he thanked her for her efforts to communicate.

Soon after getting touched by this friendly ethereal being, Bret once again saw a white misty form up toward the ceiling. He asked Gina to take some pictures in the area where he had seen it. At that moment, we captured on our digital recorder another EVP from the same woman who also replied, "OK. I'll try harder." The ghost knew that Bret had seen her and also seemed to know that we were trying to get her picture. She was letting us know that she was trying to manifest into a full-body apparition so that we could take her picture. Gina took several photos in the bedroom but unfortunately caught nothing paranormal.

As the paranormal activity began to subside in the master bedroom, we decided to leave and explore some other areas of the mansion. Bret suggested that we go down to the first-floor kitchen area. As soon as he said that we caught another EVP. This time it was a male ghost speaking and his message was more ominous. "I got you now!" the eerie voice threatened.

We have been threatened countless times by angry spirits. It comes with this type of work. We don't scare easily and proceeded down the stairs to the first floor. After exploring the rooms of the first floor of The Anchorage and not experiencing any further activity, we decided to head all the way up to the attic once again. If nothing else, we wanted to climb the rickety old stairs up into the bell tower and enjoy the spectacular view of Marietta it offered.

As we made our way back up to the third floor, we noticed that almost all of the people from the tour had left. We entered the dark, dank attic and slowly walked into the room. It was very quiet there now. We then picked up another EVP. "Get closer," the male voice demanded. We could feel the energy change as we walked into the attic area. We spotted three young men sitting in the middle of the attic floor and another lady sitting by herself near them. They all seemed to be simply observing while they waited for something paranormal to happen.

It wasn't long before they got their wish. We had sat down close the group. Like them, we sat quietly and observed our surroundings. After only a few minutes we heard movement in an adjoining room. "Did you hear that?" one of the young men asked the others. You could hear the nervousness in his voice. "What was that?" one of the other young men then asked his friends. Thankfully, everyone got quiet again as we intently listened for what may come next.

We stood up and took a couple of steps toward the direction of the sounds. We were standing there looking into a pitch black room when we clearly heard footsteps walking across that room. We weren't the only ones who heard them. Everyone did.

By this time everyone was standing up, but remaining several feet behind us. Bret then slowly approached the room and began talking to the ghost. The footsteps were light and soft. The rhythm of the steps made us think that they were the ghostly footsteps of a child.

When Bret got into the middle of the room, he knelt down and began to speak softly to the unseen presence. "Hi, my name is Bret," he said as he introduced himself to the ghost. "Can you tell me your name?" We picked up an answer on our digital recorder, but, alas, it was too faint to make out anything definite.

Gina was taking pictures as Bret was attempting to communicate. By this time the other four people had gotten their nerve up enough to approach closer, but still would not go into the room with Bret.

Bret explained to the ghost that we were only there visiting and meant it no harm. He told it that there was no need to be afraid and that it was welcome to come out into the other room with us. After a few minutes he felt it had moved, and he left the room. Everyone else was talking among themselves, excited about the events that had just transpired. Soon after their excitement died down, they left.

We made our way over to the bell tower. We climbed the creepy old staircase into the top of the bell tower. The view was magnificent! We were starting to understand why Eliza had decided to stay here after her untimely death. Wondering if she might still be in our presence, Bret then asked her, "How do you feel when you stand here and look out?" We were amazed when we heard back an EVP reply from a female voice who simply stated, "Happy." Gina then asked how many spirits were in her house, to which she replied, "seven."

It was getting late, and we knew the tour guide probably wanted to lock up the place, so we headed back downstairs. On our way out, we found a staircase that we previously hadn't seen so we took it down. It led us to some rooms we hadn't noticed earlier. So, before we left for good, we thought we'd take a quick look around the remaining rooms. We tried to hurry, but as we entered the last room we thought we would take a few minutes and do another EVP session and snap a few more pictures. We spent a few minutes conducting another EVP session and took one last series of photos. We thanked the tour guide for a wonderful evening and walked off into the chill of the night.

We had gone to The Anchorage for fun, never expecting to experience the phenomena that we did that Halloween night. We left there quite surprised at the events that had taken place.

Upon our return to our home in Tennessee we uploaded the pictures we had taken that night at The Anchorage. One after another, the pictures revealed nothing until we got to the very last photo that we had taken. Our camera was set in burst mode, which is something we often do on investigations to better our chances of catching an apparition. We were certainly glad that we had used the burst setting again that night. Had we only taken a single shot we would have missed her appearance, for there in the final picture we shot was the image of a little girl in a white dress—just as she had been described by others who had witnessed her ghost. Perhaps it was her footsteps we had heard in the attic. Perhaps she had accepted Bret's offer to come out and be with us. Had she followed us around the rest of the night? There is no way to know. However, there is one thing we do now know. The Anchorage is one very haunted old mansion. It left two experienced paranormal investigators with a Halloween surprise we won't soon forget.

Bret and Gina Oldham are paranormal researchers and founders of Halo Paranormal based in Nashville, Tennessee. Their research encompasses a wide range of subjects including UFOs, ghost hunting, and cryptozoology with special emphasis on alien abductions, and EVP and ITC communication. They have been interviewed numerous times in magazine and newspaper articles and have been featured guests on radio and TV shows in the USA and Europe. Bret is also a writer and author of the audiobook *Ghost Stories of Las Vegas*.

Bret and Gina can be reached at haloparanormal1@hotmail.com. Their website is: www.haloparanormal.com.

GHOSTLY SOUTHERN BELLES AT ROCKY HILL CASTLE

Rocky Hill Castle, an old Southern mansion, was built by Reverend Thomas Saunders near Courtland, Alabama, in 1828. Until sometime in the 1950s, the castle still sheltered Reverend Saunders' descendants—and the family ghost.

Once, when he was queried by reporters as to the reason why the Saunders family remained on the old estate for so long, Saunders replied simply that they just happened to love the place. During the interview, Saunders said that the family had, on certain occasions, heard the clanking of chains coming from the basement. Upon investigation, Saunders said, nothing was seen that could have produced the mysterious noises. On other occasions, they had heard a persistent tapping coming from the basement. It had long been a legend in the Saunders family that the sounds were the knocking of the two dead brothers who built the castle.

Mrs. Saunders recalled the time that she had seemed to sense the presence of someone in the room with her. Whenever she turned to look over her shoulder, she would see no one, but the strong feeling that someone was still with her remained, until, finally she dared the thing to speak, or go away and leave her alone. Whereupon, according to Mrs. Saunders, a voice whispered: "Sister, do not be doubting, for I am truly here."

Later that same day, Mrs. Saunders was descending the staircase when she was startled to see a woman attired in the swirling petticoats of the antebellum South standing at the foot of the stairs. A number of nearby towns were celebrating centennial observances at the time, and Mrs. Saunders assumed that someone soliciting funds for some historical project had slipped into the castle. Mrs. Saunders recalls that she did not for one moment suppose that the smiling lady at the bottom of the staircase was anything other than a living person. But when Mrs. Saunders reached out her hand to welcome her unannounced visitor, the costumed lady vanished. It was as if the voice had materialized a body to demonstrate to Mrs. Saunders that it had been "truly there."

Mr. Saunders had suffered patiently through all the weird noises in his old family mansion, but he was skeptical about his wife's account of the disappearing lady in swirling petticoats. He had never seen the family ghost, and although he was forced to accept the unaccountable noises in the basement, he did not believe in materializing and dematerializing spooks. A few days later, when Saunders was in the basement on an errand, he witnessed dramatic

Haunted mansions have become the classic domain of ghosts in literature and oral tradition.

evidence of the reality of ghosts. There, sitting on a trunk, was a Southern belle from the Alabama of long ago.

A family ghost, built up through generations of psychic reconstruction, can almost become an independent mental mechanism. Whether or not the ghost actually whispered to Mrs. Saunders or whether, because of a heightened psychic sensitivity, she was able to feel the presence of the ghost prior to its actual materialization, makes for interesting speculation.

⊸▥ʃ▥⊷

SANDRINGHAM'S CHRISTMAS GHOSTS

Servants at Sandringham, the country house of England's royal family, have been finding it difficult to sleep for many generations. According to those who have inhabited the servants' quarters, the rooms are haunted.

One maid who had spent several years in service of the royal family, said that the disturbances always begin on Christmas Eve. Once the ghost has dumped the Christmas cards on the floor and mussed up the beds, the servants can look forward to enduring the ghost's pranks for six to eight weeks.

The housemaids have known for generations that the most haunted spot is that of the sergeant footman's corridor on the second floor. Maids refuse to go there alone, and they clean and dust that corridor in small groups. The ancestral ghost is noted for reproducing the thudding of footsteps in the corridor, opening doors when no one is near them, and clicking light switches on and off. Its most grisly accomplishment, according to one sergeant footman whose lot it was to occupy a room with it, is to sound like a huge, grotesque lung breathing in and out.

Most of England's ancestral ghosts have marvelous old legends of unrequited love or grim murder to account for their presence, but researchers have been unable to determine any particular incident which could have put Sandringham's ghost in motion.

SCANDALS AND MURDER SATURATE LONGLEAT MANSION

Longleat, one of England's largest and most elegant Elizabethan mansions, has been virtually saturated with history, legend, and tragedy since its completion in 1580. Of special ghostly prominence is the haunted corridor where, in the 1730s, the Viscount Weymouth was said to have strangled his wife's lover.

There was an NBC television special on January 25, 1965, entitled *The Stately Ghosts of England*, which explored the eerie corners and shadows of Longleat. In the haunted corridor where Weymouth may have strangled the paramour, the cameras managed to capture a weirdly glowing light that came out of one door, bobbed about, moved about ten yards down the corridor, then disappeared into another door on the same side of the corridor. This light from no known source appeared on the film for nearly half an hour. Mysteriously, the usable footage had dwindled to eleven minutes by the time technicians began to edit the film for television.

In an article for the June 1966 issue of *Fate*, well-known British psychic-sensitive Tom Corbett provided readers with an account of some behind-the-scenes activity of an eerie nature which took place during the filming of the NBC special. According to Corbett, microphones went dead suddenly and inexplicably, film taken in the mansion "turned out muddy" in spite of the fact that two sets of recently inspected cameras had been used, light cords were unplugged at crucial moments, and a series of annoying minor accidents plagued the crew.

The chief cameraman, who had entered the nursery on the third floor in search of a prop, felt something oppressive and cloying envelop him. He left the nursery in extreme shock and later said that he thought he would have suffocated if he had not been able to wrench himself away. Decorated twice for

Built in 1884 and continuously rebuilt and remodeled until 1922, when its owner died, Winchester House in San Jose, California, was designed by the wealthy Mrs. Sarah Winchester. A widow who lost her husband and only child, Mrs. Winchester supposedly built the home with the purpose of welcoming spirits. Her own spirit is said to wander the home's quirky layout to this day, and tours of the mansion remain popular.

valorous service during World War II, the chief cameraman was not the sort to be easily disturbed by mysterious noises and weird shadows.

On another occasion, two young journalists had come upon the scene to have a bit of sport with the "cranks" who were making a film about ghosts. To get them out of the way, Corbett suggested that they go up to the Bishop Ken library. There, Corbett told them, they could see two pictures painted by Adolph Hitler and one by Winston Churchill. The Marchioness of Bath gave them her permission and the key, and the journalists went up to the third floor.

Corbett writes that when the young men returned, their cocky attitude was gone. After they had seen the beautiful collection of books in the library, they had locked the door and started down the haunted corridor. They had gone only about twenty feet when they both heard a key turn in the door. Startled, one of the young men shouted that he had the key. Nevertheless, they hurriedly retraced their steps and saw, to their amazement, that the handle was being turned. They fled, frightened by the realization that something was twisting the doorknob in the empty room they had just locked up.

⊲⊲⊲∭∿∭⊳⊳⊳

GHOSTS OCCUPY THE HOME OF WILLIAM LYON MACKENZIE

When people enter the front door of 82 Bond Street in Toronto, they step into a physically restored scene of the past. Mannequins in period dress stand about, and in the parlor a nineteenth-century housewife in a red shawl stands delicately poised with a red paper flower in her hand.

Oil portraits stare down at the visitor with eyes from another time and a family album resting on a tasseled velvet tablecloth offers stiff faces looking up from lozenge-shaped depressions in heavy pages.

This was the home of William Lyon Mackenzie, first mayor of Toronto, grandfather of William Lyon Mackenzie King, prime minister of Canada from 1921 to 1930, and then again from 1935 to 1948. Mackenzie emigrated to Canada in the early nineteenth century and first became a shopkeeper in York (Toronto). Possessed of a rebellious and stubborn mind, he founded the newspaper *Colonial Advocate* to provide a means of directing scathing attacks on the government. His fiery campaign made him a political hero. Mackenzie was elected to the Legislative Assembly of Upper Canada in 1828 and won reelection five times. He became Toronto's first mayor in 1834.

William Lyon Mackenzie died in 1861, but a over century later, caretakers of the historic shrine claim that the ghosts of Mackenzie and a lady—either the shade of Mackenzie's wife or daughter, Isabel—are still walking the halls of the memory-charged mansion. Some witnesses have said that they have seen a third ghost, that of a small bald man in a frock coat.

Mr. and Mrs. Alex Dobban, who assumed the position of caretakers in April of 1960, resigned after little more than a month because of the effect the place was having on Mrs. Dobban's nerves. They hadn't lived in the mansion long before they heard the footsteps of invisible feet going up and down the stairs. On another night, they were awakened to hear a rumbling noise in the basement. At first they took it to be the oil burner, but Mr. Dobban checked and found that the furnace was not on. They concluded that the noise was the old printing press that occupied one of the locked rooms in the basement. On some nights, they also heard the piano in the front room downstairs playing after they were in bed.

Caretakers Mr. and Mrs. Charles Edmunds were able to withstand the ghostly manifestations for nearly four years before they were forced to leave by the constant, oppressive presence of something. Mrs. Edmunds lost forty pounds due to the stress of knowing there was some unseen entity always watching them from behind.

On the very day the Edmundses moved into the Mackenzie Homestead, they heard footsteps on the stairs when there was no one else in the house.

One midnight, Mrs. Edmunds was awakened by something touching her on the shoulder. She opened her eyes to see a ghostly lady standing over her bed, leaning down, "like a shadow." Mrs. Edmunds said that she could see the ghost clearly. The phantom had long dark brown hair hanging down in front of her shoulders, framing a long, narrow face. She vanished after a few moments.

Nearly two years passed before Mrs. Edmunds was awakened by the lady again. This time, the ghost left Mrs. Edmunds with a physical memento of their meeting. According to the Edmundses, the lady reached out and slapped Mrs. Edmunds, leaving three red welts on her cheek and her left eye purple and bloodshot.

Mrs. Edmunds reported that she had also seen the ghost of a little bald man in a frock coat. She would see him for just a few seconds, and then he would vanish. She stated that she saw the bald man or the ghostly lady standing in the third-floor bedroom at least eight or nine times.

Charles Edmunds recalled a time shortly after they had moved into the mansion when their grandchildren, Susan, age four, and Ronnie, age three, were visiting them. To get ready for bed, the children went from the upstairs bedroom down to the second-floor bathroom. A few minutes later he and his wife heard the children screaming. Edmunds ran down to the bathroom and found both children huddled in a corner. They said a lady came into the bathroom, then just disappeared.

Although Edmunds never saw a materialization of either of the two ghosts that seemed to haunt the mansion, he often heard footsteps on the stairs—heavy, thumping sounds as if made by heavy boots.

On July 1, 1960, Archdeacon John Frank performed the rites of exorcism in the house at 82 Bond Street. *Toronto Telegram* staff reporter Aubrey Wice was on hand to observe the ritual means of laying an earth-bound spirit to rest.

The Toronto clergyman decided to consecrate all the vital spots of the haunting—places where the ghostly images of the man or woman had been seen or heard. The bedroom where Mrs. Edmunds claimed to have been struck in the face was the first stop. After the rites of exorcism had been completed, journalist Wice wrote that he felt as though the oppressive air had lifted.

A later caretaker, Mrs. Winifred McCleary, maintained that the "oppressive air" had not been lifted quite enough to suit her. She claimed that the house was still haunted and reported hearing the toilet flush by itself and seeing the hot water tap turn on by itself. "You thought you were in another world in that house," she told Gary Oakes, a *Telegram* reporter. "You knew you weren't alone." Mrs. McCleary maintained that one of the ghosts was not content just to lurk about and engage in phenomena of a mildly annoying nature. She claimed that it seemed to want to put its arms around people.

A second exorcism was ordered, and the second performance of the ritual appears to have put the ghosts to rest. I researched the mansion in the late 1960s, but later curators of the house would not answer my queries concerning any continuing phenomena. It seems that caretakers have not actually lived in the Mackenzie Homestead since around July 1967. This is not to imply that curators will not reside in the museum because it is haunted, but it does mean that no one was in the position to have experiences similar to those encountered by the Dobbans, the Edmundses, and Mrs. McCleary.

York University history professor William Kilborn, who wrote a book about Mackenzie entitled *The Firebrand*, believes the caretakers had valid experiences of some kind or other and expressed his opinion that he wouldn't go out of his way to spend the night there. And the Haunted Ontario website (http://www.ghosthuntersinc.com/haunted/ontario.htm) continues to describe the Mackenzie House as being "full of spirits. People have reported misty figures and orb-like lights. Lights go on and off. Voices are heard, as well as footsteps. One witness saw a woman in one of the bedrooms walk to the window and disappear. There have been many other ghosts and activity reported."

⊷⊶⊷

THE WHALEY HOUSE: AMERICA'S MOST HAUNTED MANSION

Old San Diego is the birthplace of California. On Presidio Hill, Father Junipero Serra established the mission of San Diego de Alcala on July 16, 1769. In the early 1820s, a small Mexican community was formed that by 1835 had evolved into El Pueblo San Diego. Because it was the site of the first permanent Spanish settlement on the California coast, San Diego is a significant part of the Pacific heritage of the United States—much as Jamestown, the first English settlement in Virginia Colony, is material to our Atlantic ancestry. The first U.S. flag was raised on Old San Diego's tree-lined plaza in 1846.

Not only have my wife, Sherry Hansen Steiger, and I found Old San Diego one of the most haunted places in North America, but the Whaley House, constructed in 1857, just might be one of the most haunted mansions in the country. June Reading, the amicable and knowledgeable director of the Whaley House who has since passed on, told us when we were researching the mansion that immediately after its completion by Thomas Whaley, the mansion became the center of business, government, and social affairs in Old San Diego. The oldest brick house in southern California, the Whaley House served as a courthouse, a theater, and a boardinghouse, as well as the family home of Thomas and Anna Whaley and their children. Located at 2482 San Diego Avenue in Old San Diego, the Whaley House has been restored; it is now owned and operated by the San Diego Historical Society as a tourist attraction.

Whaley House.

Although guests can no longer stay overnight in the Whaley House, it is still possible to tour the mansion in the early afternoon. No one is allowed in the Whaley House after 4:00 P.M., but police officers and passersby say that someone—or something—keeps walking around at night turning all the lights on. Often, while conducting tours through the old mansion, members of the society have heard eerie footsteps moving about visibly unoccupied parts of the house.

Almost every facet of haunting phenomena has been observed or encountered in this mansion. Footsteps have been heard in the master bedroom and on the stairs. Windows, even when fastened down with three- or four-inch bolts on each side, have opened of their own volition, often in the middle of the night, triggering the burglar alarms.

As they tour the mansion, people have often smelled cooking odors coming from the kitchen, the sweet scent of Anna Whaley's perfume, and the heavy aroma of Thomas Whaley's favorite Havana cigars. Screams have frequently been heard echoing through the upstairs rooms, as well as the sound of girlish giggles and the rattling of doorknobs. Once a large, heavy china closet toppled over by itself. Many people have heard the piano playing in the music room and

One of the bedrooms in Whaley House. Many visitors have said they have felt the presence of Anna Whaley there.

phantom crowds milling and shuffling about in the courtroom. The ghostly images of Thomas and Anna Whaley have been seen on numerous occasions.

Numerous individuals have sensed or psychically seen the image of a scaffold and a hanging man on the south side of the mansion. According to Mrs. Reading, ten years before Thomas Whaley constructed his home on the site, he witnessed the execution of a renegade sailor named Yankee Jim Robinson. The scaffold had stood on the spot that would later become the arch between the music room and the living room in the mansion.

In the fall of 1966, a group of reporters volunteered to stay in Whaley House to spend the night with Yankee Jim. Special permission was granted to the journalists by the historical society, and the ghost hunters settled in for their overnight stay. The wife of one of the reporters had to be taken home by 9:30 P.M. She was badly shaken and claimed that she had seen something on the upper floor which she refused to describe. The entire party of journalists left the house before dawn. They, too, refused to discuss the reason for their premature departure, but some people say that they were confronted by the ghost of Yankee Jim, still protesting the horror of his death.

In this photo, a mistlike presence can be seen by the antique couch.

The primary spirits are Thomas and Anna Whaley and Yankee Jim, but Mrs. Reading said that the other ghosts have been seen, including phantoms of a young girl named Washburn, a playmate of the Whaley children; and "Dolly Varden," the family's favorite dog. Some visitors to the Whaley house have reported seeing a gaudily dressed woman with a painted face lean out of a second-story window. In Mrs. Reading's opinion, that could well be an actress from one of the theatrical troupes that leased the second floor in November 1868.

The Court House Wing of the mansion is generally thought to be the most haunted spot in the Whaley House, due to the violent emotions of legal proceedings there in the early days of San Diego. Many individuals who have visited the old house have heard the sounds of a crowded courtroom in session and the noisy meetings of men in Thomas Whaley's upstairs study. According to many psychic researchers, the fact that this one building served so many facets of city life, in addition to being a family home, almost guarantees several layers of psychic residue permeating the environment.

Many sensitive visitors to the Whaley house have also perceived the image of Anna Whaley, who, some feel, still watches over the mansion that she loved so much. And who, according to a good number of those who have encountered her presence, deeply resents the intrusion of strangers.

June Reading told us that in 1964 the popular television talk show host Regis Philbin and a friend saw Anna Whaley as they sat on the Andrew Jackson sofa at 2:30 A.M. The spectral image floated from the study through the music room, and into the parlor. At that moment, Philbin, in nervous excitement, "dissolved" the apparition with the beam of his flashlight. Since that time, Mrs. Reading said, night visits to the Whaley mansion have not been permitted.

Numerous photographs of spirit phenomena have been taken over the years in Whaley House and many are on display in a glass case in the mansion. As a matter of fact, Sherry was able to capture a rather starting image on film. When we returned home and developed the photographs taken during our research trip of the Whaley House, we discovered to our amazement a ghostly materialization of the noose that hanged Yankee Jim Robinson. Sherry had photographed the arch between the music room and the living room, the site where the renegade had been executed before that portion of the Whaley House had been constructed. There at the top of the room, the location where Yankee Jim swung, one can see a phantom noose hanging from the ceiling.

Sherry also captured several other odd materializations that showed up on the developed photographs. In two locations of the house, where many have reported lights being turned on when no one is there, the lights were illuminated in the developed pictures—even though the lights were turned off during our daytime interview with Mrs. Reading.

THE MYRTLES: AMERICA'S MOST HAUNTED PLANTATION

According to the Smithsonian Institution, the Myrtles Plantation located three miles north of St. Francisville, Louisiana, rivals the Whaley House for the title of the most haunted house in the United States. If we add a category of "most haunted" that emphasizes "due to acts of violence," I think we may easily grant two Number One awards. Built on the site of an ancient Native American burial ground in 1794 by General David Bradford, the plantation has been the location for at least ten violent deaths. Throughout the years, owners and their guests have fled the house in the middle of the night, terrified by the appearance of frightening ghosts—and the entities continue to be sighted to this day. With the recent popularity of reality programming and documentaries on the strange and unknown, the story of Myrtles Plantation has been shown numerous times on television. But for those who may have missed the documentaries that have been featured on the History Channel, The Learning

Channel, and the Travel Channel—and for those who just plain like a good ghost story—here are the eerie details of the saga of Myrtles Plantation:

The tragic events that set the haunting in motion began when Bradford's daughter Sara Matilda married a young judge named Clark Woodruffe. Although the Woodruffes were happily married and their union had produced two daughters, when Sara Matilda was carrying their third child, Clark began an extramarital affair with Chloe, one of the house slaves.

Although Judge Woodruffe had a reputation for integrity in matters of the law, those who had knowledge of his personal life were aware that he was also promiscuous with ladies of ill repute. At first, Chloe tried to deny the sexual demands of her master, but she knew that if she fought Woodruffe's unwanted advances, she could be sent to work in the fields—and she much preferred being assigned to the duties in the mansion. While Sara Matilda suffered through her pregnancy and gave birth to another daughter, Chloe provided the release for her master's sexual needs.

Eventually, when the Judge grew tired of her and chose another house slave as his new mistress, Chloe feared that she would lose her position as a servant in the plantation house and be sent to do brutal work in the cotton fields. Desperately, she hoped that she might somehow find a way to win back Woodruffe's affections.

One evening, as Chloe stood near the Judge and Sara Matilda, pretending to go about her chores but listening for any mention of her name and any clue to her fate, Woodruffe grew irritated. He accused her of eavesdropping on a private family conversation with his wife. As punishment, the Judge ordered his overseers to cut off one of Chloe's ears. From that time on, Chloe wore a green headscarf with an earring pinned to it to hide her missing ear.

Now disfigured and dismayed that her chances of winning back the sexual attention of her master were diminished, Chloe felt certain that she would soon be banished to the cotton fields and life in the crude cabins and barracks of the other slaves. That was when the clever Chloe came up with what she believed might be the perfect means that would guarantee her status of house slave and keep her out of the fields. Ever since she was a very young girl, she had been wise in the ways of herbs and potions. She knew that it was possible to mix up a potion that would make her master love her again, but it would be difficult to find a way to make him drink it.

After much thought and deliberation, she devised a much better way to use her expertise with herbs. She would bake a birthday cake for the Woodruffes' oldest daughter and place oleander—a poison if used in large doses—into the mix. Because she would used only a small amount of oleander, the family would suddenly and mysteriously become ill. Then, the loyal maid and servant that she was, she would nobly nurse them back to health.

The spirits of former plantation slaves may still haunt the fields where they once labored for their white masters, often dying at the cruel hands of farm owners.

Tragically, Chloe inadvertently sprinkled too much oleander into the cake mix. Sara Matilda and two of her daughters became extremely ill and died within hours after the birthday party. Because neither the Judge nor the baby ate any of the poisoned cake, they survived the mysterious illness that had struck down the rest of the family.

Grief-stricken and ashamed of what she had done, Chloe confided in another slave that she had only intended to make the family ill so that she would be the one to take care of them. Chloe made a poor choice for a confidante. Rather than keeping the secret, the woman loudly tattled to her fellow slaves that the death of the mistress of the house and her two daughters had not been due to some mysterious sudden illness. Chloe had deliberately poisoned them.

An enraged mob made up of both the Woodruffes' slaves and their white neighbors chased Chloe into the surrounding woods where they caught her and hanged her. Later her body was cut down, weighted with rocks, and thrown into the river.

Judge Woodruffe closed off the room where the birthday party had been held and never allowed it to be used again while he lived. He was unable to enforce his decree for long, for Clark Woodruffe was murdered a few years later.

Since that scene of mob violence in antebellum Louisiana, the ghost of Chloe has been often sighted both inside and outside of the plantation house. She is most often seen wearing a green headscarf wrapped turban-style around her head with an earring pinned over her missing ear. Her ghost is also held responsible for stealing earrings from many guests over the nearly two hundred years since her hanging.

John and Teeta Moss, the current owners of the Myrtles Plantation, have converted the place into a bed-and-breakfast, and Hester Eby, who manages house tours of the mansion and grounds, states that the haunting phenomena continue unabated. Mrs. Moss even photographed a shadowy image of Chloe standing near the house.

According to Ms. Eby and members of the staff, of the ghosts of the two poisoned Woodruffe girls have been seen frequently; they are often heard playing and running in the halls. The spirits of the girls have also been seen playing on the verandah of the mansion and seated at the table in the children's dining room. Perhaps they are eternally partaking of that last terrible meal that featured a deadly treat of poisoned cake.

Many guests have heard a baby crying when there are no infants present in the mansion. Some witnesses of this phenomenon have associated the sounds of the infant with the manifestations of the ghost of a French woman who wanders from room to room, as if seeking someone. Perhaps she is searching for her baby.

Other ghosts include those of a woman in a black skirt who floats about a foot off the floor and who is seen dancing to music that cannot be heard by the living. Some guests have seen the ghost of a man who was stabbed to death in a hallway over an argument concerning a gambling debt. A more active spirit is said to be that of an overseer who was robbed and killed in 1927 and who angrily demands that guests leave the place and return to their own homes. Numerous guests have been awakened by an unseen pianist who plays the grand piano, but who ceases at once if someone enters the room where the piano is kept.

There is a ghost of a young girl that seems to appear only when a thunderstorm approaches. She has long curly hair, wears an ankle-length dress, and is seen cupping her hands and trying to peer inside the window of the game room.

Many guests have heard the sounds of footsteps on the stairs and have seen the image of a man struggling to reach the hallway at the top. Hester Eby says that it is commonly believed that the ghost is that of William Winter, an attorney who owned the Myrtles Plantation in the late nineteenth century. According to the story surrounding his death, he was summoned to the porch one evening by a stranger on horseback who claimed to be in desperate need of an attorney. When Winter stepped outside to see how he might be of service, the man shot him and rode away. Fatally wounded, Winter stumbled through the house, painfully climbed the stairs, and died in the arms of his wife.

Throughout the years, many residents and their employees have heard their names called by invisible entities. The haunting phenomena seems to ebb and flow, intensifying and then lessening in its manifestations. Now that the place is also a bed-and-breakfast hotel, Eby said that the staff knows when the Myrtles is having a bad night by the number of guests who call up at midnight and demand to leave the place at once.

Both employees and guests have reported seeing a candle floating up the stairs at night, bobbing up and down as if it is being carried by someone. Many believe that the candle is carried by Sara Matilda as she searches for her errant husband dallying with one of the servant girls.

One man, who was hired to be a gateman and greet guests upon their arrival at the bed-and-breakfast, was fascinated by a woman who approached his post dressed in a white, old-fashioned dress. Thinking she was merely getting in the mood for a stay in a old Southern plantation by dressing as a belle from the antebellum South, he was a bit miffed when she seemed unresponsive to his cherry greeting. In fact, she seemed to take no notice of him at all. He watched the seemingly snobbish woman until she walked up to the main house and vanished through the front door without opening it. He left his job that day and never returned to the Myrtles Plantation.

19

CREEPY CASTLES AND GHOSTLY ROYALTY

THE INCREDIBLE SUPERNATURAL SIEGE AT CALVADOS CASTLE

A Classic Case from France

All of the inhabitants of Calvados Castle were disturbed by the strange noises that echoed throughout its dark corridors shortly after midnight on October 12, 1875. The next morning, the master of Calvados thought that he knew what had caused the nocturnal knockings and thumpings. Someone was obviously trying to frighten his family away from the castle so that they might purchase the surrounding land at a fraction of its value. The scoundrels who had invaded the castle had no doubt found entrance to the interior by means of some long forgotten passage. The brigands probably thought it a simple matter to drive a man away from an old castle that he had just inherited.

He had no sooner finished discussing his theory with his coachman Emile and gardener Auguste when the three men heard the two formidable watchdogs outside in the garden howling and barking. Rushing to a window, the master of Calvados saw the dogs directing their angry attention toward one of the thickets in the garden. He smiled at the thought that their noisy midnight visitors had tarried too long and found themselves cornered by the dogs. He unlocked his weapons case and thrust rifles into the hands of Emile and Auguste. He selected a double-barreled shotgun for his own use. They would soon have the miscreants at gunpoint.

After the men had posted themselves at the edge of the garden, the dogs were urged to attack. The two brutes rushed into the thicket with vicious growls. There was a moment of silence, and then the hoarse canine rumbles of fury turned to plaintive whines and whimpers of terror. The dogs ran out of the thicket with their tails between their legs, and the master could not call them back. Cautiously, the three men entered the thicket, their firearms cocked and ready. They found nothing, not a footprint, not a shred of clothing on a branch, absolutely nothing. "But, what," the master asked of his men after they had searched in all directions, "could have frightened the dogs so?" His question was never answered to his satisfaction.

> If the strange incident with the watchdogs had not been so fresh in his mind, M. de X. may have accused his son's tutor of too much after-dinner sherry.

The mysterious disruptions at Calvados Castle that October night started of one of the most prolonged and terrifying accounts of haunting phenomena. The hauntings that took place in the old Norman castle from October 12, 1875, to January 30, 1876, were written up and published in 1893 as the *Annales des Sciences Psychiques* by M. J. Morice. Although the master of Calvados kept a diary that was later used as a meticulous record of the phenomena, he insisted that his family name not be mentioned in connection with the haunting. He is, therefore, referred to in the narrative only as M. de X. His immediate family consisted of Mme. de X., and their son, Maurice. The remainder of the household consisted of Abbe Y., tutor to Maurice; Emile, the coachman; Auguste, the gardener; Amelina, the housemaid; and Celina, the cook.

On the evening of October 13, Abbe Y. came down to the drawing room and told M. and Mme. de X. that his armchair had just moved without anyone being near it. He insisted that he had seen it move out of the corner of his eye. If the strange incident with the watchdogs had not been so fresh in his mind, M. de X. may have accused his son's tutor of too much after-dinner sherry. He tried to calm Abbe Y. down and returned with him to his room. M. de X. attached gummed paper to the foot of the tutor's armchair and fixed it to the floor. Then he gave Abbe Y. permission to ring for him if anything further should occur.

At ten o'clock that evening, M. de X. was awakened by the ringing of Abbe Y.'s bell. When he entered the tutor's room, he found the man with the covers pulled up to the bridge of his nose, peeking out at his employer like a frightened child. In a trembling voice, Abbe Y. said that the whole room had been moving about, and there had been rappings on the wall. M. de X. saw that the armchair had indeed moved about a yard, and several candlesticks and statuettes had been toppled. He heard a door open behind him and turned to see Amelina peeping out from her room across the hall. Her face was pale. She, too, had heard the rappings. The next evening, the disturbances did not confine themselves to Abbe Y.'s room. Thunderous blows were heard all over the castle. M. de X. armed his servants and conducted a search of the entire building.

They found nothing. The pattern was repeated night after night as the noisy ghost began its siege in earnest. For more than three months, the inhabitants of Calvados Castle would not know a night of unmolested slumber. The curate of the parish and Marcel de X., a relative, arrived to witness the phenomena and to try to determine the origin of the manifestations. That night, the sound of a heavy ball was heard descending the stairs from the second floor to the first, jumping from step to step. After having spent a night in the castle, the parish priest declared that the heavy tread he had heard during the night sounded like the footsteps of a giant, and he proclaimed the activity to be supernatural. Marcel de X. agreed with the priest. He had quickly concluded that this ghost would be a most difficult one to "lay," and declared that he would leave Calvados Castle to the noisy spirit. He wished M. de X. the best of luck and returned to his home.

On Halloween the ghost seemed to outdo itself with a display of paranormal prowess that kept the household from going to bed until three o'clock in the morning. The center of the activity had become the green room. The ghostly machinations seemed to always begin or end with loud rappings in the empty room. The entity's walk had also evolved. By All Hallow's Eve, its tread had begun to sound like wooden stumps repeatedly hitting the floor.

It was during a violent November rainstorm that the spirit acquired a voice. High above the howling wind and rumbling thunder, the household heard a long shriek. Amelina declared that there was a woman outside in the storm calling for help. The cry sounded again and everybody looked curiously at one another. Mme. de X. agreed that the wail certainly sounded like a woman, and she asked Celina to look out a window and see if someone was outside. Celina had just reached the window when a cry sounded from within the castle. The members of the household gathered together in the sitting room as if they hoped to seek strength from their unity. Three sorrowful moans sounded from the staircase. The *thing* was getting closer!

The men of Calvados Castle left the sitting room to inspect the castle. They found nothing. There was no woman in the castle and no sign that anyone or anything had entered the castle from the storm. They heard no further sounds until the following night, when everyone was awakened just before midnight by terrible sobs and cries coming from the green room. They seemed to be the sounds of a woman in horrible suffering. The activity seemed to become intensified as days passed by, and the cries of the sorrowful woman in the green room evolved into shrill, furious, despairing cries, "the cries of demons or the damned."

Shortly after the "weeping woman" had arrived and added to the disturbances at Calvados, a cousin of Mme. de X.'s paid a visit. The gentleman was an army officer, and he scoffed at the wild stories his family told him. Against all their pleas, he insisted upon sleeping in the green room. He told them that

Old castles have, almost like a tradition, been havens for ghosts.

he always had a revolver at his side, and that if anything should dare to disturb his sleep it would get a bullet in its hide. The officer strode boldly to the green room, left a candle burning as a nightlight, and went straight to sleep.

He was awakened a short time later by what sounded like the soft rustling of a silken robe. He was immediately aware that the candle had been snuffed out and that something was tugging at the covers on his bed. He gruffly demanded to know who was there. He attempted to relight the candle at his bedside, but as soon as he had a flame something extinguished it. Three times he lighted it, and three times he felt a cold breath of air blow it out. The rustling noise seemed to become louder, and something was definitely determined to rob him of his bedclothes. He cocked his revolver and warned his unwelcome guest that if it did not declare itself, he would shoot. The only answer to his demand was an exceptionally violent tug on the covers.

The officer decided to shoot. It was simple enough for him to determine where his silent adversary stood by the sound of the rustling and the pull on the bedclothes. He fired his revolver three times. The lead slugs struck nothing but the wall, and he dug them out with a knife the next morning. While it appeared that the shots had only hit the wall, the officer's attempt was mildly effective, as the ghost left his covers alone for the rest of the night.

Abbe Y. fared far worse than any member of the household throughout the duration of the haunting. No other room in the castle had to entertain such animated furniture. Whenever the tutor left his room, he always made certain that the windows were bolted and his door was locked. The key to his room hung by a leather strap that he kept belted to his waist. These precautions never accomplished the least bit of good. When he returned to his room, Abbe Y. would invariably find his couch overturned, cushions scattered about, windows opened, and his armchair placed on his desk. On one occasion, all of his books were scattered on the floor. Only the Holy Scriptures remained on the shelves. The tutor once tried nailing his windows closed. He returned to find the windows wide open and the couch cushions balanced precariously on the outside windowsill. The most hurtful attack on the clergyman occurred as he knelt at his fireplace, stirring the coals. Without warning, a huge amount of water rushed down the chimney, extinguishing the fire. The sparks that flew from the chimney blinded Abbe Y., and he was covered in ashes. The cleric somberly concluded that such actions could only be the work of Satan.

One night the ghost roamed the corridors of the castle and sought admittance to the rooms of each member of the household. It knocked once or twice on the doors of several bedrooms, then, true to its aggressive pattern of behavior against the tutor, it paused to deal 40 consecutive blows to Abbe Y.'s door before it returned to the green room.

When a priest from a neighboring parish ventured to stay the night in Calvados Castle, he heard the distinctive sounds of a large animal rubbing itself along the walls. Another visitor took special notice of the sounds the ghost made as it walked through the halls. He said that the steps taken by the ghost were quite unlike human steps and was sure that no animal could have walked in such a manner. He declared it sounded more like a stick jumping on one end.

When the Reverend Father H. L., a Premonstrant Canon, was sent to Calvados by the bishop, there was not the slightest sound from the noisy ghost from the moment the reverend father entered the castle until the moment he left. But as soon as the clergyman had made his departure, there was a loud thud in the first-floor passage that sounded like a body had suddenly fallen to the ground. That disturbance was followed by what sounded like a rolling ball violently striking a door. The ghost had once again begun its torment of the household in earnest.

On January 20, 1876, M. de X. left for a two-day visit to his brother, leaving his wife to keep up the journal of the haunting. Mme. de X. recorded hearing an eerie bellowing that sounded something like a bull and frightened everyone during her husband's absence. A weird drumming sound was also introduced during M. de X.'s absence, as well as a peculiar noise that seemed very much like something striking the stairs with a wand or a stick.

Upon M. de X.'s return to Calvados, the disturbances became more violent than they had ever been. The ghost charged into the rooms of Auguste and Emile and turned their beds over. It invaded the master's study and heaped books, maps, and papers on the floor. The midnight screams increased in shrillness and were joined by the furious cries of animals. Rhythmic tappings moved up and down the corridors as if a small drum and bugle corps were parading in the halls. For the first time the ghost pounded on the door of Maurice, the son of M. and Mme. de X. The force of the successive blows on his door shook every window on the floor.

On the night of January 26, 1876, the parish priest arrived to conduct the rites of exorcism. He had also arranged for a Novena of Masses to be said at Lourdes and coincide with his performance of the ancient ritual. The priest's arrival was greeted by a long, drawn-out cry and what sounded like hoofed creatures running from the first floor passage. The door to Maurice's room began to shake as if something desperately demanded entrance.

The last days of the haunting are significant in that a great deal of the activity began to center around the adolescent son. It was as though the psychic tremors of puberty had somehow set the manifestations in motion or had reactivated unseen forces that had lain dormant in the old castle. The rites of exorcism reached their climax at 11:15 on the night of January 29. From the stairway came a piercing cry, like that of a great beast that had been dealt its deathblow. Rappings began to rain on the door of the green room. At 12:55 a.m., all those present in Calvados Castle heard the voice of a man in the first-floor passage. M. de X. recorded in his journal that the voice seemed to shout twice, "Ha! Ha!" Ten powerful blows to the door of green room shook everything. After one final blow to the door, there was the sound of coughing in the first-floor passage.

The sound of coughing may very well have been the entity's death-rattle. The family rose and cautiously began to move about the castle. The priest slumped in exhaustion from the long ordeal. There were no terrible screams, no moving of furniture, no mysterious knocking. They found a large earthenware plate that had been broken into 10 pieces at the door to Mme. de X.'s room. No one had ever seen the plate before that night.

"Everything has stopped," M. de X. wrote in his journal entry for January 30, 1876. His elation was somewhat premature. Several days after the exorcism had been performed, Mme. de X. was sitting at a writing desk when a packet of holy medals and crosses dropped in front of her. It was as if the ghost had suffered a momentary defeat and was declaring that it must withdraw from the fray

The Tower of London, guarded by its famous Yeoman Warders, also known as "Beefeaters."

for a time to recuperate and lick its wounds. Toward the end of August 1876, soft knockings and rappings began to be heard again. On the third Sunday in September, the ghost arranged the drawing-room furniture in the shape of a horseshoe, with the couch in the middle. When the parish priest heard that the hauntings had returned to Calvados Castle, he was heard to moan that the devil had held council and was about to begin the spiritual warfare again.

REAL GHOSTS, RESTLESS SPIRITS, AND HAUNTED PLACES

The final cycle of the phenomena was very short-lived. The ghost had lost intensity, was less destructive, and appeared content playing the organ and moving an occasional bit of furniture about the room of Maurice's new tutor. The phenomena became progressively weaker, and eventually whatever energy had energized it during the brief cycle dissipated. Finally, the only thing that haunted Calvados Castle was the memory of those terrible months when a ghost with a thundering, hammering fist had run rampant in its corridors and manifested one of the most dramatic hauntings on record.

THE GHOSTLY LADIES AND LORDS OF GREAT BRITAIN

Anne Boleyn

Shortly before World War II, a British music hall comedian sang a song about Anne Boleyn's ghost walking through the Tower of London "with her head tucked underneath her arm," but a phantom such as Anne's is hardly a subject to jest about. Anne *does* haunt a site near Wakefield Tower, in the historic Tower of London. It has been said that her unhappy shade manifests wearing the etheric replica of the fur-trimmed robe of gray damask, crimson petticoat, white collar, and black hood she wore to her execution on May 19, 1536. Anne not only haunts the Tower of London but also Hever Castle, her old home in Kent, and Bollen Hall in Cheshire.

Not many years ago, one of the guards at the Tower of London reported to an officer that there was a strange light in the old Chapel of St. Peter ad Vincula, and that it had been seen before. On each occasion the building was known to be locked and empty. The officer obtained a ladder that he propped up near one of the high windows to peer into the chapel, and he was amazed to see a procession of men and women radiating a luminous glow. Among the figures was a woman who resembled the old paintings that he had seen of Anne Boleyn. The officer watched the ghostly scene for several minutes before it suddenly vanished.

Henry VIII

It is a wonder that Henry VIII does not haunt the Tower of London, for the nearby Chapel of St. Peter ad Vincula contains the bones of not only Anne Boleyn but also Katharine Howard and numerous other persons who were victims of Henry's wrath and the headman's axe. For centuries, King Henry's ghost has been seen in Windsor Castle. Witnesses claim that his spirit can often be heard groaning and dragging the ulcerated leg that tormented him in his later years.

"View of Hampton Court Palace" by Jan Griffier, c. 1702.

Katharine Howard

The ghost of Katharine Howard, another of Henry's unlucky wives, is associated with Hampton Court Palace. While a prisoner in the palace, she managed to escape from her room on November 5, 1541. She ran down a gallery that gave access to the king's private chapel, where her lord and master

In 1996 Britain's Queen Elizabeth II met an actress portraying Elizabeth I at the opening of the Royal Armouries Museum.

was at his devotions. She hoped to plead with him to spare her life, but as soon as she had she reached the door of the chapel, she was dragged back by the guards. After her death at the block, her phantom was said to haunt the gallery. Her wraith would appear at the far end, pass as far as the door of the chapel, stop, and then return to utter a piercing shriek, which ended in her vanishing.

Jane Seymour

Jane Seymour, the wife who followed Anne Boleyn, died in childbirth and is also said to haunt Hampton Court Palace. On very rare occasions she has been seen descending one of the staircases, a lighted candle in her hand.

Queen Elizabeth I

King George V saw the ghost of Queen Elizabeth a few years before his death, during one of his periods of illness. He was at Windsor Castle at the time and alone in his bedroom. Suddenly pictures on the wall began to move as if they were being stirred by a draft. At the same time, a woman wearing a black Tudor costume appeared out of one of the walls, crossed the room, and vanished through the opposite wall. The king felt a sensation of coldness that so frequently accompanies psychic manifestations. His nurse told how she, too, had been conscious of an invisible presence in the sick room; she had also seen the pictures stir on the walls.

The ghost of Queen Elizabeth I was also seen by a man in the king's service at Windsor Castle. He saw the ghost in broad daylight, and on comparing notes with His Majesty, came to the conclusion that they had both seen the phantom of Elizabeth Tudor.

The Brown Lady of Raynham Hall

Another great lady's ghost that has walked for many generations is that of Dorothy Walpole Townshend, sister of Sir Robert Walpole, the first prime minister of England, and wife of Lord Charles Townshend of Raynham Hall. In 1712 at the age of 26, Dorothy married her childhood sweetheart, Lord Charles, after his first wife died. When Lord Charles learned that Dorothy had been the mistress of Lord Wharton—or so the legend goes—he ordered her imprisoned in her room. Various stories say Dorothy died of a broken heart, a fall down the stairs, or of smallpox.

After Lord Charles's grandson George was made a marquess in 1786, he became known for the lavish parties he held for aristocrats at Raynham Hall, located a few miles southwest of Fakenham, in Norfolk. An added attraction for the guests was the opportunity of glimpsing the ghost of Dorothy Townshend carrying a lamp as she walked the darkened corridors of the estate. Her ghost has been seen many times wearing a dress of brown brocade, so her specter became popularly known as the "Brown Lady of Raynham Hall." When George IV visited Raynham in the early nineteenth century, he was awakened as he slept in the state bedroom by a pale woman dressed in brown. The ghost so frightened him that he vowed to never again return to Raynham.

In 1835 Colonel Loftus, a gentleman staying at the estate over Christmas, saw the ghost on two occasions in as many days. On the night of his second encounter, she was on the staircase, carrying a lamp. He made a sketch of her, making a particular note of the fact that her eye sockets were hollow and empty. Not many years later, Captain Frederick Marryat, author of numerous popular books for boys, saw the Brown Lady carrying a lamp and followed her. When she turned toward him, she smiled in a manner he deemed diabolical, and he fired his pistol at her. The bullet went right through her and was lodged in a heavy door. After this attempted assault, she vanished for about a hundred years.

When the Brown Lady reappeared again, it was in 1926 to the then Marquess Townshend, who was a boy at the time of the encounter. Ten years

The famous photograph of the "Brown Lady of Raynham Hall."

later, Lady Townshend hired photographer Indra Shira to take photographs of the interior of Raynham Hall. To the astonishment of the photographer, he saw the ghostly form of a woman descending the stairs. The photographer managed to capture the ghost on film. Shira's photograph appeared in *Country Life* magazine, December 1, 1936, and shows a woman wearing what appears to a wedding gown and a veil, or possibly a shroud.

Some psychical researchers from the United Kingdom claim that Queen Elizabeth II has seen the ghost of Dorothy Walpole on several occasions. According to members of the Queen's staff, the Brown Lady appears with a cold rush of air that makes Her Majesty's dogs start barking like mad.

In the 1950s a famous race car driver sat up all night with two dogs waiting for the phantom. He did not see her, but the dogs sensed a presence that came down a passage in the dead of night, for they suddenly appeared terrified.

The Green Lady of Louth

From the Brown Lady of Raynham, we turn to Green Lady of Louth. Thorp Hall, Louth, was once the seat of Sir John Bolle, an adventurer who set out on an expedition to Cádiz, Spain, in 1596. While there, he fell in love with a beautiful Spanish woman who wanted to be his wife, but this was impossible as he had a wife and family in his native land. Thus, she could not accompany him to England, but as a keepsake she gave him a miniature of herself wearing a green dress. Strange as it may seem, although the woman never visited England during her life, her phantom has occasionally been seen at Thorp Hall. She is usually seen under a tree in the grounds, but she always manifests wearing a green dress.

The Gray Lady of Hackwood

After ladies brown and green comes the Gray Lady of Hackwood. In the 1860s a certain legal gentleman, who was hard-headed and not easily deceived, saw the Gray Lady appear out of a wall in the bedroom he occupied as a guest at Hackwood Hall, near Basingstoke in Hampshire. At first he suspected trickery, but on investigation, a hoax was ruled out after the Gray Lady appeared twice in one night. In the morning he resolved to say nothing to his fellow guests, but on his arrival at the breakfast table they excitedly asked him if he had noticed the shadowy gray form that had followed him up the staircase the previous night.

Amy Robsart

Another famous lady who was reluctant to quit this world was Amy Robsart, wife of Robert Dudley, who was very famous at court in the days of Elizabeth I. Her husband neglected her when royal favor had come his way, and she became despondent. At that time she lived at Cumnor Place in Oxfordshire, and it was there that she met her death on September 8, 1560. The circumstances surrounding her death have always been considered strange. She had given her servants the day off so they could visit a fair at Cumnor Village, and when they returned in the evening they found their mistress dead at the foot of the staircase. Her neck was broken.

Whether she had met with foul play or had an accident will never be known, but her violent passing seemed to result in her becoming an earthbound spirit. Her phantom haunted the staircase from 1560 until the house was demolished in 1810. Twelve clergymen had tried to "lay" her ghost, but their attempts were all in vain.

After the house was pulled down, the ghost of Amy Robsart was occasionally seen in the open parkland. It was said that all who came face to face with her died within a few days of the encounter. Legend says that Amy's ghost appeared to her husband, and during her visit to him she told him that he would shortly die. This proved correct, for 11 days later he was dead.

THE GHOSTLY CASTLES AND MANSIONS OF GREAT BRITAIN

Windsor Castle

Windsor Castle, built in the eleventh century, has been christened by psychical researchers as the "Grand Central Station" for the ghosts of English royalty. Princess Margaret confided in friends that she had encounters with the ghost of Queen Elizabeth I, who died in 1603, and Charles I, who was beheaded in 1649.

King George III, England's monarch at the time of the American Revolution, tragically went mad during his reign and has often been sighted in the castle library. He appears to be studying ancient volumes, perhaps to determine the reason for his spells. He is said to mutter, "what, what," over and over again.

The Monster of Glamis

Princess Margaret was born in a haunted castle that has its own grotesque monster-in-residence. While the British Isles can boast of many spectral visitants, Glamis Castle is the only one that can claim an indestructible, flesh-and-blood monster that resides in a hidden mystery room.

Glamis is one of the most ancient of Scottish castles, and as it is purported to be the scene of Macbeth's foul murder of Duncan, there is little wonder that the old fortress shelters a number of extremely active phantoms. For centuries, inhabitants of the castle have claimed to see numerous ghostly re-

Queen Elizabeth II of Britain during 2001's Garter ceremony at Windsor Castle.

enactments of tragedies that have saturated the psychic ether of the environment. Among the phantom recreations are:

1. The erection of the scaffold used for the execution of the widow of the sixth Lord Glamis, who was hanged as a witch.

2. The accidental death of the eighth Lord Glamis.

3. The agonizing natural death of the fifth Earl of Strathmore.

4. The murder of the third Earl of Strathmore during a game of cards at the castle.

One of the more foul deeds committed by one of the lords of Glamis concerns the mass murder of a group of Ogilvies, who arrived at the castle and begged for refuge from a band of pursuing Lindsays. The Lord of Glamis pretended to be sympathetic to the Ogilvie cause and locked them up in a secret dungeon, promising to shelter them from the Lindsays. When the leader of the Lindsays arrived at the castle, Lord Glamis winked, held up the key to the thick stone door, and told the man not to worry about the Ogilvies any longer. Lord Glamis had sealed them away to starve to death.

A later Lord Glamis, who was a bit less awed by manifestations of the supernatural than some of his predecessors, led a number of servants in an investigation of ghostly noises that had been disturbing the household. They managed to trace the spectral sounds to a large room in an unused portion of the castle. Lord Glamis found a key to fit the ancient lock, and as the door swung open, he fainted. The wide-eyed servants, who caught their swooning lord, were horrified to see that the room was filled with skeletons. From the position of the skeletal frames, it was easy to determine that they had died gnawing one another's flesh.

But back to the monster. All chroniclers of Glamis agree that it resides somewhere in a secret room, and generations of servants have sworn that they have heard its shuffling feet and hideous half-human cries as it emerges for its nocturnal prowlings. According to Augustus Hare, who visited the castle in 1877, a ghastly chamber that is deep within a wall hides a secret transmitted from the fourteenth century, which is always known to three persons. When one of the triumvirate dies, the survivors are compelled by a terrible oath to elect a successor. In his famous book *Demonology and Witchcraft*, Sir Walter Scott also wrote about the ritual of the select three that have to hide their terrible secret. Scott wrote that the only people who knew the location of the hidden room were the Earl, his steward, and, upon coming of age, the heir.

According to legend, the monster is a Lord Glamis who received the brunt of a family curse while in his mother's womb. The curse dictated that he be born a half-human monster who should live in misshapen form for all eternity. When the child was delivered, it was found to be a grotesque monstrosity, and the brutish baby was hidden away by his father in a secret room. For centuries, three people have been selected to care and look after for the monster.

A persistent legend tells of one Lady Glamis who was determined to discover the location of the secret room and view the monster for herself. While Lord Glamis was away on a trip, she instructed her guests, who were all quite

Glamis Castle, Scotland.

eager to help her solve the mystery, to hang a towel from every window in the castle. The window without a towel, she reasoned, would be the secret room.

After the party had draped a towel in every visible window, they encircled the castle to see if any opening might be without a tell-tale cloth. One window remained undraped, but the searchers had no luck in locating the hidden room. They could only conclude that the secret chamber lay deep within a wall. Lord Glamis returned home to find the guests and his lady still engaged in their search for the monster. He was enraged, for he had no intention of allowing the terrible family secret to ever become public knowledge. After a violent quarrel with her indignant husband, Lady Glamis left the castle, never to return.

Culzean Castle

Culzean Castle is a picturesque and historic fortress in Turnberry, Ayrshire, Scotland. Today, much of its colorful past has been forgotten, and it is commonly referred to as "Ike's Castle" because former United States President Dwight D. Eisenhower was given a lavishly furnished apartment in the castle as a tribute to his leadership of the Allied armies in World War II.

On March 3, 1993, Brenda Ray took a set of photographs in Tutbury, Staffordshire, United Kingdom. Tutbury Castle, quite visible in the background, is home to many ghosts. When Ray had her film developed, one image showed an individual in a flowing cape walking down the middle of the road. Another photograph taken seconds later does not show the hooded figure.

Visitors and staff often mention ghostly encounters with a beautiful dark-haired girl in an evening dress who approaches them in an empty corridor. Mrs. Harriet Howard, an American tourist, told of a meeting she had with the girl in Culzean Castle. She remembered that the ghost greeted her with the words, "It rains today." Howard nodded in reply, assuming that the beautiful girl must be some kind of hostess-guide for the castle. As the corridor was quite narrow, Howard leaned back against a wall and stated that she would give the young woman some more room to pass. The girl's smile faded. "I do not require any room nowadays," she said wistfully. According to Howard, her entire right side became chilled as the girl brushed past her and continued down the corridor. "And the really strange part of it," the startled woman said later, "was that she didn't really brush up against me, she actually walked through my side."

Close up of the mysterious figure walking through Tutbury.

World's Biggest Ghost Hunt at Tutbury Castle

Walpurgis Night (April 30) has traditionally been regarded as one of the most powerful nights for ghosts, demons, and long-legged beasties. In essence, it is springtime's Halloween, though many practicing witches and occultists believe that Walpurgis Night has an even greater potential for smashing the barriers between the seen and unseen worlds.

On Walpurgis Night, 2003, hundreds gathered at Tutbury Castle outside of Derby to participate in an event publicized as the "World's Biggest Ghost Hunt." According to many of the participants, they received more than they bargained for. David Clensy, a feature writer for the *Evening Telegraph*, said that he arrived at the castle a cool, calm, and reserved skeptic. When he left, his suit was caked with mud, sweat was streaming from his brow, and he felt "somewhere near a gibbering wreck." Nobody, he said, had anticipated such violent results at the ghost hunt.

Tutbury Castle was originally constructed in 1071 by the Norman Hugh de Avranches. In 1265 Henry III gave the castle to his younger son Edmund, who was granted the title of Earl of Lancaster in 1267, and the estate has remained in the possession of the earls and dukes of Lancaster ever since. Mary Queen of Scots was imprisoned at Tutbury in the late sixteenth century. In 1646 the castle was taken by parliamentary forces during the civil war and ordered to be destroyed, leaving the ruins that exist today.

The King's Chamber, where Charles I took shelter to avoid the round-head forces, is considered the most haunted area of the castle. Ghosts frequently reported include a monk, a baby, a drummer boy, and a gray lady. Management of the castle grounds has closed portions of the ruins, including the King's Chamber, because in recent years they have had so many visitors and ghost hunters faint as they enter the room. The spirits within are quite aggressive and have been known to push, slap, and touch people.

Clensy said that although his skeptical mind tried to focus on having only rational thoughts as he entered the King's Chamber, it was hard to do after he saw a husky bouncer from Derby run from the cold, dank place. The man later told Clensy that he had felt a tapping on his shoulder that began to burn. It had left him feeling powerless and terrified. The big man admitted that he had burst into tears he had felt so frightened. And when he had run out into the light and pulled back his collar, there was a long, three-pronged claw mark on his neck that was still bleeding.

The team of four medics stationed at Tutbury Castle said that the bouncer's wounds were the most serious they dealt with that night. Most of the first-aid was directed toward the people who fainted and swooned. The medics observed that fainting was quite common when people felt overcome by strange things going on around them.

On May 3 the sponsors of the World's Biggest Ghost Hunt declared the event an unqualified success. According to Tutbury Castle and Fright Nights (<http://www.frightnights.co.uk/wbgh/>), 750 people attended the event, and nearly 200 reported strange experiences within the castle walls. In addition, dozens of individuals camped all night in the rain and reported further ghostly encounters.

PHANTOMS ON ROADS AND HIGHWAYS

We've all heard at least one variation on the Phantom Hitchhiker story. It may well be the best-known and most universal of all so-called urban legends. Here is a recap of the familiar tale to set the mood for this chapter.

A college student [or a salesman] is driving on a lonely country road late one rainy night when he is startled to see a young woman walking along the shoulder. Immediately, he pulls over, leans across the front seat to open the passenger door, and asks her if she wants a ride. She appears a bit dazed and she is soaked to the skin.

With a mumbled word of thanks, she gets inside. The college man reaches behind him, grabs his sweater from the backseat, and offers it to the hitchhiker. In the glow of the dashboard lights, he can see that she is really a very lovely girl.

She smiles her thanks and drapes the sweater over her shoulders, informing him that she has to get home to see her parents. The driver notices for the first time that her face and hands are scratched and bleeding, and he asks what happened to her. She explains that her car slid off the road and into a ditch. She had been standing there for what had seemed like hours, hoping for help, before she decided to walk the rest of the way to her parents' home.

He tells her that there is no problem taking her right to her parents' front door. She thanks him, gestures into the darkness ahead and says that the house is only a few miles ahead.

As he is summoning the courage to ask her name, she points to the lights of a house down a very short lane. She asks him to stop, and she gets out of the car. He protests that he would be happy to drive her the rest of the way, but she is already running away into the night. As he drives on, he berates himself for not asking her name, but then he remembers that she still wears his sweater. That will be his excuse to drive back to her parents' home and formally make her acquaintance.

> **Some version of the above account of a phantom hitchhiker has been told and retold with variations since the days of horse and carriage.**

Two days later, the student drives back to his mystery girl's home and knocks on the door. He is surprised when a very elderly woman opens the door and invites him to step inside. As he looks about the interior of the front parlor, he notices a framed portrait of the beautiful young girl, and he asks the woman if her granddaughter is home.

Following the student's gaze to the portrait, the woman begins to weep. Her darling daughter, she said, is still trying to come home. The student listens incredulously as the woman tells him that her daughter had been killed in an automobile accident on a dark and rainy night over forty years before.

He leaves the old woman, concluding that she must be crazy. The hitchhiker he had picked up that night was no more than nineteen years old. And she was very much alive.

As he passes a small rural cemetery, something blowing in the wind on one of the grave markers catches his eye. When he enters the graveyard to investigate, he finds his sweater draped over a tombstone that marks the final resting place of a young woman who had died forty years ago.

Some version of the above account of a phantom hitchhiker has been told and retold with variations since the days of horse and carriage. Each year I receive a number of accounts from individuals who swear that they themselves have stopped to pick up a ghostly hitchhiker—nearly always a lovely young woman.

The stories of Phantom Hitchhikers translate easily from one culture to another. For many years, taxi drivers in Naha, Okinawa, have claimed that an attractive woman in her twenties, with short-cropped hair and dressed in black slacks, often hails them for a ride on the road to the U.S. Marine Camp. When the cab driver turns to ask for a specific destination, she disappears. The phantom has been dubbed the "Nightwalker of Nago" because she most often appears on the mountain road leading from the fishing village of Nago to the marine camp.

RESURRECTION MARY, ARCHER AVENUE, CHICAGO

Chicago paranormal researcher Richard Crowe has quite a file on Resurrection Mary, a beautiful phantom hitchhiker who haunts Chicago's South

Side. "She was buried in Resurrection Cemetery on Archer Avenue, which is where she gets her nickname," Crowe explained. "During the 1930s and 1940s, Mary was often picked up at dances by various people. She would ask for a ride toward Resurrection Cemetery, saying that she lived down that way As people drove her home, she would yell at them to stop in front of the cemetery gates. She would get out of the car, run across the road, and dematerialize at the gate."

Crowe mentioned a report wherein two young men were fascinated by watching this beautiful blonde dance by them, but when she passed near them they got the strangest sensation. That night when they got home, they told their father about this woman. They'd never heard of Resurrection Mary, but their father recognized her by the description they provided.

"I investigated and found out that a week before this sighting, Mary had been seen dancing around the cemetery's fence," Crowe said.

Crowe told me that he has had numerous first-person accounts from people who say Mary has opened their car doors and jumped in, but only one person who met her at a dance and followed up by going to the street address she gave him. According to the man's report, Mary sat in the front between him and the driver. Their friend sat in the backseat. When they approached the front gate of Resurrection Cemetery, she asked them to stop and let her out. It was a few minutes before midnight, and the young men had protested, saying she couldn't possibly live there. According to the narrator of the story, Mary said, "I know. But I have to get out."

"So being gentlemen and she being so beautiful, we let her out, and she left without saying another word," he told Crowe. "She crossed the road running, and as she approached the gate, she disappeared."

The young man continued with his account: "She had given me her name and address, so early Monday morning, all three of us guys came to the number and street in the stockyards area. We climbed the front steps to her home. We rang and knocked on the door. The mother opened the door, and lo and behold, the girl's color picture was on the piano, looking right at us. The mother said she was dead. We told her our story and left. My friends and I did not pursue the matter any more, and we haven't seen her again. All three of us went into the service thereafter and lost contact with each other."

THE WEEPING BRIDE OF STOWE, VERMONT

Old-timers in the region of Stowe, Vermont state that there is a ghost that haunts the covered bridge on Hollow Road, a young bride who was left waiting at the altar by an irresponsible groom. The jilted woman quit the church, heading for her elusive lover's home near the bridge on Hollow Road. As she was crossing the bridge, something startled her horse, causing it to bolt and throw her to her death on the rocks below the bridge.

Traditionally, in the wee hours of morning, the sorrowful bride returns to search for the lover who betrayed her and humiliated her by jilting her on their wedding day. Motorists traveling the road late at night have reported seeing the image of a young woman dressed in a bridal gown driving her carriage resolutely toward the covered bridge. Some have reported making eye contact with the angry ghost and state that the experience chilled them to the bone.

Misty Miss Latta on Arkansas 64

Drive the lonely stretch of Arkansas Highway 64, especially on a rainy night, and area residents swear that you will be likely to sight the tormented spirit of Laura Starr Latta, who died a month before her twentieth birthday in 1899. Motorists have claimed to have seen Laura's small, frail frame inside a white nightgown standing on the side of the road across from the cemetery where her body lies. Some old stories say that Laura was accosted by a gang and beaten to death on the way to her wedding. Others say that she was killed by a runaway wagon or murdered by a bizarre cult. All that is known for certain is that she died a month before her twentieth birthday in 1899.

The inscription on her tombstone reads "Gentle Stranger passing by, As you are now, once was I. As I am now, so you must be. Prepare yourself to follow me."

Lady of the Lake, White Rock Lake, Texas

Most of the reports of the apparition of the Lady of the Lake come from lovers' lane couples or late-night drivers who see her appear along the side of the road. Local folklore says that she is the ghost of a woman who was killed by being drowned in White Rock Lake.

According to some who have encountered her face to face, the phantom appears to be jealous of young lovers and wishes to frighten them out of their amorous activities. One young man said that he will never forget the sight of the shimmering ghost staring in the car window at him and his frightened date. Drivers who have stopped to help what they thought was a woman in trouble, say that she leaves only a puddle of water where she had stood at the side of the road.

This photograph was taken on a rural road where strange apparitions were often seen.

THE SPIRITS OF POCAHONTAS PARKWAY TOLL PLAZA

Over the years I have received numerous reports from truck drivers who make long hauls across the Plains States and who say that they have seen some mighty strange things. Most often, they happen upon phantom hitchhikers of varying descriptions, or encounter spirits from the past—ghostly wagon trains, small bands of native tribespeople, stagecoaches, and Pony Express riders.

On July 15, 2002, the driver of a delivery truck reported seeing three Native Americans approaching the recently opened Pocahontas Parkway toll plaza on state Route 895 in eastern Henrico County, Virginia. In a report filed by the toll taker to whom he related the account, the truck driver said he had seen three warriors who were wearing breeches, carrying torches, and walking in the middle of the highway. He blasted his horn to warn two more torch-wielding men who were clearly illuminated by his headlights. He wondered if the tribespeople were staging a bizarre protest of some sort against the parkway.

The toll taker took the driver's report and added it to the list of stories from motorists who had seen strange, unexplainable phenomena. She knew that although she would report the incident to state troopers, who would definitely follow up on the case, they would find no Native Americans parading with torches protesting anything.

Troopers who patrol the graveyard shift along the Pocahontas Parkway told Chris Dovi of the Richmond, Virginia, *Times-Dispatch*, that they have responded to dozens of calls similar to the one the delivery truck driver made on July 15. The first was on July 1, then two nights later, when plaza workers reported hearing Native American drums, chants, whoops, and the cries of what seemed to be hundreds of voices. From time to time others would report seeing the vague outline of people running back and forth in the darkness.

According to his findings, there were artifacts scattered all over the site, dating back five to six thousand years.

Virginia state police spokeswoman Corinne Geller visited the toll plaza late one night in July and said that the high-pitched howls and screams were real. She told Chris Dovi (August 11, 2002) that the sounds were not the kind of screams that a person in trouble would make, "but whooping. There were at least a dozen to fifteen [voices]. I would say every hair on my body was standing up when we heard those noises."

An engineer working nights to complete the construction of the bridge in Parkway Plaza said that he and a group of workmen had seen a Native American sitting astride a horse watching them from below on the interstate. They were about to tell him to move on, that he wasn't allowed to ride a horse on the interstate, when both rider and horse disappeared.

Deanna Beacham of the nearby Nansemond tribe confirmed that none of their tribal members were engaged in any kind of protest against the plaza. Although she would not admit to a belief in tribal spirits roaming around near the plaza, she said that there were many rivers, streets, roads, and communities with Native American names in the region—so why shouldn't people see physical manifestations of that impulse?

Dennis Blanton, director of the College of William and Mary's Center for Archeological Research, did a dig at the site of the bridge's construction at the plaza. According to his findings, there were artifacts scattered all over the site, dating back five to six thousand years. Edward Halle, an area historian, agreed that the Pocahontas Parkway location had been home to tribespeople for a long time.

An area resident who owned a business less than a mile from the toll plaza said that "hooting and hollering" had been heard near the place for years and that the local Native Americans had long declared that there were many spirits there. In his opinion, the plaza had been built on a Native American burial ground.

◆⫸⫷◆

THE PHANTOM WARRIOR WHO RACED TRAINS

A traveling salesman was making the night trip from Minneapolis, Minnesota, to Butte, Montana. He had been dozing lightly in a lower berth when he was awakened by what he later described as a "damned uneasy feeling."

He couldn't put a finger on what was troubling him, he told a reporter for a Chicago newspaper in the summer of 1943. There were no strange or unusual noises in the train. He could detect nothing that sounded wrong in the steady clicking of the wheels. For some reason he decided to lift his window shade.

That was when he saw the apparition. Outside of his window, so close that it seemed as if he might be able to touch it if he lowered the glass, was an apparition of a brightly painted Native American brave on his spirited mount. The warrior bent low over the flying black mane of his horse and looked neither to the right nor to the left. He seemed to be mouthing words of encouragement to the phantom mustang as they rapidly gained on the train.

"I've seen them five or six times after that, in different parts of the Dakotas," the salesman said. "They seem to be solid flesh, but there's a kind of shimmering around them. It's like watching a strip of really old movie film being projected onto the prairie."

Railroad brakemen, engineers, and construction crews in the Dakotas and Wyoming have often spoken of the phantom Sioux and his determined race with their swift, modern iron horses. They couldn't beat the trains when they were alive, one old-timer who knew the legend behind the spectral racers commented, but they seem to have picked up some speed in the happy hunting grounds.

According to tradition, Frederic Remington, the famous artist of the Old West, sketched the Sioux brave and his mustang from life as the inexhaustible pair raced the train on which he was riding in about 1888. Many times, Remington had heard the tale of a determined warrior astride a big, bony mustang who tirelessly raced the trains as the iron horses steamed across the plains. It was as if the locomotive represented a tangible symbol of the encroaching white man, and the Sioux believed that if he could conquer the iron horses, his people could vanquish the paleface invaders.

With a marrow-chilling war whoop the warrior would come astride the train engines as they entered a wide open stretch of the prairie. The mustang would pound the plains until sweat formed on its lean, hard body. Only the greater speed of the locomotives would at last enable them to pull away from the chanting Sioux and his indefatigable mount. Even in life the two had seemed more phantom than flesh.

One can easily sense the great admiration Remington had for the spirit of the Sioux and his animal as his sensitive hands recreated the intensity he felt. Remington named his sketch "America on the Move."

⚊⚊⟭⟬⟭⚊⚊

GHOSTLY HITCHHIKING COWBOY ON U.S. 101

By J. T.

I'm a field service engineer. The electronic security company I worked for twenty some years ago required that we use our personal vehicles to perform our job. I had a pickup that I employed in this capacity. There was no camper shell on it, and it was a rather plain Jane bronze-colored Dodge four-wheel drive truck.

The drive from San Jose to Lockwood along US 101 in California passed through what was then mostly farmland. It is about a two-and-a-half hour drive. I had stopped at a roadside hot dog stand, and bought a couple of hot dogs, and a couple of cans of Coke for the drive. As I turned out of the dirt lot to head back to the freeway ramp, I looked both ways, and saw no one. I do mean no one. Not a single soul.

But when I pulled onto the road, there was this guy standing at the freeway onramp. There were no trees, signs, or bushes that could have hidden him. No other vehicles had passed and dropped him there.

As I drew near, I could see he was dressed as a contemporary cowboy—jeans, chambray shirt, boots—everything but the hat.

He could have been anywhere from fifty to his mid-sixties, at least six feet tall, clean shaven, with dark hair that was more than halfway to silver, and a tan that comes from a lifetime spent outdoors. He was what my wife refers to as "ruggedly handsome." He carried a single rather battered leather satchel. I think my father used to call them "AWOL bags," a term he learned in the army.

I remember the cowboy putting his thumb out, and I thought, "What the heck. It'll be nice to have someone to talk to on the drive."

I asked where he was headed and he said, "Jolon." It's a small town just north of Lockwood and home of Fort Hunter Ligget. I told him I was headed to Lockwood, and to hop in. He eyed the two hot dogs on the center of the bench seat, and asked if I was planning for company. I laughed and told him, "No, but you're welcome to have one and a Coke, too." He asked what I had put on the dogs, and I said just brown mustard, whereupon he beamed, picked one up, and said, "Just how I like'em!"

I'm used to wolfing down my food, especially when I'm driving. This guy was so dainty as he ate that hot dog. It was clear that he was savoring every bite. As we rolled through Gilroy, about ten minutes into the drive, I asked him how the dog was. He bobbed his head, and said he hadn't had a hot dog in a very long time, and it was nice to have one this good.

There were things about him that were just a wee bit off. Some of his physical mannerisms, some of his speech, his choice of words, and not having a hot dog in a very long time. I had grown up in an army family, and we moved around a lot. I've met lots of different people and, you know, everyone is a little off, so I didn't think too much of it.

We talked about this and that on the drive down. I learned his name was Willie and that he was going to see about a position as a foreman on a ranch down there. His languid drawl as he spoke placed me curiously at ease. I, in turn, conveyed my name and that I had just started this job not quite a year ago. I told him that I enjoyed it very much, and that I could see spending my life happily at this job.

He thought that rather odd for someone who was only twenty-two. He wanted to know why I didn't have more of a yearning to see the world. I told him of growing up as the son of an army man, and seeing more of the world than I cared to. He eyed me speculatively and just nodded sagely. As we drove down Jolon Road headed toward town, he announced that we were nearing his stop. He directed me to pull off to the side of the road near a gate. I shut off the truck and sat with this stranger in the early afternoon sun.

He was preparing to dismount, but stopped and opened his satchel. He pulled out this huge silver belt buckle. It was bigger than a large butter dish. It was obviously handmade and had to weigh ten or twelve ounces. In the center of the buckle was one of the biggest pieces of turquoise I had ever seen on a piece of jewelry.

Now, I love Turquoise. Especially that from the Sleeping Beauty Mine. It has a rich, incomparable blue color that just resonates with me. This stone just was absolutely perfect. Outstanding. I was nearly certain it came from that mine because of its color.

"Want to buy it?" he asked me.

"I can't afford something like that." I told him.

"Sure you can, I'll trade you for however much you have in your wallet."

I had fifty-three dollars in my wallet. That buckle was worth much more than that, and I told him so.

"That's fine, I'll take the fifty-three dollars, and we'll call it square."

"I can't do that to you. We both know that buckle is worth between three hundred and four hundred dollars."

He just shrugged.

"Why do you want to sell it for so little?" I asked.

"I need the money."

"For …?" I was looking at this guy intently now.

"If I don't get the job, I'll need bus fare home and hopefully something to eat along the way."

I reached into my wallet and pulled out the fifty-three dollars. "Here," I said. "Take it, and keep your buckle."

"Now that wouldn't be fair, son!"

I said, "It wouldn't be fair if I accepted your buckle in trade. You and I both know it would be the same as if I had stolen it from you."

"How am I supposed to square this if you won't accept it?"

I wasn't entirely sure of his meaning.

"I mean, how am I to repay this debt? You place me in your debt."

"If you ever come upon someone who needs a little help, remember someone helped you once, and if you can, offer to help. That is more than adequate payment." I smiled and said, "Fifty-three dollars is fifty-three dollars, but I'm young and healthy and I can earn it again."

He stared at me and made me uncomfortable. "You're much older than twenty-two, boy."

He accepted the proffered money with thanks, and got out of my truck. Once he was out, he leaned through the open window and offered his hand.

> He spoke precisely and enunciated each word in a manner unlike our earlier conversation. It was almost as if it was a proclamation.

I took it, and his strength was amazing. I don't think I could have broken that grip had I tried. He didn't crush my hand, he just locked it in place. I've never run across anyone with a grip like that. He stared in my eyes and said, "It is a rare thing to meet someone not driven by avarice and sheer greed. I don't think you have anything to worry about. I think you'll do just fine at your job."

He spoke precisely and enunciated each word in a manner unlike our earlier conversation. It was almost as if it was a proclamation. It made me uneasy for a reason I can't articulate. It was just a feeling gnawing at the back of my brain. I smiled at him and stumbled out my thanks. He released my hand and withdrew from the truck.

He stooped to pick up his bag, and I turned my attention to starting the truck. I looked up to wave at Willie, and make sure he was clear of the truck, and he was nowhere to be seen.

Where I had stopped, I could see up the road ahead of me and down the road behind me. I could see across the road into a vacant pasture, and over to the field behind the gate. I didn't see him.

Fearing that maybe he had fallen beside the truck, I turned off the engine and got out. I raced around to the passenger's side. Nothing. I looked in the bed. Empty, except for my handtruck, tools, and equipment cases.

The hair was starting to stand up on the back of my neck. I backed away from the truck, and slowly sank down and looked under it. Nothing.

I stood up and looked around. There was nowhere for this guy to go to in roughly thirty seconds. No trees to hide behind. No bushes. No ditches. Nothing.

Immediately the story about that hitchhiking girl that who would disappear from a car after giving directions popped into my head, and I felt a little sick.

I called his name a few times, and the only response I got was the wind rattling through the dry grass. I got back in my truck, took a deep breath, and got the hell out of there.

All through the job in Lockwood, my wallet burned in my right hip pocket. I couldn't pull it out and look inside to see if perhaps the money was still there, and I had imagined the whole episode. I was too fearful. I've never used drugs in my life, so I struggled with how to account for the incident if somehow the money was still in my wallet. Wild scenarios raced through my brain as I worked the afternoon away.

Upon finishing the job, I had my invoice signed, and walked back to my truck parked in the now nearly empty lot. I put my tools in the bed of the truck, and finally had enough strength to pull out my wallet. The most scared I have ever been in my life is the time some hunters mistook me for a deer and opened fire on me as I ran through the hills in the early morning. Opening that wallet was on par with that fear.

It was empty. Nothing. I had given the money to someone. There was no other explanation.

Over the past twenty years, I have often thought about the mysterious hitchhiking cowboy. I've survived three layoffs when the company was restructured three times by three different management teams. People with more seniority than I had lost their jobs each time. I'm still here even after the company was bought by a huge multinational conglomerate, and they cut nearly thirty percent of the workforce. There were two additional layoffs as they reorganized segments within our business unit. When they combined districts just a year ago, more people lost their jobs. Several people I had worked closely with have committed suicide while I have been employed here. I'm still here. I'm still happily doing a job that I love.

Did this entity bless me? I'm beginning to think so. I don't want to think about what might have happened if I had accepted that belt buckle.

***

ROUTE 666: ARIZONA'S DEVIL'S HIGHWAY

Although U.S. Route 666 was renamed U.S. Route 491 in 2003, the legend of Camino del Diablo, "the Devil's Road," will long be remembered. The original naming of the highway had nothing to do with the Number of the Beast, 666, as given in Revelation, the last book in the Bible. It was so designated because it was the sixth branch of an interstate route called U.S. 60. The section linking Chicago to Los Angeles became the legendary Route 66. And the Four Corners detour from Route 66 was renumbered 666 in August 1926.

But some say labeling the road with those numerals made it Satan's own road to perdition. The 190 miles of U.S. 666 starts at Gallup, New Mexico, wends its way through seventy miles of Colorado, then ends in Monticello, Utah. According to statistics, the ill-named highway has a incredibly high accident rate, and some people think they know a few of the reasons why this is so.

According to numerous eyewitness accounts, on nights of a full moon, a black, 1930s-vintage phantom Pierce-Arrow roadster has run scores of cars, trucks, and motorcycles off the road. The ghostly automobile has been linked to at least five deaths.

Dr. Avery Teicher of Phoenix spent ten years documenting reports of the phantom Pierce-Arrow and the howling hellhounds that materialize to terrorize anyone foolhardy enough to pull off Route 666 and admire the desert landscape. According to Dr. Teicher, two members of a biker gang had both of their arms chewed off by the fiendish ghost dogs and a third biker had ninety percent of his face eaten away.

The least threatening of all reports from the Devil's Highway are those of a phantom female hitchhiker who vanishes whenever someone stops to give her a ride.

On January 21, 2003, New Mexico Governor Bill Richardson stated his support to change the name of U.S. 666. Most people approved the plan to get rid of the negative connotation of the highway, the number of the Antichrist, the Beast.

***

A TUNNEL OF GRAYNESS ON I-80

In the late 1950s, I was driving late at night with my family heading west on I-80 near Ames, Iowa. Suddenly we entered a section of road that had the thickest fog I had ever encountered. When a large flock of sheep appeared, intermixed with the incredibly thick fog, they made the driving extremely hazardous. At last we broke through the patch of fog, to find the highway completely free of the pea soup that had so thoroughly blinded my vision. I had been moving at an extremely slow rate of speed to avoid hitting the animals that had crowded around us, so I accelerated to make up time, cussing out the farmer under my breath for allowing his sheep to run free. Iowa has no open ranges.

I thought back on the strange, unusually thick fog from time to time over the years. Mainly when talk of hazardous driving conditions arose, I would mention the really thick fog that I had once encountered. I did not really consider the event paranormal until I received this email from Kent in February 2002:

> [W]e seemed to "jump" about thirty miles up the road in an instant, and arrived at our destination a full half-hour sooner than we should have.

I play in a jazz trio around the Cedar Rapids/Iowa City area. Having an interest in the paranormal, I have found that nightclubs are a great place to collect firsthand accounts of strange events. Naturally, after a few drinks people are more willing to talk about subjects they would not normally discuss.

A second-hand account was recently related to me about a professor from Ames, who with his wife, was driving west on I-80 at about 2:00 A.M. one night. The couple supposedly had to come to a complete stop to allow a herd of "wild" horses to cross the highway! As the account went, the horses seemed to appear out of a fog and disappear into the mist on the other side of the road.

My family had a very strange incident happen in roughly the same area several years ago, and we still discuss it when we pass that stretch of road. In our case, we seemed to "jump" about thirty miles up the road in an instant, and arrived at our destination a full half-hour sooner than we should have. Also, there was a strange fog around the highway, which seemed to cover both sides of the road and obscure the scenery totally, but the road itself was clear! That was the really strange part. It was like driving through a tunnel of grayness.

SHE HANGS BY HER NECK DURING THE FULL MOON

By now, it is unlikely that anyone remembers the names of the witnesses who first saw the ghostly image of a young woman hanging from the bridge on the old country road near Mt. Pleasant, Iowa. But nearly everyone agrees that it was two truck drivers who had turned off the main highway at about midnight one night when there was a full moon. As they rounded the bend that approached the old bridge, the driver suddenly slammed on his brakes. "Look ahead!" he said to his partner. "Look in the full beam of the headlights! There's a woman hanging there on the bridge." When he really became conscious of what they were seeing, the other man said that they should cut the woman down, maybe she was still alive.

There could be few sights creepier than coming upon the swaying body of a hanged woman suspended from the girder of an old country bridge, but the two truckers knew they had to do something—whether it was midnight on an eerie gravel road or not. Their feet had no sooner touched the coarse road when the form of the hanged woman began to fade from their sight. And, by the time that they reached the bridge, the woman, noose and all, had completely vanished. The two men stared at each other with open mouths, mouths no longer capable of articulating the fear and confusion that jammed their brains. Just moments before, they had both clearly seen the wretched figure of a hanged woman swaying above the worn wooden planks of the old bridge.

The second sighting of the ghostly hanging was witnessed by a young couple coming home from a Saturday night dance, who saw the same grim apparition on the dark and eerie country road. Then other truckers and townspeople reported seeing the form of the hanging woman in the light of the full moon.

We decided when our team went to investigate the apparition that we would have to be there on a night of a full moon, for the ghost had never been sighted at any other time. So on July 19, 1970, with the moon full above us, we sat in my station wagon with the psychic-sensitive Irene Hughes and a number of others, just a few yards away from that haunted country bridge. My associate Glenn and I wanted to see if Irene could pick up on the ghost and the events that led to the hanging, so we withheld any information about what we might see. All Irene knew was that our research team had gone to the Iowa countryside and parked at a particular place.

Just a few minutes before midnight, someone whispered that Irene was in light trance. "There's someone coming down the road," she said. Two or three people agreed with the sensitive. I strained my eyes to perceive a midnight visitor, but I could see nothing more than a traffic sign advising approaching motorists about the narrow bridge and its load limit.

Irene said nothing. She seemed to be tuned into another dimension, which we others could neither see nor hear. The medium sat in silence for a few more moments, then she spoke, slowly, precisely: "I see a woman swinging in a circle. A circle of confusion. She is disturbed, confused. She feels betrayed. She feels like she wants to jump over the side of the bridge." A high, thin wail seemed to come from the direction of the bridge. Was it only the cry of some night-hunting bird, the distorted complaint of some farm animal, or the keen of a tormented soul? The frogs and crickets seemed undisturbed by any of the possibilities.

This photograph was taken at 14 Mile Creek, Raymond, Mississippi.

"I see a circle," Irene said, speaking once more. "I see a woman committing suicide from this bridge." (Again it must be noted that we had not told Irene what she might expect to see at this lonely country bridge.) "It was suicide," Irene said. "But there was another person involved. This is most unusual. Usually when someone in spirit appears, they are dressed just as they were in life. I have never had any spirit who comes to me wrapped in a sheet like so many people think spirits do. But that is just what I saw on the bridge. I saw what looked like somebody wrapped in a sheet!"

"A shroud?" I asked her.

"A shroud," she agreed. "And she tells me her name is Brown. Or maybe it was O'Brien. She was a brunette. I really don't feel that she was a sick person. I feel that this act was just a sudden thing in her life. I feel that there was a husband, but that he was not close by."

Irene sat quietly for a few moments, apparently sifting through the psychic impressions bombarding her from the bridge. "I'm hearing the name Helen," she said, resuming her reportage. "I feel that this woman was having a love affair with a doctor in the community. And I feel that you will find that there was a doctor who left the town rather quickly after this woman took her life. I don't feel that this woman was mentally ill or anything like that. I feel that her life was okay and then, suddenly, involvement with the doctor began."

A reporter who had accompanied us asked how many years ago this happened. Irene said that she had the feeling that it may not have been more than sixteen to twenty years ago, around 1950. "According to the information that I have," Glenn said "that would seem to be exactly the time that the ghost began to appear."

> **"I'm hearing the name Helen, ... I feel that this woman was having a love affair with a doctor in the community."**

"Look!" Irene said. "Can you see it? A form was very clear there for an instant."

It may be that our eyes were playing tricks on our group, but on the right-hand side of the bridge, there seemed to be a glowing figure.

"Oh, I see her so clearly," the medium said. "She's wearing a yellow dress." Irene suddenly stopped talking. Then, after several seconds of silence, she said: "She keeps telling me, 'Honey, don't talk. Honey, don't tell them.'" I asked if there was some reason why she didn't want anyone to know why she killed herself? "I think it is the doctor," Irene said. "I think she was involved with a doctor who left soon after her death."

By this time the research group had left the station wagon and were standing in the middle of the bridge. There were holes in the wooden planking, and we had to move cautiously in order to avoid twisting an ankle.

"I am getting the impression that some member of her family was from Philadelphia, but she came here from Kansas," Irene said. "I'm seeing a huge sunflower, and that is the sunflower state, isn't it?"

As discreetly as possible, we conducted a follow-up investigation after our vigil that full-moon night near the legendary bridge. Through one of our sources, we learned that there had been a young woman, originally from Kansas and fond of wearing bright yellow dresses, who had come to the area and become romantically involved with a local doctor. The young woman had committed suicide in despair over their impossible love affair, and public opinion, or conscience, had forced the doctor to leave town. While some informants believed that the ghost of the hanging woman might well be the suicidal Kansan, others said that the young woman in question had not hanged herself and that they were unaware of the legend of the haunted bridge.

It appears, then, that the spirit of the young woman in the bright yellow dress may have hanged herself at the bridge in an earlier decade than the 1940s or 1950s. Or perhaps the hanging woman is only a mischief-making spirit who takes delight in frightening motorists who travel a dark country road. Or maybe she is only an urban legend, who shall be forgotten—until some night when the moon is full moon and someone turns the bend toward the old country bridge and sees her ghostly figure hanging there.

A MONSTER'S HAIRY HANDS
GRAB THE STEERING WHEELS ON B3212
By Nick Redfern

Nick Redfern is the author of many books on the worlds of UFOlogy, cryptozoology, and the paranormal, including Final Events, There's Something in the Woods, *and* Memoirs of a Monster Hunter.

It was around the year 1910 that the weird and horrific saga of the "Hairy Hands" began on what is today the B3212 road, which can be found in the vicinity of the Dartmoor, England locales of Postbridge and Two Bridges. Somewhat disturbingly, a hairy, monstrous and unknown force would time and again violently lash out at unwary passing drivers. In one case, the altercation reportedly resulted in a tragic death. And, as will shortly become apparent, the diabolical assailant may have been nothing less than a terrifying, definitive shape-shifter.

In most of the cases, the victims of the frightening phenomenon reported seeing large, hairy, "disembodied hands" manifest out of thin air, firmly grab the steering wheel of their vehicles—or the handle-bars of their bikes—and unsurprisingly strike complete terror into their hearts. This invariably resulted in the unfortunate victims being violently forced off the country road. For a decade or so, the events were considered nothing more than a mild—albeit certainly sinister—curiosity for the superstitious locals of the Dartmoor wilderness. That situation would drastically change in 1921, however, when tragedy struck.

In June of that year, Dr. E. H. Helby, who was at the time serving as the Medical Officer at the nearby Dartmoor Prison, died on the same stretch of road. He lost control of his motorcycle and sidecar, where his two children were seated. Helby had just about enough time to warn his children to jump to safety—which they did—before he was thrown from his motorcycle and instantly killed.

Then, on the dull, foggy day of August 26 of the same year, a young British army captain—described by the local media as being "a very experienced rider"—was thrown onto the shoulder of the very same road, after he too lost control of his motorcycle. Significantly, and incredibly, the captain stated at the time, in response to media questions: "It was not my fault. Believe it or not, something drove me off the road. A pair of hairy hands closed over mine. I felt

Nick Redfern

them as plainly as ever I felt anything in my life—large, muscular, hairy hands. I fought them for all I was worth, but they were too strong for me. They forced the machine into the turf at the edge of the road, and I knew no more till I came to myself, lying a few feet away on my face on the turf."

And there was much more to come—and none of it good.

In the summer of 1924, the well-known and widely-respected Devonshire folklorist Theo Brown was camping in a trailer, approximately half a mile from the road where practically all of the ominous activity was taking place. In later life, she would detail the particularly nightmarish nighttime encounter that she experienced, and that is directly relevant to the mystery of the Hairy-Hands. Brown, the author of *Devon Ghosts* and *Family Holidays around Dartmoor*, said: "I knew there was some power very seriously menacing us near, and I must act very swiftly. As I looked up to the little window at the end of the caravan, I saw something moving, and as I stared, I saw it was the fingers and palm of a very large hand with many hairs on the joints and back of it, clawing up and up to the top of the window, which was a little open. I knew it wished to do harm to my husband sleeping below. I knew that the owner of the hand hated us and wished harm, and I knew it was no ordinary hand, and that no blow or shot would have any power over it. Almost unconsciously I made the Sign of the Cross and I prayed very much that we might be kept safe. At once the hand slowly sank down out of sight and I knew the danger was gone. I did say a thankful prayer and fell at once into a peaceful sleep. We stayed in that spot for several weeks but I never felt the evil influence again near the caravan. But, I did not feel happy in some places not far off [sic] and would not for anything have walked alone on the moor at night or on the Tor above our caravan."

Then there was the story told to the writer Michael Williams, author of the book *Supernatural Dartmoor*, by journalist Rufus Endle, who maintained that while driving near Postbridge on an undetermined date, "a pair of hands gripped the driving wheel and I had to fight for control." Luckily, he managed to avoid crashing the vehicle; the hands, meanwhile, simply vanished into thin air. A concerned Endle requested that the story not be published until after his death.

And now, it seems that decades later, the diabolical Hairy Hands of Devonshire have returned to terrorize the little villages and hamlets that, practically unchanged for centuries, still adorn the wilds of Dartmoor.

Michael Anthony, thirty-six, works for one of the largest suppliers of photocopying machines in Britain, and spends a lot of time traveling the length and breadth of the country meeting clients and promoting his company's products. Late on the night of January 16, 2008, Anthony was driving along the B3212 road when he had a terrifying encounter with the unknown, Indeed, it was an encounter that easily paralleled the many and varied reports of the Hairy Hands that surfaced in the 1910s and 1920s.

According to Anthony, it was around 11.00 P.M., and he had been visiting a customer in Postbridge who was establishing a new business in the area and who wished to rent several copiers from Anthony's company. The evening had gone very well: a deal had been struck, contracts had been signed and exchanged, and a pleased and satisfied Anthony was now homeward bound to the city of Bristol. It turned out to be a journey that he would never forget.

Anthony had barely left Postbridge, when his skin began to feel distinctly cold and clammy, and a sense of dread and fear completely enveloped him. And the fact that there seemed no logical reason for this only heightened Anthony's fear and concern. After all, he was merely making a leisurely, late-night drive home—something that usually cheered him after spending several days on the road and away from his wife and two young daughters. It would not take long before he found out what lay at the heart of this strange affair, however.

Like so many people before him, Anthony was about to have a dark, and very close, encounter with the Hairy Hands. He explained further that perhaps two minutes after the atmosphere in his car became oppressive, fear-filled, and even somewhat malevolent, he felt his hands begin to "go numb." He added: "I actually thought I was having a stroke."

Fortunately, it was no stroke. In some ways, however, it was far worse. Anthony could only look on in complete horror and disbelief when, just as had been the case decades earlier, a very large pair of hair-covered hands, "or paws," encased his own, and then suddenly attempted to violently steer the car toward the edge of the road and onto the cold, moonlit moors. To his credit, Anthony struggled valiantly with the wheel and fought off the spectral, hairy intruder three times.

Interestingly, after the third attempt, said Anthony, the hands simply vanished into thin air, amid a brief flash of light that lit up the interior of the car—and an overwhelming smell of sulfur. The shaken driver floored the accelerator and did not stop until he reached a late-night restaurant on the main M5 highway.

The mysterious hairy intruder had struck once again.

In essence, that is the story of the Hairy-Hands of Dartmoor. One might well ask (and indeed many have!), however: what lies at the heart of the puzzle? Some researchers, such as Jonathan Downes, one of Britain's leading figures in the field of cryptozoology, have suggested that perhaps the Hairy-Hands are a modern-day manifestation of a centuries-old, and decidedly deadly, shape-shifting creature from Celtic folklore known as the Kelpie.

According to ancient Scottish legend, the kelpie—or the water-horse—is a wholly supernatural creature that haunts the rivers and the lochs of Scotland and that has the uncanny ability to radically alter its form and appearance. The most common form that the kelpie takes on is that of a horse—hence the name. It stands by the water's edge, tempting any passing, weary traveler to mount it's back.

That, however, is always fatal downfall of the traveler; invariably the beast rears violently and charges head-long into the depths of the river or loch, drowning its terrified rider in the process. Very notably, the kelpie was also said to be able to transform itself into either a beautiful maiden or a large, hairy man, hide in the vegetation of the Scottish waterways, leap out and attack the unwary, and lead them to their deaths.

It goes without saying that the Hairy Hands, like the kelpie, seem to have supernatural origins rather than physical ones, and both seem to have a particular liking for attacking travelers. And, of course, the belief that a kelpie could shape-shift into a giant hairy man may be the reason some feel this legend may have some bearing on the story of the hair-covered hands or paws that sometimes fatally attack travellers near bleak, windswept Dartmoor.

As remarkable as it may seem, even in the twenty-first century, the creatures of myth, legend, and folklore of centuries past may still be with us, lurking in the shadows, and with thoughts of nothing but death and disaster upon their crazed minds....

THE HAUNTED HIGHWAYS AND
ROADS OF GREAT BRITAIN

People have been traveling about at night in carriages and coaches far longer in Great Britain than in the United States, so it is no surprise that their shadowy highways have an inordinate number of ghosts at the side of the road.

The United Kingdom's most haunted road is said to be A23 between London and Brighton, where numerous motorists have sighted a small girl with no hands or feet, a specter in a white trench coat, and a ghost dressed in cricketer's clothing.

The country road by Bosworth Battlefield (near Sutton Cheney, Leicestershire) is said to be haunted by ghostly soldiers and galloping horsemen.

* * *

On a stretch of the A465 near Bromyard in Herefordshire, villagers are concerned that the ghost of an accident from more than sixty years ago could be haunting the country road. A farmer reported as many as twenty-six drivers

REAL GHOSTS, RESTLESS SPIRITS, AND HAUNTED PLACES

Blue Bell Hill, Maidstone, Kent, United Kingdom, where phantom hitchhikers have been seen.

crashing into his fence during an eighteen-month period. Some motorists stated that they mysteriously lost control of their vehicles, that they felt their steering wheel pulled from their hands, as they approached the haunted area.

* * *

On a dark night in the 1970s, a lorry driver was traveling north up the A12 on a narrow stretch of road outside Blythburgh in Suffolk when he was horrified to see a man riding in a small cart pulled by a horse in the road straight ahead. In the split second he had to make a move, he caught sight of a woman walking beside the cart and knew what he had to do. He swerved in an attempt to avoid hitting them, but the road runs between high banks at that point, and he was forced to stay on the road.

Shaking with dread and remorse, assuming that he must surely have killed the two, the driver stepped down from his cab and began to walk back along the road, fearing at any moment to come upon the grisly remains. He found nothing. He walked back to his truck, looked underneath and around the vehicle. Nothing.

At last he drove on, baffled, but relieved that he was not leaving the scene of an accident. Later, he learned that the folk of Blythburgh often encounter the cart, the driver, and the woman crossing that piece of road, and the historians among them believe the ghosts date back to the eighteenth century.

* * *

Since 1965, dozens of drivers have slammed on their brakes to avoid hitting a pretty young woman in a flowing white dress standing in the road on Blue Bell Hill in Maidstone, England. The phantom is said to be that of a woman who was to have been a bridesmaid for her best friend, but died in a car crash the night before the wedding. Her spirit appears, still dressed in her flowing bridesmaid's gown, and still attempting to get to the wedding on time.

* * *

In October 1959, Charles Collins, a salesman for an industrial engineering firm, was returning to London when he decided to spend the night at the Spread Eagle, a small eighteenth-century coaching inn on the western edge of Salisbury. About midnight, Collins suddenly had the urge to get out of bed and look out of the window. When he did, he saw a man in eighteenth-century costume ride through the yard on a horse. He wore a mask and carried a pistol. Collins was captivated by the sight—until the man suddenly vanished.

In the morning, the landlord unhesitatingly told Collins that he had seen the ghost of a highwayman named Richard Savage, who had been hanged in 1730. Tradition said that he had sought refuge at the Spread Eagle, but the landlord turned him away. Ever since, he had returned to the inn to haunt it. Historical records of the phantom highwayman go back to 1850, and the ghost has been seen on the average of once every five years. In 1962, Savage's spirit was seen by three American tourists staying at the inn.

21
HAUNTED HOTELS, MOTELS, AND INNS

———

BENJAMIN "BUGSY" SIEGEL STILL HAUNTS THE FLAMINGO

If you had checked into the Flamingo Hilton prior to 1993 and were feeling flush enough from your Las Vegas winnings to put up $400 a night, you might have asked for the Presidential Suite and spent the evening with the ghost of Benjamin "Bugsy" Siegel.

The Presidential Suite was the place that the stylish mobster called home, and countless guests who rented the suite since Siegel's death in 1947 swore that his ghost still haunted it. The Flamingo was Siegel's desert dream come true, and the casino-resort has anchored the Las Vegas strip since the arm of the first slot machine was pulled and the first dice were thrown in 1946.

While most of the original furniture used by Siegel and his girlfriend Virginia Hill had been replaced, there were some pieces, such as an end table and bathroom fixtures, which remained. The lime-colored bidet and the pistachio-hued toilet and sink were the ones that Siegel and Virginia used. The green linoleum on the two bathroom floors was also original. In the late 1940s and early 1950s, the ghastly shade of green was considered "class" by the fashionable Siegel.

Although the pool table in the parlor area of the suite was brought in during the early 1970s to replace Siegel's original table, some guests insisted that they heard pool balls rolling around in the middle of the night and that they caught a glimpse of the ghost of the notorious mobster who created Las Vegas.

Benjamin "Bugsy" Siegel, 1941.

Today, a lavish garden grows on the grounds where the original Pink Flamingo building was located. The final wall of Siegel's desert paradise was torn down in 1993, giving way to the luxurious new casino-resort which includes a wildlife habitat and a fifteen-acre Caribbean-style water playground. In the garden there is a plaque that reads, "On this site, Benjamin "Bugsy" Siegel's original Flamingo Hotel stood from December 26, 1946 until December 14, 1993."

Some people who have followed the wandering paths of the garden after dark have reported encountering the ghost of a man that they believe is Benjamin Siegel. Although the gangster was murdered in his house in Beverly Hills, ghostly traditions have long maintained that spirits will return to the place that they held most dear. Others, who have stayed in the Presidential Suite of the new hotel, state with conviction that they have seen the ghost of Siegel making himself comfortable in the plush accommodations of the penthouse.

THE HOTEL ROOSEVELT, HOLLYWOOD'S MOST HAUNTED

If gangster ghosts are not your cosmic cup of tingle, how about the spirits of departed movie stars? Travel a bit farther west from Las Vegas and check into the Hollywood Roosevelt Hotel in Hollywood, and you just might encounter the ghosts of Marilyn Monroe, Montgomery Clift, or Carole Lombard.

Lombard shared her fabulous top-floor suite with Clark Gable, and the elegant decor is basically the way the ill-fated actress left it. The essence of romantic Hollywood is nowhere more powerful than this glamorous star's favorite hideaway. Numerous guests who have shared the romance of this suite have also experienced an encounter with the gorgeous ghost of Carole Lombard.

Marilyn Monroe posed for her first print advertisement on the diving board of the Roosevelt's pool, and she stayed often at the hotel over the years, preferring a second-floor cabana room overlooking the pool. Her favorite mirror is on display in the lower elevator foyer, and numerous individuals have

The Flamingo Hilton Hotel in Las Vegas, Nevada, as it looked in 1979.

claimed they have seen Marilyn's sensuous image near—or superimposed over—their own when they stop to look in the reflecting glass.

In December of 1990 while my wife, Sherry Hansen Steiger, and I were in the lower elevator foyer taping a "Ghosts of Hollywood" segment for a Japanese television program, a hotel guest, curious as to what we were filming,

Marilyn Monroe in front of her favorite mirror, which is now at the Roosevelt Hotel in Hollywood.

stopped to watch the proceedings. Suddenly, he stepped briskly aside as if to avoid a collision with some unseen person and stifled a cry of surprise, which interrupted the scene that we were filming. When the director asked the man what was wrong, he replied, somewhat shaken, "Didn't you see that blonde woman who just brushed by me? If I didn't know Marilyn Monroe was dead, I would have sworn it was her!'

As we quizzed him about his experience, he appeared only mildly interested when we explained that the full-length mirror in the foyer had once been a personal favorite of Marilyn Monroe. "But the woman who brushed by me was solid flesh and blood," he insisted. "She was no ghost!" The man stalked off a bit indignant, both incredulous and angry when we, together with the director and the camera crew, tried to make him understand that there had been no woman visible to the rest of us in the foyer.

Montgomery Clift lived at the hotel for three months during the final stages of filming *From Here to Eternity*. He would often pace the hall outside of his ninth-floor apartment, rehearsing his lines, and sometimes practicing bugle calls—much to the consternation of nearby guests, who were trying to get some sleep.

Kelly Green, one of the personable staff members of the Roosevelt, told us of the dozens of guests who had heard Clift's bugle blowing long after his death in 1966.

Brad and Sherry Steiger with Kelly Green at the very haunted Roosevelt Hotel in Hollywood.

In November of 1990, a witness to the ghostly bugle blasts had been interviewed for inclusion on our segment on Hollywood ghosts for Entertainment Tonight. In October of 1992, Sherry and I wanted to return to the hotel and try to catch the ghost of Clift in the act for ourselves for the new "Haunted Hollywood" segments that we were filming for the 1992 Halloween edition of HBO's *World Entertainment Report*.

The night before filming, Kelly Green made arrangements to place us in the room next to Clift's haunted room on the ninth floor. It was our intention to film in the room early the next morning, so Sherry and I were disappointed to hear a variety of sounds coming from Clift's room, as if it may have been occupied by a family with children.

We couldn't imagine that the thoughtful Ms. Green would book guests—especially a family—in a room that we wished to utilize the next morning for filming, but we really didn't feel that we could complain. It was really quite enough that she was making the room available for us to film the segment the next day. So Sherry and I went to bed sincerely hoping that the next-door guests would check out very early in the morning, which seemed increasingly unlikely when—our neighbors stayed up most of the night, moving noisily about their room. Perhaps it wasn't a family with children after all, for it certainly sounded like they were having a party, and showing little consideration for the neighbors.

Neither of us seasoned ghost hunters could suppress a small shiver that next morning when we learned that Ms. Green had indeed left orders at the desk for the Clift room to remain unoccupied for the convenience of our filming. The thumps and bumps that we had heard all night had been the ghost of Montgomery Clift and his circle of spooks welcoming us to his portion of Haunted Hollywood.

Later that day, Sherry recalled that she had been awakened sometime during the night by what she had thought at the time was one of the rambunctious kids next door blowing on a horn, but she had been too tired from the seminar that we had just completed at a Los Angeles area college for the eerie significance of the bugle blasts to register fully in her sleep-numbed consciousness.

⬤▬▬▬◖▮◗▬▬▬⬤

GHOST HUNT AT THE PICO HOUSE

By Richard Senate

The icy thing seemed to be right next to me on the stairway of the historic hotel. I reached out my hand, found it was shaking and cold, and then touched something. It was as if the thing was wrapping around, embracing my hand. I was wide-eyed, silent, paralyzed as time seemed to slip by. Was it shaking my hand? What seemed like minutes was really only seconds and then it was gone. I caught an impression, a feeling, it was a woman in a long yellow dress, an old-fashioned dress, with her hair piled high. Then the impression was gone. Had I imagined it or did I meet one of the ghosts of the legendary Pico House?

The Pico House is a historic monument today, right next to Olvera Street in downtown Los Angeles. In its prime in the 1870s it was the most lavish hostelry in southern California. It was the brain child of the flamboyant Pio Pico, the last Mexican governor of California, built in the popular Italian palace style. It was state of the art for its day, three stories tall with over eighty rooms, indoor plumbing, and an attached French restaurant. When President U.S. Grant visited Los Angeles, this was where he stayed.

Over the years stories of ghosts have attached themselves to the old hotel. Locals reported seeing faces looking down at them from windows of the unused rooms. Some people even claimed that Pio Pico himself haunted his hotel, peering down onto the street from the roof, sometimes wearing his top hat. Footsteps have been heard—some of them on the roof—and dark supernatural shadow forms have been seen within the structure.

In January of 2011, I was invited by the LA Paranormal group to join them on an investigation of the site. I jumped at the chance. They were actually the second team to investigate this hotel. The first were the fellows from the TV show *Ghost Adventures*. They had detected several ghosts here for their show, even seeing the apparition of a ghost on the third floor.

My good friend and associate Gene Dunn and I met for a tasty taco dinner at one of the Olvera Street eateries, and then at 8:00 P.M., we met the LA Paranormal group in front of the old Pico House. We were divided into teams and entered the hotel through a side door that led to a central courtyard. The courtyard was nothing but bricks now, but history records that it once held an ornate fountain and cages of exotic parrots.

We toured the site. My goal was to start at the top and work my way down so we made our way to the third floor. I detected a classic cold spot on the third floor, near a window. A woman on the team also saw an apparition of a short figure. Oddly enough, it was near the spot where the TV show people had spotted something.

Gene began to use his tools as I continued seeking another site where my equipment might chance upon something. The first thing I detected was on the stairway. Something made my equipment jump, causing a sharp spike in the electromagnetic field. There was nothing to account for it. I was alone, but I began to feel that familiar tingle that I experience just before something paranormal happens. I started downstairs, and it was between the first and second floors that I encountered the "icy woman" or whatever it was. A smile crossed my face. I then knew that all the stories were true—the Pico House is haunted.

On the second floor, Gene and a team member caught something in one of the side rooms. We tried an experiment in communication and the ghost said, through dowsing rods, that it was a boy, a newsboy, who was Italian and who was hiding from someone. A lady member of the team caught the name Stephan, and when asked, the rods indicated, "yes." We asked if it could appear for us. It said, no; then we asked if it could make sound. We heard nothing, but in later examining the recording of the session, there was a tapping sound heard. Was this in answer to our question? Who can say?

Gene took many pictures. In one there was a figure on one of the balcony stairs in the courtyard. He took this picture as we entered, so there was no one in the house or balconies at the time. It is a shadowy figure, almost a black silhouette, but you can see it is wearing a hat—a cowboy-style hat—as it walked, hunched over, going down the steps. Is this a picture of Pio Pico or perhaps one of his many guests who called this place home long ago?

We saw little of the downstairs floor, because it is closed off. The City of Los Angeles is hoping to interest a group in opening a French restaurant there, perhaps recreating the restaurant that stood there in the nineteenth century. It might serve as a counterpoint to the Mexican restaurants on Olvera Street. I believe if that should happen, the restaurant will also become the focus of many haunting experiences.

We continued our investigations at the Masonic Hall's old theater and the tunnels of the basement, but none of these locations held as much supernatural activity as the Pico House itself. We came away convinced that the place is haunted and that more investigations are needed in the future.

⸻⫘⫘⸻

THE VINEYARD HOUSE

By Henry Bailey

I first became aware of the Vineyard House when an episode of the In Search Of *television series featured psychic Sylvia Brown exploring the home, which had been renovated and opened as a bed and breakfast. According to Brown, there were at least five ghosts active at the Vineyard House, and it was, at the time, the most haunted home she had ever visited.*

I will say that although I have spent countless hours and nights in haunted locations, I have never been in one so odious as the Vineyard. Hot, electric, menacing. It was oppressive, and at least the second floor had a taint of madness to it. I was never able to sleep there at all. The one common bathroom among the eight guest rooms on the second floor did have an uncanny habit of locking people in.

Traveling through gold rush country in Coloma, California, a turn from Route 49 onto Cold Spring Road will take you to the dream house of Robert and Louisa Chalmers. Located just above the South Fork of the American River in El Dorado County, The Vineyard House still stands silhouetted against the trees a short distance across the street from the family cemetery.

Robert, along with his friend Martin Allhoff, had originally arrived in the area at the beginning of the gold rush, but met with little success in mining for gold. Returning to Ohio, the pair was determined to return to Coloma and gold country. This return trip would also include Martin's new wife, fourteen-year-old Louisa Weaver.

While riches in gold had evaded them, Martin's stake in opening a vineyard in the area led to financial and social rewards in the community. The high elevation and soil were excellent for producing fine wines. But life for Martin would soon end; he committed suicide after a variety of legal problems led to his imprisonment in 1868. Some people in town speculated that Louisa had driven Martin to suicide as much as his legal problems. Shortly after his death, she married Robert.

Robert and Louisa had begun working on their prosperous vineyard, and in 1878 they built a four-story, nineteen-room house, complete with a ninety-foot ballroom and music room. They named their home The Vineyard. The Victorian-style building was the site of the town's high society parties, and the games of the Chalmers's children.

Tragedy soon followed the family's success, as they began to lose some of their young children to illness. Robert was reported to have contracted syphilis or been the victim of some other disease of the nervous system, and, as blindness and mental illness overcame him, Louisa chained him in a windowless room in the basement of the home. Convinced that Louisa was trying to poison him with the food delivered to his cell, Robert stopped eating and died of starvation in 1880.

Henry Bailey.

The days of wealth and society also ended for Louisa as blight moved through and destroyed the grapes that had brought the family wealth and notoriety. Left with no income from the winery and unable to pay her creditors, Louisa opened the home to boarders as an inn and restaurant. Perhaps as part of an agreement with a judge who allowed her to stay in the home, the cell which once held Robert was also rented out for town prisoners, and at least a few were hanged on the oak tree by the courtyard of the house. Louisa's death in 1900 saw her buried in the cemetery across the street with Robert, the children, and others who had been placed there before her.

But death apparently did not bring an end to Louisa's occupation of The Vineyard House or at least the spirit of the woman often considered partly guilty in the death of Martin and Robert. It seems that the move to the cemetery was only temporary for Louisa, Robert, their children, and myriad guests of both the Vineyard House and the jail cells.

The home, having gone through multiple owners, was opened to the public in the mid-1970s by Darlene and Frank Herrera, who put in a great deal of effort to restore the Victorian residence and furnish it with museum-quality pieces. The jail cells had been transformed into a bar and vegetables were once again grown in the garden and served on the first-floor patio along with period entrées for dinner. Like Robert and Louisa, the new owners were proud of the restored home overlooking the small city of Coloma. Any suggestions of a haunting were kept to a whisper by the owners and staff, but who could explain cups and items in the small souvenir shop moving across the counter-top in front of guests? Unfortunately, I had decided to stay overnight in the middle of summer during a particularly hot June.

The drive to the Vineyard House takes one up a small hill overlooking the center of Coloma, a city that was once the bustling site of the California Gold Rush. The home sits overlooking the town, removed from those still-working mining claims but not removed from the history and chaos of the Gold Rush. In fact, history never quite left the Vineyard House. It is still there. The home is almost alive with it.

Darlene and Frank had done a wonderful job with bringing life back to the Vineyard House. They had completed a restoration so true to the period that they may have brought back the Chalmers family, and prior visitors—both the willing and the unwilling few who were held in the jail cells and whose last view of the home was from the prominent oak tree in the courtyard.

During my visit the home was in excellent condition and antiques from the 1800s were well arranged throughout the house, including period items in the guest rooms. The music room and ballroom had become a restaurant that featured a grand piano on a hardwood floor and a lovely chandelier in the cen-ter of the room. The stairs to the second story were carpeted with the same patterns popular during the time the house had been built. The guest rooms were all located on the second floor and shared one bathroom, while the jail cells were adjacent to the home and had been converted into a bar.

It was in the bar area where my brother, Greg, who had made an earlier visit to the Vineyard House, became extremely ill and experienced a nosebleed that sent him to his room and caused him to cancel further plans to visit the bar again. He had complained of a distinct and unpleasant pressure in the area of the jail cells, and feeling a need to escape. For many visitors that feeling extended to the bed-and-breakfast rooms in the home as well. For along with those visitors enjoying a taste of homemade cooking and a taste for history, or those planning a rafting trip on the American River, came a different and more lively set of visitors from the home's past.

At least one couple had packed up during the night and left, later that evening explaining to authorities in nearby Placerville that a murder had occurred in the room next to theirs. The police discovered nothing. Other guests have watched as their locked doors opened, and many had reported the sounds of rustling dresses, arguments, period music, and banging on walls while they were the only guests in the home. Staff members have reported see-

Vineyard House.

ing candles floating in the hallway, souvenirs moving across the counter, and beds that were just made being undone and left with an impression of a person on them. Bartenders in the old jail cell area had become used to the routine movement of glasses across the counter and the feeling of extreme cold in a certain area of the cells.

Two of the three Chalmers's children—Robert, Jr., who died at the age of three, and William, who died at age six—still seem to be present in the house, as guests have reported some of the activity as playful. Apparently, one dinner guest had a young child ask for assistance with mashing his potatoes and then requested a cracker. The lady diner did not realize until later that there were no children present at the hotel.

My own experience in room five, which I later learned had a disturbing reputation for strange activity, did not allow me any sleep. It had a palpable energy that seemed restless and quite aware of my presence. I was aware of it, too, and apparently I was not welcome. I had a strong sense of a heartbeat to the room.

Over the years, the Vineyard House has seen all manner of activity, sights, sounds, scents, and poltergeist activity. It has a reputation in Coloma and Placerville as a haunted location. It is famous for the low lying fog that seems to hang ever so close to the home and nowhere else at different times of the year. And it's also famous for driving prospective ghost hunters off the property.

Today, the Vineyard House is no longer a bed-and-breakfast. It is a privately owned property with no trespassing signs and we respect it as such. I just

The family cemetery plot at Vineyard House.

wished they had posted one of those signs in the bathroom when ghostly forces locked me in.

* * *

Highly respected paranormal researcher Henry Bailey had this to say about his path exploring the unknown:

I picked up my first ghost book at the age of fourteen. I've been visiting, researching, and investigating haunted locations since I could drive. I'm at the ripe old age of sixty-one now. I started out with an interest before we had knowledge of EVP, EMF, or other supposed equipment that would offer some evidence of ghosts. I grew up reading Brad Steiger's books, Hans Holzer's books, Richard Winer's books, Barbara Smith's books, the books by Beth Scott and Michael Norman; they and many others—including the early explorers such as Colin Wilson and Peter Underwood, not to forget Harry Price—were among my favorites. I was reading Aleister Crowley at the age of fourteen and knew Israel Regardie when he was in Studio City. I've probably forgotten more about the occult than most will know. I counted Raymond Buckland among my friends and Scott Cunningham. I've studied with Michael Harner and

Sandra Ingerman. I've met and had long discussions with Gerald Suster and Pete Caroll. I also counted Hans Nintzel as one of my friends.

My family lived in no less than two haunted homes and two haunted apartments. I believe that was what originally led me to look into the paranormal. One house was particularly disturbing. I was age fourteen when I had my first experiences with the paranormal and there were no ready explanations for it. So, with no ready answers, I set out on my own to investigate the field. Later, I discovered that I could help others. I investigated many, many hauntings in California, and many in Washington state. I decided to form the Washington State Ghost Society so others could learn and help families with questions. We worked throughout the state to assist people and to investigate hauntings. After my move to Texas, I was pretty much on my own again, but went about investigating anything I could find there as well.

Most of my writings have been on the Internet, although I did have a few brief stories published in *The Encyclopedia of Haunted Places* by Jeff Belanger. I've been on radio, TV, and local newscasts, featured in a documentary film and in newspaper articles. My favorite was the episode of *Dead Famous* TV series because we had a lot happen that night.

Everything I've done I've either done for free or it has cost me money. No regrets about any of it. I still stay as a member of the American Ghost Society because I appreciate Troy Taylor's skeptical attitude and historical research. I'm an independent investigator, helping those who ask, and doing a lot of learning myself everyday.

THE CRESCENT HOTEL

By Henry Bailey

Traveling through the Ozarks in the fall gives one a panoramic definition of seasonal changes. The multitude of trees on those winding roads and small hills offer a fabric of color rivaling any in New England. The red, yellow, orange, and purple hues dot the landscape like sheets of color laid out among the small creeks and springs. It's a living testament to change. But if you were to drive into Eureka Springs, Arkansas and look up at the Crescent Hotel, that "Grand Old Lady of the Ozarks," you might find that change does not come so easily in every area of the Ozarks, and history does have a way of repeating itself.

Plans for the Crescent Hotel were drawn up by famed architect Isaac L. Taylor in 1884 during a period when train travel had become quite popular and proper accommodations at stops along the way for wealthy guests were needed. The location of the Crescent is on the last stop of the "Trail of Tears," the forced relocation route of the Cherokee and other tribes from their ancestral homes in the East in 1838. The construction on the huge building lasted from 1884 to 1886 and was financed by Powell Clayton (the first Reconstruction governor of Arkansas), other wealthy local investors, and officials from the Frisco Railroad. They hoped to capitalize on travelers seeking rejuvenation and health from the waters of the healing springs made famous by Native American lore and Dr. Alvah Jackson. After all, they had decided to build on ground held sacred by the Sioux, Caddo, Iroquois, Cherokee, and Osage tribes. That, combined with Dr. Jackson's mail-business of selling his "Dr. Jackson's Eye Water," would bring a great deal of attention, and most importantly, paying guests to the community. Even now, although it is no longer sourced in Eureka, Dr. Jackson's miracle water is still bottled as Ozarka Water and distributed by the Perrier Group. Eureka's waters had gained national fame when they were used to treat injured combatants during the Civil War and continued to be popular for drinking and bathing.

With the plans completed and finances provided by the Eureka Springs Improvement Company, Irish stone masons from St. Louis were hired for the construction. Although some later reports state that the stone used in the building was granite, the foundation and the eighteen-inch walls of the Crescent were actually built from limestone furnished by the quarry on the nearby White River, which also provided the stones for earlier construction in Eureka Springs. The very dense limestone from the region allowed the masons to fashion the building together without the use of mortar.

And so the "Grand Old Lady of the Ozarks" rose up six hundred feet above the Crescent Springs looking down on the city of Eureka Springs. The mixed French Gothic architecture, with its many towers and balconies, created a classic look of imposing grandeur. The overly large lobby includes a huge fireplace made from locally quarried stones. The 125-room building, now consisting of seventy-six guest rooms and cottages, included a dining room designed to feed five hundred people at one sitting, and an extensive twenty-six acres of lawns, gardens, gazebos, and tennis courts. Marble floors and interior woodwork were provided by Swedish carpenters who worked their craft to create what was once referred to as the most opulent hotel in the United States. Although the Crescent has undergone quite a few renovations and it now only occupies fifteen acres of recreational land, it still dominates the landscape as it did originally.

The Crescent Hotel formally opened on May 10, 1886, under the management of G. W. Kittelle. The invocation was delivered by a Reverend McElwee, which apparently did not prevent later manifestations of the spirit of one of the workmen who had fallen to his death from an upper floor into what is now room 218. The original construction costs were to be above $100,000, a huge sum during the time, and eventually rose to $294,000. The investors were anxious to see a return on their investment, and in fact, the Crescent did a brisk business, with wealthy and middle-class tourists arriving by train and, later, automobile. The visitors came to indulge in a bit of Victorian elegance, the excellent air, and views, but mostly for the healing properties reputed to be in the waters of the local springs. Still, the hazards of winter travel and the recognition, that while quite enjoyable, the local waters offered no curative powers, reduced the flow of tourists to the hotel. The five-year lease of the Frisco Railroad System ended in 1908 and the hotel operation was taken over by Crescent Management, who had also secured a lease on the downtown Basin Park Hotel from W.M. Duncan Operations. The property was taken over by Phillips and Maddox of the Crescent group.

In 1908, in an attempt to raise the income needed to operate the hotel, A.S. Maddox and J.H. Phillips operated a school for wealthy young women as the "Crescent College and Conservatory for Young Women" during the winter and maintained the Crescent as a hotel during summer. The Conservatory operated until 1924, and again from 1930 to 1934, when it operated as the Crescent Junior College for Girls. But, even with the large sums charged for tuition, the money was not enough to offset the costs of operating and maintaining the hotel, which lacked winter tourism. The hotel closed after the 1929 season, operating only as a school, and in late 1931 the property was sold

Soldiers who died on battlefields such as Gettysburg may still linger there, generations after they met their tragic ends.

REAL GHOSTS, RESTLESS SPIRITS, AND HAUNTED PLACES

From Henry Bailey: "The historic photo I sent you of the Crescent shows the original front of the building. That is now the rear of the building and used as a veranda. The current main entrance to the Crescent used to be just across from the train tracks, tracks no longer used. If you were of the poor class you came in directly from the train into the back entrance of the Crescent. If you were of the Gentry, you were taken by carriage to the front entrance. It might be important information to add that I also learned that the hotel was on built right next to the last stop on the Trail of Tears."

to Lloyd Patterson. Due to the Great Depression, even the college closed its doors by 1933, although some accounts suggest that the school operated in some form until 1934. From 1933 until 1937 the Crescent was a languished structure that was leased from Patterson by a series of managers hoping to make a profit. None of them were successful.

It was in 1937 that a major portion of the Crescent's history would take place, as the bizarre and very wealthy Norman Baker bought the grand old Crescent and promptly painted the exterior in a bright lavender color. Baker had made his fortune with the invention of the Tangley Air Calliope or as he called it, the Calliaphone, a device that uses air instead of steam to produce its musical notes. He was also quite a self-promoting charlatan who started his own radio station and used it to rail against the medical establishment and endorse his own treatments of disease. A rather modern-day snake oil salesman, Baker, who had no medical training, believed (or at least led others to believe) that he could cure cancer. A dapper dresser, Baker often wore purple shirts with his white linen suits and had his office in the Crescent painted in purple, blacks, and reds.

He not only repainted the Crescent, but remodeled it, tearing down much of the handmade woodwork, and painting the interior in red, orange, black, and yellow. The original wood entry porch was removed and replaced by concrete and railroad ties. His other modifications included placing a calliope on the roof of the Crescent. He called it his "Castle in the Air" and its music could be heard throughout the city of Eureka Springs. Those who would later restore the Crescent reported finding secret passageways, hidden entrances and exits, and trapdoors in many of the guest room closets. Baker put the finishing touches on his office by installing a huge desk in order to attend to his many business enterprises, decorating the walls of the office with functioning machine guns, and bulletproof glass. After lavender, black, and purple drapes trimmed in gold were hung in the room, he was ready to open his Arkansas hospital and "health resort."

Baker moved his remaining patients and staff from the first hospital he had opened in Muscatine, Iowa, to the Crescent and immediately began a mail-order campaign to recruit more patients. He had been convicted of practicing medicine without a license in Iowa and the location of the Crescent and the healing waters of Eureka Springs offered a new beginning in his battle with the medical establishment. His solicitations promised cancer cures with no X ray treatments and no surgery. He also promised to be able to cure additional ailments by use of the natural spring waters and his miracle elixirs.

While the exact ingredients of his mail-order elixirs are not known, one report states that it was watermelon seed, brown cornsilk, alcohol, and carbolic acid. Baker was reported to have made close to $500,000 dollars a year, doing a brisk business selling his elixirs across the country. His most famous cure for in-resident patients consisted of five or more elixir injections a day, a mixture of ground watermelon seeds and local spring water poured directly onto the patient's cancerous sites, and bathing in and drinking the legendary waters of the area. Other homemade elixirs mixed with alcohol were also commonly used as cures.

Everything went well for Baker for the next two years. His machine guns still mounted to the walls of his office, no further charges of practicing medicine without a license, and an estimated $4,000,000 dollars of income from his mail-order business and Crescent "health resort" allowed him to enjoy life and use his radio station to claim victory over the medical establishment and the American Medical Association. He still dressed in purple and white and even drove his purple Cord automobile into town, but there was a growing unrest in town and rumors of what was taking place up the hill in the Crescent that led to speculation that Baker was far from being a healer. Patients were not returning home and the local funeral homes were quite busy.

Local rumors had begun to circulate that some of Baker's treatments included pouring his solutions directly into the brains of those who had tumors.

Some residents spoke in hushed tones, saying he was sewing good limbs from cadavers onto those who had cancerous ones amputated in order to send photos to relatives showing that they were cured. It was also suggested that he had patients write letters imploring their relatives to send money for their treatments and funeral costs, money that was pocketed by Baker. There were rumors that those in the last stages of cancer would be secretly transported to asylums and poorhouses where they would die without treatment. The suspicions increased when some vanished without a trace and many wondered why a man with no medical experience would maintain a morgue and freezer in the basement. The large incinerator was often warm and the gurney that the night nurse moved through the halls on the third floor after 11:00 P.M. could be heard on many nights by those in residence, oddly enough at the same time that most hospitals move the dead from their rooms. After all, not all the rooms had trapdoors and there was a convenient passage down to the base of the hill.

Whether it was the Calliaphone music playing at night through the town, Baker's eccentricities, or talk of the morgue, freezer, and incinerator, sentiment in the town over Baker's "health resort" soon attracted attention that would again land him in trouble with the law. In late 1939 he was charged in federal court with mail fraud. Convicted shortly after the charges were brought, he would spend the next four years in Leavenworth Prison. While Baker was never directly implicated in the deaths that occurred at his "health resort," it is certain that his promises of a cure caused early deaths. In 1944, Norman Baker, inmate 58197, was released from Leavenworth Prison and lived a comfortable life in Florida until his own death of cancer in 1958.

The Crescent again shut its doors from 1940 to 1946. From 1946 until 1997 ownership of the Crescent would change hands a few times. Each new owner would add to the restoration. After the lavender paint was removed, and the woodwork restored, the Crescent had been described by some writers and visitors as "seedily elegant." Nothing could seemingly erase the years from it. On May 5, 1997, the Crescent Hotel was purchased by Marty and Elise Roenigk and after five million dollars in restorations and a new spa, the Crescent is closely restored to its original look and condition. But, when one walks into it, the history and past scenes there do seem to come back.

Eureka Springs is a small community in Carroll County, Arkansas with an eclectic population of 2,350 people. The redeemed Crescent Hotel still sits on top of the hill among the winding roads and extensive streets and preserved Victorian landscapes. Today people visit the city for the arts and crafts, fine food, religious interests, and very often they visit the Crescent Hotel to walk the lawns or hold their wedding ceremony. Whether starting life by taking marriage vows, hoping that an education will provide a new and better life, trying to escape the end of life, or even relaxing and enjoying life, the guests at the Crescent seem to have something in common. Today, former and current

A view of the front of the Crescent Hotel.

visitors of the grand old haunted hotel are all attempting to catch the memo-ries of former times or make new ones.

Today's Crescent Hotel is a well-traveled and frequently booked hotel. Its history does repeat itself. It may be the dense but porous limestone in the construction, the legendary magnetic creeks and streams, or just the episodes of a traumatic past that have led to reports by guests, staff, and past owners that the Crescent is one of the most haunted hotels in the United States. A pleasant stay there may be nothing more than a pleasant stay—or it may include an old memory from the past or create a new memory for the current guest.

The Crescent certainly epitomizes old-fashioned elegance. A walk into the lobby, a view of the dining room and fireplace, or the scope of the lawn and grounds easily brings back the earlier part of the century—according to many visitors, that era is still alive at the Crescent. The hallways and corridors still have the feel of age and there is a little electricity in the air that does not seem to come from the Southwestern Electric Power Company.

Guests have experienced their bed being shaken at night, hands com-ing out of the bathroom mirror, screaming, shutters being slammed repeatedly while they tried to sleep, pounding on the inside of the stone walls in the room, a feeling of being watched, and both the lights and TV going on and off. The rooms in the original building have door knobs that are centered on the door, not on the left-hand side as we have today. It's not unusual for them to rotate as if someone were trying to open the door. The ghost of Dr. C. F. Ellis, the first hotel physician, is often seen wandering the building in a stovepipe hat. The odor of tobacco smoke usually announces his presence. The wife of one of the former owners of the hotel was found running and screaming down the hallway saying that she woke up in the room one night to see blood on the walls. The staff found nothing.

Room 218 is reportedly haunted by the spirit of the workman who fell from the rafters and died in the nearly completed room. The staff has given him the name Michael and he has been known to play tug-of-war with at least one housekeeper and her cart. The shutters in the room have a habit of slamming, even in a mild wind. Actual sightings of the supposed red-haired Irish workman are few, but he is described as a young man in his twenties with bushy blond/reddish hair and a short beard. The activity in room 218 has earned it the most-haunted room designation in the hotel. It seems that Michael is attached primarily to room 218 and loves to slam doors on guests as well as lock and open them, but the doors to any room on the second floor seem to have a habit of opening and closing on guests. In fact, some guests have experienced the opening and closing of doors in unoccupied rooms next to them all night.

Room 218 is far from being the only room on the second floor with poltergeist activity attributed to it. In the hallway outside of Room 219, a young boy has been seen bouncing a ball loudly enough to wake guests. He has been heard saying, "It is not fair. It's not fair." When I tried to take photos in Room 219, my camera would not work. When I set it on the dresser, it turned itself on. A photo was taken in room 202 that appears to show a ghost cowering in the closet and another photo shows the shadow of a man in a wide-brimmed hat hovering over the headboard of the bed in the room. Visitors to room 203 have reported having their bed shaken during the middle of the night, and guests have reported strange happenings in rooms, 205, 209, 210, 221, and 216. It seems that both Michael and paying guests have a lot of company during their stay on the second floor. Still, room service is reportedly excellent, as even a ghostly waiter walks the hallways carrying a tray of butter to no room in particular.

I should mention that late-night knocks on the door on any floor are not uncommon, nor are doors of unoccupied rooms opening and shutting, sometimes slamming. The third floor seems to have fewer reports of haunting activity but most certainly those staying in rooms 303, where blankets are folded and moved off and on the bed and sometimes back into the closet, might disagree. And some guests have awakened at night in room 309 to find a man in a black suit standing at the foot of their bed. It's also between the third and fourth floor where screams can be heard coming from a young woman who once attended the "Crescent College and Conservatory for Young Women" and fell to her death either by jumping or being pushed.

In the spring of 1967, a fire destroyed a third of the fourth floor of the South Wing. This required major restoration. It was reputedly on the fourth floor where Baker kept his terminally ill patients and it is on this floor that the spirit of a nurse, dressed all in white, repeatedly performs her duty of pushing a gurney. She is seen only after 11:00 P.M., the time when they used to move the deceased out of the cancer hospital; her spirit vanishes when she reaches the end of the hallway. Although there have been sightings of the nurse on her rounds, most have reported the sounds of squeaking and creaking wheels that sound like a gurney rolling down the hallway. Many of Baker's "Spa and Health Resort" guests would die in agony on the fourth floor.

When I tried to take photos in Room 219, my camera would not work. When I set it on the dresser, it turned itself on.

While the fourth-floor restaurant, nicely named "Dr. Baker's Bistro and Sky Bar" and decked out in a purple motif, seems to be relatively ghost-free, the fourth floor is famous for hauntings. Room 419 is referred to as "Theodora's" room. She was apparently a former patient of Baker's "Health Spa" and has been seen and heard by both staff and visitors staying in room 419. There is at least one tape recording made in room 419 that states in response to a quest's question that her name is Theodora. Both staff and visitors have encountered odd activities in the room. The most common encounters with Theodora include a brief appearance in which she announces she is a cancer patient looking for the key to her room. She also seems to prefer privacy since some guests and staff experienced trouble opening the door to the room or find it keeps locking on its own. She seems to enjoy locking the closet as well. Room 424 is famous for the repeated sighting of a gentleman dressed in black who casually walks through the closed door of the room and disappears into the bathroom.

The lobby, bar, and dining room also appear to be busy with return guests. While there are no records regarding the death of a black- mustached Victorian gentleman in a frock coat and frill shirt on the grounds or in the hotel, his spirit certainly seems to enjoy having a drink at the bar and following guests around. He also enjoys walking on the second floor and particularly down the hallway and by room 218. Some guests have tried to engage him in conversation at the bar but receive no response. Others have spotted him sitting down to eat a rack of lamb in the Crystal Dining Room alone, when no such meal is on the current menu. He particularly likes to haunt the lobby area and at least one staff member was at the check-in counter when the main doors opened accompanied by a very cold gust of air, followed by the appearance of a mischievous and grouchy spirit. He's also reported standing at the bottom of the staircase or by the elevator.

The Crystal Dining Room has been well restored, enough so, that often visitors to it will see or hear Victorian diners enjoying meals, drinks, dancing, and laughter. But, it seems those visitors from the past are jealous of their space. Some current diners have been pushed while seated or actually experienced the chairs being pulled out from under them. Place settings and chair arrangements have, on occasion, been known to be altered but not by the current staff. Even the kitchen staff is not immune to the antics. A young boy in period clothing has been spotted on occasion just before the hanging pots and pans start flying off the wall.

For a short time the hotel owners tried to maintain the antique switchboard that had been in the building when they purchased it, but hurried the upgrade to a new system when calls kept coming in from the building's basement. The basement housed the old recreation room, which was currently locked and unused. Visits to it after frequent calls to the desk revealed it to be tightly locked, but interestingly after every series of calls the phone in the basement was found off the hook. The locked door was the only way in or out of the basement.

> **A young boy in period clothing has been spotted on occasion just before the hanging pots and pans start flying off the wall.**

It was in the basement/recreation area, away from the terminally ill patients too sick to take part in any recreation, that Baker would have potential patients sign over their savings for a chance at life. It was here that Baker would call up his operator and have patients call relatives to send money. And, it is in the basement/recreation area that a hurried and confused Baker is still often seen. He's also seen furtively looking around at the steps of the stairs to the first floor, perhaps some part of him is still expecting the arrival of the authorities or angry relatives or longing for the sanctuary of his office and machine guns.

Some of the ghostly guests might have just stepped out of the morgue Baker maintained in the hotel. The morgue, along with the freezer for cadavers and the autopsy table, is still in the hotel and available for view as part of the ghost tour held in the hotel. The morgue is complete with old bottles of formaldehyde, surgical tools, mixing agents for Baker's homemade cures, and at least one well-photographed specter that does not like visitors and loves to upset them. And, while many guests arrive hoping to be poked, prodded, and touched by the staff at the Crescent's luxurious "New Moon Spa & Salon," some will find that this is not an exclusive service offered just by those currently employed by the spa. The proximity of the spa to the basement and morgue might make the dim-lit massage experience a little more intriguing.

During the heyday of the hotel, one could see up to seventy-five individuals riding horses on the local trails, many enjoying picnics on the lawn, playing croquet, drinking, eating, or enjoying a good cigar on the veranda. Today many guests suggest that you still can see figures from the Crescent's time of opulence walking the grounds. Whether it's the sight of a "girl in the mist" from the old "Crescent College and Conservatory for Young Women," a past visitor of the carriage set enjoying their money, or a cancer patient from Baker's "Health Spa," current guests might find that history does have that strange way of mingling itself with the present. Once, when I sat on one of the downstairs rocking chairs, a chair two down from mine began rocking along with me. It stopped when I stood up, then began rocking again when I sat down.

Another interesting thing about the Crescent is you never know where the friendly service will come from. One guest who had made reservations called to cancel them, only to be informed that they had already been cancelled, while another guest arriving home from a stay at the Crescent had placed their bags on the bed at home only to find them unpacked when they returned to the bedroom.

Is the Crescent Hotel haunted? It's been investigated by the SyFy Channel's *Ghost Hunters* and been featured in "Haunted Road Trips," in USA Today, and on the Biography's Channel's program, *My Ghost Story*. The hotel's website includes a long list of stories from guests regarding their experiences there. Guests have sent the hotel management thousands of photos of shapes and forms that are not readily explained. On many lists of haunted hotels in the United States, the Crescent occupies spots in the top ten (and even top five in some cases). Numerous paranormal groups have walked away with strange recordings and photos after a visit to the Crescent. One thing that is certain is that the "Grand Old Lady of the Ozarks" certainly has given a home to those seeking to meet the past.

For my part, a one-night stay at the Crescent, during the fall, when the Ozark tree leaves are packed with color is not enough. I still want to visit room 3500 and discover more about the lady in the Victorian lingerie who has been heard in the room and photographed as a reflection in the room's TV set. Perhaps I will get a chance to ask for a performance from pre-Word War I ballroom dancer Irene Castle, who was recently identified by a young girl as one of the ghosts of the Crescent. Either way, I'm going to repeat some history and have a Baker's Bistro Burger.

⊸⫘⟁⫘⊷

SLEEPLESS IN BELLINGHAM

The personal ghostly encounter of Sherry Hansen Steiger

In the mid–1990s, during one of our frequent speaking tour engagements—in which we lecture, conduct seminars, make local radio and television appearances and book signings—my husband, Brad, and I had just completed several events on the West Coast and were about to land at the airport in the beautiful state of Washington.

The Washington event was sponsored by our friend Benjamin Smith who picked us up from the airport, briefed us on the logistics and updates regarding the next few days of our seminars, and then with an extra twinkle in his eye enthusiastically told us of a surprise he'd arranged for our overnight lodging. Ben could hardly contain his excitement, but he made it clear that he didn't want to tell us too much about the castle where we would be guests because he didn't want to influence our opinions or experience of the place.

We had known Ben for quite some time, so during the last segue of the drive from the airport en route to our destination we chatted, sharing old times and catching up on things before getting back to the business at hand. As we neared Bellingham, it was already far later in the evening than when we had hoped to arrive. Inclement weather, flight delays, and the like had put us in past dark and served to remind us yet again why we like to arrive in a city the day before our scheduled appearances.

There was little doubt that Ben had worked long and hard to put this seminar together in his usual expert and efficient manner, so Brad and I were certain his surprise had a great deal of thought behind it as well. As we approached the "castle," Ben expressed his regret that we had not been able to view it first during the daylight hours. Any doubts he might have had regarding our approval of this overnight stay were allayed before he was able to complete the rest of his sentence by declaring, "This is it." I let out a squeal of delight as Brad simultaneously said, "Wow! You weren't kidding."

We could see why Ben referred to the bed-and-breakfast as a castle. Even through the black hues of a dark and stormy night the proud, looming structure betrayed her magnificence as she beckoned us into her Victorian elegance and enticed us with her secrets. It almost seemed destined that we should arrive on a stormy night with the stage set for an experience we were never to forget.

We entered through the kitchen where the owners greeted us warmly, expressed their delight at our being there, and graciously made us feel at home. Promising a more complete tour of the mansion the next day when we wouldn't disturb the other guests, (who were most likely already asleep), we were escorted to the room reserved for us—passing the most incredible antiques and luxurious decor at every twist and turn along the way through the halls and up many stairs.

During their many global expeditions, the owners spared no expense in acquiring some of the most elaborate and unusual antiques I had ever seen. And all these treasures had been carefully selected and transported to the Bellingham Bed and Breakfast. Representing what seemed to be every culture from the farthest corners of the earth, there was nary a square inch that didn't have some interesting intrigue or history associated with it and a story to tell. Differing themes embellished the guest rooms—each one decorated in an elaborate, unusual motif and eclectic style reminiscent of a bygone era, but styled with immense creativity.

After showing us the bathroom we would share with other rooms on our floor, they opened the door to our most amazing room. The wallpaper, drapes, bedspreads, lampshades, overstuffed lounging chairs, as well as a canopy of sorts over the head of the bed, were all done in a matching pattern with deep blue hues and an Oriental flair. Although lush, the room was illuminated by low lighting and it was somewhat dark, so it was suggested that we leave a light on all night, in case we needed to get up. We said our goodnights as we settled into our room after a very tiring day of traveling. At that time in our lives, we were traveling so much that it wasn't unusual for Brad and I to wake up during the night and forget which city we were in—so we readily agreed to the wisdom of leaving a light on. We chose the floor lamp with a large Victorian shade next to an overstuffed chair on the other side of the room from our bed.

> His demeanor was grim and it looked as if he was in a great deal of pain with his head down—cradled in his hands—almost like he was crying.

It was late and we were exhausted, and knowing we were going to be up early, we settled into the comfy feather bed and promptly fell into a deep sleep. A few hours later, I was awakened by the feel of the bed covers being pulled to Brad's side of the bed. I started to tug some back to cover me, then noticed that Brad seemed restless. Thinking he was just trying to get comfortable in a new bed, I fell back asleep.

Once again I was awakened, only this time when I rolled over and looked at Brad, I saw that he was sitting up on his side of the bed, holding his head in his hands. Thinking he must have a bad headache or not be feeling well, I asked him if he was okay. Getting no immediate response, I asked again, only a bit louder this time. Suddenly I was startled beyond belief when Brad answered me—from a prone position still under the covers and apparently not happily awakened by me!

"Weren't you just sitting up on the side of the bed" I asked somewhat confused.

"What are you talking about?" Brad muttered. "I'm trying to sleep!"

Shrugging it off as the results of being overtired, I watched as Brad pulled the covers back over his head and went back to sleep. With this movement of pulling the covers over his head I could clearly see he definitely was not sitting on the bed—now at least—and I drifted back to sleep.

Sometime later, I awakened again and saw that Brad was not in bed. Looking around the room, I saw him sitting in the chair next to the lighted lamp. His demeanor was grim and it looked as if he was in a great deal of pain with his head down—cradled in his hands—almost like he was crying.

Concerned, I cried out to him. "Honey, what's wrong? Do you have a headache? Can I get you some aspirin, water, or something?"

There beneath the covers next to me, grumbling with great dissatisfaction that I disturbed his sleep yet again, Brad uttered loudly, "I am trying to sleep, for heaven's sake!"

With the sound of Brad's voice, the solid image of the man in the chair vanished! I dared not say another word. At this point I was grateful that Brad fell asleep immediately, but I lay there for a few minutes, pondering what in the world was going on.

This strange state of affairs continued on and off on three or four more occasions. Two of the times I distinctly saw Brad—or so I thought—pacing the room, back and forth, back and forth, each time acting extremely upset and disturbed. Another time, he was sitting in the chair again, holding his head and shaking it.

Finally, it just seemed too real and I became convinced that Brad just didn't want to worry me, so I blurted out shrilly and loudly enough so that I was worried that I'd awakened the guests in the rooms next to ours: "Honey, please, please … tell me what's wrong!"

With that outburst, Brad woke up once again and, after I told him what I had been seeing and experiencing, we both had the shocking realization that the physical being I thought was Brad in distress was not him at all. Without too much further discussion, we decided if we were going to be at all coherent for our lectures the next day, we'd better try to get some sleep. We decided that maybe we both had better take some aspirin, and somehow, we managed to doze off once more.

Mercifully, another few hours passed, allowing us to sleep peacefully, until I was awakened by Brad's hand clasping mine ever so gently under my pillow. Thinking it odd that he would awaken me, yet guessing he was just reassuring me—or himself—that we were both really still there in bed, I squeezed his hand.

Dozing off, I felt the squeeze of my hand again. This time, I raised up my head from the pillow, sputtering, "Why are you grabbing my hand?" Then looking over at Brad, I saw that he was facing the other direction with his arms and hands on the opposite side. There was no way he could have just squeezed my hand; furthermore, he was sound asleep.

How I was able to drift off to sleep again, I really don't know, but I did, and thankfully, Brad didn't wake up, even with yet another of my outbursts. However, the tranquility was not to last.

A short time later, an electrical sensation pierced my entire body as I was literally shocked into feeling something or someone trying to get my full attention with yet another squeeze of my hand. This time it was with a jolt that startled me to the point of full consciousness. I was wide awake.

With total wakefulness, an awareness hit me and I absolutely knew that the hand that had been squeezing mine under my pillow was a baby's hand. I could literally feel teeny, tiny fingers wrap around mine and give a gentle squeeze. Seeing that Brad was still lying still and facing the other direction, I knew that even if he had been capable of grabbing my hand and rolling over fast in the hopes of carrying off some kind of joke, his hand was ten times larger than the one I felt clasping mine.

Just before the owners of the bed-and-breakfast had said goodnight to us after showing us to our room, they described a spectacular breakfast feast of homemade goodies that sounded too good to miss. The meal was served in a formal manner in the dining room at an appointed time, and as I glanced at the clock after this final rude awakening, I knew it was time to get ready if we were to be there

> This time it was with a jolt that startled me to the point of full consciousness. I was wide awake.

on schedule. Sitting bolt upright with the many occurrences of the night surging through my mind and body, I didn't quite know what to do next. Brad rolled over and upon seeing me sitting up said, "I guess it's time to get up if we are to make that early morning breakfast."

"Honey," I said, "I don't know how much you remember of what happened last night, but I have to tell you about it." Quickly I described the events from beginning of the evening to the present—ending with the squeeze of my hand by what I felt to be a baby's hand. I asked if he would convey my apologies to our hosts for not making the breakfast, as I had looked forward to it, but that I felt a guidance to stay and pray and meditate.

Brad's first concern was for me, that I would need to eat before our lecture and seminar, but he was persuaded that whatever was going on was indeed more important for me to figure out. Acknowledging that he remembered me waking him up with the weird proclamations about seeing him pacing, sitting holding his head, and squeezing my hand, he asked what I thought had really taken place, since it certainly was not he who had done these things. My answer was that I needed to go into prayer and find out.

Brad dressed and went on down, telling me he'd try to at least bring me coffee or something to nibble on. Telling him not to worry, I went into prayer for guidance. It came to me that there was an infant that truly was clasping onto me for help and that it was somehow "stuck" between worlds not knowing where it was. I filled and surrounded myself with light and a prayer for protection as I was urged to pray the baby into the light. Praying that God's will be done and that I be led to what to do next, I felt a baby's hand grab onto me again and then felt the arms of a blessed angel gently lift the infant with immense love and understanding and carry it off to free it from the earthly realm of confusion.

An hour and a half must have passed before Brad entered the room to find me still in prayer. His presence was exuberant as he could hardly wait to tell me of the discussion that had ensued at the breakfast table. Brad and Ben met before the others joined in, so, addressing Ben's surprise at my absence, Brad explained a few of my experiences. When the others, including the owners of the bed-and-breakfast, were all gathered at the table, Brad explained my absence by saying that I had a rather sleepless night. Ben laughed and added that he wasn't surprised at what I had picked up on, said, "Wow, that's why we wanted to put you guys in that room!"

With that, the owners of the mansion were too intrigued to wait for details, so they asked if Brad would mind sharing what had happened to me throughout the night. As Brad was recounting the rest of the discussion to me, my first impulse was that of dismay that this strange uncanny episode of mine was being made public when I wasn't even certain of what it was. But then, when Brad described what the owners had told him about what had really happened in that bedroom to the original owners and builders of the mansion, my heart skipped a beat!

The original owner's love and devotion for his wife took form in the physical manifestation of building this mansion for her, and the two of them had eagerly hoped to fill it with the laughter of children. The expectant joy on the night that his wife was giving birth to their first child was suddenly turned to horror when what seemed at first to be the normal screams of child labor, changed to screams from the midwife at something gone very wrong. As the newborn baby cried upon taking its first breath of a life, the wailing and weeping of the midwife revealed the beloved mother was giving up the last breaths of her life. The husband watched grief stricken as his dear wife's life was terminated in what seemed a sacrificial act of giving birth. It was as though this terrible scene was etched in the memory banks of the very walls of this bedroom where the terrible tragedy took place. It may have been that I had picked up on the extreme emotions of a sorrow and grief beyond measure.

It was said that the owner was in such despair that he constantly paced his bedroom, back and forth, and frequently sat in his chair, holding his head in disbelief and anguish.

The second tragedy that I may have experienced was when the child, while still an infant, succumbed to the dreaded scarlet fever and died in its crib in the middle of the night in that very room. The Father's grief was so overwhelming that he was able to do little more than pace and pace and sit on the side of the bed or in his chair, holding his head. No doubt his heart was broken.

Brad and Sherry Steiger in their room at the Bellingham, Washington, bed and breakfast where they spent a sleepless night.

Later, the owners of the mansion attended our lecture, and asked me if I would mind telling my story before we began our presentation. They found it amazing that without any prior knowledge of the history of the house or information about the previous owners, I had picked up on so many details. It was as if I had seen the events as they had occurred originally. Whether it was an experience in which I traveled back in time, or I was sensitive enough to perceive an energy that was recorded (like a record or a tape) in the ethers of time and space, or if ghostly manifestations had called my attention to their unfortunate tragedy, it was without any doubt a sleepless night in Bellingham—and one that neither Brad nor I will ever forget!

<hr />

HAUNTED HOTELS ACROSS NORTH AMERICA

There are many haunted hotels and motels in North America. Here are just a few of my favorites. Check Dennis William Hauck's Haunted Places: The National Directory *for many more:*

St. James Hotel, Cimarron, New Mexico

A glimpse of an old guest register at the St. James Hotel reads like a "Who's Who of the Wild West" : Billy the Kid, Pat Garrett, Bat Masterson, Black Jack Ketchum, Doc Holliday, Buffalo Bill Cody ....

Almost any room in this 120-year-old hotel—a favorite of gunfighters in the 1880s—will produce an active spirit encounter. According to yellowed newspaper accounts, twenty-six people have died violently at the St. James, and the dining room ceiling remains pockmarked with bullet holes. If you should decide to give the St. James a try, it would probably be best to avoid Room 18. Things got a little too wild in that room back in the 1880s, and the spirits there are too hostile and aggressive for most folks.

Bartenders and chefs in the hotel complain that food and crockery disappear from under their noses. Bottles and glasses float in the air and sometimes shatter in loud explosions.

"A lot of gunfighters checked into this old hotel," a bartender exclaimed. "But their spirits have never got around to checking out!"

The Mission of San Antonio de Padua, California

There are guest accommodations in the old Mission of San Antonio de Padua, located in the central California mountains of the Santa Lucia range, thirty miles north of Paso Robles (see additional details in chapter 18). Constructed in 1771, the Mission remains an enchanted, spiritual, haunted place. If you can make arrangements to stay overnight, you might very well catch sight of the ghosts of several monks, the benevolent spirit of Father John Baptist, and the mysterious entity that manifests as a headless woman on horseback.

The monks who reside in the Mission speak of having often seen a small colored cloud, about three feet square and about eight feet high above the tile roof over the women's guest quarters. The cloud changes color from white to green to blue, then yellow and red.

On numerous occasions in recent years, the mission has been the scene of remarkable spiritual conversions and healings. And the monks speak of such miracles as the appearance of white and purple violets on certain graves within the courtyard.

The Dorrington Hotel, Dorrington, California

The ghost of Rebecca Dorrington walks at night in this 120-year-old hotel in the tiny High Sierra hamlet of Dorrington. The town itself was named for Rebecca, the Scottish bride of John Gardener, a 1850s homesteader who also built the old hotel. Rebecca's eerie nocturnal repertoire consists of banging doors open and shut, flashing lights on and off, and shifting furniture about. Some guests have been "treated" to a ghostly reenactment of Rebecca's fatal tumble down a back stairwell, the accident that cost her her life in 1870.

The Brookdale Lodge in the Santa Cruz Mountains

The sprawling Brookdale Lodge, built in 1924 in the Santa Cruz Mountains near Boulder Creek, California, was a popular hideaway for gangland kingpins in the 1930s. Later, the lodge was a favorite of film legends Marilyn Monroe, Joan Crawford, and Tyrone Power. The colorful inn, which features a brook running through the dining room, has a number of "cold spots," which indicate haunted areas. The most frequently sighted spirit entity is that of a small girl dressed very formally in 1940s-style clothing. The ghost is thought to be that of the five-year-old who drowned in the brook sometime in the late 1940s.

Hotel Monte Vista, Flagstaff, Arizona

The picturesque old Hotel Monte Vista provides a marvelous place for an overnight stay on the way to or from the Grand Canyon. Guests who stay there may encounter the "phantom bellboy," who knocks on doors and announces, "room service," in a muffled voice. Others claim to have seen the wispy image of a woman strolling through an upstairs corridor.

San Carlos Hotel, Phoenix, Arizona

Guests have complained about the noisy children in the halls. When they are informed that there are no children running about unattended, some annoyed patrons have set about trying to prove they aren't going crazy by catching the shouting, squealing, laughing kids who are disturbing their relaxation and sleep. Some frustrated guests who have nearly grabbed one of the little rascals have been astonished to see the child disappear before their eyes.

The only explanation that some investigators have offered for this phenomena is the fact that the old San Carlos Hotel was built sometime in the late 1920s on the site of Phoenix's first adobe elementary school. Perhaps psychically sensitive guests are hearing and seeing the ghosts of schoolchildren from long ago.

The Horton Grand Hotel in San Diego, California

There are so many ghosts at the historic old Horton Grand Hotel in San Diego that the entities often get together and hold dances. Shelly D., who lived at the hotel for two years, claimed to have watched a group of fifteen to twenty ghosts dressed in the style of the 1890s, having a dance in the third-floor ballroom.

It was only after she had watched them for a while that Shelly realized that there was something very strange about the costumed dancers. No one paid the slightest attention to her. Everyone appeared to ignore her when she spoke. Then she noticed that there was something very eerie about their eyes, kind of dark and hollow. The ghostly figures didn't seem to mind the intrusion of her physical presence. Shelly wondered if she was observing the recreation of some past scene that had once occurred in the hotel. She remembered that they swung their partners round and round and seemed to be having a great time.

Room 309 receives the most nominations for "most haunted" in the Horton Grand. Research has revealed that a gambler named Roger Whittaker was murdered in that room in the 1880s.

Dan Pearson, the owner of the Horton Grand, said that he first became aware that there were strange things happening in Room 309 when he brought workmen in to renovate it in 1986. Later, as Pearson walked by the room with a psychically talented friend, the man stopped suddenly and said, "There's something going on in that room! I feel it strongly!"

Three months later, Pearson said that a guest at the hotel staying in Room 309 found her young daughter carrying on an animated conversation with someone else in the room. "Don't you see him, Mommy?" the girl asked incredulously. "Don't you see the man in our room?"

Our son-in-law, John T., a media specialist, was in San Diego a few years ago filming some of the unique architecture of various structures, when one of his technicians shared an experience that had occurred when he stayed at the Horton Grand.

"He called the front desk to complain that the people above him were making too much noise, as if they were marching up and down the hall," John told us. "The front desk clerk responded, 'Sir, there is no floor above you. Perhaps you should have read the diary on the mantle.' The technician checked and found the diary filled with guest experiences with ghosts through the years at the Horton Grand."

Hotel del Coronado, San Diego, California

In another San Diego haunted hotel, the El Coronado, where our son-in-law and his crew were filming a convention, he said that one of his technicians reluctantly admitted that an invisible someone had brushed against him when no one was around. After they had completed filming the function they were assigned to cover, the entire crew heard strange booming noises coming from a balcony loft area where there was no living, visible person.

Our son-in-law's technician may have brushed up against Kate Morgan, the Hotel del Coronado's principal resident ghost, who died of a gunshot

The Hotel del Coronado, outside of San Diego, California.

wound to the head that was officially ruled a suicide. Kate's body was found in November 1892 on an exterior staircase leading to the beach.

Although most of the sightings of Kate have occurred on the beach and in hotel hallways, Room 3327, where Kate stayed, seems to be the center of most of the other paranormal phenomena.

REAL GHOSTS, RESTLESS SPIRITS, AND HAUNTED PLACES

The Old Stagecoach Inn in Waterbury, Vermont

Margaret Spencer, a once-wealthy, vivacious beauty who died in 1943 at the age of ninety-eight, haunts Room 2 of the Old Stagecoach Inn in Waterbury, Vermont. Margaret is often glimpsed in a wispy, white shawl, and she loves to play tricks on the guests.

Fifty Ghosts Walk the Streets and Hotel Hallways of Nantucket, Island, Massachusetts

Almost any place of lodging near the town's historic section harbors its share of unseen guests. Even the Coast Guard station is haunted.

When author Peter Benchley was on the island writing his bestseller *Jaws*, he encountered the ghost of an old man dressed in eighteenth-century clothing. The entity sat in front of a fireplace in a rocking chair, and Benchley insists that he was not dreaming.

Kennebunk Inn, Kennebunkport, Maine

This two-hundred-year-old inn is haunted by a friendly ghost named Silas, who delights in levitating champagne glasses and tossing beer mugs around the bar. The phantom shade of Silas Perkins has haunted the inn since his demise in the eighteenth century, and weekend vacationers flock there in the hope of getting one of his spiritual uplifts. The Kennebunk Inn is a favorite of former President George Bush because it is near his seafront estate.

The MisFitz Inn, Southbury, Connecticut

This 165-year-old inn is haunted by a ghost known affectionately as Sadie the Lady, a prostitute who practiced her profession at the inn in the 1890s. Sadie had the misfortune to fall in love with a married patron, who claimed that he returned the heartfelt emotion. However, when Sadie approached her lover when he was dining at the inn with his wife, he denied knowing her. Two days later, Sadie was found dead in her room above the tavern, an apparent suicide. Ever since her tragic end, Sadie has been held responsible for strange noises coming from empty rooms, overturned chairs in the bar, and water being dumped on unsuspecting patrons and employees.

King's Tavern, Natchez, Mississippi

In the late 1700s, Madeline was the mistress of Richard King, the tavern's namesake, until she was murdered by his jealous wife. For over two hundred years, Madeline's restless and angry ghost has been held responsible every squeak, rattle, and rap in the tavern. Patrons regularly report seeing Madeline's large portrait swing back and forth, and some have claimed to have seen the ghost of a slender woman who stands defiantly before them, her hands on her hips. To add to the color and allure of the haunted tavern, in the 1930s a woman's skeleton was found sealed in a brick fireplace with a jeweled dagger in her chest.

The only guest suite remaining in King's Tavern is on the third floor. After the restaurant section closes, the occupants of the room are left alone in the tavern with Madeline's ghost. According to the proprietors, many guests check in, but few remain to check out in the morning.

General Wayne Inn, Merion, Pennsylvania

Located on the old Lancaster roadway between Philadelphia and Radnor, the establishment has been in continuous operation since 1704 when Robert Jones, a Quaker, decided to provide travelers with a restaurant and a place of lodging. During the Revolutionary War, the establishment, originally called the Wayside Inn, played host to General George Washington and the Marquis de Lafayette, as well as a number of their adversaries, the British Redcoats and their Hessian mercenaries. The Wayside was renamed the General Wayne Inn in 1793 in honor of a local hero, General Anthony Wayne.

The ghost of Edgar Allen Poe, a frequent guest when he was alive ..., had been reported in a room known as the Franklin Post Office.

When Barton Johnson bought the General Wayne Inn in 1970, he was well aware of its reputation for being haunted. Previous guests had claimed encounters with the ghosts of men dressed in Revolutionary-era uniforms. The ghost of Edgar Allen Poe, a frequent guest when he was alive according to the old register, had been reported in a room known as the Franklin Post Office. Employees working in the bar area, as well as the guests seated there, often saw dozens of wine and other liquor glasses in a wooden rack begin to shake violently for no apparent reason.

In 1972, New Jersey psychics Jean and Bill Quinn conducted a séance in which at least seventeen different entities declared their presence and provided a bit of their personal history. When Wilhelm, a Hessian soldier killed in the Revolutionary War, identified himself through the mediums, he explained that most of the time he liked to stay down in the cellar. As far as the restaurant's maître d' was concerned, Wilhelm could have the cellar to himself. He had seen the ghost so often that he finally told Barton Johnson that he would no longer go down into the cellar.

In addition to Wilhelm, the mediums identified a little boy ghost, who cried for his lost mother; two female entities who had worked at the inn and had died at a young age under bizarre circumstances; eight other Hessian soldiers who had once been quartered at the inn and who had died nearby in battle; a Native American who seemed primarily to be watching the other entities; and an African American who chose to remain silent. The spirits of the Hessians have been seen by many customers and employees over the years. Usually they play harmless pranks, such as blowing on the necks of young women, but one of their spectral ranks enjoys terrifying any employee whose job it is to stay after closing and clean up.

Ludwig, the spirit of a Hessian soldier, materialized for many nights in the bedroom of Mike Benio, a contractor. Ludwig appealed to Benio to unearth his bones, which had been buried in the basement of the inn, and give them a proper burial in a cemetery. When Barton Johnson returned from a vacation, Benio asked permission to excavate a certain area of the cellar that was under the parking lot. Here, Benio found fragments of pottery and some human bones. After giving the remains a proper burial, the ghost of Ludwig was at peace and no longer manifested at the General Wayne Inn.

One night, Johnson placed a tape recorder in the bar. The next morning during playback, he could clearly hear the sounds of bar stools being moved about, the water faucet being turned on and off, and glasses catching the water.

Jim Webb and his partner Guy Sileo bought the inn in 1995. Webb was found murdered in his office on December 27, 1996 and Felicia Moyse, a twenty-year-old assistant chef, committed suicide on February 22, 1997. Some people felt that the place has added two more ghosts to its roster.

A Phantom Nazi Officer Haunts a Hotel in Ontario

According to reports coming out of Gravenhurst, Ontario, in September of 1968 a deserted hotel was hosting a kind of ghost not often seen in North America. A Nazi officer wearing a German uniform with a swastika cross attached to his jacket was seen on numerous occasions. But, actually, the appearance of a Nazi ghost at this location is not as strange as it may seem because the old hotel at which the ghost has been sighted used to house German prisoners during World War II.

One girl told a story of being lifted off the ground and dropped by the ghost, and her account was backed up by the corroborating testimony of several witnesses. A teenager said that he had reached out to touch the phantom and had found the thing to be very cold. Observers have seen the ghost loitering in the dining room and strolling across the grounds. Others have seen the entity as a black cloud drifting across the yard, ranging from six to eight feet in height.

Those who observed the thing in either guise affirm that it was a creature of habit. It seemed always to appear between 11:00 P.M. and 1:00 A.M., and usually followed the same route from the dining room to a certain point on the grounds.

Thomas B. Creager, a historical appraiser working with the Historic National Trust, says that he doesn't know whether or not ghosts exist, but he admits that in his work he has seen some things that are unexplainable. On an early morning of a sunny day in April 2012, Creager was taking a picture of a stream that flows near the foundation of the Fort Worth Stockyards Hotel when he saw a face "in the mist or smoke or whatever." Puzzled, Creager sent the photograph to Henry Bailey, a highly respected psychical researcher and a contributor to this book, who sent it on to Brad Steiger with the comment that "the Stockyards was the original Hell's Half Acre, Bonnie and Clyde, among others, spent time in the Hotel there." With Creager's permission, Steiger sent the photograph to well-known investigator and photo analyst Dr. Dave Oester of the International Ghost Hunters Society, who responded, "The photo of the stockyard hotel with the white mist/smoke in it is what we call ectoplasmic vapor. This is a good example of ghost/spirit/soul energy as seen when captured with a camera. In my opinion this is a good example of a paranormal anomaly." (Photograph by Thomas B. Creager).

HAUNTED RESTAURANTS, BARS, AND THEATERS

A Moment in Time in Printers Alley, Nashville

By Bret and Gina Oldham

Bret and Gina Oldham are paranormal researchers and founders of Halo Paranormal based in Nashville, Tennessee. Their research encompasses a wide range of subjects including UFOs, ghost hunting, and cryptozoology with special emphasis on alien abductions, and EVP and ITC communication. They have been interviewed numerous times in magazine and newspaper articles and have been featured guests on radio and TV shows in the USA and Europe. Bret is also a writer and author of the audiobook Ghost Stories of Las Vegas. *Bret and Gina can be reached at haloparanormal1@hotmail.com. Their website is www.haloparanormal.com.*

Stroll down Broadway in the heart of Nashville, Tennessee, and you will feel the heart of the city. Brightly lit neon lights fill the night with color. Music is pumping out of the countless honkytonks lined up like dominos all fay up the street that ends on the banks of the peaceful waters of the Cumberland River. Just a few blocks over from the party atmosphere of Broadway is an area that was also once filled with the same energy. This area is known as Printers Alley.

This historic section of Nashville runs between Third and Fourth Avenues close to Church Street. In the early years, Printers Alley was the location of many of Nashville's first publishing and printing companies. Many of the workers who worked at these companies often went out to the alley to

Bret and Gina Oldham

cool off on their breaks, and the small alley-way became known as Printers Alley. The nickname stuck and it has been known by that moniker ever since.

The area has evolved and changed many times over the years. Unfortunately, violence and crime also became a part of its turbulent history. During the Civil War, troops occupied the buildings lining Print-ers Alley. After the Civil War, some women who had lost their husbands and had no other way to support themselves turned to prostitution. Many of them worked in the area now known as Printers Alley in the brothels, saloons, and gambling halls that sprang up to cater to the men of Nashville.

Many of Nashville's elite—including judges, lawyers, and politicians—were said to frequent the alley. In the late 1800s, it became known as "The Men's District."

As the years passed, the alley became famous for entertainment. Many music clubs opened there. During the 1950s and 1960s, several of the Grand Ole Opry stars would come over to the numerous clubs in the alley and do late-night shows after their Opry appearances.

Today Printers Alley is a tourist attraction. The old buildings with their French architecture still stand among the neon-lit signs, and the area looks a bit like the French Quarter of New Orleans.

At the end of the narrow alley there is a boarded-up building that was once home to one of Nashville's most famous nightclubs and where one of Nashville's most famous murders took place. Known as the Rainbow Room, it was located on the bottom floor of a much larger building which used to be the home of the Southern Turf. During the 1890s the Southern Turf was consid-ered the finest brothel and saloon in Nashville. Today the Southern Turf building is used for law offices.

The Rainbow Room has been closed since the murder of its former owner, Skull Shullman, in 1998. Known for his recurring role on the hit televi-sion series *Hee Haw*, Shullman was also quite a colorful character in real life. He would often sit in the doorway of the Rainbow Room wearing overalls and a belt with a large silver skull-shaped belt buckle. Skull was a smart businessman and would use his fame to entice fans into his establishment. Many times he would have several of his beloved poodles sitting with him at the doorway. He would have the dogs dyed different colors. Sometimes red, sometimes green or blue. He was known for being eccentric. He was also known for carrying large amounts of cash—which eventually led to his death during a robbery inside the Rainbow Room on January 21, 1998.

Printers Alley was a place of commerce during the Civil War, but afterwards the dark lane was the business place of prostitutes.

The Rainbow Room has been closed since the murder of Skull Shullman. Currently the blues bar next door uses it for storage. Many reports of ghostly activity have been reported there since Skull's murder. Workers from the blues club would often hear whispers while in they were in there gathering supplies. Very noticeable cold spots have frequently been felt, especially in the area where Skull's body was found. One particular bartender reported feeling a hand on his shoulder while he was retrieving glasses—only to turn around and find no one there. Other people have talked of seeing a shadowy figure walking across the room. The doorway to the old Rainbow Room is said to be the spot where the restless spirit of Skull is most seen. Some claim to have captured his ghost on film in the doorway where he used to sit every night.

Because we are paranormal investigators, we had heard many of the reports of the paranormal activity associated with the Rainbow Room. We had previously walked though Printers Alley to take a look at the mysterious doorway, but there was no way to do an investigation in the building without the proper permission, so we simply took a look around and left.

One night we had been downtown in Nashville enjoying the nightlife. This particular night we had brought along a camera to take a few photos of ourselves. We had been over on Broadway for dinner. We had stopped at several clubs to listen to music and had thoroughly enjoyed ourselves. On the way back to our car we decided to take a brief walk through Printers Alley and stop by the doorway to the Rainbow Room again.

These days, many of the clubs that once filled the alley with people and music are closed. As you get down to the end of the alley where the Rainbow Room once was there are no nightclubs open. The ambience changes immediately. You feel an awareness of the tragic past of the alley. The negative energy still resides there, and it's easy to sense that. Since we had our camera with us, we thought, just for posterity's sake, we would take a few pictures of the entrance to the old club and a photo or two of each of us standing in the door-

A ghostly presence lurks in the shadows of Printers Alley.

way where Skull's ghost has reportedly been photographed before. Both of us took a turn stepping into the old stone entrance while the other one snapped a couple of pictures. After we had taken pictures of ourselves, we took a few more of the area around the entrance and down the alley before we left.

A few days later we uploaded the photos from that night. When we got to the ones from Printers Alley that we had taken in front of the Rainbow Club, we noticed something odd in one of the photos. There was silver object in the foreground that to us appeared to be some kind of bent molten metal.

Both of us are experienced photographers. We know to not let objects that could be perceived as something paranormal get in front of the camera lens. This strange silver object wasn't hair, a zipper, or a camera strap. Neither of us had a jacket or a hat on that night so nothing like that could have produced such an image.

We couldn't debunk the object so Bret lightened up the picture to see if we could get a better look at what exactly it was. When he did, we both were shocked at what we then saw. The silver metallic object that had first captured our attention was now not our main focal point of the picture. When the picture was lightened to reveal what was in the alley with us the mysteries within the photo expanded.

Walking down the alley in front of the camera was a heavy-set woman wearing a long dress. Her hair was pulled back in a tight bun style. She was carrying what looked like a white blanket or perhaps a shawl. She seemed to be oblivious to fact that we were there. It was like we were the ones who were invisible.

Standing against the wall of one of the buildings, several feet in front of the woman was the figure of a man. He appeared to be a soldier in uniform as evidenced by his hat and the stripe down his pants. There was absolutely no one around us when we were taking those pictures that night in Printers Alley, much less anyone dressed in a uniform or long dress.

We have never figured out what the silver object close to the camera was or why these ghostly figures we caught on film seemed to be going about their business without acknowledging our presence in any way.

We now had several new questions to which we have sought the answers.

Did we just get lucky by being at the right place and the right time and simply photographed two full body apparitions? Possibly.

Were they residual energy that had left an indelible imprint on the fabric of time? Perhaps.

Was there a dimensional overlap, making both our reality and theirs exist on top of each other for a brief few seconds? Maybe.

Or had we, or had they, somehow experienced some sort of shift in the space-time continuum resulting in an image that will forever remain on film as a moment in time?

∞

TWO GHOSTS VISIT A MCDONALD'S IN YUMA, ARIZONA

The personal experience of Verne Koenig

I must relate to you a very strange or weird incident that happened to me during our winter stay in Yuma, Arizona in 1996. One weekday afternoon I stopped by a McDonald's restaurant for a cup of coffee. On the north side of the restaurant there are two doors, one going directly up to the counter, the other is further back that leads to the restrooms and then to a booth area around the corner from the counter. I bought my coffee and sat in the first booth of this area between the two north doors, looking toward the door leading to the restrooms.

I picked up a newspaper and started looking through it as I was sipping my coffee. There was no one else in this particular booth area, and I noticed just a few customers on the east side area sitting in booths. One waitress was at the counter at that time, and there were a few other employees in the kitchen area.

Very shortly, I noticed a man and a woman enter the further north door near the restrooms. I did not notice if they came from a car or they were walking. They paused, looked around for a moment, and then sat down in the first booth near the door. I couldn't help noticing them because of the way they were dressed and the way they looked. The man was dressed in a nice-looking gray suit and wearing a tie, but his complexion was that of a very sick man. He was very pale and seemed to be sweating, although it was not warm outside that day. The woman wore a Hawaiian-type dress, flowery and very colorful, and it reached down to her ankles. She was carrying a large cloth bag. They sat for a moment and then the woman reached into her bag and withdrew a large towel of some kind and began wiping the man's face, over and over again. Then she put it back, got up and went into the ladies restroom.

I was observing these things, peering over the top of the newspaper I was supposed to be reading. The woman was in the restroom for five or six minutes. When she came out, she took the towel from her bag and again wiped the man's face, neck, and head. They sat there for a few more minutes, apparently conversing, although I couldn't hear what they said.

Then the woman went back into the restroom and the man got up and walked up the aisle toward me. When he reached my booth, he stopped and I could see how pale-looking he was, very white. He asked me, "Do you have some money so I can get something to drink?"

I guess I was surprised that he would ask me for money. Both of them were so well dressed that I thought surely they would have enough money to pay for a drink. I refused him. He looked at me for a moment and then walked back to his booth by the door and sat down. Shortly after, the woman came out of the restroom again. They talked awhile, and then both of them walked up the aisle toward me. Without looking at me, they rounded the corner to the counter area.

Out of curiosity, I immediately got up to observe if they were going to buy something—when suddenly, they weren't there! They had completely disappeared.

I was dumbfounded. I went to the door on the south side of the counter area, looked out, but nobody was there. They could not have reached that door so quickly or gone out without my seeing them.

And then the weird thing! I stopped at the counter where a single waitress was on duty, and I asked her if some people had just walked by and gone outside. She looked kind of funny at me and said, "No, there was no one that just walked past here. I assure you I would have seen them."

I went outside and looked at the cars that were parked in the lot. All were empty, and there was no sign of the man and the woman I had observed, even driving off in a car.

There were only a few people in the other part of McDonald's that day, and none of them had seen the couple, only me. It's truly unexplainable. I often think what if I had given the man some money, what would have happened then? I guess I'll never know.

A Haunted Godfather's Pizza in Ogden, Utah

By Merrie Barrentine and Michael Zimmer

A research project in progress by Utah Paranormal Exploration and Research (UPER).

Utah Paranormal Exploration and Research (UPER) began its investigation of Godfather's Pizza in the fall of 1999. Traditionally, our group has avoided ghost hunting—jumping around from one site to the next—in order to better focus on a handful of more active sites. At Godfather's Pizza, we've done the standard video filming, digital and 35mm photography, and audio recording for electronic voice phenomena (EVP). We've also recorded many of the restaurant owner/manager's memories of activity over the past nineteen years, beginning with his second night there, when the jukebox suddenly began playing even after the power to that end of the building had been shut off. The jukebox kept playing even when the electrical plug was pulled.

Since that initial encounter, there have been many other events involving the paranormal. A woman, a man, and two different boys have been the most frequent visitors, seen by employees and customers alike. The tile floor in front of the counter bulged up one morning, rising approximately eight to ten inches, before returning to level. When the tile was removed later, the concrete underneath was unbroken.

Fluorescent lights have shot out of their boxes to arch across the room, as if thrown by unseen hands, until about forty lights lay shattered on the floor.

The owner has heard someone whistling in the kitchen on numerous occasions when no one else was there, and customers have seen figures walk through walls, tables, and railings. The owner said one of the ghost boys walked right through him, an event he described as "chilling."

UPER has done archive research on the restaurant and its riverside location through old books, regional history sources, and microfilm at the local library. There is fairly convincing evidence—as yet unconfirmed—that the site was once a paupers' field. Its location in relationship to the one-hundred-plus-year-old Ogden City Cemetery—just below the hill from it and right on the Ogden River—would seem to support that possibility.

UPER's best paranormal experience at Godfather's was in 2000. During an after-hours investigation, a vague mist was seen forming in the middle of the room. Although the apparition's physical appearance lasted only seconds, UPER's general manager, Merry Barrentine, was able to snap several photos of the manifestation before it disappeared. It was in one of these that the "Godfather's boy" appeared.

The restaurant's owner identified the boy as an apparition he's seen in the restaurant before, but UPER wanted a second opinion and sent the photo to a professional photographer out of state. His opinion is below.

I opened it (the photograph) in Photoshop 6, cropped the image to the area you now see, increased the resolution to 300ppi, and changed the image size to 7 inches high. Then, I used the unsharp mask filter at 100%, with a radius of 3.3, and a threshold of 0. Those were the only settings I used to clean it up. No further enhancement was done on the original image.

A photograph of the ghost that appeared at Godfather's Pizza in Ogden, Utah, in 2000.

REAL GHOSTS, RESTLESS SPIRITS, AND HAUNTED PLACES

My [observations concerning] the photo are what you've mentioned....(One), the very bottom bar is a reflection on the table by the bar above it and the form is behind it and yet there is lens flare above the form (that) suggests the form is in front of the window.

Here is what I see in the image: It appears that the figure is standing inside the room, though there doesn't appear to be anyone physically in the room itself. There is some mist-like stuff that seems to be in the area where the person would be standing, if there were someone in the image. By zooming in on the photo, I can sort of see that the person is short, appears to be a boy, though it is impossible to be certain. The person's face is in profile, the nose being obvious as is the ear. The hair seems to be parted on the person's left side, since that is the area of the head that appears in the reflection. A white starch collar is the most prominent feature of the person's clothing, leading us to assume that the figure is a male. Also, it appears that the figure is standing at the front edge of the table (the edge nearest to the camera lens) and is leaning with his/her left hand resting on that flat edge of the table. The shirt is rather blousy and is ill-defined, but is still visible.

━━◆◈◆━━

THE GHOSTS OF SANDY'S RESTAURANT, VENTURA, CALIFORNIA

An investigation by renowned psychic investigator, Richard Senate.

Sandy's is best known for its steak and seafood, but the regular customers believe this restaurant is haunted by at least two ghosts. The manager states that he has never seen anything, but he does admit that customers tell of odd happenings. Some say that they have seen a dark shadow following them into the place; still others say they hear things in the back room—things like silverware moving about with an odd tinkling sound. Several years ago, a woman witnessed a glass levitate and fly across the room, smashing against the wall. There is a persistent cold in the back room of the place that is apparent even on a hot day. Could this cold spot be evidence of a ghost?

The stories that reached me were so dramatic that I felt I needed to conduct an on-site investigation. I drove out to the very modern-looking cinder block restaurant on the corner of Saviers and Bard Streets. It was deceptively ordinary looking. When I pulled in, I started to get the impression that the stories were just so much folklore or perhaps the product of liquid spirits and nothing supernatural. But when I stepped into the place, the hair on the back of my neck shivered. It was a feeling I had felt many times when I entered a haunted site. As I was drawn into the building I felt something cold and invisible pass by me. Yes, I was convinced the stories were true—this place was haunted.

I met with George, the bartender, who confirmed what the patrons had seen. Some said they even saw a dark shadowlike form come through the bar area. The waitress, Lillian, said that a coffee pot had flown across the room and that strange crashing sounds were heard. The bartender confirmed her story and said some time back four people sitting at the bar felt something touch them, turned and looked, but there was nothing there. He when on to say that the odd events seem to take place late at night, after nine.

> As I was drawn into the building I felt something cold and invisible pass by me.

The restaurant was built perhaps forty years ago and was successfully managed by a friendly couple. When ill-health forced them to sell, the present owners purchased the establishment. The original owners passed away, and it has been from the time of their deaths that there have been reports of ghosts wandering Sandy's Restaurant. Some speculate that the phantoms are the spirits of the former owners, checking on the place they worked so hard to establish. Whatever the reason, my visit did confirm that the former owners could find little fault with the steak the present proprietors serve at the place or with the quality of the service. Perhaps that is the cause of the ghostly activity. So many people had so many good times at the restaurant, they return now that they are in spirit.

The bar area and the front lobby seemed to me to be haunted. There was a strange feeling in the last booth, as well. If you go there, order the steak, and keep an eye on the bar for moving shadows. And keep a tight grip on the water glass—just be sure it doesn't fly off by itself!

A Vanishing Restaurant Outside of Amarillo, Texas

In the early summer of 1987, Sam and Clara were traveling to Amarillo, Texas, on a business trip. Shortly after midnight, they decided to stop to eat at a quaint, rustic-style restaurant that neither of them had ever noticed on previous trips to the region. They remembered that the food was prepared in an excellent down-home country style, and that the waitress, the cook, and even the other customers were so friendly in a sincere manner that Sam and Clara truly meant it when they promised that they would stop back again.

"And we tried to do exactly that on our return drive," Sam said, "but that great little down-home restaurant was nowhere to be seen. We even looped back a couple of times, thinking we might somehow have driven on by. We even got into an argument, each of us insisting that we remembered exactly where it was. We just couldn't find it, and since the hour was getting very late, we drove on."

Because their business required a number of return visits to Amarillo, Sam and Clara traveled that route on three consecutive weekends, each time keeping a watch for the restaurant with the wonderful cooking, but it seemed as though it had simply vanished. "Since then, we have driven that route a dozen or more times," Sam said, "but we never again found that friendly little restaurant."

Indeed, Sam and Clara may have been extremely fortunate. What if the "friendly little restaurant" appeared and disappeared every few years? A kind of Texas-style "Brigadoon." They might have been lost in time and space for decades. But at least the food and the company would have been good.

A Protective Ghost at Homestead Restaurant, Jacksonville, Florida

Alpha Paynter operated a boarding house in the cabin that later became the Homestead Restaurant in Jacksonville, Florida. Alpha devoted her life to the place, and when she died in 1962, she was buried in the yard behind the building. According to many of those who have patronized the place in recent years, Alpha Paynter has never left the Homestead and remains its protector.

Steve Macri, a former owner of the Homestead, admitted to Michele Newbern Gillis of the Jacksonville *Daily Record* (September 22, 2002) that in the twenty-six years that he ran the place, there were many things that he could not explain. In October of 2001, just before he closed, there was a rash of complaints from women who claimed that an invisible someone was touching them on the shoulders. Macri also mentioned the newly-hired dishwasher from out of town who asked who the lady in the long dress was who was watching him from the top of the stairs. A young employee, who was shooting hoops during his break, ran back in the restaurant screaming that he had seen a woman in the backyard, half in and half out of the ground.

A new ownership team, which includes Kathy Johansen, whose family owned the Homestead until 1975, reopened the restaurant in September 2002. Although Johansen said that she had never seen the ghost of Alpha, she knew that over the years that her father owned the restaurant, many customers and employees had claimed to have seen her. Contractors working alone in the building after hours complain of being touched from behind. Many have left and never returned to complete their work.

According to tradition, Alpha's spirit appears most often in mirrors in various rooms in the restaurant. Many patrons have reported seeing her leaning over the fireplace in the center room.

DANZA'S IN BROOKLYN IS HAUNTED BY WISEGUYS

Danza's restaurant in Bensonhurst was once Tali's Restaurant and Lounge, headquarters of Salvatore "Sammy the Bull" Gravano, where at least two men who co-owned the place with the infamous mob informer were murdered. And now the present owner, Stephen Carroll, told Al Guart of the *New York Post* (March 10, 2002) that the place was haunted. Reports have come in about ghosts that sit down for dinner, disembodied voices, and tablecloths that fluff up and drop back down on their own.

Principal among the restless spirits that have never left the restaurant are likely to be that of Michael DeBatt, Gravano's partner, who Sammy the Bull had murdered while he was tending bar, and Joseph D'Angelo, who Sammy claimed was killed by another mobster. Roseanne Massa, DeBatt's sister, believes that her brother Michael may well be haunting Danza's restaurant because his spirit is disturbed that Gravano has never really paid for, or atoned for, killing him and eighteen others. Sammy spent less that five years in prison for his crimes as the result of a deal that he cut with prosecutors for testifying against Gambino head John "the Teflon Don" Gotti.

Stephen Carroll said that he had pretty much overlooked the bullet holes that still marked the restaurant's brick walls and the claims of ghosts until his cousin, Angela Perrone, was working alone in the basement. She said that she heard someone speaking to her and thought it was her partner. But then she discovered that he had been outside packing the car the whole time that she was in the basement.

Since that time, Carroll and other members of his staff have seen men sitting down at tables or walking toward the basement—only to vanish. Employees and customers have said that they have heard disembodied voices and had the feeling that they were being watched.

GHOSTS BELLY UP TO BAR WITH PATRONS IN AMERSHAM

At the fifteenth-century bar Boot and Slipper in Rickmansworth Road, Amersham Old Town, England, the staff is too frightened to go down in the cellar alone. They complain that the resident ghost brushes past them, says a few words that cannot really be distinguished, then places its hand on their shoulder.

Patrons say that the Elephant and Castle in Amersham Old Town is just as haunted as the Boot and Slipper. The ghost of a woman in black has been seen gliding to and fro in the kitchen. Barmaids complain that they have their bottoms pinched when there is no one else around who could perpetrate such a personal offense.

The Chequers Pub is haunted by a white-hooded figure, and numerous cold spots have been detected in the bar that was built in the 1500s. Some say that people accused of witchcraft and other crimes were imprisoned there while they waited to be burned at the stake.

> The ghost of a woman in black has been seen gliding to and fro in the kitchen.

The Crown Hotel has five ghosts, including a very inhospitable one who shouts at guests to get out. In Room 16, a more maternal spirit exists, that of an old Victorian housekeeper who likes to tuck young men into their beds. Staff members reported some men running down the stairs at three in the morning when the caring housekeeper pays them a visit.

ANDREA ROSE BED & BREAKFAST, HOT SPRINGS, ARKANSAS

By Larry Flaxman, Arkansas Paranormal & Anomalous Studies Team

On October 31, 2009, ARPAST (Arkansas Paranormal & Anomalous Studies Team) conducted an investigation at the Andrea Rose Bed & Breakfast in Hot Springs, Arkansas. The team went through their routine of setting up cameras throughout the buildings and passing out equipment for individual groups. The team then quickly got into their assigned groups and began the investigation. The first rotation went off without a hitch.

The night became interesting at the beginning of the second rotation. Investigator April Fales and her group were in a massage room in the back of the main building. The team members took their positions in the room with their equipment and began taking EMF (measurements of fluctuation in magnetic fields) and temperature readings. April was standing in the front of the room, next to the door.

As April bent over to record her team members readings, she felt a horrible sensation go down her back. It felt as if hot ashes had been thrown on her. She calmly stood up and asked team member, Robin Sisson to accompany her outside of the room. Robin raised April's shirt and discovered seven scratches going down her back, from the bottom of her neck, to the very bottom of her back. The scratches turned into large welts, and the skin on her back was radiating red.

The team then began searching the room for anything that could have possibly caused the wounds, but there was nothing to be found. There was no rhyme or reason for this to happen. There was also no evidence captured on the cameras or digital recorders. So why did this experience occur without being provoked in any way? I guess we will never know. One thing is for sure: it was absolutely one of the most dramatic personal experiences that April has had.

———◦◦◦———

Admiral Grog Heads the Ghostly Crew at the Inn

The ghost of Admiral Edward Vernon, remembered as the man who introduced watered down rum—"grog"—to the British Navy, now heads a crew of spirits at the Tuddenham Road Inn in Ipswich, Suffolk, that includes a monk, a drowned seaman, and a publican named George.

Staff members have reported seeing an ash gray figure scamper through one of the upstairs bedrooms. On one occasion, the spirit of a pony-tailed sailor appeared in the back bar and walked right through the landlord. Witnesses who saw this eerie phenomena find the back bar an extremely unpopular place to have a drink.

The Admiral himself, who was Ipswich Member of Parliament from 1741 to 1754, has been seen often, standing fully materialized and in full dress uniform. Those who have seen the ghost, say that the Admiral appears very authoritative.

———◦◦◦———

What Do You Get When a Jail Becomes a Theatre?

Employees at the Tollbooth Theatre in Stirling, Scotland, refused to work in a place that is haunted. In the restaurant portion of the building, a former jail that underwent a multimillion-pound renovation in 2002, staff members have witnessed wine glasses become airborne and door handles turn themselves. Because this was the section in the old jail where prisoners once awaiting execution were held, many employees rationalized that there should be little wonder why restless and angry ghosts should inhabit the area.

Operations assistant James Wigglesworth told reporter James Hamilton that although the building had totally changed since it was a jail, there were still things that made the hairs on the back of his neck stand up. Late at night, Wigglesworth said, one could hear things being dragged across the floor of what used to be the cell area upstairs. The bar staff regularly reported wine glasses dashing themselves to the floor, and a ticket seller quit her job when she saw the ghost of man walk across the room.

The owners of the theatre hoped they had found the reason for the disturbances when they found the skeleton of a convicted murderer under the concrete floor of the former prison entrance. According to old prison records, the remains were those of Alan Mair, who was hanged outside the Tollbooth in 1843. Mair was given a Christian burial in January 2002.

But the respect paid to Mair's bones did not alleviate the haunting phenomena. The manifestations continued to plague the staff of the theatre and the restaurant of the remodeled Tollbooth. And the hauntings even stretched beyond the confines of the building.

The postman, while on his regular route, stopped by the Tollbooth, spotted a man he assumed was an actor fully dressed in eighteenth-century costume, and gave a cheery hello. He was terrified when the man returned his saluta-tion with a resounding, "and good morning to you, sir," then disappeared.

> Late at night, Wig-glesworth said, one could hear things being dragged across the floor of what used to be the cell area upstairs.

In order to placate the nervous staff at the Tollbooth, the owners have promised an exorcism, but parapsychologist Dr. Richard Wiseman of the Uni-versity of Hertfordshire doubted that the rites would do any good. Theatres attract ghostly experiences, he said, and when they were placed in buildings that were former jails, there would be great "expectations of ghostly events going on."

THE GRAND THEATER INVESTIGATION IN WAUSAU, WISCONSIN
By Todd Roll

Research in progress by the Wausau Paranormal Research Society.

Built in 1927 to replace the old Grand Opera House, the Grand Theater has been a Wausau, Wisconsin, landmark for decades. Originally a vaudeville and silent movie house the Grand has changed functions over the years, show-ing motion pictures from 1932 to 1985. After a renovation project in 1986, the Grand became the feature performing arts theater for north central Wis-consin. Over the years the Grand has been host to numerous plays, movies, musical performances and, if the tales are to be believed, one or more ghosts.

The earliest reports of ghostly activity at the Grand are from the 1950s when workers reported movie canisters being moved from the upstairs projec-tion room to the lobby. Over the years other manifestations have been report-ed including phantom footsteps, apparitions, electrical malfunctions, cold spots, and areas that are just creepy to be in.

The Wausau Paranormal Research Society launched an investigation of the Grand Theater in July of 2001. At that time the theater was undergoing a major renovation project. The theater was to receive an addition and be

This photograph was taken inside the Grand Theater in Wausau, Wisconsin. A number of anomalies were revealed on the negative after development.

linked to two other buildings as part of the "Arts Block" project, making conditions less than ideal for an investigation, but our hope was that the project might "stir up" the spirits of the building.

During our initial research we collected reports of the following paranormal phenomena at the Grand:

- Many stagehands reported the sound of footsteps walking across the empty stage. When they would investigate the source of the footsteps could not be located.

- A worker closing up the theater for the evening saw an apparition of a man appear along the back wall of the balcony. The apparition was seen in the exact spot where the door to the projection room had been located.

- An apparition, again of a man, was seen in the lighting rack above the stage by a number of people over the years. In one case the apparition walked down the spiral staircase from the lighting rack and crossed the stage directly in front of two witnesses.

- Lights in the projection area are often turned on when no one is around.

- Various areas of the theater are reported to be "cold spots."

- During the most recent construction project, power would mysteriously shut off in one area of the basement. Electricians would test a wire and find it live, but when they tried to power equipment off of it, the same line would be dead—only to become live again moments later.

- A puddle would form in another area of the basement, when no source of water for it could be found.

- Two staff members reported hearing "voices" coming out of a room behind the balcony. A search revealed no other people in the building.

The Wausau Paranormal Research Society decided to concentrate our investigation in two areas, the balcony and third-floor offices, and the stage and lighting rack.

While taking background photos of the balcony, I snapped a photo of an anomalous blob. I was using standard 35mm 400-speed film and did not see the blob at the time the photo was taken. A photo taken seconds later did not show the blob. When checking the negative, the blob does appear on it. The photo does have some other development flaws on it, but the blob is something different. It should be noted that there was a renovation project going on at the time and the blob could very well be a dust particle.

During our third visit we recorded some electronic voice phenomena (EVP) in one of the spotlight rooms in the third-floor office area. While setting up equipment in the room, two members reported hearing "whispering" coming from the far corner of the room. After playing back the tape a voice can be heard saying "Don't come back over here." The origin of the voice could not be determined at this time.

The Wausau Paranormal Research Society plans to conduct a further investigation of the phenomena reported.

BATTLEFIELDS WHERE PHANTOM ARMIES ETERNALLY WAGE WAR

A Phantom Army in Scotland

In the mid-eighteenth century, Archibald Bell, a farmer of Glenary, Scotland, and his son were walking down a local road. Before long the noise and clatter of many feet alerted the men to the imminent approach of a marching army. As soldiers were not averse to recruiting unwilling victims to serve in their ranks, the two Bells retired hastily to a hiding place some distance above the ground.

They saw pass beneath them a vast army. There was something peculiar about the soldiers, though. They were wearing uniforms unlike any seen in the Highlands. And the cut of their breeches was in the style of another era altogether. Just as the elder Bell was noticing the absence of a ground swell of dust accompanying the soldiers, the army disappeared. The road was empty and untrodden. To their dying days, the elder Bell maintained that the vision had been one of the future, while Bell the younger insisted that they had seen an army of the past.

The Ghostly Army of Kentucky

It was an unusually warm day on the afternoon of October 1, 1863, when a small group of Union soldiers stopped at the Kentucky mountaintop home of Moses Dwyer and asked for a drink of water. Although Dwyer made it clear that his sympathies lay elsewhere, he said that he could not deny the Yankees a drink of water.

The Union sergeant thanked the mountaineer and assured him that his men would be on their best behavior if they might just rest a bit in the shade of his large porch. The members of the Dwyer family offered the troops some freshly baked cookies, and soon the civilians and the soldiers were talking and joking, forgetting about the great schism that was supposed to divide them.

After a few minutes of gentle conversation, one of the Union soldiers noticed a clump of strange clouds and pointed skyward. There, over the ridges of the adjacent hills, were rows and rows of weirdly shaped clouds, about the size and general shape of doors. They seemed to be constructed of smoke or some cottonlike substance rather than water and vapor.

Within moments, the sky had filled with the peculiarly shaped clouds.

The sergeant noted that the clouds seemed to be flying on their own. There was no wind that day, so all the soldiers and the Dwyer family were wondering out loud how the clouds could be moving in such a manner. As neatly regimented as companies of soldiers, the strange clouds sailed swiftly over the heads of the astonished witnesses on the porch of the Kentucky mountain cabin. Their numbers were so great that it required more than an hour for all of the door-sized "rolls of smoke" to pass overhead.

Moses Dwyer had just finished commenting that the sight was the darnedest thing he had ever seen in all his years in the region when suddenly, in the valley below them, thousands upon thousands of what definitely appeared to be human beings materialized, marching at double time in the same direction as the mysterious clouds.

A soldier cocked his musket nervously, muttering that the whole Rebel army was fixing to march on them. The sergeant was as pale as the next man, but he had not yet allowed himself to panic. He quieted his men and spoke to them in a harsh whisper, proclaiming that the strange army approaching them was not made up of living combatants but the ghosts of men who were once soldiers.

The phantoms all wore white shirts and trousers and marched approximately 30 to 40 "soldiers" deep. Oblivious to the attention they were receiving from the startled mountain family and the Union troops, the apparitions strode purposefully across the valley and began to ascend the steep mountain range that surrounded it.

The ghostly marchers could have passed for a mighty earthly army on the move if it had not been for their bizarre appearance. The phantoms were not of uniform size, as their companion clouds had been. Some of the eerie marchers were tall, and others appeared to be quite small. Their legs were seen to move and their arms to swing briskly. While they marched in strict military fashion, they bore no weapons of any kind. As the phantom parade began to ascend the mountain, members of the ghostly march were seen to lean forward, just as men do when negotiating steep terrain.

It took over an hour for the great parade of phantoms to march out of the valley, and the witnesses to the remarkable sight were left speechless and filled with wonder. Some of them, perhaps rightly, interpreted the ghostly marchers to represent the many men who would die in the bloody War Between the States.

Strangely enough, on October 14, 1863, a similar parade of phantoms was observed by ten Confederate soldiers and a number of civilians at Runger's Mill, Kentucky. According to contemporary reports, the phenomenon remained identical in every detail, except that the combined passage of the weird clouds and the eerie marchers took only one hour instead of two.

A PHANTOM RE-CREATION OF DIEPPE

On August 4, 1951, two young Englishwomen vacationing in Dieppe, France, were awakened just before dawn by the violent sounds of guns and shell fire, dive bombing planes, shouts, and the scraping of landing craft hitting the beach. Cautiously peering out of their windows, the two young women saw only the peaceful pre-dawn city. They knew, however, that just nine years previously, nearly 1,000 young Canadians had lost their lives in the ill-fated Dieppe raid.

Being possessed of unusual presence of mind, the young Englishwomen kept a record of the frightening cacophony of sound, noting the exact times of the ebb and flow of the invisible battle. They presented their report to the Society for Psychical Research, whose investigators checked it against detailed accounts of the event in the war office. The times recorded by the women were, in most cases, identical to the minute of the raid that had taken place nine years before.

SPIRIT MEMORIES OF THE BATTLE OF EDGE HILL

Restored battle scenes offer excellent examples of what seem to be impressions caused by the collective spirit memories of large groups of people under threat of death and the most-severe kinds of physical and emotional stress. Perhaps the best-known, most extensively documented, and most sub-

The village of Radway and the field where the Battle of Edge Hill took place in 1642.

stantially witnessed of such occurrences was the Phantom Battle of Edge Hill, which was "refought" on several consecutive weekends during the Christmas season of 1642. The actual battle was waged near the village of Keinton, England, on October 23 between the Royalist Army of King Charles and the Parliamentary Army under the Earl of Essex.

The battlefield of Edge Hill.

It was on Christmas Eve that several countryfolk were awakened by the noises of violent battle. Fearing that it could only be another clash between actual living soldiers that had come to desecrate the sanctity of the holy evening and the peace of their countryside, the villagers fled from their homes to confront two armies of phantoms. One side bore the king's colors; the other, Parliament's banners. Until three o'clock in the morning, the phantom soldiers restaged the terrible fighting of two months before.

The battle had resulted in defeat for King Charles, and the monarch grew greatly disturbed when he heard that two armies of ghosts were determined to remind the populace that the Parliamentary forces had triumphed at Edge Hill. The king suspected that certain Parliamentary sympathizers had fabricated the tale to cause him embarrassment, so he sent three of his most trusted officers to squelch the matter.

When the emissaries returned to court, they swore oaths that they themselves had witnessed the clash of the phantom armies. On two consecutive nights, they had watched the ghostly reconstruction and had even recognized several of their comrades who had fallen that day.

GHOSTS STILL DEFEND CORREGIDOR

Another area that seems to be drenched with the powerful emotions of fighting and dying men is that of the small island of Corregidor, where in the early days of World War II, a handful of American and Filipino troops tried desperately to halt the Japanese advance against the city of Manila and the whole Philippine Islands. Filipino Defense Secretary Alego S. Santos said after the war was over that the valiant defenders of the Philippines had fought almost beyond human endurance.

According to several witnesses, their ghosts continued to fight. In the 1960s the only living inhabitants of the island were a small detachment of Filipino marines, a few firewood cutters, and a caretaker and his family. And then there were the nonliving inhabitants. Terrified wood cutters returned to the base to tell of encountering bleeding and wounded men who were stumbling about in the jungle. In every instance, they described the men as grim-faced and carrying rifles at the ready.

Marines on jungle maneuvers reported coming face to face with silently stalking phantom scouts of that desperate last-stand conflict of a quarter of a century ago. Many claimed to have seen a beautiful red-headed woman moving silently among rows of ghostly wounded, ministering to their injuries. Most often seen was the ghost of a nurse in a Red Cross uniform. Soldiers on night duty who spotted the phantom have reported that, shortly after she faded into the jungle moonlight, they found themselves surrounded by rows and rows of groaning and dying men in attitudes of extreme suffering.

According to the caretaker and his family, the sounds that came with evening were the most disconcerting part of living on an island full of ghosts. Every night the air was filled with horrible moans of pain and the sounds of invisible soldiers rallying to defend themselves against the phantom invaders.

The supervisor of tourism for Luzon, Florentino R. Das, said that he and his wife had visited the island and heard for themselves the terrible sounds of men in pain. Upon his investigation, he was unable to find any physical cause for the eerie disturbances.

THE SHADOW WARRIORS OF CRETE

How long might the violent emotions of warfare saturate the psychic ether of a terrain? The phantom marchers of Crete have been parading for centuries and seem to be armored men right out of the pages of Homer's *Iliad*.

People come from all over the island to observe the ghostly army, which usually puts in an appearance during the last weeks of May and the first week of June. No trained observer has been able to put the spectral army into any precise historical context. The ghostly ranks are filled with the images of tall, proud men, who wear metal helmets of classic design and carry short, flat swords.

The native islanders call them the "shadow men" or the "dew men," because they always appear just before dawn or just after sunset. They seem to form out of the sea, march directly for the ruins of an old Venetian castle, then disappear with the growing darkness of the night or the light of day. Historians have discarded any theory of a connection between the ghostly army and the medieval castle because of the design of the phantoms' breastplates and weapons.

Many claimed to have seen a beautiful red-headed woman moving silently among rows of ghostly wounded, ministering to their injuries.

For almost a century, feature stories on the spectral army have been carried in the major newspapers of Greece. In addition to the local peasants, Greek businessmen, archeologists, and journalists have reported seeing the phenomenon. German and English archeologists and observers have also been on hand for the parade of phantoms. During the Turkish administration of the island in the 1870s, an entire garrison of Turkish soldiers sighted the ghostly marauders and were frightened into readying themselves for combat.

Most theorists have discarded the possibility that the phantom marchers are only a mirage. Mirages have maximum ranges of about 40 miles and only occur in direct sunlight. The army, as has been noted, appears only in the half-light of dawn or dusk. Then, too, a mirage is a reflection of reality. This would mean that within a range of 40 miles, such an army would truly be marching. It would seem beyond all range of imagination to suppose that an entire army of men, who enjoyed conducting annual secret maneuvers in ancient armor, could exist on the island of Crete without being detected by the populace.

THE PHANTOM HUN

My friend John Pendragon of Tunbridge Wells, England, sent me the eerie account of the "Phantom Hun" who was seen in 1916 well behind the British lines between Laventie and Houplines to the northeast of Bethune, France. According to Pendragon, the story was first made public in the 1930s, when Edwn T. Woodhall (late of Scotland Yard and the Secret Service) wrote his reminiscences.

It was the practice during World War I (*c.* 1916) to earmark numerous isolated sites for reserve dumps of explosives that could be drawn upon in an emergency. Such dumps were usually in abandoned villages or farmhouses, well away from the range of enemy guns, and were guarded by one or two soldiers, the guards being changed weekly. From the guard's point of view, such jobs were "cushy," though the loneliness of a deserted ruin could often be rather irksome.

> He challenged the figure, and receiving no reply, fired his rifle. To his amazement the figure vanished.

One such dump was located between Laventie and Houplines, and the explosives were hidden in the basement of a ruined farmhouse close to a derelict village. The guards were given rations for a week, plenty of fuel, cooking utensils, books and magazines, and perhaps a dart board. The men used to say that it wasn't so bad during the day, but nights were apt to be eerie—even if one did not believe in ghosts.

From far away there came the rumble of the guns and the frequent ascent of Verey lights. Occasionally an airplane droned over. Although they were in the midst of war, it seemed strangely remote to those in the ruined farmhouse near Laventie.

Then, gradually, stories began to circulate about the site. It seemed, according to reports, that always around the full moon, strange sounds were heard as if the guards were not the only inhabitants of the shambles of the farmhouse. Unaccountable footsteps were heard on the cobbled road that ran past the dump, and one man reported that when the moon was full he had seen a figure some 25 yards from where he stood. He challenged the figure, and receiving no reply, fired his rifle. To his amazement the figure vanished.

Since it was suspected that an enemy agent was at work, the intelligence service was informed, and an officer—Edwin T. Woodhall on the first occasion—was sent with a French policeman to augment the guard. The gendarme was chosen in case the arrest of a civilian was necessary.

The first night passed uneventfully enough. The men had a good fire, plenty of candles and food, and a couple of packs of cards, and after they had amused themselves for a while, they arranged to take turns to keep watch. It was on the second night's vigil that the strange manifestation occurred. Woodhall was taking the first two hours watch while the gendarme and the soldier slept. The latter soon settled themselves and fell asleep, but a little over an hour later they found Woodhall shaking them awake and telling them to listen.

The awakened men listened as they silently reached for their weapons. Above the cellar hideout there came the unmistakable sound of iron-shod boots on the road that ran a few yards away. So heavy and so definite were the footfalls that the vibration caused one or two pieces of plaster and earth to drop from the ceiling of the cellar.

With Woodhall leading, the three men crept to the top of the steps and into the moonlight. Instantly they saw a dark figure move from its place near a wall and vanish into the deep shadow cast by the buildings. For an hour or more, they searched the area but found nobody, not even a stray animal disturbed by the uncanny silence that had fallen upon the moonlit ruins. When daylight came, a more thorough search was made, but again there was no indication of any unauthorized person being on the site or in the derelict village beyond.

The following night brought spectacular events. Again the watch was kept, but the men who were resting did not slumber. They were too expectant and tense. At 2:55 a.m.—a little later than on the previous night—there came once again that characteristic sound of heavy iron-shod boots clumping toward them in the darkness.

Silently the three men crept to the top of the steps and, remaining in the shadows, gazed to the right towards a moonlit wall. A few yards from where they stood, their weapons ready, a German soldier knelt by the wall turning over some fallen bricks. Spellbound, they watched him. There was no doubt in their minds that he was as earthly as themselves. His spiked helmet gleamed in the moonlight. There was, nevertheless, something rather odd about the appearance of his uniform. It was heavily smeared with clay, as if it had been buried.

For more than a minute they gazed at the figure as he turned over the bricks. Then they challenged the German soldier. He responded by half-rising and turning to look at them. Then it was that all three of the men realized that before them was not a German soldier of flesh and blood but a grotesque skeleton. From beneath that spiked helmet a skull nodded while the bony hands dropped the bricks they held.

Shots from three rifles rang out, shattering the stillness of the night. Instantly the phantom vanished. The men kept watch until dawn, but the spectral German soldier did not reappear.

It must be granted that the intelligence staff investigated the case very thoroughly, but not before the explosives were removed from the dump—this being done on the day following the report being made. Acting in collaboration with the French authorities, the British pieced together the history of the village as it existed at the time of the declaration of war in August 1914. Although many of the inhabitants were dead, a number were traced and questioned, and from their various reports the following strange story was patched together.

In the late summer of 1914, the vast army of General Von Kluck swept towards Paris and the Channel ports. German infantry reached the village and overran the place, taking whatever they required but not harming the inhabitants unless they resisted.

The farmhouse was occupied by a sergeant-major and 20 or more men. The farmer had gone, leaving his wife and an infant, together with several villagers who had decided to remain. The cellar that had later been occupied by the British guards was then used as a wine store. The wine was promptly taken by the German soldiery, who settled down to a night's revel—the sergeant-major, in particular, pestering the farmer's young wife with his attentions. The situation became so threatening that the woman left the house and sought the advice and protection of an aged priest, who had remained behind with his parish. He said that he would remain with her until the Germans left, their departure being expected on the following day.

Shortly afterwards the Allies began to shell the village, forcing the Germans to retreat sooner than they had planned. All was confusion. The shouts of the men, the neighing of their horses, and the crash of the exploding shells made the place hell. The sergeant-major, according to the report of witnesses testifying later, was angry that the young mother had sought the old priest, and he denounced her as a spy. Drunkenly he first shot the child, then the mother, and finally the old priest.

The woman and child died instantly, but the cleric lingered for a few minutes, and pointing at the German he said, "Evil man, your spirit will live on, and you will return when your hour comes to haunt this place until God sees fit to absolve your soul!" Then, in the presence of witnesses, the priest died.

Running unsteadily to join his company, the sergeant-major was caught by a splinter from an exploding shell and died on the cobbled road.

The Germans departed, and the few French peasants buried the woman, the child, and the priest in one grave and the soldier in another. All the graves were close to the wall at the spot where the phantom was seen kneeling among the scattered bricks. The bodies were eventually exhumed to testify to the truth of the story.

WITNESSING A GHOSTLY RE-CREATION OF THE "WAR FIGHT"

In his article "Time Marched Backward" (*Fate*, October 1962), William P. Schramm recounts an interesting ghostly reconstruction of the past. The experience occurred to Paul Smiles, a friend of Schramm's, who was on duty with the British Army in Nairobi, East Africa, in 1942. He had taken advantage of a furlough to head for the lion country below Mount Kilimanjaro. Once there, he learned that a pride of lions had put themselves outside the protective laws by hunting native stock. A native guide named Simbia led Smiles to a shooting platform, and the white hunter was directed to await the lions, which would, according to the guide, come down to the pool to drink.

Smiles was about to drift off to sleep when he was brought fully to his senses by the roar of a lion. Just as he was bringing a large male with full, dark mane into his sights, a rifle shot split the night's silence and sent the pride of lions scattering.

The shot had come from the direction of the tree in which Simbia sat perched. The two men had agreed that Bwana Smiles should have the first shot. The Englishman was about to castigate his guide when "a bedlam of rifle fire broke loose, as if hundreds of … troopers had gone into action. Amidst this din, sharp commands rang out in both English and German. The fusillades ensued time after time, interposed with excited commands. Then came silence."

Startled and shaky, Smiles came down from the shooting platform. Simbia stood at the foot of his tree, waiting for him. He had not expected Smiles to be able to shoot a lion on that night, the anniversary of the "War Fight" that had been waged on that ground between the English and the Germans 25 years before. On the first night that Simbia had heard the sounds of phantom warfare, he had thought that he had experienced some kind of nightmare. He had never told anyone what he had witnessed for fear that they would say he was bewitched. That was why he had brought Smiles to that particular shooting platform on that night. He had wanted corroboration of his story.

> He had never told anyone what he had witnessed for fear that they would say he was bewitched.

Simbia led Smiles through the brambles until they came to the open veldt. There under the African moon, Smiles saw rows of crosses marking the graves of both British and German infantry. "Outnumbered ten to one, and maybe taken by surprise, the British regiment had been annihilated. Since then every year on the fight's anniversary night, Simbia explained, the souls of the troopers came back and fought the battle over again."

DO YOU LIVE ON BATTLE-SATURATED SOIL?

In his article "Battles and Ghosts" (*Prediction* magazine, July 1952), John Pendragon sought to establish his theory that in regard to England, the eastern part of the country produces the greatest crop of haunted sites. The late, eminent British psychic-sensitive and researcher stated that such might be due to the fact that the eastern area of the country has been the scene of most of England's battle, especially battles to stave off invasion. Pendragon also made reference to the theory that the districts may, in some unknown way, have become "sensitized" as the result of these emotional conflicts involving bloodshed.

It has for some time been suggested by paranormal investigators that great human emotion can saturate a place or an object with its own particular vibration. On that assumption, is it not possible—or even probable—that the scenes of bloody conflicts have, so to speak, "sensitized" the very soil upon which they took place?

Many readers may be living in a house that is built on the site of an early battle, recorded or unrecorded, or even the scene of a human sacrifice or a terrible murder. Perhaps you smile indulgently, but such a case is by no means impossible. Many a sedate parlor may be standing on a place that has witnessed the most grim and terrifying scenes.

> The American troops, who looked down on the charred ruins from their positions in the front-line bunkers, called Kumsong the "Capital of No Man's Land."

John Pendragon stated that eastern England is an especially haunted area, and its geological composition is composed mainly of soil types of the Tertiary and Quaternary periods, the most recent eras of geological history. The Tertiary era of rock includes marine limestone, clay, shelly sands, and gravels. In the Quaternary era one finds peat, alluvium, silt, mud, loam, and sometimes gravel.

Essex probably contains the greatest number of haunted sites in England, and Essex is 80 percent London clay, with the remainder mostly chalk. This particular county and its clay subsoil may provide a key to the problem of why certain areas are more haunted than others. The question is, are certain subsoils more sensitized than others?

The astrophysicist Robert Millikan discovered that certain soils absorb cosmic waves more readily than others, some soils acting as conductors and others as insulators. The French physicist Georges Lakhovsky noted that the highest incidence of cancer appeared to occur on clay soils and soils rich in ores, and that the lowest incidence was to be found where the soil was sand or gravel. Lakhovsky attributed this fact to the deflection of cosmic waves by the conducting soils, causing an imbalance in body cells, which, he maintained, are miniature oscillating circuits. Therefore, we may deduce that cosmic rays or the deflection of them by a soil consisting predominantly of clay does, in some way yet unknown to us, act as an aid to the production of phenomena that we call haunting by spirits.

It would seem that the clays, chalk, and alluvial soils are more sensitized than the ancient rocks, such as granite, gneiss, coal, old red sandstone, limestone, and so forth. Perhaps clay has the property of storing or deflecting the X energy, while granite and basalt do not. Subterranean water may also play a part. We might also point out that the most haunted places in England are on the "drier side" of the country. Pendragon was convinced that the reason why some areas are more haunted than others lies in a fusion of a number of factors, widely different, but that the geology of the district is one of them.

CHING, THE GHOSTLY VIOLINIST OF KUMSONG

Veterans of the Korean conflict returned with tales of a ghost town that came to life on cold, still nights. By day, Kumsong, Korea, was nothing but piles of battered rubble. The population had long since given over residence of their war-washed village to the rats. The American troops, who looked down on the charred ruins from their positions in the front-line bunkers, called Kumsong the "Capital of No Man's Land."

But, then, on some nights, soldiers would come back from their frozen bunkers with stories of music, singing, and the laughter of women that had drifted up from the ghost town. So many Allied troops heard the ghostly music that "Ching and his violin" became a reality to the front-line soldiers.

One morning the GIs awakened to find that some wit had nailed a poster to the side of a log bunker: "Come to the gala dance this Saturday night—located in lovely, convenient downtown Kumsong. Dancing partners and delicious drinks without cost."

Soldiers who scoffed at the tales of the weird phenomena were invited to put on their long-johns and join the sentries on the hill that overlooked the battered city. A sergeant with a poetic soul wrote the following to celebrate Kumsong's ghostly dance: "There's a place to dance in your combat pants,/And a place to forget the fight;/There's gals galore and no sign of war,/In Kumsong, Saturday night./It's down the line, don't step on a mine,/Far from the battle's din,/Where you can jig to the phantom music/Of Ching and his violin."

GHOSTS ON PORT HUENEME NAVAL BASE

Richard Senate, the experienced paranormal investigator, has found that the Port Hueneme Naval Base in California has many stories of ghosts. "The Officers Club, formerly the Senator Thomas Bard Mansion, has a long history of strange psychic events," Senate said. "Some believe that the ghost of Mrs. Bard walks the halls. Others report the phantom of the old senator himself haunting the second floor. Still others point to sightings of a Chinese servant as the specter that dwells in the three storied house."

Senate has found that new accounts of ghostly behavior point to the new Navy Exchange warehouse as being perhaps more haunted than the mansion. It was built on the site of a clinic, and the sightings of ghosts in that old structure date back to World War II.

"A phantom officer was once encountered late at night," Senate stated. "There were reports of whispering voices that came at a set time each day. When personnel checked, there was no one around or any logical explanation for the sounds. Years ago, two naval personnel witnessed a man run though the building late at night, wearing clothing that resembled the uniform of the Second World War. He ignored them and ran past them. It was a long moment before they the witnesses recalled that all the doors and windows were locked for the night. The man they saw looked as if he was very solid—unlike the commonly held view that ghosts are semitransparent or dressed in white."

Senate remarked that while the old building is history now, the ghosts may not have been evicted with the demolition. A young man was stocking merchandise in the new Naval Exchange warehouse before the store was open when he saw an officer in uniform standing, looking at a rack of uniforms. He got up to inform the office that the store was not yet open but he would be glad to help him. The officer turned to him and abruptly vanished.

Senate told another story about a young man who went to the vending machines in the Naval Exchange late one night for a snack. He walked away and then remembered that he forgot his change. He turned and heard a woman's voice say, "Did you forget something?" There was no one else in the building. He ran away, unwilling to return to vending machine out of fear.

Is the new building haunted? "Perhaps," Senate said. "The files of psychic research are filled with accounts of haunted buildings being torn down, only to have the structures built on the same location haunted with the older spirits."

⚉

THE FRENCH CAPTAIN GOES IN SEARCH OF HIS HEAD

In October 1965 the air force airfield of Tan Son Nhut had enough to keep it busy with Viet-cong raids and air strikes without having to worry about restless spirits, but a pesky phantom Frenchman had the nasty habit of setting off flares and keeping the men on edge.

One night staff Sergeant James Hinton of Lexington, Kentucky, an air policeman, was making his customary watch. He was out near the bomb and ammunition dump when someone triggered off one of the flares. The captain in charge of the detail immediately began to fire in the direction of the flare, thinking he saw someone in black pajamas drop into a ditch, but when the men got there, the ditch was empty. The next thing they knew, another flare went off, and there seemed to be someone up in a tree just beyond the old French tower. The captain opened up again and so did the rest of men. No one fell from the tree. The soldiers glanced uneasily at each other on the moonlit-flooded runway. What had caused the flares to go off? The adrenalin was flowing in their veins; their nerves would not be quieted.

Veteran Vietnamese guards explained to the Americans that the ghost was that of a French captain who was on duty in the tower when his outpost was overrun by Vietminh on the last day of the war waged against the French in 1954. The Frenchman put up a fierce, though vain, struggle.

When finally captured, the communists decided to repay him for the trouble he had caused them by beheading him. The French captain pled with his captors to be shot like a soldier instead of beheaded like a criminal, but the communists had made up their minds. He was clad in black pajamas and decapitated.

The Vietnamese soldiers believed that the Frenchman's body was buried in the old Buddhist cemetery out beyond the airport gates, but his head was hidden somewhere near the old watch tower. The Frenchman, now a member of the unquiet dead, must make regular forays to the old tower in search of his head if he was ever to find any rest.

The captain opened up again and so did the rest of men. No one fell from the tree.

According to Hinton, that was only the first of many spectral visits from the phantom Frenchman. As the soldiers became accustomed to these encounters, they learned to disregard the pajama-clad figure hovering around the old French tower at the edge of the main runway. Flares continued to be set off mysteriously, however.

The Vietnamese soldiers were firm in their beliefs regarding the nocturnal specter. They avoided night watch on the edge of the runway, and they repeatedly refused to allow the old tower to be torn down. When the runways were extended to accommodate fighter jets, all the other towers were removed, but not the one where the disconsolate Frenchman sought his head.

THE STERN GHOST OF THE GURKHA HAVILDAR

No sentry dares to sleep on duty at the Khamba Fort in the mountains of Kashmir. The Indian army men who guard this fort believe that they are watched over by the ghost of the Gurkha Havildar. And he is a harsh taskmaster.

In these mountains, the legend of the Gurkha ghost has become famous. Educated army officers, although disbelieving the legend, are content to let it grow because the Gurkha ghost solves many disciplinary problems in Khamba Fort. Indian troops swear the ghost prowls the fort at night, slapping the faces of sentries who aren't alert and using his best parade ground language to berate slovenly soldiers.

The ghost is said to be that of a Gurkha havildar (sergeant) who performed a heroic one-man assault on Khamba Fort during the bitter 1948 war between India and Pakistan for Kashmir. The fort, held by Pakistani forces, had fought off Indian troops for weeks. Then, the Gurkha havildar found a crack in the fort's steep, thick stone walls, and one night, armed only with grenades and a knife, crept inside. He killed all the defenders but was fatally wounded himself.

One night in June 1965, Lance Naik (Corporal) Ram Prakash said he met the ghost when firing broke out along the cease-fire line. Prakash said that a terrifying voice rose from a turret on the fort's wall: "I have given my life for this post. Why are you so slack?" Then came the sound of a face being slapped. It was learned later, Prakash said, that a sentry in the turret was nodding over his rifle and was punished by the stern ghost.

The men of Khamba Fort know the Gurkha ghost well. Each can describe in detail the clothing worn by the eerie figure that strides the ramparts at night. The troops say that the ghost invariably appears wearing only one shoe. The other apparently was lost in battle more than 50 years ago. The men agree that they are not really afraid of the ghost because they know he is on their side.

The men of Khamba Fort are very careful to put out cups of tea and sweets for the lonely Gurkha ghost who maintains his vigil throughout the night. And, they say, the tea and sweets always are gone by dawn.

24
GHOSTS IN CIVIC BUILDINGS AND PRISONS

ENCOUNTERING A NEBBISHY GHOST IN THE STATE CAPITOL

The Personal Experience of Richard D. Hendricks

Richard D. Hendricks is a researcher with a large Madison, Wisconsin, law firm, the proprietor of Weird Wisconsin (<www.weirdwi.com>), the associate director for the Wisconsin Paranormal Research Center (<www.my.execpc.com/~wisprc/>), and the Newsline editor for The Anomalist *(<www.anomalist.com>).*

"I've heard my share of loud ghost encounters. Fully dressed apparitions, water sluicing off them, materializing in showers, with bloated gray heads, blackened hollows for eyes. Smoky snake entities slithering in through the front door, baleful golden-slitted eyes nailing shock-frozen homeowners to the sofa. Aged frail women wearing yesterday's faded dresses, hair knotted in gray buns, quietly threatening to kill robust young men. Wild and weird encounters; enough to raise goose bumps on even the strongest.

"I hear these stories and rub my hands in anticipation. Maybe this house, this snug secure suburban abode, is finally the place where the screaming bloody revenant all ghost hunters secretly hope for will at last reveal itself in all its gaudy excess.

"Alas. Hours, days spent poking about, with little to show for the effort. No amorphous shape captured on video or film; no eerie voice spitting sibilants on a cassette tape; only ambiguity, and the lingering thought that, if only I had been here sooner. In my lectures, I've worked it into a standard joke: if you're afraid of ghosts, the best place to be is with ghost hunters, for only rarely do they ever encounter them.

"Even my own family has had numerous paranormal encounters, not the least of which was the haunted saloon my mother owned in northern Wisconsin. For a decade, well over a dozen members of my extended family saw apparitions, felt cold spots, experienced inexplicable electrical phenomena, heard banging noises, and puzzled over other routine spirited manifestations. But when I visited: nothing. Quiet as the grave. The closest I ever got was years before, when my grandmother phoned my mother to ask how she was doing. From upstairs, I heard my mother answer the phone—and then scream. My grandmother had been dead already for a couple of days. It was my nearest contemporaneous encounter.

"Or so I thought until a few years ago. I work across the street from the state capitol building in Madison, Wisconsin. It's a massive structure, situated on the highest point between two large lakes, built of white Bethel Vermont granite in the form of a Greek cross in the Italian Renaissance style, surmounted by the only granite dome in the United States, and only second in height as a concession to the national capitol in Washington, D.C. It's oriented to the four cardinal directions, with windows throughout, and massive Corinthian columns, carved statuary, and a gilded bronze statue, Miss Forward, symbolizing our state motto, with a stylish badger clinging to her head, atop the dome. Legislative offices, the governor's office, and the Supreme Court share space with the public, who are either visiting, advocating, or simply cutting through to save blocks of walking around its perimeter.

"It's the third building on site; two previous capitol buildings were consumed by fire. Before that, Native Americans camped here for hundreds of years, and the effigy mounds they constructed high above the glittering blue lakes were obliterated without a second thought. In the original badly constructed wooden building, James Morrison boarded pigs in the basement for safe keeping. Bored legislators goaded the hogs into squealing by poking sticks at them through the spaces between shrunken floorboards. In 1882, while two wings were being added, one collapsed, killing eight workers. If, as some people theorize, certain buildings act as enormous energy storage batteries, then this one, with its history of native spiritual practices, horrific fires, sudden deaths, partisan antagonisms, and the concentrated attention of millions of citizens from across the state, must be simmering with potency.

"Are there ghosts? For years, custodians have talked of doors opening and closing, [and of] hearing paper rustling in empty rooms, and a lucky few have encountered a distinguished, bushy-bearded, white haired man striding about. He's Moses Strong, former legislator and lobbyist for the Milwaukee Railroad in the mid-1800s. A portrait of Strong, when straightened, always settled askew, until finally it was considered such a nuisance it was buried away in a dark basement closet. I haven't yet found a reason for Strong's lingering tenancy, but his continued presence amply illustrates the lobbyist's tenacity.

"Until recently, the State Law Library was also in the building. During the hot summer of 1999, I was in the capitol on an errand to the library on the third floor. Finished, I took the elevator to ground level. I poked G, and as the brass door began closing, it abruptly stopped, stuttered, then shrugged open, as if a straggler had stuck an arm in to stop its closure. I've done this often myself; except, no one was there.

"An old building, an old elevator; some glitch, no doubt. Still, I have another old joke, on the off chance there may be someone invisible trying to sneak on. After all, it always pays to be pleasant, particularly in the presence of the unknown. I offered a greeting. 'Hi. How are you?'

"I didn't expect a response, nor did I receive one. The elevator slowly settled to ground level. I continued my gag, 'I hope you don't mind if I get out first; I'm sorta in a hurry.'

"Midway through the opening door, I swear I felt something shoulder past me. I faltered. Lurched to the right. It was weird. Of course, my rational mind immediately discounted the experience. It was the heat; I was woozy; and was still a little unsteady from recent knee surgery. I shrugged, and thought no more of it. And it would have ended there had I not been back in the building within the hour on a new errand. I was on a different elevator to the third floor. My ride was uneventful.

> I swear I felt something shoulder past me. I faltered. Lurched to the right. It was weird.

"I'm always in a hurry, even with a gimpy knee. A wide marble staircase was in front of me as the door opened. I ducked to the right, to take a hallway past legislative offices to reach my destination on the other side. Just as I rounded the corner, I nearly collided with a small nondescript man, a bit smaller than me, about five-foot-four, short brown hair, glasses, wearing a mustardy colored polo shirt, and also seemingly in a hurry.

"'Excuse me,' I blurted out, neatly sidestepping this nebbishy little man and allowing my momentum to carry me along the hallway.

"At the end of the corridor, I turned left. On my left was the gallery from which I had just come, across the wide expanse of the marble staircase. There, some 50 feet away, was the same nebbishy man I had nearly collided with, already in the act of waving at me.

"He was moving slowly, partly in profile, looking back at me, waving his right arm in an exaggerated languorous sweeping gesture, a goofy grin spread across his narrow face. Strange. At the rate he had been traveling, and from his position where we had nearly collided, he should have been well past this point, perhaps vanished. It was as if he had waited just around the bend of the hallway, and had started waving before I turned my corner, knowing that I would look back across to where I had been. As if to say, See me now?

"I immediately flashed back to my elevator ride an hour earlier. It was just flat-out weird. Was it coincidence? Did I weave a connecting narrative on the fly from two discontinuous and utterly mundane events? Or was it something more?

"I've long suspected that every individual clothes a discarnate entity in his or her own individual design. If ghosts are some form of free-floating energy, then each person particularizes it. The same energy—but one person may see a bent old man painfully hobbling down a hallway, another a girlish figure skipping merrily. And in a psychic locus, where millions of citizens project their thoughts, their desires, their dreams, their fears, their concern over faceless bureaucrats and archetypal state workers, surely something could poke up that did not have an onsite historical antecedent. Something like a scurrying nebbishy little man in a polo shirt.

"For years I've thought of this figure. Was it a ghost? It would be nice to have a loud, excessive ghost encounter—scary, then over with, and done. Paranormal? Who knows. Its ambiguity resonates through the years, making it seem more spooky. Unknown, and ultimately unknowable."

⬤⬤⬤

GHOSTS IN THE OLD STATE CAPITOL IN RALEIGH

For many years there has been talk of slamming doors, muffled voices and ghosts walking the corridors of the 164-year-old capitol building in Raleigh, North Carolina. A number of persons hired as night watchmen have quit after only one night on duty, complaining of doors opening and closing and invisible footsteps following them on their rounds. In July 2002 a staff member working late thought she heard the sounds of a reception in progress on the first floor, but when she reached the foot of the stairs, she found the rotunda empty, and all noises suddenly ceased.

Sam P. Townsend, a retired capitol administrator, recalled the state library room on the third floor as being particularly creepy. Late one night as he approached the library door, he remembered a cold, dank air falling on his head and neck, and he decided his work could wait until the next day.

Although the capitol had gone through a considerable number of watchmen who declined the privilege of working in the building after one night on the job, Owen J. Jackson, 84, stuck with the task for 12 years before he retired in 1990. He simply shrugged off the angry slamming of doors that sounded behind him and the thumping noises that followed him on his rounds.

The old State Capitol Building, Raleigh, North Carolina.

Capitol historian Raymond Beck admitted that he didn't like to work in the capitol after dark. He always made it a point to be out of the building by quitting time, because when darkness fell, he could sense the whole atmosphere changing.

In February 2003 psychic investigator Patty Ann Wilson of the Ghost Research Foundation released the findings of her group's research into the capitol conducted in November 2002. Their biggest coup, she told Lorenzo Perez, staff writer for the Raleigh *News and Observer*, was to record a spectral whisper and to photograph a ghost in Reconstruction-era clothing as it sat in the third chair in the third row of the old House chambers.

THE PHANTOM OF HARRINGTON'S CITY HALL

Jan Almquist, city manager of Harrington, Delaware, said that she had actually bumped into the ghost that walks the hallways of the city hall after dark. She remarked that it felt something like a "soft pillow," but she was able to walk right through it. At that very moment, she caught the image of a man, about five-foot six and solidly built, reflected in the window glass.

Other city employees have reported locked doors opening themselves, then slamming shut again. Some have heard unseen footsteps creaking down the hallways and treading up and down the stairs. Police officers working late on night duty frequently hear footsteps clearly sounding in another part of the building. When they investigate, they hear the noises in the area that they just left. City Clerk Norma Short said that she had seen the ghost on three different occasions. She also reported the manifestation of a gray form standing in the library that disappeared when she approached it.

Although no one can identify the ghost for certain, some residents of Harrington have nominated Millard Cooper as the mysterious specter. Before the building, which was constructed in the early 1900s, housed the city government, library, and police headquarters, it was Cooper's Funeral Home. On February 25, 1971, mortician Cooper committed suicide, and longtime residents of Harrington comment that the description of the ghost could well fit the undertaker as he appeared in life.

ARE THERE GHOSTS IN THE FEDERAL BUILDING IN JONESBORO?

For some years now, employees have claimed that there are a number of ghosts in the E. C. "Took" Gathings Federal Building and U.S. Courthouse in Jonesboro, Arkansas. While Bill Collier, who retired after 15 years as the General Services Administration building superintendent, said that he had never spotted a ghost during his period of service, he acknowledged that there were plenty of complaints of strange night noises and of objects being mysteriously moved. Collier also admitted that nearly every employee and security guard in the building had complained of unusual activities at one time or another.

Ernest Mungle, who had worked in the building as a custodian, told Larry Fugate, a reporter for the *Jonesboro Sun* (October 13, 2002), that he had once heard voices from an empty and locked jury room and even had met a ghost on the third floor many years ago. He didn't worry about its presence and had given it the nickname of Charlie.

One of the offices in the building hired a carpet installation crew to work in the evenings when the rooms were vacant. After only two shifts, the crew refused to work in the place after dark.

Two employees of the Internal Revenue Service complained of hearing rickety-ticky piano music, such as the kind that was heard in the old saloons.

When a longtime resident of Jonesboro heard the stories, he explained to the employees that a saloon had once stood near the front entrance of the downtown office building.

A TALL, MUSTACHED GHOST IN HATBORO'S BOROUGH HALL

On a Friday morning in December 2000, Viki Connolly, the administrative assistant at the Loller Building, the borough hall in Hatboro, Pennsylvania, had come to work early. Because she knew she was the only one in the building, she was surprised when she saw the tall, sad-eyed mustached man standing in the tax collector's office. There was something about him that immediately transmitted to Connolly that he was not human. As she watched from her desk, about 15 feet away, the stranger crossed the office in five quick steps and vanished.

> There was something about him that immediately transmitted to Connolly that he was not human.

Later, recreating the scene for John Anastasi, a staff writer for *The Intelligencer* on October 2, 2002, Connolly said that the ghost simply walked from one corner of the room to the opposite corner and disappeared when it got to the wall. She stated that she was not frightened by the entity, for his facial expression was "sad or sick or tired," and she felt sorry for him. She described the ghost as tall with a mustache, salt and pepper hair, wearing his long hair pulled back in a ponytail. He was dressed in a gray military uniform.

The building that currently houses Hatboro's administrative offices, council chambers, and district court was constructed originally in 1811 as a school. While no one stepped forward to admit seeing paranormal visitors in the building, District Justice Paul Leo stated that he considered Ms. Connolly to be a very credible person. Justice Leo, whose courtroom is on the second floor of the Loller Building, said that there had been evenings when he had come in the courtroom for arraignments that he had suddenly felt as if he wasn't alone, that someone stood behind him.

A JUSTICE OF THE PEACE BROUGHT A HAUNTING ON HIS FAMILY

The Classic Case of the Drummer of Tedworth

In March 1661 John Mompesson, a justice of the peace of Tedworth, England, had an ex-drummer in Oliver Cromwell's army brought before him. The former soldier, whose name was Drury, had been demanding money of the bailiff by virtue of a suspicious pass. The bailiff had believed the pass to be counterfeit, and Mompesson, who was well acquainted with the hand-writing of the official who had allegedly signed the note, judged the paper to be a forgery.

Drury beseeched Mompesson to verify his story with Colonel Ayliff of Gretenham, who, the drummer insisted, would vouch for his integrity. Mompesson responded to the drummer's pleas that he not be put into jail, but he told Drury that he would confiscate his drum until he had checked out his story. Drury begged that he be allowed to take his drum with him, but Mompesson told the man to be on his way and to be thankful that he did not sentence him to wait out the time until Colonel Ayliff could be contacted residing in a cell in Tedworth Goal (jail).

Mompesson had the drum sent to his house for safekeeping, then left on a business trip to London. When he returned, his wife informed him that the household had been frightened by noises in the night that she attributed to burglars trying to break into the house. On the third night of his return, Mompesson was awakened by a loud knocking that seemed to be coming from a side door. With one pistol cocked and ready and another tucked in his belt, he opened the door. There was no one there. But knocking sounded at another door. When he opened that door and found no one there, he walked around the outside of the house in search of the prankster. He found no one, nor could he account for the hollow drumming sound that came from the roof.

From that night on, the sound of drumming came always just after the Mompessons had gone to bed. After a month, the disturbances moved from the roof down into the room where Mompesson had placed Drury's drum. Once there, the ghostly drummer favored the family with two hours of martial rolls, tattoos, and points of war each evening.

The ghost began beating on the children's bedsteads at night, sometimes raising and lowering their beds in time with its drumming. When it would at last cease pounding the invisible drum and hoisting their beds in the air, it would lie under the beds, scratching at the floor. The Mompessons tried moving their children to another bedroom, but the drummer moved along with them. The knocking became so loud that it awakened neighbors several houses away. The Mompessons' servants also received nocturnal visits from the ghost. It would wait until they drifted off to sleep, then it would lift their beds. On occasion, it would curl up around their feet.

The unseen drummer soon had achieved such strength that it could hand boards to a servant who was doing some repair work in the house. This remarkable display of spirit energy was observed by numerous witnesses, but Mompesson stepped in and forbade the servant to encourage such familiar interaction with the demon. Perhaps Mompesson should have been more judicious in his designation of the unseen spirit's character, for the entity emitted offensive, sulfurous fumes. The stench convinced the justice of the peace that their unwelcome visitor had come directly from the pit of Hell.

A Reverend Cragg was summoned to conduct prayers and a kind of exorcism in the house. The drummer kept quiet until the minister's closing "amen," then it began to move chairs about the room, throw the children's shoes into the air, and toss objects about the room.

The drummer particularly enjoyed wrestling with a muscular servant named John. It delighted in wrapping itself around the big man and holding him fast, as if he were bound hand and foot. Only by exerting the full extent of his brute strength could John free himself from the hold of his invisible opponent.

On the night in which Mrs. Mompesson gave birth to another child, the drummer kept respectfully silent. For three

Five different entities have been seen in this photo of Tennessee's retired electric chair.

weeks, there were no sounds of drumming in the Mompesson home. The family had begun to think that the mysterious and annoying sounds had ended. But then one night the drummer began the rolls again. It was as if it had maintained a period of quiet to allow the mother to recover some strength before it began its mischief in earnest.

By January 10, 1662, nearly a year after the disturbances began, the ghost had acquired a voice and the ability to simulate the sound of rustling silk and the panting of animals. It had begun by singing in the chimney, then moved into the children's bedroom, where it frightened them with its chanting that it was a nasty witch. On a particularly cold and bitter winter's night, the ghost came to Mompesson's bedside, panting like a large dog. Even though the bedroom did not have a fireplace, it soon became very hot and filled with a stifling, disagreeable odor. The next morning, Mompesson scattered fine ashes over the bedroom floor to see what sort of footprints might be made by the obnoxious entity. The ghost entered the bedroom again that night, and on the following morning, Mompesson was baffled by the discovery of the markings of a great claw, some letters, circles, and other strange imprints.

Reverend Joseph Glanvil was attracted to the case by the reports that had reached him, and he arrived to conduct his investigation. The phenomena provided the clergyman with ample evidence of their existence from the very first moment of his arrival. It was eight o'clock in the evening and the children were in bed, suffering their nightly ritual of scratching, bed-liftings, and pantings. Reverend Glanvil tried desperately to trace the source of the disturbances but could find nothing. Later that night, when Reverend Glanvil and a friend retired for the evening, they were awakened by a loud knocking. "What would you have to do with us?" the clergyman asked the entity. "Nothing with you," a disembodied voice answered him.

On a particularly cold and bitter winter's night, the ghost came to Mompesson's bedside, panting like a large dog.

The next morning, Reverend Glanvil's horse was found in a state of nervous exhaustion. A puzzled servant pronounced his opinion that it appeared as though the animal had been ridden all night. Glanvil mounted the horse for his return trip, and it collapsed. Although the horse was well attended and cared for, it died within two days.

On one occasion, Mompesson fired his pistol at a stick of firewood that had suddenly become animated, and he was astonished to see several drops of blood appear on the hearth. The firewood fell to the floor, and a trail of blood began to drip on the stairway as the wounded ghost retreated. One wishes that a modern pathologist's laboratory could have had an opportunity to analyze the drops for blood-type.

When the thing returned three nights later, it seemed to take out its anger for Mompesson's attack on the children. Even the baby was tossed about and not allowed to sleep. In desperation, Mompesson arranged to have the children taken to the house of friends. Later that night when the ghost pounded on the door to Mompesson's bedroom, it showed itself to a startled servant. "I could not determine the exact proportion," the terrified man told his master, "but I saw a great body with two red and glaring eyes, which for some time were fixed steadily upon me."

A friend of Mompesson's, hoping to be of some assistance to the justice of the peace, had all of his coins turn black during the course of his overnight stay. His horse was discovered in the stables with one of its hind legs firmly fastened in its mouth. It took several men working with a lever to dislodge the hoof from the unfortunate beast's jaws.

About this time, Drury, the man whose drum Mompesson had confiscated, was located in Gloucester Gaol, where he had been sentenced for thievery. Upon questioning, he freely admitted putting a spell on Tedworth's justice of the peace and "witching" him. "I have plagued him," the man boasted, "and he shall never be quiet 'till he hath made me satisfaction for taking away my drum."

It is likely that the haunting at Tedworth began quite independently of the bitter ex-soldier who claimed to have put a curse on John Mompesson. It would not seem at all inconsistent with Drury's character to conjecture that after he learned of the disturbances at Tedworth, he might have taken the credit for originating the manifestations. On the other hand, one should recognize the terribly potency that some people accredit to "curses," the direction of negative suggestion.

Justice of the Peace Mompesson had Drury tried for witchcraft at Sarum, and the drummer was condemned to be transported to one of the English colonies. Certain accounts have it that the man so terrified the ship's captain and crew by raising storms that they took him back to port and left him on the dock before sailing away again.

With the drummer either on his way to the colonies or set free from jail to do as he would, the manifestations in the Mompesson house ceased. By the time a king's commission had arrived to investigate the alleged haunting, the phenomena had been quiet for several weeks. The cavaliers spent the night with the family, then left the next morning, pronouncing their consensual verdict that the entire two-year haunting had been either a hoax or the misinterpretation of natural phenomena by credulous and superstitious individuals.

Whatever the truth of the manifestations in the Mompesson home, the demon of Tedworth is so much a part of the legend and folklore of England that ballads and poems have been written in celebration of the incredible series of events.

Later, Reverend Joseph Glanvil wrote *Saducismus Triumphatus*, his account of witnessing the phenomena at Tedworth while it was in progress. Expressing his frustration with the king's investigators and their final verdict regarding the phenomena, Glanvil wrote: "It was bad logic to conclude a matter of fact from a single negative against numerous affirmatives, and so affirm that a thing was never done.... By the same way of reasoning ... the Spaniard inferred well that said 'There is no sun in England, because I was there for six weeks and never saw it.' This is the common argument of those that deny the being of apparitions. They have traveled all hours of the night and have never seen any thing worse than themselves (which may well be) and thence they conclude that all ... apparitions are fancies or impostures."

THE WHITE LADY OF SHEPTON MALLET

On Tuesday, January 17, 1967, the British press carried the story of six prison warders who complained of frightening experiences while on night duty at Shepton Mallet, Somerset.

In 1988 Lars Thomas was on a guided tour of the Viaduct Inn's cellar, which used to be cells of London's notorious Newgate Prison. He took a photograph inside one of the empty cells, but when he developed the film, this figure appeared on the photograph.

The guards told of a "chilling atmosphere" and a "weird presence" that seemed to permeate the tiny, blue-tiled duty room. Each of the men testified that he had heard unaccountable bangings and the sound of heavy breathing, and had had the feeling that something or somebody was in the room with him. One of the guards told a reporter that he personally would not do another night in the duty room for a thousand pounds.

The warden of the prison, Barry Wigginton, sent a full report to the home secretary, Roy Jenkins, stating that he had been unable to find any satisfactory explanation for the happenings. Wigginton said that he had spent a night in the guard room and had found nothing unusual. He had also called in two chaplains to calm his frightened staff. By the time the story had appeared in the British press, the incidents had ceased, but some prison officers were still reluctant to spend the night alone in the duty room.

One senior warder told a journalist that they had all been scared stiff and nobody had yet come up with an explanation. Someone brought up the legend of a "white lady"—a woman who was beheaded in 1680—that had been known to haunt the 360-year-old prison in autumn and winter.

"If this has been the white lady doing this," a prison officer commented, "and she comes back again, the night duty staff is going to wear thin."

⊸◅▨◖▨▻⊷

An Eerie Visitation at Pentridge Prison

From the Ghost to Ghost Website <www.ghosttoghost.com>:
The Personal Experience of Karen Linstrom, Governor (Retired),
HM Prison Service, Victoria, Australia

"I worked in the Victorian Prison Service, Australia, for 16 years. I began my career at HM Pentridge Prison, Coburg Victoria. The site, now partially torn down, was home to 1,200 male and female prisoners at any one time. The ghostly encounter that I am going to describe took place in 'D' Division, originally constructed for female prisoners in 1880 but currently the remand facility for 320 maximum security male prisoners.

"One night, a young male prisoner had slashed his wrists and arms in a suicide attempt. He had lost a life threatening amount of blood, and six of us were desperately trying to stem the flow while waiting for the intensive care ambulance to arrive. At one point, the Senior Prison Officer requested that I run out of the infirmary, up a shot landing to call [your equivalent of 911] to get an ETA on the ambulance.

"As I ran up the stairs I hit what felt like an ice wall and was momentarily stopped in my tracks. The air around me became instantly chilled, and although this was in the middle of summer, I was cold and could see my breath. I was then able to get up the last six steps, but when I turned around, I saw an opalescent fog crystallize into the form of a woman. She wore long skirts, a cap on her head, and when she turned her face towards me, I got the impression of a woman old before her time, with uncountable horrors and sorrows written in the depth of her startling blue eyes. She then vanished, and the air around me returned to its warm and humid state.

"I have never forgotten her face, and that five to ten second interlude. I went in search of files and possible photographs to try and find this restless soul. I now have it narrowed down to three possible women, all transported from England, all of Irish extraction, all for seven to 14 years hard labor for crimes such as stealing one shilling's worth of bread.

"She saved me from annoying an already busy emergency service, and made me acutely aware of how much of us we leave behind for other people to learn from."

⊶⊷

THE RESTLESS SPIRIT OF A MONK WHO VISITED A PRISON CELL

A Classic Case from Germany

On a September night in 1835, Dr. Henry Kerner was confronted by a problem that had never been outlined in textbooks or explained by men under whom he had studied. That night he left his room near the Weinsberg prison grounds and walked to a cell where he intended to shut himself in with a 38-year-old female inmate who appeared to be suffering from strange delusions. The prison guards let him pass with a nod, and the turnkey opened the cell of Mrs. Elizabeth Eslinger.

Dr. Kerner asked the woman how she felt before he removed his cloak and sat in the cell's single chair. She replied that she was fine, and Kerner knew her answer to be the truth, for he had examined her himself that afternoon. The minutes passed slowly until an hour had elapsed, then another. Finally, at 11:30 Kerner heard a sound as though some hard object had been thrown down on the side of the cell opposite where the woman sat.

Mrs. Eslinger immediately began to breathe more rapidly and informed the doctor that the ghost she had seen for so many nights had appeared in the cell again. Dr. Kerner put his hand on the woman's forehead and told the evil spirit to depart. Immediately, there sounded a strange rattling, cracking noise all around the walls of the cell, which finally seemed to go out through the window. The woman said the spirit had departed.

Thus, for Dr. Kerner, the reality of the woman's story was established beyond a doubt. He had been decidedly skeptical when he had first heard of the prison ghost, but after examining the woman and hearing the testimony of her fellow prisoners, Dr. Kerner decided that he must investigate the phenomena personally before he could write his report.

According to Mrs. Eslinger, the ghost was the shade of a Roman Catholic priest of Wimmenthal, Germany, who had lived in 1414 and had committed many crimes. In particular, he and his father had worked a fraud upon his own brothers. Since his death, the monk had existed as a spirit in despair. His presence was often accompanied by groans and moans and sometimes by an earthy smell. Although he could not be touched when Mrs. Eslinger reached for him, she claimed that she could feel his hand, which became warmer as time passed and his visits increased.

Prison officials considered the particular cell block to which Mrs. Eslinger had been confined to be nearly impenetrable. With no windows and thick walls on the first floor and only closely barred, narrow windows on the second, they felt that no person could enter the block without passing the guards who were on duty 24 hours a day. Yet the apparition visited the cell nightly, and its presence had been attested to by Mrs. Eslinger's fellow prisoners.

Mrs. Eslinger told Dr. Kerner that the spirit had been sorely troubled when the doctor had called it an evil spirit, protesting that it deserved pity. It had entreated Mrs. Eslinger to pray for it nightly.

For more corroboration (and perhaps to protect his reputation), Dr. Kerner brought his wife to Mrs. Eslinger's cell on October 18. Once again, the woman's breathing quickened, and this time, the doctor asked quite gently that the spirit trouble the woman no longer. The same noises rattled around the cell, then down the passageway.

On October 20 Dr. Kerner again stayed in the cell, this time with Justice Heyd. At midnight Dr. Kerner saw a yellowish light come through the window that had been shut tight against the weather. Simultaneously, he felt a cold breeze and smelled a strong odor. The same sensations awoke Justice

Heyd, who had been dozing, and Dr. Kerner described his face feeling as if ants were running over it. Mrs. Eslinger had fallen to her knees next to her cot and had begun to pray fervently. While she prayed, the men saw the light move up and down the cell, then heard a moaning, hollow, resonant voice that Dr. Kerner could not ascribe to any human.

On December 9 the doctor and the wife of the prison deputy warden, Madam Mayer, were again in the cell. Suddenly a small cloud of light about the size of a small animal, like a cat, came into the cell and moved across it. At the same time there came such a noise at the window that Dr. Kerner thought the panes of glass inside the bars would surely be broken. Mrs. Eslinger told her guests that the ghost had seated itself on a stool in the cell. After the ghost had arrived they heard footsteps, as if someone paced up and down on the floor. Although they saw nothing, Dr. Kerner again felt a cold wind, and a little later he and Madam Mayer heard the same hollow voice say, "In the name of Jesus, look on me!"

Both Dr. Kerner and Madam Mayer could then see a light surrounding them. Once again they heard footsteps and the voice asking, "Do you see me now?"

Dr. Kerner for the first time perceived the form of the being. The ghost was dressed in the loose robe of a medieval clergyman. Dr. Kerner saw it several times again that night, often standing near Mrs. Eslinger as she prayed. Once it approached Madam Mayer, and she commanded it, "Go to my husband in his chamber and in his chamber leave a sign you have been there."

> **D**r. Kerner put his hand on the woman's forehead and told the evil spirit to depart.

The voice replied that it would accept the challenge. The door to the cell, still locked and bolted, swung open easily, then fell shut again, and a shadow seemed to float down the hall while the sound of footsteps filled the quiet block of cells. Fifteen minutes later, it had returned near the window, and when asked if it had completed its task, a hollow laugh filled the cell. Later in the morning, without prompting, Deputy Warden Mayer remarked that the door to his bed chamber, which he was certain not only had been locked but also bolted, had been standing open when he arose.

In concluding his report, Dr. Kerner did not attempt to explain away what he had observed, but he re-emphasized the fact that he and other witnesses had indeed seen *something* in Mrs. Eslinger's cell, and whatever it was, he knew of no natural explanation for it.

The published report, with its admirably objective viewpoint, created a great stir throughout Germany. The report had influence not only among the general public but among scientists as well, and many learned men sought entrance to the Weinsberg prison to investigate the phenomena. In all, over

The administration building of the former Ohio State Reformatory, photographed in 2002. The prison was closed in 1990 and reopened for tours in 1996.

50 men of science visited Mrs. Eslinger, and nearly all of them observed some unexplainable phenomena. Although many of them tried to duplicate the manifestations, none were successful. The bars that rattled so easily at the passing of the ghost could not be shaken by the effort of many men, nor could the awesome voice be duplicated. Two German surgeons claimed that they had heard a sound as if gravel were falling to the ground while they awaited admittance, and that upon entering the cell, the sound was repeated for them by the ghost at their request.

Another time two physicists, Dr. Sicherer and Dr. Fraas, visited Mrs. Eslinger and described a thick cloud that hung near her head. They also heard a loud pounding noise and observed the phenomenon of the locked cell door swinging open, then clanging shut with great violence. These strange occurrences repeated themselves eight times during the night in which they stayed in the cell.

All during the remainder of Mrs. Eslinger's prison term, the ghost continued to haunt the cell block. On Mrs. Eslinger's release, the ghost promised to return to the cell and did so two nights later, whereupon it manifested new sounds at the request of Mrs. Mayer.

The ghost did not bother Mrs. Eslinger after her release from prison, but during the months it had been with her in the cell, it had asked her many times to journey to Wimmenthal to pray for its soul. After much deliberation, Mrs. Eslinger went to Wimmenthal, and witnesses said that when she prayed, the form of a man appeared, accompanied by two small specters. When Mrs. Eslinger ended her prayer, she fell into a faint. After she had been revived, Mrs. Eslinger said that the ghost had asked for her hand. She extended it after taking the precaution of wrapping it in her handkerchief. When the ghost had touched her hand, a flame shot from the cloth. Finger-like marks were scorched into the handkerchief, providing physical proof of the ghost's presence.

The Weinsberg Prison ghost was front-page news in Germany for six months and is certainly one of the best-documented manifestations in the annals of psychic research. It is interesting to note that the prison files on Mrs. Eslinger made mention of the fact that she claimed always to have been a "ghost-seer," although her first actual communication with a ghost did not occur until the specter of the Catholic priest began to appear to her during her internment in Weinsberg Prison.

It would seem that Mrs. Eslinger had long had mediumistic abilities and would, therefore, be of the proper mental makeup to serve as an energy center for a restless spirit. How and why the ghost of the priest became attracted to the imprisoned widow is beyond speculation at this point.

SPIRITS SEEK REDEMPTION AT SHAWSHANK PRISON

The old Ohio State Reformatory at Mansfield, Ohio, made famous by the motion picture based on Stephen King's novella, *Rita Hayworth and the Shawshank Redemption*, is said to be haunted by the ghosts of inmates and guards alike, all of whom seem to be seeking some kind of spiritual redemption and peace.

When the reformatory was constructed in 1886, the architect Levi T. Scofield intended his Romanesque-Gothic design to be one that would uplift, inspire, and overpower people. It was Scofield's intent to build a prison that would fulfill the ideals of the mid-nineteenth century—to teach the incarcerated individuals a skill, instill within them a fear of God, and return them to society as contributing citizens. The prison has the largest freestanding steel cellblock in the United States, with cells stacked six tiers high, 593 cells designed for 1,200 inmates. The idealistic precepts held by the architect and

A cell inside the former Ohio State Reformatory in Mansfield, Ohio.

the wardens were realized in the early days of the reformatory's existence. Historical records indicate that more than 65 percent of the inmates did not return to its cells. But as the early ideals of reformation faded, recidivism rose, and eventually prisoners were crammed four to a cell that had been designed for two.

The state of Ohio abandoned the old reformatory in 1990. In 1995 the Mansfield Reformatory Preservation Society convinced the state to rehabilitate the sprawling, castle-like prison. In 1999 the society was permitted to purchase the reformatory and 17 acres for one dollar.

After the motion picture *The Shawshank Redemption* was released in 1994, the reformatory became popular both with movie fans and with ghost hunters. Among just a few of the restless spirits reported in the Ohio State Reformatory are the following:

1. The inmate in Cell 17, who killed himself by dousing himself with lighter fluid then lighting up his own body.

2. The inmate in Cell 35, who had his head crushed when someone slammed a steel door shut on him.

3. The inmate who had his throat cut with a straight edge razor in the barbershop.

4. The wife of warden Arthur Glattke, who died under suspicious circumstances in 1950.

5. Arthur Glattke himself, whose spirit has been seen in numerous spots in the reformatory.

6. Urban Wilford, a guard who was killed during a prison break attempt in 1926.

Writing in the October 13, 2002, issue of the *Detroit Free Press*, travel writer Gerry Volgenau described the spirit manifestations of the reformatory: "Ghostly images appear. Faces emerge in the shadows.... Visitors hear voices, sometimes singing.... Most unnerving of all, people say they've been touched: a flick to the ear, a finger poke in the shoulder, a push from behind, an ankle grabbed on the stairwell. And ... they were utterly alone. Or were they?"

25

PHANTOMS SEEN ON SEAS AND LAKES

⟜⟜⧓⟜⟜

THE GHOST OF THE HMS *EURYDICE*

March 24, 1878, was a clear spring day, and inhabitants along the west coast of England were basking in the good feeling of another winter gone. Suddenly a large cloud, coming from the northwest and heading southeast toward the Isle of Wight and the English Channel, appeared on the horizon. The cloud was estimated to have been 24 miles in length and a half a mile in depth. And though there was no wind that day, the cloud passed overhead with unusual speed.

The sky through which the incredible mass passed was clear and calm, but watchers below heard a steady roaring from within it, not unlike the sound of tornado winds, and they felt a numbing cold. Snow flurries could be seen occasionally within the cloud. When the cloud had passed, though, no trace of the wind or cold remained, and the springtime weather returned.

Cruising the English Channel at the time of the appearance of the strange cloud were two sailing vessels, the HMS *Eurydice*, a 921-ton naval training ship with 360 men aboard her, and, about a mile behind her, the merchant schooner *Emma*.

Five-hundred-foot-high cliffs along the coast of the Isle of Wight hid the approaching cloud mass until it was almost upon the *Eurydice*. Her captain had no time for emergency preparation. Just as the order to take in the sails was given, the tornado winds of the weird mass hit the defenseless vessel. A howling darkness descended upon the *Eurydice*, and she was lashed by heavy snow and icy spray.

For a full half hour the hapless ship wrestled beneath the mysterious energy mass, until finally the badly battered vessel ceased to struggle, capsized, and sank beneath the channel. Only two of the 360 men aboard her survived. Meanwhile, only a mile behind the *Eurydice*, the *Emma* breezed by, completely untouched by the violent sudden storm that had sunk her sister ship beneath the waves.

For more than 200 years, seamen have claimed to have seen the ghost of the HMS *Eurydice* on rainy nights at sea, and the mystery of the sudden storm that swept out of nowhere and destroyed the vessel has haunted many a sailor on night watch. Then, on October 17, 1998, the *London Mirror* reported that Prince Edward and a motion picture crew saw the ghost ship while filming the second installment of his *Crown and Country* television series on the Isle of Wight. According to Edward, he had been telling the story of the HMS *Eurydice*, the 26-gun frigate that had capsized and sank in Sandown Bay during a sudden and mysterious blizzard in 1878. The crew had been discussing how they might illustrate the incident when a three-masted schooner suddenly appeared.

Excited to be able to film a vessel similar in appearance to the HMS *Eurydice*, the cameramen began to focus on the schooner. And then it disappeared. Robin Bextor, the program's producer, told reporter Gerry Lovell that they had filmed the vessel for a while, then decided to wait so they could catch it sailing off into the horizon. "We were pleased at our stroke of luck at seeing it because it would save us time and money getting footage of a similar vessel. We took our eyes off it for a few minutes, but when we went to film it again, it had gone."

Officials of the Sail Training Association added to the mystery by saying that they knew of no vessel in the area at the time Edward and his television crew saw the ghost ship. The officials stated that they did have two three-masted training ships, but on that particular week they were both away.

Prince Edward said that he was convinced that as far as ghosts were concerned, "there are too many stories, coincidences, occurrences, and strange happenings. There is definitely something out there.... I cannot believe it is just people's imagination. There is more in it than that."

And in this particular sighting of a phantom ship, the television crew had the good fortune to have captured it on film.

⊶⊷

VANISHING GHOST SHIPS

The ghost image of a British gunboat that was sent to harass the French forts along the eastern seaboard of Canada puts in sporadic appearances at

Cape d'Espoir in Gaspe Bay. Observers of the phenomenon down through the decades have stated that ghostly crewmen line its decks, and at the wheel stands a man with a woman at his side. As the vessel approaches the shore, its lights gradually go out, and it appears to sink at exactly the same spot where the British gunboat sank 200 years ago.

In 1647 a ship was seen to vanish in full view of a crowd of people who had been awaiting its arrival at New Haven, Connecticut. Five months earlier, the ship had put out from New Haven and had been feared lost. When her sails and rigging were spotted coming into the harbor, the word quickly spread, and a crowd of eager friends and relatives gathered to welcome the ship home. Then, before their startled eyes, the vessel became transparent and began to slowly fade from view. Within a few moments, the astonished crowd was left staring at the empty harbor.

The ghost ship commonly referred to as "The Flying Dutchman" is one of the best-known in the world.

THE LEGEND OF THE *PALATINE*

Dozens of reputable witnesses claimed to have heard the terrible screams that issued forth from the ghost ship *Palatine* just five miles off the coast of Rhode Island. John Greenleaf Whittier committed the legend to poetry, and the story of the ghostly ship has found its way into several formal histories of New England. Although the ghostly recreation of the disaster was last officially reported in the 1820s, there are several old-timers in the Block Island area who can relate the details of the phantom ship.

The story of the tragic ship *Palatine* and her final voyage goes back to November 1752. With a full passenger list of immigrants, all bound for the prospering districts around Philadelphia, the vessel set sail from a Dutch port. The immigrants carried everything they possessed with them, for none planned to return to the Old World.

The voyage was uneventful until the *Palatine* reached the vicinity of the Gulf Stream, at which point it seemed as if all the fury of the North Atlantic was hurled upon them. Storm after storm smashed the ill-fated ship, driving her far off course into uncharted seas.

The captain had become ill shortly after the *Palatine* had set out, and the turbulence of the storm soon drove him to his bed. With their captain in quarters, the ship's crew began to slack off. For weeks the little vessel was mauled by the vicious sea while the crew did little to get her on course. Without their captain to drive them, the seamen stayed below and let the sea rule the *Palatine*.

When the captain died, all hope was lost for the ship's passengers. Ambitious young officers, backed by the crew, seized control of the provisions. To those passengers who could pay their exorbitant prices, the greedy officers doled out meager rations of food and water. Those without money starved to death and were cast overboard.

The supplies gave out around Christmas time. The crew took to the lifeboats and abandoned the *Palatine* and its surviving passengers to the whims of the sea. The vessel drifted for several more days, until it finally ran aground on the sandy shoals of Block Island. Most of the surviving passengers left on board had suffered mental breakdowns.

Residents of Block Island removed the survivors to the safety of village homes. One woman had become so crazed by her suffering and by the death of her loved ones that she refused to leave the ship. She maintained that she had to stay aboard to await the return of her family so they could all disembark together.

The islanders decided to allow the woman to remain on board and selected a committee that would be responsible for providing her with food and water. The *Palatine* was towed into a cove, and the villagers planned to salvage any usable cargo and to dismantle the ship at their convenience. Perhaps by that time, they reasoned, the poor woman might have regained her senses.

One day while the islanders were working on the *Palatine*, the ship was blown adrift by a sudden storm. In his haste to leave the ship, one of the workmen accidentally tipped a brazier of coals. Flames began leaping upward from the dry timbers, and the work crew scrambled for their boats. As they rowed toward the shore, the islanders looked back at the *Palatine*, its deck enveloped in flames. Then the men heard the agonizing screams lifting from the flaming vessel. The "daft woman" had been left behind.

The workmen were filled with shock and pity. They knew the flames were too intense to risk going back to the *Palatine*. There was nothing they could do for the trapped victim except to offer a prayer for her soul. They watched, horrified, as the rising wind slowly pushed the blazing vessel out to sea.

In flames, the *Palatine* sailed into legend. There are some people in the area who claim that the ship returns every year on the anniversary of her destruction. Others contend that the *Palatine* came back only as long as any member of her original crew remained alive. Historians found dozens of witnesses who claimed to have seen the image of the burning ship and to have heard the terrible screams of the dying woman.

Dr. Aaron Willey reported having viewed the lights of the *Palatine* on several occasions. His story exactly paralleled other reports: a blazing fire the size of a ship appears near shore, then slowly recedes until it is only a tiny light on the horizon.

PHANTOMS OF THE *QUEEN MARY*

During the years that the 1,019-foot luxury liner the *Queen Mary* was in service (1936–1967), there were 41 passengers and at least 16 crew members who died on the high seas of various illnesses and accidents. In addition to the deaths that occurred directly in her cabins or on her decks, the *Queen Mary* was responsible for the deaths of 300 seamen during World War II. This latter tragedy occurred when the liner was painted gray and was pressed into military service as a transport to carry American troops to and from Europe. Nicknamed the "Gray Ghost," the ship's great speed helped it to elude Nazi U-boats, but it was also that speed and power that accidentally sliced her escort ship HMS *Curacao* in two and drowned most of its crew.

Since the *Queen Mary* was permanently docked in Long Beach in 1967, hundreds of visitors have claimed to have seen materialized ghosts, moving objects, and eerie lights floating through its hallways. Disembodied voices are frequently reported, and many individuals say that they have heard screams and the harsh sound of ripping metal in the bow area, terrible echoes of the night the Gray Ghost tore the *Curacao* in half.

While there have been reported sightings of ghostly officers, crew members, and soldiers, perhaps the most often seen apparition is that of an 18-year-old crewman who was crushed to death deep among the pipes and girders of the engine room by hydraulic door no. 13 during one of the luxury liner's final voyages. Many witnesses claim to have seen a young man in coveralls on the catwalks of the engine room who vanishes before their eyes. Others have met him in narrow walkways and have even stepped aside to let him pass, only to see the young man disappear after a few steps.

THE USS *HORNET*: THE SHIP OF SOULS

The USS *Hornet* has a distinguished record of service for her country. The massive aircraft carrier has a flight deck that is 894 feet long. It weighs

Psychical researcher Loyd Auerbach.

41,000 tons and is outfitted with a full hospital, three barbershops, a tailor shop, a cobbler shop, and seven galleys. During World War II as many as 3,500 sailors served aboard her at one time, and the aircraft carrier won nine battle stars during naval action. Because of the many battles that she endured during her years of service (1943–1970), there may have been as many as 300 military personnel who died during combat or shipboard accidents.

In 1969 the *Hornet* retrieved the Apollo 11 astronauts from the sea after their return from the Moon. In 1995 she was docked at Alameda Point, outside of Oakland, California, named a National Historic Landmark, and opened to the public as a museum.

Among the ghosts most commonly sighted on the *Hornet* is that of a khaki-clad officer who is often seen descending the ladder to the lower deck. Some witnesses claim to have followed him, fully believing him to be a member of the museum staff or a visiting naval officer, only to have him disappear before their astonished eyes. Understandably, most of the ghosts that have been seen are male because of the World War II term of service of the aircraft carrier. Some witnesses have sworn that they have recognized the ghost of Admiral Joseph James ("Jocko") Clark, who commanded the ship during the years of heavy fighting during World War II.

Well-known psychical researcher Lloyd Auerbach has conducted a number of investigations on the *Hornet* with the psychic Stache Margaret Murray, and researchers David Richardson, Fred Speer, and Dinny Anderson. Of the many decks, compartments, nooks, and crannies on the huge aircraft carrier (Auerbach says it's like investigating a small city), the team of researchers located 27 different areas that they assessed as "hot" and a number of others that were "lukewarm" on the ghost scale. Because of the great range of spirit activity on the *Hornet*, Auerbach has christened it the "Ship of Souls."

The researchers deemed two locations as psychically interesting: the medical bay and hangar bay no. 3 in the stern of the ship. One can imagine, Auerbach suggests, the emotions that would be absorbed in a place where medical personnel treated those individuals suffering from war-time wounds.

The feelings felt by the psychically sensitive could be "downright oppressive." Interestingly, Auerbach writes in the October 2000 issue of *Fate* magazine that the two psychics on their team "picked up … a feeling that there were spots we needed to stay away from, at least until we were fully accepted by the ghosts."

In the area of the hangar bay, Auerbach felt as though he was walking through a heavy curtain of thicker air, and he immediately felt nauseated. When he backed out of the area, he felt fine. The psychics and other members of the team sensed negative energy in the "nausea zone."

"Just outside, in hangar bay no. 3, is an area where several apparitions have been seen," Auerbach says, "and an area where I felt 'something' very strong on one of my first visits. Also, at the end of the hangar bay is the fantail section.… It too is a spot where people have reported activity."

ADRIFT AT SEA BUT KEPT ALIVE BY A LOVING, LOYAL GHOST

In the summer of 1991, three fishermen—Tabwai Mikaie, Nweiti Tekamangu, and Arenta Tebeitabu—set out on a fishing trip from their South Pacific island of Kiribati, in the Republic of Kiribati. Not far from land, off a coral atoll called Nikunau, they were suddenly pummeled by a powerful, unexpected cyclone that capsized their 12-foot boat and tossed them into the sea. Although the men lost their outboard motor, they managed to climb safely back into the boat. However, since they were no longer able to power the tiny vessel, they began to drift farther and farther out into deeper waters, thus commencing a voyage that at times must have seemed endless.

Incredibly, the three men remained adrift for 175 days and nearly a thousand miles. By using a spear and a fishing line, they were able to survive on fish. From time to time they achieved some variety in their diet when they were able to snare a coconut floating by. To supplement their meager water supply, they collected rainwater. On numerous occasions, razor-jawed sharks circled their boat, but the fishermen turned the tables on the monsters and caught and ate no fewer than 10 of the voracious predators during their six months adrift. Tabwai Mikaie, 24, said that they prayed to God four times a day, asking for his tender mercies to save them.

Tragically, after a seeming eternity of helpless drifting, Nweiti Tekamangu, 47, died when they were at last in sight of land. Although his friends wept and pleaded with him to hold on for just a few days longer, Tekamangu's heart simply gave out after such a strenuous ordeal, and his sorrowful companions had no choice other than to cast his body overboard.

In 1924, while the oil tanker SS *Watertown* traveled down the West Coast of the United States on its way to the Panama Canal, two men died in an accident on board and were buried at sea. For several days following their burial, two faces were seen following the ship.

The survivors, Mikaie and Tebeitabu, were now terrified by the thought of the formidable ordeal that lay before them. Since they were now only a few days from the mountainous island of Upolu in Western Samoa, they would soon have to maneuver their little 12-foot boat through some of the most treacherous reefs in the South Pacific. In their weakened condition, the task seemed impossible.

Tekamangu, the oldest of the tiny crew, had also been the most experienced and by far the most accomplished navigator. If he were still alive, he would have been able to guide them to a safe harbor. Mikaie and Tebeitabu began to resign themselves to what appeared to be their certain destiny: They, too, would perish before they reached land.

Just as it seemed certain that the boat would be shattered into a thousand pieces of driftwood, the two men were astonished to see the spirit of their dead friend rise from the depths of the turbulent sea. The ghost of Tekamangu told them to listen to him and they would be safe. Although there were sharp and treacherous reefs on each side of their weather-beaten and sea-battered boat, Mikaie and Tebeitabu placed their complete confidence in the commands of their ghostly comrade, who masterfully guided them through the murderous offshore rocks to the safety of the beach on Upolu. Soon the two half-dead fishermen were being lifted from their little boat and taken to a hospital.

Later, while authorities and journalists decreed the feat of their having survived six months adrift at sea as a miracle, Tebeitabu and Mikaie testified that it was only the supernatural presence of their friend that had enabled them to live. In their statements to the authorities, they declared that if Tekamangu's love and loyalty had not sent his spirit back to help them, they would surely have been dashed to splinters on the reefs of Upolu.

<hr>

LEGEND OF YAQUINA BAY LIGHTHOUSE

The Yaquina Bay Lighthouse in Newport, Oregon, was built in 1871 and used for only three years until the Yaquina Head Lighthouse was constructed.

According to legend, one dark and stormy night a hundred years ago, a group of teenagers crept into the abandoned lighthouse to explore its empty hallways, but one of them never came out. All that was left of the young lady was her bloody handkerchief at the bottom of the third-floor staircase. Ever since that girl met her mysterious fate in the lighthouse, people have seen an eerie light in the upstairs window and heard cries and moans issuing from the darkened interior.

In November 1998 Cathy Kessinger, writing in *MidValley Sunday*, quoted Walt Muse, who oversees the lighthouse for the state parks department, as stating that there wasn't a "shred of evidence to support the spooky tale of the young woman who disappeared, leaving only a bloody handkerchief and a few drops of blood behind." Muse said that he had heard all the stories about people seeing lights on in the lighthouse and hearing and seeing strange things to support the legend. He himself was surprised one night to see a single light in the third-floor window. After a careful examination, he concluded that the source of illumination must have been light escaping from the beacon above.

Muse said that he is continually surprised by tourists who want to visit the haunted lighthouse. He often hears people saying that they "feel something" within its walls. Some people have sent Muse pictures they took while touring the lighthouse that purport to show something passing in front of the camera, like an apparition.

Perhaps the expectations of hundreds of people over the years have created a spirit and a mysterious light at the Yaquina Bay Lighthouse, and these same expectations have kept the "ghost" alive for more than 100 years by feeding it with their collective psychic energy.

⊶⊷

"WILLIE" HAUNTS BIG BAY POINT LIGHTHOUSE

As far as Norman and Marilyn Gotschall were concerned, one need not bother with theories of collective psychic energy and expectations when it came to "Willie," the ghost that haunted the 18 rooms of the historic lighthouse at Big Bay Point, Michigan. When they moved into the place in December 1986, Norman said that he did not believe in ghosts. After a few nights in the lighthouse, he changed his mind.

On the very first evening of the Gotschalls' arrival, the wind suddenly began to howl and shutters started banging. From the sounds of things, there was a terrible storm brewing on Lake Superior. But when Norman and Marilyn looked outside, it soon became apparent that the only storm was inside the lighthouse. Later, they figured that weird phenomena was just Willie's way of welcoming them.

"Willie" was William Pryor, a former military man who manned the lighthouse in 1896. A perfectionist who took his position very seriously, Pryor was thrown completely off balance when, after a few years on the job, his 20-year-old son committed suicide. A week later, in his grief and shame, Pryor hanged himself.

Marilyn Gotschall said that on one occasion shortly after they took up residence in the lighthouse, she heard someone calling her name from one of the upstairs rooms. Believing it to be Norman, she walked upstairs to find the area completely empty. "Willie" called her name two more times, then, seemingly satisfied with her friendly nature, he was quiet.

In 1990, when the Gotschalls were in the process of converting the lighthouse into a motel, one of their early guests claimed to have seen a man in a military uniform with bright gold buttons standing at the foot of her bed. The man told the guest that he was upset by all the commotion at the lighthouse and said that he wouldn't be content until all the restoration work was completed. Then he vanished, leaving the guest more confused than frightened.

The Gotschalls explained to their guest that Willie was their resident ghost and that he was a bit particular about the condition in which they managed the lighthouse.

THE GIRL GHOST OF WHITE ROCK LAKE

Texans who live near White Rock Lake in Dallas have reported the nocturnal visits of a girl ghost in a dripping wet evening gown who appears on the lakeshore. Young couples, who have parked beside the lake to take full advantage of the bright moon reflecting on the placid waters, have told some hair-raising tales about the phantom. One young man said that he would never forget the sight of the shimmering ghost looking in the car window at him and his frightened date.

Frank X. Tolbert, a columnist for the *Dallas Morning News*, dealt with the legend of the alleged girl ghost and received hundreds of letters and phone calls in response to his article. Apparently the apparition had been seen and firmly attested to by a good number of people.

Mr. Dale Berry told Tolbert that he and his family had purchased a home near White Rock Lake in September 1962. On their first night in their new home, Berry hurried to the door to answer the ringing of the bell. There was no one there. The bell rang a second time. In spite of Berry's rapid dash to the door, whoever had rung the bell had vanished by the time he opened the door.

The third time the bell rang, Berry's daughter answered the door. Soon the entire family was clustered around the front door in response to the girl's screams. There, on the porch, were large puddles of water, as if someone dripping wet had stood there. There were large droplets of water on the steps and the walk leading up to the front door, yet the sprinkler system had not been turned on, the rest of the yard was dry, and the night was clear and cloudless. Moreover, the neighbors were not the sort to indulge in practical jokes.

It appeared that the girl ghost of White Rock Lake had been trying to pay the newcomers a visit to welcome them.

White Rock Lake in Dallas, Texas.

DID THEY DISCOVER A LAKE RESORT FOR GHOSTS?

The Personal Experience of Roy

"We drove into the bush one day and paddled up a river for 45 minutes or so to a small lake, totally inaccessible, except by a canoe. There are no roads or trails to it, and the canoe route was only accessible by small boat because of the shallowness of the river and many beaver dams.

"It was my first visit to the lake. My cousin had urged me to go with him as he had been shown the lake by his father but had never fished it, although it was rumored (correctly) to have very large northern pike. When we finally arrived at the lake, my cousin was totally surprised that a very large and beautiful log home, complete with large dock, had been built on the north shoreline. The building was not a small log cabin but a large and well-crafted log home. And as the lake is only a pothole of a lake and only a few hundred feet across at its largest point, the building stood out clearly and magnificently in the natural setting.

"My cousin marveled at how someone had somehow built such a large structure in such a short time, and we wondered how all the building materials could have been brought in. I suggested that the lake couldn't have much fish if there was a large building on it with people coming and going. It was early in the evening when we arrived there, and there seemed to be a strange kind of static in the air. We soon left, convinced that the lake couldn't hold big fish if people were visiting regularly and living on it.

"Eventually, we decided to give the lake another chance, and packed up our gear and returned. Incredibly, on the *exact* spot where we had seen the

"The Sculpture of the Ghost" is located in Klaipeda, Lithuania. Built in 2010, it commemorates the legend that on February 19, 1595, at 9 o'clock in the evening, the guard of the old castle Hansas fon Heide saw a ghost that warned that the city may run out of wood and grain.

building, there was nothing except unspoiled nature. There were not the slightest indications that anything had ever been there except for a beaten down lean-to a few feet in size that had obviously been there for years and years and [that was] probably the remnant of a trapper's shack! There were no trees cut down, no old stumps, no rubble or garbage. In fact, there were old trees on the spot! The lake was exactly as it had been when my cousin had gone there originally ... without any sign of human habitation or activity! We have wondered about this for about 30 years now. My cousin muses that maybe one day we will go there and such a building will have materialized and that somehow we were looking at the future."

⊶⫘𝄐⫘⊷

A MOST UNUSUAL FISHING COMPANION

On April 26, 2000, during the *Jeff Rense Program*, a woman named Jenny called in to tell Jeff and me that she had had a most perplexing experience occur to her some years before when she lived in Arizona c. 1986. But what began as a colorful anecdote told by an articulate and charming woman suddenly took a sharp detour into a rather chilling ghost story.

Because her husband was out of town a great deal of the time on business, Jenny was attempting to be both mother and father to their young son. Although she had never really been fishing before, she bought rods and reels and all the other necessary equipment and took her son to a lake outside of Tucson, because that was the kind of thing that a father and son would do.

No one else was near their spot on shore that afternoon, and Jenny was having difficulty putting the worms on the hook for her son and casting the line far enough from shore to attract the fish. As she grew increasingly frustrated with the whole idea of fishing in order to please her son, a man in his mid-twenties came up behind her and offered to help her bait the hook. He told her that she had to make a knot in the worm so it would not come off the hook, and he demonstrated the art of baiting the hook and casting the line.

The man stayed with them through the entire afternoon, and the three of them had a great deal of fun fishing together, and they even managed to catch some fish. At the end of the day, Jenny invited him to come back with them to the picnic area where she planned to have a barbeque. He accepted the invitation, and they all ate heartily of the burgers and other food that she prepared. It was the perfect ending to a wonderful day, and Jenny took a picture of the man and her son as they posed for the camera.

The next day, Jenny took the film to a one-hour photo shop to be developed, and when she saw the man's beautiful smile, she was touched with the manner in which he had unselfishly shared his day with them. He had no doubt come there to do some serious fishing, and he had diverted his own precious free time away from the office to help make the afternoon more meaningful for Jenny's son. She decided that she would send him a copy of the photograph as a thank-you for the fishing lessons.

Several times during the previous afternoon he had told them his full name and the place where he worked, so Jenny got the telephone number from information and called the store. When she asked for him, the receptionist connected her to a man who rather brusquely asked why she wished to speak with him and what her business was. Rather impatiently, Jenny explained the circumstances and her wish to send a photograph in an effort to repay the man for his kindness.

The man on the telephone asked her to describe their fishing companion. When Jenny did, the man gasped and said that she had described perfectly his younger brother who had drowned at that lake five years before.

Stunned, Jenny at first thought the man was playing a cruel joke on her, but she verified his account by checking newspaper records at the public library. Thinking the man would want to see her proof of his brother's spirit on the photograph, she sent him a copy. But the letter was returned to her, unopened. She put the picture away in a drawer, but it appeared again on the top of her desk. She grew increasingly uncomfortable with the picture in her possession. No matter what she did with it, it would return to a place where she could not ignore it. She even tried ripping it up and burning it, but it kept materializing and returning to her.

At last Jenny drove out to the lake where she had met the man and spoke into the lake, as if she were addressing him face-to-face. In a solemn manner, she said that she felt that it was time that he went into the Light, that it was not right for him to remain around the lakeshore any longer. She would pray for his soul to be at peace.

Jenny drove back home and went to bed. At three o'clock in the morning, the telephone rang at her bedside. With her husband traveling away from home, she feared an emergency call. When she picked up the receiver, she heard a great deal of static, as if the call were coming from a great distance away, then a male voice said, "Thank you," and hung up.

Jenny told Jeff Rense and me that the next day, she could not find the photograph of the man. It was gone at last, and it has never reappeared.

TALES OF MONSTERS AND DEVILS IN THE SEA AND LAKES OF HOLLAND

Contributed by Theo Paijmans

Geographically speaking, the Netherlands, also called Holland or the low countries, is a peculiar country. Most of it actually lies below sea level, as expressed in the meaning of the words "nether" and "low." Throughout the centuries, the Dutch have always had an intense relationship with the sea, and friendly though she may seem most of the time, we know from experience that she is a harsh mistress. Dutch folklore features many legends concerning the waters that surround us. We have legends of sunken towns with the bells of their church towers tolling in the deep, dark lakes on stormy nights. Dutch lore is rich in tales of mermaids, too, and river and sea spirits. We have had fiery portents flying through our skies since the earliest times. That memorable master of the anomalous, Charles Fort, would have a field day here. And after all, he was from Dutch stock. All aspects of the global canon of ghostlore and paranormal manifestations are found here as well, recorded in old legends and folk tales. Sightings of phantom-like black dogs, headless ghosts, poltergeists and haunted houses, witches and apparitions of the devil, all feature in the ghostlore of the Netherlands.

One of the most famous legends, that of the Flying Dutchman, features a Dutch Captain Van der Decken, who closes a pact with the devil and is meted out a terrible punishment. There are also the legends of the devil who comes for those who have sold their souls to him. There was the tale of a skipper in Harderwijk who had sold his soul in order to have a good cargo. One night, during a storm, the boat's mate saw the skipper drinking and throwing dice with a stranger in his cabin. That same night the skipper disappeared. The devil had wrenched him through a porthole. The glass was missing from the porthole and blood and strands of hair were sticking to the woodwork. No matter how thoroughly the blood stain was cleaned and the woodwork repainted, the blood stain kept on reappearing. The entire porthole needed to be replaced.

The devil did not only steal souls. In the church library at the Dutch city of Zutphen a book can be found chained with heavy iron shackles on a desk: this was done to prohibit the devil from stealing the book, as he had often tried. In the stone floor one clearly sees the imprints of very large dog's paws that the devil left behind. The trail of imprints is named Duivelsvoet-stappen or Devil's Footsteps.

To a fisherman from Harderwijk who was in the habit of uttering loud curses, the devil appeared on board of his ship one night. The skipper saw something vaguely resembling a sea lion, "a horrible creature," climb aboard. It had paws like giant bat's wings. "Gigantic and sluggish the creature lumbered on the deck of the ship and it was so heavy that the ship nearly sunk.... The creature drooled a brown slime...." While the creature chased him, luckily the skipper remembered that a Christian can withstand the devil. After having called unto God, the creature slid back into the sea with a terrible scream.

26
GHOSTS ON TRAINS, PLANES, AND AUTOMOBILES

GHOST TRAINS THAT COME AND GO

The Phantom Train of Pittsfield, Massachusetts

Several Pittsfield, Massachusetts, residents are convinced of the existence of a phantom train and swear that they have seen the specter on a stretch of track between the North Street bridge and the junction, and passing the Union Depot. One of the most impressive sightings occurred one afternoon in February 1958, when John Quirk and several of his customers in the Bridge Lunch saw the phantom train of Pittsfield go by.

Regardless of what anyone else would try to tell them, Quirk told reporters, the phantom train consisted of a baggage car and five or six coaches. Quirk and his customers could describe that locomotive down to the last bolt. It was so clear and plain that they were even able to see the coal in the tender.

Railroad officials replied that they had operated no steam engine on that line for years. There has definitely not been a train that has passed Union Depot or the junction at the times when certain witnesses claim to have seen a locomotive in the area.

At 6:30 A.M. one frosty March morning, Bridge Lunch employees and customers caught another glimpse of the ghost train. The place was full of customers and every one of them saw the ghost train, according to waiter Steve Strauss. "Just like every time before, the steam engine pulled a baggage car, five or six coaches, and was high barreling east toward Boston."

Cover of *Railroad Stories,* June 1933.

A Phantom Train in Texas

Thomas Phillips of Pasadena, Texas, told of the time when, on a business trip in the 1960s, he stopped for a train between Belleville and Sealy, Texas. He first saw the train coming off to his right, about 300 feet ahead. Strangely enough, the train, pulled by an old style locomotive, had seemed to move out of a cloud of fog.

As he drummed his fingers impatiently on the steering wheel waiting for the train to pass, Phillips suddenly realized that there were no crossing lights, signs, or signals. As the freight cars passed slowly in front of him, he also noticed that the train seemed to be lighted by a source entirely apart from the lights of his car. When the last boxcar passed before him, Phillips saw to his surprise that there was no sign of a railroad bed, not even a break in the pavement where one ever had been.

A Ghostly Engineer Looks for His Head on the Tracks

For more than 80 years, the people in the town of St. Louis, Saskatchewan, have been seeing the light from a phantom train and the subsequent light from a lantern, as the ghost of a Canadian National Railway engineer seeks his lost head. According to the story, a CNR engineer was checking the tracks near St. Louis when he was struck by a train and decapitated.

Mayor Emile Lussier told CBC News on November 1, 2001, that he was present when a scientist came to the site to investigate the mysterious appearance of the ghost light. According to Lussier, the scientist left baffled by the maneuvers of the engineer's lantern. The light would appear behind them, but when they turned around, the ghostly illumination appeared right at their heels.

Haunted Railway Sites in Newfoundland and Labrador

Dale Jarvis, a columnist for the St. John's, Newfoundland, *Telegram,* often features paranormal subjects. In his column for December 4, 2002, he discussed a number of railway ghost stories across Newfoundland and Labrador. Among the haunted trains or railway sites he listed were the following:

1. A ghostly conductor who manifests on the Port Union and Bonavista branch line.

2. The spirit of a young girl who haunts the railway trestle in Clarke's Beach.

3. The phantom train that materializes on the company rail line built by the American Smelting and Refining Company.

Strange Disturbances at the Tamaqua, Pennsylvania, Train Station

They say that light bulbs won't stay lit in the 1874 Tamaqua, Pennsylvania, train station. Many people attribute this phenomena—and several others, including sudden icy drafts and the sighting of ghosts—to the spirits of five members of the Molly Maguires, a group accused of taking violent action on behalf of mine workers' rights. On June 21, 1877, known as "Black Thursday" and the "Day of the Rope," 10 alleged members of the Molly Maguires were hanged. Five of those bodies were kept packed in ice overnight inside the Tamaqua train station, then only three years old.

THE PILOT CAME BACK TO CLEAR HIS REPUTATION

In May 1913 a small group of pilots and mechanics near a workshop hanger at Britain's Montrose Air Training Station were inspecting a newly arrived airplane on the grounds. The man most interested in the craft was the pilot who would fly it for the first time, Lt. Desmond Arthur, a black-haired young Irishman who was enthusiastic about what he considered the advanced lines of the airplane. The senior mechanic agreed that the craft was nice to look at, but he was skeptical about its ability to bear any extra strain.

"We'll find out now," Arthur said confidently, stepping into the cockpit. A mechanic spun the prop, then jumped away as the motor caught. Without hesitation, the young pilot taxied the plane into the wind, then picked up speed. The plane lifted from the ground.

The spectators watched carefully as the accomplished pilot took the plane to nearly 4,000 feet before he leveled off and began to test the new model's maneuverability with a series of stunts.

In the middle of a twisting roll, the plane heeled over on its back, then shed a wing. The machine and the pilot dropped to the ground like a falling stone. By the time the men of the Montrose Station arrived at the scene of the crash, Desmond Arthur was dead.

The tragedy did not receive official comment until 1916, when authorities blamed the accident on misjudgment by the pilot. The official report based its findings on the immediate investigation by military authorities after the accident and their evaluation of the testimonies of witnesses to the crash.

There were those, including the senior mechanic, who protested that the crash was due to faulty construction of the aircraft, but the investigators' assessment discounted such testimony.

A few weeks after the report was published, a mechanic at Montrose Station learned that the Desmond Arthur tragedy could not be dismissed so easily. While working on the inside bracing of an airplane, he noticed an officer in flight clothes approaching the craft. The mechanic continued work until the officer came very close and stood directly over him.

Becoming a bit uneasy at the man's silence, the mechanic finally asked, without looking up, if the officer wished to fly the craft. When the officer did not reply, the mechanic slid out from under the brace, and looked up at the silent man.

The officer's face was contorted with rage; his lips moved furiously and he gestured as if he were shouting, but he made no sound. The mechanic fell away from the strange flier; the wrench he had been holding clattered to the floor. Before the mechanic could turn and flee, the officer disappeared. Terrified, the mechanic ran until he came to Flight Sergeant Wilkens.

"I've seen him," the man gasped, out of breath. "The ghost of Desmond Arthur! The officers were right. He's come back."

The Montrose ghost first appeared in August 1916, to Second Lieutenant Ralph Peterson. Peterson had entered his room and found a fellow airman leaning against the wall. Surprised by the officer's presence, Peterson had just begun to question the man when the visitor melted into the wall. When Peterson reported the incident, Colonel James Rutherford dismissed it as imagination and warned the junior officer of the hazards of alcohol.

A few days later, two officers, whose testimony the station commander could not question, saw the same strange flier. Major Jenkins and Captain Edward Milner, two senior officers who shared a room, had just retired. The bed lamp had not been off more than a few minutes when the sound of footsteps caused both officers to sit up in their beds. Before either of them could move, their door swung open and a young man in flying kit entered. He gestured wildly and seemed to be shouting at the two officers, neither of whom could testify that any sound issued from the angry visitor.

When one of the officers switched on the light, the figure faded before the astonished eyes of the two officers. They quickly had the building secured and ordered all exits guarded. Guards reported that no person had attempted to leave the building. After the officers had conducted a bed check, they were convinced that their visitor had not been a living man.

The next officer to see the restless ghost recognized its form. Lieutenant Edwards, the station adjutant and an officer in the regular army, swore that he had seen Desmond Arthur come into his room. Edwards had known Arthur well, and he, too, described a man who seemed to be shouting at the top of his lungs, yet made no sound.

The Montrose ghost added a bizarre note to the aviation news, but in 1916, aviators did not receive much good press. The high cost of World War I was bearing hard on the British, and it had become fashionable to take pot shots at the fledgling air corps and its personnel. It was in this spirit that the report on the Desmond Arthur crash had been compiled, and even though a few devoted airmen had fought to remove the blight from Arthur's otherwise clean record, their efforts had been overpowered by a rising tide of criticism against the corps. In addition to the great cost of the war, British air losses reached their peak in 1916, and Parliament appointed a committee to investigate the matter. The air corps cringed under the double obligation to reduce costs and increase efficiency at the same time.

But the ghost of Desmond Arthur seemed determined to bring about a change in the record the report had left of him. The story gained momentum, and soon the tale of the ghost of the airbase spread to the Continent and even to the enemy. In one instance, a German soldier, shot down behind Allied lines, asked almost immediately for news of the Montrose ghost.

Meanwhile, the parliamentary committee had found that to increase Britain's aviation efficiency would entail increased, not lowered, costs. Machines arriving at French bases were ill-equipped, seldom outfitted with essential parts, and the personnel arriving in the war zone often came prepared with only a few days' training.

It was at this point that C. G. Gray, the editor of the British aviation magazine the *Aeroplane*, took up the reinvestigation of the Desmond Arthur case. "With training and machines in such bad shape now," Gray wrote, "imagine what [conditions] would have been in 1913."

With the aid of a friend, Commander Perrin, one of Britain's earliest fliers, Gray prodded the authorities into a reinvestigation. In a few weeks, the Royal Air Club's Safety and Accident Investigation Committee announced that Desmond Arthur had not, after all, been guilty of an error in judgment. With the help of influential men in Parliament, these findings were finally incorporated into the parliamentary record on November 12, 1916.

About two months later, the Montrose ghost appeared for the last time. The phantom materialized first to Lieutenant Edwards, then to Major Jenkins and Captain Edward Milner. All three claim that the ghost smiled broadly at them. The Montrose ghost had vindicated his memory, and he has not been seen since that day in January 1917.

THE LEGEND OF BRICK BARTON

Here is one of my favorite ghost stories from World War II. It may be a legend from the war, but as a child of those years of conflict who had a cousin flying P-51s out of England, and two uncles in B-24s—one out of England, the other out of Italy—it has always spoken to me of the heroism and sacrifice of the aviators of that period in our nation's history.

Captain Brick Barton of Auburn, New York, was a pilot of a B-24 bomber out of an English base during World War II. One day Barton and his crew had just completed their mission over Frankfurt, Germany. The copilot confirmed that all targets had been approached and all bombs dropped. Now they could go home.

> **"D**on't worry, kid," Barton told him, managing a weak grin. "You just take control, and I'll give you instructions on how to get us home.

Barton nodded. They had completed their mission successfully. It would be good to get back to the base. As Barton was in the process of turning the bomber back toward England, a German fighter made a strafing pass at the B-24. The pilot's compartment was riddled, and several bullets struck Barton.

The copilot, seeing that his captain had been hit, took immediate control of the plane. He heard the harsh chatter of the bomber's machine gunners, and he knew that he would not have to worry about the German fighter any longer. But how, he asked himself, was he going to get this giant airplane back to England all by himself.

"Don't worry, kid," Barton told him, managing a weak grin. "You just take control, and I'll give you instructions on how to get us home. I'll be with you all the way."

As the B-24 neared the base in England, the copilot radioed the tower and told them to prepare an ambulance for Barton. When the relieved young officer stepped out of the plane, the flight surgeon complimented him on a safe landing.

"Thank you, sir," said the copilot, "but I couldn't have done it without the help and advice of Captain Barton. He kept talking to me and giving me pointers from the moment he was hit over Frankfurt. You had better see to him right away."

The flight surgeon hurried into the pilot's compartment. A few minutes later, visibly shaken, he left the bomber and approached the copilot.

"You say Captain Barton spoke to you, that he helped you land the airplane?"

"That's correct," the copilot acknowledged, frowning his bewilderment at the surgeon's strange barrage of questions.

"Well, that's impossible," the surgeon said. "Captain Barton died instantly, and he's been dead for almost an hour."

<hr />

REPORTS OF A CAR ACCIDENT THAT WASN'T REVEALED A FATAL CRASH THAT WAS

It is doubtful that the dispatcher at the police station who took the call from motorists reporting a crash off the A3 in Surrey at 7:20 p.m. on Wednesday, December 11, 2002, realized that he was actually taking down a report of a chilling ghost story. The witnesses all told the same story: a car had swerved off the road at Burpham, near Guildford, its headlights blazing, and crashed in the undergrowth off A3. When officers investigated, they found no sign of the alleged accident. It was apparent because of the thick undergrowth off A3 that no vehicle had crashed through it.

This photograph was taken at the Henry Ford estate. Although no one was sitting in this classic car when the photograph was taken, the image of a man is clearly visible in the driver's seat.

A close-up of the ghost in the classic car.

But witnesses persisted that they had seen a car that had veered off the A3, headlights brightly burning, crashing into the undergrowth. Police officers returned in the daylight and began foraging in the thick and twisted undergrowth. They were amazed to discover a wrecked Vauxhall Astra automobile, nose-down in a ditch, invisible from the road. However, it could not have crashed with headlights blazing on the night before. The car had been hidden there for a good while. So long, in fact, that it contained a decomposed body. Puzzled, the officers kept searching, but they could find no signs of a recent crash, only one that had obviously taken place some months ago.

On December 13, 2002, the authorities revealed that the corpse was that of Christopher Chandler, who was being hunted for an alleged robbery. He was reported missing by his brother on July 16. Surrey police stated that it was obvious from the physical evidence that the accident that had claimed Chandler's life had occurred in July, not December, and that the body and the Vauxhall Astra had remained undiscovered for five months, just yards from the dual carriageway that was used daily by thousands of motorists.

The question that will never be answered to everyone's satisfaction is whether the motorists who witnessed the crash in December saw a ghostly replay of the accident that had actually taken place unnoticed in July.

GHOST AUTOMOBILES ON THE HIGHWAY

Mary Passed a Car That Disappeared

Mary of Portland, Oregon, writes to say that she was driving east out of Bend on the Bend–Burns Highway early one morning. "The road is raised up somewhat banked from the desert, and it is a long, easy slope down from Horse Ridge. I wasn't going very fast, just enjoying the drive, when I came upon a black sedan moving slowly. I hit my passing gear and zoomed past. As I passed, I looked in to see if there was anyone I knew in the sedan. There was just an older man and woman who looked back at me."

But when Mary glanced in her rearview mirror, just as soon as she had passed the black sedan, there was no car behind her. "The highway behind me was empty."

Mary had a frightening thought that the older couple had somehow gone over the bank, which, at that point, was several feet high. "I came to a quick stop at the edge of the road and got out. I went to the back of my car and looked and looked, but I couldn't see the black sedan anywhere. There were no access roads around or any other cars around. Besides, the car was only out of my sight for a couple of seconds."

As Mary stood there looking around for some sign of the mysterious black sedan with the older couple inside, "a light breeze sprang up and blew across me, and I can tell you that the hairs on the back of my neck and my arms stood up. I jumped in my little car, locked all four doors, and got out of there. I was both frightened and puzzled. I guess I still am. I still get that creepy hair-rising-on-back-of-neck-and-arms feeling whenever I recall the car that disappeared and the breeze that sprang up out of nowhere."

Max Encountered the Ghost of a 1941 Chevrolet

Early on a Sunday evening in 1991, Max was driving with his family outside of Albany, New York, when he became impatient with the way an old car, which he guessed to be a 1941 Chevrolet sedan, was slowing traffic. Max figured that the car was going to or coming from some antique auto show or rally and he wanted to be tolerant, but they were returning from a family outing at Lake George and he wanted to get home to do some paperwork.

"I had to be at work early the next morning with my presentation ready to go, and I had some factors that I needed to sharpen," Max said. "As I approached nearer to the Chevy, I was surprised that it didn't have those special license plates that owners of those old cars are supposed to display. I hated to be a jerk, but I really leaned on my horn, something I usually don't do when following a slow-moving vehicle."

Max recalled that he could see the driver of the Chevy turn around and look at him with what appeared to be shock. "I expected an angry, hostile look, and maybe an obscene gesture or two, but this guy looked as if I had genuinely startled him. As if he had somehow imagined himself to be driving all alone on the highway."

Mary had a frightening thought that the older couple had somehow gone over the bank.

Then, before the startled, incredulous eyes of Max, his wife, and their three children, the old Chevrolet sedan in front of them began to fade away. "It was as if it were some old photograph dissolving bit by bit before us, just fading away until there was nothing left to prove that it had ever been there. The antique Chevy and its driver had completely disappeared in about 30 seconds."

A Wagonload of Hay from Another Dimension

Inez M. of Ely, Minnesota, reported her experience during the winter of 1924, when she and four others found themselves stalled in the snow near an old country school house near Embarrass, Minnesota. As they were shoveling their way free, they looked up to see a wagonload of hay pulled by a team of horses fast approaching them on the narrow road. Two men sat on top of the hay, seemingly unconcerned with the plight of those in the stalled automobile.

As the wagonload of hay came abreast, Inez said, she jumped aside on her side of the road. Her friend Martha jumped to the other side. Then, just as the team drove between them, it disappeared. Where moments before Martha and she had been unable to see each other from the sides of the road because the hayrack was in the way, they now stood facing each other in amazement. When they recovered somewhat from the shock, they looked for a trail to show them where the wagon had been, but they found none.

A Phantom Car Approaches Their Front Porch

Deborah from Montana wrote to say that her friends in Montana have a ghost car that goes by their front porch. "Their driveway (which ends on their property) used to be the county road," she said. "The county road used to pass by their front porch (about 30 feet from their front porch) and continue up through their pastures and on into the rolling hills. I have sat on their front porch and heard cars come down their driveway, past their front porch and into the pastures. I can never see the cars, but I can certainly hear them crunch on the gravel.

"I have heard the car(s) on just about every trip I have made to their ranch. My friend, who does not believe in ghosts, says it is only the wind, but I have never heard the wind crunch gravel as does a car."

⊸⫘⫘⫘⊸

THE PHANTOM CAR THAT COMES TO A MIDWEST FARM AGAIN AND AGAIN
The Personal Encounters of Mark

"**I** was listening to a past Halloween show with you and Jeff Rense, and you told a story about a phantom car that hit home. I live with my family in the rural central Midwest. I grew up here until I graduated high school in 1974, then I moved to Illinois to farm. With lowering prices and more government involvement in the farming industry, I quit farming five years ago and went to write and design for a magazine. I was the production supervisor there until I left a couple of years ago.

"My father retired from farming, and he and my mom moved into my grandmother's house, across our pasture, and my wife and I moved back to my childhood home. The old two-story farmhouse we live in is over 100 years old, and my mother and uncle also grew up here.

"As far back as I can remember, we have been visited by a phantom car. It comes a few times a year but is most noticeable in the summer. (With the windows open you can hear the engine and the tires crunching the gravel.) The

Mark's photograph of the car that he believes still visits his family's farm.

phantom car can be seen just after dusk as it turns off the highway and into our long gravel lane. You can see and hear the car coming up the lane clearly and solidly. It appears to be a car from a different era, as it has large round headlights on either side of the car's hood like they are sitting on fenders. The car drives all the way up the lane and stops in front of our house on the circle drive. Then the engine shuts off, the lights turn off, and two car doors open and close.

"As the 'occupants' come crunching across the gravel, their footfalls stop. Nothing is ever out there! This phenomenon has been seen by everyone in my family, and a couple of times by a whole house full of people celebrating birthdays.

"My wife had a visit by it one night while on the phone with my dad. She told him that I had just driven up. She went outside with the remote phone and told my dad that nothing [was] here, but she [knew] she had just been watching me drive up and thought I had someone with me because she heard two car doors open. I had never told her about the car.

"I found the attached picture over at my mom's. It is a picture of our house from April 1937. It was taken from the sky, as you can see. The original photo was brown with age and faded. I scanned the photo into Photoshop and turned it back into a grayscale picture and adjusted the levels so it is clearer.

"What struck me in the photo is the car sitting on the circle drive. It is in the exact position that the phantom car is in when it stops, the engine shuts off, the lights turn off, and two doors can be heard opening and closing. The sounds of walking also match the spot it is sitting in! I know very little of the cars from that period. But if it had large headlights on either side and an engine that had the underlying sewing machine sound, it could be the phantom car.

"I found out from my mom that my grandparents were married in 1916 and moved into this house in 1918. The house was originally one story. My grandfather built the second story in 1929. (Yes, during the depression.) I had told you in an earlier e-mail that I thought my grandparents were also visited by the phantom car. I was wrong. The earliest my mom remembers [seeing it] is in the 1960s. My grandfather died in the late '50s when I was three or four years old.

"This doesn't solve the mystery, however, because two doors open and shut and two people are heard walking. (My grandmother lived to be 100 years old.) It makes me wonder if the car in the drive is actually my grandparents' car or someone who came to visit (and continues to come to visit).

"The latest on the phantom car (April 2, 2003) is that its visits are becoming more infrequent, but it does still make the journey. Now perhaps only once every three or four months at least that we see it. (As you can imagine, that makes it even harder to out-guess it and get any photos, etc. It tricks us into thinking we are getting company every time it appears, and it is gone about the same time we realize what it is.)

"The last sighting of it was at a time when I was waiting for someone to come to our house. So I did watch its whole 'performance.' I realized what it was just when it stopped on the circle drive. No interior lights come on as the doors open. In fact, you can't tell by watching that they do open, but you hear them shut distinctly. It does appear to be the car in the old photo, or one very similar.

27

WHEN GHOSTS VISIT STORES AND OFFICE BUILDINGS

THE GHOST OF LADY MARTHA

A business acquaintance of mine in a nearby city called to inform me that he had found what seemed to be a classic haunting. According to the information he had gathered, the ghost of a strong-willed woman was haunting an entire office complex. The woman, whom everyone respectfully had called "Lady Martha" in life, was, according to certain startled witnesses, even more imposing in death.

Before she had passed on, Lady Martha had strongly opposed smoking, and she was bold enough to walk up to a total stranger on the street, slap a cigarette out of his mouth, and deliver a blistering lecture on the evils of nicotine. If cigarettes aroused her ire, beer and liquor drove her into an absolute frenzy. Those who had known Lady Martha and her opinions said that her oratory on temperance and prohibition were well-known in the community.

Some time after Lady Martha's death—so went the story that was told to my friend—an executive in the office building which Lady Martha owned and in which she had maintained a top-floor apartment shook a cigarette out of a pack on his desk. He hung the cigarette on his lower lip and reached for a match—but before he could light the tobacco, the cigarette and the pack on his desk had vanished. A thorough search of the office could not turn up even one crumb of the man's tobacco. Word began to spread that Lady Martha's no smoking rule still held firm in her office building, and what is more, the lady herself was somehow still around to enforce it.

A clothing store located in the same building had been experiencing a series of peculiar happenings which seemed to reach a bizarre kind of climax one night after work when some of the sales personnel decided to have a few relaxing beers in a basement storeroom. Since the salesmen were married and the saleswomen were young coeds from the local college, a decision was made to bolt the fire door behind them so that someone would not happen upon their after-work libation, misinterpret the innocent amusement, and report the scene to the men's wives.

[T]o their immedi-ate astonish-ment and their subsequent fear, a shimmering replica of Lady Martha drifted into the storeroom and shook a scolding finger....

As the beer was being distributed, one of the men jokingly commented that it was a good thing that Lady Martha was in her grave or she would be able to smell the booze in her basement. According to all those in attendance on that occasion, the words had scarcely been uttered when the bolted door swung open with a violence that slammed it against the wall. Then, to their immediate astonishment and their subsequent fear, a shimmering replica of Lady Martha drifted into the storeroom and shook a scolding finger at each participant in the after-hours beer bust.

When my friend began to hear repeated accounts of such ghostly confrontations in Lady Martha's office build-ing, he called me and asked if he might arrange for me to visit the scene of the manifestations. I agreed with his assessment that he had uncovered a haunting with interesting investigative potential, and I asked him if he would tape-record an interview with some of the witnesses of the phenomena so that I might better evaluate the material before I made arrangements to travel to his city.

My friend earnestly complied with my request, but it was that simple act of tape recording that led to the witnesses fearfully squelching my visit to the haunted office building of Lady Martha. At first the businessmen had no objections to taking time to give my friend an interview regarding the phe-nomena which they had witnessed and they had no objections to my plans to conduct an investigation in the basement storeroom where Lady Martha's ghost had so dramatically and forcefully appeared. But then, as a courtesy to them, my friend offered to play what he had recorded on the tape so that they would be able to hear their comments before he mailed the cassette to me.

Unexplainably, anytime one of them mentioned Lady Martha's name, the tape went blank,so that it was full of such lines as, "Yes, I remember the time that _____ stopped me in my office to lecture me about smoking. Boy, could _____ ever preach against man's enslavement to tobacco."

And that was that. Before my friend left that evening, the businessmen were no longer eager to have an investigator of the strange and unknown visit their building. They had enough of the strange and unknown happening about them every day, thank you, and that little demonstration that evening had convinced them that Lady Martha did not wish to have any spook hunters prowling around her building. More than one of the men expressed his concern that if things had been weird up to then, think what it would be like if Lady Martha really got angry with them for bringing in an outsider.

"Brad, we have a situation in which a group of normally hard-nosed, tough-minded businessmen are actually afraid of a ghost," my friend summed it up over the telephone. "I'm sorry I blew it," he apologized. "I never should have played the tape for them."

I told my friend that he could hardly be held responsible for the strange malfunctioning of his tape recorder, which may have presented us with a most peculiar audio proof of life beyond the grave. As difficult as it may be for the skeptical reader to believe, even in our twenty-first-century world of science and technology, scores of sensible, well-educated, practical men and women still fear the supernatural. Moviegoers may enjoy being cinematically frightened and titillated by horror films and afterward engage in bold laughter and self-conscious analysis of the manner in which they were able to temporarily suspend reality and enter into the frightening illusion of the eerie motion picture. But take these same individuals, place them in an environment of moss-covered crypts, moldering mansions, and mournful midnight sighs floating up circular stairwells and some peculiar atavistic mechanism transforms them into shuddering, haunted men and women.

And when ghosts come to the office or store, they seem to be playing out of bounds. Ghosts should be hanging out in spooky houses and cemeteries, not bothering anyone at work.

━━◦▥∿▥◦━━

THE NOISY GHOST IN THE ARMY SURPLUS STORE

When Mr. A. M. Sharp took over the Lancashire, England, army surplus store on that Monday morning in the spring of 1952, he was still puzzled by the former owner's odd behavior and the weird story that he had told as he handed over the keys on the previous Friday. The man had actually seemed reluctant to allow Sharp to take ownership of the store, not because of any regrets about selling the place, but because he seemed to fear for Sharp's well-being.

His story had been strange. He told Sharp that as he readied the store for new ownership, he had heard peculiar noises coming from the upper floor. It had seemed as though someone was walking around up there—and the longer the fellow walked, the bigger and heavier he became. By late afternoon, the footsteps sounded as if they were those of a giant. The man was certain that there was no one upstairs and that there had been no one up there all day. When it came time for him to catch the evening train, he realized that he had left his coat on the upper floor. He started for the stairway, then as a particularly violent bump sounded from above, he bolted and left the store on the run.

This bewildered Sharp; he had known the man for several years and was aware that he was an ex-commando who had taken part in some of the bloodiest campaigns of World War II. It was indeed difficult to imagine the man running from some silly bumps on the floor. Obviously the poor fellow was breaking up. It was a good thing that he had decided to retire.

Sharp was soon to learn, however, that whatever his friend had heard clomping around in the upper room could hardly be written off lightly as a case of nerves. He later told journalists that it was shortly after he had taken over the store and was working late one evening that he distinctly heard the steady tread of footsteps on the floor above. He knew that he was alone in the shop. He ran out of the store to see if there was anybody about next door. The place was deserted.

Sharp was determined to find out what was going on, and he started to run up the stairs. Suddenly, as he reached the third step, his legs seemed to freeze. He looked up and sensed, more than saw, a figure walking along the small passageway at the top of the stairs. At this point, Sharp admitted that he was really frightened.

The next morning when Sharp opened up the surplus store, he was dismayed to find that several shelves of army ankle-boots, which had been carefully stacked the previous afternoon, had been scattered about the shop. His first thought was that a burglar had broken into the shop and, finding only a few coins in the cash register, had decided that this must instead be an act of vandalism. Sharp checked the back door and all the windows, but he could discover no way by which an intruder might have gained entrance to the store.

It wasn't until he discovered the boots dumped about the floor a second time that Sharp began to connect the mysterious noises on the upper floor with the senseless violation of the shelves. The pattern was repeated on several mornings, and Sharp began to plan on his picking up the scattered boots as a matter of course.

One night, when he stayed after the closing hour to catch up on some book work, Sharp was startled to feel the pressure of a hand on his shoulder. He spun around on his chair, but there was no one there—only the sound of retreating footsteps.

Eventually, rumors of strange goings-on in the army surplus store began to reach the ears of inquisitive journalists. With the permission of Sharp, some reporters from the *Lancashire Evening Post* decided to conduct a vigil in the shop one evening. One reporter assured Sharp that there was a perfectly normal explanation for the seemingly odd occurrences and that they would have uncovered the cause of his "walking boots" by the following morning.

One of the journalists carefully inspected the upper rooms and found them to be completely empty. Because of his reluctance to enter the area after dark, Sharp had long since ceased using the area for storage. The reporters were also careful to test the rooms for loose boards, noisy shutters, or gnawing rats.

Throughout the evening, the journalists heard a great variety of sounds, especially heavy bumping and thumping sounds. At other times there were noises like metal scraping the floor. It was just after midnight when they seemed to hear the sound of a chain being rattled across the floor. By this time, the journalists were all quite nervous.

This bureau was photographed for a trade furniture dealer. Photographer Montague Cooper could not explain the hand that mysteriously appears in the photograph.

They had become convinced that they were not hearing rats and mice, nor the antics of some jokester.

Shortly after midnight, most of the journalists left the noisy upper floor for the comparative quiet of the shop area. With the coming of dawn and the cessation of the activity, the reporters made another inspection of the storage rooms. They were amazed to discover a long chain lying in one corner of a room. They all agreed that there had been no chain in any of the storage rooms when they made their first inspection. Upon opening a closet door, a reporter called the attention of his fellow journalists to a broken, three-legged chair that they had previously noted as hanging from one of a series of wall pegs. It now dangled from one of the other pegs on the closet wall.

Each of the journalists accused the other of having crept upstairs and moved it. While they were arguing over which one had played ghost, Sharp arrived and put the clincher on their debate. He swore that when he had left that previous evening, there had been no chair at all on the upper floor. Nor, he insisted, had he ever seen that particular chair before in his life.

When the journalists left the army surplus store that morning, they had to confess that rather than solving the mystery, they had merely recognized its complications.

Although the ghost that inhabited the upper floor had contented itself with producing mild amusements for the journalists during their overnight stay, by the next morning it had reverted to raising havoc with Sharp's merchandise once again. The harried shopkeeper opened his door that next day to find boxes emptied of their contents, army boots strewn about the shop, shirts unpinned and draped across shelves, and trouser legs tied together in knots.

Frank Spencer, a British clairvoyant, paid a visit to the haunted army store and later told reporters that he had seen a number of entities inhabiting the building. Each of these entities had wailed of an injustice or a great sorrow that kept it earthbound. An investigation later revealed that the surplus store had been built on the site of an ancient jail. An unused section of the basement was found to be paved with flagstones and contained an old room that may very well have been an old cell.

> An investigation later revealed that the surplus store had been built on the site of an ancient jail.

When last interviewed in the spring of 1952, Sharp was less concerned about who or what was causing the disturbance in his store than he was with why they insisted upon making such a terrible mess of his surplus store. Eventually, after a few more months of havoc, the disturbances ceased.

VOICES OF THE AFTERLIFE?

By Frank Joseph

In a paranormal sense, "electronic voice phenomena" (EVP) are the typically brief or curt statements, words or sounds generated by disembodied entities (human or otherwise, but usually attributed to persons), whose consciouness continues to survive their physical passing into an undefined afterlife. Because death has supposedly transformed these individuals into an electromagnetic condition of some kind, they are alleged to sonically interface with electronic receivers—- televisions, radios, computers, telephones, but most effectively, digital recorders—back on Earth.

Although my wife, Laura, and I had heard something about EVPs for many years, we tended to dismiss them as the results of stray radio transmissions, hoaxes, apophenia, or auditory pareidolia.

These last two explanations are less well known. The former is mistakenly hearing meaningful arrangements or connections in random and accidental sounds, a result of our all-too-human tendency to find deliberate designs in everything around us. A man who believes in nothing (he refers to himself as a "nontheist"), Michael Shermer, founder (not surprisingly) of "The Skeptics

Society," coined his own apopheniac term—patternicity—to define EVP as "the tendency to find meaningful patterns in meaningless noise."

A variation of apophenia is auditory pareidolia—the perception of imaginary, significant sounds in random stimuli. A good example of this is commonly experienced by bathers taking a shower and hearing a nonexistent telephone ring, because it and the noise of water splashing in a confined space share a parallel auditory frequency thus detected and confused by the human brain.

Laura and I were satisfied at face value with any one (or a combination) of these eminently rational explanations for all paranormal claims on behalf of EVPs. But after the turn of the last century, we were forced to deal with a series of evidently poltergeist-like activities while living at our previous, home in Minnesota, as described in chapter 1. These experiences led us to at least consider alternative possibilities for electronic voice phenomena.

As a test, a personal acquaintance and the proprietor of a late-nineteenth-century building in the old Mississippi riverboat town of Wabasha, about eighty milies south of St. Paul, allowed us to carry out our experiment in his seldom-used basement and even less frequented second-story apartments. He closed up his first-floor business, handed us the keys, and we entered the building on a weekday evening a few hours after sundown, when Wabasha was itself already fast asleep.

Our only equipment comprised a pair of flashlights and one, common, handheld, cassette tape recorder. Making no pretense to professionalism of any kind, we hoped the creaky structure through which we carefully picked our way past musty sofas and peeling, faded wallpaper had acquired enough spectral energy during the previous 120 years to make some impression on our battery-operated Sony. We felt foolish addressing the vacant air, trying to converse with hoped-for entities in moldy, dark rooms, where no otherworldly presence could be felt, nothing to make the hairs on the back of our necks stand up could be seen, and no response to our questions concerning their identity or state of being was heard. Following an equally unproductive descent into the basement, Laura and I locked up the place, and drove home, where we reviewed our tape of the night's rambles. We laughed to hear our silly voices mixed with our shuffling feet and legs clumsily banging into unseen objects strewn across the torn carpets and floors of delapidated, ill-lit apartments.

At a point in the recording we both associated with our passage through a front room overlooking the street below occurring less than an hour before, an older woman's voice surprised us by whispering very clearly, "Paul." Three seconds later, she repeated somewhat louder, with firmer emphasis, "Paul!" It did not sound like a stray radio transmission, and was plainly distinct from any parallel sounds which could be the result of either apophenia or auditory pareidolia. There was a Paul Busch Auto Center, Inc. at the end of the same block contiguous with the store-front apartment building in which the female voice was recorded. But what connection, if any, this establishment might have had with an invisible woman was beyond knowing. Perhaps she was interested in purchasing a Rolls Royce "Ghost."

In any case, while her audible contribution was intriguing, a single specimen proved nothing and was hardly definitive. I felt nevertheless sufficiently intrigued by our experience to further pursue the line of investigation we had begun with another EVP attempt at the most obvious place I knew, with the highest presumed chance of success. Sadly, my wandering and lingering among various tombstones of the local cemetery, the same Sony recorder at hand, left all my inquiries into the open air unanswered. Another self-evident target area—- the Cathedral of Saint Paul—- was just as unproductive. Given the high number of funerals and prayers that cavernous interior has experienced since its massive, bronze doors first opened to admit parishoners in 1915, I expected more than unrelieved silence.

> **[A]n older woman's voice surprised us by whispering very clearly, "Paul."**

Thereafter, my enthusiasm for further experiments with electronic voice phenomena cooled until 2008, when I began working part-time at a Wabasha store, the next block over from the location of our first EVP effort five years earlier. Part of my general assignments included cleaning out piles of various trash and debris that had accumulated over what must have been many years in the narrow space between my boss's establishment and the next building. Almost sandwiched between their walls in an area no more than four feet wide, I labored several days straight, hauling out all manner of wind-blown or deliberately tossed refuse. While thus engaged, I noticed that the old, brick wall on the west belonging to my boss's store was covered with dozens of inscribed names, many severely worn, all of them apparently cut into the aged, red bicks very long ago, perhaps as far back as the 1880s, shortly after these sagging, old structures were constructed.

One name, carved in particularly deep letters somewhat below my chest height, stood out: "Arnold." I wondered what Wabasha looked like when he made his mark, perhaps more than one hundred years ago. Maybe an EVP would be worth trying here.

Although my manual labors between walls had by then been completed, I returned the next day with my faithful Sony, put the fingers of my right hand on the engraved letters that spelled out "Arnold," and, alone, began asking questions into the confined space. After some ten minutes, my boss happened to march past on the sidewalk just outside, and stopped in mid-stride the moment he caught sight of me: "What are you doing?!," he demanded.

Unable to tell him he interrupted my most recent effort at communicating with the dead, I lied my way out with a tale—deliberately prepared in advance as a contingency for such a possible intrusion—of searching for a nonexistent, albeit momentarily useful, lost pen. (In this world, at any rate, there are moments when truth is inconvenient.) So, my brief attempt had been aborted, and I returned home with my recorder, virtually certain its cassette had not been allowed enough time to capture anything. I nevertheless reviewed it, half-listening, hearing my inquiries earlier that day answered only by a passing breeze, some dog barking across the street, or passing cars, until I asked Arnold, just moments before my boss showed up, "Are you happy?"

Almost immediately thereafter, a young, male voice replied—not through a faint whisper, but in clear tones—"I'm happy!" The inflection suggested, "Well, of course, I'm happy! Isn't it obvious?"

His response was what is known among paranormal investigators as a "Class-A" EVP, sometimes even referred to as "the Holy Grail of electronic voice phenomena," when a disincarnate entity actually supplies a direct, pertinent answer to a specifically addressed question. The perfect aptness, clarity and timing of the response definitively ruled out all possibilities for stray radio transmissions, auditory pareidolia, apophenia, patternicity or anything else that congenitally myopic mob of self-styled skeptics disconnected from the real world choose to call it. Someone I never knew, who passed away, probably long ago, was generous enough to assure me, a perfect stranger, that he is alive and happy in another dimension. In so doing, he freely gave me a great gift; namely, the hope that I, too, after my own death, might actually be alive and happy in a future I presently cannot imagine. If Arnold made it, maybe the rest of us can, too!

Thereafter, Laura felt urged to try her hand at the same kind of communication, particularly because she sometimes felt herself being faintly touched at our home—built in 1926 and, since then, occupied successively by at least four or five different families before we moved in—by the hands of someone she never saw. Our faithful Sony had by then been replaced with a more modern digital recorder that she now used to question the spring air around the back of our house. A few, unresponsive days passed, until Laura documented what sounded like a middle-aged or older woman whispering pronouncedly and very clearly to her, "I just love you!"

Neither Laura nor I recognize the voice, though we are happy to have captured such a sentiment. But it signaled the end, forever, of our EVP adventures. We wanted to quit while we were ahead, as it were, having learned of too many unpleasant examples so-called "ghost-hunters" typically encounter. More importantly, we do not want to inadvertently contact possibly negative energies less easily disposed of than attracted. Even so, whenever I happen to pass along the sidewalk by that narrow space between buildings where I recorded my Class-A EVP, I always say, "Hello, Arnold!"

Copies of *Opening the Ark of the Covenant: The Secret Power of the Ancients, the Knights Templar Connection, and the Search for the Holy Grail* by Frank Joseph and Laura Beaudoin, with Foreword by Brad Steiger (288 pp.gs, 50 original photos and illustrations), are available for $17.99 (plus $3.00 shipping & handling) from Ancient American Book Store, PO Box 370, Colfax, WI 54730; orders taken by phone usingat our 24-hour, toll-free number,telephone (877) 494-0044; or by email: wayne@ancientamerican.com.

Also, hear Frank Joseph narrate his first audio book, *Alien Revelation: 2012*, a *"Novel of our Time"* based on a true story, at www.mysticvalleymedia.com.

THE POLTERGEIST THAT TRASHED A COURT REPORTER'S OFFICE

When Jim Hazelwood, editorial writer for the *Oakland Tribune*, arrived at the office of court reporter George W. on Franklin Street on June 15, 1964 the ghost had already been active for two weeks. The first manifestations, according to Mrs. Helen R., concentrated on the telephones in the office. The row of lights on each telephone base would light up in rapid succession, but there would be no one on the line. The telephone company insisted that there was nothing wrong with the instruments.

Next, the disturbances centered on the electric typewriters. The coil springs beneath the keys began to go limp, twisted together, and balled up. When the repairmen came to take the typewriters away, they left replacement machines so that work in the office might go on without interruption. The springs on the loan machines, however, began to suffer from the same mysterious mechanical affliction. When the original typewriters were returned to George W's office, their springs once again began to twist and bend.

Bob G., a sales representative for the typewriter company, told Hazelwood that the typewriter springs in question normally lasted for the life of the machine. They hadn't replaced more than three of the springs in the last ten years. But during the past few days, they had replaced about one hundred in George W's machines. They had practically exhausted the stock of springs in the San Francisco Bay area.

Hazelwood arrived at the office about fifteen minutes after Officer Charles N. had completed an inspection tour of the suite. The inhabitants of the besieged office had decided to suffer in silence no longer. The staff members of George's office included: his wife, Z., court reporters Robert C. and Calvert B., and two transcribers, Helen R. and John O. Hazelwood quickly surveyed the office and saw that it was in a shambles. A cracked ashtray littered the floor along with a pile of smashed crockery. A puddle of water had seeped out of a broken flower vase that rested against a corner of George's desk.

Officer N. told Hazelwood that when he had first arrived, the broken vase had been on a shelf eighteen-inches deep. It flew across the room and made a right turn to smash itself on the floor. While the policeman spoke, he was interrupted by a banging sound from the room on the left. One of the telephones had fallen to the floor. Hazelwood later wrote that they had quickly become tired of picking up telephones. While he was in George W's office on June 15, all eight of the phones kept sliding off the desks and falling to the floor with monotonous regularity.

Jim E., a staff photographer for the *Tribune*, arrived and asked John O. to pose beside a pile of debris. Jim snapped the picture, and the two men turned to leave. Their attention was brought sharply back to the room when they heard a loud crash behind them. The floor was now covered with white powder from a large jar of cream substitute that had jumped out of the coffee cupboard and smashed on the floor.

[T]he broken vase had been on a shelf eighteen-inches deep. It flew across the room and made a right turn to smash itself on the floor.

The phenomena called a halt to its unwelcome activities that afternoon at precisely four o'clock. George W. announced that he was going to move some of his equipment into an empty office downstairs in an attempt to escape the wild thing that had mysteriously beset them. It was imperative that the staff get caught up on work that had been accumulating because of the ghost's rampages.

The next day, George's frustrations were multiplied when he learned that the ghost had followed them into the new suite. In addition, other offices on the second floor had been afflicted by the phenomena. Ralph and Jeanetta R., who ran an engineering insurance service, had their typewriter fly off a desk and several coffee cups explode. Their telephone hurled to the floor and was broken. In another office on the second floor, dental technician Frank B. was mixing some paste when an asbestos board suddenly tore loose from the nails holding it to the wall.

Reporter Hazelwood arrived shortly after ten o'clock and went up to the third-floor office where some of the staff were still trying valiantly to conduct business. The journalist resolved to keep a logbook of the occurrences for one hour. During those sixty incredible minutes a metal Dictaphone foot pedal with cord wrapped around it flew out of the cabinet, struck a wooden counter and fell to the floor, light bulbs broke in the stairwell between the third and fourth floor, paper cups were strewn around the water cooler, a metal card index file fell to the floor, a typewriter top flew out an open window to the street below, and a two-pound can of coffee left the cabinet and landed ten feet away.

Later that day, a thirty-pound typewriter leaped off a table in an empty room and fell to the floor. A large electric coffee percolator slid off a table and several coffee cups exploded. Bob G., the harassed typewriter repairman, saw a heavy wooden filing cabinet turn sideways and fall over.

The noted expert Dr. Arthur Hastings, who at that time was a professor at Stanford University and who had already gained an excellent reputation as an investigator of the unusual and unexplained, offered his opinion that the office was the scene of a genuine poltergeist phenomenon. Dr. Hastings told Hazelwood that this was the first time that he had ever heard of a poltergeist case taking place in an office. But the phenomenon was real enough to convince even the most hard-nosed skeptic that this particular poltergeist preferred the typewriters and filing cabinets of an office to domestic surroundings.

On Wednesday morning, June 17, the phenomena reached a climax shortly after Cal B. and John O. opened the office. In rapid succession, the water cooler tipped over, soaking the left office and covering the floor with broken glass, a large wooden cabinet of office supplies came thudding down, and a movable counter flipped over onto its back.

Dr. Hastings predicted that the phenomena would not return. "This is usually the pattern with the poltergeist phenomena," he told Hazelwood. "They start slowly, build up to a climax, and then stop altogether. I don't think we'll see any more of these occurrences. Of course," he added, "I could be wrong."

It appeared at first as though Dr. Hastings' prediction had been accurate. The poltergeist was quiet for nine days, then, on June 26, it once again caused havoc at George W's office. George W's wife said that she tried to prepare for it as soon as the first tell-tale signs showed up. When springs started breaking in all three typewriters, she knew that it had come back. Mrs. W. started placing breakable objects on the floor. She had no sooner set a cup down and turned her back when the cup leaped eight feet across the room and shattered against a filing cabinet. Almost simultaneously, two glass ashtrays smashed to the floor, and a stapler bounded from a desktop. Mrs. W. said that they didn't know what was systematically attacking their office, but whatever it was, they were sick and tired of it.

Dr. Hastings said that he still believed that the "eye of the storm" had passed on and that only the weaker manifestations remained. It appeared that this time Dr. Hastings was correct. After that last dramatic manifestation, things at the office seemed to quiet down for good. But both Hazelwood and Hastings were shocked when John O. confessed to the police that he had caused all the objects to fall by "flipping them behind his back."

Hazelwood had been away on an assignment in San Francisco on June 29, the day that the police had called the press conference to air O's confession. John had asked to speak first with Hazelwood, but the police convinced him that he should make his confession public before reporters from all media. At the press conference, the police had outlined the twenty-year-old court transcriber's confession, and John O. soberly nodded his head and agreed to the charges that the police read. The story of the young man's admission of guilt and trickery went out over all the wire services and was broadcast live on television. Another poltergeist case was "exposed" as the work of a hoaxer.

Immediately upon his return from San Francisco, Hazelwood started for John O's apartment, taking Leo C., a staff photographer, along as a witness. Hazelwood said that he knew and John knew that he couldn't have thrown all those things around the office. Almost in tears, John said that of course he wasn't responsible, but it was easier to admit to the disturbances and get the police off his back. The police interrogators kept suggesting ways that he could have caused things to fly and typewriters to break down. At the same time, they assured him that he would probably not be prosecuted. At last, to end the incessant interrogation as quickly as possible, John had simply agreed with them. The two journalists informed the police of John O's repudiation of his confession, but the police were adamant—they had solved the case to their satisfaction and great relief and were unwilling to stir things up again.

Dr. Hastings said that John O. could conceivably have caused some of the accidents by trickery, but that there were too many aspects of the case that could not be explained by sleight of hand or by any natural causes.

Although the classic poltergeist formula usually involves a young person who is in the throes of puberty, it was pointed out by reporter Hazelwood that John O. was emotionally high-strung and sensitive. He was upset to the point of illness that the police should even consider him guilty of the disturbances. It should also be noted that John had been recently married. Poltergeists have been known to plague those making marital adjustments as well as those entering puberty.

Hazelwood remained convinced of John O's innocence and of being consciously responsible for the chaos in George W's office. In a letter dated July 30, 1965, Hazelwood told me: "I suspected him (John O.) almost from the first and would have loved to have been able to expose him as the trickster. It was just not possible to do so. At the same time, all activity ceased the moment John O. left the building. This happened on several occasions.... In fact, he was out of the room, but not the building, more often than not when the events occurred. I went into this as a hard-nosed reporter with almost twenty years in the business. I was prepared to scoff, expose, disbelieve. I came out of it absolutely convinced that the poltergeist phenomenon is a real one which cannot be explained by our present knowledge of natural laws."

THE OLD BERNARDSVILLE LIBRARY
By L'Aura Hladik, Founder-Director of New Jersey Ghost Hunters Society, www.njghs.net.

Today this building, located at 2 Morristown Road in Bernardsville, New Jersey, is home to an upscale home furnishings and decorating store known as

Debra Blanchard heard that the building she was purchasing for her business was haunted, but she did not realize just *how* haunted until she moved in.

Meli Melo. Current owner Debra Blanchard has been here since 2008, and although she had heard before going into business in this building that it was reported to be haunted, she had no idea just how haunted.

The origin of the main ghost here traces back to January 1777. At that time, the Vealtown Tavern was owned and operated by Captain John Parker. He had the assistance of his lovely daughter, Phyllis. In addition to being a tavern, Captain Parker had extra rooms that he rented out to boarders. One of the boarders was the young and handsome Dr. Byram. Phyllis fell in love with Dr. Byram and they were engaged to be married.

Subsequent to the Battle of Princeton, General Anthony Wayne stayed at the Vealtown tavern. He had important papers to deliver which were stolen from his room. Upon discovering the stolen papers, General Wayne asked Captain Parker to account for everyone staying at the tavern. Dr. Byram and his horse were gone, but, as Captain Parker explained, it was typical for the doctor to take off for few days at a time to treat his patients. General Wayne demanded to know more about the doctor and positively identified him as Aaron Wilde, a Tory spy, once Captain Parker produced the miniature portrait the doctor had given to Phyllis.

Wilde was caught with the stolen papers in his possession in nearby Basking Ridge, New Jersey. Wayne's orders were to hang the spy for treason immediately. Prior to his execution, Wilde requested that a note be given to his precious Phyllis and that Captain Parker provide a decent burial for his body. Shocked and upset by the news of Dr. Byram's hanging, Captain Parker had the body delivered to the tavern while he arranged for its burial. He specifically requested that this news be kept from Phyllis. Perhaps he was waiting for the right time and place to tell her the sorrowful news?

Unfortunately, Phyllis figured it out for herself. She might have overheard the soldiers discussing the matter through the thin walls or she had a gut feeling that something bad had happened to her fiancé. Either way, she crept downstairs during the night and found the pine box in the kitchen. By the light of a candle, she proceeded to hack away at the box with a hatchet until she made the horrific confirmation that her beloved Dr. Byram was dead. Her agonizing scream shattered through the stillness in the tavern and soldiers and servants rushed to find her collapsed on the floor with the hatchet next to her. She was sobbing uncontrollably and it was noted that the "light of reason had left her eyes."

One hundred years later, what paranormal investigators today call a residual haunting, took place at the tavern. However, in January 1877 the former tavern was a private residence. A nameless woman recounted her experience to the *Newark Sunday News* in February 1903. She explained that her husband was working late one night, and she had locked up the house. Her baby was asleep upstairs. She was at her sewing machine which was very noisy, and yet she could hear distinct, heavy footsteps on the back porch. She would stop sewing in order to listen intently and she would hear nothing. She'd resume sewing and start to hear the footsteps again. By the third pause in sewing, she heard the heavy, labored footsteps in her kitchen making their way to her dining room. Once in the dining room, she heard a loud thud as if a heavy wooden box had been dropped to the bare floorboards. Then, she heard the sound of marching footsteps as they exited back out the kitchen. She was content to ignore all this and continue with her sewing, but next she heard the chopping sounds of wood being pulled from wood, and nails falling to the floor.

Paralyzed with fear, she was able to break free from the sewing machine and race upstairs once she heard her baby's cries. As she bolted her bedroom door and collapsed on her bed with her baby, she heard what she described as the shrillest, most agonizing woman's scream followed by moans and sobs that seemingly echoed throughout the entire house.

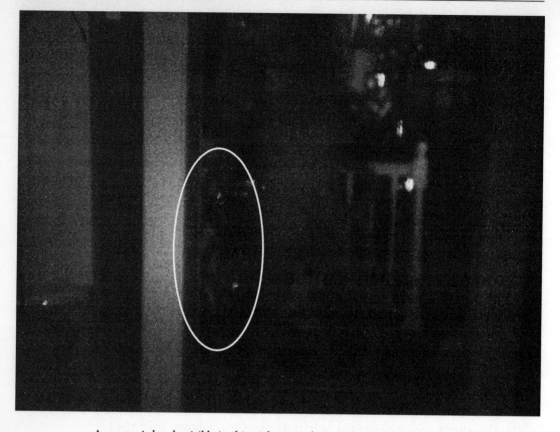

A spectre is barely visible in this night time photo in the former Bernardsville Library.

One hundred years after the news of Wilde's hanging was ordered suppressed by General Wayne, that this woman unknowingly experienced a residual haunting of Wilde's body being dropped off for burial.

Phyllis' ghost made another appearance on January 29, 1974. At this point, the building was the Bernardsville Library. Teenager Wendy Wright worked part-time at the library and arrived there ready to get to work. From the parking, looking through the library window, she noticed a woman looking through books. She figured it was her boss Geraldine Burden.

She approached the front door and knocked to be let in, and Mrs. Burden did not respond. Wendy went around the side to peer through the window and saw the woman standing and stretching. Wendy went back and knocked again on the front door, figuring Mrs. Burden did not hear her the first time. Again, no answer came.

As Wendy started to walk around the building again, she met Mrs. Burden. Wendy explained that she thought the library director was inside this

A face is clearly visible in this interior photo.

whole time ignoring her knocks at the front door. Mrs. Burden explained that she had just arrived. Together they entered the library to look for the woman Wendy saw through the window. The library was empty.

Currently, Bernardsville has a brand new library on adjacent property to this haunted building on Morristown Road. They retain a library card on file for Phyllis Parker and to her credit she has no overdue books.

The New Jersey Ghost Hunters Society (NJGHS.net) investigated this two-hundred-year-old building in 2004 when it was Sandra John Interiors. Nothing was captured definitively on video. Photography yielded some bizarre streaks of light on a Sony digital camera. They would appear in response to a question posed prior to taking the picture. If the investigator remained silent and simply took pictures, no anomaly appeared. An interesting, yet inherently questionable, orb picture was taken outside the building at the conclusion of the investigation.

In July 2011, a team of investigators named New Jersey Researchers of Paranormal Evidence (NJROPE.com) spent four hours investigating the location. Equipped with full-spectrum cameras, digital audio recorders, and various other tools of the ghost-hunting trade, they were able to achieve results that are impressive. Frank Lazzaro, the founder and director of the group, said they took a total of 1,135 photos, fifteen hours of video, and twenty-five hours of audio. While they experienced some sporadic spikes on their K-2 meter in the cash register area of the building, no other evidence was captured to substantiate these K-2 "hits." Frank said they have twenty-two viable EVPs collected from both stationery devices, and dedicated EVP sessions with questions and prompts offered by the investigators. They have three positive photos: a shadow figure, a figure peering through the doorway, and a ghostly face appearing by a lampshade. The psychic investigators on the team determined there to be a male and female entity present. In fact, the one psychic investigator determined the name of Clara for the female spirit.

Days after NJROPE delivered and reviewed the report of findings with Debra, a bizarre message appeared on the store's computer screen. It said, "I am Clara! Please help! Help!" This message appeared a second time, and a store employee was able to take a picture of it with her cell phone.

Deb was not at the store each time this message presented on the computer screen, but she can attest that neither she nor any of her employees had access to create and program a display like that one.

NJROPE researched further to discover that "Clara" was Clara Ormiston, a librarian during the 1950s and 1960s. While it is an eerie computer message and the name has been verified, it is not solid enough evidence to conclude that the spirit of Clara sent that message.

But whether you are hunting with a digital full-spectrum camera for ghosts, or hunting with your debit card handy, a trip to Meli Melo is worth it.

⬤⬤⬤

THE HAUNTED ARTS AND CRAFT STORE IN SCAPPOOSE, OREGON

An investigation by Dr. Sharon A. Gill and Dr. Dave R. Oester.

Since this contribution by Sharon and Dave appeared in the first edition of this book, they have become Drs. Sharon and Dave Oester. Dr. Sharon A. Gill is a licensed and ordained minister and holds a doctorate in metaphysical counseling from the University of Metaphysics. Her thesis was on grief counseling. Dr. Dave R. Oester is a licensed and ordained minister who holds a Doctor of Divinity and a Doctor of Philosophy in Religion through his religious affiliation. Dr. Gill and Dr. Oester's ministries focuses on teaching people how to confirm that there is life after death, and they believe the spirits of the dead are the evidence that life exists beyond the grave. They have appeared on many prime-time television shows and specials on the History Channel, the Discovery Channel, The Learning Channel, Arts & Entertainment, Fox, and ABC. Their website, www.ghostweb.com, is one of the most popular and the largest ghost-hunting websites on the Internet. They have over nine thousand ghost photos and three hundred Electronic Voice Phenomena ghost voices posted on the site.

Dr. David Oester begins the narrative:

In 1994, Sharon and I had moved from the quiet little coastal town of Seaside to Warren, Oregon, along the Columbia River. We moved into an old house built in 1928 that had many of the original features, including the lead-pipe plumbing. It was a wonderful old place with lots of character. It also seemed as though the original tenant had remained there to share our home. Her name was Amelia, and she let us know when she was around in terms that were unquestionable. We coexisted there with her for over three years.

Dr. Sharon Gill and Dr. Dave Oester.

Before we moved to the area, we had been driving over to Scappoose for two years to visit my Mom. When visiting the town, we would frequent the local arts and crafts store. It was the only one around, and it usually carried the supplies we were looking for. I had been there many times prior to our move and knew the store well. Once we moved to the area, I got to know the owner and his family. Something very strange was taking place in the store yet the owner, a young man, was not talking about it.

Ghosts were the farthest thing from the young man's mind. Yet after he closed the store and retired to his apartment on the second floor, things would happen. Often he would catch sight of a shadow moving and turn quickly to see if it was one of his cats. Nothing was there. His cats would react to things that he could not see, and it unnerved him, not knowing what was taking place. The activity picked up when he started to redecorate the apartment, and things were happening down in the store, too. Finally he consulted us about the strange occurrences.

We were able to meet Chris, the mother of the young man who owned the store, and who often worked in the store herself. She was very talkative and shared stories of many of the ghostly hauntings that were taking place in the store. Each time we came into the store, she would relate another experience about their ghost.

Our interest was piqued, so we decided to investigate the history of the building and determine if any other stories about a ghost surfaced. Sharon and I visited the local library and searched for historical records relating to the building. The crafts store was next-door to a tavern and behind the tavern in the same building was an abandoned doctor's office.

After some research, we found some local residents who recalled going to this doctor, over fifty years ago. They remembered that a ghost had haunted

Doc's office. That portion of the building had documented history of a haunting. Now we had established evidence of a historical haunting that had spanned some fifty years, important information since the crafts store and the abandoned doctor's office are in the same building.

The top floor of the crafts store was adjacent to the old ballroom above the tavern. This ballroom was a favorite of the locals on Saturday night. According to newspaper accounts, a fire destroyed the ballroom and also resulted in people burning to death.

During one conversation with Chris, she had mentioned that she had heard people upstairs laughing and thumping around, almost like they were dancing country-western style. When she investigated, she would find nothing out of place and no living person upstairs. The newspaper accounts of the fire and the deaths may provide clues that account for the sounds that Chris was hearing upstairs; some of the people killed in the fire were still dancing away in the ballroom.

Since Sharon and I had established that the building had been haunted some fifty years ago by a ghost, we arranged a time after the store closed for us to go down to the store to investigate. The owner had mentioned that, while upstairs in his apartment, he would hear crashing sounds down in the store, yet he would find nothing disturbed. He would go downstairs in the morning to open the store and find that cans of paint that had been neatly arranged on a top shelf were now sitting on the floor, yet no one had been in the store since he had closed it the night before. One morning he found an entire display sitting at the foot of the stairs. Everything had been moved during the night while he slept. His first thought was that someone had broken into the place, but there were no signs of an intruder.

A family member who worked in the store agreed that something very strange was going on, and we were looking forward to being able to investigate and maybe learn more about the spirit who remained there. We took our cassette recorders and cameras one evening at 7:00 P.M. and met Chris and her grandson in the old building. We spent the first hour talking with them, learning about what had been taking place for quite some time. Dr. Sharon Gill picks up the storyline:

> It was during the interview that I heard music playing. It sounded like a music box playing softly in the background. Since the music had caught my attention, I had to find out where it was coming from. The grandson, about ten years old, heard it too, so we went deeper into the store to find the source.

We found nothing in the store itself, though we searched thoroughly. I decided to go upstairs to the apartment to find the music. I followed David up the dark stairs, slowly, as they were steep. When I was almost to the top, I turned and snapped a picture down the stairway. I can only explain that the reason I took the picture at that moment stemmed from a feeling I had. After we had investigated the apartment, David said he had felt a cold draft come by him, as though it was rushing past us down the stairs. I had not felt the cold, but I had felt the need to take a picture.

The resulting picture was the first vortex captured by us and is the photograph on the cover of our second book, *Haunted Reality*. When taking the picture, the camera strap on the Pentax UC–1 was around my wrist. It has always been my policy of to use the camera strap to prevent dropping the camera and to keep the strap away from the lens.

At the end of the evening, we suggested to Chris that she give the ghost a name. When things started to happen again, she could talk to it and tell it to put an end to the pranks and stop scaring the animals. Chris named the ghost, Billie. We asked her why the name Billie, but she didn't know why. It was a name that just came into her mind.

While working in the store during the day, the bell on the front door would ring, alerting the clerks to customers coming in. The bell rang regularly, but the clerks found that no one had entered. It was something that started to get on their nerves, because they would drop everything to see who had entered.

The problem was complicated after the story of Billie had come out in our second book. The media had filmed the story for television, and folks were coming to the store to see the ghost. The owner feared that they would start to go upstairs to his apartment without his knowledge. He decided to install a security system at the bottom of the stairs to alert him to anyone going up to his living quarters.

The security system included a motion sensor that would ding like a doorbell if someone walked in front of it. The only trouble with the security system was that they had not accounted for such a playful ghost. Billie enjoyed setting off the motion sensor almost immediately, and some days it would ding almost constantly. The constant dinging occurred, but there was no living person triggering the sensor. Finally, giving up on the whole idea, the owner decided to have the system removed, because it was driving the clerks crazy while they tried to work in the store. We all enjoyed a good laugh when hearing how the ghost had outsmarted modern technology.

Late one afternoon, one of the clerks was upstairs in the warehouse putting stock away. She had a bag filled with Pogs in her hand and though she was aware of Billie and the antics, her mind was on getting her work done. She knew the warehouse well, as she had been up there a hundred times. On this particular day, however, something happened that she never expected. As she looked up from where she was putting the Pogs on the shelf, she saw a mist at the end of the aisle. It moved around the shelves to the other side of where she was standing. At that moment, she screamed, Pogs flew everywhere, and she took off running back out through the apartment, down the stairs, and into the store below.

As she told Chris what had happened, she calmed herself. It was not so much that the ghost scared her; rather, she had reacted to the surprise of seeing the mist. She and the other clerks had felt cold spots down in the store, saw items moved from one location to yet another location, and heard things banging upstairs on many occasions. On this day, Chris and the clerk went back up the stairs to the warehouse. They had to see if Billie would show herself again.

As they entered the warehouse, they saw the Pogs all over the floor. They walked the aisles, but found no mist or sign that Billie had been messing around. Chris told the clerk to pick up the Pogs, and she went back downstairs to tend to customers. The clerk finished her job upstairs and the rest of the day was uneventful.

One evening remains clearly fixed in my mind. We were at the store purchasing a few items and another customer was in line, holding yarn that she wanted to purchase. As Chris was adding up our bill, we spoke about Billie and recent events. The woman standing in line behind us was listening to the conversation. Suddenly she threw down the yarn and said the store had demons, and she was not going to buy anything there.

I looked at Chris who had experienced a lot in the store and had come to understand Billie and had actually become very fond of her. The tear in her eye said it all. Billie was no more a demon than any one of us standing there, but the woman had no understanding of the spirits that remain on this physical plane. Many people judge ghosts as something demonic, which can not be farther from the truth in most cases. There are ghosts with attitudes and ghosts who are negative, but they are not demons.

We have worked with hundreds of people and helped them to understand the nature of ghosts. They remain here for a purpose, which we may or may not understand. They are people without physical bodies who have unresolved issues or things left unsaid or undone at the time of their deaths.

Billie continued to make herself known to the owner and his employees. She became an accepted part of the old building. By understanding Billie, the owner coexisted with her and set limits to her antics. The cats would still react at times, but mostly they calmed down and just watched as Billie moved about the room.

The owner sold the building a few years later, and we learned that it is now a restaurant. The new owners do not believe in ghosts, so whether they have experienced Billie or not, we will never know. They refuse to discuss the subject.

A photograph of the "vortex" inside the crafts store in Scappoose, Oregon.

The events that took place at the arts and craft store were real to those who experienced them. The photograph validated to us that there was at least one spirit at the store. We learned a lot from investigating and sharing that story. The reversed "J" -shaped anomaly captured on film was coined a "vortex" by us. The vortex captured on film cast a shadow on the wall, meaning that it was dense in nature and the flash did not penetrate through it. We did not see anything on the stairs that night, yet the camera recorded the energy moving behind me. David had felt its chill as it moved by him. The interesting aspect of the photo was that the vortex's shadow was at a forty-five-degree angle from the vortex, instead of directly behind the vortex.

In July 1996, we posted this vortex photo on our website: www.ghost web.com. The response to the photo was remarkable and by November of 1996, we had established the International Ghost Hunters Society on the Internet.

28

MYSTERIOUS ENTITIES AND DARK, HOODED BEDROOM INVADERS

In recent years, dozens of men and women have sent me accounts of their mysterious encounter with a dark-robed hooded entity. Some believe that this increased interaction between spirits and humans is due to the barriers between the two worlds becoming thinner, as our physical world approaches nearer to a great time of transition. Others theorize that these hooded beings come from some dimension that occasionally rubs up against ours and believe that these entities are curious about our species. Still others speculate that the mysterious nocturnal visitors are aliens from an extraterrestrial world who invade human bedrooms in order to conduct certain physical and mental tests to learn more about what it is to be an earth-dweller.

My own experience seemed more in the nature of a spiritual teaching mechanism in which the hooded entity imparted certain information to me and subsequently assumed the role of a kind of spirit guide.

THE AUTHOR'S ENCOUNTER WITH A HOODED ENTITY

I was awakened one night in 1972 by an unusual kind of buzzing sound, and I sat up to encounter a dark, hooded figure standing at my bedside. In the dim light issuing through the shades and curtains from an outside streetlight, I could see that the unexpected bedroom intruder, who looked very much like a cowled monk, was waving his arms over me in a peculiar manner.

Interpreting his movements as threatening, I was instantly wide-awake. I rolled out of bed, stood up, and prepared to deliver as solid a punch as I could manage right into the face of the person who had invaded our home and posed a threat to my sleeping wife and four children.

My blow never landed. I felt all the strength drain from my body. My arms dropped limply to my sides—and this was back in my iron-pumping, jogging days. But at that moment, I had never felt so weak, so helpless. I collapsed in a heap back on the bed. I remember that I actually began to weep in fear and confusion. I was completely at the mercy of whoever or whatever had come into our bedroom.

It was then that the hooded being spoke. "Don't be afraid," it said in a quiet whisper. "We won't hurt you."

And the next thing I knew, the morning sunlight was making me squint into wakefulness. There was no physical trace that a hooded entity or anyone else had been in our bedroom during the night, but strangely, within my mind there had been planted the seed of an idea for a book about the contemporary revelatory experience. I had dreamed concepts for books before, but I had a peculiar kind of feeling that the cowled monk was not simply a character in a bizarre nighttime vision meant to inspire me. As I reflected on the incident throughout the day, I became more and more convinced that an actual visitation had occurred and that some kind of entity had come to our bedroom in the night.

The next evening, I was just falling asleep when I became aware of a peculiar buzzing that sounded like the noise a metallic bumblebee might make. I realized at once that it was just such a sound that had awakened me the night before when the hooded being invaded our bedroom.

I was instantly wide-awake. When I focused my attention on the open door to the bedroom, I perceived a greenish-colored light emanating from somewhere in the stairway. My pulse quickened as I saw a green globe of softly glowing light moving down the hallway toward our bedroom.

On one level of consciousness, I knew that somehow the glowing orb was associated with the hooded entity. The being was returning for some purpose I had not yet ascertained. But I resolved that on this, his second visit, I would not under any circumstances allow him to "knock me out" the way he had done on the preceding visitation. I would stay alert and mentally analyze every moment of the experience.

The greenish globe entered the bedroom and hovered near the bedside, and I heard a deep, but very pleasant, male voice command me: "You will listen!"

I perceived only a glimpse of the hooded figure as he somehow extricated himself from the glowing orb—then, at once, my physical self and my questioning brain were silenced.

Once again, my next conscious memory was that of the morning sunlight streaming through the bedroom windows. But I now had bursting within the creative corridors of my psyche the passionate conviction that my next book was to be about the experiences of men and women who had entered into spiritual contact and communication with a higher intelligence. And I knew that I would entitle the book *Revelation: The Divine Fire*. I also realized that my cowled after-midnight visitor had not come to frighten me but to inspire me.

Revelation: The Divine Fire was published in 1973 by Prentice-Hall. Wherever I have lectured or presented seminars in the past 30 years, there have always been a number of individuals who will tell me that that particular book was the one that turned their lives around or that gave them the spiritual tools they required at a particular time in their lives. I tell them that I can only take credit for having been a competent stenographer for the book.

It was nearly eight years later before the hooded figure appeared to me again. This time I was permitted to remain conscious as my spirit teacher presented me with the exact information for which I had been seeking to complete a very important project. He also told me that his name was Elijah, and he allowed me to see his face—a countenance that shone with a spiritual light, framed with long gray hair and a full beard.

About a year later, Elijah, my cowled spirit mentor, came to me when I was suffering with painful boils and skin eruptions that covered a good portion of my body. I lay miserable on my bed, unable to bear even the touch of a sheet on my skin. Elijah took pity on my suffering and gave me certain specific instructions of a seemingly bizarre combination of ordinary food to ingest. Within two or three hours, all traces of the horrible boils had vanished from my body, never to return.

> It was nearly eight years later before the hooded figure appeared to me again. This time I was permitted to remain conscious....

In 1987 a most important visitation from my hooded advisor occurred in my apartment in Scottsdale, Arizona, when he confirmed that Sherry Hansen was to be the one with whom I was to walk together on a mutually rewarding spiritual and physical life-path. He has not appeared to me since that time.

THE ANGEL OF LIFE

As the following account demonstrates, one aspect of the mission of the hooded bedroom invaders may be to tell the recipient of their visits some things about their lives that they need to know in order to better carry out their own mission on Earth.

An Observation from Mark

"I saw something on our local television news program on Halloween (2000) morning that made me consider the actuality of those hooded figures that you've been reporting that appear to people in their bedrooms or other places.

"A reporter was interviewing children and adults who were dressed in Halloween costumes. She stopped to speak with a little fellow who was no more than four to six years old. He was dressed in black hood and long black robe and it looked like he didn't have a face, as he had a black, opaque nylon covering the opening in the hood.

"The reporter asked him who he was supposed to be, and the little boy said, 'I'm the Angel of Life.' Now remember, he was dressed all in black, the universal color for death.

"The reporter then asked him who the Angel of Life is. The boy replied, 'The Angel of Life is someone who comes to talk to you. He tells you things about your life.'

"The boy's mother had a helpless, embarrassed look on her face as she explained that she had no idea where her son ever came up with such thoughts. The conviction in the little boy's face and the non-hesitant way in which he explained who he was has me thinking that, at some time, he actually had talked to the Angel of Life."

HOODED ENTITIES PROLONGED HIS MOTHER'S LIFE AND GAVE HIM A HEALING

The Personal Encounter of Douglas Stingley

"I was for 17-plus years the medical caregiver for my mother. During the early summer of 1991, a short time after my mom's first major stroke, she got better for no apparent reason. [Previously] she had a profound speech impediment and a total lack of ability to reason or to focus on mental tasks. It was that way until a single day when her problems stopped all at once with a near total return to normalcy. Around three years after that period of time, I had a dream recall of what really happened to make my mother's quality of life so much better before her death. I was sitting in the family room, watching the last part of *Late Night with David Letterman* on television, when I saw the hall light go on. My mom had already gone to bed around an hour before. I got up and went to the west end of the dining room and looked down the hall. Her door was closed, and everything was quiet.

"Something made me sit down at the dining table and look down the hallway. Out of the third bedroom, a couple of creatures of humanoid form came out and moved through the wooden door of mom's bedroom without opening it. They came in and out of her bedroom for what seemed to be a period of two and a half to three hours. They always returned to the third bedroom as their staging area. They wore light hooded robes [that were] dark brown, with tan accents. They were too thin of body compared to their height. But what was shocking was their faces—solid black without eyes, nose, mouth, or ears, and no indication of such. Their head was like an egg colored with a black felt marker. They did not walk as much as they glided across the floor.

"Whatever they did in that room restored my mother to a near-normal state. They carried whatever they needed inside small gray-colored boxes no larger than large rectangular tissue boxes. One odd note about this is that they paid no attention to me to the point that one could wonder if I was even on their plane of existence. Also during this period, our pet cat Mitzi could not be seen. (Mitzi was lined up at her feed dish the very next morning, like nothing had happened.)

"[T]hey paid no attention to me to the point that one could wonder if I was even on their plane of existence."

"A next follow-up is on Mom. She suffered a massive stroke that totally destroyed all memories of me or anyone in 1997. However, due to those creatures, she had an additional six years of peaceful retirement.

"I myself had a healing by the hooded ones some years ago. This was when I was a 13-year-old boy in 1971. During that summer, the Willamette Valley of Oregon was struck by a strep epidemic that had hospitals filled to the brim. It was a very hard-to-treat strain. I got this infection and was hospitalized for a life-threatening kidney infection that despite all the drugs used seemed to get worse instead of better. I think I was close to death. None of the antibiotics seemed to work.

"A 'nurse' wearing a grayish white hooded robe came to my bedside at Salem Memorial Hospital. Somehow I could sense that inside the robe was the body of a chubby, round of body, older-type person. I looked at her face in the dim room light, and it was covered by plastic-like skin. Her nose was only a V-shaped ridge. She implanted thoughts into my head instead of talking to me, and she gave me the information that she had a solution to my problem. She said not to look at what she was doing. She then moved her arm down as if to give me an injection, but I felt no needle, only a cold pressure like an ice cube pressed against my body.

"I began to get better within 24 hours. I asked a day-shift nurse about this 'nurse,' but was told there was no one like her working there. I think now her face must have been some sort of mask."

<hr />

"Inside the Hood Was Only Blackness"

The Personal Encounter of Judith

"Back in 1973 in Fountain Valley, California, I had become extremely psychic, and at the same time had developed a habit whereby it always took me a long time to fall asleep. Restless and unusually agitated, with my eyes closed I visualized that I was looking out the bedroom window at the neighborhood.

"The night was quiet, due to the late hour, and I 'saw' no activity in the neighborhood with my mind's eye until my attention was directed to a corner of the street where I saw two men dressed in monk habits with hoods over their heads wearing odd looking pointed-toe slippers. Their unusual footwear attracted my attention, and only then did I realize that they were not walking, but floating, a few inches above the sidewalk. My view of them was long-ranged, yet detailed.

"I watched one lone monk figure reach our house, float up the walkway, pass through our closed and locked door, move up the entry hall, make the sharp left through the open bedroom door, and stop at the foot of the bed. Throughout the entire perception my eyes had been closed, and I had become increasingly stressed and frightened. Now I had to open my eyes to prove that the astounding horror in the cold, dark room really was not there. When I opened my eyes, I was wrong. It was!

"The monk-like figure had moved around the room to stand beside my bed. He towered over me. I thought I would die from heart failure when he bent over me to stare into my face. But inside the hood, instead of a face, I saw only empty blackness. And then, the next thing I knew, it was morning."

<hr>

THREE STRANGE ENCOUNTERS WITH HOODED BEINGS

The Personal Encounters of Michael G.

"I do not recall the month, but I will never forget that Sunday afternoon in 1999. I had been to church, and I was full of energy on this beautiful, sunny afternoon. About a half an hour after getting home, I still felt energized but I began to feel a sensation around my forehead as I have many times since. I suddenly felt weak. I went in and sat at the foot of my bed. I remember feeling light-headed, then I fell back slowly on the bed and passed out. I have never been given to fainting or passing-out spells, but I didn't fall asleep—I passed out cold.

"When I woke, I had no concept of time. My first reaction was that I had fallen asleep and woke up later that night, as it was pitch dark. But things were different. I was now wide awake, and I was aware that I was naked and lying on my back on what felt like a metal table. As I looked upward, I noticed two very tall dark figures standing in front of me in black-hooded robes.

"At this point my normal first reaction would have been to shake myself into consciousness, as I would have thought it to be some kind of nightmare. But then I felt intense pain, and I realized that it was the pain that woke me in the first place. I struggled to get up, but could not move an inch. The two creatures just stood and watched as if they were observing my response to the pain. However, I could tell that they were responsible for the pain.

"I lost track of time. Soon my eyes started to adjust to the dark, and I could start to make out small images around the room. I couldn't tell if they were machines or people—it was still too dark. I was very scared, but I gathered the courage to stretch forward what little I could. I looked closely into the face hole of the hoods. I just started to get focused on some sort of facial features when the creature to my left waved his hand (which seemed to have longer fingers than should be normal) in front of my face—and I passed out cold again.

"**When I looked over at my sleeping wife, I saw a tall, dark hooded figure standing right beside her.**"

"I woke later in my apartment on my bed, but not quite in the same position. If I had to take a guess, I believe I was gone/out/whatever for about an hour, maybe a little more. When I was back I saw the sun was still out, and I got up and felt fine—but I was somewhat sore. I don't know where those creatures took me or what they did—or for what reason—but I do know I was nowhere near my home. This was the first time in my life I 'remember' encountering these strange creatures.

"Regarding my second encounter, I had not seen or heard anything from the beings since that initial experience, and I had no desire to meet them again. It was late one night in February 2003. I recall being startled suddenly awake. As I woke, I remember feeling as though all my senses were heightened. When I looked over at my sleeping wife, I saw a tall, dark hooded figure standing right beside her.

"I couldn't see much detail because it was dark and we sleep with the blinds shut, but I could make out the round hood facing me. It stood very tall. Maybe seven or eight feet. The hooded entity looked as startled—momentarily at least— to see me as I was to see it. When it saw that I saw it, it turned to the side quickly. I sat still, not really knowing what to do, but ready to react if it tried to harm either my wife or myself. As it turned to the side it moved very fast two steps forward toward the wall at the foot of the bed and then vanished.

"I did make out its form before it disappeared. It was tall, dark and wearing a hooded shroud of some sort. It had small arms that protruded out of its sleeves, and I could only make out four fingers. The thing I noticed most was its shape. The entity's form seemed to be that of a large snake dressed in a dark hood and gown. I was wide awake when I saw the physical shape of it, and it had blocked my view of the mirror behind it—so I know that at least for a few moments it was a solid figure.

"The third time (so far) that I have experienced these beings was just as unexpected as the first two. The Saturday after the second encounter, I was working at my job in an office supply store. It was late and not terribly busy when I was walking about five aisles down in the middle row. I looked over in aisle two—and there was one of those creatures. It saw me look at it and jumped behind a shelf and disappeared into thin air. This one was a little shorter than the previous creatures that I had encountered—maybe only seven feet this time. I asked the guy in the back if he had seen anyone, but he hadn't.

"I am truly at a loss to explain who these beings are and what they want, but I know for a fact they are real."

SOME GHOSTLY MANIFESTATIONS MAY BE ANGELS— OR EVIL SPIRITS

The Personal Experience of Journalist Michael Shinabery

"Ghostly manifestations, be they God's angelic messengers or evil spirits, are not uncommon throughout history. Jesus walked on the water and calmed the storm, and so afraid were his disciples huddled in the boat that—at first—they called Jesus a ghost. In the Bible, Satan perverts everything that is of God. Therefore, it is no stretch to believe in ghostly, even malevolent, manifestations—because if there is a Holy Spirit, there must be evil spirits.

"On June 30, 1995, a long-time friend in Colorado awoke one morning, padded from her bed to the living room, and went down, dead, on the floor. [She was] only 43; a heart attack ended her life on Earth. Ironically, the house's previous owner, an older woman, fell dead of a heart attack in the exact same spot.

"Not long after the funeral (which I attended), her daughter called me late one night, waking me from sleep. Terror was unmistakable in her voice. Her husband, brother, and my friend's six-year-old son had gone to the house to gather up my friend's belongings. Pulling dinnerware from kitchen cabinets, they were unnerved when they heard heavy pounding from the basement. It was an area of the house my friend had said made her feel uneasy.

"The brother, husband, and her son fled the house when blood bubbled up from the cabinet's wood shelves. The daughter had one frantic request: pray. Please. Prayers can be easily spouted. Persuasive prayers in the face of such oppression are another challenge. My prayer was in the Spirit, or praying in tongues.

"I do not know how long I prayed, lying in bed, but—as is not always the case—I did pray with what the Bible terms 'understanding.' The Holy

Spirit was clear in what happened to my friend. In recent months, she had been sliding from her faith, delving into areas and things that made me uncomfortable, and I had told her so as delicately as possible. From the 'understanding,' my friend, an influential Christian, was demonically oppressed to lead others astray. Delving into occult areas had opened the door to that influence. Others with less or no faith would see her as a devout woman involved in this and that occult practice, and because they knew she was Christian, it must be OK.

> **P**ulling dinnerware from kitchen cabinets, they were unnerved when they heard heavy pounding from the basement.

"Ergo, the spirit that persecuted her—including tempting her over time with substances (drugs and alcohol) and foods that weakened her heart—was there to use her further, but not cause her death so soon. Yet in its fervor the effect was final. Its subsequent rage at having failed, thus worsening its own eternal state, was taken out on the three who entered the house that night.

"I have no idea how far I was into my prayer, lying in bed, when the attack turned to me. The demonic laughter was undeniable, and suddenly I could not breathe because my chest was being so tightly squeezed. So tight that I could not utter a word.

"Just before I thought I was going to lose consciousness, however, I squeezed out the name 'Jesus,' then struggled to repeat it slowly, like a mantra, until the attack diminished and finally subsided.

"Talking to my friend's family soon after, we realized that about the same moment I conquered the demonic attack, the manifestations that night in Colorado stopped. The family reentered the house over several days, boxed up her belongings, and never went back.

"Over the next several months, though, I struggled with late night manifestations. I would be awakened from sleep, unable to breathe, hearing demonic laughter. Only speaking 'Jesus' with great effort would stop the nocturnal attacks."

THE HAUNTED GUITAR

Today, Patrick Cross is a recognized paranormal researcher who travels throughout Canada and the United States, investigating ghosts and hauntings. Cross grew up in a house in Rexdale, Toronto, built on a murder-suicide site, and he recalls mysterious blood spots appearing and reappearing on the basement floor. There was an organ upstairs that would play eerie music— even when unplugged.

"When I was only five or six years old, ghosts scared me all the time," Cross recalled, "then I just tried to live with them. I wanted to find out what was happening and why. I began researching the paranormal."

In 1995 Cross, who is also an accomplished musician, bought a white electric guitar in the shape of a "V," a copy of the more famous guitar made by Gibson, called a Gibson "Flying V." The guitar purchased by Cross was made of heavy maple wood and looked like it had been passed down by various musicians.

"It was made in 1989, and it was in very good shape considering it was used," Cross said. "Other than a slight crack on the top of the neck of the guitar, as if it had been dropped, it played well—or so I thought. The guitar had come from a fire in a Michigan bar, where a band was playing and a fire broke out. Everything in the bar was burned to a crisp—all except the guitar, which survived without any burn marks and fully intact. Apparently, someone in the band had died in the fire, and the guitar was sold, ending up in Oakville, Ontario."

Cross recalled that he was strangely drawn to the guitar. "It was as if it called to me saying, 'play me.' As soon as I picked it up to play, I felt a tingling electric sensation, like it knew I wanted it and it was right for me. I didn't even check out the other guitars, since I couldn't put this one down. It was an odd feeling, but most musicians will understand.

"The guitar played fine in the store, jamming to some bluesy rock riffs and some classic chords, but when I got it home, it seemed to go out of tune when I picked it up to play it. I thought this was odd, since it played fine before—and now it started de-tuning itself. When I started playing something like 'Smoke On the Water,' by Deep Purple, and 'Purple Haze,' by Jimi Hendrix, the guitar played back in tune. It felt like it really liked a dark, heavy sound, and it played better than ever. I put the guitar away and went about my business."

After two days, Cross began to hear weird sounds in the apartment. "The noises seemed to be coming from the closet in the second bedroom where the guitar was stored. I opened the closet door, heard nothing, looked at the guitar, looked around, didn't see anything—but I heard what sounded like men's voices arguing with each other. It was as if an argument was going on in the closet between two men. One sounded Spanish, the other Mexican, and they were talking about money. I heard this from the front room, then went into the bedroom to the closet to look. Again, everything stopped."

As the days passed, weird things started happening around the inside of Cross's apartment: "My car keys would disappear, then re-appear sometime later. I saw shadows move on the wall, heard footsteps and bangs or knocks. Cupboard doors opened and closed on their own. Lights turned back on after I shut them off. The television set was on when I would come home, even though I remembered turning it off before I went out. My cat would look in

Patrick Cross (right) and his "Flying V" electic guitar.

the air, as if she saw something move in the air, and then look in the other bedroom as if she could see someone walking around. If the guitar was left out, I could feel a chill around it—like cold air or cold wind."

As Cross began to use the guitar in his rock band, "SCI-FI Prodigy," strange things would also happen at music rehearsals and band performances. "We experienced power failures on our equipment and heard weird voices coming through the music amplifiers. Lights would go off and on and blow out and on several occasions, actual fires started from the floodlights in the room for no reason. The drummer experienced his cymbals falling off and his drums go out of tune every time he started to play. The band members also heard other people talking in the room around the guitar when we were out of the room.

"As we started playing our songs, the haunted guitar would go out of tune on the fifth and sixth strings, repeatedly. I had to put it down and play my other guitar, because the Flying V could not be played. If we started playing songs with negative lyrics or heavy metal, the guitar would play perfectly fine. The guitar particularly liked one song I wrote and played called, 'Something Is Out There,' which is all about ghosts and evil entities with emphasis on something coming to get you. It's an X-Files type of feeling. This was one of the very few songs during which the guitar would stay in tune.

"The guitar had a presence of evil—a bad aura around it. It seemed to be three feet of cold presence. Other people, including Rob McConnell from the *X-Zone Radio Show* and Janet Russell from *Beyond the Unexplained*, also felt this."

More things of a paranormal nature occurred to Cross as time went on. "I had a series of bad luck, which I believe was related to the guitar being in my apartment. I lost my job; my health started to suffer; rashes and sores appeared on my legs for no apparent reason. My car would shoot out flames from the top of the engine every time I started it, even though there was no mechanical reason to account for this.

> I saw shadows move on the wall, heard footsteps and bangs or knocks.

"At times, there was a stench that seemed to come from the guitar—like a burnt dead smell. Then the terrible odor would go away as quickly as it appeared. I could hear heavy breathing around my amp and guitar when it was out in the bedroom. Yet when I walked back into the room, the sounds faded away."

Cross began to take pictures of the guitar and investigate why all these bizarre happenings and bad luck occurrences should be taking place. He captured some "ghost orbs" around the guitar many times, and on occasion he could see a misty presence.

"It always felt cold when I would pick up the guitar, and I would get small electrical shocks even when it wasn't plugged in," Cross said. "Everywhere I went with the guitar, it seemed to cause things to happen. On one occasion in London, Ontario, where our band was performing, a fire broke out in the bar area. Glasses filled with water would shatter as they passed near the table where the guitar lay."

On May 16, 1999, Cross was a guest speaker at a UFO-ghost conference, the X Zone Symposium, in St. Catharines, Ontario. He brought his haunted guitar along to see if he could find some individuals who could psychically channel anything that might explain the phenomena surrounding it.

"Psychics said that they felt weird around the guitar and expressed their opinion that it contained an evil presence," Cross recalled. "Two people who said they could help were psychic-sensitives Janet Russell and Eugenia Macer-Story. Eugenia proceeded to channel the guitar and found out it had a living entity attached to it. The entity was inside the wood of the guitar. She found it had a controlling effect on me and anyone who touched or felt it. It seemed to have intelligence and was clearly talking to Eugenia, saying it did not wish to be put on display, but wanted to cause evil and destruction. It wanted to fly like a condor with large wings, and it called itself, 'Eye of the Condor.' We later found out this was a popular song in Mexico and South America, where condors do live. The guitar wanted to start fires. It wanted me to kill with it. Actually use it to kill, swinging it like an axe. This was its way of having me worship and glorify it."

Cross felt sickened when he heard these words being channeled by Eugenia, for many times, he had had frightening images enter his mind of wanting to kill when he was around the guitar. He had also experienced very vivid dreams of going out to commit murder, using the instrument as if it were an axe.

The entity that possessed the guitar went on, saying that it had started many fires and survived while all else burned. It said it had been spawned by the Devil, and it was here to rise up to do its father's bidding in the world. It wanted to fly free, like a condor, spreading evil throughout the world.

"Eugenia found the guitar had the most powerful of Voodoo hexes, EXU (pronounced 'Echu'), placed on it by previous musicians who had owned it," Cross said. "The hex was supposed to bring wealth to anyone who owned it and did its bidding. The EXU hex back-fired on the owners who were involved with drug money and they were killed."

The spirit inside the guitar wanted to be released into human form in order to kill and destroy. It liked Cross to play only dark, evil music and said it de-tuned itself if the music was good, happy, or up-tempo. The entity said that it never wished to become good. It only wanted to commit evil acts.

"It used profanity, swearing, and vulgar language as it spoke to Eugenia, trying to latch onto her," Cross said. "The spirit said that it wanted to come into her body and kick out her soul. Eugenia felt the presence coming into her, and she let go and moved away from the guitar as it tried to possess her."

Eugenia confirmed that many of Cross's personal problems were from the "Devil-guitar." She said the only way to fix the problem was to bless it or to destroy it completely. When she asked the guitar if it wanted to be blessed, the entity responded by saying no, and speaking in Spanish, began blaspheming Christ and God.

On the advice of Eugenia, Cross put the guitar in its case and covered it with salt to contain the energy. Then he wrapped the outside of the case with a light blue cloth in an effort to keep the negative spirit energy from leaving the case.

"On Sunday night after the conference, I took the guitar to destroy it," Cross said. "I didn't want any more bad things to happen, and I wanted to get rid of the guitar for good. I took the guitar to a remote park just after 9:00 P.M. I found an area that was secluded with a steel garbage can. I took the guitar out of its case, doused it with lighter fluid and gasoline, and put it in the garbage container. Before lighting the guitar aflame, I poured salt all around the garbage can to stop the entity from escaping or attempting to attach itself to me. I recited the Lord's Prayer three times and told the entity to go back where it came from. I demanded it to leave in God's name.

"After I said these things, I saw a misty cloud of air rise up inside the garbage can. There was wind all around me. Minutes before, it had been calm. I attempted to light the guitar, but the fire kept going out. I poured more gasoline all over it. I found some wood to put around it. Finally, after 25 minutes, it was on fire. It started to burn at last.

"As the flames went higher, I heard a high-pitched shriek coming from the burning guitar. It sounded like a sick, wounded animal. I was standing there, watching it burn, adding more gasoline to the fire, when some of the flames jumped on my arm. Now I was on fire, and as I tried to put it out, I dropped the full can of gasoline. I was horrified—because now the whole can of gas could explode and engulf me in flames.

"I panicked, but somehow I managed to put out the flames that had begun to burn my clothes. I breathed a sigh of relief as I watched the guitar burn away, into a charred chunk of wood.

"After an hour, I made sure the flames had burned out. I poured more salt over the burned up guitar, just to make sure it would contain whatever spirit energy was still left. I left the guitar in the garbage can and took the case, closed it up with salt inside it, and wrapped the blue cloth back around the case. I was shaking, but I felt good that I had destroyed the evil entity. Hoping that it wouldn't haunt or possess anything else again, I left the park around 10:30 p.m."

Immediately after returning home, Cross felt a sense of relief. He didn't hear any voices or see or feel any more ghostly activity around him. The next day, Monday, everything immediately changed for the better. "I had a phone call for a new job, my health was coming back, my sores and rashes had all disappeared, and my plants came back to life," he said. "I won $150 on a Bingo scratch ticket, there were no more power failures on my TV, and my car started normally. Miraculously, everything that had been going bad changed over night since getting rid of the haunted guitar."

Since 1999 Cross has investigated all sorts of hauntings and ghost activity, but he has never had anything happen as bad or bizarre as when he owned the haunted guitar.

⬤═══◈═══⬤

TOUCHED BY AN APPARITION

In October 2001 Barry Conrad, a psychic investigator and documentary filmmaker (*California's Most Haunted*), went to a woman's home in San Diego to film and interview her. She had reported being touched and held

This photograph was taken by Lisa McIntosh after she felt something touch her back and realized that no one was standing behind her.

down in her bed and said that her small son had been seeing an apparition of a soldier that would appear in his room.

"While we were there, my girlfriend, Lisa McIntosh, was standing off by herself, snapping pictures, when she later told me she felt a hand go across her back. She turned and finding no one there, took pictures of the area she was standing in." Attached is a picture of McIntosh and one of the pictures she snapped of the area behind her; this latter photo is similar to the photos taken during the Entity case (a famous case investigated by Conrad and a team of investigators, including the well-known parapsychologist Barry Taff and documented in the film *Unknown Encounter*).

For her part, McIntosh noted that "When we first arrived at this woman's home, the first thing that gave me a very strange feeling was that there were no sounds at all outside. No birds, crickets or anything. It was as if the ground her house stood on was 'dead.' It was also an area that was in complete darkness around her home. There were no street lights or anything like that because she was very far from a main road.

Lisa McIntosh.

"After entering her home all of a sudden I had mixed emotions about being there. I felt like something was with us in every room we went in. Going in to her home the first time, I did not know how vicious the attacks on her had been. While Barry started to film her, she began telling about the events that had been taking place in her home. I was listening, but was off by myself and was standing near some sort of vent on the floor taking pictures of her and just snapping random shots when all of a sudden, I felt a hand go across the lower part of my back. At first I thought someone had walked up behind me, so I turned around only to discover there was no one there or anywhere around me. I felt stunned, frozen and although instinct dictated to run, being a ghost researcher, I decided to take more pictures where the incident happened. Never in my wildest dreams did I think I would capture what developed.

"I was not touched again the remainder of the time we were there but before I ever took the first picture in this house, I felt an uneasiness that is hard to put into words. I think for some reason I dreaded to have to be there but I didn't know why.

"The woman eventually had to move from this home and has reported to me that her tenants renting the home are beginning to have trouble there as she did."

STRANGE BEINGS THAT MASQUERADE AS HUMANS

There is a category of ghosts that I consider among the very strangest of all, because they seem to function as some sort of independent entities who masquerade as human beings for some unknown reason. These mysterious spirit beings literally walk among us, sometimes pretending to be us to achieve some goal that is at present beyond our ability to ascertain.

If, when we encountered these entities, we might come away from the experience concluding that we had met angels unaware, higher beings who were trying to teach us something or who were cleverly guiding our footsteps along the path to higher spiritual awareness, we could justify their incomprehensible actions by rationalizing that they were working to fulfill a greater plan than we are capable of comprehending as material beings. But their agenda not only lies beyond our knowing, it in fact seems designed to confuse us rather than enlighten us.

⚬━━⟊∩⟊━━⚬

FIVE STRANGE CUSTOMERS IN A TOBACCO SHOP

The Personal Encounter of Rick Aiello

"I had finished shopping for groceries with my wife and stopped next door at the tobacco store to buy her some cigarettes. I walked in as usual, but I stepped into a scenario for which I was not prepared. Standing in front of the counter were five people, all about in their mid-twenties. They all had their backs to me but one. The one facing me was standing at the end of the counter right in front of me.

"What struck me as odd right away was the way he was dressed. First let me say that he was tall and very thin and wore strange, small black frame glasses. He was very white and pale complexioned. He had on a black suit with a black tie and the brightest, whitest shirt that I have ever seen. As I was standing there waiting for my turn, I noticed him fidgeting with something in his hand. He had a gold, 1940-ish type, thin cigarette case open in his hand. He was putting white candy cigarettes in the gold case and talking about how important it was that he had them.

"Strange ... but the whole impact had not hit me yet. I was still waiting for my turn, and at that moment of impatience tried to see why I was having to wait. The four others still facing the woman behind the counter had been talking to her. She had just finished seeing all their IDs, and I caught her asking, 'Where are you people from?' They all had identification from different states, and at one point the clerk said, 'Come on!' like they had fake IDs or something. Then she asked, 'What are you people up to? Who are you?'

"I've been going to this store for five years, and I have come to know this woman. I had never heard her ask such questions or act that way. I do know that she knows her stuff when it comes to IDs. Here in New York, accepting a false ID is no excuse for selling tobacco products to minors, and the state takes it very seriously.

"Anyway, now I'm tuned in and really watching these five strangers and taking a real interest in what the hell is going on. Now I really look the people over. They all [wore] odd clothing, some articles that were stylish in the 1940s. One of the group, the only female, wore a very large ribbed corduroy jumper-type dress and a pair of real leather, white 1960s go-go boots. She wore a cotton/wool '40s type coat the like you have not seen since watching the movie *It's a Wonderful Life*. Now I'm tingling from the energy in the room. The three others also wore very old-style clothing. No Nikes ... nothing from the present ... nothing!

"After taking all this in so far, I start to look at their faces and listen to them talk. They all had very pale faces, and in retrospect, they all acted peculiarly. I think the more I felt they were not 'right,' the more they tried to act more casual. They all acted very friendly in a kind of superficial way.

"None of the five answered any more of the clerk's questions after she appeared to sense something odd about them. They paid for a couple of cigars and seemed overly cheerful to avert our attention from their strange appearance and off-kilter behavior. After the clerk took their money, they turned toward me and started toward the door. For the first time I noticed that at the door are five suitcases that belong to them. They assembled at the door, grabbed their individual suitcase, and walked out the door.

"Each suitcase was individually just as strange as the people were. Remember the old-fashioned type that looked as if they were made of fabric, with a kind of basketweave design? Okay, that was one suitcase. The rest were equally dated, as if they were from the 1930s or '40s. Not one of the suitcases was even modern enough to be made of plastic, like a seamless Samsonite type. All of them were very, very old styles, but they looked like they were only about a year old—leather straps and all.

"When they were out the door, I felt my body buzz and tingle, as if it had been touched with electricity. I turned to the woman behind the counter, and she [was] as white as a sheet. I asked her what was the matter, but she didn't answer. I asked what they had said to her, and she replied that she didn't know what they were talking about. She said she remembered them standing there at the counter, but she could not remember what had been said.

"Puzzled, I reminded her that I had been standing in line and could see that they had engaged her in conversation. I said that she had certainly appeared to be intent on what they were talking about. The clerk said that she didn't even notice me come in until they left.

"I told the clerk that I had heard her ask the five weird strangers what they were

Ricardo Pustanio

The strangers seemed benevolent, though oddly dressed. They had an attractive appearance, but there was a sense that this was merely a façade and something more sinister lay beneath.

up to and where they were from and that they had answered that they 'came from afar' and they needed the cigars for a play. None of the five had made eye contact with me all the while they were in the tobacco store. Nor did they turn and look at me when I came in as most people would. Even after I stood right behind them up in line, they acted as if I was not there.

"After the five bizarre people walked out of the tobacco shop, they began to cross the parking lot, which [was] empty except for my car and some others way down the plaza. The smoke shop is at the end of the plaza, and unless someone is getting cigarettes or cigars, that end is empty. I had a clear view of them, and as they [were] walking away I asked the clerk again what it was they talked to her about. She was still confused and scattered, but finally she said, 'I don't know what those people are up to but they are not who they look like.' That was all she could say.

"As I was talking to her, we both watched this strange group cross this wide open lot, and I wondered where their car was. At that point, they disappeared! POOF! At two o'clock in the afternoon in broad daylight, they vanished.

"I blurted out to the clerk that the five strangers who were in her tobacco shop just disappeared into thin air, but she did not appreciate the statement. She was still freaked from whatever happened in there.

"I left the store, wondering if my senses had somehow deceived me, and rejoined my wife, who had been sitting right out front waiting for me. She was annoyed, because she thought I was in the smoke shop shooting the breeze with the clerk and not concerned about how warm it was for her in that parked car. (Remember, I told you those people had 1940s-style winter coats on? And it was a hot afternoon.) She angrily wondered why it had taken me so long in the tobacco store.

"When I told her that the store was busy with five customers who were there before me, she really got steamed. 'Are you telling me that you had to wait for five people?' she demanded. 'Well, I've been sitting here waiting for you to come out and *nobody* has come out since you went in.'

"Incredulously, I asked her if she hadn't seen those five strangely dressed people with suitcases walking across the parking lot. 'They had to walk right in front of you,' I said. My wife, who really is not normally pushy, said, 'I've been here for ten minutes and was about to come in to see what the holdup was. No one has come out of that store.'

"Then I told her the whole story. She swore that she was glaring at the door, waiting for me—and nobody came through the door. The funny part emotionally for me was a sense of well-being after leaving the store. I was kind of tickled to think that I was part of something special of sorts. Maybe for just a moment I had rubbed elbows with higher energy beings. Why do I say that? They left me with a very good feeling. I was elated and smiling, because the more I reflected on the incident, the more I picked up on details of the exchange.

"The five out-of-place strangers seemed benevolent in a funny way, and the manner in which they were dressed seemed to indicate that they didn't appear on this plane often. They all looked very young, but no one in their early twenties would wear those 'uncool' clothes, especially the shoes, which were definitely off style and appearance. And winter coats? It was 78 degrees outside. The suitcases were the icing on the cake. Right out of Hollywood props. That's the story, and the experience will be with me a long time."

Perhaps some readers who have considered Rick Aiello's encounter with the spirit masqueraders might suggest that we are dealing with entities from another dimension of time and space—perhaps even time travelers from a distant future who wanted to explore life in the twenty-first century but who didn't read the guide book closely enough when it described the items of apparel that would be in vogue in our time.

Or maybe the five strange entities, who bought candy cigarettes to place in a gold case and who bought cigars as part of a role in a play, really were angels, higher spirit beings, just playing at life as a material being for a few hours before they vanished back to their dimension of spirit. Perhaps that was why Rick felt such a strange sense of well-being and elation after his encounter with the fantastic five.

The experience of Jerry and his girlfriend Kelly indicate that these bizarre beings might be from some other dimension of reality, but their motives are suspect and less than angelic.

⋘⦿⋙

A Spirit Imposter Tried to Woo His Girlfriend

Jerry told me that during a two-week period in 1997, his girlfriend, Kelly, received a number of telephone calls from someone or something pretending to be him. The first time that Kelly received a call from the entity posing as Jerry, he asked her to meet him at a park on the edge of town as quickly as possible. She was getting ready and would soon have left her apartment when Jerry knocked on her door. She was puzzled when she opened the door to admit him.

> The phony Jerry let out a high-pitched scream and literally disappeared.

Jerry had come directly from his job at the dry cleaners, and he had stopped by to see if Kelly wanted to take in an early movie. Kelly wanted to know why he suddenly changed his plans. He had just called 20 minutes ago and asked her to meet him at the park on the edge of town. When Jerry adamantly denied making such a call, they assumed it was some friend trying to pull a prank on them. So they laughed it off and went to the movies.

The next evening, however, when Kelly knew Jerry would be working very late, she answered the telephone and heard her boyfriend's familiar voice. But she was baffled when he asked where she was the night before and why she hadn't met him at the park.

Kelly grew impatient and told Jerry that he wasn't funny. Whereupon Jerry, who never raised his voice in anger, snapped at her and warned her not to get "sassy" with him. In addition, he called her a "little twit."

When Jerry continued to rage, Kelly hung up the telephone. It was only after she had calmed down that she began to play back the rude conversation in her mind. "Twit"? Where had Jerry come up with that one? And "sassy"? The more she analyzed the whole weird telephone call, the less it really sounded like Jerry's voice.

Who was the spirit imposter pretending to be Kelly's boyfriend?

Kelly picked up the phone and called Jerry at work. She knew his boss didn't like Jerry to receive personal calls at work, especially when the employees were putting in overtime, but she considered this an emergency. Jerry nervously came to the phone, gently remonstrating with her for calling him at the dry cleaners when he was on overtime. He laughed ironically when she asked if he had called her apartment earlier that night. In fact, if he didn't get off the phone immediately, he said, his boss would have a seizure.

Kelly was satisfied that it hadn't been Jerry on the telephone calling her a twit. But two hours later when the telephone rang again, she wasn't quite so certain. It was Jerry again, asking her to drive her car to meet him out by Miller's Pond, near the old mill.

Kelly protested that it was late and that he must be tired from working such long hours overtime. Jerry responded that seeing her, his little pigeon, would wake him up. Kelly heard the warning buzzer go off in her mind. Jerry had never called her a "little pigeon" before. This could not be the real Jerry.

"Whoever you are," she said calmly, keeping her voice even and under control, "leave me alone."

The voice at the other end pleaded with her. If she would not meet him at Miller's Pond, wouldn't she at least come down to the corner and speak with him.

She knew that she may have been acting foolishly, but Kelly gave the voice a "maybe." She kept watching the corner for any sign of a man she might suppose was the person pretending to be Jerry on the telephone. She wanted to get all the weirdness resolved. If it was a friend of theirs playing a joke, she would give him a piece of her mind. Amazingly, around midnight, she saw Jerry walk slowly up to the street corner in front of her apartment building and look up at her window. He waved and smiled, and she waved and got her sweater.

When she got about six feet away from him, she stopped and looked very carefully. He did look an awful lot like Jerry, but he was wearing some kind of heavy work boots, a baseball cap, and a brown leather jacket, kind of like the type she had seen in old movies that pilots wore in World War II.

He reached out his hand and asked her to come with him. The light from the streetlamp was fairly bright, and she could clearly see that, except for the way he was dressed, he certainly did look like Jerry.

But then she said, "Jerry, you always told me you hated to wear baseball caps." When he took off the cap, the imposter had a crewcut, a hairstyle that Jerry would not have in a million years.

Kelly started to run back into the apartment building. At that same moment, the real Jerry pulled up in his car next to the imposter. The phony Jerry let out a high-pitched scream and literally disappeared.

"Whatever this thing really was," Jerry said, "it tried to contact Kelly just once more, about five days later. Kelly thought for sure she was talking to me until 'he' asked her to drive out to the park and meet me for a picnic after work. The park is four miles out of town, and Kelly knew that I knew that her car was in the garage for a few days. She screamed at the false Jerry to leave her alone and never to call again. And, thank the Lord, he never has."

Neither Jerry nor Kelly have any theory to offer as to why this spirit masquerader wished to appear as him or why it was so persistent in attempting to pursue her. They soon became engaged and were married four months after their bizarre experience. Could the interloper from another dimension have been sent to play a weird version of Cupid in order to insure and hasten the union between Jerry and Kelly to fulfill some larger purpose?

HARASSED BY SPIRIT MASQUERADERS FOR 20 YEARS

Some years ago I received a fascinating account from a young professor in the graduate department of a major university. There seemed no purpose in the nightmarish experience that Jim had with spirit masqueraders other than sadistic harassment. His adventure across the murky borders of the supernatural began when he was 17.

Jim's father had been a senior sales representative for an import company based in the South Pacific, and from March 1964 to May 1968, they had lived in New Zealand. In March 1967, shortly after he had turned 17, Jim had gone on holiday at the beach near the little New Zealand ocean town of Kawhia and had been swimming around a section of shoreline that was not usually penetrated by tourists. It was here that he found a flat, smooth metallic object under a tidal rock.

The object was oval-shaped, rounded at the edges, and engraved with peculiar symbols. It weighed about one pound, and when Jim found it, it had been tightly wedged between two tide-level boulders that were only exposed at low tide. The object looked very old. Algae and other sea deposits encrusted it.

When such objects are found in New Zealand, they are most often taken for Maori relics, which are in high demand. Jim's father immediately advised him to take the oval-shaped object to a knowledgeable Maori to have it examined. Two weeks went by, during which time the object passed from hand to hand among Maoris who were experienced in appraising the relics of their people. At last the consensus was delivered to Jim: the object did not come from any time in their culture and they did not recognize what it could be.

Jim could not later recall if a metallurgical analysis of the object had ever been made, but he did remember that the curio ended up in a dresser drawer in their home in Te Awamutu, where it was to remain until his father received orders to move to New York in May 1968. As Jim recalled, that was when he first discovered that the object was missing. When he came to pack it for moving, it was not there. It had disappeared.

As they waited for the flight from Auckland International Airport in May, Jim's parents were saying good-bye to some friends at some distance from him when he was approached by two young Polynesian men, who claimed to be from New Zealand Inland Revenue. They asked him if he were taking anything illegal out of the country, and they were especially interested in learning if he had any relics, art objects, or the like.

The two men intimidated Jim, and he did his very best to explain that he had no relics in his possession—but then they insisted that he go with them to a hotel to undergo a private baggage check. It was at that point that he called for his father, who demanded to see their identification and asked why they couldn't examine his son's baggage right there in the airport. When their answers didn't make sense, Jim's father summoned a patrolling constable to intervene. His mere arrival seemed to frighten the two men away.

That fall, back in the United States, Jim enrolled at Columbia University for his freshman year. Shortly after the term began, he was approached by an art dealer who said that he had heard that Jim had spent some time in New Zealand and indicated that he was interested in purchasing any relics or curios that Jim might have brought with him. Although the alleged art dealer was polite and businesslike, he was annoyingly persistent. In spite of Jim's repeated denials that he had any such relics to sell him, the man approached him three times before the winter holidays.

Through correspondence, Jim learned that three of his closest friends in New Zealand had been questioned by men who seemed to fit the description of the two strange men who had attempted to search his luggage at the airport. In one instance, the New Zealand police had to be called in to block continued harassment. In another case, a girl's life had been threatened. According to their letters to Jim, each of his friends had been questioned about whether or not he had given them anything to keep before he left New Zealand. They all used words like "spooky," "weird," and "creepy" to describe the men who had persistently troubled them.

In 1970 Jim transferred to Stanford University. He had no sooner moved into his apartment and had the telephone installed when he received a call warning him never to return to New Zealand. During a later call, a woman with a high-pitched voice informed Jim that he was being kept under surveillance by a group who felt that he had acted unjustly in the past by not returning things to their proper owners.

In 1972 Jim decided to teach high school for a time before he continued with his graduate work. That summer, a few weeks before he was to begin his first job in the Sacramento school system, he was vacationing in San Francisco. Late one night, the telephone rang in his hotel room, and Jim answered it to hear a voice tell him that he had acted wisely by not returning to New Zealand.

> They all used words like "spooky," "weird," and "creepy" to describe the men who had persistently troubled them.

Jim emphasized to me that he had led a very quiet life as an undergraduate. Yet at both Columbia and Stanford he probably received 30 or more telephone calls from anonymous voices advising him not to return to New Zealand. In other instances, the voices reprimanded him for having taken something that did not belong to him. Jim said that he didn't carry a sign with him declaring that he had lived in New Zealand, and he seldom discussed his life there with any but a few of his closest acquaintances. Who could possibly have cared about his finding that metallic slab? And who could possibly have taken such a long-term interest in him because of a casual act committed a few days after his seventeenth birthday?

About the third day after classes had begun in the suburban community of Sacramento where Jim had accepted a high school teaching position, a student unknown to him stopped by his classroom to say hello. Jim knew that such an act was hardly unusual, since students will often do this to look over a new teacher, but from the first moment he stepped in the room, the boy acted strangely inquisitive.

Jim was astonished when the teenager stepped to the blackboard and drew the same design that he had first seen on the mysterious metallic object that he had found in New Zealand. He smiled at Jim, then asked if he knew what the symbols meant. When Jim pressed the boy, in turn, for some answers, the student erased the design, laughed, and said that he was just fooling around, that he didn't mean anything by it.

REAL GHOSTS, RESTLESS SPIRITS, AND HAUNTED PLACES

Jim never saw the alleged student again. He described him to a couple of the teachers and to a bunch of students, but no one was able to identify him. Jim doubted very much if he actually went to the school at all.

After four years of high school teaching, Jim was awarded a teaching assistantship at a major university and arrived in the fall of 1976 to begin his doctorate program. He hadn't been at the university more than four days when someone rang his room and scolded him for taking things that didn't belong to him. The voice told Jim that he should always leave things where they were.

At the time that Jim contacted me in the mid-1980s, he was receiving only an occasional mysterious telephone call in which the voice at the other end chastised him for taking that strange metallic object from where he found it. If the 17-year-old Jim had discovered a strange key to other dimensions, the entities had long since reclaimed it. But apparently, some spirit masqueraders were determined that he should never forget the day he disturbed an artifact from another level of being.

⚬⚬⚬

"WE ARE ALL RELATED"

When Kent was a student at a midwestern university, he may have received some kind of clue to the identity of at least some of the spirit masqueraders. One day he was out driving in the countryside, trying his best to clear his brain and prepare for an important test in economics the next afternoon. As he drove farther away from the city, he became aware that he was passing through a tiny village that presently supported a general store, a gas station, a couple other buildings of indeterminate use, and lots of apparently deserted business locations. However, on the outskirts of the village, there appeared to be some kind of celebration in progress on the grounds of an old country church. Kent heard polka music and saw a small crowd of people playing games and lining up beside what appeared to be a generous smorgasbord table.

The college student couldn't resist pulling his car over to the side of the road, getting out, and walking over to the cheery partygoers. Suddenly his way was blocked by a big man who glared at him with ice-cold eyes. And then a tall, smiling man stepped between the brute and the student. He introduced himself as Erik and inquired of Kent his full name. When the student answered, Erik's face lit up, and he asked if Kent were related to the G. family of Boscobel, Wisconsin. When Kent said that he was, Erik loudly called to everyone at the picnic that he was distantly related to them and to make a place for him. With his arm around Kent's shoulder, Erik took him around to various people and introduced him. What Kent had so fortuitously stumbled into, Erik explained, was a gathering of the descendants of the early immigrants who had settled the little dying village that he had just found that afternoon.

Kent admitted that for him the high point of the afternoon was meeting Kari, a beautiful, blue-eyed blonde who appeared to be about his own age. After only a few moments at her side, he found her completely enchanting. While other members of the gathering came from all over the United States for the annual reunion of settlers' families, he was delighted when Kari said that she was a local resident.

After many hours of dancing to polka music with Kari, Kent asked to see her again. Although she had seemed so warm and friendly during the afternoon and had seen to it that he had received generous portions of the lavish smorgasbord, she now appeared cool and indifferent. Whenever he pressured her for her telephone number or address, she turned away and told him that it would not be wise to pursue a relationship.

Kent knew that it was time for him to get back to his studies. And all around him the families were packing up their things. Looking around in puzzlement, he asked where they had parked their cars. Erik explained that they had all left their vehicles in the village and had walked out to the picnic grounds. That was part of the annual ritual they observed.

Kent got back in his car and waved good-bye to Kari, who returned his wave with an expression of sorrow, which he took to be a sign of encouragement that she already missed him and wanted to see him again. Later that night, Kent found that study was impossible. He spent half the night disturbing his roommate, as he tried to write a paper for an English literature class, regaling him with his descriptions of the wondrous Kari.

In the local telephone book, Kent found many listings under the last name that Kari had given him, but when he rang the numbers, none of the families said that they had a daughter named Kari. Determined to find her, he drove back to the small village and inquired of all the present residents about Kari. But none of them gave him the slightest satisfaction as to her whereabouts.

Perhaps as disconcerting as his inability to find Kari was his discovery of the charred remains of a church—exactly where he thought that he had danced polka after polka with the girl of his dreams. When he asked when the church had burned, a farmer looked at him suspiciously and refused to answer. Kent concluded that he had been mistaken about the location of the celebration. It had to have been at another country church.

Persistent to the bitter end, on his next excursion to the locale, Kent drove down the long lanes of every farm within a radius of 15 or 20 miles, seeking somehow to find the beautiful Kari.

One night, several weeks later, Kent was seated at the counter in an all-night diner when he looked up to make sudden eye contact in the large counter mirror with Erik, who was sitting in a booth directly behind him. Kent was startled to see him there, for he was certain there had been no one else in the diner but one other man seated at the far end of the counter. Erik beckoned for Kent to join him.

Erik told Kent that he and his friends had really liked him, but he should stop trying to find Kari. A relationship with her was out of the question. When Kent asked about Erik's statement at the picnic that he was related to him, Erik smiled and said that was true.

"We are related, but not in the way that you probably understand it," Erik tried to explain. "We are related to you as companions, as friends. There are those among us some who have some resentment toward your kind because truly, we were here first, and sometimes we feel supplanted by you and your kind. But hear me now, young man, because we feel a true affection for you, we are telling you to give up your search for Kari. What you hope for, can never be."

The waitress yelled that Kent's hamburger was ready, and when he turned away from the counter, Erik had vanished. Kent ran out in the street because he had so many questions that he wanted answered, but Erik was nowhere to be seen.

Three years later, when Kent was visiting a friend in New York, he was certain that he saw Kari and Erik walking amidst the crowd in Times Square as he rode in a cab.

"Like an idiot," Kent said, "I rolled down the window and shouted their names. I know they saw me and heard me, for they looked directly at me, then turned quickly away and stepped into the lobby of a movie theater. I cannot help wondering how many 'Eriks,' 'Karis,' and all of our other 'relatives' walk among us, skillfully blending in with the crowd, carefully shielding their true identities and their true purpose from us."

Many years ago, in his book *Adventures with Phantoms*, British author Thurston Hopkins wondered similarly about the mysterious entities that he had encountered while walking the streets of London. Hopkins thought these beings were "not fully quick, nor fully dead." In his opinion, these entities mimic us and pretend to be as we are, but they are not truly of our kind.

"They are creatures who have strayed away from some unknown region of haunted woods and perilous wilds," Hopkins wrote. "They dress like us; pretend that they belong to mankind and profess to keep our laws and code of morals. But in their presence we are always aware that they are phantoms and that all their ideas and actions are out of key with the general pitch and tone of normal life."

Appendix

CITIES, TOWNS, AND VILLAGES IN
NORTH AMERICA HEAVILY POPULATED BY GHOSTS

There is not a single city, town, village, or hamlet in the world that does not have its own stories of ghosts, apparitions, phantoms, and haunted houses. In this directory, I have selected only a handful to illustrate the commonality of human interaction with the world of spirits.

Albuquerque, New Mexico

- Back in the 1800s, the building housing the Job Corps Center was a convent where the nuns looked after small children. One day, a sister went insane and began to kill her young charges and throw them down the well. The awful, terror-filled cries of children are frequently reported, and some witnesses have seen the ghost of a woman dressed in black.
- The Kimo Theater had its opening night in the autumn of 1927, and many spirits from that era were so impressed that they return again and again.
- Guests at the Desert Sands Motel on W140 report cold spots, ghostly voices, and doors that unlock and open of their own volition.
- Glowing lights, mysterious black-robed figures, and the sound of crying voices manifest in the Carrie Tingly Children's Hospital.
- The lobby and certain rooms on the bottom floor of the Ramada Hotel are haunted by a woman who was murdered by a lover who had grown tired of her.
- At the Radisson Hotel, screaming can be heard issuing from vacant rooms. Female guests complain of being shaken awake by the hands of ghost children.

Anchorage, Alaska

- Room 201 of the Courtyard by Marriot is haunted by a man who was found dead in that room. Another ghost named Ken roams the parking lot and the courtyard. A phantom cat is often reported in rooms 103 and 107.
- Spirits disturbed by the construction of the Diamond Center mall over sacred tribal burial grounds are frequently seen by customers in the restrooms and corridors.

- The ghost of a young girl is seen by custodians and students in the hallways of Hanshew Middle School.
- The Historic Anchorage Hotel, the city's oldest hotel, is haunted by the sound of footsteps on the stairs, a young girl in the second floor hall, and water faucets turning themselves off and on in rooms 215 and 217.
- Weird humanoid monsters that may be the spirits of forest creatures that once roamed the land where West High School was built are seen in the basement and auditorium.

Asheville, North Carolina

- The ghost of a man who was murdered in the pantry of the Old Battery Park Hotel, now an apartment building, is still seen by residents.
- When the Clyde Erwin High School was built just outside Asheville in the 1970s, the Old County Home Graveyard was disturbed, thereby causing many restless spirits to haunt the new building.
- The Lady in Pink takes spectral delight in ticking the toes of guests who stay at the Grove Park Inn.
- Visitors to the sprawling Biltmore Estate commonly report the sightings of ghosts and the sounds of voices, screaming, and maniacal laughter.

Bakersfield, California

- A lady with a long, flowing robe is seen walking along the canal in Central Park in the hours just before dawn.
- The ghosts of a girl in a prom dress and a boy wearing a football letter sweater are seen in the top row of the bleachers at Bakersfield High School.
- Witnesses have seen the ghost of a workman who was killed during the construction of Harvey Auditorium at Bakersfield High falling from the rafters to the basement below.
- Overly familiar spirits have pushed, groped, and grabbed customers at the bar in Club Paradise.
- Melodrama Musical Theatre is haunted by the ghost of the former owner of the building.
- Visitors to Pioneer Village frequently report seeing ghost children in front of the old school building.

Baltimore, Maryland

- Fort McHenry shelters a host of ghosts who still vigilantly guard Baltimore. Lights, shadowy figures, and voices have been reported for many decades.
- A floating lady and man who walks out of his grave are regularly seen by witnesses who visit the Gardens of Faith Cemetery.
- Todd's farm is home to numerous ghosts, including a lady who sits by a candle in the attic window, awaiting the return of her soldier lover.
- North Oakes Retirement Community was formerly Mt. Wilson State Hospital, a sanitarium for tuberculosis patients, whose moans and cries for medical help can still be heard.
- The house of Edgar Allan Poe is said to be haunted by the spirit of a rather rotund female dressed in gray. Those wishing a glimpse of the ghost of the master of the macabre are said to have a better chance at Westminster Church graveyard, where Poe is buried beside his wife, Virginia.
- The ghosts of three sailors who were killed in action aboard the USS *Constitution* remain on duty.

Boston, Massachusetts

- The ghost of a mayor of the city has been seen many times in the seat where he died at the Emerson Majestic Theatre (built in 1903).
- Numerous ghosts have been reported by employees and guests at the Parker House Hotel. Most of the apparitions sighted have been from the early 1800s.
- Boston Commons is the home for many ghosts, including two aristocratic women in nineteenth century attire who vanish when witnesses approach them.
- The Pilot House was originally built in 1839 as a dormitory for visiting pilots and captains. For many years, witnesses have heard the sounds of men laughing and talking and doors opening and closing.
- A lady in black haunts Fort Warren, which served as a prison during the Civil War.

Burlington, Vermont

- Among the numerous restless spirits that seem to have enrolled for eternity at the University of Vermont are the following: A female ghost in 1890s era clothing appears in the Agriculture Department; poltergeists disturb the Center for Counseling and Testing; Converse Hall is haunted by the spirit of student who committed suicide; Redstone Hall has a ghost that runs through walls and frightens female students; Coolidge Hall harbors a number of ghosts, including one who awakens sleeping residents by standing over their beds and staring at them.
- An employee who committed suicide haunts the basement and kitchen area at the Carburs Restaurant.
- Objects in an abandoned building on the outskirts of the Castleton State College campus houses antiques and museum pieces that continually get rearranged and tossed about—although no one ever enters the place.

Calgary, Alberta

- Grace Hospital is haunted by a woman who died in childbirth in one of the delivery rooms.
- The ghostly form of a woman is seen walking in the shallow area of the Bow River, where she is said to have drowned around 1910.
- Heritage Park visitors have seen the spirit of a beautiful woman holding her baby and smiling at them.
- Witnesses claim the woods next to St. Mary's College are haunted by weird entities.
- The ghosts of the victims of acts of murder and suicide are sighted in the upstairs bedrooms at the Deane House.

Chicago, Illinois

- For years now, witnesses have seen the ethereal form and heard the sobs and cries of the Sobbing Woman of Archer Woods Cemetery.
- Witnesses over the decades have sighted more than 100 glowing ghosts in Bachelor's Grove Cemetery.
- S-M-C Cartage Company was the building in which Al Capone held a gory Valentine's Day party in 1929 for seven of Bugs Moran's men, who were lined up against a brick wall and killed. Over the years, many witnesses claim to have seen seven shadowy spirits and heard screams and machine gun fire. Although the building has been torn down, people still believe the site to be haunted.

- Patrons of the Dome Room nightclub claim that haunting phenomena occur nightly in the building that once housed a morgue.
- Guests and employees have reported a large number of paranormal occurrences at the Congress Hotel.

Cincinnati, Ohio

- Security guards report an extremely tall entity that frequents one of the mummy sarcophagi at the Cincinnati Museum of Art.
- Employees and guests at the Country Hearth Hotel have noted mysterious phenomena occurring in room 331 and in room 431, directly above it.
- The ghost of a little blond, blue-eyed girl in a blue dress haunts King's Island theme park. She is said to be joined by spirits haunting the observation deck of the Eiffel Tower, the roller coaster, and the Octopus ride.
- Sister Mary Carlos haunts the school auditorium at Mother of Mercy High School.
- Cincinnati Zoo remains the stalking ground of the spirit of a lioness, whose glowing eyes have stared unblinkingly at many patrons from shadowed areas.

Colorado Springs, Colorado

- Employees and guests at the Broadmoor Hotel claim to hear the screams and cries of desperate victims of a fire that occurred there many years ago.
- The spirits of laborers who died building Gold Camp Road, originally a railroad line from Colorado Springs to Cripple Creek, are often sighted by those who travel the road.
- The sorrowful ghosts of a traffic accident in which a bus filled with elementary school children and their driver were killed are seen in and around the Camp Road tunnels.
- Pioneer's Museum is haunted by the spirit of a manager who was murdered by an employee over a salary dispute in the late 1950s.

Dearborn, Michigan

- Many witnesses have reported the sighting of a ghost in an old-fashioned uniform at the Henry Ford estate that some believe to be Ford's butler.
- A construction worker fell from a scaffolding when a new gym was being added to Divine Child High School, and witnesses say the building is haunted by his spirit.
- Firefighters at Fire Station #2 claim that the tall, shadowy figure they see in the station after dark is a fireman who won't allow death to force him into retirement.
- Crestwood High in Dearborn Heights has experienced a wide range of haunting phenomena, including objects being moved, sightings of ghosts, and the sound of voices echoing through empty hallways.

El Paso, Texas

- Shortly after midnight, an area of Concordia Cemetery that contains the graves of dozens of children, the victims of an early smallpox epidemic, reverberates with the sounds of children laughing and playing.
- The ghost of cavalry troopers have been seen in Fort Bliss, including that of a hanging soldier who swings from the rafters in Building 13.
- On the outskirts of the city, many witnesses claimed to have seen "El Muerto," the "dead one," galloping through the desert with his head hanging by a rawhide throng from the saddle of his ghostly steed.

- The J.C. Machuca Apartments were built over a tribal burial ground, and residents complain of shadowy figures in their rooms.
- Ysleta High School is haunted by the ghosts of a cheerleader who committed suicide in a restroom and by a small boy who died when he fell off the stage in the auditorium.

Gainesville, Florida

- The "Blue House" of the Sweet Water Bed and Breakfast Inn has a ghost that may hearken back to the days when the place was a plantation. The maids complain of furniture moving around, and some guests feel the spirit pressing down on their chests at night.
- The ghost of a female patron who was killed in the upstairs restroom of the Purple Porpoise is often seen or felt. On occasion, the hostile spirit of her murderer also manifests and molests female guests.
- A female student who jumped to her death from Beatty Towers at the University of Florida haunts the halls and some of the rooms in the towers.

Galveston, Texas

- Many of the unique shops in Galveston's historic Strand area were used as morgues during the destructive 1900 hurricane, and employers have reported problems convincing their workers to stay late. Lights switch off and on. Footsteps are heard in upstairs rooms that are empty.
- Some residents and tourists who walk the beaches at night claim to have encountered the ghosts of Jean Lafitte's pirate crew. Others testify to seeing the spirits of Civil War prisoners and plague victims lying in darkened streets.
- The ghost of a young police officer named Daniel, who was gunned down during a robbery in 1920, still defends the bank he was guarding at 2401 Strand Street, which is today the Mediterranean Chef restaurant. Waiters and waitresses have claimed to have caught glimpses of a ghost in an old-fashioned police uniform.

Gettysburg, Pennsylvania

- There are many reports of visitors witnessing spirit re-enactments of segments of the great battle that took place near here on July 1-3, 1863. Frequently cited are areas near Devil's Den, Cemetery Hill, and Gettysburg National Military Park.
- Farnsworth House Inn is considered by many to be among the most haunted houses in the United States. Among the numerous ghosts seen are a midwife attending to a young woman in labor; three Confederate soldiers at their post in the garret of the house; and the voice of a soldier singing to comfort his dying friend.

Houston, Texas

- Motorists on Christman Road look out for the phantom female hitchhiker in a purple dress.
- Jefferson Davis Hospital was built upon the final earthly resting place of 3,000 Civil War veterans and victims of yellow fever epidemics. Certain hallways and rooms are teeming with the spirits of nurses, doctors, and patients.
- Beer mugs and plates loaded with food fly across the room at the Ale House Pub and Eatery.

- Although Klein Collins High School is new, it was built over an old burial ground, thereby provoking many mysterious sounds and paranormal experiences in its rooms and hallways.

Indianapolis, Indiana

- Nighttime security officers at the Old Central State Hospital and Asylum claim a nightmarish cacophony of screams, groans, and cries for help and sightings of people who vanish.
- The House of Blue Lights on Meridian Street is haunted by the spirit of a beautiful young wife who lay in state in a special glass coffin by a sorrowing husband who couldn't bear to bury her.
- The ghost of a young firefighter who in the early 1990s died trying valiantly to extinguish the flames at the Indianapolis Athletic Club often awakens guests in the middle of the night.
- There are those who claim to have seen a spirit re-enactment of the 1960s murder of a witness in an elevator at the Indianapolis City County Building.

Jerome, Arizona

In the early 1900s, Jerome, ninety miles north of Phoenix, was a boomtown, home to 15,000 copper miners, and known as "the wickedest city in the West."

- The sounds of men suffering from lung problems have been reported issuing from the United Verde Hospital that sits high on Cleopatra Hill. Witnesses have also seen the dim shapes of bodies lying in a hallway in another older hospital farther down on Cleopatra Hill.
- The ghost of "Headless Charlie," the spirit of a miner who was decapitated in a grisly mine accident, is often reported.
- Not far from Spook Hall, a one-time dance hall where the crude shacks that housed the "working girls" in Jerome's red-light area, the ghost of a hooker appears walking near the Little Daisy Hotel.

Kansas City, Missouri

- According to witnesses, there are eight ghosts in the Donaldson House/Kansas City Art Institute, but only one is a friendly spirit.
- The ghosts of young girls in long white dresses have been sighted merrily playing together in Elmwood Cemetery.
- Many individuals claim that the entire shoreline around Houston Lake—with emphasis on the beach area—is haunted by some very bizarre entities.
- Some guests in room 505 at the Hotel Savoy have made the mistake of wishing to take a bath at the same time that the ghost of Betsy Ward manifests in the tub.
- Strawberry Hill has evolved from a mansion into an orphanage and, currently, a museum. The ghosts of the couple that built the mansion have been sighted, as well as two nuns who attended the children when the place was an orphanage.

Laredo, Texas

- The building that currently houses La Posada Hotel was formerly a convent. That fact explains the spectral nun that guests often see in the halls, but nothing can truly interpret the actions of a ghost that assumes the exact image of employees for the purpose of tricking the staff and management.

- The Civic Center is said to be haunted by the spirit of a custodian who was killed by falling curtain weights on the stage.
- When Martin High School was built, no attention was given to the task of moving the bodies from the old cemetery site on which the building would rest. Consequently, strange sounds are heard throughout the school and shadowy figures haunt the gym.
- The ghost of a mud-caked woman in a white dress is said by many witnesses to walk in the water near the banks of Zacate Creek.

Los Angeles, California

- Belmont High School is haunted by the spirit of a young girl who died in a fire in the early 1900s, when Belmont was a private school for girls.
- Strange phenomena at the Southwest Law School building, formerly I. Magnum/Bullocks department store, built in 1929, is attributed to the spirit of a little girl who was said to have been pushed into an elevator shaft sometime in the 1930s.
- Apparitions of weird entities haunt the eighteenth floor and the parking garage at the Los Angeles Airport Marriott. Guests have reported strange odors and sounds and being engulfed by feelings of absolute terror.
- Employees and security officers report three ghosts at the Neutrogena, Johnson & Johnson Corporation. Neutrogena founder's wife and son were murdered execution style in the building, and those individuals working late have sighted a woman in white and a child in the factory. The third entity has not been seen, but a menacing growl signals its arrival.
- Westchester High School is haunted by a student who fell and crushed his skull and broke his neck while playing basketball. Two other spirits, a boy and a girl, are sighted in various places in the school.
- The performances never end at the Palace Theatre. Over the years, employees and psychic researchers have determined that as many as twenty-four ghosts of actors, stage hands, and audience members haunt the building.

Louisville, Kentucky

- The ghost of a girl in a prom dress is seen at the top of the hill on Mitchell Hill Road, near the spot where she and her date are said to have been killed on prom night.
- The Deaf Community Center was once a private mansion inhabited by the Hampton family. The sounds of the many lavish parties and balls that the Hamptons hosted can still be heard, and Mrs. Hampton herself can be seen walking the hallways.
- The ghost of a male student who was shot and killed in the lobby of Meyzek Middle School has haunted the school since the 1930s.

Milwaukee, Wisconsin

- Perhaps because the Stritch dormitory at Cardinal Stritch University was a former convent, today's students often encounter the ghosts of nuns in their rooms and in the halls.
- Students residing in Humphrey Hall at Marquette University must learn to live with the ghosts of children who died in the building when it served as the Milwaukee Children's Hospital. Even the security monitors have picked up images of singing, laughing, screaming children.
- The bar area in The Walker House is haunted by the ghost of a horse thief, who was hanged from a tree outside the establishment.

REAL GHOSTS, RESTLESS SPIRITS, AND HAUNTED PLACES

- Customers and security guards at the Grand Avenue Mall are perplexed by the figure of a dancing ghost on the second floor.

Minneapolis/St. Paul, Minnesota

- Among the most well-known ghosts who haunt the Twin Cities are those who appear dressed in flashy 1920s attire in the Wabasha Street Caves, 215 Wabasha St. South, St. Paul. Originally a mushroom factory, the Caves became a speakeasy and a dancehall during the years of Prohibition. According to historians of the era, a number of mobsters were gunned down in the Caves during the Roaring Twenties. Today, guests have reported hearing dance music on Swing Nights after the live band has stopped playing. Calling to a bus boy for service might cause him to disappear before your startled eyes. Asking a woman dressed like a flapper from the Twenties for a dance may precipitate a similar vanishing act. Unexpected and uninvited "guests" often appear on wedding photographs.
- Forepaugh's Restaurant, once a big, elaborate gothic mansion, was owned in the 1890s by Joseph Forepaugh, a successful businessman who committed suicide because of his failing finances and the shame of his wife discovering his affair with their maid. After Forepaugh took his own life with a revolver, Molly, the maid, hanged herself from a chandelier. Today, employees often report seeing the strange image of a large arrogant man stalking through the restaurant, looking as if he owned the place. The chandelier from which the maid hanged herself is often seen to rock back and forth independent of any apparent force that might have set it in motion.
- Ghosts seem to have a peculiar affinity for theaters, and Minneapolis's famous Guthrie Theater appears to have a resident spirit who patrols the place after the last stage lights have gone down. Eerie figures have been sighted on catwalks, elevators, and tunnels. Even stranger, some patrons have reported being ushered to their seats by a slim young man dressed in a uniform more suitable for the 1960s. The sightings of the young usher have given rise to the explanation that the Guthrie Ghost is that of a teenaged boy whose very existence centered around the theater. After his social life had plummeted from bad to worse, he shot himself in his automobile while dressed in his usher's uniform. His last wishes were that he be buried in that same revered uniform.

New Orleans, Louisiana

- Some guests craving a ghostly encounter choose the third-floor rooms of The Castle Inn. The bed and breakfast is haunted by the playful spirit of a little girl and by a black man who burned to death in one of the wood sheds.
- Numerous ghosts appear at various places in the French Quarter, but locals warn of a handsome specter of an alleged real-life vampire who still takes delight in assaulting women.
- Le Petit Theatre du Vieux Carré is said to be haunted by the ghost of a young bride who fell to her death in the courtyard below, the specter of an old man seated in one of the theatre rows, and spirits who touch actors backstage with cold, unseen hands.
- According to tradition, at least four spirits haunt O'Flaherty's Irish Channel Pub—two victims of a murder-suicide and two former owners.
- The Morgue Bar and Lounge is well named for the building in which it is housed served as the city's first integrated mortuary during the Yellow Fever epidemic of 1853. Paranormal activity has been reported throughout the place, but the ladies' restroom is particularly active.

- During the Civil War, the Hotel Provincial was converted into a hospital. Numerous guests and employees have reported viewing spirit re-enactments of the terrible days when wounded troops lay screaming in pain and frantic doctors and nurses worked desperately to save lives.
- The LaLaurie House at 1140 Royal Street ranks among the most haunted in the United States. Behind the gentility of Madame LaLaurie and her third husband, Louis, was a nightmare reality rarely surpassed for tales of gruesome tortures dealt to their slaves. When a fire broke out on April 10, 1834, firemen discovered the horror of dozens of slaves chained in a secret attic. Horrible mutilations had been perpetrated, and human body parts lay scattered about the ghastly torture room. Madame and her husband fled, perhaps to France, and in 1842 an angry mob lay waste to the once elegant mansion. In those years before its present restoration, the mansion has served as a saloon, a girl's school, an apartment building, and a furniture store. A wide variety of ghostly entities and scenes have been reported in and around the mansion. For a brief period, the LaLaurie House was owned by actor Nicholas Cage.

Portland, Oregon

There is something so frightening in the basement of the Lotus nightclub that most employees refuse to venture down alone.

- The ghost of a hanged horse thief and his dog haunt the campground at Scapponia Park.
- The Fairmount Apartments was once a grand hotel built in 1905 to celebrate the centennial of the Lewis and Clark expedition. Residents on the lower floors report a sinister presence.
- The ghost of a young woman dressed in Victorian era clothing haunts the theatre at the University of Portland.
- The Villa St. Rose School for Girls is haunted by the spirits of small children who died there when the place was an orphanage maintained by nuns.

Salt Lake City, Utah

- The City County Building harbors ghosts on all five floors. According to employees and visitors, there are the spirits of two children, who were killed accidentally during construction; a woman who seems to be searching for lost children; and a former judge and a former mayor of Salt Lake City.
- Even nonbelievers in the spirit world are creeped out when they read that Lilly's tombstone in the Salt Lake City Cemetery decrees that she was a "victim of the Beast 666."
- Several murders in bygone days have afflicted many buildings with poltergeist phenomena in the West Temple and 2nd South area.
- A lady in a purple dress seems to head a veritable community of spirits at the Utah State Historical Society building.

San Antonio, Texas

- The atmosphere is heavily melancholy at the Alamo. Some sensitive people have viewed spirit re-enactments of segments of the fierce struggle between the defenders and the attacking Mexican forces.
- Shadowy figures are often sighted moving in the halls and rooms of Brackenridge Villa Mansion. The construction in the 1840s was begun on a site held sacred by Native American tribespeople.

- The spirits of soldiers and tribespeople are often reported walking at the side of Old Nacogdoches Road.
- Our Lady of the Lake University is haunted by the ghost of a former janitor who dwells in the basement of the library and the spirits of nuns who walk the halls.
- Through the years—and at various times—employees, staff members, and guests have claimed to have encountered as many as thirty-eight ghosts at the Menger Hotel, including Teddy Roosevelt and a number of his Rough Riders.

San Diego, California

- A woman in white appears in the shadows at a table in the corner of El Fandango Restaurant.
- The sound of marching ghosts and a number of haunted rooms have kept many a guest awake throughout the night at the Horton Grand Hotel.
- The ghost of Kate Morgan haunts room 3312 and the beach area in front of the Hotel Del Coronado.
- Yankee Jim, Thomas Whaley, and an entourage of spirits both welcome and unnerve visitors to the Whaley House.
- Your prayers for the peace of her soul will please the ghost of "Amanda," a tall former model who committed suicide in room 325 while depressed over her addiction to drugs.

San Francisco, California

- A headless man, thought to be the ghost of a victim of the 1989 earthquake, knocks on the windows of cars driving towards Oakland on the Bay Bridge.
- Before the Queen Anne Hotel offered the elegant, Victorian style accommodations that it provides today, it served as a school for girls. Guests and employees frequently encounter the spirit of the headmistress, who died heartbroken when the school was closed.
- The spirit of a young woman, who in the 1920s sought to hide her unwelcome pregnancy from her parents by leaping into Stowe Lake, can be seen walking in despair around Strawberry Hill in the Stowe Lake Golden Gate Park.
- The San Francisco Arts Institute attributes its various restless spirits to the possibility that it was built over a graveyard of earthquake victims in the early 1900s.
- Known as "the Rock," Alcatraz, the twelve-acre penal island in San Francisco Bay, was the last stop for 1,576 mobsters, murderers, and malcontents until the prison closed in 1963. Today, security guards employed by the National Park Service and visiting tourists report strange sounds issuing from the deserted cells. Some visitors and guards have also claimed to have felt the sensation of hands touching, even pinching, them.

Savannah, Georgia

Many researchers claim that hundreds of hotels, inns, and private homes harbor ghosts in Savannah, Georgia's oldest city, settled in 1733, the scene of a fierce Revolutionary War battle, three deadly yellow fever epidemics, and a harsh Civil War period of occupation.

- Before guests may stay in room 204 at the 1790 Inn, they must sign a waiver at the front desk stating that the management is not responsible for any items of clothing stolen by "Anne," the ghost who haunts the inn.
- Hanging Square derived its name quite logically by being the place where the city's criminals were executed. Spanish moss will not grow on the bough where Anna Reilly, a

teenaged murderess who was the first woman hanged in Georgia, was dispatched—and a stiff, cold breeze is always felt around the tree.

- The Hamilton-Turner Inn was built by Samuel Hamilton, a wealthy jeweler and former mayor of Savannah, in 1837. Many guests at the inn have soon learned that the "ghost bird" carvings on the roof will not keep away the spirits within, who open and close doors and windows and direct cold drafts on them.

- The Forsyth Park Inn, built in 1896 as a private residence, is haunted by the ghost of Lottie, a young girl who murdered a woman she suspected of being her uncle's mistress by poisoning her tea—then learned to her dismay that she had killed the wrong woman. Lottie's mother is also said to haunt the stairway and hallways of the inn.

- The eighty-eight-room Marshall House on Broughton Street has been used as a hospital three times, twice during Savannah's yellow fever epidemics and during the Civil War by the Union Army. Guests have encountered ghosts in the hallways and even in their beds.

Seattle, Washington

- Both employees and guests complain of the loud party taking place on the ninth floor of the Claremont Hotel, which stops abruptly whenever anyone investigates. Witnesses say that it sounds like a party from the Roaring Twenties, judging from the music that blares forth from the unseen merrymakers.

- The spirit of a Native American woman haunts the Pike Place Public Market, walking the area that was once sacred ground to her tribe.

- Footsteps and voices issue from the upper floors when the University YMCA is known to be devoid of human occupants. An eerie presence is often felt in the basement.

- The Hunt Club Bar in the Sorrento Hotel plays host to the antics of entities that enjoy moving objects, especially glasses, across the room.

St. Louis, Missouri

- A noisy ghost named George, who is often seen in a white suit and white hat, haunts the Powell Symphony Hall.

- The Lemp Mansion has a wide range of haunting phenomena, including numerous cold spots and pervasive feelings of being watched and touched.

- Although the Old City Hospital has not been used since the 1960s, witnesses report shadowy figures moving across the non-boarded windows and screams issuing from the vacant building.

- Six Flags Theme Park is home to the ghost of a little girl, a spirit named Stella, and a bizarre entity that makes an eerie squealing noise, much like a pig.

- Witnesses have claimed to have heard babies crying in Coopers Cemetery. Others report the ghost of an old man carrying a lantern.

Toronto, Ontario

- Custodians and security guards who draw night duty have reported the sounds of voices and electrical appliances that turn themselves off and on at the Goodwill Executive Offices on 108 George Street.

- The spirits of a number of soldiers who capsized their boat and drowned in Grenadier Pond in the 1800s are sighted on nights with stormy weather.

- The Mackenzie House has a wide variety of poltergeist and spirit activity, including misty, glowing figures.

- Chairs, dishes, and other objects become airborne due to the ministrations of a ghost with a nasty disposition that inhabits the Mynah Bird Coffee House.

- The Lady in Red mysteriously appears and disappears—and sings a bit of a tune—near the Old Bay Street Subway Station.

Tucson, Arizona

- The ghost of a woman in a long white dress, who often pushes employees off balance, haunts Centennial Hall. The more benevolent spirit of man seems to be on duty to assist anyone who might be harmed by the nasty entity.
- The Fred G. Acosta Job Corps Center is haunted by the ghost of a young girl who committed suicide in the restroom on the second floor.
- The rebuilt Pioneer Hotel is said to be haunted by the spirits of those who died in a fire in the building in the past.
- Ghostly miners with their lighted headlamps have been sighted in the San Miguel Magma cooper mine.
- The victim of a jealous boyfriend haunts the room at the Radisson Hotel where she was discovered with another man. Another female spirit is heard weeping in the ballroom area.

Winnipeg, Manitoba

- The Fort Garry Hotel is haunted by a ghost that takes delight in crawling in bed with the guests. Maids have claimed to have seen blood on the walls of 202, the room in which a despondent female guest hanged herself.
- The spirits of three hanged men haunt the parking lot of Little Mountain Park.
- Watchful presences are sensed and clearly audible voices are heard among the ruins of the old St. Norbert Monastery.
- Some researchers feel that the spirits of actors Laurence Irving and Mabel Hackney may be responsible for many of the ghostly phenomena at the Walker Theatre. The couple died in 1914 after less than a week of their run at the theatre. They may have felt cheated by fate and continue to perform in spirit.
- The old St. Vital Hotel appears to be haunted by the ghost of a man who was murdered outside the back door in the 1970s.

Resources:

Hauk, Dennis William. *Haunted Places*. New York: Penguin USA, reprint edition, 1996.

————. *International Directory of Haunted Places*. New York: Penguin, 2000.

Haunted Cemeteries. www.zerotime.com/ghosts/cemet/htm.

"Homegrown Hauntings." Interview with Chad Lewis. *Minnesota Daily*, October 25, 2007.

Kerman, Frances. *Ghostly Encounters: True Stories of America's Haunted Inns and Hotels*. New York: Warner Books, 2002.

Mead, Robin. *Haunted Hotels: A Guide to American and Canadian Inns and Their Ghosts*. Nashville, TN: Rutledge Hill Press, 1995.

Norman, Michael, and Beth Scott. *Historic Haunted America*. New York: Tor Books, 1996.

————. *Haunted Heritage*. A Forge Book, Tom Doherty Associates, 2002.

Obiwan's Ghosts, Hauntings, & Other Strange Phenomena. www.ghosts.org.

Shadowlands. www.shadowlands.net.

Smith, Susy. *Haunted Houses for the Millions*. Los Angeles: Sherbourne Press, Inc. 1967.

————. *Prominent American Ghosts*. New York: Dell, 1969.

Taylor, Troy. *Beyond the Grave*. Alton, IL: Whitechapel Productions Press, 2001.

Wlodarski, Anne Powell, and Robert James Wlodarski. *Dinner and Spirits: A Guide to America's Most Haunted Restaurants, Taverns, and Inns*. iUniverse.com, 2001.

Index

Note: (ill.) indicates photos and illustrations.

Q